Civil Society and Political Theory

Civil Society and Political Theory

Jean L. Cohen and Andrew Arato

The MIT Press, Cambridge, Massachusetts, and London, England

To Julian and Rachel

Fourth printing, 1997
First MIT Press paperback edition, 1994

This book was set in New Baskerville at MIT Press and was printed and bound in the United States of America.

Library of Congress Cataloging-in-Publication Data

Cohen, Jean L.
   Civil society and political theory / Jean L. Cohen and Andrew Arato
     p. cm. — (Studies in contemporary German social thought)
   Includes bibliographical references and index.
   ISBN 0-262-03177-9 (H), 0-262-53121-6 (P)
   1. Civil society. 2. Civil society—History. I. Arato, Andrew.
   II. Title. III. Series.
   JC336.C65 1990
   306.2—dc20   90-46723
                                                   CIP

Contents

Preface

This book is meant as a contribution to democratic theory. Unlike other approaches to the topic, however, ours does not focus directly on political institutions. Nor is it restricted to the domain of normative political philosophy, although both institutions and philosophy have their place in the text. Our goal, rather, is twofold: to demonstrate the relevance of the concept of civil society to modern political theory and to develop at least the framework of a theory of civil society adequate to contemporary conditions. In the process we hope to fill a rather glaring lacuna in recent work in the field of democratic theory. Every theory of democracy presupposes a model of society, yet no one has addressed the question of which type of civil society is most appropriate to a modern democratic polity.[1] To put it another way, the relation between normative models of democracy or projects of democratization and the structure, institutions, and dynamics of civil society has remained opaque, in part because there is no sufficiently complex theory of civil society available to us today. The task of this book is to begin the construction of such a theory.

The concept of civil society, in a variety of uses and definitions, has become quite fashionable today, thanks to struggles against communist and military dictatorships in many parts of the world. Yet it has an ambiguous status under liberal democracies. To some, it seems to indicate what the West has already achieved, and thus it is without any apparent critical potential for examining the dysfunctions and injustices of our type of society. To others, the concept belongs to early modern forms of political philosophy that have become irrelevant to today's complex societies. It is our thesis, however, that the concept of civil society indicates a terrain in the West that is endangered by the logic of administrative and economic mechanisms but is also the primary locus for the potential expansion of democracy under "really existing" liberal-democratic regimes. In advancing this thesis, we shall demonstrate the modernity and normative/critical relevance of the concept of civil society to all types of contemporary societies.

There are good arguments for each of these three positions, and we shall address them in detail. We shall try to show that the first two sets of arguments draw their strength from inadequate versions of the concept that have been unreflectively revived in the discussion so far in Latin America, Eastern Europe, and the West. One common ambiguity concerns the relation between the terms "civil" and "bourgeois" society, a distinction that cannot even be made in German (*bürgerliche Gesellschaft*) or in some East European languages. This is not simply a terminological problem, for the program of "civil society vs. the state," challenging statist dictatorships that penetrate and control both the economy and the various domains of independent social life, seems to stand for the autonomy of both the civil and the bourgeois. To be sure, the democratic movements in the East rely on the strengths of new autonomous forms of discourse, associations, and solidarity, i.e., on the elements of civil society. But they have not sufficiently differentiated between the task of establishing viable market economies (whatever form of ownership replaces state property and control), on the one hand, and the project of strengthening civil society vis-à-vis the state and the liberated market forces, on the other. Yet, as we know from the history of the West, the spontaneous forces of the capitalist market economy can represent as great a danger to social solidarity, social justice, and even autonomy as the administrative power of the modern state. Our point is that only a concept of civil society that is properly differentiated from the economy (and therefore from "bourgeois society") could become the center of a critical political and social theory in societies where the market economy has already developed, or is in the process of developing, its own autonomous logic. Otherwise, after successful transitions from dictatorship to democracy, the undifferentiated version of the concept embedded in the slogan "society vs. the state" would lose its critical potential. Thus, only a reconstruction involving a three-part model distinguishing civil society from both state and economy has a chance both to underwrite the dramatic oppositional role of this concept under authoritarian regimes and to renew its critical potential under liberal democracies.

Let us start with a working definition. We understand "civil society"[2] as a sphere of social interaction between economy and state, composed above all of the intimate sphere (especially the family), the sphere of associations (especially voluntary associations), social movements, and forms of public communication. Modern civil society is created through forms of self-constitution and self-mobilization. It is institutionalized and generalized through laws, and especially subjective rights, that stabilize social differentiation. While the self-creative and institutionalized dimensions[3] can exist separately, in the long term both independent action and institutionalization are necessary for the reproduction of civil society.

It would be misleading to identify civil society with all of social life outside the administrative state and economic processes in the narrow sense. First, it is necessary and meaningful to distinguish civil society from both a political society of parties, political organizations, and political publics (in particular, parliaments) and an economic society composed of organizations of production and distribution, usually firms, cooperatives, partnerships, and so on. Political and economic society generally arise from civil society, share some of its forms of organization and communication, and are institutionalized through rights (political rights and property rights especially) continuous with the fabric of rights that secure modern civil society. But the actors of political and economic society are directly involved with state power and economic production, which they seek to control and manage. They cannot afford to subordinate strategic and instrumental criteria to the patterns of normative integration and open-ended communication characteristic of civil society. Even the public sphere of political society rooted in parliaments involves important formal and temporal constraints on processes of communication. The political role of civil society in turn is not directly related to the control or conquest of power but to the generation of influence through the life of democratic associations and unconstrained discussion in the cultural public sphere. Such a political role is inevitably diffuse and inefficient. Thus the mediating role of political society between civil society and state is indispensable, but so is the rootedness of political society in civil society. In principle, similar considerations pertain to the relationship between civil and economic society, even if historically, under capitalism, economic society has been more successfully insulated from the influence of civil society than political society has been, despite the claims of elite theories of democracy. Nevertheless, the legalization of trade unions, collective bargaining, codetermination, and so on witness the influence of civil on economic society and allow the latter to play a mediating role between civil society and the market system.

Second, the differentiation of civil society from both economic and political society seems to suggest that the category should somehow include and refer to all the phenomena of society that are not directly linked to the state and the economy. But this is the case only to the extent that we focus on relations of conscious association, of self-organization and organized communication. Civil society in fact represents only a dimension of the sociological world of norms, roles, practices, relationships, competencies, and forms of dependence or a particular angle of looking at this world from the point of view of conscious association building and associational life. A way to account for this limitation in the scope of the concept is to distinguish it from a sociocultural lifeworld, which as the wider category of "the social" includes civil society. Accordingly, civil society refers to the structures of socialization, association, and organized forms of communication of the lifeworld to the extent that these are institutionalized or are in the process of being institutionalized.

Finally, we want to stress that under liberal democracies, it would be a mistake to see civil society in opposition to the economy and state by definition. Our notions of economic and political society (which admittedly complicate our three-part model) refer to mediating spheres through which civil society can gain influence over political-administrative and economic processes. An antagonistic relation of civil society, or its actors, to the economy or the state arises only when these mediations fail or when the institutions of economic and political society serve to insulate decision making and decision makers from the influence of social organizations, initiatives, and forms of public discussion.

The Structure of This Book

We shall argue that what is at stake in the debates animating political and social theory in both East and West[4] is not simply the defense of society against the state or the economy but which version of civil society is to prevail. There is, however, another issue underlying these debates. Max Weber's disillusioned insistence that we moderns are living in an age of disenchantment appears to be more true now than ever before. Secular political utopias seem to have gone the way of the great mobilizing religious world views of the previous age. The demise of the most important radical-democratic and socialist utopia of our time, Marxism, has already led thinkers to proclaim the end of history and the worldwide triumph of a rather uninspired version of liberalism. Now that the revolutionary rhetoric of communism has at last (and deservedly) been discredited, the question confronting political theorists is whether utopian thought and corresponding radical political projects are conceivable at all. Or are the mobilizing ideals embedded in earlier utopias consigned to the dustbin of the history of ideas?

The great ideals generated in the age of democratic revolutions—liberty, political and social equality, solidarity, and justice—were each embedded in totalistic and mutually exclusive utopias: anarchism, libertarianism, radical democracy, Marxism. Sober reflection on the history of the past century and a half should dissuade responsible persons from seeking to revive any one of these utopias in their original form. However, a society without action-orienting norms, a society without political projects, is equally undesirable, for the civil privatism or "realism" that would result would really be just another name for egoism, and the corresponding political culture would lack sufficient motivation to maintain, much less expand, existing rights, democratic institutions, social solidarity, or justice.

It is our thesis that the revival of the discourse of civil society provides some hope in this regard. For this discourse reveals that collective actors and sympathetic theorists are still oriented by the utopian ideals of modernity—the ideas of basic rights, liberty, equality, democracy, solidarity, and justice—even if the fundamentalist, revolutionary rhetoric within which these ideals had once been articulated is on the wane. Indeed, civil society itself has emerged as a new kind of utopia, one we call "self-limiting," a utopia that includes a range of complementary forms of democracy and a complex set of civil, social, and political rights that must be compatible with the modern differentiation of society. It is this utopian ideal that plays a fundamental, if regulative, role in the construction of our book as a whole, as well as in its individual parts.

Parts I and II analyze the major theories and criticisms of the concept of civil society that have emerged in the nineteenth and twentieth centuries. In the introduction we present an overview of the theoretical importance of the problem of civil society by situating it in terms of three central debates in contemporary political theory: between elite and participatory democracy, between liberalism and communitarianism, and between critics and defenders of the welfare state. For the most part, this discussion draws on American sources. Our intention here is not to prove that the concept of civil society can resolve all the relevant debates and antinomies but rather to show that it opens up new and unexpected possibilities for synthesis in each case.

But which concept? Bracketing the working definition just provided, chapter 1 introduces the concept of civil society in a deliberately nonsystematic manner, by reproducing its heterogeneous current usage by intellectuals in or close to a number of social and political movements. Since our interest is in politics, we believe we must first learn from contemporary discourses in order to contribute something to them. We start our examination of the political motivations relevant to our task with a presentation of four ideal typical discourses: Polish (the democratic opposition), French (the "second left"), German (the realist Greens) and Latin American (the new democratic left). In each case, the concept and categories of civil society have become central to efforts to articulate normative projects for liberalization and democratization. We do not assume that the discourses we reproduce are fully representative of what is available, and even less that they in themselves can provide or substitute for a political analysis of the four contexts. Only in the Eastern European case do we return to analyzing, this time on the basis of a variety of primary and secondary sources, the fate of the intellectual project in the face of complex constraints. We complete this part of our analysis by comparing and contrasting the four different discourses of civil society, and only then do we raise the question of whether a unified conception of civil society with a critical thrust can be developed from intellectual contexts related to contemporary forms of action. The chapter shows how these heterogeneous and unsystematic attempts differ, what they have in common, and why it makes sense to link them together.

The revival of concepts of civil society notwithstanding, it could be argued that twentieth-century developments render key dimensions of the concept irrelevant. The norms of civil society—individual rights, privacy, voluntary association, formal legality, plurality, publicity, free enterprise—were, of course, institutionalized heterogeneously and in a contradictory manner in Western societies. The logic of capitalist private property and the market often conflicts with plurality and free association; that of bureaucratization, with parliamentary will-formation. The principles of a representative, inclusive, political process of legislation controlled by society conflicts with new forms of exclusion and domination in society, in the economy, and in the state. Moreover, given structural changes over the last century, any attempt to equate "state" with "the political" or " civil society" with "the private" seems anachronistic. If this is so, can a category of early modern political philosophy have any continuing relevance to the contemporary world?

In chapter 2, we present a short conceptual history of early modern versions of civil society and a theoretical analysis of Hegel's masterful synthesis. These steps belong to what we take to be the necessary prolegomenon for a theory of civil society on the level of the history of theory. Indeed no one could seriously contest Hegel's position as the most important nineteenth-century predecessor of and inspiration to twentieth-century analyses of civil society. The categorial richness of the concept of civil society can be recovered only through an analysis of Hegel's framework, which gathered into itself all available interpretations of the concept. We cannot, of course, pretend to examine the evolution of Hegel's political philosophy, the whole body of his relevant work, or even the full range of secondary literature dealing with the most important text for us, *The Philosophy of Right*. Nevertheless, the Hegelian theory is crucial because it reconstructs civil society in terms of the three levels of legality, plurality and association, and publicity and because Hegel sees the link between civil society and state in terms of mediation and interpenetration. As chapter 1 shows, no contemporary discourse of civil society has managed to add even a single fundamental category to *legality, privacy, plurality, association, publicity*, and *mediation*, except that of social movements, and the most sophisticated contemporary authors—Michnik, O'Donnell, and Cardoso, for example—work with *all* of these levels.

Hegel's own ambiguities concerning civil society, and perhaps even his recurring statism in face of the alienation of the system of needs, can be traced to his inclusion of the economy as one of the levels of civil society. The importance of Gramsci and Parsons for our framework is their demonstration that the basic Hegelian conception can be improved by introducing a three-part model differentiating civil society from both economy and state. We argue in chapter 3, however, that both Gramsci's and Parsons's analyses suffer from the fact that they introduce these three domains in terms of overly monistic and functionalistic forms of theory. In Gramsci's case, this led to a deep ambivalence toward modern civil society and its future in a free socialist society. In Parsons's case, on the other hand, the flat combination of normative and functionalist approaches leaves us with an explicitly apologetic theory of the contemporary American version of civil society. We wish to make the reader sensitive to the dangers of both versions of functionalism.

Together, the first three chapters show that the concept of civil society continues to inform major paradigms of contemporary social and political theory. Chapter 3 in particular shows that the theoretical aims of Hegel's synthesis are better served if we abandon his own statist bias and if we differentiate civil society from the system of needs more sharply than he did. Gramsci and Parsons thus point beyond economism and statism within the terms of Hegelian political philosophy.

Twentieth-century usages of the concept of civil society are not without their critics. Indeed, many have argued that the concept of civil society is anachronistic, normatively suspect, or both. Accordingly, in part II, we reproduce and assess four fundamental types of criticism to which we believe all currently available conceptions of civil society are more or less vulnerable. To be sure, there would be other ways of schematizing critical approaches, and other critics to include—no analysis can avoid selectivity. We have chosen to divide critical perspectives according to four models: the normative (chapter 4), the historicist (chapter 5), the genealogical (chapter 6), and the systems-theoretic (chapter 7). With the exception of the historicist model, where we refer to three authors, each approach is typified by a single theorist. We use this procedure to produce as coherent a case for each perspective as possible. For the same reason we bring to bear our own criticisms immanently in each instance, leaving our own position until later. As we proceed, though, we note that several of the critics have reconstructed one dimension of the classical concept of civil society as inherited from Hegel even as they battled against the conception as a whole. In addition, each critic has helped to weaken the case of at least one of the others. This was the case for Arendt's notion of the public sphere as a genuinely political concept (vs. Schmitt), for Habermas's rediscovery of the bifurcation of the public in a model of mediation (vs. Arendt), for Foucault's genealogy of modern power relations (vs. all functionalist models), and for Luhmann's notion of differentiation (vs. Schmitt and Habermas).

Part III is more systematic and less expository than the first two parts. Keeping in mind the difficulties that have emerged from contemporary political discussions and from the four types of criticism of the concept of civil society, we have produced four theoretical studies. These are meant to respond to the most important objections left over from the critical confrontation of the critics with each other, to outline a reconstructed theory of civil society, and to reconnect this theory to politics through analyses of social movements and civil disobedience.

Chapter 8 starts to work out the normative foundations of a theory of civil society, using the discourse ethics developed by Habermas and his colleagues. The presentation of the discourse ethics has a double function. First, it responds to the normative and genealogical critics by showing how a convincing justification for civil society can be provided today. Second, it shows that the project of the institutionalization of discourses is possible only on the ground of modern civil society. It is in this context that we hope to give a more comprehensive solution to the antinomy of rights-oriented liberalism and communitarianism discussed in the introduction, taking into account the claims of participatory democratic theory as well. The thesis of chapter 8 is that the plausibility of rights and democracy depends on their conceptual and normative interrelation despite the apparently antithetical character of the two theoretical paradigms in which each is articulated and defended.

Because every normative theory of democracy, and every liberal theory, implies a model of society, it is incumbent on political theorists to add the dimension of social-structural analysis to normative political philosophy. Of course, those who are convinced of the universality of hermeneutic methodology would need do no more to demonstrate the validity of contemporary theoretical uses of the concept of civil society than reconstruct the contemporary discourses of civil society in a normatively coherent theory. On such a view, the fact that the concept of civil society informs the self-understanding of social movements is enough to show that it remains an adequate basis for the symbolic orientation of collective action. But the "discourse of civil society," including even the best philosophical reformulation of it, could be merely ideological. Whatever the intentions of social actors, the functional requirements of modern economic and political systems may make projects based on the concept irrelevant, corresponding identities unstable, interpretations one-sided. Given the challenges to the very model of differentiation that is at the heart of the discourse of civil society, it is essential to provide a systematic reconstruction of its structural presuppositions. Without a social-scientific analysis of the structure and dynamics of modern society, we have no way of evaluating the generality of a given identity or the global constraints operating behind the back of social actors.

In addition, the relation between civil society, the economy, and the state requires elaboration. This is the goal of chapter 9, which starts by mapping out the three-part model of civil society introduced by Gramsci in terms of the Habermasian distinction between the lifeworld and the economic and political subsystems. We then attempt to demonstrate the modernity of this construct. Chapter 9 must be read as a sympathetic revision of the Habermasian framework. Our main addition is to integrate the concept of civil society into the overall model, making the necessary adjustments. Convinced that the theory of communicative action represents the most advanced contours of critical social theory today, we try to unfold the implications of the whole conception on the level of political theory. Indeed, our reconstruction of civil society should be seen also as a political "translation" of Habermasian critical theory, one that has been guided by the dramatic struggles of our time under the aegis of his own values and ours: freedom and solidarity. We argue, against Luhmann, that a model of differentiation and modernization cannot do without an ultimately cultural substratum, where the rationalization of normative action coordination occurs. We also show that our model has the advantage of being able to accommodate the negative phenomena associated with modern civil society in the genealogical criticism, and much more. We discuss the contradictory institutionalization of the norms of civil society while insisting both on the utopian implications of the model and on its alternative forms of development. Chapter 9 concludes by outlining a proposal, based on the three-part model, for the reflexive continuation of both the welfare state and the democratic revolution.

The last two chapters formulate this politics by referring to social movements and to one of their key forms of contestation: civil disobedience. We do not wish to imply that the politics of civil society can only take the form of social movements. Normal institutional forms of political participation—voting, becoming active in political parties, forming interest or lobby groups—are part of this politics. But the utopian dimension of radical politics can be found only on the level of collective action. Thus, in chapter 10, we address the relation between collective action and civil society from a slightly different point of view than that of chapter 1. Instead of focusing on the discourse of activists, we take up the major theoretical paradigms that have evolved since the 1960s in order to analyze social movements and show that they each presuppose (in some cases implicitly, in others explicitly) the concept of civil society. Moreover, we demonstrate that civil society, beyond all functionalist and pluralist models, should be seen not only passively, as a network of institutions, but also actively, as the context and product of self-constituting collective actors. We then try to demonstrate that our tripartite structural model is the best framework with which to approach "new" and old forms of collective action.

We conclude by reflecting on the question of what is and what should and could be the relationships among societal plurality, individual autonomy, social movements, and a liberal, democratic political system. Social movements are not always internally democratic, and they often engage in action that violates the democratic procedures or laws generated by a nonetheless legitimate political order. What mode of political voice, action, and representation is legitimate for social actors in *both* society and state? What is the proper locus of political activity and how should boundary lines between public and private be drawn? How can the danger of permanent mobilization be avoided? Our discussion of civil disobedience in chapter 11 responds to these questions. Above all, our argument on civil disobedience seeks to demonstrate that social movements and citizen initiatives are capable of influencing policy and molding political culture without entry into the field of power politics and without necessarily endangering liberal or democratic institutions. Thus (implicitly returning to the first debate in our introduction), we provide for a framework of democratization in the contexts of elite democracies, without falling into the traps of fundamentalist theories of participation. We also take up once more the debate between rights-oriented liberals and participatory democrats, this time from the perspective of the appropriate forms of noninstitutionalized politics of civil society. We hope to provide, if not the solution to the antinomies of contemporary political and social theory, then at least to a way to begin rethinking them.

Acknowledgments

Each chapter of this book was extensively discussed by the authors before drafts were written. The preface, introduction, and chapters 6, 8, 10, and 11 are primarily the work of Jean L. Cohen; chapters 1, 2, 3, and 7 are primarily the work of Andrew Arato; chapters 4, 5, and 9 are collaborative efforts.

We received support for this project, individually and jointly, from more people and institutions than we can mention here. We start with our separate acknowledgments.

Jean L. Cohen would like to thank the Russell Sage Foundation for the intellectual and institutional support received there while I was a Post Doctoral Fellow in Residence in 1986–87. I would also like to thank the Department of Political Science at Columbia University for a leave of absence that enabled me to carry on this research. Special thanks to the Councils for Research in the Humanities and Social Sciences of Columbia University for summer fellowships in 1987 and 1988 that enabled me to conduct research abroad. The École des hautes études en sciences sociales, and in particular Claude Lefort and Pierre Rosanvallon, deserve special mention for allowing me to work as Directeur d'études associé in political and social theory in 1989. While in Paris, I presented several lectures based on the book and received very helpful criticisms. My deepest thanks to Jürgen Habermas for sponsoring a two-month research fellowship at the Max Planck Institut für Sozialwissenschaften in Starnberg in 1981; there I was able to familiarize myself with his recent work, which has had the greatest influence on my thinking and on this book. I would like to thank the American Council of Learned Societies for funding my travel to Dubrovnik, Yugoslavia, in 1984 and 1985, to present lectures at the Course on Philosophy and Social Science. There, too, I aired my ideas on social movements, discourse ethics, and civil society and received invaluable feedback. Finally, thanks are due to the Vienna Institut für die Wissenchaften vom Menschen, and in particular to Krzysztof Michalski and Cornelia Klinger, who invited me to lecture at their summer school program in Cortona, Italy, in 1989 and 1990. There I gave seminars on the theme of civil society to an interesting group of graduate students from the United States, Eastern Europe, and the Soviet Union, and I profited greatly by their responses.

Andrew Arato would like to thank the Alexander von Humboldt Stiftung for its support in 1980–1981, and the Max Planck Institut für Sozialwissenschaften in Starnberg for providing a work base during this time. I very much appreciate the help I received from Professor Habermas, then director of the institute, and his colleagues in getting to know the framework of the Theory of Communicative Action, which is often utilized in this book. I would further like to thank colleagues at the Institute of Sociology of the Hungarian Academy of Science, for their interest in my work on civil society and for the many interesting discussions we have shared. I owe a great debt to the Graduate Faculty seminars of the New School for Social Research at which I had a chance to discuss topics from this book—in particular, the democracy seminar, the staff seminar in sociology, and the philosophy colloquium. Conferences at the Cardozo Law School on Hegel and Luhmann have provided excellent opportunities to refine my ideas. I wish, finally, to thank all my students who have so actively participated in courses related to the problems of civil society.

Many friends and colleagues have given us useful critiques of drafts of the manuscript and interesting suggestions in the course of conversations. We would like to mention, in particular, Ken Baynes, Robert Bellah, Seyla Benhabib, György Bence, László Bruszt, José Casanova, Cornelius Castoriadis, Juan Corradi, Drucilla Cornell, Ferenc Fehér, Carlos Foreman, Alessandro Ferrara, Jeffrey Goldfarb, Claus Guenter, Jürgen Habermas, Elemér Hankiss, Agnes Heller, Dick Howard, George Kateb, János Kis, György Márkus,

Maria Márkus, Alberto Melucci, Sigrid Meuschel, Claus Offe, Guillermo O'Donnell, Alessandro Pizzorno, Carla Pasquinelli, Ulrich Preuss, Zbigniew Pelczynski, Pierre Rosenvallon, Bernhardt Schlink, Phillippe Schmitter, Alfred Stepan, Ivan Szelényi, Mihály Vajda, Jeffrey Weintraub, and Albrecht Wellmer.

We owe a special word of thanks to our series editor, Thomas McCarthy, as well as to our editor at MIT Press, Larry Cohen. Without their help this book would certainly not have been possible.

We dedicate the book to our children, Julian Cohen Arato and Rachel Arato.

Introduction

We are on the threshold of yet another great transformation of the self-understanding of modern societies. There have been many attempts from various points of view to label this process: the ambiguous terms "postindustrial" and "postmodern" society reflect the vantage points of economic and cultural concerns. Our interest is in politics. But from this standpoint, the changes occurring in political culture and social conflicts are poorly characterized by terms whose prefix implies "after" or "beyond." To be sure, for a variety of empirical and theoretical reasons the old hegemonic paradigms have disintegrated, as have the certainties and guarantees that went with them. Indeed we are in the midst of a remarkable revival of political and social thought that has been going on for the last two decades.

One response to the collapse of the two dominant paradigms of the previous period—pluralism and neo-Marxism—has been the attempt to revive political theory by "bringing the state back in." While this approach has led to interesting theoretical and empirical analyses, its state-centered perspective has obscured an important dimension of what is new in the political debates and in the stakes of social contestation.[1] The focus on the state is a useful antidote to the reductionist functionalism of many neo-Marxian and pluralist paradigms that would make the political system an extension, reflex, or functional organ of economic (class) or social (group) structures of selectivity and domination. In this respect the theoretical move served the cause of a more differentiated analysis. But with respect to all that is nonstate, the new paradigm continues the reductionist tendency of Marxism and neo-Marxism by identifying class relations and interests as the key to contemporary forms of collective action. Moreover, the legal, associational, cultural, and public spheres of society have no theoretical place in this analysis. It thereby loses sight of a great deal of interesting and normatively instructive forms of social conflict today.

The current "discourse of civil society," on the other hand, focuses precisely on new, generally non–class-based forms of collective action oriented and linked to the legal, associational, and public institutions of society. These are differentiated not only from the state but also from the capitalist market economy. Although we cannot leave the state and the economy out of consideration if we are to understand the dramatic changes occurring in Latin America and Eastern Europe in particular, the concept of civil society is indispensable if we are to understand the stakes of these "transitions to democracy" as well as the self-understanding of the relevant actors. It is also indispensable to any analysis that seeks to grasp the import of such changes for the West, as well as indigenous contemporary forms and stakes of conflict. In order to discover, after the demise of Marxism, if not a common normative project between the "transitions" and radical social initiatives under established liberal democracies, then at least the conditions of possibility of fruitful dialogue between them, we must inquire into the meaning and possible shapes of the concept of civil society.

Admittedly, our inclination is to posit a common normative project, and in this sense we are post-Marxist. In other words, we locate the pluralist core of our project within the universalistic horizon of critical theory rather than within the relativistic one of deconstruction. At issue is not only an arbitrary theoretical choice. We are truly impressed by the importance in East Europe and Latin America, as well as in the advanced capitalist democracies, of the struggle for rights and their expansion, of the establishment of grass roots associations and initiatives and the ever renewed construction of institutions and forums of critical publics. No interpretation can do these aspirations justice without recognizing both common orientations that transcend geography and even social-political systems and a common normative fabric linking rights, associations, and publics together. We believe that civil society, in fact the major category of many of the relevant actors and their advocates from Russia to Chile, and from France to Poland, is the best hermeneutic key to these two complexes of commonality.

Thus we are convinced that the recent reemergence of the "discourse of civil society" is at the heart of a sea change in contemporary political culture.[2] Despite the proliferation of this "discourse" and of the concept itself, however, no one has developed a systematic *theory* of civil society. This book is an effort to begin doing just that. Nevertheless, systematic theory cannot be built directly out of the self-understanding of actors, who may very much need the results of a more distanced and critical examination of the possibilities and constraints of action. Such theory must be internally related to the development of relevant theoretical debates. At first sight the building of a theory of civil society seems to be hampered by the fact that the stakes of contemporary debates in political theory seem to be located around different axes than the nineteenth-century couplet of society and state. It is our belief, however, that the problem of civil society and its democratization is latently present in these discussions and that it constitutes the theoretical terrain on which their internal antinomies might be resolved.

Three debates of the last 15–20 years seem to tower above all the rest. The first continues an older controversy within the field of democratic theory between defenders of elite vs. participatory models of democracy.[3] The second, for the most part restricted to the Anglo-American world, is between what has come to be called "rights-oriented liberalism" and "communitarianism." While it covers some of the same ground as the first controversy, the terms of the second discussion are quite distinct for, unlike the first, it occurs within the field of normative political philosophy rather than between empiricists and normativists.[4] The third debate, pitting neoconservative advocates of the free market against defenders of the welfare state, has animated discussion on both sides of the Atlantic.[5] Its context is, of course, the notorious crisis of the welfare state that intruded on political consciousness in the mid-1970s. These debates are interrelated, and, as already indicated, there are overlaps. Nevertheless, each of them has culminated in a distinct set of antinomies leading to a kind of standoff and increasing sterility. What no one seems to have realized, however, is that the relatively unsystematic and heterogeneous discourse of the revival of civil society can be brought to bear on these debates and indeed can provide a way out of the antinomies that plague them. Accordingly, we shall briefly summarize these debates in this introduction and show how our book provides a new paradigm for thinking about the issues they raise.

Debates in Contemporary Political Theory

Elite vs. Participatory Democracy

It would not be an exaggeration to say that the debate between elite and participatory models of democracy has been going around in circles ever since Schumpeter threw down the gauntlet to the normativists in 1942.[6] Schumpeter's claim that "the democratic method is that institutional arrangement for arriving at political decisions in which individuals acquire the power to decide via a competitive struggle for the people's vote"[7] has formed the core of the elite model of democracy ever since. Democracy is defined not as a kind of society or as a set of moral ends or even as a principle of legitimacy but rather as a method for choosing political leaders and organizing governments. The elite model of democracy claims to be realistic, descriptive, empirically accurate, and the only model that is appropriate to modern social conditions.

Far from indulging in utopian illusions about the possibility of either conjuring away the phenomenon of power or the gap between rulers and ruled, this approach assumes that no society, and certainly no modern one, could function without both. A "realistic" appraisal of democratic societies must grant that the motor of the political system is power just as the motor of the economy is profit. The struggle to acquire and use power is at the heart of the political. What distinguishes democratic from nondemocratic societies is thus the way in which power is acquired and decisions are arrived at: So long as some core set of civil rights is respected and regularly contested elections are held on the basis of a universal franchise, so long as alternation in power is accepted by elites and occurs smoothly without violence or institutional discontinuity, so long as decision making involves compromises among elites and (passive) acceptance by the population, a polity can be considered democratic. The main concern here is obviously with the ability of a government to produce decisions, to have them accepted, and to ensure orderly transitions, i.e., stability.

The elite model of democracy prides itself on providing an operationalizable and empirically descriptive account of the practices of polities considered to be democratic. There is no pretense here that voters either set the political agenda or make political decisions; they neither generate issues nor choose policies. Rather, leaders (political parties) aggregate interests and decide which are to become politically salient.[8] Moreover, they select issues and structure public opinion. The true function of the vote is simply to choose among the bids for power by political elites and to accept leadership. The voters are consumers, the parties are entrepreneurs offering alternative packages or personnel; it is they who create demand, bowing to consumer sovereignty only with regard to the yes/no decision by the voters about who among the preselected candidates will be their "representatives" (using the latter term very loosely indeed).[9] In short, the empirical theories of democracy (elite, pluralist, corporatist, and rational choice models) tend quite openly to reduce the normative meaning of the term to a set of minimums modeled on a conception of bargaining, competition, access, and accountability derived more from the market than from earlier models of citizenship.

Competitiveness in acquiring political power and in making policy decisions is, of course, the core of this model of democracy. The competitive element is deemed to be the source of creativity, productivity, responsibility, and responsiveness. The ultimate sanction of the vote, together with the necessity on the part of elites to compete for it, will supposedly keep things fair, encourage authorities to be responsive to a multiplicity of demands and accountable to the citizenry, and foster their willingness to compromise with one another. To be sure, this model of democracy rests on certain preconditions that it supposedly should be able to reproduce: high-quality leadership with a tolerance for differences of opinion, a restricted range of political decision,[10] and an elite political culture based on democratic self-control.[11] These preconditions are predicated in turn on the fact of social pluralism or cleavage, which the democratic method institutionalizes into non-violent competition for office and influence. A final precondition, deemed indispensable for a stable political system to be able to make decisions, is that it must be shielded from too much partici-pation by the population: Citizens must, as it were, accept the division of labor between themselves and the politicians they elect.[12] Accordingly, this model of democracy argues that the secret ballot, civil rights, alternation, regular elections, and party com-petition are central to every modern conception of democracy if democracy is to have any place at all in complex modern societies.

We find this last statement to be quite convincing, so far as it goes. But the normativist critique of the elite model of democracy is also convincing. It is especially compelling against the elite model's tendency to extol apathy, civil privatism, and the necessity to shield the political system from "excess" demands of the population as *democratic* principles, the meaning of this excess to be determined by the elites alone.[13] The normativists correctly point out that what makes for stability and continuity in a polity is not identical with what makes it democratic. From the standpoint of participation theory, the elite model of democracy is both too broad and too narrow. To define a polity as democratic if it periodically holds contested elections and guarantees civil rights, regardless of what sorts of public institutions or private arrangements exist, is to extend democratic legitimacy to an enormously wide range of societies while simultaneously shielding them from critical scrutiny.[14] At the same time the concept of democracy at play here is too narrow, for it is defined by procedures that have little to do with the procedures and presuppositions of free agreement and discursive will formation.[15] Indeed the participation theorists argue that the "realistic" model has denuded the concept of democracy of so many of its elements that it has lost any connection with its past meaning.[16] What is left if one drops the ideas of self-determination, participation, political equality, discursive processes of political will formation among peers, and the influence of autonomous public opinion on decision making? In short, the price of the elite model's realism is the loss of what has always been taken to be the core of the concept of democracy, namely, the citizenship principle.

Moreover, by restricting the concept of democracy to a method of leader selection and to procedures regulating the competition and policy making of elites, this model sacrifices the very principles of democratic legitimacy on which it is nevertheless parasitic. It loses all criteria for distinguishing between formalistic ritual, systematic distortion, choreographed consent, manipulated public opinion, and the real thing.[17]

The participatory model of democracy maintains that what makes for good leaders also makes for good citizens—active participation in ruling and being ruled (i.e., in the exercise of power) and also in public will and opinion formation. Democracy in this sense would allow all citizens, and not only elites, to acquire a democratic political culture. For it is through political experience that one develops a conception of civic virtue, learns to tolerate diversity, to temper fundamentalism and egoism, and to become able and willing to compromise.[18] Hence the insistence that without public spaces for the active participation of the citizenry in ruling and being ruled, without a decisive narrowing of the gap between rulers and ruled, to the point of its abolition, polities are democratic in name only.[19]

For the most part, however, when it comes to conceptualizing alternatives, participation theorists offer institutional models that are meant to substitute for rather than complement the allegedly undemocratic (and/or bourgeois) forms of representative government that exist today.[20] Whether the theorist harkens back to an idealized model of the Greek *polis*, to the republican tradition of the late medieval city-state, or to the new forms of democracy generated within the milieus of the workers' movement (council communism, revolutionary syndicalism), in each case the alternative is presented as the single organizational principle for society as a whole. Accordingly, the underlying thrust of these models is the dedifferentiation of society, the state, and the economy. Small wonder that participationists in turn are accused by their opponents of utopianism and/or antimodernism.[21]

To sum up, this debate leaves us with the following antinomy: Contemporary democratic theory involves either some rather undemocratic adjustments to the "exigencies of complex industrial societies" coupled with an abandonment of the normative core of the very concept of democracy, or it proffers somewhat hollow normative visions that cannot be reconciled with the institutional requirements of modern society.[22]

Rights-Oriented Liberalism vs. Communitarianism

The debate between political liberals and communitarians reproduces some of the arguments described above but on a different terrain. In one respect, both sides in this debate challenge the elite/pluralist model of democracy.[23] Both reject the antinormative, empiricist, utilitarian strain in this model and both seek to develop a convincing normative theory of democratic legitimacy or justice. The dispute is over how to formulate such a theory. Despite this shift in emphasis, however, this debate also culminates in a set of antinomic positions from which it seems unable to extricate itself.

At the center of the controversy are two interrelated issues, one epistemological, the other political. The first revolves around the question of whether it is possible to articulate a formal, universalistic (deontological) conception of justice without presupposing a substantive (historically and culturally specific) concept of the good.[24] The second revolves around the question of how freedom can be realized in the modern world. At issue here is whether the idea of freedom should be explicated primarily from the standpoint of individual rights or of the community's shared norms.[25] Each side comes up with a different, indeed opposed, set of responses as to what constitutes the legitimating principles of a constitutional democracy. In the process, however, the very conception of liberal democracy disintegrates into its component parts.

Liberal theorists see the respect for individual rights and the principle of political neutrality as the standard for legitimacy in constitutional democracies. The core premise of rights-oriented liberalism is that individuals qua individuals have moral rights that serve as constraints on government and on others—constraints that are under the control of the rights holder. They have these rights not on the grounds of some social convention, aggregate common utility, tradition, or dispensation from God, but by virtue of their having some "property" (moral autonomy, human dignity) that constitutes them as bearers of rights.[26] The liberal sees individual autonomy, moral egalitarianism, and universalism as inherent in the idea of moral rights.[27] As such, rights constitute the heart of a conception of justice that makes plausible the claim to legitimacy of any modern polity. Law and political decisions are binding to the degree to which they respect individual rights.[28]

The communitarian critique of the rights thesis focuses on its individualist presuppositions and universalist claims. With respect to the first, communitarians argue that the liberal ideals of moral autonomy and individual self-development are based on an atomistic, abstract, and ultimately incoherent concept of the self as the subject of rights.[29] This allegedly leads to a focus on nonpolitical forms of freedom (negative liberty) and an impoverished conception of political identity, agency, and ethical life. Accordingly, the communitarians invoke a set of empirical and normative arguments against these assumptions. First, they argue that individuals are situated within an historical and social context; they are socialized into communities through which they derive their individual and collective identity, language, world concepts, moral categories, etc. Hence the empirical primacy of the social over the individual is asserted against the alleged priority of the asocial individual to society. Second, on the normative level, communitarians charge that liberals fail to see that communities are independent sources of value and that there are communal duties and virtues (loyalty, civic virtue) distinct from duties to others qua their abstract humanity. Indeed, duties of loyalty and membership are and must be primary.

As far as universalism goes, communitarians claim that what the liberal sees as universal norms grounded in the universal character of humanity (dignity or moral autonomy) are in fact particular norms embedded in shared understandings of specific communities. The individual cannot have a firm basis for moral judgment without getting it from a community to which one is committed. The strongest claim is that there are no duties pertaining to abstract man but only to members: The proper basis of moral theory is the community and its good, not the individual and her rights. Indeed, individuals have rights to the degree to which these flow from the common good. Accordingly, the idea of moral rights is an empty universalism that mistakenly abstracts from the only real basis of moral claims, the community. Only on the basis of a shared conception of the good life, only within the framework of a substantive ethical political community (with a specific political culture) can we lead meaningful moral lives and enjoy true freedom.

For those communitarians who see themselves as democrats,[30] the concept of freedom thus has to do not with the idea of moral rights but with the specific way in which agents come to decide what they want and ought to do. Taken together, the empirical and normative criticisms of the rights thesis imply that freedom must have its original locus not in the isolated individual but in the society that is the medium of individuation: in the structures, institutions, practices of the larger social whole. Civic virtue rather than negative liberty, the public good as distinct from the right, democratic participation unlike individual rights (and the concomitant adversarial political culture), involve a communal practice of citizenship that should pervade the institutions of society on all levels and become habitualized in the character, customs, moral sentiments of each citizen. By implication, and on the strongest version of these claims, a society in which claims of individual rights proliferate cannot be a solidary community but must be alienated, anomic, privatized, competitive and lacking in moral substance.

This debate also leads to an apparently unresolvable antinomy. On the one side, the liberal tradition itself, with its focus on individual rights and its illusions about the possibility of political neutrality, appears as the source of egoistic, disintegrative tendencies in modern society and hence as the main impediment to achieving a democratic society predicated on civic virtue. The other side counters with the contention that modern societies are precisely *not* communities integrated around a single conception of the good life. Modern civil societies are characterized by a plurality of forms of life; they are structurally differentiated and socially heterogeneous. Thus, to be able to lead a moral life, individual autonomy and individual rights must be secured. On this view, it is democracy, with its emphasis on consensus, or at least on majority rule, that is dangerous to liberty, unless suitably restricted by constitutionally guaranteed basic rights that alone can render them legitimate in the eyes of minorities.

The Defense of Welfare State vs. Neoconservative Antistatism

The debate between defenders of the welfare state and its neo-laissez-faire critics has also been going around in circles, albeit for a shorter time than the controversy plaguing democratic theory.[31] Arguments for the welfare state have been made on both economic and political grounds.[32] According to Keynesian economic doctrine, welfare state policies serve to stimulate the forces of economic growth and to prevent deep recessions by encouraging investment and stabilizing demand. Fiscal and monetary incentives for investors coupled with social insurance, transfer payments, and public services for workers compensate for the dysfunctions, uncertainties, and risks of the market mechanism and contribute to overall stability. High growth rates, full employment, and low inflation should be the result of this policy.

The political aspects of the welfare state would also increase stability and productivity. On the one side, legal entitlements to state services and transfer payments simultaneously aid those who feel the negative effects of the market system while removing potentially explosive needs or issues from the arena of industrial conflict. On the other side, the recognition of the formal role of labor unions in collective bargaining and in the formation of public policy "balances" the asymmetrical power relation between labor and capital and mitigates class conflict.[33] The overall increase in social justice would lead to fewer strikes, greater productivity, and an overall consensus of capital and labor that they have a mutual interest in the success of the political economic system: Growth and productivity serve everyone. The welfare state would finally deliver on the claim of liberal capitalist societies to be egalitarian and just, by supporting the worst off and by creating the preconditions for a true equality of opportunity, which in the eyes of defenders of the welfare state is the only context in which civil and political rights can function in a universalistic manner. Instead of being concerned by the anomalous status of the so-called social rights, for a theorist such as T. H. Marshall these represent the highest and most fundamental type of citizen rights.[34]

Certainly the remarkable growth rates, relative stability, and increase in the standard of living in postwar Western capitalist economies have, until recently, made the arguments for state intervention convincing to all but a very few. In a new context of more limited possibilities for growth, neoconservative defenders of a return to "laissez-faire" criticize both the economic and political claims of the welfare state model. Unfortunately for the latter, their arguments also carry weight. Indeed, it was not difficult for these critics to point to the high rates of unemployment and inflation and low growth rates that have plagued Western capitalist economies since the 1970s as proof that state-bureaucratic regulation of the economy is counterproductive. They can also point to successes in these domains where their own policies have been applied.

On the economic front, three claims are made against the policies of welfare states: that they lead to a disincentive to invest and a disincentive to work, and that they constitute a serious threat to the viability of the independent middle class.[35] The burden imposed by the regulatory and fiscal policies on capital together with the power of unions to extract high wages allegedly contribute to declining growth rates and, in a context of severe competition, lead to the perception that investment in home markets will be unprofitable.[36] The disincentive to work is attributed to extensive social security and unemployment provisions that allow workers to avoid undesirable jobs and to escape the normal pressure of market forces. The quantity of available workers shrinks as whole sectors of the working class are turned into welfare state clients, while the work ethic declines as workers become simultaneously more demanding and less willing to spend effort on their work. Finally, the independent middle class finds itself squeezed by high rates of taxation and inflation. The emergence of the "new middle class" of civil service professionals and higher-level bureaucrats only exacerbates these problems because these strata have an interest in reproducing and expanding the client population on which their jobs depend. Welfare state economic policies are thus antinomic in more than one respect: Policies meant to stimulate demand undermine investment, policies meant to provide economic security for workers undermine the willingness to work, the policy of tempering the undesirable side effects deriving from unregulated market forces creates even greater economic problems in the form of a vastly expanded, expensive, unproductive state sector.

On the political front, neoconservatives argue that the very mechanisms introduced by welfare states to resolve conflicts and create greater equality of opportunity, namely legal entitlements and the expanded state sector, have led to new conflicts and have violated the rights and liberty of some for the sake of others. By impinging upon the core right of liberal market systems, namely, private property, state intervention and regulation undermine both the liberty of entrepreneurs and the incentive to achieve on the part of the working population. Far from increasing social justice or equality of opportunity, welfare undermines the preconditions for both of these. In short, it rewards failure rather than success. In the name of equality, moreover, state intervention in the everyday lives of its clients poses a severe threat to liberty, privacy, and autonomy.

In addition, these mechanisms have allegedly generated a set of rising expectations and increasing demands that lead to an overall situation of ungovernability.[37] Indeed, the very institutions of welfare state mass democracy that promised to channel political conflict into acceptable and harmless forms (the end of ideology) and to integrate workers especially into the political and economic system of late capitalism (deradicalization)—i.e., the competitive (catchall) party system based on universal suffrage, interest group politics, collective bargaining, and extensive social rights—lead to a dangerous overload of the political system and a crisis of authority.[38] In short, the rights explosion that so irritates democratic communitarians is even more alarming to neoconservative critics of "statism." By placing obligations upon itself that it cannot possibly fulfill,[39] the state creates rising yet unsatisfiable expectations, becomes overexpanded and weak at the same time, and suffers from a dangerous loss of authority. Indeed, on this view, there is a central political contradiction inherent in the welfare state: In order for the performance capacity of the state to be enhanced vis-à-vis the number of demands, the very freedoms, modes of participation, and sets of rights associated with it would have to be curtailed.[40]

The neo-laissez-faire economic and political alternatives, however, do not escape the fate of becoming merely one of the untenable sides of an antinomic structure. "Supply-side" economists seek to dismantle the welfare state in order to eliminate the "disincentive" to invest, but to do so would be to abolish precisely those "buffers" that stabilize demand.[41] If the socioeconomic supports for workers and the poor are terminated in the name of refurbishing the work ethic, the compulsion of the market will certainly return, but so will the gross injustices, dissatisfaction, instability, and class confrontations that characterized the capitalist economies prior to welfare state policies.

Of course, the attack on the welfare state is predicated on the idea that there is an unlimited growth potential for marketable goods and services that would be unleashed once the state is pushed back into its proper, minimal terrain. Privatization and deregulation would allegedly restore competition and end the inflation of political demands. However, the political presuppositions for such a policy conflict with its goals of social peace and social justice. Necessarily repressive policies regarding the right to associate and efforts to abolish social rights ranging from social security to unemployment compensation, not to mention welfare, are scarcely conducive to consensus. While the "freedom-threatening" dimensions of state intervention, namely the regulation of proprietors, the supervision and control of clients, and the spiraling cycle of dependency, would end, so would all of the gains in social justice, equality, and rights. Moreover, efforts to restore state authority by limiting its scope and by shielding it from popular demands would not reduce state activism but would simply shift it from the political to the administrative terrain. For, if one reduces the ability of democratic institutions such as the party system, elections, and parliaments to provide for the articulation of political conflict, alternative channels, such as the neocorporatist arrangements proliferating in Western Europe, will develop. While these arrangements successfully shield the state from excess demands, they hardly indicate a shift from state to market regulation. Thus the neo-laissez-faire alternative to the "crisis" of the welfare state is as internally contradictory as the illness it purports to cure.

We are accordingly left with the following antinomy: Either we choose more social engineering, more paternalism and leveling, in short, more statism, in the name of egalitarianism and social rights, or we opt for the free market and/or the refurbishing of authoritarian social and political forms of organization and relinquish the democratic, egalitarian components of our political culture in order to block further bureaucratization of everyday life. It seems that liberal democratic market societies cannot coexist with, nor can they exist without, the welfare state.

Revival of the Concept of Civil Society

The early modern concept of civil society was revived first and foremost in the struggles of the democratic oppositions in Eastern Europe against authoritarian socialist party-states. Despite different economic and geopolitical contexts, it does not seem terribly problematic to apply the concept also to the "transitions from authoritarian rule" in Southern Europe and Latin America, above all because of the common task shared with the oppositions of the East to constitute new and stable democracies. But why should such a concept be particularly relevant to the West? Is not the revival of the discourse of civil society in the East and the South simply part of a project to attain what the advanced capitalist democracies already have: civil society guaranteed by the rule of law, civil rights, parliamentary democracy, and a market economy? Could one not argue that struggles in the name of creating civil and political society especially in the East are a kind of repeat of the great democratic movements of the eighteenth and nineteenth centuries that created a type of duality between state and civil society which remains the basis for Western democratic and liberal institutions? And isn't this an admission that the elite theorists, the neoconservatives, or at best the liberals are right after all? Put this way, the revival of the discourse of civil society appears to be just that, a revival, with little political or theoretical import for Western liberal democracies. And if this is so, why would a civil-society-oriented perspective provide a way out of the antinomies plaguing *Western* political and social thought?

Several interrelated issues that have emerged in the current revival go beyond the model of the historical origins of civil society in the West and therefore have important lessons to offer established liberal democracies. These include the conception of self-limitation, the idea of civil society as comprised of social movements as well as a set of institutions, the orientation to civil society as a new terrain of democratization,[42] the influence of civil on political and economic society, and finally an understanding that the liberation of civil society is not necessarily identical with the creation of bourgeois society but rather involves a choice between a plurality of types of civil society. All these notions point beyond a restriction of the theory of civil society merely to the constituent phase of new democracies.

The idea of self-limitation, all too often confused with the strategic constraints on emancipatory movements, is actually based on learning in the service of democratic principle. The postrevolutionary or self-limiting "revolutions" of the East are no longer motivated by fundamentalist projects of suppressing bureaucracy, economic rationality, or social division. Movements rooted in civil society have learned from the revolutionary tradition that these fundamentalist projects lead to the breakdown of societal steering and productivity and the suppression of social plurality, all of which are then reconstituted by the forces of order only by dramatically authoritarian means. Such an outcome leads to the collapse of the forms of self-organization that in many cases were the major carriers of the revolutionary process: revolutionary societies, councils, movements. Paradoxically, the self-limitation of just such actors allows the continuation of their social role and influence beyond the constituent and into the constituted phase.

This continuation of a role of civil society beyond the phase of transition can be coupled with domestication, demobilization, and relative atomization. That would mean convergence with society as the Western elite pluralists see it. But in the postauthoritarian settings actors who have rejected fundamentalism and raised civil society to a normative principle show that we do have a choice. While the total democratization of state and economy cannot be their goal, civil society itself, as Tocqueville was first to realize, is an important terrain of democratization, of democratic institution building. And if East European oppositionals were driven to this alternative at first only by blockages in the sphere of state organization, there is certainly a good chance that the idea of the further democratization of civil society will gain emphasis in the face of the inevitable disappointments, visible above all in Hungary, (East)

Germany, and Czechoslovakia, with the emergence of the typical practices of Western democracies. Thus, the actors of the new political societies would do well, if they value their long-term legitimacy, to promote democratic institution building in civil society, even if this seems to increase the number of social demands on them.

The idea of the democratization of civil society, unlike that of its mere revival, is extremely pertinent to existing Western societies. Indeed, the tendency to see extrainstitutional movements and initiatives in addition to settled institutions as integral parts of civil society is found earlier in Western than in Eastern experience, to which it is rapidly being extended primarily by new and old movements and initiatives. It is quite possible that some of the emerging Eastern constitutions will embody new sensitivity to an active civil society, a sensitivity that should in turn influence Western constitutional developments. These potential normative gains will confirm, in the East as well as the West, the idea that there can be very different types of civil society: more or less institutionalized, more or less democratic, more or less active. Discussions in the milieu of Solidarity in Poland raised these choices explicitly as early as 1980, along with the choice of political vs. antipolitical models of civil society. In the current wave of economic liberalism in Poland, Czechoslovakia, and Hungary, another question inevitably arises concerning the connection between economy and civil society and the choice between an economic, individualistic society and a civil society based on solidarity, protected not only against the bureaucratic state but also against the self-regulating market economy. This debate, too, will be directly relevant in Western contexts, as it already has been in Latin America, and conversely Western controversies around the welfare state and the "new social movements" should have much intellectual material to offer Eastern radical democrats hoping to protect the resource of solidarity without paternalism.

The aim of our book is to further develop and systematically justify the idea of civil society, reconceived in part around a notion of self-limiting democratizing movements seeking to expand and protect spaces for both negative liberty and positive freedom and to recreate egalitarian forms of solidarity without impairing economic self-regulation. Before turning to this task, we would like to conclude this introduction by illustrating the important, and perhaps decisive, contribution of our theory of civil society to the three theoretical antinomies mentioned above.[43]

Civil Society and Contemporary Political Theory

It might seem that our position is already anticipated by one of the six theoretical traditions involved in the debates depicted above, namely the pluralist version of the elite democratic tradition of political theory.[44] Indeed, the pluralists' addition to the elite model of democracy is precisely a conception of a "third realm" differentiated from the economy and the state (what we call "civil society").[45] On the pluralist analysis, a highly articulated civil society with cross-cutting cleavages, overlapping memberships of groups, and social mobility is the presupposition for a stable democratic polity, a guarantee against permanent domination by any one group and against the emergence of fundamentalist mass movements and antidemocratic ideologies.[46] Moreover, a civil society so constituted is considered to be capable of acquiring influence over the political system through the articulation of interests that are "aggregated" by political parties and legislatures and brought to bear on political decision making, itself understood along the lines of the elite model of democracy.

Although we use many of the terms of this analysis in our work on civil society, our approach differs in several key respects from that of the pluralists. First, we do not accept the view that the "civic culture" most appropriate to a modern civil society is one based on civil privatism and political apathy. As is well known, the pluralists value involvement in one's family, private clubs, voluntary associations, and the like as activities that deflect from political participation or activism on the part of citizens.[47] It is this which allegedly makes for a stable democratic polity. Moreover, it makes no difference to this model what the internal structure of the institutions and organizations of civil society is.[48] Indeed, in their haste to replace "utopian (participatory democratic) principles" with realism, the pluralists tend to consider attempts to apply the egalitarian norms of civil society to social institutions as naive.[49]

We do not share this view. Instead, we build upon the thesis of one of the most important predecessors of the pluralist approach, Alexis de Tocqueville, who argued that without *active* participation on the part of citizens in *egalitarian* institutions and civil associations, as well as in politically relevant organizations, there will be no way to maintain the democratic character of the political culture or of social and political institutions. Precisely because modern civil society is based on egalitarian principles and universal inclusion, experience in articulating the political will and in collective decision making is crucial to the reproduction of democracy.

This, of course, is the point that is always made by participation theorists. Our approach differs from theirs in arguing for more, not less, structural differentiation. We take seriously the normative principles defended by radical democrats, but we locate the genesis of democratic legitimacy and the chances for direct participation not in some idealized, dedifferentiated polity but within a highly differentiated model of civil society itself. This shifts the core problematic of democratic theory away from descriptive and/or speculative models to the issue of the relation and channels of influence between civil and political society and between both and the state, on the one side, and to the institutional makeup and internal articulation of civil society itself, on the other. Moreover, we believe that the democratization of civil society—the family, associational life, and the public sphere—necessarily helps open up the framework of political parties and representative institutions.[50]

Indeed, these concerns open the way to a dynamic conception of civil society, one that avoids the apologetic thrust of most pluralist analyses. Far from viewing social movements as antithetical to either the democratic political system or to a properly organized social sphere (the pluralists' view), we consider them to be a key feature of a vital, modern, civil society and an important form of citizen participation in public life. Yet we do not see social movements as prefiguring a form of citizen participation that will or even ought to substitute for the institutional arrangements of representative democracy (the radical democratic position). In our view, social movements for the expansion of rights, for the defense of the autonomy of civil society, and for its further democratization are what keep a democratic political culture alive. Among other things, movements bring new issues and values into the public sphere and contribute to reproducing the consensus that the elite/pluralist model of democracy presupposes but never bothers to account for.[51] Movements can and should supplement and should not aim to replace competitive party systems. Our conception of civil society thus retains the normative core of democratic theory while remaining compatible with the structural presuppositions of modernity. Finally, while we also differentiate the economy from civil society, we differ from the pluralists in that we do not seal off the borders between them on the basis of an allegedly sacrosanct freedom of contract or property right. Nor do we seek to "reembed" the economy in society. Instead, on our analysis, the principles of civil society can be brought to bear on economic institutions within what we call economic society. The question here, as in the case of the polity, is what channels and receptors of influence do, can, and ought to exist.[52] Indeed, we are able to pose such questions on the basis of our model without risking the charges of utopianism or antimodernism so frequently and deservedly leveled against worker-based versions of radical democracy.

It is also our thesis that the tensions between rights-oriented liberalism and, at least, democratically oriented communitarianism can be considerably diminished if not entirely overcome on the basis of a new theory of civil society. While the idea of rights and of a democratic political community derive from distinct traditions in political philosophy, today they belong to the same political culture. They need not be construed as antithetical, although on an empirical level the rights of an individual may conflict with majority rule and "the public interest," necessitating a balancing between the two sides.[53] Nor is it necessary to view these as based on two conflicting sets of principles or presuppositions, such that one could accommodate the first set only insofar as it is instrumental to the achievement or preservation of the other. On the contrary, we contend that what is best in rights-oriented liberalism and democratically oriented communitarianism constitutes two mutually reinforcing and partly overlapping sets of principles. Two steps are necessary to argue this thesis and to transcend the relevant antinomies. First, one must show that there is a philosophical framework that can provide a political ethic able to redeem the normative claims of both rights-oriented liberalism and radical democracy. Second, one must revise the conception of civil society as the private sphere, shared by both theoretical paradigms, in order to grasp the institutional implications of such an ethic.

We also defend the principles of universality and autonomy to which the rights thesis is wed, but we deny that this commits us either to the liberal notion of neutrality or to an individualist ontology. The communitarians are right: Much of liberal theory, especially the contract tradition from Hobbes to Rawls, has relied on either one or both of these principles.[54] However, the Habermasian theory of discourse ethics, on which we rely, provides a way to develop conceptions of universality and autonomy that are free of such presuppositions. On this theory, universality does not mean neutrality with respect to a plurality of values or forms of life but rather refers, in the first instance, to the metanorms of symmetric reciprocity[55] that are to act as regulative principles guiding discursive processes of conflict resolution and, in the second instance, to those norms or principles to which all those who are potentially affected can agree. The procedure of universalization defended here involves an actual rather than a hypothetical dialogue. It does not require that one abstract from one's concrete situation, need interpretations, or interests in order to engage in an unbiased moral testing of principles. Instead, it requires that these be freely articulated. It also requires that all those potentially affected by institutionalized norms (laws or policies) be open to a multiplicity of perspectives. Accordingly, universality is a regulative principle of a discursive process in and through which participants reason together about which values, principles, need-interpretations merit being institutionalized as common norms.[56] Thus, the atomistic disembodied individual allegedly presupposed by procedural (deontological) ethics is most emphatically not the basis of this approach. Assuming that individual and collective identities are acquired through complex processes of socialization that involve both internalizing social norms or traditions, and developing reflective and critical capacities vis-à-vis norms, principles, and traditions, this theory has at its core an intersubjective, interactive conception of both individuality and autonomy. It is thus able to accommodate the communitarian insights into the social core of human nature without abandoning the ideas of either universality or moral rights. Indeed, discourse ethics provides a philosophical basis for democratic legitimacy that presupposes valid rights, even if not all of these rights are derivable from it.[57]

While it is of course individuals who have rights, the concept of rights does not have to rest on philosophical or methodological individualism, nor, for that matter, on the idea of negative liberty alone. Although most liberal and communitarian theorists have assumed that such a conception of freedom and of individualism is presupposed by the very concept of rights, we believe that only some rights involve primarily negative liberty while none requires a philosophically atomistic conception of individuality. It is here that a revised conception of civil society, together with a new theory of rights, must enter into the analysis. For every theory of rights, every theory of democracy, implies a model of society. Unfortunately, communitarians and liberals also agree that the *societal* analogue of the rights thesis is a civil society construed as the private sphere, composed of an agglomeration of autonomous but egoistic, exclusively self-regarding, competitive, possessive individuals whose negative liberty it is the polity's task to protect. It is their assessments and not their analysis of this form of society that diverge.

But this is only one possible version of civil society and certainly not the only one that can be "derived" from the rights thesis. Only if one construes property to be not simply a key right but the core of the conception of rights—only, that is, if one places the philosophy of possessive individualism at the heart of one's conception of civil society and then reduces civil to bourgeois society—does the rights thesis come to be defined in this way.[58] If, however, one develops a more complex model of civil society, recognizing that it has public and associational components as well as individual, private ones, and if, in addition, one sees that the idea of moral autonomy does not presuppose possessive individualism,[59] then the rights thesis begins to look a bit different. In short, rights do not only secure negative liberty, the autonomy of private, disconnected individuals. They also secure the autonomous (freed from state control) *communicative interaction* of individuals with one another in the public and private spheres of civil society, as well as a new relation of individuals to the public and the political spheres of society and state (including, of course, citizenship rights). Moral rights are thus not by definition apolitical or antipolitical, nor do they constitute an exclusively private domain with respect to which the state must limit itself. On the contrary, the rights to communication, assembly, and association, among others, constitute the public and associational spheres of civil society as spheres of *positive freedom* within which agents can collectively debate issues of common concern, act in concert, assert new rights, and exercise influence on political (and potentially economic) society. Democratic as well as liberal principles have their locus here. Accordingly, some form of differentiation of civil society, the state, and the economy is the basis for both modern democratic and liberal institutions. The latter presuppose neither atomistic nor communal but rather associated selves. Moreover, on this conception the radical opposition between the philosophical foundations and societal presuppositions of rights-oriented liberalism and democratically oriented communitarianism dissolves. This conception of civil society does not, of course, solve the question of the relation between negative and positive liberty, but it does place this issue within a common societal and philosophical terrain. It is on this terrain that we learn how to compromise, take reflective distance from our own perspective so as to entertain others, learn to value difference, recognize or create anew what we have in common, and come to see which dimensions of our traditions are worth preserving and which ought to be abandoned or changed.

This brings us to the heart of our differences with the neoconservative model of civil society. The neoconservative slogan, "society against the state," is often based on a model in which civil society is equivalent to market or bourgeois society. Another version of this approach does, however, recognize the importance of the cultural dimension of civil society. We have serious objections even to this second version, whose strategies for unburdening the state are aimed in part at the institutions involved in the formation and transmission of cultural values (art, religion, science) and in socialization (families, schools). An important component of the neoconservative thesis of "ungovernability" is the argument that the excessive material demands placed by citizens on the state are due not only to welfare institutions themselves but also to our modernist political, moral, and aesthetic culture. The latter allegedly weakens both traditional values and the agencies of social control (such as the family) that tempered hedonism in the past.[60] In this view, we need to resacralize our political culture, revive faltering traditional values such as self-restraint, discipline, and respect for authority and achievement, and shore up "nonpolitical" principles of order (family, property, religion, schools), so that a culture of self-reliance and self-restraint replaces the culture of dependency and critique.[61] The cultural politics of neoconservatism that accompanies the policies of deregulation and privatization are thus based on the defense or re-creation of a traditionalist and authoritarian lifeworld.[62]

Our conception of civil society points to a different assessment. First, we try to show that the resources for meaning, authority, and social integration are undermined not by cultural or political modernity (based on the principles of critical reflection, discursive conflict resolution, equality, autonomy, participation, and justice) but, rather, by the expansion of an increasingly illiberal corporate economy as well as by the overextension of the administrative apparatus of the interventionist state into the social realm. The use of economic and political power to shore up (or worse, re-create) the "traditional" hierarchical, patriarchal, or exclusionary character of many of the institutions of civil society is, on our view, what fosters dependency. We agree that certain features of the welfare state[63] fragment collectivities, destroy horizontal solidarities, isolate and render private individuals dependent on state apparatuses. Unrestrained capitalist expansion, however, has the same destructive consequences. But appeals to family, tradition, religion, or community could foster the destructive fundamentalism of false communities so easily manipulated from above, unless the achievements of liberalism (the principle of rights), democracy (the principles of participation and discourse), and justice (a precondition for solidarity) are first defended and then supplemented with new democratic and egalitarian forms of association within civil society.

Moreover, to opt for the preservation of traditions, if accompanied by a denial of the universalist tradition of cultural and political modernity, implies fundamentalism. Accordingly, the question that flows from our model becomes: Which traditions, which family form, which community, which solidarities are to be defended against disruptive intervention? Even if cultural modernity itself is just one tradition among many, its universal thrust is the reflexive, nonauthoritarian relation toward tradition—an orientation that can be applied to itself and that implies autonomy (allegedly cherished by the neoconservative) rather than heteronomy. Indeed, traditions that have become problematic can be preserved only on the terrain of cultural modernity, i.e., through arguments that invoke principles. Such discussion does not mean the abolition of tradition, solidarity, or meaning; rather, it is the only acceptable procedure for adjudicating between competing traditions, needs, or interests that are in conflict. Accordingly, our model points toward the *further* modernization of the culture and institutions of civil society as the only way to arrive at autonomy, self-reliance, and solidarity among peers allegedly desired by the neoconservative critics of the welfare state.[64]

Our conception of civil society seeks to demystify the other strain within neoconservatism, namely, that the only alternative to the paternalism, social engineering, and the bureaucratization of our lives typical of welfare state systems is to shift steering back to the magic of the marketplace (and of course to renounce distributive justice and egalitarianism). This "solution" is not only politically untenable and normatively undesirable; it is also based on the fallacious assumption that no other options exist. Our framework, however, allows in principle for a third approach, one that does not seek to correct the economic or state penetration of society by shifting back and forth between these two steering mechanisms. Instead, the task is to guarantee the autonomy of the modern state and economy while simultaneously protecting civil society from destructive penetration and functionalization by the imperatives of these two spheres. For now, of course, we have only some of the elements of a theory that can thematize both the differentiation of civil society from state and economy and its reflexive influence over them through the institutions of political and economic society. But we believe that our conception has the best prospects for future theoretical progress and for integrating the diverse conceptual strategies that are currently available. The project it implies would avoid correcting the results of state paternalism by another form of colonization of society, this time by an unregulated market economy. It would seek to accomplish the work of social policy by more decentralized and autonomous civil-society-based programs than in traditional welfare states and the work of economic regulation by nonbureaucratic, less intrusive forms of legislation, "reflexive law," focusing on procedures and not results.[65] In our view this synthetic project should be described not only by Habermas's term, "the reflexive continuation of the welfare state," but also by the complementary idea of the "reflexive continuation of the democratic revolution." The former arises in the context of Western welfare states, the latter in that of the democratization of authoritarian regimes. The two ideas can and should be combined. Thus far, the recent revival and development of the concept of civil society has involved learning from the experience of the "transitions to democracy." The idea of the reflexive continuation of the welfare state and of liberal democracy should, however, open the way for enriching the intellectual resources of democrats in the East by what has been learned in a double critique of already established welfare states and of their neoconservative discontents. A theory of civil society informed by such ideas should also inform the projects of all those in the West who seek the further democratization of liberal democracies.

I

The Discourse of Civil Society

1
The Contemporary Revival of Civil Society

Phrases involving the *resurrection, reemergence, rebirth, reconstruction,* or *renaissance* of civil society are heard repeatedly today. These terms, indicating the continuity of an emerging political paradigm with essential trends of early modernity, are misleading in one important respect: They refer not only to something *modern* but also to something significantly *new.* A simple chronology derived in part from Karl Polànyi might, in an extremely preliminary way, indicate what is at stake. According to Polànyi, during most of the nineteenth century, forces representing the capitalist self-regulating market economy were on the offensive, claiming an identity with the liberal society that was in the process of emancipating itself from the absolutist and paternalistic state. Polànyi, however, rightly stressed that in the late nineteenth century and through much of the twentieth century a reversal had taken place. Now, elites representing the logic and goals of the modern state were successfully claiming to express the interests of a heterogeneous set of social groups and tendencies resisting and challenging the destructive trends of capitalist market society. Not even Polànyi, however, foresaw that the statist phase would also have its limits. For a period of more than a decade and a half now, citizen initiatives, associations, and movements have increasingly oriented themselves toward the defense and expansion of a variously described societal realm, the forms and projects of which are clearly distinguished from statism.

Two crucial ambiguities remain from the orientation "society against the state." First, while increasingly significant groupings of collective actors reject any representation of their program in terms of communitarianism, others continue to defend an idealized *Gemeinschaft* or premodern network of communities, traditional solidarities, and collectives against modernity itself. Second, there are various neoconservative, neoliberal, and libertarian initiatives (rarely movements, but with significant force behind them) that identify "society" with market economy. Both of these trends are regressive versions of antistatism. The first wishes to retreat behind the modern state, thus eliminating an essential precondition of modernity itself; the second wishes to repeat the already failed experiment with the fully self-regulated market economy of classical capitalism. There is no chance of the first trend registering even temporary successes, although it will continue to have a role within most social movements. The second trend, wherever successful, threatens to transform history into oscillation between economic liberalism and paternalist statism.

We believe there are today important elements of a third project for retrieving the category of *civil society* from the tradition of classical political theory. These involve attempts to thematize a program that seeks to represent the values and interests of social autonomy in face of *both* the modern state and the capitalist economy, without falling into a new traditionalism. Beyond the antinomies of state and market, public and private, *Gesellschaft* and *Gemeinschaft*, and, as we shall show, reform and revolution, the idea of the defense *and* the democratization of civil society is the best way to characterize the really new, common strand of contemporary forms of self-organization and self-constitution.

Problems of self-reflection and self-understanding within the movements and the initiatives themselves sometimes prevent them from clearly recognizing their own difference with communalism or libertarianism. At best the difference represents a stake that must be internally contested. Behind the many ambiguities of meaning tied up with the concept of civil society stand such conflicts. In company with many participants, our book takes a clear stand in these conflicts on behalf of a *modern* civil society capable of preserving its autonomy and forms of solidarity in face of the modern *economy* as well as the state.

Such a project emerges from contexts of social and political conflicts themselves. In this chapter we present the idea by examining several discourses that have revived the category of civil society (albeit in different versions) in order to critically interpret the political contexts of East and West, North and South. Without aiming at a complete presentation of all related views within each context, we deliberately stress perspectives in each that can be compared with those in the other contexts. We shall attempt to identify the common strands, the alternative models, the significant differences as well as the conceptual unclarities in these forms of interpretation and self-interpretation. The rest of this book will, we hope, contribute to the further development of the discourse of civil society and thereby benefit the actors and interpreters we present in this chapter.

The Polish Democratic Opposition

The opposition of civil society and state made its most dramatic return in East Europe, particularly in the ideology of the Polish opposition from 1976 to the advent of early Solidarity and beyond. The juxtapositions are well known: society *against* the state, nation *against* state, social order *against* political system, *pays réel against pays légal* or *officiel*, public life *against* the state, private life *against* public power, etc. The idea was always the protection and/or self-organization of social life in the face of the totalitarian or authoritarian state. Adam Michnik provided the theoretical elaboration of this conception under the heading of "new evolutionism."[1] He also discovered the historical conditions of its possibility: the failure of a potentially total revolution from below (Hungary in 1956), and the demise of a process of reform from above (Czechoslovakia in 1968).[2] Michnik drew two lessons from these defeats. First, the transformation of the Soviet-type system of East Central Europe was possible only within limits whose thresholds were the alliance system (threatened in Hungary in 1956) and the confirmation of the control of state institutions by a Soviet-type Communist party (challenged in different forms both in Hungary and in Czechoslovakia in 1968). Second, neither revolution from below nor reform from above would work as the strategy for achieving what was in fact possible.

The point of view of civil society in this context aims at a twofold reorientation. First, the juxtaposition of society against the state indicates not only the battlelines but also a shift concerning the target of democratization, from the whole social system to society outside of state institutions proper. Thus, while the conception surely implies a pushing back of the state-administrative forms of penetration from various dimensions of social life, it has, nevertheless, the idea of self-limitation built into it from the start: The leading role of the party in the (albeit shrinking) state sphere will not be challenged.

Second, the conception also indicates that the agent or the subject of the transformation must be an independent or rather a self-organizing society aiming not at social revolution but at structural reform achieved as a result of organized pressure from below. These two aspects are brought together by the term "self-limiting revolution" coined by Jacek Kuron in the period of Solidarity. At that time, the new conception truly came into its own, showing its formidable powers in promoting the self-understanding of new types of social actors. Nevertheless, it should be noted that the "new evolutionism" or the "self-limiting revolution" represented both a strategic and a normative break with the revolutionary tradition whose logic was understood to be undemocratic and inconsistent with the self-organization of society.[3] All major revolutions from the French to the Russian and the Chinese not only demobilized the social forces on which they originally depended but also established dictatorial conditions that were meant to block the reemergence of such forces at their very root for as long as possible. The project of "self-limiting revolution" has, of course, the opposite goal: the construction from below of a highly articulated, organized, autonomous, and mobilizable civil society.

Leaving aside for now the overall theoretical cogency of the conception, we must note some serious ambiguities in its elaboration in the milieu of the Polish democratic opposition.[4] Are the terms "society" and "civil society" the same? After all, they both refer to a plurality of forms of independent groups (associations, institutions, collectives, interest representations) as well as forms of independent public opinion and communication. Put another way, how can civil society be both the agent of social transformation and its result? One could, of course, try to resolve the difficulty by distinguishing between society and civil society. The latter would represent a version of the former, institutionalized by legal mechanisms or rights, as in the Gdansk and subsequent agreements of August and September 1980.[5] But the ambiguity would remain, because "rights" in an authoritarian state-socialist setting (lack of independent courts; lack of a clear, unambiguous legal code; lack of an organized legal profession) are easily revocable not only in principle but also in a political practice that depends on constant demonstration of this revocability. Moreover, institutional continuity can apparently be achieved by public enlightenment and self-organization even without rights, as witnessed by the durability and growth of autonomous forms of culture in the twelve-year period after 1976.[6]

Another set of conceptual difficulties revolves around the interpretation of the notion of society, of social self-organization in a supposedly totalitarian setting. Here one view (Michnik) stressed the obliteration of all social solidarities and the resulting social atomization, except for carefully defined institutional complexes (the church) or historical periods (1956, 1970–71, and after 1976). Another position, more consistent with the theory of the new evolutionism, insisted on the failure of totalitarianism, whatever its intentions, to truly atomize society, or to completely disorganize families, face-to-face groups, and cultural networks.[7] This position, however, would have required the working out of a paradigm to replace the totalitarianism thesis as the theoretical framework of the "new evolutionism," something never actually attempted.

More serious in principle is the lack of clarity regarding the type of civil society that is to be constructed or reconstructed. The conceptual confusion derives above all from a common unwillingness to take an openly critical attitude toward the liberal model of civil society, despite participation in a solidaristic workers' movement that is, in many respects, incompatible with this model. In the 1980s more and more people (e.g., Krol, Spievak, the editors of *Respublica*) came to champion a version of the liberal model, based on economic individualism and freedoms of property and enterprise as the central rights. Even within the milieu of those close to Solidarity in its first great period (1980–81), there were disagreements over the various conceptions of civil society. Cultural models (Wojcicki) were counterposed to political conceptions (the Committee for the Defense of Workers, or KOR), on the one hand, while the level of democracy needed in popular movements and institutions was hotly debated, on the other. Whereas it was generally recognized that the new civil society was to be pluralistic,[8] the need for a single, all-encompassing organization to respond to the interest of this plurality was temporarily accepted.[9] But once such an organization emerged and managed to survive in the face of "totalitarian" power, could its unitary and all-encompassing tendency be easily disposed of?

Formulating a dualistic civil society and state framework proved even more difficult, especially in practical politics. Was civil society, as represented by Solidarity, to be entirely apolitical, disinterested in "power," or was it to be expanded as a self-governing republic making a state in the old sense more or less superfluous? Sometimes aspects of each conception are to be found even in the same author.[10] Would a self-coordinating system of society not negate the idea of self-limitation if the party-state were left only as a representative of Soviet power, in charge of military, police, and foreign policy and partially converted into an expert bureaucracy?[11] If, on the other hand, the dualistic conception requires institutional mechanisms of compromise between societal organizations and party-state institutions, does the idea of building a hybrid system based on a new type of society next to an unreformed party-state make sense? And if a reform of official institutions, especially the party itself, must be hoped for and even promoted, if party pragmatists could be looked upon as partners even if not allies, could the much insisted-upon independent identity of the social movement be maintained?[12] What would be the point of this if on many issues party pragmatists and sectors of the movement are closer to one another than potentially different elements of the antistate opposition? It is insufficient to reply that only an organized society, conscious of its identity, is capable of compromise, for just this unity tended to demobilize potential partners in the party. The deep identity problems of the ruling party could hardly be solved in the face of an organized society successfully reclaiming all legitimacy. Without a new party identity, party pragmatists lost all freedom of action. And for the party leadership, without legitimacy, the only freedom of action left was the exercise of raw sovereign power.[13]

Many of the difficulties touched upon here pointed toward the failure to rebuild civil society or at least a stable version of it. Yet the failure itself produced a new set of social relations that could again be reinterpreted in terms of a new model of opposition between state and society. Thus in the context of the failure of "normalization," the original "new evolutionist" conception remained the basic form of orientation for theorist-activists such as Michnik. Undoubtedly the fact that it was now the turn of the martial law state to practice (reluctant) self-limitation reinvigorated the idea that an independent society could somehow be defended. "Independent civil society" was not, according to Michnik, annihilated. "Instead of resembling a Communist system after victorious pacification, this situation resembles a democracy after a military coup d'état."[14]

Despite the reappearance of martial metaphors such as "a dramatic wrestling match between the totalitarian power and a society searching for a way to attain autonomy" and "the stationary war between an organized civil society and the power apparatus,"[15] the new situation was nevertheless one that indicated the coming into its own of the cultural model of independent society. The major independent activities were publishing, lecturing, discussing, and teaching. For several years, the hope seems to have been the building of the moral bases of democratic structures and practices, i.e., a democratic political culture. While the army-state seemed powerless against these trends, it was rather successful in marginalizing its major political opponent: underground Solidarity. The latter, however, linked to the mechanisms of independent culture, continued to survive and play a role.

Nevertheless, in this context, the democratic opposition moving within the paradigm of civil society had to face the question of how and when the survival and even the dramatic expansion of an independent culture, more and more pluralized ideologically, could be a foundation for the reemergence of aboveground political organizations capable of making effective demands. The regime's inability to deal with the same economic crisis that was used in 1980–81 to help erode the resistance of the population provided new opportunities for the opposition. The strategy to restore the regime's legitimacy through a relatively free referendum, and thereby to recover freedom of action to impose an austerity program, failed in 1987 in the face of an only partially organized opposition. In this context and that of the strike movements during the spring and summer of 1988, it became clear that the regime needed partners to be able to initiate significant policy, and that only a reconstituted Solidarity could command sufficiently wide loyalty to become a credible partner.

From the point of view of Solidarity's leadership, given the economic crisis and the prospects of simultaneously weakening both regime and opposition in a continuing process of polarization, it would certainly have been counterproductive not to promote and utilize reforms from above, as long these involved real gains in institutionalizing a genuine civil society.[16] After the negotiated "resolution" of the second strike wave, the issue seems to have been the following: Could the regime yield enough concessions that would be adequate trade-offs for legitimizing the deep austerity measures required for successful economic reform? While such concessions even minimally had to involve legalizing elements of civil society, it was not at all clear that a version sufficiently democratic for the population and still acceptable to elements of the regime could be found. It was not clear, furthermore, whether the minimum unity of a society with different interests and increasingly differentiated ideologies could be maintained even in an emergency situation in which there were no longer any alternatives other than radical change or social decay. But could radical change still be conceptualized within the framework of opposing civil society to the state?[16a]

The Ideology of the "Second Left" in France

It is not only under authoritarian regimes that the problem of democratization gets posed in terms of the reconstruction of civil society. The category was revived in France in the mid-1970s as a prime referent for democratic projects on the part of significant groups of intellectuals and a variety of collective actors.[17] Of course it was here that the critique of totalitarianism and sympathy for East European dissidence had the greatest intellectual importance.[18] And here, too, totalitarianism was defined as the absorption of independent social life of "civil society" by the party/state, involving the replacement of all social ties by statized relations. It seems clear that the French "discourse" of civil society derived from a sympathetic understanding of developments in the East. But could a category so derived be made applicable to a Western capitalist society with a multiparty parliamentary state?

In France three arguments have been used to justify this theoretical move. First, and most like the East, the political culture of the French left (and not only the Communist party) is seen as deeply connected to the totalitarian phenomenon, i.e., a statist political culture deriving from an idea of revolution based on the fantasy of a society without division or conflict.[19] Paradoxically, a left that represents in its very existence societal diversity, conflict, and opposition denies just these presuppositions while hoping to use the state as the instrument of progress and as the agent of the creation of the good society beyond conflict.

Second, the actual role of the centralized, modern state in French political life is traditionally greater than in most Western democracies. With a good deal of exaggeration, one could speak here of a "totalitarian" statist tendency suppressing many dimensions of an independent "civil society."[20] Third and finally, recalling the thesis of Herbert Marcuse, or its more sophisticated French counterpart in the writings of Cornelius Castoriadis in the 1950s and early 1960s, one might also claim—again with significant exaggeration—that "capitalism has become more 'totalitarian,' engulfing all spheres of social activity under the single dimension of economic activity."[21]

The last two theses concerning the state and capitalism converge in another thesis asserting that all autonomous social solidarity is destroyed under the impact of the administrative penetration of society by the (capitalist) welfare state. Of course, this line of argument does not theoretically assimilate France to a paradigm derived from the analysis of the East. P. Rosanvallon and P. Viveret warn us that even the three theses taken together do not add up to a conception of capitalist democracies as totalitarian in the sense of Marcuse. But the limitation turns into an advantage: Whereas in the East, in fully totalitarian society, no internal opposition is allegedly possible, the totalitarian trends of French society can be met head on by countertrends involving the reconstruction of *civil* and *political* society.

It is noteworthy that the French discussion has preserved a three-part Tocquevillian distinction among civil society, political society, and state. *Civil* society is defined in terms of social associations cutting across class relations: neighborhood groups, networks of mutual aid, locally based structures providing collective service.[22] More dynamically, civil society is seen as the space of social experimentation for the development of new forms of life, new types of solidarity, and social relations of cooperation and work.[23] *Political* society, on the other hand, is understood as the space in which the autonomy of groups and the articulation of conflict among them are defended and the discussion and debate of collective choices occur.[24] The concept of political society thus includes the public sphere as its major dimension, but, given the stress on conflict (and negotiation and compromise), it is not entirely reducible to it.

Nor are civil and political society to be reduced to one another. To eliminate political society in the conception, or to treat it as civil, is to juxtapose civil society rigidly to the state. This alternative is variously (and somewhat confusingly) described by Viveret and Rosanvallon as a choice among liberalism, apolitical and utopian anarchism, or corporatism as alternatives to statism.[25] Without political mediations, however, the integrity of civil society in face of the state cannot be indefinitely stabilized; the model prefigures a new statist outcome. However, to defend and extend *only* political society, to seek to politicize all civil structures themselves, leads to an overpoliticized democratic or *autogestionaire* (self-management) utopianism of which political anarchism and council Communism have been the representative historical conceptions. It is, however, doubtful that the forms of self-organization of political society can be maintained without the protection and development of independent but apolitical forms of solidarity, interaction, and group life.

The rigid conceptual division of civil and political society is difficult to maintain in the specific form in which it is used in the French discussion. Solidarity and conflict, as well as structures of public communication, are to be found on both sides of the divide. Politically, however, the distinction makes good sense because it implies a reorientation of democratic politics away from the state to *society* without promoting the overpoliticization of society. Thus the exact translation of the revolutionary tradition into the language of democratic theory is avoided: Viveret and Rosanvallon attempt to think both democratization and the self-limitation of democracy. In other words, core components of the liberal model of civil society as the sphere of private, voluntary association secured by rights are retained in a model that also includes the "democratic" dimensions of publicity and political influence of nonprofessional actors, i.e., citizens.[26]

The point, however, is not simply to recommend a move (typical of social democracy) from revolution to democratic reformism. Both poles of the old duality, revolution or reform, oriented themselves through a structure of demands to the state[27] and to a society understood in terms of a class dichotomy. The reorientation to civil and political society relocates the locus of democratization from the state to society and understands the latter in terms of groups, associations, and public spaces primarily. As Claude Lefort argued, the actors the strategy banks upon are not classes but social movements constituted in civil society.[28] These attain a political status in the conception of Viveret and Rosanvallon through the mediations made available in political society: the reconstruction of *political parties* (replacing the no longer ideological catchall party) and the renewal of *public forums* of discussion and debate (ending the hegemony of the established media and of political communication that has been reduced to measuring nonpublic opinion, i.e., polls).

The conception of Viveret and Rosanvallon was designed to promote the self-understanding of one dimension of the French left: the so-called "second left"—oriented to the Rocard group of the 1970s in the Socialist party and to the CFDT labor union. As the original conception was further developed, the reconstruction of civil society received an even more central role in terms of the political history of the period in which the watershed was the Socialist party's coming to power. Civil society's integrity had to be preserved now even in the face of a socialist-controlled state and political society. Logically, however, since political society was understood in terms of mediation between civil society and state, its reorganization presupposed the rebuilding of more fundamental social ties. One strong strand in the then triumphant French socialism could be easily understood to endanger exactly this level through its connection to a Keynesian form of statism. As Pierre

Rosanvallon has forcefully argued, the welfare state disorganizes above all social networks, associations, and solidarities, replacing these by state-administrative relations. Not only has the welfare state in the countries of its highest development proved to be an increasingly inefficient and ineffective strategy of societal steering; more importantly, its earlier success has implied a veritable crisis of solidarity replacing forms of mutuality, self-help, and lateral co-operation by systemically organized functions. Thus, the reification of human relations in the context of social statism fully matches the effects of the capitalist market economy; a civil-society-oriented program must therefore represent not only a third way between social statism and neoliberalism but a way qualitatively different from the other two, which, despite their opposition, are seen as resembling each other in their effects on solidarity relations.

What is extremely vague in the analysis is the nature of the civil-society-based alternative, beyond the demand for a "thicker civil society" involving the creation of new networks, new forms of intermediation and association, as the sources of local and face-to-face solidarity. Evidently such a general premise is compatible with very different forms of civil society. Rosanvallon notes the failure of the communitarianism of the 1960s and 1970s and seeks to avoid a corporatist version of the return to society.[29] He is, however, skeptical concerning the very possibility of a theoretical answer to the problem of reconciling individual autonomy and new spontaneous forms of solidarity, i.e., concerning a model beyond statism, neoliberalism, corporatism, and communitarianism. In general, he convincingly asserts a complementary relation between a (nonregressive) reduction of demands on the welfare state and the building of new forms of sociability. His list concerning the latter, however, is limited. He notes the existence and importance of new forms of privately based collective service and of underground forms of nonmarket, non-state-oriented structures of economic life,[30] but he understands these as only the first and most primitive forms of what is required. The need for new types of socially generated legal structures, neither statist nor individualist, is powerfully asserted, but we find out little about the nature of such law or its relationship to existing private and public law. The projects of building new social norms, new cultural identities, and a new public sphere are vaguely postulated, but we do not find out much about the relationship of new social actors (movements) to any of these. Moreover, there is some serious ambiguity here about the relation of solidarity and conflict in constructing a new form of sociability.

The analysis is more convincing in its treatment of the problem of compromise. Rosanvallon postulates the need for compromise (1) with capitalist entrepreneurs (exchanging rationality and mobility in the use of capital for self-management and free time), (2) with the bureaucratic state (exchanging reduction of demands for the recognition of forms of autonomous collective services), and (3) within society itself, involving the construction of new, democratic forms of public debate, negotiation, and interest aggregation. It remains unclear, though, how the two post-welfare-state, post-Keynesian, post-social-democratic projects mentioned, regulation by self-management and intrasocial regulation, would have a fundamental effect capable of generating the force behind those forms of compromise. The relationship of these projects, presumably representing political (self-management) and civil (intrasocial regulation) society, respectively, is highly unclear. Here political society is introduced not so much as a political rearticulation of civil society but rather as a competing model altogether. But the notion of political society oscillating between public discussion and self-management shows its problematic nature, since the latter notion threatens to assimilate political society to the world of work or, at best, to industrial democracy. Correspondingly, the idea of intrasocial regulation oscillating between individualistic and solidaristic conceptions of civil society threatens to surrender part of what has been achieved: the critique of the statist logic of individualism. While the protection of individual rights has its legitimate place in the normative conception of a modern civil society, just as industrial democracy can be reconceived in a way perhaps analogous to a democratic political society,[31] the moments that need to be stressed in the context of the critique of the statizing and economization of society, as Rosanvallon recognizes, are solidarity and publicity. Unfortunately, it is their all too crucial relation that is left underdetermined by the tradition of French analysis we associate with the term "the second left." It may very well be the case that the eventual emergence of forms of neoliberalism in this milieu can be traced among other things to the theoretical weakness of the original conception, i.e., to the difficulty of formulating adequate concepts of civil and political society and their relationship.

A Theory for the West German Greens

A direct intellectual relationship to "antitotalitarian" or antiauthoritarian struggles for democracy is not entirely indispensable for interpreting the politics of Western democracies in terms of the category of civil society. A good case in point is West Germany, where, unlike France, the Eastern dissidents have had only a slight and ambiguous impact. There was also no need here to differentiate radical politics from that of an authoritarian mass party in the Leninist mold. To be sure, even in West Germany one could insist upon some impact of the thought of the French "second left" (especially through the writings of Gorz), and one could also stress the statist-authoritarian and even repressive political culture of the German Social Democratic Party.[32] Nevertheless, in our judgment two related developments, common to all the Western democracies including the United States, link the German rediscovery of civil society to the somewhat earlier one in France: the crisis of the welfare state, and the emergence of a neoconservative critique of "social statism."

The welfare state has often been understood not only as a mechanism of the repoliticization of the economy but also as a dissolution of the sharp boundaries between state and society. However, the crisis of the welfare state raises doubts concerning the continued effectiveness and legitimacy of state intervention into the capitalist economy as well as into the various spheres of civil society: the family, schools, cultural institutions, etc. As a whole series of radical left writers of the 1970s indicated, state intervention in the capitalist economy creates insoluble fiscal and administrative problems in the long run, while political intervention *on behalf of the capitalist economy* (especially in the context of decreasing effectiveness) is not easily legitimated in the context of democratic norms.[33] These projections turned out to be devastatingly accurate and were in fact taken up by conservative opponents of the welfare state under headings such as decline of productivity, profit squeeze, dissolution of tradition and authority, and ungovernability.[34] However, the original political alternative proposed by some of the same radical writers, a democratic statism that would exploit the repoliticization of economy and society but break its link with the private accumulation of capital, was abandoned just around the time when the diagnosis concerning the end of the welfare-state-guaranteed processes of growth was confirmed. In Germany, at least, the reason for this surprising development in the self-understanding of one key writer, Claus Offe, was the emergence of two distinct programs of society against the state: the challenges to the welfare state by neoconservatives and by the new social movements. What the two trends have in common are many aspects of an economic analysis of what went wrong with the welfare state. More importantly, each challenge was ready to move beyond a critique connected to inefficiency and dysfunction to develop a distinct, normatively based critique exploring the negative consequences of the welfare state, even at its most successful.

Leaving the economic analysis to the side,[35] the two programs of civil society against the state that emerged offer sharp contrasts. The neoconservative analysis stresses the erosion of authority as a result of the political manipulation of the nonpolitical spheres of society, leading to the introduction of conflict and controversy into the very sources of legitimacy. Authority can be refurbished, accordingly, only if *uncontestable* economic, moral, and cognitive standards are restored. Civil society is to be restored in this program, but its restoration is understood not only as a defense against the state but also, more importantly, against politics. The neoconservatives thus have in mind a model of depoliticized civil society.[36] In this interpretation of neoconservatism, the stress is on their identifying the freedom of civil society with that of the market. What remains outside the market must be reintegrated through a conservative retraditionalized cultural model and lifeworld that itself will help to integrate market society. However, it is also evident that their model seeks to strengthen the state, specifically an authoritarian version of it.[37] The boundaries of state and society are to be redrawn in their model in order to provide for a smaller but stronger state streamlined for fewer but far more effective and authoritarian forms of action. Despite explicitly aiming at such an outcome, the neoconservatives have managed to channel and focus a good deal of antiauthoritarian political sentiment produced by the various consequences of the welfare state for different spheres of life.

An alternative program for the restoration of civil society, according to Claus Offe, must begin by recognizing that "social statism" or "welfare statism" did indeed have disastrous consequences for whole strata, for forms of life, for forms of participation, solidarity, and autonomy. Here his analysis duplicates those of French "second left" critics of statism. The program of the new social movements for the reconstitution of civil society that Offe calls one of nonstatist socialism[38] makes no concessions to economic privatism or to statist authoritarianism. This program

seeks to politicize the institutions of civil society in ways that are not constrained by the channels of representative-bureaucratic political institutions, and thereby *reconstitutes* a civil society that is no longer dependent upon ever more regulation, control, and intervention. In order to emancipate itself from the state, civil society itself—its institutions of work, production, distribution, family relations, relations with nature, its very standards of rationality and progress—must be politicized through practices that belong to an intermediate sphere between "private" pursuits and concerns, on the one side, and institutional, state-sanctioned modes of politics, on the other.[39]

Two not entirely consistent features of this conception need to be stressed. Behind it lies a defense of modern but postmaterial values inherited from the new left of the 1960s that contrast participation, autonomy, and solidarity with consumption, efficiency, and growth. Thus the model of civil society here is that of a culturally defined framework of the social, to be distinguished from economic and political models. On the other side, however, is a model of a civil society inherited from the antiauthoritarian dimension of the Marxian tradition, involving a democratization mainly of the world of work. This model is one that French writers tended to call that of p*olitical* society, and Offe's defense, unlike theirs, separates the case for *political* and *civil* society in terms of alternative and opposed left and neoconservative scenarios. *Civil* society in the sense of

Rosanvallon and Viveret is here identified with the private, and correlatively anything not left to the private is to be politicized. Moreover, the new "political" society is understood by Offe to represent a model of democracy alternative to the institutions of liberal democracy, even if it remains unclear whether we are to see the two as opposed or potentially complementary.

The program for the restoration of civil society that Offe represents has, to a greater extent than that of the writers of the French second left, preserved its links to the classical Marxian conception that places political economy within civil society. The model of politicized civil society recapitulates Marx's early stress on the reinterpretation of political democracy and everyday life. Even more important, Offe operates within the terms of the Marxian critique of liberal democracy. In his conception, liberal democracy represents a mediation between state and civil society that is in our time on the verge of failure. Here civil society, however, means capitalist bourgeois society, and liberal democracy (a particular version of "political society") is identified also as a mediating principle between two supposed incompatibles, capitalism and democracy.[40] Following Macpherson, Offe points to the competitive party system as the specific mechanism that accomplishes mediation between state and civil society, reconciling democracy and capitalism in the process. Along with the crisis of the welfare state, however, the major contemporary institution of the competitive party system, the catchall party, has entered into crisis: it never could (unlike its forerunners) generate collective identities, and in a zero-sum society it can decreasingly satisfy the interests of its diverse constituency when this happens.

The conflict between democratic legitimacy and nondemocratic economic order can be resolved in one of two "extrainstitutional" directions,[41] one (representing governing elites) antidemocratic; the other (representing ordinary citizens) radical democratic. Neocorporatism represents the first type of solution for the articulation and resolution of conflict outside liberal democratic channels. With private organizations taking on public functions, Offe depicts neocorporatism as a higher degree of fusion between state and society, public and private, than state interventionism itself.[42] This idea parallels the view of Viveret and Rosanvallon, according to whom neocorporatism means the disappearance of political society as such, i.e., all mediations between civil society and state stabilizing their differentiation.

The radical democratic "extrainstitutional" solution for the failure of liberal democracy has the opposite consequence: redifferentiation rather than fusion. The revitalization of political society or of a political version of civil society in the form of citizen initiatives and social movements represents a renewed model for the differentiation of state and society. Offe variously and somewhat inconsistently depicts this option as a response either to the failure of the party system or to the success (but exclusionary tendencies) of neocorporatism. In either case, however, we can speak of the reconstitution of civil (or political) society *outside* an established institutional framework that has threatened the disappearance of all independent forms of social life.

The bases on which (political) civil society is reconstituted, if a fusion between the spheres of *state* and *society* has already occurred, remains unclear in this analysis.[43] Since no revolutionary rupture is being contemplated, one must somehow discover the foundations of the new independent structures in the old society on the level of norms and/or nonstatized forms of association.[44] Offe's model of the reconstitution of civil society is more emphatically movement-centered than the other two forms of analysis we have so far depicted. Social movements play a major role in all of them, but only in Offe's model is there a shift of emphasis toward movement politics from two directions: nonpolitical associations, institutions, forms of life on the one hand, and liberal democratic, parliamentary politics on the other. While the issue may be one of stress rather than omission, the relationship of a political version of civil society to its nonpolitical associational substratum is hardly explored (though without this the origin of movements cannot be thematized), while that of the two paradigms of politics is explored only in an inconclusive way.

Along with the realist faction of the Greens, Offe, of course, presupposes in practical politics the complementarity of party and movement forms of organization, of parliamentary and grass-roots forms of politics. His earlier critique of liberal democracy, however, oscillated between a conception that asserted an outright contradiction between liberalism and democracy and another positing liberal democracy as a deficient democratic bridge between the will of citizens and the state. Both versions still leave the way open to the secret hope of the classical Marxian theory: a political society embodying all economic and political powers in a single institutional framework.[45] Such a utopia beyond the dualism of state and civil society needs no bridge between the two poles, least of all a liberal democratic one. Under the impact of the new self-limitation of contemporary social movements, which seek to limit but not abolish the existing version of the modern state, Offe no longer seems to hold this particular utopian view. His critique of majority rule[46] allows him to thematize the relationship between the "extrainstitutional" political impulse of the new social movements and the need for constitutional change within the structure of liberal democracy. Since this critique is actually aimed at the centralized forms of majority rule represented by the liberal democratic nation state, Offe proposes to supplement majority rule not so much with the classical liberal forms of the protection of minorities as with various federal, decentralized, quasi-aristocratic (in the sense of self-elective bodies of those most concerned), and elsewhere also functional representative forms. Of course, all of these supplementary forms of democracy would have to rely on some form of majority rule. What remains unclear about the analysis is again the problem of the relation of the two political societies, this time the centralized and the supplementary ones, and, in particular, how the official, institutional, centralized form is to be transformed or at least made receptive to and capable of being *influenced* by the other forms. While the suggestion to make majority rule reflexive about its own boundaries through a reinstitutionalization of the *pouvoir constituant* is important, this (still vague and possibly impractical) proposal bypasses the question of the structure of parliamentary, party democracy. We are left with the impression (also present in some of the other analyses we have presented) that while liberal democracy is admittedly dangerous for the autonomy of a political version of civil society, because of its depoliticizing tendencies, civil society cannot in the long run be institutionalized without some of the structural possibilities that, in the West at least, are carried by liberal democracy.

Civil Society in the Transition from Latin American Dictatorships

The concept of civil society has also emerged under several "bureaucratic-authoritarian" regimes as a key term in the self-understanding of democratic actors as well as an important variable in the analysis of the transition to democracy.[47] This discussion has been the richest, most open-ended, and most synthetic among the ones so far discussed. We can, of course, only trace forms of discourse that we believe indicate the beginnings of a new political culture; it is beyond our competence to integrate this discourse into the diverse political and social contexts involved. Nevertheless, we are struck by the remarkable unity of the discussion and by its parallels with developments elsewhere.

The main concern of Latin American theorists and their collaborators has been the transition from a new type of military-bureaucratic authoritarian rule: First, involving a period of "liberalization" (defined as the restoration and/or extension of individual and group rights); and second, a stage of "democratization" (understood in terms of the establishment of a citizenship principle based on at least a "procedural minimum" of participation). But these transitions are seen as strongly dependent on the "resurrection of civil society."[48] Here, civil society stands for a network of groups and associations between (in some versions, including) families and face-to-face groups on one side and outright state organizations on the other, mediating between individual and state, private and public. Different from clan, clique, cabal, and clientele, the associations of civil society have themselves a public, civic quality related both to "a recognized right to exist" and the ability "to openly deliberate about . . . common affairs and publicly act in defense of justifiable interests."[49] Others significantly add the notion of self-expression to that of the representation of interests, and they propose to include movements along with recognized associations in the concept.[50] It is often suggested that the "resurrection" of civil society culminates in the highly mobilized and concentrated form of "mass mobilization" and "popular upsurge," in which the various layers and strata of civil society develop, if temporarily, a single collective identity.

The category of *mass* is misleading here for two reasons. First, the analysts tell us that in liberalized authoritarian states, civil society typically comes into motion in distinct and successive layers: intellectual groups, middle-class organizations, human rights organizations, professional associations, movements of industrial workers, etc. (not necessarily in this order).[51] Even in contexts of high mobilization, in the recent transitions to democracy the different groups, associations, and organizations do not coalesce into one mass, as was characteristic of the earlier "populisms" that often led to dictatorships. Second, the forums of resurrected civil society are typically "public" as against "mass," ranging from intellectual discussions in universities, bookstores, cafés, etc., to popular forms of association and assembly, which together represent new contexts in which "the exercise and learning of citizenship can flourish in deliberations about issues of everyday concern."[52] High levels of mobilization against recent dictatorships typically used rather than bypassed these public forms. This is understandable, since after the authoritarian reduction of public discussion to state-controlled, restricted "codes and terms," the restoration of this sphere achieved high significance, for a while at least making the simplifications involved in populist discourse less attractive. All the same, the distinctions between higher and lower levels of mobilization, as well as between unified and more particularized collective identities in civil society, remain important.

Leaving aside some differences among the relevant authors concerning the very meaning and the relative importance of the concept of civil society, some important puzzles and ambiguities characterize the whole line of analysis. According to an interpretation characteristic of the most repressive regimes, such as Argentina, authoritarian regimes atomize, depoliticize, and privatize society, creating a purely manipulated and controlled public sphere.[53] According to another, in some contexts at least (such as Brazil), civil society or its residues survive authoritarian rule in forms of interest associations, autonomous agencies, local government, and church life.[54] According to a third line of interpretation, the "resurrection of civil society" that pushes the democratization process forward is possible in either case, with or without surviving forms of recognized association, with or without memories of earlier mass mobilization.[55] As Francisco Weffort from Brazil puts it, "we want a civil society, we need to defend ourselves from the monstrous state in front of us. This means that if it does not exist, we need to invent it. If it is small, we need to enlarge it. . . . In a word we want civil society because we want freedom."[56] In this interpretation, which recalls arguments made in Poland, the social foundations for civil society, starting with family and friends and continuing with the church, never disappeared in any of the southern dictatorships.

The strategy of "inventing" and "enlarging" is favored by the fact that bureaucratic-authoritarian regimes never manage to solve their problems of legitimacy.[57] The constitution or reconstitution of elements of civil society, indirectly promoted by reducing both fear and the costs of autonomous activity, becomes a means to address these fundamental problems.[58] While this effort from above is always expected to stay within careful limits, it cannot amount to a complete farce if the goal of legitimacy is to be attained, and the elements of actual democratization that are established in this way are by definition unpredictable and cannot be kept within any given predefined limits.[59]

It is still unclear, however, what difference the state of development of civil society under authoritarian rule makes in terms of the process of transition or the stability and character of the outcome. It seems likely that the character of a mobilized civil society itself is affected by the alternative patterns: more homogeneous where no previous structures existed or were preserved, more pluralistic and structured where civil society did not have to be created after a high degree of atomization. And this difference has many potential consequences.

It may be helpful to distinguish, in relation to transitions, processes of *initiation, consolidation,* and *completion.* The exact role of civil society in the process of initiating the transition remains in some dispute. The dominant thesis stresses, on the basis of much comparative data, that the beginning is primarily a function of internal splits in the authoritarian regime, although all analysts concede that if such a split leads to an "opening" or to liberalization, the resurrection of civil society cannot be easily contained and will play an important role in all succeeding steps.[60] However, some interpreters seem to argue that where mobilization plays a role in the end of an authoritarian regime, the whole process of the "over-throw" or "self-dissolution" from the very beginning is very much a function of the regime's relationship to civil society.[61] The notion that the problem of legitimation is the Achilles heel of the post-1945 authoritarian regimes[62] seems to imply that the instability of the regimes and the impetus for liberalization should be sought in the relationship of the rulers to groups and opinion outside of them.

The features of civil society are as important to potential rollbacks, in particular military coups, as to the process of initiation and acceleration. While some analysts fear overmobilization as a pretext for coups and a motivation for reunification of the ruling elites, the dominant position seems to stress the costs of a conflict with mobilized civil society as a deterrent to hard-liners that reformers can use.[63] One might add here that not only the level of mobilization but that of structure formation is important because it is easier to suppress a society without deep organizational roots than a highly articulated one, even if the former is superficially mobilized.

Equally important is the issue of whether or not the pressure of civil society, once mobilized, is capable of pushing to the end a process of transition to democratic politics. It seems obvious that an evolutionary strategy involves important negotiating and bargaining processes with those authoritarian rulers who are able and willing to moderate their rule, while at a later stage any transition to democracy must involve organization for elections. It is not obvious in either of these contexts, however, how civic associations, social movements, grass-roots organizations, or even media of communication can substitute for the differentiation of a political element capable of strategic considerations. In fact, a strategy from below on its own has nowhere succeeded.

Aside from ideologies of reform from above, two forms of discourse are available to participants seeking to understand the place of political organizations in the transition from authoritarian rule; one is dialectical and the other more analytical. According to the former, since bureaucratic-authoritarian regimes suppress or se-riously deform all types of mediation between the private sphere and the state (including popular organizations as well as institutions for political citizenship), the task of democratization is primarily to reconstitute these.[64] Indeed, the dialectical version of the discourse of civil society often comes to identify democratization with the reconstitution of these mediations. In this version, the political actors capable of interposing themselves between society and state emerge from the process of organizing new social associations and movements as their organic continuation. But in their search for legitimacy, the regimes themselves often initiate the process of reconstituting mediations beyond the semipolitical, state-constituted "bureaucratic rings or clusters" of "social interests" that have failed as effective replacements for societal pressure groups.[65] As a result, those in opposition find themselves having to choose between "the imbecility" of refusing degrees of social autonomy simply because they are offered or even accepted by governments and "the opportunism" of accepting limited autonomy too quickly, entering into a predetermined and coopting game without testing the actual possibilities of democratization.[66] One option beyond these two seems to be the attempt to organize and defend the new sphere of civil society not as mediation but as an end in itself, as in itself *political*: "If politics was to have a new meaning, a new sphere of freedom for political action had to be developed. For political Brazil, civil society, previously either ignored or seen as an inert mass, began to signify that sphere of freedom."[67] From this point of view, it is natural to treat even political parties and associations as undifferentiated parts of the heterogeneous field of self-organization.[68] In an extreme antipolitical version in Brazil, combining the views of "lay anarchism and Catholic solidarity thought," parties are to be more feared than trusted because of their propensity to enter the game of the state. To the extent that self-organization had to be complemented by policies and legislative measures, these were to be achieved by movements of direct participation organized around single issues of intense concern to their own constituencies.[69]

In the face of intact authoritarian power, however, a high level of mobilization without mediations, symbolized by the figure of civil society as "the political celebrity of the *abertura*,"[70] could have demobilizing consequences. Unable to go beyond polarization, civil society can defeat state initiatives without generating a comprehensive alternative of its own. As in the cases of both Brazil and Chile, fear of the regime can easily be replaced by society's fear of itself, fear of the consequences of its own impotent power.[71] Both in theory and in practice, a second strategy comes to stress the need for an orientation to political society to complete the transition to democracy. This strategy is intellectually analytical in that it does not see the institutions of political society—parties, electoral mechanisms, forms of bargaining, and legislatures—as either parts or as organic continuations of the processes of the self-organization of civil society.[72]

While it seems misleading to identify civil society primarily with liberalization, and political society primarily with democratization, it is certainly right to insist that "full democratic transition must involve political society."[73] Without political society, neither the necessary negotiation for transition nor the mechanisms of societal control of postauthoritarian states can be established. This has been shown through analyses of elections and political parties. In those dictatorships where electoral mechanisms were maintained, even if greatly restricted, it has been possible to channel social pressure in the direction of substantial, if gradual, political change ("decompression"),[74] even in the context of an intact authoritarian order that has not been weakened from the outside. This was the case in Brazil. Similarly, the continued, if restricted, existence of political parties represented in several countries, from Brazil to Uruguay and (most recently) Chile, the natural focal point for negotiated transitions.[75] Indeed, parties and elections represented opportunities for the remobilization of civil society in several contexts where phenomena of demobilization occurred after failures of early challenges against authoritarian rule.[76] Wherever it has been possible, the activation of political society seems to have been the key to avoiding polarized, zero-sum, or even negative-sum confrontations between organized civil societies and authoritarian regimes that have maintained some continuity with the past.[77]

Whatever its necessity, *the turn to political society has potentially demobilizing consequences with respect to civil society*, as many participants and observers have noted. In this context, Cardoso justly calls attention to the double nature of political parties: Their mediating role is made possible by, but cannot overcome, the contradictions within them of movement and administration, of participation and elitism, of democratic norm and strategic calculation.[78] At two points, however, the elitist, administrative, and strategic side may dominate: pacts and elections. Often possible and necessary as "undemocratic" halfway stations, pacts are rightly stressed by many as important means of avoiding violence and its risks in the transition to democracy.[79] It does not seem completely justified, though, to claim that, where they are possible, pacts between the parties of the opposition and elements of the regime are also desirable, especially when it is a little too quickly admitted that they are as a rule exclusionary, nonpublic, and aimed at drastically curtailing conflict in the political system. Their violation of the norms of democracy[80] can have long-term negative consequences for a political culture. With this said, it should perhaps be added that pacts in which certain interests of the existing rulers are guaranteed have different possible consequences for civil society, depending on their timing. Coming early in a process of transition, pacts can secure elements of liberalization, making possible the reconstitution of civil society. In this case, with the emergence of new actors and the activation of public spaces, the chances are good that the initial pact will eventually be swept aside.[81] If a pact comes late, however, after the resurrection and possibly the upsurge of civil society, and especially if it guarantees power positions to all contracting parties, including some of the opposition, its very aim involves an exclusion and demobilization that may be successful for a long period. Often the consequence is a revival of populism rather than processes of further democratization.

The only "late" pacts that seem to avoid this trajectory are those in which oppositional groupings ask for no concessions for themselves but only for society as a whole. Above all, pacts that arrange elections and electoral rules can have this character. But elections, even when they themselves do not incorporate strongly exclusionary rules, can be ambiguous from the point of view of mobilizing civil society.

Several analysts ask the partially rhetorical question, Why should ruling elites agree to elections that are likely to abolish their rule? The answer given is that these elites expect to channel politics "away from the ebullience of civil society" and perhaps even to win elections by dividing the opposition and being rewarded by the electorate.[82] When elections are only gradually decontrolled, as in Brazil, the hope is to slow down the rate of change while still achieving procedural legitimacy. The hopes of victory and legitimacy are generally frustrated, but not those of demobilization and, where pertinent, gradualism.[83] The move to electoral parties with their less intense, more inclusive, more abstract form of political identification and their lower degree of direct participation tends to devalue and replace movements and associations with their more particular, but also more intense and participatory, forms of organization. Although this depends on the specific electoral rules enacted, the tendency of modern elections is to reduce the number of political parties capable of effectively participating in elections. In turn, and especially in periods of uneasy transition, potentially successful parties will often restrain movements of civil society that might jeopardize the outcome or even the possibility of elections.[84] The major parties, moreover, share a common interest in obtaining a larger than representative share of votes for forces close to the authoritarian regime, to avoid an overly great victory for the opposition.[85] Thus, it can be said not only of the processes leading to unrestricted electoral contests that end dictatorships but also of the elections themselves that they are implicit negotiations between regimes and oppositional parties that provide space and time to "redefine their respective roles."[86] And while the weak legitimacy and the plebiscitary possibilities of partially restricted elections can indeed lead to societal mobilization and to learning processes outside the official framework, the liberal democratic legitimacy of open confrontation provides much less of a chance for such an outcome. It is possible that where civil society is underdeveloped and passive, or is in the process of contraction, elections might draw otherwise uninvolved strata into organized politics; in the context of a highly mobilized civil society, the reverse may very well occur, with parties turning out to be "not only, or not so much, agents of mobilization as instruments of social and political control."[88]

There is little doubt after the experience of several countries that the highest level of a mobilized civil society cannot be maintained for long.[89] But is civil society equivalent to such mobilization? Is it not a mark of its weakness that it can exist in some countries only in this form? There is some serious theoretical uncertainty concerning what comes or can come after demobilization. The question is whether there is anything left of a "resurrected civil society" after selective repression, co-optation, manipulation, internal conflicts, fatigue, disillusionment, and the channeling of opposition into the party and electoral systems take their toll and demobilize "the popular upsurge."[90] Here one interpretation stresses depoliticization, reprivatization, and the emergence of political ghettoes, which together will endanger democratic consolidation and weaken the society's ability to resist renewed authoritarianism. The idea that in some countries, notably Chile and Uruguay,[91] an overdeveloped system of parties contributes to a dependent and underdeveloped civil society is more consistent with this line of argument than is the stress in the case of other countries on the survival of civic associational life even under authoritarianism. If one identifies demobilization with the atomization of civil society, it is hard to see how one can speak of a transition to democracy rather than a return to cycles of democracy and dictatorship, neither of which can be stabilized, in part because of the cycles of politicization and depoliticization of civil society *within* each form of rule. The idea of finally leaving the cycle[92] must therefore point beyond the alternative of a fully mobilized and fully depoliticized and privatized civil society.

Logically, at least, the demobilization of a popular upsurge is not necessarily the end of a politically relevant civil society. Nor is it necessary that everything learned in previous cycles be forgotten. In this context, it is significant that some interpreters see the emergence of a new form of differentiation between de facto societal pluralism and democratic pluralism as a change in values, as the transformation of the collective identity of groups and institutions.[93] The former type of pluralism has been present in most of the societies in question, but the latter has been a product only of the recent struggles against authoritarian regimes that have led to the replacement of the imagery of the *via revolucionaria* by democratic ideologies.[94] After the failure of illusory revolutions and the experience of dictatorships, democracy came to be increasingly viewed as an end in itself rather than a means for the realization of sectoral interests.[95] But for it to become an end also for nonelite groups, a reorientation to civil society had to and actually did occur. "The discovery of the value of democracy is inseparable, within the opposition, from the discovery of civil society as a political space."[96] The question inevitably arises, What will happen to the value of democracy as the space of civil society shrinks to the benefit of political society?

Actually, one should distinguish three possibilities: (1) a civil society that loses its value for social actors with the restoration of democracy, a process in which political society has come to play the major role; (2) an overpoliticized civil society that implicitly, on behalf of various of its sectors, seeks to abolish societal plurality itself and/or devalues mediations between itself and the state; and (3) a civil society that has become reflexive to itself through its self-thematization and self-normatization, as well as its self-limitation vis-à-vis political society.

The self-reflexive model of civil society involves not only the idea of the self-limitation of civil society but also its own strengthening. This has consequences for both civil and political society. The model is incompatible with the liberal-individualistic concept of civil society that implies both its full depoliticization and its dependence on the forces of the market economy: "the social inequality and the fragility of the individual before business and the bureaucracy." Cardoso proposes an alternative combining the radical democratic stress on collective subjectivity and self-organization (without, however, abandoning individual rights) and a reform democratic acceptance of the necessity of the state. This "dualistic" synthesis leads to the start, admittedly needing further development, of a proposal for greater social responsibility on the part of the management of firms and the bureaucracy, with increasing public control over their processes. Without this, civil society remains defenseless and "private in the strict sense of the word."[97]

This redefinition of the relationship of state and civil society in a democracy yet to be created alters the model of political society as well, and along with it that of political parties. Their task now becomes building "movable bridges on both sides of the antinomy."[98] The idea is not well enough explained in terms of the notion of "countering the widespread idea that the parties are 'inauthentic' and incapable of serving as a filter for the aspirations of the electorate."[99] What seems to be involved instead is the rejection of a choice between the elitist and the radical-democratic, between the strategic and the normative-democratic dimensions of the ambivalence of modern parties. Rather, it seems to be this ambivalence made conscious that could allow both the sensitizing of civil society to the need for strategic considerations *and* the introduction of elements of democratic decision making into state and firm.[100]

Sketchy as it may be, Cardoso's outline for the development of democratic theory has several virtues. It is a model of the goal of transition that does not lose sight of the preconditions of consolidating democracy and remobilizing in its defense. It corresponds well to the institutional requirements for O'Donnell's notion of building a civil-society-based democratic political culture. Finally, the model points beyond restricting democracy to the political sphere (i.e., beyond elite democracy or elite pluralism) to the possibility of exiting the historical cycle in a way that allows the issue of "more democracy" to be raised without being a subterfuge for a dictatorship of the left or the pretext of the dictatorship of the right.

Revisiting Eastern Europe in the Late 1980s

As indicated above, the rediscovery of civil society in Poland was the product of two negative learning experiences: the failure of total, revolutionary change from below (Hungary in 1956) and of comprehensive reform from above (Czechoslovakia in 1968). Polish reformers decided that a radical change of society was still possible if a third route was followed. This would have two components: The agent would be organized society "from below," and the target would be civil society rather than the state, within a program of self-limitation. Note that by its own standards the new strategy was itself open to the test of new learning experiences. After the repression of Solidarity in December of 1981, the question inevitably arose of whether the third and seemingly last route had also been proved impossible in Soviet-type societies. (Apparently last on the basis of a dualistic conception that rigidly juxtaposes state and civil society.)

Within Poland the dualistic formulation has been subjected to stringent critique by Jadwiga Staniszkis. Here we will outline and expand her general line of attack:

1. The polarization of society vs. the state in Poland is connected to a political history in which three foreign imperial governments represented the state.

2. Polish culture survived the age of partitions by preserving its own traditions, mentalities, practices, system of education, and religion in isolation from the state(s).

3. The strategy was, however, always a purely defensive one and is not suited for real social change.

4. The post-totalitarian state is more subtle and penetrating, more invisible and corrupting, than the openly repressive states of the past. Thus the isolation of state and society is in principle not possible.

5. The unity of society is illusory on the empirical level, and a populist and solidarist uniformity imposed on society (allegedly the case during the sixteen months of Solidarity) is undesirable.

6. The unity of the party-state is also illusory and, from a strategic point of view, hardly desirable. The notion of inherent opposition between society and state makes it impossible to exploit internal cleavages and tensions in state and party. Reformist attempts from above and within the ruling structure must then be taken as a priori illusory, and compromise can be understood only as strategic, i.e., in principle unstable. Party oppositions are continually driven back into the party.

7. Popular mobilization and conflict under the aegis of the dualistic conception can amount only to ritualized forms of channeling opposition; they will not be able to produce any significant change in the existing system.[101]

Staniszkis was wrong about the mobilizing power of the dichotomous conception of society against the state. Indeed, the conception was in many respects self-realizing: While Solidarity was legal (1980–1981), Polish society was at least tendentially organized around the fault lines of the dichotomy of civil society and (party) state, despite conflicts within each pole of the duality. In retrospect, however, one implication of Staniszkis's analysis was fulfilled: The dichotomous conception reinforced a type of polarization in which compromise solutions became impossible, however much desired by the sector of Solidarity led by Lech Walesa. For compromise one needs partners, presumably reformists, and also (political) institutions of mediation. In a context of radical polarization, actively sought by sectors of the regime but favored by Solidarity's ideology, neither could emerge. The normatively and affectively successful dualistic conception of the original project of the self-liberation of civil society was thus part of the constellation that led to strategic failure.

In the 1980s this project was, amazingly enough, not only not abandoned but extended to two other countries: Hungary and the Soviet Union. Two reasons, aside from that of the inherent normative validity of the basic ideas, were responsible. One was geopolitical: Important shifts had occurred in the international economic and political environments in which the project had originally led to stalemate. The other was theoretical, involving an expansion of the original framework by introducing the category of political society.

The change in the international environment followed from the crisis of the Soviet model of economic development both on the periphery and even in the center of the imperial system. The Soviet Union had exhausted the possibilities of extensive development based on continuous expansion of the resources of raw materials and labor and was being decisively challenged by the threat of unlimited technological-military competition with the United States, a competition the Soviet Union could not win.[102] Aside from economics, the new situation was marked by three new processes: the failure of normalization in Poland, the emergence of reformism from above in the Soviet Union, and the beginning of the crisis of Kadarist consolidation in Hungary.

The reference to the Soviet Union already indicates that, given the change of environment, the strategy of reform from below as well as from above has made a comeback, despite the expectations of Polish oppositionists in the late 1970s under the influence of the Czech experience and the atmosphere of the Brezhnev era. Remarkably, the strategy of reform from above, initiated by segments of the ruling party, was now complemented by another one: the reconstruction of independent civil society. Indeed, it is this complementarity that was often seen as the mark of the difference between *radical* reform and mere reform. According to this line of thought, attempted changes in the Soviet economy failed in the past because (1) they targeted only the economy, (2) they did not go far enough even in relation to the economy, and (3) their only agent was the ruling institution above, excluding all forces from below.[103] All these points belong together. Assuming that the goal was first and foremost an economic reform that went "far enough" to work, elite reformers now argued that this is possible only if other areas of life were transformed and other actors than the party-state participated in the overall project. In effect, the claim is that civil society is a part of the environment needed for a new type of economic coordination that could not be created without movements for, and in, civil society.

The thesis applied not only to the system inherited from the conservative Brezhnev era by the Gorbachev team, where even the formal abolition of the command structure would require the mobilization of pressure outside the ruling apparatus. It applied as well to the reformed Kadarist system, whose successes were due more to partial privatization than to the transformation of the command system into one of informal bureaucratic controls.[104] From the writings of Hungarian economists, legal scholars, political scientists, and sociologists it becomes clear why civil society was implicated on two levels in what was supposedly required for "radical reform."

First, we have learned that the introduction of reforms exclusively from above cannot, because of conservative-bureaucratic resistance, be formulated or implemented in a sufficiently consistent manner.[105] Nor is such a process protected against rollbacks initiated by bureaucratic counterattacks in contexts of even minor leadership realignments. Thus, independent actors are needed for more consistent and determined pursuit of economic reform. However, since social movements are not likely to be the agents of economic reforms (because of the sacrifices involved), political trade-offs for movements (unions, forms of industrial democracy, ability to strike) and the institutionalization of collective economic actors (legality of interest representations, new forms of property) are necessary.[106]

Second, both the relevant trade-offs and the institutionalization of actors point to laws, rights, and associations of interest representation. These features of civil society are also needed to counter spontaneous reinvasion or repenetration of the economy, freed from the prerogatives of direct economic command, by informal, extralegal types of bureaucratic regulation that reinforce the weaknesses of the inherited "economy of shortage."[107] Laws and rights consistently formulated and made entirely public are needed, along with independent courts and judicial procedures, to provide predictability and regularity for economic actors and to protect them against the discretionary power of the existing apparatus operating through legal inconsistencies and the gaps and loopholes within the law.[108] But laws and rights alone would be powerless against administrations whose practice is to bypass all formal regulation through their control of the execution and implementation of the laws. They must be backed up by established interest associations and an open public sphere. These are also needed to provide a counterweight against the already established, monopolistic lobbies (themselves rooted partly in the apparatus and partly in the moderately decentralized structures of industry) that now control the bargaining processes involving investment, subsidies, tax exemptions, and even prices and that reinforce the resource-constrained and built-in wasteful character of the economy of shortage.

When the reconstitution of civil society was promoted as a component of reform from above, especially in the Soviet Union, it was supposed to stay within carefully defined limits. The only institutions of civil society that were to be reconstituted were those most relevant to economic rationality; the independent actors were to accomplish only the strictly necessary tasks. But both aims were self-contradictory. Economic laws and rights become such only in the context of *Rechtsstaatlichkeit* (constitutionalism), with far more general implications. Associations genuinely competent to exert open economic pressure are also able and motivated to address other social and political issues. A public sphere that allow criticism of economic waste, corruption, and resistance to change cannot

easily be prevented from taking up other issues. All these departures presuppose the reduction of fear in society, and the reduction
of fear becomes the stimulus for new departures. Finally, movements that can be easily restrained cannot play an important role
in overcoming resistance to reform, while those that can play such
a role cannot be controlled and are unpredictable. The constant
fluctuation in the Soviet Union between measures that lead forward and those that revive past practices, between democratization
and authoritarian centralization, is best explained in these terms.
The regime wants radical reform, it unleashes and even prods the
revival of civil society, but it also wants to press its prerogative to
determine the limits of what can and cannot be changed, including
the structure and dynamics of civil society itself.

Nevertheless, the process of social mobilization and the building
of at least some dimensions of what the actors themselves call civil
society continues amidst the fluctuation. The level of societal self-
organization today would have been unthinkable a couple of years
ago. But it is not at all clear that the result will be radical reform
rather than hopeless polarization and stalemate.[109] If the pathology
of reform from above is that it replaces a formal command system
with one of informal bureaucratic regulation, the step to civil
society supplies only the necessary but not the sufficient condition
of its cure. As the Poles discovered, even an organized and mobilized civil society cannot, especially in the context of self-limitation,
act directly on an unchanged party-state and overcome the resistance
of a political-economic apparatus whose last major stronghold
becomes the unreconstructed bureaucratic economy.

This was the lesson that inspired those who imported the Polish
project of radical reform into Hungary, especially after martial law.
Key elements of the Hungarian opposition[110] reformulated the
program in terms of a radical minimalism that nevertheless implied
that changes in society must be complemented by necessary, if less
radical, change in the party-state sphere. At first, this meant
redefining as rights the elements of already conceded openness
and differentiation in Hungarian society and redefining the discretionary state (*Massnahmenstaat*) as an authoritarian *Rechtsstaat* that
is self-limiting, at least with respect to the rights it grants. The
second version, developed at the time of increasing crisis and some

success in involving intellectuals in oppositional activity, proposed to independent social forces that they demand pluralism in the sphere of private law (civil society) and a fully developed *Rechtsstaatlichkeit* in the sphere of public law.[111] Finally, in 1987, at the time when the foundations of the Kadarist system were already cracking, a detailed model of radical reform was proposed. Appearing under the name *Social Contract*, this involved the restoration of civil society in all its dimensions and a reform of the political system to include elements of genuine parliamentarism, a responsible government, and a reconstruction of the place and role of the Communist party that would preserve some of its prerogatives, but only within a framework of constitutional legality. It is the structure, rather than the exact formula, that is important to us, for it represented a call for discussion, negotiation, and compromise. The partisans of the *Social Contract* approach attempted to reconstruct the dualistic project inherited from Poland in terms of a model linking the radical reconstruction of civil society with a less radical but nevertheless principled reform of the political sphere. The idea was not to abandon the goal of parliamentary democracy but to combine two different rates of change, one in civil society and one in the state sphere, in a mutually reinforcing way, and to provide at the same time the necessary change of "environment" for institutionalizing a genuine market economy.

The *Social Contract* retained an important link to the Polish politics of the "new evolutionism" by maintaining, against other approaches of the time that still addressed the regime or its reformist elements,[112] that groups, associations, and indeed movements outside the official institutions would have the primary task of pushing the reforms through. In Hungary, though, the idea was paradoxical, given the absence of anything resembling the Polish level of societal self-organization.[113]

Oddly enough, the political results in Hungary turned out to be more radical than in Poland. Indeed, after the removal of Kadar in May 1988, the Hungarian Communist party made a number of rapid concessions: a de facto open public sphere, a law of association and right to strike, and a law that allowed the formation of parties, though not initially as electoral organizations. Moreover, by February 1989 the party conceded the need for early competitive and unrestricted elections, and in June 1989 it entered into negotiations concerning electoral rules and procedures with eight or nine protoparty formations represented by "the roundtable of the opposition."

There are two ways of reading the logic of these changes. The first (F. Köszeg) takes the point of view of the fledgling organizations of independent society and points to the inner dissolution of the ruling party (due to economic crisis as well as the destabilizing effects of the Soviet hands-off policy) that made it too weak to resist even a relatively small degree of social pressure. Certainly the thesis seems to be confirmed by the history of several key concessions, which began with proposals intending merely co-optation, continued with intense public criticism, and ended with the regime backing down.[114] But this reading does not leave enough room for an important actor outside the opposition, namely the reform groupings within the party, which played an active role in several of the same concessions.

The second reading (J. Kis) sought to correct this underestimation by stressing the attempt on the part of the increasingly dominant reformist faction to find legitimate, viable partners in society for instituting economic reforms along with new austerity programs. The search for partners might itself have led only to an attempted co-optation of the social forces in formation, but the necessity of viable partners, given the decline of the regime's legitimacy, required genuinely independent entities operating in an open, competitive political terrain.[115] In this analysis, the search for partners led the regime, or its dominant faction, to the opening of the space for the emergence of political society.

It is instructive to compare this situation to the 1980–1981 period in Poland. Then it was Solidarity that sought a "historic compromise" with the regime, unsuccessfully, involving the creation of institutions of mediation.[116] Its own polaristic conception, and the regime's belief in the possibility of "normalization" and in its powers to enact economic reform, played major roles in the failure of compromise. Perhaps at that time, as opposed to 1988, Solidarity, having behind it all of society, was so strong that the regime could not allow it any genuine role in the making of policy. By 1990 important elements of the old regimes themselves both in Hungary and Poland had accepted the idea of far-reaching compromise with relatively weaker opponents, and this involved the creation of institutions of mediation that required the participation of independent actors. For this reason, they turned to the actors of civil society, actively promoting their transformation and in the process stimulating the emergence and consolidation of political agents (they hoped) without any (or weakened) roots in civil society. To make such a change in the existing pattern of oppositional politics worthwhile, competitive political procedures leading to elections were conceded. Given the risks of elections for the survival of the established regimes, the elites that reluctantly opted for this process sought their own survival by introducing elements of restriction into the compromise (Poland) or by taking up roles as members of the new political society in formation (Hungary).[117]

Our interest is not in the correctness of such calculations but in the effects on civil society of the turn to political society. Four ideal types of significant change operate in East Europe today: reform, radical reform from below (or the "new evolution"), political transition to a new system, and what has been recently called "revolution."[118] Each has its actors, its pathologies, and its potential form of self-correction. Each takes up a different dimension of the problem of civil society. The strategy of reform, still dominant in the Soviet Union, has as its agents modernizing state actors. The pathology of this path is that it replaces formal bureaucratic discretion with its informal variants, which do not on the whole improve economic functioning and, as in the current Soviet case, may actually weaken it. The imagined corrective is the turn to civil society, which would involve in the reform process collective actors (groups, associations, movements, and publics) outside the state sphere. In the Soviet Union, even the turn to the electoral mechanisms typical of political society bypassed and for a while even blocked the emergence of independent *political* actors, though it helped the self-organization and mobilization of informal actors of civil society. Thus the elections of early 1989, and the contradictory and inconsistent sessions of the Congress of Peoples' Deputies,[119] tended to lead not to mediation but to a form of mobilization that is already polarizing and will turn out to be more so as the economic reform continues to stagnate. In the absence of both violent repression and parliamentary mediation, the conflicts will more and more take place in the streets.

Polarization, as we have seen in Poland, is the specific pathology of the turn to civil society and its actors, in spite of the dramatic consequences of this turn for societal learning processes and, specifically, for the building of a democratic political culture. Linked to polarization in Poland has been an overunification of civil society in which a single movement has been the vehicle for heterogeneous and even competing social interests and identities, somewhat blocking (even if against the intentions of the participants) the emergence of societal and, later, political pluralism. In a nationally divided society such as the Soviet Union, a second form of polarization—between competing ethnic or national groups, or between democratic and national movements—has been an even more negative consequence of a civil-society-oriented strategy.[120] In this context, the emergence of political groupings capable of negotiation, compromise, and genuine parliamentarism represents a small hope for mediation, which can work only if the institutional means are found to link them to the deepening lines of social conflict involving national, economic, and political issues. The question is how the increasingly mobilized groups of civil society will be able to manage their conflicts with the regime and each other. In this context, there does not seem to be an alternative to the rule of law and multiparty parliamentarism other than an increasingly destructive polarization that, in the Russian center of the crumbling imperium, could eventually take either the form of a stalemate between societal forces and a state they cannot overthrow or a clash between democratic and conservative-nationalist movements, or even a combination of these outcomes.[121]

In Poland and Hungary, the supposed corrective for polarization has already been promoted in the form of the turn to political society. This implies that the agents of the process of transition will increasingly be the actors of political society, at least initially including the reformists in the Communist party. Does this model have its own potential pathologies, and if it does, what are its correctives?

As we have seen in the case of Latin American transitions, one of several reasons governmental elites turn to or revive political society is to help demobilize civil society. They do this both to protect themselves and the transition from an excess of economic demands and to exclude from the political process actors and forms of mobilization that could lead to their own exclusion. While the elites of the old ruling parties, or rather their reformist parts, do not have the social support to become actors of civil society (with the very questionable exception of trade union bureaucracies), they hope that by self-conversion into electoral parties with social democratic ideologies they can become actors in the new political society. Thus, clearly, the turn to political society has as its pathology the demobilization of civil society and the failure to replace its mobilized forms by institutionalized ones. This is a serious matter in Eastern Europe, where atomization and the disruption of social ties, solidarities, and associations far surpassed anything under even the recent bureaucratic-authoritarian regimes, and where civil society seems to exist for the moment only in a mobilized form whose contribution to the restoration of social integration has been limited. For this reason a constellation that bypasses institution building in civil society would be highly unfavorable for the development of a democratic political culture, and conversely, where this type of culture continues to develop, it could lead to serious legitimation problems for new political elites.

The attempts by the reformist elements of the old elites to depoliticize and even fragment civil society are quite understandable. For them, the issue involves not only maintaining their free hand at making economic policy but also their survival as a political force. The root of the difficulty goes deeper, of course, and may have to do with basic tendencies linked to modern political society composed of parties and parliaments. Arising from civil society and preserving some of the marks of their origin, and having resisted the label "party," the new leading parties of Hungary, Poland, and Czechoslovakia have nevertheless given rise to expectations that they would be able to resist the "oligarchic" tendencies of modern political parties.[122] They are nevertheless (or as a result) often criticized for replacing one elite rule by another, for disregarding civil initiatives and social movements and even intensifying state controls over local government and the public sphere, and for bypassing social consultation before making major economic decisions.[123] Significantly, attempts to refute such charges by reference to parliamentary sovereignty have only led to new charges of parliamentary absolutism and even the exaggerated accusation of multiparty dictatorship.

Even if an elite democracy in which popular participation is restricted to periodic votes is not the ideal of the major elements of many of the parties and groups involved, the present context in many respects points in this direction. Once again, the requirements of economic transition, which some rigidify in terms of a nonsolidaristic, individualist version of civil (i.e., bourgeois) society, are in part responsible.[124] In Hungary even more than in Poland, such trends are reinforced by conceptions of parliamentary sovereignty based on the so-called Westminster model, which are present in all of the major parties. But will a population used to social guarantees easily accept the legitimacy of decisions involving new austerity merely on the basis of the arrangements of elites, irrespective of their formal possession of an electoral mandate? There is ample experience from the history of Latin American populisms that it will not, election or no election. There is a danger that populism, which has strong roots in Eastern Europe, will be the response to elitism on the part of demobilized or undeveloped, semiatomized, unsolidaristic civil societies.

Some Comparisons and Some Problems

It would be illegitimate to try equating the projects just surveyed. The models of civil society that have emerged in these differing contexts have shown important variations. Indeed, there are obvious difficulties with any single interpretive framework that seeks to interrogate the meaning of, and provide orientations for, these varying constellations of structure and history. Yet a theoretical framework that can anchor what is in the end a common discussion across boundaries is indispensable. A false unification would provide only illusory solutions, and we must therefore explore the whole range of discourses available today. Before doing so, however, we should at least justify our presentation of the different projects for reconstructing civil society as a single set, beyond the obvious use of the same terminology in different contexts. We shall do this in two steps.

First, we argue for a common intellectual background on the level of the circulation of forms of discourse. In the milieu of critical social thought, there is noticeable today a post-Marxist intellectual turn, producing a discussion of civil society that is truly international. Second, we present two intellectual positions, related to the crisis of Marxism but not reducible to it, that are shared by social actors in the four political contexts, as our "case studies" demonstrate. These are (1) critique of the state and (2) the desire to go beyond the alternative of reform and revolution, in the classical sense of these terms.

The crisis of Marxism is a worldwide phenomenon today, for a variety of local and global reasons. In the advanced capitalist countries, the continuing inability of Marxist theory to explain the relative stability and repeated reconstruction of the existing system is one major reason. Another is the decisive end to the era when it seemed possible (not to mention desirable) for the working class—or any other single social stratum or grouping—to play the role of the global subject of social change. In Latin America, the decisive factor was Marxism's association with a revolutionary road that not only failed to produce any kind of socialist commonwealth but also directly and in some cases deliberately contributed to the end of liberal democracy and the rise of right-wing dictatorships. Where so-called socialist revolutions succeeded, the results are hardly such as to inspire imitation. The Soviet model in the East, in the hour of its fall, is now almost universally recognized as inefficient and dehumanizing. This development, reflected in the actions and intellectual views of dissidents, has discredited in advance the goals of most Western and Southern Communist or ultraleft groupings that have inherited the mantle of Marxism. Significantly, Marxian theories and forms of analyses have repeatedly failed in their attempts to understand the structure of Soviet-type societies and to outline plausible orientations for actors seeking to transform them.[125]

It has always been possible, of course, to move from Marxism to any position from liberalism and neoconservatism to religious fundamentalism. But if one desires to avoid replacing a Marxist dogmatism by an anti-Marxist one, if one refuses to exchange apologetics for one form of domination with that for another, one has to grant the possibility that Marx did establish some critical vantage points that cannot be abandoned as long as capitalist society persists. In many cases, this means reinterpreting or reconstructing some of his major concepts, leading to theoretical projects going far beyond the normative and analytical implications of any version of the classical Marxian theory, including the neo-Marxisms of Lukács, Gramsci, and the older Frankfurt school. It is these theoretical projects that we wish to describe under the heading of *post-Marxism*.[126] A common position of all post-Marxisms, in spite of different terminologies, is a revision of Marx's identification of civil and bourgeois society as well as his various political projects aiming at the reunification of state and society.[127] Post-Marxists not only register, as did Gramsci,[128] the durability of civil society under capitalist democracies and the consequent implausibility of revolution in the classical Marxian sense, but maintain the normative desirability of the preservation of civil society. Yet post-Marxism can be distinguished from all neoliberalisms (which in their own way also identify civil and bourgeois society) by their attempts to thematize the radical democratic or radical pluralist transformation of existing versions of civil society.

We maintain that the concept of civil society, as our various sources so far have used it, belongs to the intellectual world and even political culture of post-Marxism (and perhaps of "post-Gramscianism"). The contemporary discourse of civil society was internationally disseminated, at least initially, by the circulation of post-Marxist ideas. The wide reception of such a concept for the first time in our recent history, allowing for a dialogue between social critics East and West, North and South, has been possible because of shared problems and projects among those contexts.

Two such problems/projects can be found in the sources we have cited already. First and foremost, there is the critique of the state and the search for a "poststatist" politics. The inability of Soviet-type regimes, Latin American dictatorships, and even welfare states to solve all or some key social problems, and the undesirability of the solutions that have emerged, is thematized in all the relevant sources. There was a time when the answer to similar diagnoses was a more rational state—a dictatorship of the proletariat, i.e., of the left rather than the right—or (in the case of the welfare state) simply more state, "nationalizing" more spheres of life. It seems that after our recent experiences with dictatorships, nationalizations of big industries, and the consequences of the penetration of social life by central bureaucracies, none of the old answers can carry their earlier weight. It is increasingly impossible to regard the state as either a passive synthesis of a plurality of social forces or a neutral instrument in the hands of whatever class holds the socially dominant position or manages to have its party elected to governmental power. "Bringing the state back in" should mean recognizing that the modern state has its own logic and that it constitutes an independent constellation of interests.[129] Contrary to the spirit of the great nineteenth-century rebellion against the self-regulating capitalist market economy, the state cannot be a neutral medium through which society can act upon itself in a self-reflective fashion.[130]

Second, the alternative of reform or revolution has been discredited because both reformist and revolutionary parties have had a share in our present crises. All of our case studies reveal, explicitly or implicitly, the same renunciation of the utopia of revolution, of the dream of a single, imposed model of the good society that breaks completely with the present, that is beyond conflict and division. Such a model is not compatible even in principle with any modern notion of democracy. At the same time, what the case studies express is more than merely incremental reform; at the very least, structural or radical reformism is implied. Yet even these terms coined by A. Gorz[131] do not exhaust what is at stake. Revolution and reform are both today widely understood in terms of (and condemned for) their statist logic, and the idea of somehow combining them, as the term "radical reformism" still suggests, now becomes unacceptable. The term "new evolutionism" is too vague to serve as a replacement, but either "self-limiting revolution" or "self-limiting radicalism" seems appropriate. The idea here, worked out by analysts as diverse as J. Kuron, A. Gorz, N. Bobbio, and J. Habermas, is that the object of radical reconstruction and also its (multiple, nonunified) subjects shift from the state to society. Correspondingly, with regard to the existing structures of state (and, in the West, capitalist) economies, a new kind of self-limitation would have to be and even ought to be practiced. This idea survives in the two temporalities of change referring to state and civil society, as proposed by *Social Contract*, and even in the turn to political society that implies a consciously nonrevolutionary slowing down of the rate of change through negotiations and elections. In a Western version, the same idea is expressed quite well by Rosanvallon's juxtaposition of the rebuilding of civil society with necessary compromises on the structures of the state and the economy. Civil society can help change those structures but must not abolish all aspects of their autonomous operation.

Interestingly enough, it is in the most anti-Marxist of our three constellations, Eastern Europe, that the term "revolution" is most often used to indicate transition from authoritarian rule. It must be said, however, that the sense of the term differs from those established by the French and Russian revolutions. The search for the perfect and transparent society associated with these revolutions is explicitly rejected as state-strengthening and even unavoidably terroristic. Some authors redefine the term in a more conservative sense, seeking to preserve still existing (or imagined) older political cultures or traditions threatened by Sovietization, or conserving someone else's tradition (e.g., classical liberalism).[132] Others, building on the single case of the defeated Hungarian Revolution of 1956, seek to understand the transitions in the making as a pure "political revolution" leading to the establishment of a new form of democratic sovereignty, a *novus ordo seclorum*.[133] The first of these lines of thought, in part returning to the premodern notion of revolution as an attempt to reestablish a previous state of affairs, tends to miss what is genuinely new in the present-day projects of transformation. It can lend credence to views referring to "restoration" or "counterrevolution." The second misses their explicitly self-limiting and evolutionary character. This has been repeatedly manifested in the search for compromise and transitional solutions and the deliberate acceptance of the slowing down of the rate of change. Amazingly enough, given the nature of the previous regimes, their successors seek neither a general personal expropriation of the members of earlier elites nor their total exclusion from political or professional activity. Indeed, these options are avoided in a reflective and conscious manner even in the face of repeated efforts to convert powers of the past into those of the future. The self-limiting revolution avoids the total destruction of its enemy, which would inevitably mean putting itself into the place of the sovereign,[134] thereby depriving society of its self-organization and self-defense.

The term "self-limiting revolution" (as well as its partial synonyms, "peaceful" and "velvet" revolution) avoids the weaknesses of both the ideas of "conservative" and "popular" revolution. Instead of retreating behind the modern meaning of "revolution" or repeating its totalizing thrust, this idea extends the self-reflexive and self-critical discourse of modernity to its most important political concept, namely, revolution.[135]

We have already noted that the more or less common posture of antistatist, self-limiting revolution that we discover in our diverse sources is not expressed in terms of a single categorical framework or a single model for reconstructing civil society. At times we find several variants are proposed within a single cultural-political context, and of course the projects vary even more significantly across contexts. The common core of all the interpretations, though, is the concept of civil society, or rather some of the components of this concept. All agree that civil society represents a sphere other than and even opposed to the state. All include, almost always unsystematically, some combination of networks of legal protection, voluntary associations, and forms of independent public expression. A very few conceptions seem to include families and informal groups. Some include movements and even equate civil society with the presence of social movements; others (such as that of the Polish writer Wojcicki) exclude and even fear this possibility as a form of unacceptable politicization. In the texts concerning the four political projects, however, we have found no comprehensive treatment of the relation among the categories of civil society or, for that matter, of the nexus between civil society as movement and as institution. But there is no question that the stresses in the various contexts and texts are often quite different, even if little has been added to (or explicitly subtracted from) the classical list of laws, associations, and publics.[136]

There are two major issues that produce important shifts in categorial frameworks. First, should the economy be included or excluded from the concept of civil society (the Hegelian vs. the Gramscian model)? And second, should one seek to differentiate civil and political society (the Tocquevillian vs. the Hegelian model)? Neoliberals and residually neo-Marxist writers tend to agree on including the economic sphere within civil society, albeit for opposite reasons. The former, whether in the West or now increasingly in the East, reaffirm the identity of the civil and the bourgeois, fear a model of rights in which property is not in the primary position, and reject the politicization of society and the formation of social movements that would demand economic redistribution from the state. While legitimately concerned about the consequences of the link between populism and statism, this intellectual tendency forgets the destructive effects of the self-regulating market on the cultural fabric of society, described so well by Karl Polànyi. Those in Eastern Europe who forget this lesson because of their hatred of all forms of state interventionism seek in effect to rejoin Europe not as it is today, facing ecological and social problems generated by the capitalist economy, but as it once was, inviting the repetition of already known disasters.

The second approach, the residually Marxist one typified by André Gorz and to an extent even by Claus Offe, presupposes these destructive effects but does not sufficiently consider the disastrous results of eliminating economic rationality in the process of politicizing production and distribution. While neoliberals reduce civil society to economic society, neo-Marxists either reduce the future (postcapitalist) economy to political society or propose, in the manner of utopian socialists, some kind of socially reembedded economy. In Gorz's *Farewell to the Working Class*, these two recipes are combined. In the (to us, preferable) realist Green formula of Offe and his colleagues, an economic sphere based on reciprocity, mutuality, and self-activity (*Eigenarbeit*) is combined with a macro-economically steered but nevertheless genuine market economy. In this formula, economic activities in the substantive sense are (at least in part) included in civil society, but economy as a formal process is outside of it.[137]

When civil society in the shape of a social movement is in the process of organizing and institutionalizing itself, however, few authors argue for its unity or even continuity with economic society. There is no question of such reductionism, for example, in the writings of Michnik and Kuron. Instead, they have consistently argued for the autonomy of legal structures, free associations, and genuine public life conceived in terms of the promise of a solidaristic civil society. Undoubtedly the fact that a minor chord in their argument is the liberation of the economy from state controls played a major role here. Beyond the utopia of the complete democratization of production that Kuron still proposed in the mid-1960s, the writers of the Polish democratic opposition are forced to face the harsh reality that only the restoration of the market, beyond any model of social reembedding, could master the Polish crisis and produce a viable, modern economy. Even if industrial democracy plays a role in their proposals, it is recognized that this must be made compatible with the needs of expert management operating in an environment that allows rational calculation. Understandably, in the East European context, the harmful effects of a fully autonomous capitalist market economy on social solidarity, denied by neoliberal writers, was not directly thematized by the main authors of the democratic opposition. Nevertheless, the Solidarity movement, because of its social nature as well as its ties to a Catholic syndicalist tradition, has been to an extent sensitive to just these dangers.

Significantly, the intellectual and political journey made by Latin American writers like O'Donnell and Cardoso is in many respects similar to that of Kuron and Michnik. As late as 1978, O'Donnell still used "civil society" in the neo-Marxian sense of bourgeois society. The mediations he then proposed between civil society and the state (nation, pueblo, and citizenship) corresponded only to the underdeveloped structure of societies plagued by cycles of populist unification and authoritarian atomization. Under the impact of new forms of self-organization and struggles for democracy in the next decade, O'Donnell and P. Schmitter fully changed their terminology and began to use "civil society" to describe a sphere between economy and state, characterized above all by associations and publics. The failure of populist-authoritarian efforts, moreover, led to the rejection of the reverse subsumption, that of the economy by social or political institutions. In Cardoso's subtle analysis, the role of industrial democracy seems to be to establish vantage points of social control without impairing economic rationality.

On the whole, in neither Latin America nor Eastern Europe has the "interface" of civil society and market economy been adequately analyzed.[138] Such an analysis, however, is a precondition for any really serious conceptual alternative to the dangers of economic liberalism and the false promises of utopian socialism.[139] Without such an alternative, one can expect more vacillation between market and state as agents of liberation and renewed neglect of the destructive effects of both on social solidarity and individual autonomy.

Equally important is the division of opinion on the interface between civil society and state. The French writers we have described tend to consider civil and political society as two spheres, the second mediating the relations of the first with the state. In this conception, both civil and political society must be reconstructed to preserve and renew the foundations of associational life and to be able to make those effective vis-à-vis the state. In most of the East European analyses coming from the democratic opposition, and in at least some Latin American writers (e.g., F. Weffort), the category of civil society includes and subsumes the levels of its political mediations. Finally, in yet other models, the two categories "civil" and "political" appear more as alternatives of the type of civil society that is desirable or possible. In the writings of Claus Offe, for example, the choice seems to be between neoconservative (depoliticized) or radical democratic (political) civil society. In the argument of O'Donnell and Schmitter, there is a succession of temporal phases, with depoliticized civil society representing the normal phase that can survive even authoritarian rule, while political civil society is only the exceptional phase of mobilization or upsurge. Here the cycle of types of civil society represents another version of the political cycle of authoritarian and democratic regimes. The move from demobilized to mobilized civil society implies the end of the authoritarian regime; demobilized civil society, implies first the stabilization of democracy and only eventually the possibility of a return of dictatorship. Even in some Eastern European analyses, a choice between unpolitical and political interpretations has been proposed (in Poland, by Catholic intellectuals) to highlight the alternative of antipolitics in a society deeply tired of previous forms of politicization.

Assuming for the moment that the stark alternative between political and civil society is a function of either undesirable political polarization, in which the neoconservatives have had the initiative, or an equally undesirable cycle, we are still left with two competing models that express the need to combine prepolitical levels of social life with political forms that can provide for public life outside the framework of public political authority, i.e., the state. These involve, on the one hand, a model of civil society that includes a political public sphere among its categories and, on the other hand, a framework within which civil and political society are clearly differentiated. To some extent, the choice is a question of inherited intellectual traditions. The German tradition stemming from Hegel and Marx represented a culmination of the differentiation of the classical *topos* of political or citizen society into state and depoliticized civil society. This tradition has room for mediations between civil society and state within each domain but not for an independent domain between them with distinct institutions and dynamics. In contrast, the French tradition derived from Tocqueville never totally dissolved the old category of political society but instead established it alongside civil society and state. Finally, and most confusingly, the Italian tradition going back to Gramsci uses all three terms but tends to identify political society with the state, echoing the traditional premodern usage.

Current political requirements are equally important in the choice between the two types of categorization. In both Latin America and Eastern Europe, the juxtaposition of civil society and state was a conceptually dualistic outcome of a period of societal self-organization that led to polarization between democratic and authoritarian forces. Independent society was strong enough to survive and even to challenge the legitimacy of the authoritarian state. But it was not strong enough to compel genuine compromise or to secure a transition beyond authoritarian rule. With the emergence of real possibilities of negotiation and compromise, and even agreement, concerning the dismantling of authoritarian governments in favor of electoral scenarios, the category of civil society seemed to many writers (Cardoso, Kis, Stepan) to be unsuitable to depict the organized social forces entering into processes of political exchange with state actors. This led to the resurrection of the category of political society (or its stand-ins) even where the influence of Hegel, Marx, and Gramsci was strong. Some writers offer normative reasons for the shift, insisting that the turn to political society allows a desirable pluralization of the opposition, whose location on the level of civil society is said to involve monolithic unification within the one great movement of society.[140]

Thus, the choice between the two frameworks cannot rest on intellectual history, current political requirements, or even their combination; it presupposes additional systematic considerations that we shall outline later in this book. For now, we note only that a choice of either approach has been insufficiently motivated thus far. In particular, the structures and forms of action that would correspond to civil as distinct from political society have not been systematically analyzed by those who presuppose the sharp differentiation of these two domains. To make their case, defenders of differentiation would have to have recourse to something like the old distinctions of movements and elites, as well as of influence and power, to flesh out the difference between the "civil" and the "political." This they may not wish to do, however, for tacit normative or ideological reasons.

Indeed, the two frameworks seem to have different relations to analytical and normative considerations. From an analytical point of view, the distinction between civil and political society helps to avoid the sort of reductionism that assumes that political activities with a strategic dimension are easily generated by societal associations and movements or are somehow unnecessary. Paradoxically, an undifferentiated concept of civil society gives us a stark choice between the depoliticization of society (where the political is assigned to the state) and its overpoliticization (where all dimensions of civil society are held to be political or are to be politicized). The distinction between the civil and the political, on the other hand, highlights the fact that neither of these domains is automatically reconstituted when the other is. Indeed, there could even be opposition and conflict between the requirements of the two projects.

From a normative point of view, treating political society as a mediation within a many-leveled civil society has the possible advantage of establishing the priority of nonstrategic domains of solidarity, association, and communication. Differentiating the civil and the political seems to put the domains on an equal normative footing. While this latter approach does not make the reconstitution of civil society an automatic function of the existence and activity of political organizations, it nevertheless tends to relieve the actors of political society from the normative burden of having to build or fortify civil institutions that may limit their own freedom of action. This is a serious problem, because although the actors of civil society seem to learn by their failures that they cannot achieve their own goals without recourse to political society, the reverse is unfortunately not the case, as the history of elite democracies shows.[141] It is only in the long run that the viability of a democratic political society may depend on the depth of its roots in independent, prepolitical associations and publics.

Given the complementary normative and analytical advantages of the two conceptions, one treating political society as mediation and the other stressing analytical differentiation of the civil and the political, we propose to use both conceptions and at times to combine them. We believe that this is appropriate because our methodology combines hermeneutic and analytical approaches.

The issue of the relationship between civil and political society is connected to the question of the locus of democratization. All of our relevant sources view liberal democracy as a necessary condition for bringing the modern state under societal control. They also assume that liberal democracy is incompatible with a democratic pyramid whose base is direct participation. They have, moreover, broken with the old dream of abolishing the state. Nevertheless, in the West this new emphasis tends to be coupled with an old one: awareness of the elitist character of contemporary liberal democracies. This set of positions, together with a certain deemphasis (though not abandonment) of the idea of industrial democracy, has led many authors in the West to shift the project of "democratizing" elite democracy from the state to civil society.[142] In the program of the Greens, as represented by Offe, this change has also been articulated on the organizational level, in the attempt to combine party-based with movement-oriented strategies. In general, those who seek to democratize civil society understand this domain as comprised of movements as well as institutions.

This has been also true of Eastern Europe and Latin America, where movements have tended to be far more global and comprehensive than in the West. Under dictatorships, though, there was something constrained and artificial in the shift of the project of democratization to civil society: The sphere of the state (not to mention the economy) and of potential parliamentary mediation was placed off limits not by normative choice but by strategic necessity. The long-range goal of parliamentary democracy was as a rule affirmed, with the exception of those appealing to a different (deficient or superior, as the case may be) political culture and tradition. When the crisis of the regimes made this a possible short-term goal, for many the project of democratization shifted to political society. Some authors even tried to juxtapose "liberalization," oriented to civil society, and "democratization," whose locus was to be primarily political society.[143] In Eastern Europe, the elite theoretical understanding of Western European liberal democracy was either forgotten or abandoned in favor of a civics textbook version. The revival of economic liberalism also increased suspicion of societal organizations capable of making demands on new political elites that might translate into unacceptable economic costs. Many who seek to restrict democratization attack social organizations such as Solidarity for being undemocratic. Some hold that societal democratization inhibits the creation of a truly modern state capable of effective decision making.[144]

There are, of course, countervailing tendencies rooted in the movement character of the Polish and also, in part, the Hungarian opposition. There is a tendency to articulate, more in practice than in theory, a dualistic strategy that sees the different forms of democracy and democratization in civil and political society as complementary, each indispensable for a project of "more democracy." Cardoso, in Latin America, has come the closest to articulating such a program explicitly. Initially, at least, the dualism of union and party in which the victorious Solidarity movement articulated itself favored a similar formulation. Even after the split of this movement-party, the two new organizations that have emerged, the liberal-democratic ROAD (Civic Movement–Democratic Action) and the right-wing Center Platform, seem to share this dual heritage, as do all the dynamic new organizations of

Hungary (MDF, SzDSZ, Fidesz) and Czechoslovakia (Civic Forum, Public Against Violence). The organizational models of these new political "parties," none of which is formally named as such, have at least initially brought them close to the dualistic model sought, generally unsuccessfully, by some of the new social movements of the West, especially the Greens.

Today's trend nevertheless is to professionalize and "partify" the new parties. Some still talk, though, of developing more complex ties to the forms of civil society within the framework of increasing differentiation from them. Such ties would presuppose both a programmatic openness of the political to the civil and a sufficient strengthening of the latter to allow it to function in institutionalized forms. What is needed, in other words, are programs that not only establish an ongoing process of political exchange with organizations and initiatives outside the party political sphere but also strengthen civil society with respect to the new economic society in formation.[145] Only such a program could offer something genuinely new with respect to present models of Western politics, thereby transcending the bad choice of either economic liberalism and elite democracy or direct democratic fundamentalism.

But even if such a new civil-society-oriented strategy whose roots can be discovered in the varieties of political discourse explored here were to emerge, it is not yet clear why it should be preferred to a renewed liberalism (very much on the rise) or a radical egalitarian democracy (at the moment on the decline). And if it could be shown to be normatively preferable to those options, it may well be the case that more complex theoretical considerations would show precisely what is attractive about the politics of civil society is incompatible with the development of modernity. To examine these issues with sufficient seriousness, we now take our leave of the discussions of contemporary actors and turn to theoretical reconstruction and critique of the concept of civil society.

2

Conceptual History and Theoretical Synthesis

A Sketch of Early Modern Conceptual History

Present-day political models that use the concept of civil society not only contradict one another but are also relatively poor in categories. Furthermore, their links to a rich tradition of interpretation are not clear. Since this tradition is not thematized, the differences between the new versions of the concept and their historical predecessors are also left unexplored. Thus, a theoretical scheme inherited from the past (or even several pasts) is simply assumed, but not demonstrated, to be adequate to modern conditions.

In our view, a conceptual history of the term "civil society" is an important way to begin to address these tasks. Such a history should, first of all, deepen and extend the relevant categorical frameworks in use today. Second, it should allow us to distinguish premodern and modern layers in the concept, indicating what versions have become questionable and inadequate today. While conceptual history cannot remove the contradictions among contemporary usages, it can help us see what is at stake in these contradictions and what options have become, at least historically speaking, implausible. Finally, a conceptual history can help root the usages of a concept of civil society in a political culture whose motivational power has not yet been exhausted: the political culture of the age of the democratic revolutions. Conversely, the revival of the concept today helps validate this particular political culture.

The first version of the concept of civil society appears in Aristotle under the heading of *politike koinonia*, political society/community. It is this term the Latins translated as *societas civilis*. The concept represented the definition of the *polis*, understood as the *telos* of the human being as a political animal, *zoon politikon*. *Politike koinonia* was defined as a public ethical-political community of free and equal citizens under a legally defined system of rule. Law itself, however, was seen as the expression of an *ethos*, a common set of norms and values defining not only political procedures but also a substantive form of life based on a developed catalogue of preferred virtues and forms of interaction.[1] Today we can symbolically represent our distance from the Greeks by pointing to the absence of a series of distinctions and oppositions in the concept of *politike koinonia*. First of all, the Aristotelian notion did not allow for our distinction between state and society. The *polis-oikos* duality may seem to indicate the contrary, but the *oikos*, household, was understood primarily as a residual category, the natural background of the *polis*. *Politike koinonia* was logically only one *koinonia* among many (including perhaps the *oikos*, but more generally all forms of human association from occupational groupings to groupings of friends, etc.); it was more deeply understood as the all-encompassing social system with nothing except natural relations outside of it.[2] Thus, there could be no question of the *polis* and the *oikos* representing two *systems* of (different) social or political relations. First, the *oikos* was not a legal entity: It was regulated not by law but by the despotic rule or domination of its head. Second, the plurality of households represented no system: They related to one another (in theory) only through the *polis*; indeed, through their heads they were *in* the *polis*. Economic relations beyond the household were considered merely supplementary and, beyond a maximum point, pathological.[3]

The resulting concept of *politike koinonia* was paradoxical. It indicated one *koinonia* among many and, at the same time, the whole, a whole with parts outside itself. The paradox could be resolved because of the absence of a second distinction: that between society and community. *Koinonia* in general denoted all forms of association irrespective of the level of solidarity, intimacy, or intensity of interaction. In the case of *politike koinonia*, this allowed for a conception that already presupposed the existence of a plurality of forms of interaction, association, and group life; hence, something of our concept of "society." Yet plurality and differentiation were dramatically integrated in a model that presupposed a single, homogeneous, organized solidary body of citizens capable of totally unified action—closer to our notion of community, a "community of societies." In theory at least, *politike koinonia* was a unique collectivity, a unified organization with a single set of goals that were derivable from the common *ethos*. The participation of all citizens "in ruling and being ruled" represented a relatively small problem in theory, given this assumption of a shared set of goals based on a single form of life.[4]

There is hardly any doubt about the idealized nature of the Aristotelian conception.[5] But what is important for us is that it was *this* conception that entered into the tradition of political philosophy. We leave to the side the first Roman translations of *politike koinonia* as *societas civilis*, because, as far as we can tell, here the concept played only a minor role. More important were the medieval Latin adaptations following the translations of Aristotle by William of Moerbeke and Leonardo Bruni. While some of the earlier utilizations by Albertus Magnus and Thomas Aquinas tended to restrict *societas civilis* to the medieval city-state (as the closest available equivalent of the ancient *polis*),[6] such a prudent use of the concept could not be maintained for long, perhaps because the Greek notion also referred to the overarching level of sovereignty. Only in Italy, however, did city-states approach the status of full sovereignty, and even here only in fact and not in law. As a result, when the Greek conception was more generally utilized, the feudal order of fragmented sovereign units (patrimonial rulers, corporate bodies, towns, etc.) as well as medieval kingship and empire, all came to be described in different sources as *societas civilis sive res publica*.[7] Unnoticed, this usage introduced a level of *pluralization* into the concept that could now hardly be unified under the idea of an organized, collective body, the notion of *respublica Christiana* notwithstanding.

A second important shift, one of *dualization*, occurred when the concurrent revival of monarchical autonomy and public law favored the adaptation (however implausible) of the ancient idea of republic (with which *societas civilis* was identified) to the *Ständestaat* that balanced the new powers of the prince with that of the organized, corporate estates that assembled all those having power and status in feudal society. The dualism here was, however, as Otto Brunner has tirelessly insisted,[8] not between state and society: Civil or political society was understood as a type of state dualistically organized with the "prince" on one side and "land" or "people" or "nation" on the other, with the latter terms denoting the privileged estates. If we accept Marx's 1843 judgment that the old corporate society was immediately political, then the history of the concept of civil society before absolutism belongs at least in this sense to the fundamental pattern established by the Greek prototype of *politike koinonia*, despite enormous differences among the social formations in question.

The development toward absolutism represents the watershed between traditional and modern meanings of "civil society." We see the reasons for this in two well-known and complementary developments. First, the development of princely authority from the *primus inter pares* of a plurality of power holders (classical feudalism) and the senior partner of a dualistic system of authority (*Ständestaat*) to the monopolistic holder of the legitimate means of violence laid the foundations of the modern state. Second, the depoliticization of the former power holders, the estates and corporate bodies, did not destroy their organized and corporate status. Instead, it produced a veritable society of orders. To be sure, the transition to a duality of state and nonpolitical society could be and was indeed achieved by other, at times complementary, routes: the emergence of autonomous religious bodies tolerated by a more secular state (North America)[9] as well as the rise of new forms of private economic activity outside the policies of the mercantile state (Great Britain). In our opinion, however, the shift from the corporate entities of the *Ständestaat* to those of the depoliticized society of orders was not only historically prior but was also more important, for the European continent at least. Before the absolutist state could disorganize and level its corporate rivals in the name of the universal status of the subject of the state, a countermovement already began to reorganize "society" against the state through associations and forms of public life that may have drawn on the resources of estate independence, religious dissent, and economic entrepreneurship but that embodied new egalitarian and secular principles of organization.[10] There is no doubt, at least as far as we are concerned, that the "society" of the Enlightenment, constituting a new form of public life, was the prototype of the early modern concept of civil society.

Of course, political philosophy that sought to preserve the identification of civil and political society did not immediately register the emergence of a new form of societal public sphere. Three or four alternatives were developed. First, one could try to continue, as did Jean Bodin, in spite of decisive historical changes best registered by himself, the *ständestaatliche* conception of *res publica sive societas civilis sive societas politicus*. Reapplied to the constellation of absolute monarchy and society of orders, this conception falsified the new type of duality now in formation, a duality Bodin otherwise defended. Nevertheless, the model persisted into the German eighteenth century.[11]

Second, one could identify the modern state itself with the commonwealth or civil/political society. This was the option of Hobbes, who of course believed that sovereign power supplied the only "social" bond of naturally unsocial yet rational individuals.[12] In Hobbes's theory, the social contract creates a state, not society. The fusion of society is accomplished only by the power of the state. While Hobbes merely came close to the Greek view that construed the concept of a political society as an undivided system of power, he soon came to realize that the ancient concept relied on a notion of moralized law rooted in *ethos*, rather than positive law limited only to enactment or command. Thus the later construction in the *Leviathan* more or less left out the whole concept of civil society (i.e., the normative idea of free and equal citizens comprising the body politic). Nevertheless, the identification of state and civil society is preserved down to our own day in some Anglo-American literature.

The third option involved a breaking up of the old formula *societas civilis sive politicus sive respublica* by retaining the identity of political and civil society but distinguishing both from the state. Locke's specification of the product of the social contract as "political or civil society"[13] seems to continue on the path of the early Hobbes, representing no break with the tradition. At first sight, his conception even includes an apparent identification of the body politic with government.[14] Locke, however, does clearly seek to differentiate between "government" and "society." He distinguishes between surrendering power to society and to the government "whom society hath set up over itself"[15] and even more emphatically (unlike Hobbes) between the "dissolution of the society" and "the dissolution of the government."[16] Characteristically, however, in this context Locke stays close to the ancient concept when he speaks of the "*one politic society*" in terms of "the agreement to incorporate and act as one body." This ability to become and to act as one body is still assigned to the legislative power of government. The dissolution of the legislative power is proposed as the end of a society, but Locke inconsistently assigns the possibility of providing for a new legislature to the same society when the legislature is dissolved, or even when it acts contrary to its trust.

Montesquieu's conception was more historically sensitive. It united the eighteenth-century notion of two contracts (social and governmental) with the Roman law distinction of civil and public law (here "political law").[17] Whereas political law regulates the relationship of governors and governed, civil law regulates the relations of members of society to one another. Accordingly, Montesquieu, following the Italian writer Gravina, distinguishes between government (*l'état politique*) and society (*l'état civile*).[18] Montesquieu's conception of society appears under a shifting terminology. In the context of monarchical government (which represents the *modern* state for him!) it meant, alternatively, the "intermediate powers," "the political communities," or "societies or communities" inherited from the epoch of estate dualism.[19]

Thus, Montesquieu's antiabsolutist strategy relied more on a society constituted by a hierarchic traditional society, one that he wished to repoliticize, than even Locke's notion of political society, which contained at least the notion of an initial equality of status. With regard to the Enlightenment conception, Montesquieu anticipated, however inconsistently, the differentiation, for polemical reasons, of state and society, while Locke redefined the notion of society itself in terms of the idea of formal equality derived from universal natural law. Despite the ideological features of their conceptions (in Montesquieu's case, still expressing the world view of privileged but depoliticized orders; in Locke's, that of a new status order increasingly based on private property), these two philosophers provided important conceptual preparation for the modern redefinition of civil society. Their constructions pointed beyond the ideological limits of the original presentations.

It was Hegel who synthesized much of late-eighteenth-century thought on the subject, in effect weaving together the somewhat divergent strands of "national" development. It would, however, be erroneous to credit Hegel alone with redefining the concept of civil society.[20] Before turning to his synthesis and its fate, then, we pause to note some of these other contributors.

(1) The conception we have referred to as the Enlightenment notion of "society" (as contrasted with the state) rapidly developed beyond its origins in Locke and Montesquieu. Paradoxically, the new notion often coexisted with the more traditional identification of civil and political society with the state, as in the case of Rousseau (and then Kant).[21] In France, these two trends both shared in the growing opposition to both societal pluralism, in the sense of group or collective rights identified with social orders, and monarchical absolutism. Thus, one might say that, as the polemical conception of "society against the state" was fashioned in the salons, coffeehouses, lodges, and clubs of the time,[22] both the rhetoric of antiabsolutism (Montesquieu) and opposition to privilege (Voltaire) were united in a single conception of a (civil) society opposed to a state whose components were formally equal, autonomous individuals as the sole repositories of rights. This conception fully came into its own in a series of revolutionary conceptions of natural law. Thomas Paine's *Common Sense*, the various American bills of rights, and the French *Declaration of the Rights of Man and Citizen* clearly juxtapose an individualistic, egalitarian society to government (even a constitutional state!), with the society becoming the sole source of legitimate authority.[23]

(2) In England after the Glorious Revolution, Locke's ambiguous separation of society from government was slowly eroded. What counted as "society" was now organized as a state that involved a gradual fusion between parliamentary representation and the

executive.[24] The term "society" as distinct from "the state" came to be reserved for high or polite society, a custodian of manners and influence, but not of any kind of political project. In general, the term "civil society" preserved its traditional identification with political society or the state. A new component was added to this identification by the thinkers of the Scottish enlightenment—Ferguson, Hume, and Smith, among others—who came to understand the essential feature of civil or "civilized" society, not in its political organization but in the organization of material civilization. Here a new identification (or reduction) was already being prepared: that of civil and economic society, reversing the old Aristotelian exclusion of the economic from *politike koinonia*.[25]

(3) The French and British conceptions had a strong influence in Germany, in the works of Kant, Fichte, and a whole series of lesser figures. A certain intellectual conservatism, however, in political as well as intellectual history, also played a historically important role in Germany in preparing the way for Hegel's theory. We have in mind the preservation of the Montesquieuian stress on intermediate bodies or powers in the notion of a *neuständische Gesellschaft* in which *Stände* or estates (in particular, *der bürgerlicher Stand*) would be based on occupational mobility and merit, rather than birth and inheritance, as well as a form of a constitutionalism that represented a modernization rather than the abolition of the dualism of the *Ständestaat*.[26] Nevertheless, the attempt to modernize the notion of estates was overshadowed by the influence of Kant's redefinition of civil society as based on universal human rights beyond all particularistic legal and political orders. In Kant's philosophy of history, a universal civil society based on the rule of law was postulated as the *telos* of human development. Kant explicitly rejected (in the spirit of the French Revolution) any compromise with the corporate and estate powers of the absolutist era.[27] Instead of the old concept, Kant and then Fichte put forward the notion of a citizen society, *staatsbürgerlicher Gesellschaft*, which they interpreted in the spirit of the French *Declaration* of 1789.[28] In Fichte especially, according to Manfred Riedel, two specifically modern notions appear for the first time: the sharp separation of state and society, and the understanding of society itself in individualist and universalist terms. In making this shift, the young Fichte moved from liberalism to radical democracy.

The two strands of the German discussion of civil society—the universalism of Kant and Fichte and the pluralism of more the conservative line of thought—come together in Hegel. But Hegel also brought other strands into his great synthesis: in particular, the Scottish notion of civilized or economic society. While Hegel's *conception* of civil society may not be the first modern one, we do believe that his is the first modern *theory* of civil society. Moreover, the theoretical inspiration of Hegel's synthesis is in our view not yet exhausted. Despite some views to the contrary (Riedel, Luhmann), we shall argue that several important theoretical traditions that emerged after Hegel, with or without conscious reference to him, continued to move within the terms of analysis that he has brought together. For this reason, we would like to present Hegel not in the context of a conceptual history that analyzes the hermeneutic structure of our concepts but rather as the most important theoretical forerunner of several later approaches that have preserved their potential to provide more global, intellectual orientation even in our own time.

Hegel's Synthesis

All strands of the history of the conception of civil society so far presented meet in Hegel's *Rechtsphilosophie.* He is the representative theorist of civil society because of the synthetic character of his work and, even more, because he was both first and most successful in unfolding the concept as a theory of a highly differentiated and complex social order.

It is by now a commonplace that Hegel attempted to unite, in a scheme that was to be both prescriptive and descriptive, a conception of ancient *ethos* with one of the modern freedom of the individual. But it should also be stressed that in his conception, the modern state did, could, or at least should also reconcile dimensions of the ancient, homogeneous, unified political society with the late medieval plurality of autonomous social bodies. The ancient republican dimension in his conception, drawn from Aristotle and other classical thinkers, was to rest on the twin pillars of ethical life (*ethos* or *Sittlichkeit*) and public freedom. The medieval dimension drawn from Montesquieu and a whole series of German sources involved a renewed stress on intermediate bodies in the face of the modern state.[29] The specifically modern component was to rest on three major features. First, Hegel took over from the natural-law tradition and from Kant the universalist definition of the individual as the bearer of rights and the agent of moral conscience. Second, he generalized the Enlightenment distinction between state and civil society in a manner that also involved their interpenetration. Third, he took over from Ferguson and the new discipline of political economy the stress on civil society as the locus and carrier of material civilization. Astonishingly, he succeeded in building all these elements into a unified framework, albeit one that was not free of antinomies.

One contradiction that permeates Hegel's work is that between systematic philosophy and social theory. This is expressed politically as the antinomy of statist and antistatist positions running through both the doctrine of civil society and that of the state.[30] Hegel's social theory presents modern society both as a world of alienation and as an open-ended search for social integration. His philosophical system, conversely, pronounces that this quest has ended in the modern state. It is never entirely clear, though, whether he means a possible and desirable, or a not yet existent but necessary, or an already existing state. But even in the weakest version of this argument, when he identifies the possible and desirable form of the state with a modernizing and constitutional version of a bureaucratic monarchy, the statist implications of Hegel's system building become clear. Yet, at the same time, Hegel's recurring arguments against monarchical absolutism and revolutionary republicanism revive an antistatist stress on intermediary bodies limiting bureaucratic sovereignty and providing a locus for public freedom. This trend in his thought is compatible only with the repeated implicit (and nowhere systematized) denial that the search for social integration can end in institutions like "our modern states," which can only provide citizens with "a limited part in the business of the state."[31]

The contradiction runs through Hegel's analysis of civil society in the form of two interrelated questions: (1) Is *Sittlichkeit* or ethical life possible only as inherited and unquestioned *ethos* to which individual subjects must conform in order to be consistent with their very identity, or is it possible to think of ethical life in a truly modern form, permitting and even requiring its own questioning and criticism as well as a plurality of normatively valued forms of life? (2) Is civil society to be conceived as *Sittlichkeit* or *Antisittlichkeit* or as a dynamic combination of both "moments"?

The two questions are of course deeply related and may indeed be ultimately the same. To answer them, we must begin with some of the basic categories of the *Rechtsphilosophie*. Hegel differentiated objective spirit (*objektiver Geist*), rationally reconstructed intersubjective structures of meaning ("spirit") embodied in institutions ("objective"), in three dimensions: abstract right, morality, and *Sittlichkeit* (ethical life). The differentiation among them is not so much that of contents (though these do get progressively richer as we move through the three levels) but among three levels of moral argumentation. Abstract right represents a form of argument on the basis of dogmatically assumed first principles, as in natural-rights theories. Morality, a level clearly referring to Kantian ethics, represents the self-reflection of the solitary moral subject as the proposed foundation for a universalist practical argumentation. Finally, *Sittlichkeit* represents a form of practical reason that, through self-reflection, is to raise the normative content and logic of inherited institutions and traditions to a universal level. Only *Sittlichkeit* allows the exploration of normative questions (including "rights" and "morality") on the level of concrete, historically emergent institutions and practices that represent, at least in Hegel's view of the modern world, the institutionalization or actualization of freedom.[32] Ethical life is itself differentiated in a way (entirely unique to Hegel) that combines the two dualities of *oikos/polis* and state/society in the three-part framework of family, civil society, and state.[33] Civil society (*bürgerliche Gesellschaft*) is defined variously, but most revealingly as ethical life or substance "in its bifurcation (*Entzweiung*) and appearance (*Erscheinung*)."[34]

To understand this definition of civil society, we must examine the notion of *Sittlichkeit* more closely. Charles Taylor is surely on solid foundations in at least one dimension of Hegel's text when he interprets the content of this notion "as the norms of a society's public life . . . sustained by our action, and yet as already there."[35] According to Taylor, "in *Sittlichkeit* there is no gap between what ought to be and what is, between *Sollen* and *Sein*."[36] Hegel's overall scheme repeatedly stresses the total identity of the (rational) will of the subject with laws and institutions,[37] making any clash between particular and universal will, subject and object, right and duty, impossible or at least irrational.[38]

Taylor is on less solid ground when he interprets *Moralität* and *Sittlichkeit* merely in the form of opposition. Modern ethical life as Hegel unfolds it is distinguished from all ancient *ethos* because it contains the other two ethical dimensions—rights and universalist morality—on a higher, i.e., an institutionalized, level. Indeed, according to Hegel, an institutional space is created for private morality that should not become "matter for positive legislation."[39] On this basis, Hegel could have gone on to recognize the possibility of institutionalized conflict between theory and practice, norms and actuality, as the greatest achievement of the modern world. That he did not do so allows Taylor to interpret him primarily as an "ancient," entirely against Hegel's own intentions. Of course, Taylor focuses on only the main strand of Hegel's conception, not the antinomic whole. Hegel's own definition of *Sittlichkeit* involves a greater stress on its production and reproduction through self-conscious action.[40] Are the bases of such action to be found in *Sittlichkeit* alone, or in *Moralität* as well, or at least, for the modern world, in a form of ethical life that has incorporated morality, along with the tension between *is* and *ought?* When we say that *Sittlichkeit*, as the norms of a society's public life, is already there, Hegel's authority takes us only so far as to register the institutional existence of the norms in question, possibly in forms of discourse only, or as legitimations and ideologies. Their often "counterfactual" character is noted by Hegel himself, for example, in the case of the principles and practice of positive law. Unfortunately, Hegel did not discover that modern civil society is characterized by the conflict not only of moralities (which he at times seemed to note) but also of the normative conceptions of politics itself. Thus he did not see that it was possible to establish a new form of *Sittlichkeit* containing a plurality of forms of life; this would make consensus possible only on the level of procedures, but even such a consensus can lead to some shared substantive premises and even a common identity. He certainly does admit the possibility of conflict between institutionalized norm, the actual basis of moral opposition, and the practice of institutions. Primarily for this reason, his thought and the social world he describes are open to immanent critique.

Because of the internal division of its institutional sphere, civil society is the framework par excellence where the tension between *is* and *ought* emerges. Our aim is to show that this division hardly disappears in Hegel's theory even in the state sphere, which is supposed to be the one in which all antinomies are reconciled.[41] Although Hegel periodically implies that no actually existing state should be considered already rational, he nevertheless holds that ethical (*sittliche*) substance defined in terms of the identity of rational self-reflection and actualized institutions is the "*wirkliche Geist einer Familie und eines Volks.*"[42] The absence of civil society and the presence of the family and the state, the latter only as people, are the notable features of this definition of *Sittlichkeit*. Consistently enough, civil society reappears in the next paragraph only as an "abstract" and "external" version of *Sittlichkeit*.[43] The section on the transition between the family and civil society speaks of "the disappearance of ethical life" and its reemergence only as a "world of ethical appearance."[44] Hegel goes on to speak of civil society "as a system of ethical life lost in its extremes."[45]

Thus civil society is a level of *Sittlichkeit* where the oppositions of ought/is, subject/object, right/duty, and even rational/actual would all reappear. But it would not be difficult to argue that this level of *Sittlichkeit* is its very antithesis, a *Gegen-* or *Antisittlichkeit*.[46] Much of Hegel's discussion of civil society emphasizes the disintegration of the supposedly natural form of ethical life represented by the family in a world of egotism and alienation. Nevertheless, when he speaks of the ethical roots of the state, he speaks of the family and the corporation, the latter "planted in civil society."[47] Here is the real sense of seeing civil society as the "bifurcation of ethical life," as *both Sittlichkeit* and *Antisittlichkeit*, where the unity of substantial ethical life (according to Hegel's final judgment on civil society) is attained only in appearance.

By following Hegel's unfolding of the categories of civil society from the system of needs and system of laws to the police (general authority) and corporations, and even beyond to the estate assembly and public opinion, we gain a depiction of modern society as a dialectic of *Sittlichkeit* and *Antisittlichkeit*. Only the illusions of system building put an end to this movement in the (highly inconsistent) depiction of the state as fully realized but no longer naturally given ethical life.[48]

We should stop to consider the great importance of a two-sided understanding of Hegel's concept of civil society. If we were to interpret it only as alienation, social integration would have to be conceived exclusively on the levels of family and state. In relation to civil society, then, the prescriptive or critical dimensions of the theory would come to the fore, but a transcendent version of critique[49] would have to take the form of romantic communalism, with face-to-face relations as its normative standard, or of statism, whose self-legitimation could take various republican or nationalist forms. If civil society were interpreted exclusively in terms of the forms of social integration that emerge here, however, the descriptive and tendentially conformist elements of the theory would come forward, and the negative aspects of bourgeois civil society that Hegel was one of the first to point out in detail would be lost from view. The richness and power of Hegel's social theory lies precisely in his avoiding both a transcendent critique of *civil* society and an apology for *bourgeois* society.

Many interpreters of Hegel see the integration of modern society as a series of mediations between civil society and the state. However, this way of putting the issue is already a hostage to the statist dimension in Hegel's thought. If we are not to accept from the outset that the only important line of thought in Hegel assumes the state (but which element of the state?) as the highest, most complete and universal level of social integration, the issue of mediation should be put differently. On a more abstract level, it should already be clear that mediation is between *Antisittlichkeit* and *Sittlichkeit*. On a more concrete level, however, it is the distance between *private* and *public* that is to be mediated, if we understand the former as the vanishing point where the social integration of the family is dissolved before the mediations characteristic of civil society begin. Thus it is our thesis that the mediation of *Antisittlichkeit* and *Sittlichkeit* culminates in a notion of public life that Hegel only inconsistently identified with state authority.[50] After Marx's early critique of Hegel's philosophy of the state, little would be left of this identification, except for the small detail of the role of statism, in the critiques of the capitalist market economy in the next century and a half, including those by Marx's own followers.[51] In both Hegel's and Marx's work, however, the statist trend is in a powerful tension with antistatist options.

As any reader of Hobbes knows, the road to statism is prepared by the identification of society outside the state with egotistic competition and conflict. Such is also the outcome of the well-known Marxian identification of civil and bourgeois society.[52] The traditional German translation of *societas civilis* as *bürgerliche Gesellschaft* is not the only basis of this theoretical move. Hegel himself repeatedly identifies *bürgerlich* as *bourgeois*,[53] and nowhere does he use the adjectival form in the classical sense of *Bürger* or *citoyen*. When he states that individuals as *Bürger* of civil society, the "external state,"[54] are private persons,[55] he participates in a fundamental shift in the concept of civil society away from the original meaning of citizen society. At the same time, if the bourgeois were to be understood as *homo oeconomicus*, then clearly it would represent only one dimension of what Hegel defines as the subject of civil society, the concrete person.[56] Of course, the latter is first defined as "a totality of needs and a mixture of natural necessity and arbitrary will (*Willkür*)." But this is only Hegel's starting point: The system of needs is the first level of civil society. As the argument proceeds through the next levels—"the administration of law" and "general authority and corporation"—we encounter the concrete person again under new headings: legal person, client of general authority, and association member.[57] It is only on the level of the system of needs, the description of which Hegel derives from political economy,[58] that a radical depiction of civil society as *Antisittlichkeit* is consistently upheld. For example, when Hegel defines civil society as a system of *Sittlichkeit* "split in its extremes and lost,"[59] he has in mind a condition where egoistic individualism— one extreme—is integrated by means of an abstract generality (universal interdependence)—the other extreme—that is entirely foreign to the will of individuals. Accordingly, civil society as "an achievement of the modern world"[60] involves the creation of a new type of market economy that integrates the "arbitrary wills" of self-interested economic subjects by means of an objective and "external" process that achieves a universal result unintended and unanticipated by the participants.[61] This objective process can be reconstructed by a science specific to the modern world, namely political economy, that Hegel regards as being entirely parallel to the sciences of nature.[62]

Hegel's model of integration on the level of the system of needs takes off from Adam Smith's description of the self-regulating market as an invisible hand linking self-interest and public welfare. But his arguments are less economic than sociological, even if the tremendous process of economic growth implied by the modern market economy underlies the whole thesis.[63] He sees three levels of integration in this context: needs, work, and "estates." Needs in modern society become more and more abstract in the form of money, which makes everyone's needs commensurable. It is monetarization that makes the general recognition and satisfaction of needs possible. Hegel also sees the underside of the process: The abstraction of needs allows for their tremendous expansion. And the result of the limitless expansion of needs can only be great luxury and extravagance alongside permanent want, i.e., the inability of some to satisfy even basic needs.[64] Work in modern society mediates particularity and universality through the process of value creation (the particular work of the individual creating products that are commensurable with the products of all others) and the division of labor, leading to the "dependence of men on one another and their reciprocal relation."[65] Again Hegel sees the underside of the process, this time in "the dependence and distress of the class" that is tied to forms of increasingly one-sided and restricted work that "entail inability to feel and enjoy the broader freedoms and especially the intellectual (*geistigen*) benefits of civil society."[66] Finally, Hegel has a theory of stratification according to which the differentiated social strata of civil society that he still calls *Stände* (estates or orders) integrate individuals as members of "one of the moments of civil society" with its own rectitude and status honor (*Standesehre*).[67]

Hegel insists that his estates are modern, and that individuals become part of them freely, through their own achievement, rather than ascriptively.[68] Nevertheless, it is clear that he has only partially discovered the specifically modern principle of stratification, namely socioeconomic class.[69] The working class, to which (as

Avineri showed) he restricts the new term class (*Klasse*), is not included in his scheme of agricultural, business, and universal (i.e., bureaucratic) estates.[70] This is a serious omission, especially because Hegel claims that his estates correspond to economic differentiation. In fact, however, he did not discover the specifically modern form of stratification based on socioeconomic divisions of interest and lines of conflict because he did not adequately distinguish between differentiation and integration. Thus, his theoretical instruments failed him when he confronted an increasingly differentiated class, the victim of poverty and the alienation of labor, that he therefore (as it turned out wrongly) considered only as being unable to integrate into, and unable to contribute to the integration of, civil society.

Strictly speaking, integration through estates does not belong to the level of the "system of needs," where integration is the function of objective, unwilled processes. This is shown by the fact that the analysis simply duplicates what Hegel elsewhere assigns to the family (the agricultural class[71]), to the corporation (the business class[72]), and to the general authority (the class of civil servants[73]). It is only what Hegel considers the underside of this process of the emergence of new, nonascriptive status groups that belongs to the socioeconomic level of his analysis. Accordingly, the working class represents a form of inequality produced by civil society[74] in which the absence of inheritance and otherwise unearned income, as well as a specific form of life, makes estate membership inaccessible and exposes individuals to the hazards of economic contingencies beyond their control.[75]

Taken together, need, labor, and differentiation achieve a level of universality in civil society only at great social cost. Hegel is acutely conscious of this even if he does not and cannot notice the level of the corresponding potential of conflict. Unlike some political economists he knew (in particular, Ricardo), he did not readily thematize the problem of conflict in relation to the working class,[76] perhaps because of his belief that estates (i.e., new types of status groups) alone constituted the modern principle of stratification.[77] Nevertheless, he did understand the "system integration" of civil society to be highly unstable, though he did not pose this issue in terms of action- theoretic categories. Even so, more than any political economist, he understood that social integration must occur outside the system of needs in order for the market economy itself to function. Unlike early modern political philosophers in the natural-law tradition, however, he does not confine this level of integration to the exercise of sovereign power, to the sphere of the state, or to the family, another possible choice. It was in conscious opposition to these theoretical options that he developed a theory of social integration that constituted one of the founding acts of modern sociology, or at least of the paradigm developed by Durkheim, Parsons, and Habermas, among others.

Hegel's theory of social integration moves through six steps: legal framework (*Rechtspflege*); general authority (*Polizei*); corporation; the (bureaucratic) executive; the estate assembly or legislature; and public opinion. While the first three of these are developed as parts of the theory of civil society, and the second three belong to the theory of the state, or rather constitutional law, the argument turns out to be essentially continuous.[78] We should perhaps think of these as two lines of argument, even if Hegel's movement back and forth between them is so constructed as to avoid the appearance of such differentiation. It is this double argument concerning social integration on which we shall concentrate.

As we have shown, the system of needs in Hegel's theory is itself integrated, but in a manner that is "external" (outside of will and consciousness), incomplete (less than fully universalist), and self-contradictory. Integration beyond the system of needs operates according to two different logics: the logic of state intervention into society, and that of the generation of societal solidarity, collective identity, and public will within civil society itself. Through most of the text, the unfolding of the two logics can be clearly differentiated: One series—universal estate, general authority, crown, executive—expresses the line of state intervention; another—estates, corporation, estate assembly, public opinion—follows that of the autonomous generation of solidarity and identity.

Only in the "administration of law" is it difficult to separate the two lines of argument. In Hegel's exposition, this level represents the possibility of the universally (or at least generally) valid resolution of the clash of particulars in civil society. The overcoming of *Gegensittlichkeit* as the division of particular and universal begins here, but in a form that is capable of generating only a limited collective identity. The legal person identifies with the collective only in the form of abstract obligations. Hegel not only recognizes the noneconomic presuppositions of economy in the modern sense, in the law of property and contract,[79] but he also sees that their implications go far beyond the economy. In particular, the publication of the legal code and, even more, the publicity of legal proceedings are changes of universal significance and validity that make possible the emergence of a universalist sense of justice.[80] This argument becomes fully intelligible in the context of Hegel's understanding of the concept of the public (*Öffentlichkeit*) that goes beyond the Roman law dichotomy of public and private. We shall analyze this concept in detail below, but here we simply stress that Hegel sees a functional relation between modern law and the system of needs: Each is necessary for the emergence and reproduction of the other. He also insists, however, that the institutionalization of subjective right and objective law protects the freedom and dignity of modern subjects in a way that private persons rather than isolated individuals brought together in a public process can mutually recognize.[81] To Hegel, the institutionalization of right as law requires both state action (he strongly prefers statutory codification to precedent-based adjudication[82]) and autonomous cultural processes. He is neither a legal positivist nor a natural-law theorist nor even a historicist. For Hegel, universal rights have more than just a historically restricted validity even if they emerge in cultural development and can be universally recognized only through a process of education (*Bildung*) that has become possible in civil society.[83]

Universal rights do not, however, attain objective existence without being posited as law (*gesetzt als Gesetz*), which involves legislation, codification, and administration by public authority (*öffentliche Macht*). Without autonomous cultural processes that create them, rights cannot acquire validity or recognition. But without the various necessary acts of the state and its organs, neither true definition nor a systematic relation to other rights is possible.[84] Only the combination of the two yields obligatory force. Hegel wisely recognizes the possible discrepancy of the two moments,[85] cultural and political, "between the content of the law and the principle of rightness."[86] Yet within the analysis of law, he can offer only some formal and procedural requirements that legislators and judges should not violate, in particular the requirement of publicity and the formal generality of law. Presumably he expects a closer fit between the principle of right and positive law regarding substantive legal rules through the ability of the other institutional mediations of his theory to create law.

Integration through the State

Hegel cannot maintain the complementarity between societal and statist strategies of social integration beyond his analysis of the administration of law. From this point on in the argument,[87] the two types of strategies become identified with different institutional complexes. The statist trend in Hegel's thought, anticipating Marx and especially Marxism, is clearly connected to the notion of civil society as *Gegensittlichkeit*, rooted in the analysis of the system of needs.[88] The pathological consequences of the system of needs, involving extremes of wealth and poverty, want and luxury, as well as a severe threat to the humanity and very existence of the class of direct labor, call for measures that allow Hegel to anticipate features of the modern welfare state.[89] In particular, a state bureaucracy (the universal class, the class of civil servants) is called upon to deal with the dysfunctional consequences of the system of needs, in two forms.

(1) The universal estate is called upon as the key mechanism to deal with the antagonism of estates. Here the analysis suffers from a lack of reference to the class Hegel knows to be both the product of the modern economic order and the most endangered by it. Nevertheless, the assumption that estates produce both integration within strata and antagonism between strata does represent an important opening to a sociology of conflict. In this context, Hegel maintains that the status-honor and economic condition of the estate of civil service imply that particular or "private interest finds its satisfaction in its work for the universal."[90] The salaried condition of the official, the requirement for open access to offices, and the limits against turning offices into private patrimonies all inhibit the formation of the sort of self-interested, closed estate that

characterized most traditional bureaucracies. The education of the public servant makes the idea of public service conscious and deliberate.[91] Thus, according to Hegel, the universal estate is in a unique position to resolve the antagonism of estates.

There is no need to repeat Marx's brilliant 1843 critique of the pretensions of Hegel's view of the universal estate, which pinpointed its particular interests and status consciousness. Hegel managed to delude himself on this score partly because of the statist strain in his thought, and partly because he did not see any reason to consider the social antagonism implied by the existence of the "class of direct labor." Being incapable of intraclass integration, workers in this view do not seem to be capable of interclass conflict. The dysfunctional consequence of the plight of this class is seen in the existence of an anomic mass, the *Pöbel*, whose integration requires measures that aim at individuals (i.e., clients) rather than integrated groups. But with the poorest stratum removed from the field of analysis, the idea that the bureaucracy represents a general interest needs to be reconciled only with the interests of the landed classes.[92]

Hegel's discussion of civil servants takes place in two sections of his analysis: those on the system of needs of civil society and the executive of the state. This is justified by the fact that the bureaucracy is both a social stratum and a state institution.[93] But Hegel's theoretical decision disguises the fact that this estate differs from others in two respects. First, it is constituted by the state and not by the societal division of labor. Second, in the state the bureaucracy finds its institutional place in the executive rather than in the estate assembly. Thus, Hegel's argument concerning the fortunate double meaning of the German term *Stände*,[94] referring both to social orders and to a deliberative assembly, does not apply. By calling the bureaucracy a *Stand*, Hegel misses the opportunity to discover the second, primarily modern, form of stratification whose constitutive principle is political power. Even more importantly, he disguises the statist principle of the form of social integration under consideration.

The way the bureaucracy is to accomplish the integration of antagonistic estates reveals at least some of the consequences. The state executive or political bureaucracy has the role of "subsuming the particular under the universal" by applying the laws. Hegel accepts the parliamentary assumption that an estate assembly is capable of generating a public and general will. But he believes that in civil society all the particular interests will reappear, and that for this reason outside the state sphere proper the bureaucracy must be the agent of universality. The fact that he feels compelled to admit that the authority of local communities (*Gemeinden*) and corporations is needed as a "barrier against the intrusion of subjective caprice into the power entrusted to the civil servant"[95] shows, though, that Hegel is aware that reality can be quite different from his idealized depiction. Presenting the bureaucracy as an estate of civil society is thus not only a way of disguising the actual level of state intervention he advocates but is also a way of deflecting the responsibility for dysfunctional or even authoritarian intervention from the state to a social group and to the subjective caprice of its members.

(2) The model of integration through state intervention is further developed in the theory of police or general authority (*Polizei* or *allgemeine Macht*). Unfortunately, the modern term "police" does not cover Hegel's meaning here. In accordance with earlier absolutist usage, he means more than the prevention of crime and tort and the maintenance of public order.However, Hegel also uses the term "general authority" in senses not covered by the section on the *Polizei*. Thus, it may be best simply to list his actual uses of this concept: surveillance (linked to crime and tort);[96] intervention in the economy in the form of price controls and regulation of major industrial branches;[97] and public welfare in the form of education, charity,[98] public works,[99] and founding of colonies.[100]

The idea behind linking these apparently diverse areas is not quite coherent. The functioning of the system of needs is linked in Hegel's conception to two rather different factors: a centrifugal dysfunctionality based on the subjective caprice and carelessness of individuals, *and* systematically induced effects largely based on worldwide competition and the division of labor. The police represent state penetration into civil society to serve the interests of justice and order by compensating for *both* of these phenomena without eliminating their basic causes, which lie in the dynamism of the system of needs. As a result, the centrifugal and anomic consequences of conflict are diminished but not entirely done away with. "Crime prevention" and the punishment of criminals do not eliminate crime but keep it within tolerable limits. Provisions for social welfare and public education do not abolish conflict and alienation, but they can prevent the decline of the class of labor to the status of a rabble (*Pöbel*). In these cases and also in the case of price and production controls, the goal Hegel espouses is compensation for the dysfunctional side effects of the new type of market economy, a core dimension of modern civil society. The details of his analysis do not always make clear whether he is defending precapitalist forms of paternalist intervention or anticipating features of a modern welfare state. The general conception, however, involves reactive compensation for the effects of a genuine market system more than proactive, statist substitution for market functions.

The statist feature of the doctrine of the police lies elsewhere. Hegel does not systematically distinguish between state intervention in the form of economic steering (e.g., price controls in a system of market prices) and intervention in noneconomic spheres of life (e.g., surveillance). While from the point of view of market dysfunction, each of these measures represents post facto compensation, surveillance and other forms of social control are proactive from the point of view of noneconomic forms of life, substituting, as Tocqueville noted, statized relations for horizontal social ties.[101] A similar proactive character can be noted in the roles of general authority dealing with trusteeship and education.[102] The problem, of course, is not that Hegel hopes to prevent orphans and the children of the poor from falling into poverty, but that he defines the remedies in terms of a "right" of society as a whole rather than the rights of the individuals, families, and communities concerned. Once again Hegel replaces horizontal social interaction and solidarity by vertical ties based on state paternalism. Even if it were true that civil society destroys the family ties that protected individuals in premodern society, the idea of the general authority (the state) "taking over the role of the family for the poor"[103] is a mystification of measures that do not produce but replace social solidarity.

Social Integration through Civil Society

Hegel does not claim that on this level the state produces a thoroughgoing unification of society. Moreover, the kind of universality it achieves here amounts to a form of "external" imposition and control.[104] In civil society we encounter the state only in the form of externality, and the metaphor of civil society as "universal family" is entirely misplaced in the theory of the police or general authority. This metaphor belongs instead to the second strand of Hegel's conception of social integration, the solidaristic strand that runs from the family to the corporation, the estate assembly, and public opinion. But, since Hegel (wrongly) considers the integrating role of the family to be negated in civil society,[105] the corporation becomes the starting point of the self-integration of civil society. As in the case of the police and the estates, one can legitimately question whether Hegel's theory of the corporation revives a premodern form of social life or anticipates a postliberal form of social integration. We shall return to this question, noting here only that Hegel was both harshly critical of the revolutionary and liberal attacks on the old corporate entities and in favor of a form of corporate organization significantly different from that of the old regime.[106] Indeed, he proposed and defended a version of the corporation that was open to entry and exit, that was based on no ascriptive or hereditary principle, that was voluntary and not all-inclusive, and that did not imply any suspension of the individual rights of members with respect to the corporate body. Unlike the case of a modern union, however, both employers and employees would be members of corporations in the economic sphere. Moreover, Hegel does not restrict corporate organization to that sphere: Learned bodies, churches, and local councils are also included in the concept.[107]

The primary functions of the corporation in Hegel's theory are socialization and education. The business association in particular is meant to combine vocational training with training for citizenship. Thus all of corporate life, assuming the already mentioned modernization of its structure, helps to overcome the gap civil society produces between bourgeois and citizen by educating individuals to internalize the common good and develop civic virtue. In the process, solidarities are expected to develop that would affect the motivational structure of individuals, substituting collective concerns and identifications for egoistic ones. In this context, Hegel's problem was the same as Rousseau's, namely, how to move from the particular to the general, given modern individuality. But his answer is significantly different, because Hegel did not believe that the reality of the modern large-scale state or of a modern civil society with a dynamic system of needs could or should be imagined away, or that individuals who are entirely egotistical in private life can attain the general in the political sphere. In his view, generality can be attained only through a series of steps that incorporate something of the public spirit in what is juridically the private sphere. The corporations that Rousseau, his natural-law philosophical forebears, and his revolutionary republican successors sought to banish from social life, replace the particularity in Hegel's theory with a limited form of generality on a level where resocialization is actually possible.

While the corporation represents a crucial step in the development of the strand of Hegel's thought that stresses the self-integration of society, the antinomy of his political position is nevertheless visible in it. Like Montesquieu before him and Tocqueville after him, he sought an intermediate level of power between individual and state; he feared the powerlessness of atomized subjects and sought to control the potential arbitrariness of the state bureaucracy.[108] But at the same time, in line with his doctrine of the state, he wants to defend a model of socialization that will make the transition to a state-centered patriotism plausible. In this context, Hegel's aim is to provide a smooth transition based in everyday life from the *Geist* of the corporation as the schoolhouse of patriotism to the *Geist* of the state where patriotism is to achieve its full "universality."[109] Much depends, of course, on whether the conception of the state implied here is based on a public, parliamentary generation of identity or a bureaucratic-monarchic imposition of unity. But since the antinomy is not resolved on the level of the state, the role of the corporation in political education also becomes ambiguous. This, in turn, affects the the relation of the corporation to the general authority; as Heiman shows, Hegel was never able to decide between a medievalist doctrine involving corporate independence and legal personality and a Roman law conception stressing state control and oversight.[110]

Whatever the ambiguities of Hegel's corporate doctrine, the different center of gravity here when compared to the concept of the police cannot be overlooked. Both police and corporation are at times identified as the individual's second family. They also share some functional assignments, such as education. Furthermore, the normative justifications produced for each are equally convincing. The corporation is a second family small and determinate enough in its purpose to allow genuine participation by its members. These members, however, include only a part of the population; while it appears general with regard to its members, the corporation inevitably represents a particular interest with respect to other groups and those not "incorporated." Nevertheless, the corporation is capable of creating internal motivations, and it does not depend on external sanctions guaranteeing compliance. On the other hand, the regulation of the police is universalist and ought not to allow the formation of particular clusters of interests. However, the activity of the police does rely on external sanction, involves no participation of those concerned, and does not lead to the formation of autonomous motivation.

As the comparison of police and corporation shows, statism in Hegel's thought is linked not only to some kind of political opportunism but also to the idea of universality, without which no modern conception of justice is possible. Hegel has good reasons not to make a definitive normative choice between police and corporation, between abstract universality and substantial particularity. These moments are sundered in civil society, and it is Hegel's thesis that they can be reunited only in the state. It would be only on this level that the corporation, as the second ethical root of the state (after the family), would achieve its universality.

Our reconstruction of Hegel challenges interpretations suggesting that the antinomies of civil society are resolved on the supposedly higher level of the state. Instead, we would argue that it is more fruitful to interpret Hegel's thought as dualistic or antinomic on both levels. What we crudely label as "statist" and "solidaristic" trends in his thought appear in the analysis of *both* civil society and state. Accordingly, the doctrine of the state itself can be analyzed in terms of these two trends. *Thus, it would be a mistake to oppose to the statist dimension of Hegel's thought a quasi-liberal conception according to which civil society, as opposed to the state, is the only source of genuine norms.* Such a view would be all the less defensible because of the unavoidable element of particularism attached to the important intermediary bodies of civil society. Thus, the transition to a key norm of modernity—universality—cannot occur without some participation of state institutions. Even if we were to note that the protection of the individual rights of members can be written into the charters of modern corporations, the establishment of universal rights as positive law presupposes, as we have seen, the activity of the state. But which dimension of the state? The question we must consider is whether, in Hegel's theory, the estate assembly and *public* opinion or the executive bureaucracy and *public* administration is the locus and source of the highest level of social integration and will formation.

In Hegel's conception, we should recall, the police represent the penetration of the state into civil society. Analogously, the estates assembly represents a penetration of civil society into the state. However, the civil society represented in the state through the estate assembly is already organized; to Hegel the presence of an atomized civil society in the state would be most regrettable. According to the free but convincing translation of Knox:

The circles of association in civil society are already communities. To picture these communities as once more breaking up into a mere conglomeration of individuals as soon they enter the field of politics, i.e., the field of the highest concrete universality, is *eo ipso* to hold civil and political life apart from one another and as it were to hang the latter in air, because its basis could then only be the abstract individuality of caprice and opinion.[111]

This conception directly links the estates and corporations of civil society with the assembly of estates. While Hegel at first stresses the link of estates to the legislature, as indicated by the German term *Stände*, the more important theoretical foundation of the assembly is in fact the corporation, the existence of which is the only real evidence provided for the claim that organization and community are possible in an otherwise atomized civil society. The deputies of civil society are "the deputies of the various corporations."[112] Earlier, this statement is limited and expanded. Atavistically, the agricultural estate (suddenly meaning only the nobility) is to be directly present, as in the assemblies of the *Ständestaat.* The business estate, on the other hand, is represented by the deputies of associations, communities, and corporations (*Genossenschaften, Gemeinden, Korporationen*), which are all incorporated forms of association. Hegel does not even feel the need to indicate and justify his exclusion from political life of the one class, direct labor, that is supposedly totally disorganized.[113] More important than the conformist and conservative elements in his thought, however, are his reasons for recommending his particular version of representative government. According to Hegel, when civil society elects its political deputies, it "is not dispersed into atomistic units, collected to perform only a single and temporary act, and kept together for a moment and no longer."[114] Rather, in the process of deliberating and choosing deputies, the associations and assemblies of social life acquire a connection to politics in the same act that gives politics a foundation in organized social life. It is precisely at this level, at the point where civil society and the state interpenetrate, that Hegel rediscovers and integrates, without explicitly saying so, the ancient *topos* of *political* society.

The estate assembly has the role of completing the job begun by the corporation, but on a societywide level of generality that he (and especially his English translator) often refers to as "universality." This job is to bring public affairs and, even more, public identity into existence.[115] Again parallel to the doctrine of the corporation, the legislature is regarded as a mediating organ, this time between the government (*Regierung*) and the people, differentiated as individuals and associations.[116] The former is thus prevented from becoming tyrannical and the latter from becoming a mere aggregate, a mass with an unorganized and therefore dangerous opinion. Hegel of course stresses the role of the estate assembly in legislation and even constitution making,[117] but his main interest throughout is in the constitution of the agent of legislation and, even more, its proper medium. The category of publicity indicates that only the genuine representatives of the public are legitimately entitled to make the laws. The laws they enact are to be considered legitimate only if the procedures of public deliberation are rigorously followed. Since Hegel insists on genuine and unconstrained discussion and deliberation, he emphatically rejects the *imperative mandate*, the principle of the traditional *Ständestaat*. The assembly must be "a living body in which all members deliberate in common and reciprocally instruct and convince one another."[118]

Hegel's vehement insistence on genuine publicity in the legislature (as well as the courts) has other important grounds. He wishes to promote knowledge of public business in society and (however inconsistently) to make the estate assembly susceptible to the influence of public opinion. Quite like Tocqueville, Hegel is ambivalent concerning public opinion. Defined as "the formal, subjective freedom of individuals to express their own judgments, opinions, and recommendations concerning general affairs whenever collectively manifested,"[119] public opinion is internally contradictory and "deserves as much to be respected as despised (*geachtet als verachtet*)."[120] Respect is due because of a hidden strain of rationality that is, however, buried and inaccessible to public opinion's opinion about itself because of its concrete, empirical form of expression. Interpreting public opinion is thus the role of intellectual and political elites.[121] In order to promote the formation of public opinion, Hegel supports extensive freedom of public communication (especially speech and press), and he worries only slightly about possible excesses. Indeed, he believes that the genuine publicity of legislative debates has a good chance of transforming public opinion and eliminating its shallow and arbitrary components, rendering it harmless in the process.[122] Nevertheless, it is also implied here that the debates of the assembly can transform public opinion precisely to the extent that its essential content and elements of rationality are raised to a higher level. In this sense, not only does the political public of the legislature *control* public opinion (Hegel's stress), but a prepolitical public sphere plays an important role in constituting public life in the political sense.

The concept of public opinion developed by Hegel is not free of the antinomies of his political thought. The statist trend in this context is expressed in the concern to control and disempower public opinion in order to make it compatible with the management of the state. The solidaristic trend, on the other hand, involves the raising of public opinion to a higher level of rationality in a parliamentary framework between state and society, itself exposed to the controls of publicity. From the first point of view, public opinion is ultimately a threat, and the proper relationship to it on the part of political (including parliamentary) elites is manipulative. From the second point of view, public opinion is the condition of possibility of political public life, and the proper relationship to it on the part of elites would have to be one of public dialogue in which truth would be an open question to be decided by the more convincing arguments rather than the a priori possession of one of the sides. The public sphere of the estate assembly plays a role in enlightening and educating public opinion precisely because truth here is not known in advance but rather emerges during the debate itself, along with the virtues that can serve as examples to the larger audience.[123] One trend in Hegel's thought implies that in those states where the life of the legislature is genuinely public the structure of public opinion will itself change: "What is now supposed to be valid gains its validity no longer through force, even less habit and custom, but by insight and argument (*Einsicht und Gründe*)."[124] At other times, however, the dialogue model of rational political deliberation is restricted to the parliamentary public sphere. In these contexts, the statist trend in Hegel's thought, supported by the false analogy between the search for scientific truth and the attainment of normative truth in politics, stops him from extending the model to the public sphere as a whole.

At issue here, as well as in Hegel's political theory as a whole, is the ultimate locus and nature of public freedom. We accept the interpretation according to which Hegel sought to develop a political doctrine in terms of a whole series of mediations that relativize the Roman law distinction between private and public law.[125] But we accept it with two reservations.

First, we see the mediations as two distinct series: civil servants/police/executive/crown, and estates/corporation/estate assembly/public opinion. The two express the conflicting trends in Hegel's thought. Indeed, the very manner in which they mediate the spheres regulated by private and public law is significantly different in each case. The first series involves public law categories taking on both private and public roles. The second indicates private law entities developing structures of publicity and taking on public functions rooted in these structures.[126] This second pattern is the same as the model in which constitutional rights constitute the public law rights of private subjects.[127] Once these two patterns are separated, however, the meaning of the public sphere in Hegel becomes uncertain. Is its primary paradigm that of public authority or that of public communication? And if he maintains both paradigms, what is to be their relationship?

Second, we do not accept the implicit identification of state and public presupposed by the interpretation, or the idea that each succeeding step in Hegel's exposition represents (even in terms of his own argument) an unambiguously higher level of public life than the one before. For Hegel, undoubtedly the highest purpose of public life is to generate a rational universal identity that he equates with the patriotic ethos of the state. What remains unclear is whether the generation of this ethos is assigned to a state sphere dominated by the executive and linked only to the projections of the state into civil society, or to a sphere dominated by a legislature drawing on autonomous societal resources such as the corporation and public opinion. The issue cannot be decided if we stress the problem of mediating between private and public realms alone— most categories of Hegel's theory of *Sittlichkeit*, beginning with the system of needs, provide such mediations. But it can be decided if we link the process of generating a modern, rational collective identity to the concept of public freedom that Hegel repeatedly uses in this context, that is, to a process that allows the effective participation of individuals in the free shaping of the meaning of a "we." Obviously, public freedom is quite a bit more than the kind of freedom available to the agents of the system of needs, who cannot participate in the formation of any collective identity whatsoever. But Hegel also registers serious doubts about whether the modern state as such can be the locus of public freedom, doubts that run completely contrary to the statist strain in his thought.

We should note once again that, while Hegel nowhere systematizes a conception of the public sphere (*Öffentlichkeit*), the categories of public authority, public freedom, public spirit, public opinion, and publicity play key roles in his work. Let us recall Ilting's thesis that the *Philosophy of Right* seeks above all to synthesize the negative freedom of modern liberalism and the positive freedom of ancient republican thought. The categories of the public sphere represent important ways in which republicanism could be sustained in Hegel's thought after his supposed conservative turn. But even here there is an essential difference with ancient republicanism. Instead of restricting the formation of public freedom to a single social level—political society—Hegel works out a modern republican theory in which a whole series of levels have key roles to play, including the public rights of private persons, the publicity of legal processes, the public life of the corporation, and the interaction between public opinion and the public deliberation of the legislature. Not all of these processes have a public political purpose. Yet they are the stages of learning leading to the formation of public identity. What is common to all of them is the free public participation of those concerned in the formation of decisions.[128] The public purpose of the acts of the police, at times identified as general (*allgemeine*) and even public (*öffentliche*) power, is beyond doubt for Hegel. The same is true of the acts of the executive and, in a *Rechtsstaat*, of the crown as well. Yet in these cases Hegel speaks neither of the formation of public spirit nor of the actualization of public freedom. In fact, it has been noticed that Hegel's most explicit discussion of public freedom juxtaposes the corporation, belonging to civil society, to the modern state:

In our modern states (*modernen Staaten*) citizens have only a restricted part in the general (*allgemeinen*) business of the state; yet it is essential to provide men—ethical entities—with activity of general character over and above their private business. This general activity which the modern state does not always provide is found in the corporation.[129]

In this passage Hegel not only registers the tension between the modern state and public life but identifies a different locus for public freedom than did classical antiquity. The corporations are, in his words, "the pillars of public freedom (*öffentlichen Freiheit*)."[130] Yet for Hegel the public freedom possible in the corporation, involving a relatively high level of participation, cannot be primary in society as a whole. Pelczynski and others are surely right when they argue that Hegel believed that he had proved that "the [modern] state is the actuality of concrete freedom."[131] This argument is supported, in general, by the greater universality of the estate assembly, this veritable corporation of corporations, over the inevitably particularistic societal associations. But it also disguises the reality of the modern state as a hierarchy of offices, as the monopolistic possessor of the means of violence, and as a compulsory association. By reversing the sociologically obvious hierarchy of the modern state, making the legislature primary and the executive secondary, Hegel is constructing a legitimation both in the sense of counterfactually justifying a structure of authority and in the sense of establishing a set of normative claims open to critique. These critical potentials come into view, for example, when the assembly from which the normative claims of state are drawn is depicted as its penetration by civil society.

Hegel, the peerless social theorist of his time, was clearly aware of the sociology of the modern state. We are fortunate to have at our disposal Ilting's careful reconstruction of Hegel's turn from an earlier conception stressing the freedom of the citizen in the state to one stressing the freedom of the state.[132] The shift may well have had independent intellectual motivations, which were then reinforced by Hegel's reaction to the reactionary Karlsbad decrees. Hegel knew and rejected both absolutist and revolutionary statism, as so much of the *Rechtsphilosophie* demonstrates. Is it too far-fetched to assume that a reactionary turn in Prussian politics made him realize (as did Tocqueville soon after) that features of two supposedly aberrant versions of the modern state belonged to its ideal type instead? If this were so, the shift to institutions of civil society as the pillars of public freedom would be logical and also indispensable from the point of view of strengthening this dimension in the parliamentary institutions of the state. Thus, Hegel in his mature text not only restricted the possibility of the citizen's freedom in the state but also expanded, in Ilting's words, the liberties (*Freiheitsrechte*) of civil society into rights of participation (*Teilnehmerrechte*).

The most obvious objection to our reading of Hegel would be that he himself did not admit and, for systematic reasons, would have rejected the idea of two unreconciled strands in his thought. We are not particularly concerned with this criticism (in any case, it is refuted by Ilting's reconstruction) or with the systematic aims of Hegel's work. We are interested only in rebuilding Hegel's conception around what may well be a subtextual antinomy in his political philosophy so that we can trace a new theory of civil society back to the institutionally most elaborated conception from which we can still learn. Thus, a more serious objection to our reconstruction would insist, as did the young Marx in 1843, that the dimensions we bring into special relief represent elements in Hegel's thought that are not modern, in contrast to the modernity of his conception of the system of needs, on the one side, and the bureaucracy, on the other. In this reading, Hegel's "corporation" is an attempt to save *medieval* corporate doctrine; his estate assembly, the institutions of the *Ständestaat*; his notion of public opinion, the *early bourgeois* public sphere; and perhaps the very idea of public freedom, the *ancient* city-states. Accordingly, if we are to look for the modernity of Hegel's social theory, we would do better to focus on the critical aspects of his depiction of the capitalist economy (Lukács) or his anticipation of the welfare state (Avineri).

Of course, each interpreter favorable to Hegel tries to interpret him through a specific conception, and even to enlist his alliance. The theory of civil society we are trying to develop is no exception to this rule. Nevertheless, we believe, in the context of both subsequent social and intellectual history, that the categories we stress were not mere atavisms in Hegel's time and have become even less so in the postliberal (and now also the poststatist) epoch. In this context, the history of social theory offers an important, if hardly conclusive, proof. While the theory of the system of needs was fruitfully developed by the Marxian tradition, and the theory of bureaucracy became a cornerstone of the works of Weber and his followers, the idea of civil society as the central terrain of social integration and public freedom was to become just as fruitful in a line of theoretical development that had its beginnings in Tocqueville, its continuation in Durkheim, in English, French, and American pluralism, and in Gramsci, and its culmination in Parsons and Habermas. In our opinion, this tradition of interpretation has shown at the very least that the basic categories of Hegel's *Rechtsphilosophie* can be thoroughly translated into modern terms. If we are to believe the testimony of social actors East and West, North and South, such reconstructed terms of analysis have not yet exhausted their critical and constructive potential.

3

Theoretical Development in the Twentieth Century

The untenability of the Hegelian synthesis and the collapse of its systematic assumptions do not represent the end of the theory of civil society. Subsequent theorists, however, tended to focus only on specific dimensions of the multilayered Hegelian concept, developing these to the exclusion of all others. Marx stressed the negative aspects of civil society, its atomistic and dehumanizing features; but in so doing, he managed to deepen the analysis of the economic dimensions of the *system of needs* and went far beyond Hegel in analyzing the social consequences of capitalist development.[1] Tocqueville removed the ambiguities from the discussion of *publicity*, discovered in voluntary associations a modern equivalent of the anachronistic corporation, and demonstrated the compatibility of civil society and democracy, albeit in a context (America) that he considered to be an uncharacteristic version of modern society. Gramsci reversed the reductionist trend of the Marxian analysis by concentrating on the dimension of *associations* and *cultural intermediations* and by discovering modern equivalents of Hegel's corporations and estates. Finally, Parsons focused on the dimension of *social integration* in terms of a whole series of institutions constitutive of what he called "societal community." More like Hegel in his systematic aspirations than any of the others, Parsons attempted to synthesize the normative claims of tradition with those of modernity. His concessions to ideology, again reminiscent of Hegel, were the price he paid for the failed attempt.

In this chapter our primary interest is in two twentieth-century attempts to develop theories of civil society on the foundations provided by Hegel. This seems to us the best strategy to test the viability of a form of theorizing originally attached to the problems of early modern states and industrial society and based on a mode of empirical generalization whose plausibility rested on surviving ideologies and institutions from premodern constellations such as city-states, *Ständestaaten,* and societies of orders.

The combination of Parsons and Gramsci is easily justified. Both are influenced by Hegel, and yet both correct him by differentiating civil society from the economy as well as the state. The one overcomes liberal, the other Marxian, reductionism. Both are inclined to interpret civil society in functional terms, as the sphere responsible for the social integration of the whole. At the same time, both are aware, even if ambiguously, of the normative achievements of modern civil society. The crucial differences between them, linked to their different theoretical traditions and political assumptions, can be found in the way they combine normative and functional theory. Parsons identifies the normatively desirable with the actual functioning civil society of the present, thereby falling into an unconvincing apology for contemporary American society. Gramsci, focusing on the normative desirability of a future (socialist) civil society, tends to treat the civil society of the present only in terms of its function for a system of domination he completely rejects. His combination of an excess of utopia with an excess of realism does not allow him to adopt a genuinely critical attitude to the Soviet Union, the country of the revolution where not only bourgeois but all civil society was suppressed. In the end, then, neither is sufficiently critical of his own ideological tradition, and as a result, neither is fully able to thematize the duality of modern civil society—its liberating promise as well as its links to heteronomy.

Parsons: Civil Society between Tradition and Modernity

The classical sociological tradition brought to completion by Talcott Parsons rarely used the concept of civil society, for it was undoubtedly considered a remnant of pre-social-scientific discourse about human affairs. All the more remarkable is the reappearance of the concept in Parsons's work. To be sure, it appears both in a new disguise and in the context of a new model of differentiation.

Parsons's concept of a societal community that is distinguished from the economy, the polity, and the cultural sphere represents a synthesis of the liberal concept of civil society as differentiated from the state with the stress on social integration, solidarity, and community that typifies the sociological tradition initiated by Durkheim and Tönnies. This synthesis, in which both individuation and integration are central, involves, remarkably enough, a partial and conscious return to the Hegelian theory of civil society.[2] While (unlike Hegel but similarly to Gramsci) Parsons differentiates the societal community from the economy as well as the state, the continuities between the two conceptions are more striking than the differences.

For Parsons, as for Hegel, modern society is structured by normative frameworks of plurality (associations) and legality. Publicity and participation are also present, but as in Hegel's work, they are deemphasized. Moreover, Parsons, like Hegel, is ready to pronounce a single version of modern society (in his case, the United States) as more or less the highest realization of the potentials of modernity. "The completion of the society . . . called modern" will take place when the integration problems of *this* society or type of society are resolved. Finally, Parsons is conscious of the debt that modern society bears to the historical project of the age of democratic revolutions, even if he considers this project to be fully accomplished (and hence annulled as a project) by the developed Western societies: "The more privileged societies of the late twentieth century have to an impressive degree, which would have been impossible to predict a century ago, successfully institutionalized the more 'liberal' and 'progressive' values of that time."[3] As far as these societies are concerned, the struggle for democratization is, on the whole, relegated to the nineteenth century.[4]

This last thesis concerning the actual accomplishment of the values of the age of revolutions opens Parsons's concept of modern society to the charge of "bourgeois apologetics" leveled at all post-1848 usages of the "utopia" of civil society.[5] Parsons, though, is ideological only in the sense that Hegel was, namely, in the extent to which he mixes normative insight with mystifications concerning existing institutions. Yet, and again like Hegel, the theory points beyond ideology insofar as it links these normative insights to the potentialities of existing society, even if Parsons himself does not recognize that these are actualized only partially and selectively.

Parsons's division of the social system into four functions or subsystems appears distinctly unhistorical next to Hegel's specification that it is modern development that produces the differentiation between state and civil society. But Parsons, too, insists that in earlier societies, undifferentiated institutional complexes carried out more than one, and possibly all, of the major social functions. For example, in tribal societies, kinship was the key social, cultural, political, and economic institution; the feudal bond in the High Middle Ages organized social, economic, and political relations; and the absolutist-mercantilist state was a political and economic entity. The development of modernity is thus conceived as the differentiation of what had been implicitly there in all societies, in institutions that may have had dimensions linking them to all functions but whose center of gravity was tied up with a single function. This teleological interpretation of history may well involve an impermissible projection of modern Western categories to premodern and non-Western societies, so that the universal applicability of a category such as differentiation is therefore open to doubt.[6] The relevance of this category to modern development itself is, nevertheless, highly plausible.[7]

To Parsons, the societal community is the integrative subsystem of society: Its function is to integrate a differentiated social system by institutionalizing cultural values as norms that are socially accepted and applied. The differentiation of the societal community from the cultural, economic, and political subsystems was accomplished, according to Parsons, by the three modern revolutions: the industrial, the democratic, and the educational. Each of these is represented as a step in "the societal community's declaration of independence" from the other subsystems, which, however, also acquire their differentiated institutions in the process.[8] Actually, in Parsons's analysis, the differentiation of the societal community was begun in the major English antecedents to the three revolutions: (1) the coming of religious plurality and toleration, which differentiated religion and the state from one another while to some degree freeing the societal community from a religious definition of full membership; (2) the establishment of purely economic relations through a market economy freed of social, if not yet political, restraints; (3) the development of an aristocratic form of representative government that differentiated government and its constituency (primarily the aristocracy and the gentry) and stabilized their relations through parliamentary representation; and (4) the development of a form of law that helped to carve out a societal sphere not open to arbitrary intervention even by the state itself. In presenting these antecedents, Parsons simplifies by linking steps in the differentiation of each of the four subsystems to a single process, even if the step has consequences for other subsystems as well. Thus, for example, the development of the rule of law, which he links to the institutionalization of the legal profession and the stabilization of a system of independent courts, is also the most important preparation for a differentiated societal community.

Significantly, Parsons considers that the process of differentiation of the societal community would have been incomplete without all three revolutions. In one version of his argument, these revolutions represent the differentiation of the integrative subsystem from one other subsystem in each case.[9] In another version,[10] Parsons insists that each revolution actually strengthened the other subsystem: the economic in one case, the bureaucratic-administrative in the other. There is no inconsistency here, however, because Parsons sees differentiation as a reciprocal and non-zero-sum process that involves institution building in all the relevant spheres. But there is one major inconsistency in his account: The differentiation of the societal community from the market economy is nowhere provided for in the doctrine of the three revolutions, in spite of general claims to the contrary. As a result, the argument must surrender its parallel structure; in particular, the dramatic process in which the societal community declares independence from the state, vividly portrayed by Parsons, does not have a parallel in the relationship of the societal community to the new type of market economy. We might suggest that Parsons here came up against a problem he sought to deemphasize: the problem of capitalism and a century of socialist responses to it, symbolizing, as Karl Polànyi noted, society's self-defense against the economy.

In Parsons's conception, the democratic revolution, whose center was France, certainly did lead to a tremendous strengthening of the state power that was first built in the epoch of absolutism. Nevertheless, from the point of view of the societal community, the original contribution of this revolution was the creation of a new type of solidary, national collectivity whose members have equal claim to political rights in addition to the civil rights already affirmed in English development.[11] The emergence of this new type of collectivity involves a reversal of primacy with respect to the absolutist era: "The societal community was to be differentiated from government as its superior, legitimately entitled to control it."[12] Again, no inconsistency is involved in affirming the simultaneous strengthening of state power and the development of a more autonomous society capable of defending itself against this power, because Parsons rightly does not consider power to be a zero-sum game.[13]

Obviously, Parsons thought of the industrial "revolution" as entirely parallel to the democratic one. This is true, however, only if we take the relationship of polity-economy to be the the central axis of interest. Accordingly, the industrial revolution, whose center was Great Britain, completed the trend of earlier capitalist development by enormously extending the division of social labor (in Durkheim's sense) and by differentiating an economically defined society from the state (in Polànyi's sense), leading to the complementary growth of both subsystems (as both Durkheim and Polànyi noted).

So far the parallel between the two revolutions works. But if we choose as our axis economy–societal community, as did Polànyi (on whom Parsons otherwise greatly relies), the parallelism stops. Instead of differentiation and complementary expansion, the industrial revolution produced an economic society (the market economy) that threatened to subsume and reduce autonomous social norms, relationships, and institutions. While one would hardly expect Parsons to be sensitive to the Marxian discussions of reification and commodification, it is indeed surprising that he does not examine Polànyi's thesis that a self-regulating market produces an "economization" of society, against which a program of the self-defense of society emerged in the nineteenth century.

Indeed, this program had many features parallel to the eighteenth-century liberal confrontation of society and state to which Parsons's conception of the democratic revolution in part refers.

Aspects of Polànyi's stress on society's self-defense against the destructive trends of classical capitalism do, of course, return in the discussion of features of the twentieth-century welfare state and unionism.[14] But, characteristically, Parsons considers the issue solved with the development of the welfare state. Indeed, the latter seems to "transcend" both capitalism and socialism. Uncharacteristically, however, the problem is not considered in the context of the thesis of differentiation. One suspects that this thesis could not have been applied in a consistent and convincing fashion to the economy–societal community axis.

The thesis of the educational revolution addresses the same issue once again, though this time in a rather futuristic perspective. Curiously, it is in this context that we find some of Parsons's most critical remarks with respect to classical capitalist development:

> The capitalist alternative emphasized, first, freedom from the ascriptive past, then protection from governmental "interference." The socialist alternative proposed the mobilization of governmental power to institute fundamental equality, ignoring almost completely the exigencies of economic efficiency. . . . Both failed to ground themselves in adequate conceptions of the societal community and of the conditions necessary to maintain its solidarity.[15]

The American-centered educational revolution, abstractly located on the axis culture–societal community, implies, according to Parsons, a more consistent freeing of the social structure from all ascriptive patterns of stratification than could be provided for by private property (capitalism) or governmental office (socialism), providing equality of opportunity (though not ensuring equality of results). Even more importantly, he maintains that the central institutional complex of this revolution, the university, provides for the development of an associational pattern of social organization that is to be distinguished from and counterposed to the bureaucratic and individualistic forms promoted by the state and the market economy, respectively. Thus, he sees the educational revolution, amazingly enough, as a solidaristic corrective not only to socialism and capitalism but also to the democratic and industrial revolutions. It promises, in short, a potential completion of modernity capable of securing the autonomy and integration of the integrative subsystem, the societal community, alias civil society.

Parsons's claim that the modern university provides an alternative model of organization to both market and bureaucracy would be bizarre if it were not simply a special case of his general argument about the associational character of contemporary American society. Before turning to his ideological mystification of aspects of this society, however, we must highlight another deficiency in his conception.

We have already noted that at least one strand of Parsons's conception, apparently contradicted by another, makes the emergence of the modern societal community a residual result of the self-differentiation of the other subsystems in the three revolutions. Within a purely functionalist scheme, such a depiction leads to no internal contradictions, but Parsons can continue to operate within such a scheme only to the extent that his evolutionary model denies itself the possibility of explaining the actual mechanisms of social change involving action and conflict. He can do this only as a sociologist; as a historian, he repeatedly runs into the problem of social movements and conflicts. But the functionalist sociologist is ready with his answer: The radical democratic movement, the socialists, and the new left are depicted as the fundamentalist wings of the three revolutions[16] whose projects apparently involve the sort of short-circuiting of processes of problem solving ascribed to "value-oriented movements" by Neil Smelser.[17] Parsons, however, forgets Smelser's other type of movement, the "norm-oriented movement" that is capable of positively influencing social change. This omission on the level of theory is all the more odd given that Parsons himself depicted the civil rights movement in the United States in terms of this paradigm.[18]

As a result of the theoretical short circuit in Parsons's approach to social movements, there are two issues that he cannot even raise, much less resolve: the problem of the agencies involved in the self-constitution of the new type of societal community he describes, and the problem of the resistance of an increasingly modern societal community to trends threatening its differentiation. We shall address these in turn.

With regard to the first issue, in Parsons's analysis, agency can apparently only short-circuit social change that is caused by objective processes. In the case of the other subsystems, however, the state-makers and jurists, the entrepreneurs and managers, the educators and fiduciaries are never described as fundamentalists of any kind. Thus, action in the service of social change is possible, but only on the part of elites and for subsystems other than the societal community whose differentiation does in this sense become residual.

With regard to the second issue, with the democratic movement, the working-class movement, and the student movement all described as fundamentalist, we get the impression that their forms of action as well as their goals aimed at dedifferentiation in each case, that is, the absorption of the modern economy, state, and educational system into a solidaristic societal community whose own modernity would thereby be placed in doubt. All of these movements did indeed have some elements and ideologies that were fundamentalist in exactly this sense. However, Parsons failed to see that other dimensions of the very same movements struggled precisely for social autonomy and, therefore, for the differentiation of the societal community, along with its norms and institutions. This is simply the other side of his failure to take into account the tendencies of the modern state, the capitalist economy, and even modern science to dedifferentiation, that is, the absorption and penetration of the other social spheres. A theory of modern society that fails to see these trends necessarily turns ideological and apologetic.[19]

Parsons's theory of the societal community is an excellent object of immanent criticism because he both elaborates the normative achievements of modernity and represents these as if they were already institutionalized. Indeed, he facilitates the job of the critic by pointing to integration problems that implicitly throw much doubt on the claims of successful institutionalization. The conception of societal community represents yet another answer to Hobbes and Austin, maintaining the existence of a normative order without the deus ex machina of sovereignty.[20] The concept itself, bringing together Tönnies's well-known pairing *Gemeinschaft/ Gesellschaft*, consciously aims at the same kind of synthesis of ancient and modern categories as did Hegel in his doctrine of civil society. If anything, Parsons's model seems to put greater emphasis than Hegel on elements that modern and traditional societies have in common. He defines the societal community in terms of the two dimensions of "normativity" and "collectivity." The former is a system of legitimate order produced by the institutionalization of cultural values; the latter is the aspect of society as a single, bounded, organized entity. We should note that Parsons, like Hegel, is ready to see the whole as a "politically organized" collectivity of collectivities: "Perhaps the prototype of an association is the societal community itself, considered as a corporate body of the citizens holding primarily consensual relations to its normative order."[21] But in the case of a modern society, equal emphasis is placed on the multiplicity of often conflicting groups, strata, loyalties, and roles; the modern societal community is at best a "collectivity of collectivities." Such an overarching collective solidarity, which is sufficient to produce a capacity, as well as motivations, for effective collective action,[22] is possible because of loyalty to norms based on consensus. Here, too, Parsons assumes a kind of unification hardly characteristic of modern societies; his notion that ultimately "values are mainly legitimized in religious terms" tends to commit him to the view that a legitimate social order rests on shared substantive values. But, once again, he is ready to try to modernize the conception by (inconsistently) referring to a "relative consensus," one that is only "a matter of degree,"[23] which, however, could hardly play the role of representing the decisive forum that resolves the conflict of loyalties among individuals, and even within each individual. A mere matter of degree cannot provide that "high position in any stable hierarchy of loyalties" that Parsons seeks to ascribe to loyalty to the societal community itself.[24]

If the overall contours of the conception are open to the charge of insufficiently representing modern society, in its detail the argument is capable of dealing with this objection. Once again there are uncanny similarities to Hegel, this time in terms of the very architectonic of the presentation: Modern societal community is understood above all as a framework of laws and associations. As we have already argued with respect to Hegel, there is one notable absence—the system of needs—and a notable presence—the citizenship complex. The latter, understood in terms of three categories of rights, is in fact an outgrowth of the system of laws.

For Parsons, the most important step in the emergence of a modern legal system is the transition from law as an instrument of state policy to law as the "mediating interface" between state and societal community, formally constitutive of their differentiation. Such a legal system puts the state in "the dual position of defining and enforcing certain legally embodied restrictions on its own powers." This paradox could be sustained on the bases of judicial independence, the corporate integrity of the legal profession, and especially the openness of the boundaries of the legal system "permitting tentative approaches to consensus before full 'legalization' of a norm and its enforcement" based on appeals to "collective solidarity, moral standards, and practicality."[25] While Parsons assigns definite priority here to the development of the common law with respect to continental variants, quite evidently the development of "constitutionalism," that is, the enforceability of constitutions even against state policy, was everywhere structurally related to the differentiation of a modern societal community and the state.[26]

The citizenship complex, an outgrowth of constitutionalism and the rule of law, represents its further development in three areas. (1) Embodying universal norms, modern rights anchor constitutions in principles higher than the traditions of particular societies. (2) Representing a move from objective law to subjective right, modern citizenship makes constitutional claims actionable on the part of individuals and groups. As a result, (3) the citizenship complex not only further differentiates societal community and state but establishes the priority of the former over the latter in the sense of both normative principle and political action.

Parsons's definition of "society" as the social system having the highest level of self-sufficiency is resolutely in terms of politically delimited territorial units, generally "nation-states."[27] The normative structures that define the identity of a society thus are never free of a dimension of particularism, even if the cultural value orders in which the legitimacy of norms is rooted often transcend the limits of any given society.[28] The modern citizenship complex, with its egalitarian tendency to free membership from all ascriptive characteristics, is rooted in an important attempt to base the norms of modern societies in not only transsocietal but actually universal values, of which the first version was the doctrine of natural rights. Constitutional rights thus become normative embodiments of universal principles that represent limitations on the power of the state tied to the interests of a particular politically organized society in the name of something higher. The democratic revolution, in Parsons's conception, attempted to turn such philosophical claims for the superiority of the societal community, "the nation," into actual political primacy. The citizenship complex in this argument consists of three sets of components, civil-political-social, that represent the project of institutionalization of such primacy. He considers the "structural outline" of modern citizenship "complete, though not yet fully institutionalized."[29]

For Parsons, citizenship in the modern sense signifies equal conditions of membership in the societal community rather than in the state.[30] Its civil or legal component consists of equal rights guaranteeing autonomous forms of action with respect to the state—in other words, "negative liberties." Rights involving property, speech, religion, association, assembly, and individual security along with substantive and procedural equality before the law were first formulated in the natural-law tradition and are enshrined in the French *Declaration of the Rights of Man* as well as the American Bill of Rights. In Parsons's presentation, they represent the principle of constitutionalism reformulated as subjective rights of private persons; as such, their function is to stabilize the differentiation of societal community and state.[31]

Political rights are positive rights of equal participation rather than "freedoms" or "liberties"; they involve both indirect participation in representative government through the franchise and rights to *influence* policy. It is significant that Parsons, at least in the first statement of his position, included here again the rights of free speech and assembly.[32] The overlap means that the rights of participation, especially when so strongly linked to negative rights, do not mean dedifferentiation, but rather the emergence of new mediating structures[33] that indirectly contribute to differentiation through interpenetration as well as new forms of integration. It is these structures that are supposed to establish the primacy of the societal community, going beyond the constitutional state (*Rechtsstaat*) already established by negative rights.

Finally, the social components of citizenship, not called "rights" by Parsons, consist of the "resources and capacities" required for implementing rights, for "realistic" rather than merely "formal" opportunities for their equal utilization. At issue are "adequate minimum standards of 'living,' health care and education." Although Parsons mentions here some sort of "equality of conditions," his real concern is to defend a genuine, as against an "empty," version of the "equality of opportunity." Whether he does this in a convincing manner is a question we must now ask.

According to Parsons, "In one sense the 'social' component of citizenship is the most fundamental of the three."[34] We are not told in exactly what sense this is true of this temporally latest addition to the citizenship complex. In any case, Parsons elsewhere notes a lack of parallelism between the "citizen" and the welfare "client."[35] The fact that he does not speak of social rights, that he does not note an overlap here with other parts of the citizenship complex as in the case of political and civil rights, indicates his awareness of a fundamental lack of symmetry. He does make a good case on behalf of the need for a social component of citizenship. The theoretical problem is only that this case does not primarily belong to the problem complex of the differentiation of societal community and state and the stabilization of this differentiation. While one could argue that the autonomy of the societal community depends on the resources and capacities of its members, the threat to these comes not only from the modern state but also from the modern capitalist economic order. And while at least in one context Parsons mentions the "social" component of citizenship in relation to the differentiation of economy and societal community,[36] the discussion goes nowhere because Parsons wants to deny the functional necessity or even plausibility of both rights and forms of participation with respect to the modern economic order.[37] This unwillingness definitively links the "social" component to the role of client, one that clearly does not belong to any citizenship complex. Even more, this role actually contradicts the idea of citizenship, which cannot be made consistent with any form of paternalism.

Parsons is, in general terms, very much concerned with the differentiation of societal community from both economy and state, but while he argues for a principle of organization specific to the societal community, thus establishing the pattern of differentiation, the structure of mediation he provides stabilizes this differentiation only between the societal community and the polity. We have already noted that Parsons considers the principle of association to be the form of organization of the societal community, parallel to bureaucracy in the case of the polity and the market in the case of the economy. The depth structure of associations is linked to the mutual solidarity of members, and this is what distinguishes the societal community from the different individualistic patterns of the market and the bureaucracy. Indeed, together with the third type of individualistic pattern represented by the citizenship complex, the solidaristic dimension of the societal community is the secret of the various syntheses stressed by Parsons, between modernity and tradition, individualism and collectivism, *Gesellschaft* and *Gemeinschaft*.

In Parsons's conception, an *association* represents a corporate body whose members are solidary with one another, in the sense of having a consensual relation to a common normative structure.[38] Parsons believes that this consensus, generally established by prestige and reputation, is the source of the "identity" of the association, of its becoming a "we." The associational principle involves not only a solidaristic basis of identity but also a different determination of collective action: Here basic decisions emerge from the organization itself and are not merely applied by it, as in the case of the bureaucratic principle. To Parsons, all organized frameworks have associational components, but only in cases where this is dominant (unlike the modern firm, or authoritarian governments) can we speak of an association.[39] In his view, the contemporary trend in organization is toward associations rather than bureaucracies, and he maintains that this trend emanating from the societal community penetrates government and business firms as well, though in the latter case (concerning which Parsons is inconsistent) without becoming primary.

The emergence of consensus through appeals to prestige and reputation, deliberately counterposed to the acceptance of valid argumentation,[40] points to less than fully modern associations. Indeed, in several contexts, such as the role of the associational principle in voting, Parsons explicitly speaks of "traditionalism" as against rational action.[41] Nevertheless, for the contemporary societal community, he is interested in working out the specifically modern type of association. Even in relation to voting, he maintains that associational mobility and the possibility of belonging to a multiplicity of associations partially counteract the traditionalist implications of all associations (with the possible exception of the family).[42] These characteristics are functions of the first specifically modern principle of associations: *voluntariness*, allowing relatively easy entry and exit, based in the normative principle of the freedom of association. The second such principle is the *equality* of members, constituting a horizontal as against a hierarchical pattern of organization. The third is *proceduralism*, in the sense both of providing definite, formal rules for regulating discussion and of voting. Since the framework of discussion and deliberation is understood as the locus of consensus building through persuasion, it is possible to see these three principles as the application of the great modern triad of liberty, equality, and solidarity to the model of association.

Again, the modernity of the model depends on the interpretation of the terms "consensus," "persuasion," "solidarity," and "influence." Parsons, as a student of Durkheim, is obviously aware of the difference between traditional and modern solidarity. Solidarity achieved through consensus is in some contexts identified specifically with the ideal type of voluntary association.[43] But Parsons also notes the importance of another, *Gemeinschaft* type of solidarity, "a mutual relation of diffuse solidarity" based on "common belongingness."[44] The two models thus seem to be (1) the achievement of solidarity through discussion and deliberation among individuals who freely choose to participate in an association, and (2) the generation of consensus among individuals on the basis of a preexisting, diffuse solidarity that is not open to questioning or thematization. Unfortunately, the key concept of influence tends to submerge the first model in the second, and the two are treated almost interchangeably as the basis of having influence.

The concept of influence has a major structural role in Parsons's theory of the differentiation of the societal community. Along with money, power, and value-commitments, influence is one of the four generalized symbolic media of interchange that replace relations of direct negotiation or "barter" in the four subsystems, regulating their internal relations as well as their exchanges with one another.[45] While Parsons is less insistent than Niklas Luhmann on the historical processes of the evolution of media-regulated forms of action, his theory does also imply that the real importance of the media emerges in the modern, differentiated societies they help to constitute. In relation to the modernity of influence as a medium, there are, however, three unresolved tendencies in his thought. First, the analogy with money and power, and the idea that influence is fully exchangeable with these media, points to a modern principle of integration that reduces communication to the production and reception of codes and action to an adaptation to interconnections established "behind the backs of actors." This conception cannot ground the difference between the organizing principle of the societal community and those of the economy and the polity, and it treats integration through solidarity as a form of control.[46] Second, the argument that influence "must operate through persuasion . . . in that its object must be convinced that to decide as the influencer suggests is to act in the interest of a collective system with which both are solidary"[47] points to a model that is specifically modern, yet significantly different in principle from money and power. The difference is clearly indicated by the idea that, whereas money and power work through altering the situations of actors, influence (along with value-commitment) works by one person's having an effect on another's intentions.[48] Finally, while Parsons is unable to make up his mind about how influence as a "generalized medium of persuasion" actually works,[49] his stress is clearly on the reputation and prestige of influential individuals and not on the "intrinsic" validity of their argumentation. Here the model easily slips into one of traditional integration of action unless, more consistently than Parsons, one were to specify that the ultimate foundations of an individual's reputation, with respect to the given issues, must be capable of defense as well as challenge in terms of argumentation. While this idea is present in Parsons,[50] it is incompatible with another, namely, that the ability of one person to influence another is rooted in a background of diffuse, *Gemeinschaft*-type solidarity.

Parsons, of course, fully assumes that he does succeed in grounding the differentiation of the modern societal community from the state and the economy in terms of his categories of association and influence. He thus faces Hegel's problem of thematizing the relevant mediations. With respect to the societal community–state axis, these turn out to be the classical ones the pluralist tradition inherited from Hegel and Tocqueville: the public, the lobbies, the political parties, and the legislature, which are the channels for societal influence on the administration of the state.[51] Their effective operation, according to Parsons, presupposes the system of mass communications that he pronounces the "functional equivalent of some features of *Gemeinschaft* society," again running into all the ambiguities that characterize his theory of influence. Throughout this strand of his argument, he presupposes that social constituencies communicate with instances in the political system in ways that are entirely undistorted by money and power, and that there is a symmetrical relationship of exchange between "public support" and "public influence."

Since Parsons's exploration of the problem of the differentiation of societal community and economy is unsatisfactory, it is not surprising that he does not realize that his theory, unlike Hegel's, needs a series of mediations in this context as well.[52] Such mediations do make a limited appearance in various essays. We learn, for example, that the associational trend also penetrates the economy in the form of professional associations and fiduciary boards. In the case of the modern firm, however, we also find out that the members of the association (the stockholders) have a passive role, while the board is assimilated to bureaucratic management.[53] As far as workers are concerned, Parsons rejects any model of democratic participation in management,[54] and he restricts the role of unions, in the gap between household and workplace, to that of improving the economic position of the working class.[55]

Parsons's discussion of the relation of the societal community to the economy raises existing capitalist practice to the level of norm, or at least of functional necessity. His theory of the societal community as a whole, however, consciously (though unsuccessfully) aims at a model that goes beyond the alternatives that might be described as capitalist economism and socialist statism. The astonishing part of this theory is the claim that such a postcapitalist, postsocialist model is not only the counterfactual normative construction of a social-political project but is already actualized, even if not yet completely, in contemporary American society. Once again, the rational is the real, the real is the rational:

The United States' new type of societal community, more than any other single factor, justifies our assigning it the lead in the latest phase of modernization. We have suggested that it synthesizes to a high degree the equality of opportunity stressed in socialism. It presupposes a market system, a strong legal order relatively independent of government, and a "nation state" emancipated from specific religious and ethnic control. . . . Above all, American society has gone further than any comparable large-scale society in its dissociation from the older ascriptive inequalities and the institutionalization of a basically egalitarian pattern. . . . American society . . . has institutionalized a far broader range of freedoms than had any previous society.[56]

The United States, in Parsons's view, is not only the proper home of the educational revolution with its emphasis on the "associational pattern," but also the most successful synthesis of the results of the democratic and industrial revolutions. American models of representative government and federalism yield the highest level of differentiation between state and societal community. This is the case because this society is the freest from ascriptive and political definitions of membership and (much less plausibly) this political system is least encumbered by social restrictions on participation at any level. Representative government makes all societal members its proper constituency, but the separation of powers provides the political system proper with broad freedom of action. The structures of representation, national and federal, adequately mediate, according to Parsons, between the state and the societal community.

Parsons is less able (but, given the inconsistency of his normative conception, less compelled) to claim a similar degree of differentiation between the societal community and the economy. He does seem to admit that since the "social component of citizenship" in America lags behind that of European welfare states,[57] market economic rationality has a greater power over social life. Nevertheless, he maintains that American society is also beyond the obsolete, failed alternatives of capitalism and socialism, which he defines primarily in terms of an absence of governmental controls on the economy versus total governmental control.[58] To be fair, Parsons's analysis does contain the suggestive notion that neither capitalism nor socialism is grounded "in adequate conceptions of the societal community and of the conditions necessary to maintain its solidarity." However, his depiction of America as a postcapitalist, postsocialist society is focused primarily on the emergence of the mixed economy, and he is apparently unaware of the possibility that modern interventionist welfare states are also capable of threatening and displacing social solidarity. It may be that Parsons assumes, in this context at least, that overcoming the dysfunctional effects of capitalism through state regulation and redistribution, within the limits of the market economy, establishes social control over the economy. And perhaps he sees such a control operating through the secondary mediation of representative government, which provides a more direct form of control over the state. However, the asymmetry between the two forms of supposed control is obvious. Any identification of social control with state regulation implicitly violates Parsons's own stress on the differentiation of these spheres. And even the idea that representative government is the medium of social control would bypass, in an illegitimate way, Parsons's depiction of the internal differentiation of the political system and his stress on elites as providing the actual mechanism of rule.

To be fair, Parsons also affirms the existence of structural positions from whose point of view an analogous control over state and economy could be conceived. American society is understood as the most hospitable terrain possible for the principle of associationism, which Parsons presents as the alternative to both capitalism and statism, symbolizing respectively a modern economy and a modern state free of any social controls. Continuing the line of analysis began by Tocqueville, Parsons roots the importance of a pluralistic version of associations deeply in American history. The organization of American Protestantism has favored both pluralism and associationalism, the latter by the internal structure of organization of many of the churches, the former by the multiplicity of denominations and the relatively long history of toleration.

But secular patterns contributed greatly to these trends, in particular an exceptionally long history of voluntary associations and a later, but even more important, pattern of inclusion in American society of a whole series of ethnic groups that were nevertheless able to preserve their individual identities. The struggle of American blacks for civil rights, concerning which Parsons wrote one of his best essays, represented for him a great culmination precisely of the preexisting normative and organizational patterns of American history.[59]

In this one context, Parsons could see that movements in contemporary modern societies did not necessarily imply fundamentalism but could actualize universalist, normative potentials (here the premises of the democratic revolution) in a manner capable of creating and preserving particular identities. Unfortunately, though, he seemed to expect that associationalism would be generalized not by new movements following in this pattern but only through the social implications of the so-called educational revolution and its supposedly collegial pattern of organization. Parsons did not, however, explain how the associational forms of the university are to transform bureaucratic structures in the rest of society or how these forms can be protected against penetration by economic wealth and political power. One reason why this issue does not come up, despite Parsons's obvious familiarity with contemporary universities, is that he identifies it with the claims of supposed fundamentalism. He insisted, for example, on seeing only the fundamentalist, communitarian side of the New Left and the student movement, and not the side that demanded university democracy (and associational rights) as well as autonomy and differentiation with respect to economic and political institutions. By dogmatically rejecting these movements, he closed himself to an important discourse that is in many respects continuous with his own.[60]

This issue is important because Parsons fully recognizes that "associationism" today cannot be defended on the nineteenth-century ground of small-town America, which even Tocqueville considered to be somewhat atavistic.[61] But his various attempts to provide adequate modern alternatives all fail because he never takes into account the negative potentials of contemporary institutions. While he is right to notice, beyond the elite theory of democracy, the element of social control inherent in representative institutions, he is wrong to bypass their oligarchic trends and to stylize existing political elites as the "functional equivalent of aristocracy" that "democracies urgently need."[62] He is right in insisting on the important normative implications of the pluralistic traditions of American society, but his dismissal of the specific selectivity and asymmetry built into the existing practice of pluralism is both unsophisticated and misguided.[63] Finally, he is right in not taking the mass-society thesis too seriously, as well as in insisting on the continued importance of "kinship and friendship" along with "associational activities and relationships,"[64] but he is wrong to think that this removes the ground from another distinction, that between "public" and "mass culture." Indeed, his views concerning mass culture and mass media could have been based on fleshing out the insight concerning the existence of two trends identifiable with this distinction, one toward manipulation and the other toward democratic communication.[65] Instead, after noting the possibilities of overconcentration, manipulation, decline of cultural standards, and political apathy as possible consequences of the modern mass media, he dismisses, or at least vastly deemphasizes, the relevance of these trends to American society! And after presenting the system of mass communications as a kind of market,[66] he inconsistently declares that this system represents "a functional equivalent of some features of *Gemeinschaft* society."[67]

Given his difficulties in basing his theory of association on specifically modern trends, it is not surprising that Parsons seeks a functional equivalent of *Gemeinschaft*. In this context, however, his choice of the mass media can amount only to a tacit admission of defeat. In Parsons's theory, this implicit defeat appears in his thematization of integration problems in contemporary American society, the solution of which would complete modernity itself. Indeed, we should note that he does not admit that the differentiation of the societal community and its associational form of organization are in any respect incomplete. Nor does he consider the cultural values of modern societies to be in any sense deficient or contradictory. Rather, his thesis is that successful differentiation and reorganization have produced integration gaps or lags that have not yet been successfully addressed because norms capable of generating sufficiently high levels of motivation, legitimacy, and solidarity have not been adequately institutionalized. As a result, the societal community is "the storm center" of future conflicts that cannot be dealt with through the control of money and power. On the other hand, the demand of new movements for participation and community, considered exclusively in their fundamentalist versions as signs of integration strains, can provide solutions only at the cost of massive dedifferentiation and regression. Between these two extremes, the direction in which Parsons himself would look for a solution remains quite unclear.

Abstractly, his theory commits him to the view that only the generation of new forms of influence could lead to a normative consensus that could provide symbolic resources capable of integrating the societal community (solidarity) as well as regulating its interchanges with the state (legitimacy) and the economy (motivation). Unfortunately, because his theory of influence is indeterminate, it is hard to see possible solutions to problems of social integration that could derived from it. The assimilation of influence to money and power leads, for example, to the technocratic solution of planning and manipulating its sources and conditions of application, presumably through the mass media. Alternatively, an interpretation of influence as rooted in prestige and reputation linked to traditional solidarity leads to a neoconservative option that would hope to restore an authoritarian and possibly religious foundation for norms that would be closed off to questioning and criticism. Finally, an understanding of influence in terms of rational argumentation as the "intrinsic means of persuasion" leads to a democratic alternative that would have little plausibility unless democratization were continued as an open-ended process carried on, in part, by social movements, a possibility that Parsons explicitly rejects. Indeed, he seems unaware that all these different options are compatible with one or another of the contradictory substantive value-complexes inherited by modern societies, or that their different forms of institutionalization would presuppose unavoidable organizational changes. Above all, he does not see that they imply the projects of three alternative versions of the modern societal community or civil society, among which social actors may in fact choose. One suspects that Parsons never makes up his mind among these alternatives, that he affirms all of them, or rather a combination of them in which the respective weights are unclear. Thus, he is open to the objection that the democratic elements in his theory imply only a legitimating window dressing for a traditional model of civil society that has become impossible, or for a technocratic model that is the culmination of the genealogy of unfreedom.

Actually, though, the situation may have been the reverse. Perhaps the traditional and apologetic elements in Parsons's thought interfere with his genuine insights into the critical place of civil society in modernity. This reading is suggested by his last two published essays.[68] Here Parsons demonstrated that his reconstruction of the concept of civil society did not represent a dead end and was capable of further development. The context, though, was not system construction but immanent critique, namely of R. M. Unger's important book *Law in Modern Society.* Unger offers a critique of both formalist, market-oriented and substantialist, state-interventionist structures of law from the point of view of the endangered values of solidarity and mutual recognition. In the face of older models of liberal and contemporary welfare-state capitalism, he seeks to justify a third, communitarian form of organization combining substantive justice with a morality based on face-to-face relations. Yet Unger cannot save his model from the charge of primitivism. He concedes that while the welfare state has in a sense returned to earlier, bureaucratic forms of law, his own alternative also completes a historical cycle by returning to customary law. Calling this movement a spiral rather than a circle does not alleviate the difficulty.

Despite his own ambiguities with respect to a traditional organization for the societal community, Parsons will have nothing to do with communitarianism, which he identifies as the absolutization of the dimension of social integration (in a highly misleading way, he speaks of "the absolutism of law").[69] But he is willing to take up Unger's challenge to push the critique of formal law (and thus liberal capitalism) and substantive or purposive law (and thus the welfare state) to the point where the outlines of a third option become visible. We should notice, even if he did not, that the two criticized options are not, as in his earlier work, liberal capitalism and socialism, with the welfare state representing their final synthesis. Without noticing, he took from Unger's critical theory the premise that critique must aim beyond all contemporary formations.[70] The crucial point, from the point of view of his own conception of civil society as the societal community resting on norms and associations and counterposed to both the economy and the polity,[71] is that he is here able to formulate a two-sided critique of market and state in terms that avoid all regression to historically obsolete structures of law and society.

He finds the Archimedean point in Unger himself, who distinguishes between substantive and procedural patterns of the deformalization (rematerialization) of law. Substantive law involves interventions whose purpose is to bring about specific social results benefiting specific interests; procedural law ("the great intermediate and mediating category"), however, aims only at the equalization of partners whose negotiation under carefully determined procedures is to reach agreement concerning means and ends. Unger's preference, like that of many defenders of the welfare state (such as T. H. Marshall), is for substantive law; he considers procedural law to be still within the tradition of formal law because of its preservation of the principle of legal generality on the "meta" level of procedure. To Parsons, of course, this element of continuity that preserves the status of law as a limitation rather than an instrument of sovereign power is attractive: The differentiation of the societal community from the polity depends on it. Procedural law, moreover, preserves the possibility inherent in contract law, recognized neither by legal positivism nor for that matter by Unger, that law can be created by social entities other than the state.

Equally important, Parsons discovered the link of procedural law to his own concept of associationalism, contrasted with both the bureaucracy and the market. He goes too far, though, and identifies all institutions governed by procedures as the domain of procedural law, from courts and parliaments to elections and voluntary associations. In this manner, even the very corporatism that appears to Unger as a danger to the public and positive features of the law is recast by Parsons as an instance of independent law-making by society. From a supposed indication of the decomposition of autonomous law, he thus obtains the proof of essential continuity. It is a pity that this initially promising analysis has such a flat outcome.

What goes wrong? First, Parsons vitiates his own important point concerning the link of procedural law and associations by confusing procedure and procedural law. While all manner of institutions can be regulated by procedures, including undemocratic and hierarchic ones, procedural law in Unger's provocative definition is in effect reflexive and deals with procedures (of equalization) that have other procedures as their objects. Thus, to give an example accessible to neither Unger nor Parsons, while the associations participating in corporatist bargaining may and generally are regulated by procedures, procedural law would target these procedures to produce internal democracy and the protection of individuals and minorities. Again, while the secret bargains of a limited number of associations might be arrived at under fixed procedures, procedural law might seek to make this process public and open to other interested parties. Thus, procedural law does not merely reflect the existence of associations, as Parsons suggests, but aims at the democratization of their internal life as well as their interrelations.

There are two reasons for Parsons's analytical error. First, he identifies procedural law as "a cooperative . . . framework within which 'parties,' whether they be individuals or groups, can be 'brought together' to adjust their interests with each other under a normative order."[72] This definition captures only half of what is meant by procedural law, because it brings procedures under the rule not of procedures but of a higher normative order that is not further defined. If that order were legal norms, then the definition would beg the question with respect to the type of law (formal, procedural, or substantive) that these entail. But we have good reason to think that what Parsons has in mind is not law at all, but the higher normative (religious-moral) order of society. With the meta level thus occupied, Parsons apparently sees no important reason to distinguish between procedures themselves and the procedures that produce or regulate procedures. In other words, he cannot discover the meaning of procedural law as a specifically modern, reflexive, and intersubjective regulation of the production of norms, because for him agreements and perhaps laws can be produced only as the institutionalization of what is already there on a higher normative level.

Second, while he does not notice that through an immanent critique of Unger he has implicitly been brought to a position critical of all existing societies, he definitely seeks to escape this implication on a more concrete level. As always, he is in a rush to pronounce existing American society to be the resolution of all antinomies, this time of liberal capitalism and the welfare state, at least from the legal point of view. If procedural law is the solution of the riddle, as he insightfully notes within Unger's text, then the bulk of American law must be procedural law. This apologetic claim can be sustained, however, only through the misidentification of procedural law and procedure. Once again, his discovery of the potentially critical terrain of civil society, this time on the level of legal theory, is vitiated by his apologetic treatment of American society as representing some kind of "end of history." In this respect, Parsons remained a through-and-through Hegelian to the end of his life.

Gramsci and the Idea of Socialist Civil Society

If Parsons can be said to represent a twentieth-century rehabilitation of the Hegelian idea of *Sittlichkeit* in social-theoretical terms, with inevitably apologetic consequences for contemporary civil societies, Gramsci can be said to reflect a modern renewal of the left radical critique of civil society. This characterization should not be taken to imply, however, that he simply follows the classical Marxian analysis and criticism of civil society. Although a follower of Marx, Gramsci generated his own conception of civil society directly from Hegel.[73] And unlike Marx, he turned not to the system of needs but to the doctrine of corporations for his inspiration. Undoubtedly aware of the Marxian use of the term *bürgerliche Gesellschaft*, Gramsci's interpretation of Hegel was thus at the same time an implicit critique of that of Marx and Engels. Although he did not know Marx's text that denounced the concept of the corporation as so much medievalism, Gramsci was keenly aware of such an interpretation. Nevertheless, reading Hegel's conception primarily on an abstract analytical level, he was convinced that the contents drawn from the world of the old regime could, were, and had to be given modern replacements. Accordingly, Gramsci recognized the new forms of plurality and association specific to modern civil society in modern churches, unions, cultural institutions, clubs, neighborhood associations, and especially political parties.

The most decisive departure of Gramsci from *both* Hegel and Marx is his highly original option for a three-part conceptual framework. Against Hegel's version, and more convincingly, Gramsci located both family and political culture on the level of civil society. Unlike Hegel and Marx, however, he did not include the capitalist economy on this level. We can only speculate about the reasons for the second of these moves.[74] Gramsci was essentially a political thinker who was interested in theory for the sake of political orientation. In this he confronted two great and, for him, decisive problems: the failure of revolution in the West and its (supposed) success in Russia. In neither context did the *economistic* reduction of civil society to the political economy, so prevalent in Marxism, allow the problem of transition to a genuinely democratic society to be seriously posed. In the West, the reduction led to the disappearance of the defensive "trenches" of the existing system: forms of culture and association that protect bourgeois society even when the economy is in crisis and the power of the state has crumbled.[75] Only the "methodological"[76] differentiation of civil society from both the economy and the state allowed a serious thematization of the generation of consent through cultural and social hegemony as an independent and, at times, decisive variable in the reproduction of the existing system.

In the Soviet Union, where "the state was everything" and civil society was "primordial" and "gelatinous," the collapse of the state did make revolution possible. But given the fact that that the new revolutionary power constituted itself in a statist ("statolatry") and even "Caesarist" or "Bonapartist" and "totalitarian" form, the project of creating a free society that could absorb state power was put in doubt. The very constellation that made revolution possible was apparently the greatest roadblock for developing a free society. Thus, in this context as well, Gramsci came to focus on the problem of civil society as independent of economic development and state power.

There were, of course, other reasons for Gramsci's stress on civil society. One certainly has to do with the peculiarities of the Italian situation. An acute analyst of Italian history and social structure, Gramsci was aware of the failure of liberalism to attain "hegemony" after the Risorgimento. In this assessment he was directly influenced by the great Italian philosopher and historian, Benedetto Croce. Like Croce, he attributed this failure, in part, to the power of the church in Italian cultural and social life. Although the church no longer had direct political power in the Italian *state*, its power within civil society remained impressive. Indeed, through its organization of everyday social life in "civil" institutions such as church functions, education, neighborhood festivals, and its own press, the Catholic church was able to occupy many of the trenches of civil society and to constitute a powerful barrier to the formation of liberal, secular bourgeois, hegemony on this terrain. Accordingly, Italian civil society was prevented from becoming fully modern. At the same time, like many other intellectuals of his day, and more specifically under the influence of Georges Sorel, Gramsci believed that Italy and the West as a whole suffered from a general crisis of culture. He related the contemporary "wave of materialism" to the crisis of authority that resulted from the ruling class's inability to organize consensus (hegemony) and the corresponding detachment of the masses from their traditional ideologies. (The ruling class was thus only dominant, not hegemonic.) "The crisis consists precisely in the fact that the old is dying and the new cannot be born."[77] In other words, the moment for the triumph of liberal ideology had been missed, while the old action-orienting world views had become anachronistic and were being increasingly undermined by social and structural developments. Thus, civil society, and especially its cultural institutions, appeared as the central terrain to be occupied in the struggle for emancipation.

Gramsci's conception is presented in a notoriously confusing terminology.[78] Civil society is variously defined as the counterpart of the state (which is said to be either identical with political society or its main organizational form), as a part of the state along with and counterposed to political society, and as identical with the state. The idea that runs through all these attempts at a definition is that the reproduction of the existing system outside the economic "base" occurs through a combination of two practices— hegemony and domination, consent and coercion—that in turn operate through two institutional frameworks: the social and political associations and cultural institutions of civil society, and the legal, bureaucratic, police, and military apparatus of the state or political society (depending on the terminology).[79] It may be helpful here to recall Norberto Bobbio's insistence that Gramsci battled two forms of reductionism, one reducing the superstructure to the base and the other, cultural processes to coercion. Within the framework of classical Marxian historical materialism, Gramsci sought simply to assert the independence and even primacy of the superstructure. We would go further than Bobbio, arguing that, against Gramsci's intentions, this shift rendered the whole doctrine of base and superstructure irrelevant.[80] And yet, this irrelevant dualism, now in the form of an idealist reversal, could have biased Gramsci at times to treat the two dimensions within the supposed superstructure, civil society and state, either as somehow one or at least as expressing the same principle and logic. One of his terminologies, the one integrating both civil and political society in the state, seems to express this option. Nevertheless, when he was forced to confront the consequences of reducing social integration to political coercion, he postulated that the opposition between civil and political society (here meaning the state) was indeed one of two different principles, hegemony and domination.[81] One might say, therefore, that Gramsci developed his doctrine of civil society in terms of two "declarations of independence," one from the economy and the other from the state, and that the resulting trichotomous conception, however inconsistently, burst the bounds of historical materialism.

As a theorist, Gramsci surely traveled a road from Marx to Hegel, even though his political project remained a Marxist one.[82] Of course, the Hegel of the *Philosophy of Right* also proved inadequate for his purposes. Not only did he want to use a trichotomous conception different from Hegel's, one that could not lead back to either economism or statism,[81] but he considered the corporate doctrine, which he located as the heart of the Hegelian theory of civil society, to be hopelessly obsolete in the form in which it was originally developed. Gramsci notes that Hegel's "conception of association could not help still being vague and primitive, halfway between the political and the economic; it was in accordance with the historical experience of the time, which was very limited and offered only one perfected form of organization—the 'corporative' (a politics grafted directly on the economy)."[84]

Thus, like Marx, Gramsci is fully aware of the modern state's destruction of the older forms of corporate life that constituted a "dual power" in the late medieval world (in the *Ständestaat*, that is). He is even aware, like Tocqueville, of the existence of an intermediary form—the absolutist state and the depoliticized society of orders[85]—from which the contents of Hegel's model are drawn. More importantly, however, unlike Marx or even Tocqueville, Gramsci thoroughly understood that the efforts of Jacobin and bureaucratic statemakers to the contrary, the older corporate forms were capable of modern replacements. He stresses in particular the rise of modern unionism and cultural associations.[86] And while modern churches, surrendering their earlier role in the state, also became institutions of the new type of civil society, modern political parties gradually replaced them as the main organizational form for intellectuals.[87]

Although he is clearly aware that modern statemakers seek to abolish all intermediary associations, Gramsci does not stress the obvious point that their reappearance in modern form had to be at least partly the result of what used to be called the struggle of society against the state. Instead, he tends to argue, in a more or less functionalist manner, that the demand of the state for consent, and its tendency to organize and educate such consent, is the major reason for the emergence and stabilization of new types of associations.[88] Of course, Gramsci viewed the particular content and form of civil society as the outcome and object of a class struggle. From this point of view, the outcome depends on which social group has been or is becoming hegemonic. Where the bourgeoisie is hegemonic, civil society is bourgeois society, and its constitutional guarantees (rights) and political expression (parliamentary representation) are window-dressing for bourgeois rule.

It is worth noting that the associational forms that replace Hegel's corporations can, for Gramsci, turn into key vehicles for social movements, even if Gramsci does not emphasize the state/ society opposition in this context. Indeed, he not only discovered the modern replacements for the corporation but also added the dimension of social movements to the concept of civil society, giving it a dynamism in addition to and independent of the system of needs. What is given with one hand is, however, taken away with the other, for the dynamism of civil society as the terrain of social movements lasts only so long as the working class is in opposition. Once civil society becomes socialist, the raison d'être for social movements, that is, for class struggle, will have disappeared. As we shall show, one tendency in his thought, namely the functionalist reduction of the political culture (representative democracy and rights) and of associational forms of modern civil society (clubs, interest groups, bourgeois political parties) to the reproduction of bourgeois hegemony and/or to the creation of socialist hegemony (unions, communist parties), locks Gramsci into an overly schematized conception that is at once too realist and too utopian.

We have already noted Gramsci's conviction that the associations and cultural institutions of civil society in the developed capitalist countries, as the inner "trenches" of the established system, have added immeasurably to the stability of this form of domination. At the same time, he notes their abolition under contemporary dictatorships. It is for just this aspect of their rule that he dubs them "totalitarian."[89] Thus, Gramsci seems to register five phases of relation between the state and civil society: (1) medieval corporatism and dualism (the *Ständestaat*); (2) the absolutist dualism of state and depoliticized, privileged orders; (3) the early modern dissolution of the older corporate forms that, strictly speaking, exists only in revolutionary terror; (4) the dualism of the modern state and new forms of associations; an finally (5) the totalitarian *Gleichschaltung* of modern associations and cultural forms. What is most significant in this typological reconstruction of the history of civil society is that "totalitarianism," as against earlier statist forms, is depicted as the dissolution and atomization of *modern* forms of social and cultural integration! But why and how are effective forms of social integration, of the organization of consent, dissolved? And if it is dissolved under totalitarianism, does civil society have a second chance of being reconstructed?

These questions are difficult to resolve because of three systematic ambiguities or "antinomies" in Gramsci's analysis. The first comes from his application of the term "totalitarianism" to both "progressive" and "regressive" versions; the second comes from his discussion of the normative status of civil society, which sometimes implies the consolidation of a system of domination through the organization of consent and at other time the weakening and even eventual abolition of domination; and the third comes from his conception of a free society, which alternates between a pluralistic civil society and a unified state-society.[90] All three antinomies are linked to the attempt to work out critical theories of two very different societies: Soviet Russia (of which Gramsci remained supportive) and contemporary capitalist societies and their totalitarian variant (to which he was unalterably opposed).

Without disguising anything about the form of social organization and repressive political practices in the Soviet Union, Gramsci nevertheless tries to distinguish between "regressive" and "progressive" versions of totalitarianism, both of which involve abolishing the independence of the institutions of civil society.

A totalitarian policy is aimed precisely (1) at ensuring that the members of a particular party find in that party all the satisfactions that they formerly found in a multiplicity of organizations, i.e., at breaking all the threads that bind these members to extraneous cultural organisms; (2) at destroying all other organizations or at incorporating them into a system of which the party is the sole regulator. This occurs (1) when the given party is the bearer of a new culture—then one has a progressive phase; (2) when the given party wishes to prevent another force, bearer of a new culture, from becoming itself "totalitarian"—then one has an objectively regressive and reactionary phase.[91]

The policies of the two totalitarianisms with regard to civil society are depicted as being exactly the same; both suppress cultural meaning, social solidarity, and forms of organization outside a unified party-state, thus ending social divisions. But their intentions are supposedly completely different. In this context, the defense of the Soviet Union by an antifascist must seem bizarre. Leaving aside Gramsci's political commitments, however, the whole argument does in fact follow consistently from his functionalist depiction (still tied to classical Marxism) of the institutions of civil society in the advanced capitalist countries as forms of organization of consent whose role is exclusively the stabilization of domination—its social integration, as it were. Given this interpretation, smashing these institutions by subordinating them to a monolithic party-state can be represented as at least part of the negative work of social emancipation. (We shall return to the question of what was supposed to be the positive part of this work.) Totalitarianism is regressive or reactionary in this reading only when its purpose is to block "progressive" totalitarianism, rather than create a new culture, in a context where the inner trenches of civil society are sufficiently weakened to raise the prospects of their progressively motivated abolition. All in all, Gramsci seems to indicate only three possible political positions: a conservative defense of the existing version of civil society whose function is the social integration of capitalist domination; a totalitarian-revolutionary abolition of this civil society for the sake of building a new culture; and a totalitarian-revolutionary abolition whose purpose is to conserve the existing structure of domination.

It is also possible to detect in Gramsci the foundations (or at least its traces) for yet a different version of "progressive" politics, one that is radically reformist rather than totalitarian-revolutionary. Bobbio develops such an interpretation on the basis of Gramsci's stress on building a new cultural hegemony by the socialist party in civil society.[92] The obvious contrast is between the cultural work of building a new consensus that would erode the old forms of consent and a program of revolutionary overthrow using violent means.

It is difficult to pinpoint such a strategy in Gramsci because of his second "antinomy": a Marxian-functionalist conception of civil society as the locus for producing the hegemony that will stabilize bourgeois domination, and a conflicting theoretical conception of a terrain where two alternative strategies for hegemony building contest one another.[93] In the context of the first position, a strategy for building counterhegemony would simply integrate the working class into the established institutional network of civil society, which would have to be totally abolished in order to break with the existing system of domination. In the context of the second, however, which postulates the possibility of building a cultural hegemony incompatible with the existing system, the institutions of civil society would themselves have a double structure, linked to both domination and emancipation. A radical-reformist strategy would have to build on this dual structure.

In the terms of the functionalist version of Gramsci's theory, a strategy of hegemony building could be, and most of the time probably was, entirely instrumental, given the difficulties the trenches of bourgeois civil society place on the route to direct revolutionary transformation. The aim, in this interpretation, is to erode the existing forms of social integration, to create alternative associations, and to prepare the subject of revolutionary politics. Given the negative assessment of the existing civil society in this interpretation, however, the associations and forms of a counterhegemony would have to be regarded instrumentally: The independent parties and unions of the working class would have the function of producing dysfunction within the existing form of social integration, helping to produce a crisis in which the opposing side would have to rely on domination alone. In this interpretation, therefore, a revolutionary rupture, with force facing force, must complete the internal work of transformation.[94] More important for our argument, in this context at least, there would be no reason why the independent organizations involved in building a counterhegemony should play any role after the revolution. Gramsci supports this view, especially when he assigns the task of constructing a new society and civilization primarily to the state and when he states that it is essential that the old mechanisms of producing bourgeois hegemony be eliminated. Within the functionalist interpretation, this would of course mean the end of a pluralistic system of parties, unions, and churches.

The alternative, conflict-theoretical view of hegemony building in civil society implies (even if Gramsci never explicitly drew such a conclusion) a *positive normative attitude* to the existing version of civil society or, rather, to some of its institutional dimensions. Clearly, a principled version of radical *reformism* could be based on such an attitude. Gramsci's unwillingness or inability to develop such a conception is apparent in the presence of a more developed functionalist-revolutionary option in his thought. Indeed, one might say that the more explicit development of the radical reformist option would have presupposed a political choice Gramsci never made: a thoroughgoing critique of the Soviet Union's version of totalitarianism. It would not be possible to choose a strategy of building new institutions of associational and cultural life as alternative bases of hegemony in the existing society *and also* as the core structures of a new society, while on the whole accepting the ruthless eradication of those new institutions along with the old under a revolutionary statism.

To sum up so far, while Gramsci avoids economic and political reductionism by differentiating the associational and cultural dimensions of civil society from the economy and the state, the functionalist trend in his thought combined with his strategic political goals and allegiances lead him to construe the institutions of civil society in a one-dimensional way. Although autonomous, the associational forms (types of political parties and unions), cultural institutions, and values of civil society are precisely those most adequate to reproducing bourgeois hegemony and manufacturing consent on the part of all social strata. They are, in short, not dualistic but thoroughly bourgeois. This version of civil society must therefore be destroyed and replaced by alternative forms of association (workers' clubs, the new proletarian party form, or the "modern prince"), intellectual and cultural life (the idea of the organic intellectual), and values that would be help create a proletarian counterhegemony that might eventually replace the existing bourgeois forms. Yet even the strategy of building a counterhegemony is just that, a strategy. Gramsci never sees the institutions and cultural forms of counterhegemony as ends as well as means, because he is unwilling to concede that, within bourgeois civil society, some immanent possibilities extend beyond the established framework of domination. Thus, in itself, the focus on cultural means (the organization of consent) in civil society, as against the coercive means of the state, does not imply that a radical reformist project has replaced the revolutionary one. We are still dealing with a theory that seeks the total replacement of one form of society by another.[95]

Furthermore, Gramsci's doctrine of civil society is never advanced in terms that would imply an uncompromising hostility toward statism. This attitude, too, is consistent with the functionalist strain in his thought. While at times he conceives of hegemony as a product of civil society, just as coercion is a product of the state, so in other formulations both hegemony/consent and domination/coercion are functions of the state, the former pair operating on the terrain of civil, the latter on that of political society. It is this second formulation that is consistent with the functionalist reduction of civil society.[96] According to its logic, one must regard hegemony not as autonomously produced within civil society but as one of the forms in which state power functions effectively. The forms of the establishment of counterhegemony within the old society can then be seen primarily as marking the way to a new state power that would have to establish on an entirely new basis the terms of its own operation, including a new basis in "civilization" for consent. Gramsci's remarks on the "civilizing" mission of the state support this interpretation.

Gramsci stresses the notion of the state as civilizing agent in two contexts in particular: the historical failure of Italian unification, leading to the Risorgimento of the nineteenth century, and the problems of Soviet development in the twentieth century. For our present purposes, we are interested in his analysis of the Soviet context, which he also used for comparisons with fascist Italy. Like other Marxists, Gramsci built on Marx's analysis of Bonapartism ("Caesarism") to analyze the structural similarities of modern dictatorships, all of which use a more or less autonomous form of state power to organize an otherwise unstable system of domination. Unlike Trotsky, however, Gramsci did not argue for a specific difference in the case of the allegedly progressive version of Bonapartism that would come from the working class, somehow dominant and yet not ruling, on behalf of which state power would act. Instead, he explicates the difference in terms of building a new culture or preserving the old. But what is the meaning of this new culture? Gramsci offers two interpretations, only one of which is consistent with the thrust of his own theory. First, he argues that, for a progressive form of statism, "the point of reference of the new world in gestation" is "the world of production; work," i.e., the organization of "individual and collective life . . . with a view to the maximum yield of the productive apparatus."[97] This argument, in line with both historical materialist premises and rather shortsighted apologetics for Soviet society, is consistent with the acceptance of the obliteration of the existing version of civil society in the name of a "progressive" agenda. Indeed, Gramsci speaks in this context of the repressive activity of the state, its rationalization and Taylorization of society, and its reliance on punitive sanctions.[98] The argument, however, is inconsistent with the antieconomistic turn in Gramsci's social theory: If the base does not determine the superstructure, how can the character of a new culture and a new society be determined simply by the transformation of the economic structure? And while Gramsci may have believed that in some contexts the social sphere should be reduced by the actions of the state to a mere complement of economic transformation, it is entirely unclear how this was to be the source of a new culture, especially one leading to a free society.

This last point becomes especially striking in light of the second interpretation, which presupposes Gramsci's own original position within Marxism. Here the positive role of the state that can justify even "statolatry" is said to be "the movement to create a new civilization, a new type of man and even a new citizen . . . the will to construct within the husk of political society a complex and well articulated civil society, in which the individual can govern himself without his self-government coming into conflict with political society—but rather becoming its normal continuation, its organic complement."[99] This criterion of what constitutes the progressive version of statism is very different from the first, namely, the creation of a complex, well-articulated civil society capable of self-government as the hallmark of a new culture. Given the totalitarian obliteration of civil society, however, the thesis is highly paradoxical. It may be that Gramsci had in mind the historical experience of many early modern states that abolished the institutions of traditional European corporate society only to allow and even promote the emergence of a modern structure of civil society. But the analogy does not quite work. Abolishing the old society of orders was the joint work of the state and democratic efforts from below that also maintained their distance from state power. Thus, it is almost impossible to locate historically in most Western European countries (except perhaps in the Reign of Terror) that vanishing moment in which the old associations have disappeared while the new ones have not yet emerged. On the contrary, when totalitarian governments abolished civil society, dissolving already modern rather than traditional forms of culture and association, they specifically disallowed the formation of new types of associations independent from themselves, including even, and perhaps especially, the independent social organizations and movements that had helped overthrow the old regime. How convincing was it, then, to expect that a form of statism that was more uncompromisingly hostile to civil life than any of its predecessors would create from above a "complex, and well-articulated civil society" that would be able to govern itself more or less independently? And what might be the forms of this new type of civil society that would be created from above, as different from the modern one as this latter was from its traditional predecessor? This second question is important because the analogy Gramsci seeks to construct with past statisms fails if we are to assume merely that a "totalitarianism" that dissolves a model of civil society is progressive if it recreates from above more or less the same model, or even one of its variants.

Gramsci does argue that a statolatry "abandoned to itself" or "conceived of as perpetual" must be subjected to criticism. How strong this criticism should be, and what its political consequences might be, he does not say. And yet one gets the strong impression that he is aware of what must have been a disturbing implication of his own thought, namely, that a left totalitarianism would not be normatively different from one of the right if it made no contribution to the reconstruction of civil society. And of course only a fool (of whom there were many in the 1930s, though Gramsci was not one) could have thought that Stalin's Russia satisfied the normative criteria here assigned to progressive dictatorships.

In this context, it is possible that Bobbio is right in arguing that Gramsci was at least on the verge of recognizing that abolishing civil society is not the best way to reconstruct it, even if one seeks to create a new type of civil society. If there actually was a radical reformist strand in his thought, it would have been based on the insight that the institutions through which a radical movement can build its hegemony are part and parcel of any meaningfully conceived modern form of social self-government and, as such, have value in and of themselves. It would have been based, in other words, on a recognition of the dualistic character of at least some of the core institutions of modern civil society. In short, Gramsci would have had to acknowledge that the norms and organizational principles of modern civil society—from the idea of rights to the principles of autonomous association and free, horizontal communication (publicity)—are not simply bourgeois or functional to the reproduction of capitalist or any other hegemony. Rather, they constitute the condition that makes possible the self-organization, influence, and voice of all groups, including the working class. Accordingly, the task of radical reform would be to expand such structures in a direction that reduces the chances of their being functionalized to the purposes of economic or political power. But such a stance would have led to an outright rejection of totalitarian revolution, a step Gramsci, unlike many of his heirs, did not make.

Aside from the undoubtedly decisive political reasons why Gramsci did not make this move, what we have called his third antinomy also stood in the way of his reevaluating the problem of civil society from a normative point of view. This antinomy is between a conception of a free society in terms of a pluralistic, democratic civil society and one in terms of a unified state-society. The first of these models, consistent with the conflict-theoretical strain in his thinking, and especially with the conception of the dual structure of existing civil society, potentially tempers utopia with an imagery of partial institutional continuity. Here, utopia is the realization of existing but blocked normative possibilities. The second model, consistent with functionalism (the one-dimensional critique of bourgeois civil society and the call for total revolutionary rupture), suffers from an excess of utopianism and potential links to authoritarianism. One might say that the strain in Gramsci's thought involving the relentless "unmasking" of the role of the institutions and political culture of bourgeois civil society in reproducing capitalist relations of domination helped to prepare the way to an authoritarian position vis-à-vis civil society in general.

In our view, it is this second strain that is dominant in Gramsci's thought. Here, one cannot blame the timidity of Gramsci's critique of the Soviet Union, because, in spite of his overall sympathy and reluctance to drive his criticism too far, he may have had real doubts whether a genuinely free society would be created there.

Therefore, in contrast with the totalitarian project in which civil society is absorbed by the state, Gramsci returns to the Marxian program of abolishing the state, which he calls, with some variation on the original formula, "the reabsorption of political society into civil society."[100] Marx, in his most explicit critique of *bürgerliche Gesellschaft* (in "Zur Judenfrage"), wrote only of an absorption in "society."[101] The difference appears to be all the more significant because, as Gramsci imagines "the coercive elements of the state withering away by degrees," he postulates the corresponding emergence of "ever-more conspicuous elements of regulated society (or ethical state or civil society)."[100] Thus, his identification of the new form of social organization that he most often calls "regulated society" with at least a version of civil society is quite deliberate.

Regulated society, a society without a state, seems to be defined by two premises: (1) a premise of equality and (2) a premise of the replacement of law by morality. In other words, the new society is to be characterized by a spontaneous acceptance of law by free and equal individuals without any coercion or sanctions whatsoever. This notion comes perilously close to the self-deluding Marxian utopia of a society without institutions.[103] But the transition to regulated society that Gramsci has in mind seems different. He refers to a phase in which the state will indeed be a nightwatchman, in the sense of safeguarding the "continually proliferating elements of regulated society" and in the process progressively reducing "its own authoritarian and forcible interventions."[104] This process is supposed to be identical to the construction "within the husk of political society" of a complex, well-articulated, self-governing civil society. Thus, it is hardly an exaggeration to argue that Gramsci's reformulation of the idea of the road to socialism consists of the construction of a new type of self-governing civil society that would gradually take the place of all state control over social life, leading to a withering away of the state as well as political society. Nevertheless, and amazingly enough, he does not believe that the new type of civil society in formation and its forms of self-government would enter into any conflict with the state whose powers it is to erode and replace. Instead, civil society would become the "normal continuation" and "organic complement" of what he calls "political society," namely, the state.[105]

There are two images here that do not mix. On the one hand, we have a notion something like the emergence of dual power: Two forms of social organization exist side by side; one based on democratic self-government and social solidarity is to replace another based on administrative sanctions and coercion. On the other hand, Gramsci leaves us with a notion of a state power gradually converting its form of domination into an equally effective form of social control through the institutions of civil society. Thus, the antinomy between civil society as a consolidation or normalization of domination and civil society as a genuinely alternative principle to domination returns once again. This time, the two notions appear as one because the utopian idea of the total absorption of the state by civil society would logically eliminate the distinction between a state power acting through the institutions of civil society and a form of self-government based on these institutions. Until society reaches utopia, however, the ambiguity would remain, and the elimination of conflict from the model certainly seems to imply that Gramsci's supposed transition to a free society is ultimately only a statist authoritarianism with a human face.

The utopia of a (modern) civil society absorbing political society and the state, the supposed *telos* that would resolve the most important of Gramsci's antinomies, is incoherent even on its own. First of all, it remains unclear which absorbs the other in the relationship between civil and political society. Here, the stress in Gramsci's sparse descriptions seems to be on "political society" as understood by Tocqueville, for example, as political organizations rather than the state (as in Gramsci's use of the term). Regulated society is self-governing, even if its "laws" are enforced as internalized moral rules that do not need to appeal to external sanctions. This highly unrealistic postulate has authoritarian implications, at least in the modern world, that its advocates rarely confront. Even if we suppose that a period of statist transition has eliminated older forms of heterogeneity and plurality, Gramsci's regulated society would have no social space for an opposition consisting of new minorities and pluralities that may be willing to obey the laws but cannot identify with them and may wish to organize themselves in order to reverse them.[106] With the sphere of prepolitical association eliminated or fused with that of political association, such an organization could not take place in principle. Indeed, the model of moral rather than legal enforcement eliminates the space in which such an opposition could emerge at all: autonomous conscience, which is always to some extent in conflict with the laws. The postulate of a morally based acceptance of law in itself tends to presuppose social homogeneity and to exclude pluralistic organization.[107] By definition, "pluralism" means some conflict over policy and is therefore incompatible with internalized acceptance of the decisions of majorities. Thus, it is not clear how, and on what normative and empirical bases, individuals and groups could have rights against Gramsci's monolithic regulated society.

The issue could be addressed from the point of view of the modernity of Gramsci's idea of regulated society. Can a civil society be a modern society if state power is abolished or absorbed? Does not the duality of civil society and state (of which Gramsci is a major analyst), not to mention the differentiation between civil society and the economy, constitute the modernity of both terms? It would seem that abolishing the state, which is impossible in fact but certainly imaginable, would lead not to an autonomous, plural, civil society in other ways resembling its modern forerunner but to a restoration of traditional political-civil society without modern administration but also without a modern structure of rights and liberties carving out autonomous spaces from the world of politics.[108]

Given an already established, sturdy, and complex structure of civil society, albeit of the bourgeois model, Gramsci's regulated society can be established only through a revolutionary totalitarian rupture. Most of the established institutions, including those of the working class, would otherwise militate against it: The existing plurality of forms of life, culture, and association, presupposing social conflict, needs a structure of laws and rights linked to sanctions. It also requires the mediating and interest-aggregating outputs of a modern state. No radical reformist strategy would in itself reduce this complexity, and indeed the organization and mobilization of new social actors would add to the heterogeneity of interests and increase the conflict potential of society. Unfortunately for Gramsci's thesis, a revolutionary-statist destruction of the existing version of civil society would have even less of a chance to usher in the regulated society. The choice Gramsci actually faced was not between radical reformism and revolutionary democracy prepared by a totalitarian abolition of civil society.[109] Rather, it was between civil society *tout court* and an authoritarian system that would certainly attempt to perpetuate itself. Gramsci supplied important concepts to those who would militantly challenge later versions of such a system, but this was something he neither intended nor even anticipated. And those who were to undertake the challenge could postulate the value of an independent civil society only when they completely divested themselves of the radical democratic utopia of the regulated society whose deepest roots involved, as Marx knew but Gramsci apparently forgot, a hatred for modern civil society.

Excursus on Gramsci's Successors: Althusser, Anderson, and Bobbio

Gramsci's antinomic intellectual position allows two distinct and opposed roads for continuation. While different combinations among his alternatives are possible, there is a more than elective affinity among an apologetic attitude toward the Soviet Union, a functionalist reductionism with regard to the existing version of civil society, and a utopian project (or a normative countermodel) of a unified state-society. With an emphasis on the functionalist-reductionist component, this combination marks the path of Louis Althusser and his followers, who insist on maintaining intact the Marxian project of revolution. Similarly, the internal relation is equally strong among critique of the Soviet Union, a conflict-theoretic and dualistic conception of the existing civil society, and a pluralist democratic normative model of civil society. This combination is pursued by Norberto Bobbio, who has recently focused on civil society as the proper framework for contemporary radical reformist projects of democratization.

Althusser entirely disregards the version of Gramsci's theory that involves an opposition between state and civil society and resolutely focuses on the secondary version in which civil and political society, hegemony, and domination are all functional aspects of the state.[110] Political society here becomes the "repressive state apparatus" defined in terms of a supposedly unitary structure of government, administration, army, police, courts, and prisons. "Civil society" (his quotation marks) in turn becomes a differentiated framework, with the "ideological state apparatus*es*" consisting of religious, educational, family, legal, trade-union, communications, and cultural components. Althusser has notorious difficulties in showing that all these domains belong to the state.[111] He dismisses, in part rightly, the objection that their status is private, as distinct from the public "repressive apparatus" of the state, as so much bourgeois legalism masking the actual *functions* of institutions. But this strategy only justifies a differentiation from the private, economic sphere, not an inclusion in the structure of the state. To argue that the ruling class holds state power, the ideology unifying the various institutions in question, by which they "massively and predominantly function," is the ideology of the ruling class, and "ideological apparatuses" are *therefore* state institutions is both logically fallacious and empirically questionable. It is logically fallacious because, even if the state were the instrument of the ruling class, the two terms would still not be identical, which is what Althusser's "syllogism" presupposes. And it is empirically fallacious because, as we know from the history of social democracy for example, many nonbourgeois strata and groups can occupy state power in capitalist societies, and because the institutions to which Althusser refers are characterized by great ideological diversity, internally (Catholic vs. Protestant churches, Christian vs. syndicalist unions, etc.) and among one another. Despite these seemingly obvious problems, this argument has had extended influence.

More important for us is Althusser's own inability to stick to a consistent version of this functionalist position. He rightly repeats the Gramscian position according to which no form of power can be stable for long without "hegemony over and in the State Ideological Apparatuses."[112] But this thesis is not interpreted according to his own version of functionalism when he argues that the function of the apparatuses and the ideology they supposedly produce is to reproduce the existing relations of production.[113] This latter argument separates civil society from the state and functionally links its institutions, along with those of the state, to the reproduction of the capitalist economy. Once freed from the absurd burden of having to make civil society a dimension of the state, Althusser can pronounce the ideological state apparatuses, i.e., the institutions of civil society, as "multiple, distinct, `relatively autonomous' and capable of providing an objective field to contradictions, which express, in forms that may be limited or extreme, the effects of clashes between the capitalist class struggle and the proletarian class struggle."[114] Not only does this argument implicitly shift between the two functionalisms (statist and capitalist) available in Gramsci; it is also on the verge of rediscovering the other, conflict-theoretic and pluralist-democratic, position traceable in Gramsci's work.[115] However, since he is so much more dogmatic and traditional in his revolutionary and state-socialist commitments than Gramsci, Althusser is even less able to travel this road than his predecessor. Even in a highly modified form, the functionalist road chosen by Althusser cannot lead to a genuine reevaluation of the normative double nature of civil society.

The brilliant interpretation of Gramsci by Perry Anderson, who was once a follower of Althusser, is a case in point.[116] Anderson devastates Althusser's reconstruction of Gramsci both textually and politically. Politically, he calls the reconstruction disastrous because it cannot distinguish between fascist-authoritarian and liberal democratic versions of capitalist society: Only the former absorb social institutions of cultural reproduction within the state.[117] But it is also textually wrong to the extent that it focuses on a secondary conceptual strategy in Gramsci's work, disregarding the primary usage that differentiates state and civil society.

Anderson argues that Gramsci developed this secondary usage, in which civil society is absorbed in the state, because of difficulties with his primary one. It is not civil society alone that wields cultural legitimacy; the state does as well, in particular through its educational and legal institutions (mentioned by Gramsci) and its parliamentary structures (omitted by Gramsci but strongly stressed by Anderson). Gramsci's answer was to make coercion and hegemony functions of both civil society and the state. The difficulties of this conception, which threatens the definition of the modern state as the monopolist of legitimate violence, supposedly led Gramsci to include civil society in the state or even to identify the two spheres with one another.[118]

Anderson's own solution, which in a sense combines those of Gramsci and Althusser, is to maintain the separation of civil society and state but to insist that, while the institutions of civil society produce only cultural hegemony and consent, the structures of the state—because of the all-important role of parliamentary institutions—produce consent as well as coercion. This idea assimilates the Althusserian notion of ideological state apparatuses but maintains the Gramscian stress on the production of ideology outside the state as a secondary one. By this conceptual move, Anderson in effect overcomes the bad option between an overly schematic differentiation between state and civil society in the main version of Gramsci's arguments and the complete absence of differentiation in the secondary version. In the process, he inadvertently comes close to the Hegelian notion of parliament as an institution of mediation between civil society and state, as the place where simultaneously civil society penetrates the state and a unified political will is formed. He comes close to such a view but, as we shall see, not close enough.

The new argument, in fact, does not overcome the limitations of Marxian functionalism. Anderson is quite clear: Civil society as we know it belongs only to the functional reproduction of capitalist society; "the 'private' institutions of civil society" have no place in "any social formation in which the working class exercises collective power."[119] With this assumption in mind, he is entirely consistent in fearing and rejecting the whole Gramscian strategy of trying to build a counterhegemony within the existing version of civil society, certainly more consistent than those who hope to use such a strategy as a road to the revolutionary establishment of a unified state-society. Anderson shares the latter dream and therefore rejects a radical reformist road that implicitly assumes the preservation of key dimensions of existing civil society. Because such a strategy is powerless against the ultimate guarantee of the existing system, the possession of the means of violence and repression, it can serve only to integrate the working class into the established society.[120]

The reference to violence and repression already indicates a shift to the level of the "state apparatus." A key reason why the building of counterhegemony in civil society must fail is that the main instance of the ideological reproduction of the existing system is exercised by parliament, within the sphere of the state. This instance, however, is reinforced by its links to potential violence and cannot be simply bypassed or displaced by alternative institutions. As long as parliamentary institutions are not overthrown, their primacy in the production of consent cannot be successfully contested. Such, according to Anderson, is the real answer to Gramsci's puzzle concerning the stability of liberal democracies.

This answer cannot escape the antinomy between Gramsci's two views of civil society, one monistic-functionalist and the other dualist and conflict-theoretic. The problem lies in parliament's peculiarity as a mediating institution in the Hegelian sense—in the fact that it appears as the institution through which the state is "penetrated" by civil society. Because Anderson does not fully recognize this, he is ambushed by the consequences of his own argument. Why, he asks, are parliaments so successful in generating consent? Why are they so rarely radically challenged under liberal democracies? To his credit, Anderson is suspicious of doctrines of cultural manipulation, of the generation of passivity in the work place, and even of the ability of welfare-state benefits to buy consent.[121] Parliaments do not rely on consent produced by cultural, social, and economic institutions but generate their own. They do so by presenting individuals who are unequal and unfree in civil society with an imagery of equality before the state and, by way of their representatives, active participation in the formation of political will. This imagery in turn produces the ideological code (equality, freedom, etc.) on which the secondary activities of the generation of consent all depend.[122]

The idea of parliament as the center of ideological integration brings Anderson close to the Althusserian doctrine of "ideological state apparatuses,"[123] which he finally manages to make coherent by pointing to a process actually originating in the state that produces the ideological unity of the different "apparatuses."[124] But Anderson is even less able to remain consistently within the functionalist mode than Althusser. On the one hand, the general ideological code emanating from parliament is said merely to mask prevailing forms of inequality and unfreedom. On the other hand, "The code is all the more powerful because the juridical rights of citizenship are not a mere mirage: On the contrary, the civic freedoms and suffrages of bourgeois democracy are a tangible reality, whose completion was historically in part the work of the labor movement itself, and whose loss would be a momentous defeat for the working class."[125] Anderson goes on to describe the autonomy of parliament, which makes all such bodies *double*, expressing both the functional needs of the cultural reproduction of capital and the still potent historical achievements that express the ideals of the revolutionary bourgeoisie.

Anderson may admire these ideals, but he implies that he does not share them. He certainly rejects the quasi-Gramscian strategy of using them and the spaces they provide for building an alternative hegemony. It is unclear, however, what he would put in their place, how he would abolish them without promoting yet another "momentous defeat for the working class" whose members are admittedly still attached to equality and liberty in the sense of contemporary parliamentarism. Anderson proposes that this attachment can be broken only in the postrevolutionary experience of proletarian democracy, "in parties or councils [sic]" where "the real limits of bourgeois democracy" can be learned and historically surpassed.[126] Unfortunately, he tells us little about this alternative democracy; more importantly, his thesis implies that its principles cannot even be convincingly presented to those who now experience democracy in terms of the established procedures. The link between the two democracies would thus have to be in principle an antidemocratic one, a rather strange recommendation to those who presently value the benefits of liberal democracies. One is asked to accept a revolutionary strategy on the basis of a faith that somehow it will lead to a qualitatively different, yet untried and within the present society entirely untriable, form of democracy.

That there is no such alternative form of democracy is the best-known thesis of Norberto Bobbio. And yet Bobbio is a left socialist theorist of democratization. Though he is no mere follower of Gramsci, his justly famous interpretation of the *Prison Notebooks* is the key to his own distinctive theoretical position on the question of democracy. According to Bobbio, Gramsci fought a two-front war against those who sought to assimilate civil society (and the state) to the economy (economic determinists) and those who sought to subordinate it to the state and the cult of force. He wanted to transcend not only the conditions of bourgeois society but also "the false way of transcending these conditions."[127] In this way, somewhat ahistorically of course, Bobbio seeks to distinguish Gramsci from both social democratic and Leninist politics. To Bobbio, as we have already argued, Gramsci was a strategist of "reform," in the strong sense of wanting to transform not only politics and economics but also "customs and culture." Indeed, the whole stress here is on the building of an alternative cultural hegemony that must precede the conquest of power, involving not only the political party but also, and especially, the activity of all institutions of civil society involved in the production and diffusion of culture.[128] Thus, the center of the radical strategy in this interpretation is entirely relocated from the state to civil society, where a protracted "war of position" for the conquest of cultural hegemony would be fought.

In his famous article on Gramsci, Bobbio seemed to notice no inconsistency between this radical, civil- society-centered strategy and the goal of a regulated society in which civil society absorbs the state,[129] nor even that, on this point, Lenin's views of the distant future (though obviously not Soviet reality) coincided with the essence (though not the terminology) of Gramsci's position. Nevertheless, the Gramscian vision of a monolithic, regulated society in which civil society would absorb the state is not to be found the theory of democracy and democratization that Bobbio developed in the 1970s and especially the 1980s.[130] On the contrary, his works of this period rejected in the strongest terms the idea of a monolithic direct democracy. Instead of the radical substantialist approach, Bobbio insists that the normative procedural principles of representative democracy constitute the necessary, though admittedly not the sufficient, criteria for any state to be considered democratic. The real problem for radical democratic reform, then, is to identify the reasons why liberal democracies have not succeeded in keeping their promises, and to articulate a program for their further democratization.

Accordingly, Bobbio states what he takes to be both a normative and a realistic (feasible) definition of democracy. Every democratic government has three basic prerequisites: participation (or collective and general involvement, even if a mediated one, in the taking of all decisions applying to the whole community); control from below (on the basis of the principle that all power not so controlled tends to be abused); and freedom of dissent.[131] Bobbio is, of course, under no illusion regarding the realization of the these principles in existing liberal democracies. He argues that these promises have not been kept even in states where democratic institutions are the most fully and formally developed. Here, too, as in every modern society, there are at least four paradoxes of democracy that make it difficult to realize its principles adequately: "In a nutshell, these four enemies of democracy—where I am taking democracy to mean the optimum method for making collective decisions—are the large scale of modern social life, the increasing bureaucratization of the state apparatus, the growing technicality of the decisions it is necessary to make, and the trend of civil society toward becoming a mass society."[132]

In sum, we moderns seem to be demanding more and more democracy under conditions that are increasingly unpropitious. Moreover, these paradoxes seem to be exacerbated in representative parliamentary systems. The phenomena of political apathy and participation distorted and manipulated by elites with a monopoly on ideological power have militated against the promise of participation. Control from below is emptied of significance as the center of power shifts away from those institutions that citizens succeed in controlling: The significant instruments and centers of real power, such as the army, the bureaucracy, and big business, are not subject to democratic control. Finally, the right of dissent is severely restricted in capitalist societies in which the dominant economic system never offers the possibility of a radical alternative.

What, then, is the sense of calling contemporary Western societies "democratic"? By identifying the (minimum) defining principles of democracy with the classical (broken) promises of democracy, Bobbio's works in the 1970s tended to make this question unanswerable. In the 1980s, he confronted the issue with a procedural turn in his thought, differentiating minimum definition from normative promise. He now defined democracy in terms of a procedural minimum that includes (1) participation of the largest possible number of those concerned, (2) majority rule in decision making, (3) the existence of real alternatives (persons and policies) to choose from, and (4) the existence of guarantees of free choice in the form of basic rights of opinion, expression, speech, assembly, and association.[133]

Modern democracy is thus *liberal* democracy by definition, even if Bobbio believes that there is also a built-in conflict between democracy and those dimensions of economic and political activities calling for a strongly limited government.[134] Equally important, modern democracy is also a form of elite or oligarchic, pluralistic, particularistic, and deficiently public mass democracy whose democratic character is limited to the space of politics alone. These characterizations amount, in Bobbio's view, to a series of broken promises with respect to the classical model of democracy, even in its early modern, liberal restatements, all of which involved a relativization of the distinction of ruler and ruled along with varying emphases on individualism, universalism, publicity, and an educated citizenry.[135] Despite a heterogeneous set of causes diminishing the democratic character of modern polities—the survival of secretive or invisible political practices, the capitalist character of modern economies, the elective affinity between democracy and bureaucracy, the overload of demand produced by democratic party politics, and the increasing role of technical expertise in modern life—even these violations of the classical promise of democracy do not eliminate the minimally democratic character of the existing liberal democracies, which is procedurally defined by majority rule, electoral competition, and civil liberties.[136] This point, however, could be reversed: The procedural minimum apparently cannot diminish the elite, particularistic, nonpublic, and depoliticized form of democracy in modern societies.

Bobbio is certainly not satisfied with this conclusion. He stresses the socializing aspect of the procedural minimum of democracy, which promotes values of toleration and nonviolence in conflict resolution and, less convincingly, those of solidarity and openness to radical cultural learning experiences.[137] More importantly, he strongly believes that the further democratization of existing democracies is possible. This issue is addressed on three levels: the possible place of direct democracy; the role of alternative forms of representation; and the possibility of expanding the space of democracy from the state to civil society.

Already in the 1970s, Bobbio insisted that there is no full-fledged, realizable alternative to representative democracy that would satisfy the classical promise of democracy better than the existing model does.[138] In a manner quite reminiscent of Roberto Michels, Bobbio shows convincingly that neither of the individual institutions of "direct democracy"—referenda, local committees or assemblies, the binding mandate—nor even their combination offers a feasible replacement for the representative system. Referenda are simply infeasible for all the issues that must be debated and resolved collectively in complex modern societies. The problems that a local committee or assembly is competent to discuss are hardly identical to those confronting a national polity. Binding mandates already exist where strong party systems are in effect (party discipline being the functional equivalent for the *mandat imperatif*), and where they are not in effect, the question remains as to the nature of an acceptable authority able to revoke a mandate. Finally, an alternative model of "socialist" democracy based on the dual strategy of structural reform and the widening of participation would run up against two additional difficulties. First, a structural reform that radically affects the economy is hard to imagine without invoking violent means, which have never led to an increase of democracy. Second, the widening of democratic participation in the sphere of economic power comes up against what appears to be a permanent feature or countertrend common to socialist as well as capitalist states, namely, the removal of economic power from the province of democratic control from below. While it is debatable whether the conditions favoring autocratic power in this sphere are historically determined or objective, Bobbio maintained (at least in the 1970s) that there are good grounds for suspecting that the progressive widening of the democratic base will eventually run into an insuperable barrier when it tries to pass the factory gates.[139]

But should representative and direct democracy be seen as exclusive alternatives? In the 1980s, Bobbio began to see them as potentially complementary. First, there was a possibility of mixed or intermediary forms such as representation with binding mandates. Second, one could also include direct democratic forms such as referenda, recall, and local assemblies into representative democratic constitutions.[140] Bobbio remains skeptical toward the intermediary forms he mentions, and he rejects any further extension of the already abused imperative mandate. Moreover, he considers the role of complementary direct democratic devices important but necessarily limited. He sees the referendum. for example, as appropriate only when a relatively few issues of uncompromisable principle are at stake. Thus, his own model of democratization relies primarily on extending new representative rather than direct forms.

Within the sphere of state institutions, ideas of functional democracy have often been proposed as extending the logic of democracy to a level that has become more important in modern society (according to Emile Durkheim, the most famous exponent) than the territorial one. The best-known proposal for such representation—articulated by the guild socialists and Austro-Marxists, among others—involves an additional parliamentary chamber representing professional associations outside of the party system. To Bobbio, such a scheme implies a poor and even dangerous alternative to territorial representation. Such representation of interest groups would simply deliver parliament to lobbying by special interests and to the deals they would make. To the extent this is already a "degenerative" tendency of the existing forms of parliamentarism, it should not be made worse by being raised to a principle and an institution. While Bobbio does not believe that anything like a general interest emerges in contemporary parliaments, he nevertheless claims that the political parties that dominate these structures represent a superior form of mediation between the individual and state than do interest groups. To the necessarily rigid pattern of the representation of group interests he counterposes general visions available in political movements leading to the potentially creative and flexible handling of issues. Political parties thus represent the differently interpreted, multifaceted interests of citizens, as against the narrow and inflexible interests of group members.[141] To choose a party means to choose a general framework of interpretation based on political opinions. On the other hand we do not choose our interest group; our relation to it is ordinarily not political but is defined by shared social and economic interests.

Only in this polemical context do we get such a glorified description of the logic of representation through the party system. Yet the idealized picture distorts what could have become a more differentiated analysis and proposal. Bobbio could have stressed the possibility of a form supplementing rather than replacing representative democracy as it is now officially practiced. Good arguments and models are available for such proposals. If neocorporatist bargaining already characterizes contemporary political processes, as he repeatedly admits, there may be some significant virtue in bringing such negotiations into the light of the public sphere, thereby diminishing their corporatist character, to which Bobbio, in light of the fascist experience, is understandably allergic.[142] Moreover, a second parliamentary chamber could take on a secondary role in relation to the first; it could be overruled on the basis of a qualified majority in the territorial chamber, and its functions could be limited to certain types of issues. All of this is important because, as we shall see, Bobbio's alternative strategy of democratizing civil society may be futile if the channels enabling democratic associations, organizations, and movements to influence the political system are not increased with respect to the ordinary practice of party political elite democracy.

Within a general program of democratization, Bobbio's emphasis is on the expansion of forms of representative democracy beyond the sphere of politics. He hopes in fact to redeem two "promises" that were not inherent in either the classical or the liberal model of democracy: expanding the space of democratic decision making and exploiting the potential of pluralism. In this context, he mentions a variety of roles that can be democratized (in particular, familial, occupational, educational, and client roles) as well two major institutions that are not at present organized democratically: the school and (inconsistently) the work place. His justification for choosing these is the one used by Durkheim for his theory of functional representation, namely, that it is here that "most members of modern society spend the majority of their lives."[143] At issue is not the invention or re-creation of new and direct forms of democracy but the "infiltration" of new spaces, the spaces of civil society, by "quite traditional forms of democracy, such as representative democracy."

Interestingly enough, Bobbio's earlier doubts concerning the democratization of economic life are not dispelled; the prospects here are still pronounced uncertain, as they are for the sphere of administration. Nevertheless, he insists that while the process of democratization of civil society has only just started, considerable progress has already been made in areas such as schooling, where he stresses the participation of parents in school councils, apparently a relatively new experience in Italy. On the basis of such examples, Bobbio maintains that the new index of democratization in the future will be provided not "by the number of people who have the right to vote, but by the number of contexts outside politics where the right to vote is exercised."[144]

This conclusion seems premature on the basis of the empirical support Bobbio provides, but he has a more theoretical line of reasoning to back it up. He argues that pluralism, although not democratic in origin, provides both a reason and an opportunity for democratizing civil society. Bobbio insightfully demonstrates the origins of modern pluralism and democracy in two different polemical situations. Originally opposed not so much to autocracy as to monocratic forms of power, pluralism or polyarchy is in conflict with monolithic models of democracy, whether ancient or modern. In other words, given the dominant models of democracy in the early modern period, pluralism was antidemocratic. And yet Bobbio is right: Pluralism, based on the heterogeneity of conflicting interest constellations, cannot be eliminated in complex societies. As far as he is concerned, this fact represents a violation of the promise of democracy because nondemocratically organized centers of power bring particular interests to bear on processes of decision making and also remove these important centers from democratic controls. Yet antipluralist, individualist forms of resistance on the part of democracy would of course be futile under genuinely modern conditions. Democracy can counterattack only by bringing extrastate and even nonpolitical centers of power under its own logic. In the context of pluralistic society, the promise of democracy can be redeemed only through the extension of processes of democratization through the whole fabric of human association. And this requires not a fundamentalist program of direct democracy but the introduction of representative democracy in the relevant polyarchic centers of society.

So far the argument is convincing. But Bobbio also claims that the greater distribution of power characteristic of pluralism itself "opens the door to the democratization of civil society."[145] One is hard-pressed to find an explanation in his text for how a pluralistic organization provides targets for democratization and even facilitates such process, although he does at one point refer to dissent promoted or shielded by pluralistic organizations. The claim is, moreover, implicitly contradicted by the following assertion:

The process of democratization has not even begun to scratch the surface of the two great blocks of descending and hierarchical power in every complex society, big business and public administration. And as long as these two big blocks hold out against pressures from below, the democratic transformation of society cannot be said to be complete. We cannot even say whether this transformation is possible.[146]

It seems, then, that some of the most important centers of power greatly resist their own democratization. It is unfortunately the case that if we measure democratization by the extent to which a single set of procedural standards extends into different spheres of society, the results will inevitably be mixed, and nondemocratic spaces or centers of power are likely to remain "so numerous and so large, and their importance so great"[147] as to place the whole project in significant doubt.

Without wishing to replace Bobbio's somewhat pessimistic conclusion concerning democratization by a more optimistic scenario, we believe that a few critical remarks may help elucidate the reasons why his own civil-society-centered program has reached an impasse. First, Bobbio does not consistently operate with the Gramscian notion of a civil society differentiated from the economy.[148] As a result, he cannot clearly distinguish spheres whose internal logic facilitates radical democratization from spheres whose reproduction is consistent only with subsidiary forms of democratic participation. His overly procedural definition of democracy does not serve him well in this context: It makes him demand too little of elites in some spheres (e.g., political parties) and too much of elites in other spheres (e.g., capitalist managements).

Second, Bobbio does not pose the question of the internal relations of different democratized spheres. As a result, his prognosis, according to which spheres of society can be democratized in an order that more or less reverses their general social importance, seems to reduce unduly the stakes of democratization. What is needed is a demonstration of how and under what conditions newly democratized spheres can influence the less democratic spaces of society. In this context, his general pessimism concerning the introduction of new structures into existing versions of political democracy does not serve him well.

Finally, Bobbio does not distinguish between pluralism as a context of institutions that can and should be democratized and the plurality of collective actors that are to carry out the work of democratization. His remarks on social movements and civil disobedience do not indicate much confidence in "extrainstitutional" actors as agents of democratization.[149] We are therefore left with the suspicion that he entrusts such processes to the elites presently ensconced in the relevant pluralistic institutions, including the parties of the political system. Such a position would be reason enough for pessimism; the work of democratization cannot ordinarily be entrusted to the beneficiaries of less democratic or even nondemocratic arrangements.

We do not share Perry Anderson's critique of the left socialist appropriation of Gramsci. In our view, it makes little sense to criticize Bobbio on the ground that his strategy cannot lead to a radical rupture with the institutions of parliamentary democracy, since he specifically and rightly rejects the idea of rupture. Nor does he make a transition to socialism the goal with respect to which democratic politics can be reduced to a mere means; in general, it seems that the very meaning of socialism is transformed here into that of the radicalization of democracy.[150] With all of this, we are in agreement.

Our criticism of Bobbio has to do with the unfinished nature of his program of democratization, which in part is linked to the undeveloped and even ambiguous nature of his conception of civil society. But even this criticism should not disguise our fundamental agreement with two of the most important features of Bobbio's conception: his displacement of the terrain of democratization from the state to civil society, and his insistence on a nonfundamentalist program in which formal and representative democracy provides the general model that should be followed in the various spheres of society. These achievements, based on a specific interpretation of Gramsci, link Bobbio to the most important strategies of emancipation of the 1970s and 1980s. And yet it remains doubtful that his conception could provide such initiatives with an adequate framework of orientation and self-understanding. At issue are not only his ambiguities with respect to the concept of civil society, his somewhat too generous concessions to the elite theory of democracy, his one-sided conception of pluralism, and his deemphasis of social movements in favor of political parties. These imperfections could be corrected within the terms of his theory. On a deeper level (and this is a difficulty he shares with the forms of discourse within social movements), it is not automatically obvious that the concept of civil society taken over from Hegel and other nineteenth-century authors can with only a few corrections sustain a program of democratization and yet avoid the ideological utilization with which Parsons's theory culminates. Bobbio never considers the possibility that the whole conceptual strategy may be intimately linked to now obsolete nineteenth-century conditions before the "fusion" of state and society; that even in its original utilization it may imply not only antistatism but depoliticization as well; that it might represent only a set of institutional masks for deeper and more refined authoritarian strategies; and finally, that the model of social differentiation it presupposes is a false and unsophisticated one that is inadequate to the realities of complex societies.

In our view, the kind of theory Bobbio seeks to develop cannot be constructed until these criticisms are considered in detail. We believe further that the several paradigms of the critique of civil society associated with Carl Schmitt, Hannah Arendt, Reinhart Koselleck, Jürgen Habermas, Michel Foucault, and Niklas Luhmann will yield important contributions to our attempt at theory construction. It is to these critiques that we now turn.

II

The Discontents of Civil Society

4

The Normative Critique:
Hannah Arendt

One of the most challenging, and certainly the most passionate, critiques of modern civil society has been presented by Hannah Arendt in a whole series of books and essays.[1] Arendt's main, though barely mentioned, antagonist is Hegel. Her attack is concentrated specifically on the concept of "society" as an intermediate realm between private and public, between family and political life. "Society" is a realm of mediations where private interests, activities, and institutions assume public roles, while public institutions take on private "housekeeping" functions. Thus, to Arendt, institutions such as Hegel's corporations and police do not stabilize and regulate the differentiation of public and private but rather dissolve the sharp line between them and threaten the integrity and autonomy of both. Unlike Hegel, Arendt does not seek a synthesis of modern society and ancient republicanism. Instead, she resolutely defends the model of classical political society, *politike koinonia*, along with its sharp separation from the *oikos* or private sphere, against modernity, particularly against the modern state (bureaucracy) and modern (mass) society. Her critique is a normative one based on what she takes to be the values of classical public life (political equality, public discourse, and honor) and private life (uniqueness, difference, individuality). Unlike that of the young Marx in 1843, whom she in many respects resembles, Arendt's is not an immanent criticism. The actual political reemergence and reinstitutionalization of these values requires an almost total rupture with all existing institutions. A history of decline from the emergence of "society" to mass society, seen as more or less inexorable, deprives modernity of its one admitted achievement: the development and enrichment of the private sphere as a sphere of intimacy. Thus, like Walter Benjamin, Arendt consciously practices a form of redemptive criticism that, for the sake of a possible future, attempts to save some valued aspects of the past from the perceived disintegration of tradition, including the tradition of early modernity.[2]

We examine Arendt's critique in detail for several reasons. First, she will help us counterbalance the Parsonian conception by providing rich insights into the dark side of the institutionalization of modern civil society. Second, the internal contradictions of her analysis will help us show that not even Arendt was able to base a modern theory of freedom on the abolition of civil society; she, too, is forced to assume, however unwillingly, the necessity of its preservation. Third, a comparison with the early work of Reinhart Koselleck and Jürgen Habermas will allow us to show that in the modern world one can make sense of Arendt's normatively based project, which revolves around the concept of the public sphere, only if it is relocated around the intermediary sphere of the social that she sought to banish.

The concept of the social in Arendt's work corresponds to the Hegelian topos of *bürgerliche Gesellschaft* and is, in fact, counterposed to both the political society of the ancients and the civil society of the modern liberals. While these two conceptualizations emphasized the public sphere in the case of the ancients and the private in the case of liberalism, "the social realm," a creation of modernity occluded by these two political philosophies, involves a mixture and interpenetration of the two realms and their constitutive principles.[3] To understand the mixture, we must first analyze its components.

Arendt's theory of the public sphere, although systematized around a theory of action, is derived from her understanding of the model of ancient republics. She conceives of the *polis* as "the organization of the people as it arises out of speaking and acting together."[4] Action in turn is understood as the self-disclosure and even self-renewal of the actor through the medium of speech, possible only in presence of others who see and hear and hence are capable of establishing the reality of subjective expression.[5] Action is therefore always interaction that both confirms the plurality of unique experience and personality and establishes a common world, "relating and separating" human actors at the same time. This common world is the public sphere.

One striking difficulty of Arendt's conception is that it describes both an anthropologically constitutive condition of human life and a historically specific and unique constellation: the ancient city republic (and its alleged, but admittedly exceptional, modern revivals). In this she follows the prejudices of the Greeks, and she tries to escape the resulting difficulty through her conception of power.

Action, or rather interaction, is constitutive of the public sphere,[6] but it is supposedly only power that can keep it in existence.[7] Power in turn is defined as acting in concert, on the bases of making and keeping promises, mutually binding one another, covenanting.[8] While Arendt's model of action stresses the striving of the actor for the fame and even "immortality" that can be achieved through dramaturgic self-presentation based on the rhetorical skill "of finding the right words at the right moment,"[9] her concept of power points to action oriented to normative principles that derive their force from the depth-structure of a form of communication based on mutual recognition and solidarity.[10] Thus, the concept of action can be understood as a general anthropological constituent of the "human condition," but the concept of power, and along with it a fully institutionalized public sphere, seems to require a republican model for its full actualization. And Arendt does in fact link power more closely to political speech than to action in its primordial, "rhetorical" sense.[11]

The public sphere in Arendt's view presupposes a plurality of individuals unequal by nature who are, however, "constructed" as politically equal. According to her, the meaning of the *polis* as *isonomia* (literally, equality in relation to law) is that of "no rule," in the sense of an absence of differentiation into rulers and ruled within the citizen body.[12] Thus, the public sphere establishes a model of interaction characterized by noncoercive discourse among citizens who initially hold and freely exchange a genuine plurality of opinions.[13] This model turns out to be rather restrictive. Based on her differentiation between action and work, *praxis* and *poiesis*,

Arendt at times goes along with what she takes to be the Greek exclusion of legislation, decision by voting, and even the founding of cities from the properly public, political activities.[14] When she made her journey from Greece to Rome, however, in *On Revolution*, she made the act of foundation—the making of constitutions or the exercise of *le pouvoir constituant*—the public political activity par excellence. Yet she kept an important consistency between the two positions, namely, the view that public life must be seen exclusively as an end in itself. Thus, genuine republican constitution making in the later view ought to have no other purpose than to institution-alize the public sphere itself.[15] Arendt therefore strongly rejected, as contrary to the very principle of publicity, the idea that actors bring into their common deliberations the interests, needs, and concerns of their private lives and households.

Arendt describes the all-important relationship of public and private in terms of differentiation, complementarity, and conflict. She starts by differentiating principles described variously in terms of action vs. labor and work, constructed reality vs. natural reality, uniqueness vs. real difference, freedom vs. necessity, no rule vs. domination, or equality vs. inequality.[16] For Arendt, an actual and thoroughgoing institutional differentiation is required for the operation of the principles of both private and public for two reasons. First, the complementary role of the private vis-à-vis the public can be performed only in context of their separation. Second, in each other's terrain the two principles have a strong tendency to vitiate and even abolish one another.

Abstractly, the freedom of public life requires the conquest of necessity, the task of the private in its economic capacity, as *oikos*.[17] Thus, the organization of the household was such as to provide its head with sufficient time for the exercise of public freedom. But Arendt's stress is on the conditions required for the emergence of the citizen as an independent subject, possessing substantial and independent opinions. The institutional form of the private as property (in contrast to mobile wealth) guarantees this indepen-dence by setting up "external" boundaries among citizens and households; its "interior," by offering a hiding place from the light of publicity, is the precondition for nurturing the unique aspects of personality without which life becomes entirely "shallow."[18]

In spite of the importance of a differentiated private realm for the public, the latter also involves fear and suspicion of the former. This is based on the possible distraction of the citizen by a model of private happiness, but even more on the temptation to impose on the *polis* the despotic forms of rule, inequality, and differentiation characteristic of the *oikos*.[19] While in this context Arendt speaks of the "permanent threat" of the private to the public, elsewhere she maintains that in the ancient world the greater danger was "the tendency of public power to expand and to trespass upon private interests." This possibility, "inherent in republican government," could be checked only by institutionalizing private property and eventually by the modern alternative, born in renewed republican experimentation, of framing laws that publicly guarantee the "rights" of privacy, that is, the creation of constitutional rights.[20]

While Arendt always maintains her staunch support for such rights, she nevertheless argues that they do not sufficiently protect the differentiation of public and private under modern conditions. In particular, neither the specifically modern forms of the invasion of the public by the private nor the resulting assaults on privacy and intimacy by a new and corrupt form of "public" life can be counteracted by public rights of private persons. Arendt connects both tendencies to a single phenomenon: the rise of the social.

Even if she thus admits tendencies within the public and the private to invade one another's domains, Arendt consistently claims that the ancient republics managed to maintain the differentiation that belonged to their own constitutive conditions. The actual interpenetration and even fusion of the two is a product of modernity, of the rise of the social realm that constitutes the target of Arendt's critique of civil society. The interpenetration, in line with latent tendencies of both the public and the private spheres, goes both ways. The *state* (i.e., the modern territorial compulsory association) takes over functions of material reproduction, or "housekeeping," while collective life, in the shape of the *nation*, takes on the structure and forms of behavior of a superhuman family. Arendt's formula for the political form of the rise of the social, the *nation-state*, expresses this two-sided interpenetration.[21]

The result of mutual interpenetration of public and private is the disappearance of any stable boundaries between "two realms [that]

. . . constantly flow into each other."[22] In the new topos, however, an entirely novel type of hybrid structure comes into being that will become the dynamic center of a process leading to the eventual disappearance of both public and private.

The origins of this social realm are analyzed in quite different terms in Arendt's various works. At least three points of origin are distinguishable among these: the early modern political or national economy; the depoliticized court society and the emergence of salon society; and the modern democratic revolution. In each case, the role of the early modern state, created by absolutism, is central. The first explanation, which comes closest to the Marxian tradition,[23] stresses the self-organization of the absolute monarchy "as a tremendous business concern" that failed, according to one version of the argument, to find an adequate class basis.[24] In this version, it was the state that elevated matters of mere housekeeping into the public realm, in the process deforming that realm with concerns that were incompatible with its basic principles.[25] It should be noted that in this context "the social" becomes synonymous with "political economy." Its supposedly almost unrestrainable expansion is associated with the modern phenomenon of unlimited economic growth. Here the step to an economy-centered neo-Marxist argument is a rather small one, and Arendt actually takes this step when she describes limitless economic growth as the expansion of the private realm at the cost of the public.[26]

The second train of argument is, in part, Tocquevillian. The thesis is that absolutism destroyed its own class basis by depoliticizing the *Ständestaat* in the form of a society of orders whose model and preeminent institution was courtly society.[27] This argument stresses conformism, secret manipulation, and intrigue as the results of "depoliticization" rather than "economization." The most important consequence was that the French nobility was reduced to insignificance. In other words, this development of the social occurred at the expense of political society.

These two arguments may indeed be compatible, but they share a common flaw: Both seem to imply that, before the process of absolutist depoliticization and/or economization, differentiated public and private realms existed, each operating according to its own proper logic. Because she relies on a normative model derived from the ancient city republics, however, Arendt explicitly contra-dicts this implicit claim. Rightly or wrongly, she posits the loss of the Greek understanding of politics in the medieval period and *the absence* of a public realm in the secular sphere of the feudal epoch. Since she depicts medieval corporate life as having patterned all human activities on that of the household, it is hardly feasible that she could consider the *Ständestaat* based on it as a model of public life, in her sense of this concept.[28]

Arendt's third line of argumentation, developed in *On Revolution*, proposes a model that avoids this difficulty, but in the process she throws into doubt the historical relevance of the other two theses. Here Arendt solves the problem of what precedes depoliticization by crediting the "republican" moment of the modern revolutions with re-creating the classical model of the public. It then makes sense to argue that it was the failure to institutionalize this moment and/or the emergence of the "social" question led to the subsequent dedifferentiation of public and private and their decline. In the case of the French Revolution, however, the argument concerning the rise of the social is an entirely new one. According to Arendt, the revolution in its radical phase opened the political realm to the poor, to the multitude driven by material need, in the process making matters public that by their very nature belonged to the private realm of housekeeping and could be solved not by public-political but only by administrative means.[29] Thus, once again, despite the republican ethos of the revolutionaries, government turned into administration. Of course, the turning of government into administration was anticipated by the monarchic absolutist founders of the modern state. Recalling her earlier argument as a counterpoint, Arendt now states that if in the old regime economic and financial problems could be said to have "intruded" into the public sphere, "the people" violently burst upon it.[30] And if "high society" imposed its mores and moral standards on politics, reducing it to intrigue and perfidy, the society of the poor, driven also by its earlier exclusion from society, transformed public life into its very negation: brutality and violence.[31]

Evidently, then, and somewhat inconsistently, Arendt sees the mercantilist economization of politics, the absolutist depoliticization of the aristocracy, and the revolutionary socialization of public life as successive and increasingly destructive forms of the rise of the social realm, which will be followed by the successive forms of mass society and totalitarianism, involving the complete eradication of both public and private. Her analysis of the American Revolution, however, indicates that the overall trend implied by the thesis of the rise of the social does not require the stages just depicted. American history knows only failed attempts at mercantilist economization and even more so at absolutist depoliticization. In particular, Arendt argues that the social question did not burst upon the public-political stage in America and that here, unlike all other revolutions, the institutionalization of a differentiated private sphere protected by constitutional rights was fully successful.[32] And yet exceptionalism in these respects obviously did not prevent the United States from developing its own brand of mass society, indeed for many the paradigmatic model.

Like other analysts, Arendt had difficulty perceiving the reality of the modern state behind the institutions of American federalism and pluralism. Yet this reality does make an appearance when Arendt analyzes the American failure to found lasting institutions of republican freedom. The reasons for this included a failure to institutionalize small-scale structures of direct political participation and an increasing identification of freedom as well as the aims of government with the negative freedoms of private life protected by constitutional rights. But these points are not on the same level as the arguments dealing with the rise of the social sphere; indeed, they imply only the strengthening of the private at the expense of the public.

Nevertheless Arendt maintains that the retreat to the values of private as against public happiness, and the reduction of freedom to civil liberties alone, along with the rise of utilitarian criteria in politics and the domination of public life by a uniform, homogeneous public opinion, correspond also in America "with great precision to the invasion of the public realm by society."[33] As for this invasion, we get only two related reasons, which do not add up to an explanation on the level of the rest of Arendt's thesis. To begin with, she speaks of "rapid and constant economic growth" equivalent to the "constantly increasing expansion of the private realm" at the expense of the public.[34] This is a simplified version of a classical Marxian thesis that does not in itself explain the emergence of the new structural topos, the social realm. For this realm, Arendt, unlike Tocqueville,[35] is able to discover only European origins. According to an entirely unconvincing train in her argument, the immigrant poor of Europe, confronting American riches based on economic expansion and technological innovation, brought over the social question from its originally European home. We are led to believe that it was for this reason above all that the American dream of the "foundation of freedom" was converted into that of the fulfillment of all material desires.[36] Thus, immigration in America supposedly played something like the role of the radical phase of the French revolution; that is, it converted inadequately instituted republican structures and practices into the rule of a public opinion whose ultimate interest was in satisfying needs proper to the private sphere—the needs of consumption.

Irrespective of the problem of origins, Arendt depicts the "hybrid" sphere of the social as an extremely dynamic one with devastating consequences for both public and private. Even to those who, like ourselves, judge her analysis to be highly one-sided, the depiction yields an impressive analysis of the underside of the institutionalization of modern civil society matched only by Marx before her and Foucault after her.[37]

The key terms in Arendt's analysis of the deformation of the public realm are bureaucracy, welfare state, public opinion, and political corruption. We note that the first three correspond with some precision to the categories of Hegel's analysis of civil society and state that mediate between private and public: civil service, "police," and public opinion. The category of corruption in turn leads to a critique of interest representation in the party system that is implicitly a modern variant of the fourth Hegelian mediation, the corporation.

According to Arendt, bureaucracy is the "social" form of government *par excellence* because the social question which is to say questions of collective welfare, can have only administrative solutions.[38] Arendt does not, in fact, deny the need for civil service or administration under modern forms of government. She argues only that when questions of welfare become the predominant or even exclusive questions in the life of the state (as in the *Sozialstaat* or welfare state), the result is bureaucracy, in her terminology the rule *of* the administration, which can become the most tyrannical form of all.[39] Bureaucracy is an especially arbitrary form of government because it involves rule by decree, with the holders of discretionary power becoming anonymous and invisible behind the facade of other, apparently more political forms of deliberation and decision making. If tyranny is "government that is not held to give account of itself," then bureaucracy, as rule "by Nobody," goes so far as to hide the agents who might be held accountable.[40] Such, according to Arendt, is the case in modern welfare states, where the idea of democracy is converted from that of public participation to the achievement, through the most efficient administrative means possible, of the goals of public welfare.[41]

The procedures of public participation are not, however, merely deformed from above; they are also hollowed out from within. The social form of politics is the corruption of politics: It takes three forms linked to status, wealth, and need, respectively. Members of the depoliticized aristocratic orders of the old regime continued to act together in court society to improve their status, but they could not do so in the properly political sense of relying on open speech. Thus, public deliberation and persuasion were replaced by the "pull, pressure and the tricks of cliques," the result being mores and moral standards that open the door to intrigue and perfidy.[42] The peddling of influence replaced the generation of power. The same pattern occurred in salon society. Indeed, the eighteenth-century Rousseauian attack on "society," reproduced by Arendt, was an attack on the hypocrisy of the court and its analogues, the aristocratic salons, and the hypocritical, unnatural power of women.[43] But Arendt does not restrict the notion of the corruption of politics to this obvious example. For her, it is as part of a genuine public life that property owners emerge from a protected private realm to pursue public affairs. When, however, property is replaced by "wealth," and the pursuit of political goals by the defense and generation of ever-expanding wealth, the corrupt forms of acting together generated by aristocratic society become the best means also for the "bourgeois" to pursue private goals that cannot by their very nature be validated publicly. Finally, the popular response to the corruption of status and wealth, the brutality of people driven by need, itself corrupts politics and is corruptible by "politicians." Here, too, the proper medium of political conflict and competition is replaced by a principle wholly at variance with it: instead of the secret interaction of cliques and mafias, the violence of those unable to use political speech.[44]

What ties these examples of political corruption together, in the context of the depoliticizing bureaucratic rule by Nobody, is the quasi-political interaction of people in their private capacity who lack the institutions of a public sphere that could establish their capacities as citizens. It is nonetheless part of Arendt's thesis that the eighteenth-century revolutions sought to establish precisely such institutions. Their failure was not simply a result of the intervention of bureaucracy and private wealth into the public sphere, problems that even the ancients had to face, as Arendt well knew. The *core* of her thesis about the specifically modern decline of republican politics therefore depends on the effect of the social on the very structure of the public: the transformation of public spirit into public opinion.

Once again, Arendt assigns a pioneering role to "high society," to the absolutist court and its extension in the aristocratic salon.[45] Indeed, it is this cultural development, unlike the problems of bureaucracy and poverty, that is unique to modernity and thus a pivotal point in the analysis. It is here, in a space neither private nor political, dominated by status consciousness and empty uniform conventions, that public life first acquired, according to Arendt, the forms of interaction characteristic of a unified, conformist, corrupted, collective opinion. All those who sought to enter "high society" or "society" were forced to submit to this logic, producing conformity and assimilation.[46] Courtly and salon society, character-ized by the basest pursuit of private interests, intrigue, unnatural pretentiousness, concern for status and style, and corruption (in the sense of utter lack of concern for the *res publica*) became the model of behavior that was emulated by the rest of society.[47]

But what is the dynamic of the dramatic extension of this logic beyond "society" in the narrow sense, the beginnings of which can be ascribed to the absolutist suppression of politically meaningful speech and of the plurality of political opinion within the aristocracy? To Arendt, the revolutionary transfer of the notion of sovereignty from king to people and the concomitant rise of the politics of interest are the best symbolic representations of the relevant trends.[48] The "compassionate" response by the radical revolutionaries in France to the multitude driven by need led them to substitute will for consent, unity for plurality, and a single opinion for the conflict of opinions, because any accommodation of consent, plurality, and conflict seemed to compromise the most urgent and desperate measures required to solve the "social question." The mythological sovereignty of the people, in the sense of a collective will whose only object was a unified general interest, thus became the foundation of a public opinion that could only be threatened by independent public life, including the new, decentralized, and inevitably plural institutions of the popular strata themselves.[49] And while the dictatorial embodiment of this supposedly general will did not arise from an actually unified or uniform public opinion, it was in a position to create such an opinion.[50]

While the fact of nationalism allows Arendt to extend her critique of sovereignty beyond dictatorial-populist regimes, the argument again does not work well enough for the United States, where nineteenth-century critics such as Tocqueville uncovered a public opinion of unrivaled uniformity and assimilating power. Arendt does recall a part of Tocqueville's argument contrasting democracy and republics. A democratic society involves the kind of social leveling that could open up the way to a new kind of plurality, one of opinion, only in context of creating genuine republican institutions based on free communication even at the micropolitical level. This effort having in large part failed, democracy in America came to reveal some of the despotic characteristics feared by the founders, with the public spirit, based on a multiplicity of opinions, replaced by a unified and homogeneous public opinion. Arendt insists that this trend was checked politically through the survival of some republican institutions on the national and state levels. Nevertheless, the rise of a politics of interest, common to both Europe and America, tended to complete the destructive process.

Interest as against (genuine) opinion is politically relevant only when belonging to a group, indeed a large group. The representation of interest more or less binds the representatives and interferes with the genuine exchange and formation of opinion. The modern party system in particular, by focusing on interest representation, ends up replacing parliamentary discussion by the competing collective opinions of disciplined party blocks. The hierarchic and oligarchic structure of the party thus becomes the model of contemporary politics. The welfare state may be democratic in representing the interests of the many, but it is oligarchic in the sense of drastically curtailing participation on all but the highest levels of the state.[51] The Hegelian attempt to mediate private and public spheres through intermediary social-political bodies thus winds up reducing the space for public freedom within the structure of the state.

The situation is made all the worse, in Arendt's assessment, because the decline of the public does not benefit the private; the social tends to destroy the private sphere as well. In this context, Arendt distinguishes between private property, which constitutes the outer shell of the protection of privacy, and wealth. The latter is a means of deforming the public realm but is incapable of protecting the private.[52] Because of its fluidity and absence of stable location, wealth is supposedly unable to guarantee a sphere in which the individual is free from any external gaze or penetration. More convincingly, Arendt argues that, the object of wealth being its own accumulation and consumption, its pursuit commits individuals to uniform trends, reflected by a behavioral science, of not only economic production and distribution but daily life as well. Not only does laboring activity become mindless and uniform, but the life of the home is invaded by a process of homogenization and commodification that destroys the possibility of any authentic private life. In our unlimited drive to consumption, we finally consume the material framework of the private.[53] Mass society, the society of job-holders and consumers, presupposes the absorption of the immense variety of family life into a uniform, homogenized social realm that becomes a family writ large.[54]

The private sphere resists this absorption by a specifically modern creation: intimacy. On the level of a small circle of interpersonal relations, intimacy involves a tremendous deepening of the private sphere, in the sense of an intensification and enrichment of "subjective emotions and private feelings."[55] This form of privacy is structured in terms of an opposition not to the public but to the social. Despite its immense contribution to the culture of modernity, though, the intimate sphere does not represent a reliable substitute for the protection to privacy offered by property. The intimate sphere cannot defend itself against the modern pattern of "unnatural growth" of the social, because the intensification of subjectivity cannot yield a stable and intersubjective or institutionalized "world."[56]

Without tracing any further the Arendtian thesis concerning the decline of public and private, leading at least ideal-typically to a full-fledged "mass society" and to totalitarianism, we should note the structure of her view of modern society. In this theory, the complex of the social, constituted by modern bureaucracy and political economy, confronts two realms on which the reproduction of authentic human life depend: the public and the private. These realms do appear in modern society, even if in a situation that threatens their very existence. Any reconstruction of the human condition, then, would obviously depend on a new or renewed institutionalization of both public and private. Arendt's theory of the modern revolution, understood broadly, explores the chances of such a double reinstitutionalization. In the process, she not only revives the spirit of ancient republicanism but is forced to do so in ways that require taking yet another look at the modern topos of a differentiated civil society.

In another context, Arendt links the idea of a differentiation of state and society, already associated with "the rise of the social," to the rise of a "modern" form of republicanism. She explicitly notes that the early modern (especially Lockean) version of social contract theory refers to two contracts and to the origin of two differentiated entities: "society" and "legitimate government." We should not be misled, however; Arendt explicitly defends only the principle of the first contract, resting on reciprocity, mutuality, and equality and rooted in promising and making covenants. Moreover, she interprets the first contract in terms of a constitution of bodies politic locally, regionally, and, ultimately, on a federal level, leading to a multiplication of power. She does not, in other words, see that the principle of horizontal covenanting establishes an intermediate sphere between the strictly private and the political public, whose very principle would be voluntary association.[57] Significantly, she is skeptical regarding the second contract, whose principle she understands as submission and surrender of power and the creation of a relation between ruler and ruled, only supposedly "legitimated" by mere consent. Indeed, unlike the tradition of natural rights to which she refers, she seems to consider the two contracts as mutually exclusive.[58] But does the mere existence of the second contract really vitiate the first? And is the first contract sufficient unto itself in founding a body politic? The model of differentiation Arendt entertains here is in fact that between *political society* and state, and if one takes her analysis as a whole, it is not entirely clear whether differentiation thus understood sustains or undermines a modern political society. The dilemmas of modern republicanism that she is forced to note do indeed lead her back to a model of differentiation, rather than away from it.

Arendt's revival of ancient republicanism, of the ideal of civil society as *politike koinonia*, in the contexts of modern revolutions from Paris to Budapest, is deservedly well known. Juxtaposing direct participation to representation, and federalism to unified sovereignty, she presents us with a model of pyramidally organized "small republics," "councils," or "wards" capable of institutionalizing a framework of public freedom and establishing a form of government at all levels linked to the paradigm of the communicative generation of power—a veritable "great republic."[59] She is conscious of this idea's link to the ancient model of *politike koinonia*; referring to colonial America, she speaks of the self-constitution of "civil bodies politic" that were "political societies" open to federalism but hostile to the depoliticization that would accompany a centralized state with unified sovereignty.[60] As against the contemporary constituted bodies of the European old regime ("diets and parliaments, orders and estates"), the American political societies were not tied to privilege, birth, or occupation and opted from the outset for status in public rather than private law.[61] Thus, rather than resembling the political societies of the age of absolutism or even the *Ständestaat*, the small American republics consciously returned to the ancient model of an incorporated citizen society, a genuine *res publica*. It is emphatically this conception that remains normative in Arendt's political project. And yet, the very egalitarian universalism that differentiates these two conceptions of political society derived from something new, namely, the constitutive principles of civil society, as Tocqueville knew well.

While insisting on the continuous history of her model of political society from the age of revolutions to our own day, Arendt is forced to concede the repeated failure of permanent institutionalization. Unlike Tocqueville, though, she does not seem to be aware of the contradictions of what she knows to be an aristocratic model of the political self-selection of elites in a "democratic age."[62] But she does note three areas as sources of this repeated failure: (1) internal limits of the historical attempts to build council governments; (2) the difficulty of stabilizing an instituted or constituted power in a model based on the act of instituting or constituting; and (3) the clash between republicanism and liberalism, between models of public and private happiness.

The first problem area revolves around the encounter between the council model and the modern economy and the modern state. Arendt repeatedly laments that all council experiments after the American revolution became mired in the social question (e.g., the Parisian societies) or in impossible attempts to democratize the world of work (e.g., workers councils from St. Petersburg to Budapest). Arendt's dismissal of any sort of industrial democracy flows from the dogmatics of her conception, from the automatic institutional translation of her separation between action and work. Her caution about deriving utopian models of workers' control from a monolithic concept of democracy is well founded, of course, although it is certainly wrong to pose the question of industrial democracy as an all-or-nothing proposition. Moreover, her notion that revolutionary councils should have focused exclusively on the questions of establishing and preserving the new political regime is quite unrealistic, even if one accepts her thesis of the primacy of the political rather than the social moment in modern revolutions. In this context, her hard-headedness concerning the constraints implied by the modern state is surprising, if welcome. She admits the need for a modern administration in a modern society and rightly criticizes the inability of the council experiments to come to terms with the "enormous extent to which the government machinery in modern societies must indeed perform the functions of administration."[63] Thus, she is forced to return to precisely the model of differentiation that she rejected in her discussion of the two contracts. Unfortunately, however, she turns once again to an overly rigid version of this model, confusing differentiation in principle with that of the concerns of actual institutions. As a result, the iron-tight division of functions she suggests between the political action of councils and the administrative work of a civil service represents no solution whatsoever to the task indicated.

Her attempt to deal with the second problem is also only partially successful. Arendt is fully conscious of the difficulty or even self-contradiction inherent in a project aiming at the embodiment of the revolutionary spirit in enduring institutions.[64] Without hesitation she renounces the politics of any kind of permanent revolution based on the continuous functioning of a *pouvoir constituant* that inevitably produces its own tyrannical opposite.[65] But how, then, can the revolutionary spirit be embodied at all? The aim of revolution, according to Arendt, must be the creation of foundations for a new political order, a new constitution. She maintains that such a constitution, as against any liberal or even "constitutionalist" interpretation, must establish power rather than limit it. The juxtaposition is misleading, however, because the establishment of an unlimited power, inevitably returning us to a model of permanent revolution, could not yield any institutionalization of stable political foundations. And indeed Arendt attributes this dimension of institutionalization to the rule of law rather than the exercise of power.[66] But what is the source of a law that could lend stability to a constitution if our *positive* laws are founded in the constitution itself? How are we to escape the vicious circle inherent in constitutional lawmaking itself? What is the source of the legitimacy of a constituent assembly, and if it is legitimate, what can justify its self-dissolution? Arendt does not believe that any version of a return to the eighteenth-century theory of an absolute natural law, prior to and above constitutions, can supply the answer to these questions today.[67] As a result, she has a great deal of difficulty in distinguishing between the source of law and that of power, precisely the dilemma that, in her analysis, leads to the radical instability of constitutions. Her only answer, in the spirit of Roman rather than Greek antiquity, is that the constitution as an act of foundation can replace the absolute source of law if it develops, as it did in the United States, into a tradition of a new type. In such a context, the vicious circle of constitutional law will apply only to the foundational moment. Subsequently, the constitutional tradition itself, authoritatively interpreted by a body without power, will supply the sanction for a law capable of stabilizing the framework of the exercise of power. But is the making of constitutional authority a matter of tradition compatible with the pursuit of public freedom as our highest end? Can a freedom whose vehicle is public communication and discourse stop at the limits constituted by a supposedly sacred foundation? The deep tension between civil religion and public freedom is built into this model from the outset, a tension only exacerbated when the concept of public freedom is replaced, as in the actual historical trend, by that of the private.

The third reason for the difficulty of establishing institutions of public freedom in Arendt's analysis is represented by the clash of ancient republican and modern liberal principles, by the subversive implications of the goal of private happiness for public freedom. In this context, Arendt finds that she cannot give a self-contained republican answer to the challenge of the liberal model of civil society based on the separation of a valued society and a state without norms. This comes about primarily because she holds the public and private spheres to be, in their differentiation, constitutive for one another. She does maintain with approval that the "actual content of the [U.S.] constitution was by no means the safeguard of civil liberties but the establishment of an entirely new system of power."[68] But she also makes repeatedly clear that, without the safeguard of civil liberties, at least in the modern world, public political life cannot be maintained. She is left in the end with the precarious position that, while the establishment of civil liberties represents a very real, though unfortunately all too exceptional, gain in revolutions, too great a focus on rights and the private happiness they can secure tends to devalue public happiness and freedom.

Arendt is well aware of the origins of civil rights in the modern sense. On one side, the modern sovereign state represented an entirely new type of threat to individual autonomy; on the other, the more or less contemporary erosion of the traditional, religious, and corporate forms of protection made individuals increasingly defenseless. The paradox of "human rights" from Arendt's point of view is that while protection is needed in the face of the modern state, only within the framework of a state is such protection plausible at all. Outside the body politic, the most fundamental right, namely, the right to have rights based on the ability to assert and defend rights publicly, cannot be secure. Thus, modern rights should be understood as *citizen* rights guaranteed by constitutions.[69] This early strain of her argument seems to make civil rights functions of a public sphere to be established in the face of the modern state.

Arendt soon came to understand that rights, even if they could be stabilized only as rights of citizens, must be defended even in face of a citizen body, if need be. Given the tendency, always present, of public power to absorb private interests, and given the modern erosion of a form of property capable of carving out a private space of protection for citizens, *civil* rights are needed to stabilize the private sphere. It is at this point that Arendt most clearly concedes the fundamental liberal claim that in a modern society, freedom is not possible unless *civil* society and state are differentiated by mechanisms of civil rights.

Arendt then immediately moves from the liberal thesis to one inspired by Marx. While civil rights can indeed protect the private sphere from penetration by the modern state, they cannot do so in the face of the modern economy.[70] Arendt does not in this context consider the possibility that an expanded and reorganized catalogue of rights could actually have an analogous relationship to both state and economy. Whatever hope she has concerning the restriction and control of economic forces and growth therefore depends on the existence of a public realm redifferentiated from the social one, independent of "political economy." Yet here, too, civil rights must play a role to the extent that a differentiated private sphere remains the sine qua non of the emergence of personalities capable of participating in the public sphere itself. Whatever success the American revolution had in establishing republican institutions is related to the preservation of civil rights, while the failure of all other great revolutions in this respect is linked to their systematic violations of rights.[71]

Thus, in Arendt's conception, the differentiation of civil liberty protected by rights and public freedom secured by the exercise of political power helps to establish each. But at the same time, the erosion of the line between them tends to destroy both. This restatement of her conception of public and private in terms of democracy and rights is not, however, the end of Arendt's consideration of the problem of civil liberties. She also maintains that, from the moment of its establishment, the model of freedom based on rights remains a threat to the model based on power.

According to Arendt's interpretation, the U.S. Bill of Rights sought only to control and limit republican power instead of trying to replace its aims by nonpolitical ones, as was the case with the French *Declaration of the Rights of Man and Citizen*.[72] And yet even here, a reversal was to occur in which public freedom came to be subordinated to civil liberties, the citizen to the private individual. At stake are two different models of happiness leading to two different understandings of "constitutionalism." In Arendt's overall diagnosis, the shift from the values of public happiness, freedom, and civic spirit to private happiness and the corresponding negative model of freedom tend to be ascribed fundamentally to the rise of society. But since her analysis of the rise of society, especially in the American context, is never really adequate, she is also at times tempted to reverse the causal nexus. She maintains, in other words, that a liberal component stressing private happiness (the cultivation and enjoyment of one's private concerns) as the highest end of life tended from the beginning to undermine, in the philosophical self-understanding if not the practice of the American revolution, the republican component linked to the idea that public happiness based on political participation is the highest good.[73] Thus, the model Arendt defends not only fully differentiates public and private but also asserts the motivational primacy of the the former. With private happiness achieving primacy, freedom was redefined: Instead of meaning the positive freedom to act, it came to mean negative freedom from the action of others. Even more decisively, the aim of a constitution—"constitutionalism"— shifted from the establishment of a new form of genuinely public power to the protection of individuals from the exercise of power. Political freedom came to be understood not as a function of an increase of power, but as one of a limitation of power. This liberal ideal of constitutionalism came to mean a distrust regarding all forms of power and an increasing indifference toward the form in which power was exercised, so long as civil liberties (themselves not powers) as the bulwarks of private happiness were protected.[74] This version of constitutionalism, however, proved to be quite compatible with a bureaucratic form of government expressing the logic of the "rise of the social." In the end, a rights-centered politics could not defend even the private sphere itself against the destructive trends of the modern state and society.

Arendt's understanding of rights itself suffers from a lack of differentiation reflecting her unwillingness to take seriously the idea of mediation between private and public. The ambiguous status of the rights of assembly and association in her work proves this point. On the one hand, these rights are classed with negative liberties, that is, freedom from unjustified restraint. Even in the American Bill of Rights, the right of assembly was, according to her, only "the right to assemble in order to petition." What the individual gains from such a right is "liberation" rather than "freedom"; at most, the ability to petition collectively may lead to some restraining influence over, but never participation in, a government.[75] On the other hand, the rights of assembly, association, and speech are also referred to as the most important truly political freedoms, as contrasted with apolitical freedoms such as that of enterprise.[76] While she argues that this status was reached through a development beyond the limits of the Bill of Rights, for example,[77] she does not clarify whether and how this supposed development produced a new status for what remained juridically a constitutional liberty. In any case, even the discussion admitting the status of the right of assembly as a political freedom culminates with a declaration that "political freedom, generally speaking, means the right 'to be a participator in government' or it means nothing."[78] This declaration sets up standards that can rarely be satisfied by what the right of assembly actually guarantees in even its most developed versions.

The issue goes deep in Arendt's conception of rights and reflects her ambivalence concerning the ultimate foundation of rights. Indeed, she has two conceptions concerning the core of a system of rights. One links "the right to have rights" to access to a public sphere in which rights can be asserted and defended.[79] The other isolates the right to carve out a private sphere linked to private property as the basic model of all rights. Accordingly, the right of assembly is interpreted in each of these ways, as a dimension of political participation and also as part of the private to be protected from the public. The first conception would make the rights of assembly and speech the most fundamental rights. The second conception, however, tends to assimilate these "rights of communication" to the model of property right, depriving them of any special importance in the catalogue of rights. This ambiguity does in fact reveal something about the peculiarly double nature of the rights of communication. But, characteristically enough, what does not arise at all in Arendt's conception is that the right of assembly is both civil and political, both private and public. In other words, Arendt has no room for the concept of a right of juridically private persons who can thereby attain public-law status and even exercise an important public role, thus mediating between private and public spheres.

The absence of the very possibility of mediation between public and private in Arendt's work is all the more serious when the exercise of the rights of assembly and association turns explicitly political, in particular in the case of social movements. Indeed, social movements could have played a constitutive role in Arendt's theory in the context of a problem she could not adequately deal with. Since movements have empirically demonstrable life cycles, she could have cast them as embodiments of revolutionary spirit that do not imply a permanent revolution. Indeed, she could have interpreted them as extrainstitutional instances of the generation of power that in the long run presuppose and promote rather than interfere with institutionalization.[80] Arendt is, of course, aware of the role of movements in the emergence of council-republican experiments; above all, she examines the workers' movement, which "has written one of the most glorious and probably most promising chapters of recent history."[81] Working outside the economically oriented labor unions and the socially oriented "political" parties, the movement of the industrial working class repeatedly reinvented the genuinely political project of constructing new, republican institutions. According to Arendt, this was possible whenever the class of labor, not yet admitted to society ("class society"), suddenly appeared on the public political stage.[82] Her argument is entirely fictitious, though, since the movements from 1848 to 1956 to which she refers cannot be represented as having no social and economic interests and demands, and even less as not playing a major part in the economic reproduction of society. And indeed Arendt herself is forced to admit this implicitly when she argues that interest in workers' control of industry, ever present in the movements under consideration, was a major reason for the downfall of council experiments.[83]

Arendt's linking of the movement form with republican experiments is, in her own view, relevant to a phase of modern history already past. With the emergence of "mass society," a form of "society" capable of absorbing all classes including that of labor, no movement can hope to claim a status that is exclusively political, rather than social or economic. Now the labor movement becomes a pressure group like any other.[84] Since interest articulation and interest representation (parties) are, at best, the "politics" of civil society, they substitute for real political participation, replacing political society and discursive opinion formation with bargaining and deals. Because interest groups and party politics destroy the parliamentary public space, they are in fact inferior to the administrative processing of interest claims.[85]

How does this square with the persistence of the movement form in our time? Could it be that the despised terrain of the social could after all become the scene of repoliticization in the context of movements that constitute a new public sphere and thereby mediate between the private and the public? Arendt certainly argues that the movement form itself does not disappear along with the classical workers' movement. Indeed, she assumes that their terrain is the social realm between what is left of the private and the public. Adopting a radicalized version of the pluralist critique of mass society that uses totalitarian movements as its paradigm, however, Arendt is convinced that *social* movements accelerate and complete the social realm's destruction of the public and the private. That is, social movements proper feed off and help to create and perpetuate the atomization and depoliticization characteristic of mass society. Under conditions of the modern party system and the deep distrust engendered by it, Arendt sees fertile soil for the emergence of extraparliamentary and extraparty movements. The more glaring the failures of the party system, the easier it is for movements to arise and to appeal to wide constituencies. But in the absence of genuine public institutions, movements either organize masses or turn those they organize into masses. Social movements are mass movements, and mass movements carry on the work of the social principle by invading and leveling all hitherto private domains of life, including family, education, and culture.[86] Thus, social movements are proto-totalitarian, and the totalitarian completion of the rise of society is not possible without them.

Given their starting point in society and their mobilization of social needs and motivations, movements cannot reinvent forms of public life. This thesis, we must note, coincides with the conception of social movements dominant in the early post–World War II paradigms that studied social movements under the names of collective behavior and mass society.[87] Arendt's radical democratic political philosophy distinguished her work from these paradigms. But by partially buying into them, probably under the impact of her own experience with totalitarian movements, she deprived her political philosophy of any possible politics.[88] If movements today, because of the inevitably social terrain of their emergence and existence, cannot reinvent or extend the public sphere, and if rights-oriented collective action is a threat to the love of public freedom, then it is not at all clear that in our epoch the experiments of the working-class movement in creating political institutions can have any continuation whatsoever. If Arendt is right about social movements as such, her dream of the revival of republicanism should be pronounced finally dead.

The Historicist Critique: Carl Schmitt, Reinhart Koselleck, and Jürgen Habermas

The Origins of the Liberal Public Sphere: Carl Schmitt and Reinhart Koselleck

Hannah Arendt failed to demonstrate that her normative ideal of the public sphere is compatible with modernity. We have argued that this failure was strongly linked to her uncompromising critique of the social sphere of mediation, which she had identified as the specifically modern dimension of institutional life. Thus, it is of great importance that there is an alternative tradition of interpretation focusing on the problem of the public sphere. The approach of Jürgen Habermas and his followers counterposes a *socially rooted* form of the public sphere to the ancient model identified with the state.[1] Remarkably, this second tradition goes back to Carl Schmitt, who sought to defend a conception of "the political" based on a model of war against what he took to be an apolitical conception based on public discussion, a model that was to define the deepest impulses of both Arendt and Habermas.[2]

According to Schmitt, one of the best ways to understand modern liberalism is by focusing on its "political" expression, namely, parliamentarism. The principle of the latter is open public discussion or deliberation.[3] Beyond mere negotiation and bargaining, what Schmitt has in mind is a model of discussion in the sense of

an exchange of opinion that is governed by the purpose of persuading one's opponent of the truth or justice of something, or allowing oneself to be persuaded of something as true and just. . . . To discussion belong shared convictions as premises, the willingness to be persuaded, independence from party ties, freedom from selfish interests. . . . [T]he essence of parliament is therefore public deliberation of argument and counterargument, public debate and public discussion.[4]

Thus, a common political will results from the process of the genuine and open confrontation of different opinions. This process is supposed to be public in two senses: by referring to the work of an autonomous public body free to deliberate without any external compulsion imposed upon its members, and by being genuinely open to the outside. In both of these senses, modern parliamentarism is definitively contrasted with its forerunners, the estate assemblies, which were based on the imperative mandate and closed sessions. Under modern parliamentarism, instead of the direct pressure of constituencies or any form of bound or mandated representation, public opinion is supposed to "influence" the parliamentary public only through argumentation and persuasion that presupposes rather than suspends the independence of the representatives.

Schmitt anticipates and ascribes to liberal parliamentarism both the Arendtian defense of opinion against interest and the Habermasian model of genuine argumentation as distinct from strategic and rhetorical uses of political speech. Unlike both of them, however, he treats the discussion model as deeply apolitical, linking it to the fundamental liberal faith that unrestricted competition, which takes the form of discussion in the intellectual realm, produces harmony.[5] According to Schmitt, this liberal model of the parliamentary public sphere is taken over from moral and intellectual discourse on the one side and from economics on the other. It turns a "politically united people" into a culturally interested public or an industrial concern operating in a market, in the process depoliticizing and demilitarizing the political sphere, turning the state into society.[6]

Schmitt is keenly aware that the state and politics in his sense do not thereby disappear in liberal society. The principle does not, need not, and cannot fully correspond to the actual practice. As he puts it in somewhat obscure language, "there is heterogeneity of purposes . . . but there is no heterogeneity of principles."[7] The principle of open public discussion is actually a principle of legitimation, a normative and even metanormative principle. As such, its immediate importance is that it is the basis for the validity of other norms. Schmitt particularly stresses that the norms of the independence of representatives, their freedom of speech and immunity, and the openness of proceedings all receive their validity from the principle of public discussion as the only legitimate method for attaining a collective will.[8] Even the twentieth-century claim that parliament is the "best" method for the selection of elites draws its legitimacy from the discussion model (or what is left from it in a framework of increasingly rhetorical interaction), since the valid testing of leaders is identified with performance in debate and with having the ability to persuade others successfully.[9]

Schmitt is well aware that the principle of publicity was capable of operating only in a world different from that of its own assumptions, involving a reduction of all politics to discussion. While the deepest striving of liberalism, in theory at least, was to reduce the state to society in either the economic or the cultural sense, in fact liberalism presupposed and could not survive without a state, or without the dualistic coexistence of state and society. Moreover, and this is the important point, Schmitt, unlike Arendt, realizes that the principle of discussion belongs to the level of society rather than that of the state. Quite in the spirit of Hegel's *Rechtsphilosophie*, parliament is thus seen as the penetration of society into the state, reproducing in effect the society-state dualism in the state sphere itself, thereby "mediating" the split between the poles of the duality.

Schmitt's modernized reconstruction of the Hegelian framework is much cruder than that of the master whose conception of the "estate assembly" he cites.[10] In particular, he does not distinguish between the system of needs and the other levels of civil society, nor does he recognize any mediation other than that of parliament between society and state. For him, all the fundamental political polarities of the epoch of constitutional monarchies (prince vs. people, government vs. popular representation, administration vs. self-administration), under which he (inconsistently) subsumes classical liberalism, express one fundamental dualism: society vs. the state.[11] This dualism is, in turn, a function of the "polemical" attitude of social forces (economic, intellectual, and religious) toward the bureaucratically unified military-administrative state inherited from the epoch of absolutism.[12]

But it was also a function of this state to remain independent and strong enough to stand above the other social forces: to be a strong enough threat to motivate the relativization of other forms of social (economic, confessional, cultural) opposition and conflict and also the resulting self-constitution of a more or less unified "society." At the same time, this state had to be self-sufficient enough to undertake and survive (and perhaps also be strengthened by) a policy of nonintervention and self-neutralization vis-à-vis the societal spheres, allowing these spheres (economy, culture) to unfold their autonomous logics.

The stability and the equilibrium of the resulting duality is achieved by the mediation of parliament. "Popular representation, parliament, the lawmaking body is conceived as the stage (*Schauplatz*) where society appears in the face of the state."[13] On this stage, state and society are "integrated into" one another. In terms of form, the result is dualistic, comprising a "legislative state" and an "executive state," with the former, the *Gesetzgebungsstaat*, gradually achieving primacy as the nineteenth century proceeds. This development corresponds to the ideology of parliamentarism already discussed, according to which only decisions achieved through "discussion and the conflict of opinions" are legitimate. The idea only apparently contradicts Schmitt's notion that the principle of discussion is social and indeed apolitical. The metaphor of a stage seems to indicate that what actually occurs here is a mere play or show, necessary for integrating social forces and legitimating the real decisions that are taken elsewhere and in another manner.

The polemical attitude of society against the state implies that such a state of affairs cannot be accepted. This is especially the case when the idea of the self-organization of society is democratized. For democratic forces that identify with their parliamentary representation, the residual nonparliamentary decision-making power of the executive, which bypasses the plurality of social opinions instead of integrating them, must seem illegitimate. The goal of a completed legislative state cannot be achieved, though. What is at issue here is not that a pure parliamentary state cannot be found in reality, any more than can other pure state types. Rather, the parliamentary state, unlike other forms, represents the ideal of the state as the self-organization of society, as the organization of the state according to the societal principle of discussion. According to Schmitt, as this ideal nears realization under the impact of democratization, paradoxically the parliamentary principle of integration loses its foundations, and the state itself, deprived of another principle of unity, is threatened with disintegration.

In Schmitt's conception, the ability of those outside parliament to identify with their representatives rests on a polemical attitude to the state that guarantees the unification of a society otherwise potentially divided by conflicts of both opinion and interest. But this is not the whole story. The forms of the self-constitution and self-protection of parliament vis-à-vis the executive actually turn out to be identical to the mechanisms differentiating society and state. Clearly, parliamentary discussion would be meaningless without the freedoms of opinion and speech as well as the immunity of representatives; these are presuppositions of the constitution of a genuine public body. But Schmitt also indicates that a parliamentary public sphere implies the freedom of public life outside of parliament.[14] Interpreting Guizot, he asserts that the openness of parliamentary procedures would be meaningless without general freedoms of opinion, speech, and the press. Without these freedoms, all forms of social control over parliament, which are required for the parliamentary representation of society in the face of the state, would disappear. Since Schmitt's model presupposes and requires the ability of private individuals to acquire and communicate their opinions freely, it seems that some other freedoms, such as those of assembly and association in their extraparliamentary forms, also represent "life-and-death questions for liberalism."[15] But Schmitt pays no attention to the social consequences of these latter freedoms, which provided for Hegel the possibility of mediations other than parliamentary between individual and state. Finally (and consistently), Schmitt makes no mention of any fundamental rights that cannot be derived from the principle of parliamentary publicity, whatever their importance may be for the liberal epoch (e.g., property). This consistency, however, only permits him the preposterous formulation that, with the decline of parliamentarism, "the whole system of freedom of speech, assembly, and the press, of public meetings, parliamentary immunities, and privileges loses its rationale," which is based on the belief that "just laws and right politics can be achieved through newspaper articles, speeches at demonstrations, and parliamentary debates."[16]

Schmitt's analysis leads to this conclusion, irrespective of his political predilections, because his perceptive recognition of the social foundations of the model of discussion is coupled with a conception asserting more than the claim that the existence of parliaments in the modern sense presupposes the differentiation of society and state. He also affirms the converse, namely, that the unity and differentiation of society is structurally dependent (at least in the long term) on the existence of a parliamentary representation in the face of the state, to which he, unlike Hegel, reduces the whole problem of mediation. Yet he notes in passing that there are not many people "who want to renounce the old liberal freedoms, particularly freedom of speech and press," even when their political efficacy has become doubtful.[17] In Schmitt's entirely political analysis and critique of liberalism, however, it is quite unclear why, with their political efficacy gone, anyone should cling to these norms.

There are, to be sure, hints in his analysis that the society-state opposition and even the constitution of a public sphere are not identical to the issue of parliamentarism, indeed, that they actually predated it historically. He writes:

public opinion attained this absolute character first in the eighteenth century, during the Enlightenment. The light of the public is the light of the Enlightenment, a liberation from superstition, fanaticism, and ambitious intrigue. In every system of enlightened despotism, public opinion plays the role of an absolute corrective.[18]

This thesis, relatively unimportant in Schmitt's own work, was powerfully expanded by a historian he strongly influenced, Reinhart Koselleck, in his *Kritik und Krise* (1959).[19] According to Koselleck, the absolutist state on the European continent, formed as a response to religious civil war, created the foundations for a political dualism by freeing itself from all norms in line with the doctrine of *raison d'état*.[20] The resulting separation of politics and morals, as well as the increasing disinterest of the state (anticipated by Hobbes) in controlling private, individual conscience, created a possible foothold for the constitution of a new formation, "society," first apart from and later against the state. The old regime, of course, never created a completely monistic, statized society: The older estates, now depoliticized, preserved their corporate existence. There were, moreover, new organizational forms of an emerging, bourgeois class composed of the beneficiaries of the first truly national economic policy in European history. Out of these two strata, combining with elements of intellectual and judicial elites, came the social bases of the enlightenment, one possessing money, social recognition, and intellectual influence, but not political power.

Nevertheless, the "society" of the enlightenment *was* organized, with the private salon, the café, the club, the library, the Masonic lodge, and later the secret society as its major forms. According to Koselleck, many of these unpolitical forms of assembly and association were, in fact, protected by officials of the absolutist state.[21] In spite of such protection, they would take an antistate turn as the eighteenth century progressed.

The support of enlightened state officials is relatively easy to explain, since the new formation "society," as typified by the Masonic ideology, was egalitarian in its ethos and opposed to the privileged society of aristocratic and ecclesiastical orders, itself the main enemy of "enlightened absolutism." Moreover, society was not supposed to be a threat to the state because its self-understanding was moral rather than political. Precisely on the ground of the absolutist understanding of politics as *raison d'état*, moral virtue was defined as freedom from politics. This expansion of the Hobbesian freedom of private, individual conscience was, however, no longer compatible with the internal logic of absolutist depoliticization. Following Schmitt, Koselleck implies that the unity of the heterogeneous elements of "society" could be maintained only in opposition to the state. Indeed, as his analysis of the Masonic movement shows, such an opposition was made possible by the fact that weapons of the established powers were utilized, at least initially, for the self-organization of society: The secrecy of the absolutist regime and the hierarchical organization of the social orders were the glue behind the ideology of fraternity and solidarity.

Of course, the enlightenment became both more public and more egalitarian as it became a broad movement. According to

Koselleck, such a transformation, leading to a polarization between society and state, was already implicit in the rigid juxtaposition of morality and politics. The very constitution of a "society" based on morals represented a judgment over and a rejection of absolutist sovereignty, without any visible attack on state institutions. The rejection of politics was at the same time the establishment of a moral vantage point for criticizing and judging politics. The moral pressure emanating from "society," creating a whole system of values alternative to the established ones, could not avoid being a source of influence over action and therefore becoming an indirect form of political power. Morality was directly unpolitical, but exactly for this reason it could put an amoral state into question and thus become, after all, political, if indirectly so.[22]

The radicalization of the program of society against the state postponed the appearance of an entirely unpolitical program. In Koselleck's presentation, this program went through the stages of taking a distance from politics, critique, judgment, and execution. Since the absolutist state could not be eliminated, self-limitation had to be practiced. Initially this self-limitation contained a component that was, because of the overwhelming disparity of power, merely strategic. But it also had a normatively validated antipolitical component based on principles. The latter, however, was self-negating to the extent that even an antipolitical morality had difficulty reconciling itself with immorality in the world of politics. In the radical enlightenment, then, the moral sphere constituted itself, in secret, as another, alternative, political one. The aim of this political society was no longer coexistence with the state but rather its dissolution and replacement. The methods of education, schooling, propaganda, and enlightenment were no longer adequate for the new purpose, and this implied that even strategic self-limitation had to be seen as merely temporary.

In this way, Koselleck convincingly revives the idea of an intrinsic connection between enlightenment and the crisis of the old regime, and between this crisis and the coming revolution. It is in this context that he seeks to locate the Schmittian topos of the emergence of the liberal public sphere, here representing the political turn of society in opposition to the state. Pierre Bayle's idea of a republic of letters, according to Koselleck the model for Rousseauian radical democracy, indicates what is at stake. On the one side, this "republic" is still to be based on the contrast between a powerless moral law and an amoral power. On the other, this contrast is interpreted as the confrontation of the *règne de la critique* with the rule of the state, indicating that critique, the weapon par excellence of the public sphere, has turned political.

This transformation carried risks. Taking the point of view of the state, Koselleck argues that the idea of critique, turning inward to society itself, must fail as a means of social integration and must ultimately lead to a reappearance in the private sphere of the civil war suppressed by absolutism. Here the deeply apolitical potential of the liberal idea of the public sphere, as in Schmitt's doctrine, shows itself. At the same time, as long as the state as "enemy" exists, the critical, polemical contestation of its legitimacy provides the cohesion of the "friend" component of the polarity, the alternative political society. This contestation is carried out in the medium of public criticism. In the public realm, critique becomes the means of amplifying public opinion, exposing everything, destroying all taboos, and depriving its political enemies, organized around the state, of legitimacy and means of cohesion.[23] Effectively built to counter the criticism of weapons, the absolutist state fails against the weapon of criticism, which, because of its supposedly unpolitical nature, disempowers a properly militant political response.

Because it is concerned with the rise of the dichotomy of state and society, Koselleck's analysis stresses the political dimension of the liberal public sphere rather than the potentially apolitical implications that, in Schmitt's conception, characterize the triumph of society over the bureaucratic-military state. Nevertheless, these apolitical potentialities appear in Koselleck's picture in the tendency of the agents to hide the political dimension of their actions not only from the state but also from themselves. Paradoxically, it is this refusal of politics by political agents that leads not only to the dissolution of the absolutist state but also to an inability to establish a new model of the political. Even before the collapse of the old regime, by insisting on recognizing only its own moral motivation, critique falls prey to hypocrisy.

Koselleck's conception of the hypocrisy of enlightenment antipolitics adopts the point of view of the state itself. The critique of power and the attempt to limit it are unhesitatingly qualified as hypocritical, although the author does not make up his mind whether he seeks to indict the will to power of critical reason or its implicit drive toward civil war. This ambiguity can also be found in Schmitt. While Koselleck goes beyond Schmitt in discovering the enlightenment roots of liberal parliamentarism, in his own Schmittian analysis all we get is an anticipation of the rise and decline of the political public sphere in the logic that leads to revolution. Indeed, it is difficult to connect this prehistory in France, where the collapse of the old regime did not initially lead to a stable parliamentary outcome, to the history of parliamentarism as analyzed by Schmitt. The connection can be made only when one recognizes that the enlightenment dualism, with the public sphere as its central mediation, was not merely a strategy for the disempowering of the state by politically weak competitors with a relentless power drive, but could also be institutionalized as a new political alternative.[24]

Koselleck comes close to such a thesis only when he uncharacteristically uses Marxian arguments to bolster an essentially Schmittian position. For example, he argues that the bourgeoisie constituted itself as a new elite precisely through the dualistic figure of thought. Yet even here the argument is that the dualistic conception, as preparation for the taking of power, served only to eliminate all dualisms. Unfortunately for Koselleck, neither the normative achievement of the liberal public sphere nor even its possible and eventual institutionalization can be thematized in such an argument. Both are, however, insisted upon by Jürgen Habermas, in an analysis in many ways indebted to, yet quite distinct from, Koselleck's.

From a Literary to a Political Public Sphere: Jürgen Habermas

The Schmittian thesis concerning the foundation of parliamentarism in the differentiation of society and the state can be seen as a narrow version of the Hegelian conception. In particular, the problem of mediation is reduced to a single component, the political public sphere, which is in turn presented in a normatively aggressive fashion entirely disinterested in public discussion as an end in itself. Habermas's conception, on the other hand, attempts to go beyond this reduction in two respects: first, by recapturing a richer set of mediations between civil society and state, and second, by reemphasizing and revalorizing the normative claims of the public sphere. Habermas's analysis also takes up the Hegelian project of bringing together the normative achievements of both the ancients and the moderns (and does so more successfully that Hannah Arendt's).

Habermas's original theory of the public sphere, worked out in the intellectual milieu of the older Frankfurt school, represents a species of *Verfallsgeschichte*, a history of decline. This similarity to Arendt's conception tends to disguise the entirely different relation of the two schemes to history. As we have seen, Arendt's public sphere, modeled on an idealized conception of Greek or Athenian politics, is paradoxically said to decline with the rise of modern society, state, and economy, even though she admits that the original model had long since disappeared. Moreover, Arendt is not at all inhibited by her theory of decline from postulating the repeated, but always temporary, reemergence of experiments in public freedom during modern revolutions. It is as if freedom and unfreedom moved in two separate and only occasionally connected temporalities; freedom, in other words, is always (but also only) possible whenever the dialectic of history stands still.[25]

Habermas, on the contrary, inserts the emergence and decline of a new type of public sphere *into* the history of modern society. While Arendt associated only the decline of the public with the rise of modern state and economy, in Habermas's conception the rise, contradictory institutionalization, and subsequent decline of this sphere are all related to this event. The new public sphere is accordingly seen as *bourgeois*, because in it independent owners of property, divided in their competitive, egoistic economic activities that have grown vastly beyond the limits of the household, are capable of generating, at least in principle, a collective will through the medium of rational, unconstrained communication. But it is also *liberal*, in that the sets of rights deemed necessary to secure the autonomy of this sphere (freedoms of speech, press, assembly, and communication), together with those dimensions of individual autonomy that it presupposes ("privacy rights"), simultaneously constitute the public and private domains of civil society and serve as limits to the reach of state power. Indeed, the new public sphere is also *democratic* in principle: The emergence of a new form of unified, depersonalized, bureaucratic public authority, the modern state, is to be checked, supervised, and even controlled not only by the rule of law but also by a second political public sphere (emerging within society and penetrating the state in the form of parliaments) that challenges *raison d'état* as well as *arcana imperii*. The tendency of the modern state to level and dismantle all corporate and estate organizations of a formerly divided sovereignty is countered by the emergence of a different, normatively grounded reason operating in the full view of all concerned, within new societal institutions that come to penetrate the domain of politics itself.[26]

Habermas's depiction of the emergence of the institutions of a new type of public life, polemically juxtaposed to both the absolutist state and the privileged society of orders, draws heavily on Koselleck's picture of the organization of the enlightenment. However, three dimensions of Habermas's conception differ from his predecessor's:

First, Habermas believes that the peculiar logic of the new public is continuous with, and constitutes a projection of, the form of interaction of the new intimate sphere of the bourgeois family, a sphere that Arendt considered to be the most characteristic product of modernity.

Second, he distinguishes not only between the literary and political public spheres—a distinction played down by Koselleck, who suspects hypocrisy in every antipolitical claim—but also between the small-group interaction represented by the salon, the café, the table society, and the lodge and the extension and generalization of public discourse through the media of communication, above all the press.

Finally, Habermas distinguishes among at least three national variants (English, French, and German) of the institutionalization of the political public sphere, in the process showing the development of common norms in the context of a heterogeneous set of political projects difficult to reduce to a single one, especially to the will to power of the weak.

We shall start with these three points and then turn to a more systematic analysis of Habermas's conception.

1. Habermas's depiction of the force field between individual and state, unlike that of Schmitt, involves at least three levels of mediation: family, literary public, and political public spheres. These levels are not identical to the corresponding Hegelian categories, and the choice changes the theoretical role of "mediation." The category of family has great importance in this context. In Hegel's scheme, the family is the precondition of bourgeois individuality, and as such it is prior to and outside civil society for primarily logical reasons that are sociologically nonsensical under conditions of modernity.[27] For Habermas, the early modern, small-scale, bourgeois, patriarchal family is not only (as for Hegel) the place of origin of *bürgerliche Gesellschaft*. Nor is it even what it could be in a sociologically extended orthodox Hegelian conception, namely, one of the levels of integration of egoistic individuals into the culture of the state. In Habermas's version, the intimate sphere of the small-scale bourgeois family also represents the establishment of a principle counterposed to those of both the modern economy and the state. It is not that he neglects the Hegelian idea that the family represents the background of socialization that is the condition of possibility of the existence of individuals of civil society; rather (and more in the Arendtian sense), he converts this background from a point of origin to an institution that continues to participate in social life and to which individuals can continually return as their home. For this reason, the family prevents the dissolution of individuality on the various levels of collectivity. Thus, as in Arendt's theory, it represents a private sphere without which a public sphere based on autonomous individuals would not be possible. But whereas Arendt sees the complementarity of private and public as possible only because of their radically different principles, conceived along the lines of the ancient duality of *polis* and *oikos*, Habermas uses the Arendtian notion of the intimate to generate a single principle for both, one that is normatively adequate to the modern ideal (though not the reality) of the family: interaction free of domination and of external social constraint. This ideal, leading to a new conception of humanity, is further analyzed[28] into the components of voluntariness, emotional community, and cultivation: "It appears that the family is established and maintained voluntarily by free individuals without

constraint; that it is based on the lasting emotional community of the partners; that it guarantees the development of all capacities that signify a cultivated person as ends in themselves."[29] It is not hard to recognize specific versions of the ideas of liberty, solidarity, mutual recognition, and equality in such a conception of humanity.

In line with the classical Marxian critique, Habermas is quick to point out the counterfactual character, and even more the legitimating function, of the ideal he depicts. He stresses its clash with the real economic functions of the new family type, as well as with its patriarchal forms of subordination, both of which also penetrate the intellectual elaboration of bourgeois utopias.[30] All the same, following a famous analysis by Horkheimer from 1936, Habermas maintains that the ideal is not mere ideology. The new solidaristic norms that play a role in legitimating the arrangements of a competitive and nonsolidary private economy are always in tension with what is established, promising a this-worldly transcendence of all states of affairs incompatible with freedom, solidarity, and cultivation. Thus, these norms represent both ideology and the foundations of the critique of ideology.[31] Moreover, the family, although incapable of eliminating the constraints of the economic world or even of freeing itself from its own patriarchal heritage, nevertheless defends the intimate subjective experience and intersubjective ties of its members, qua human beings, in the face of external powers. Equally important, it is the living source of experiences of passionate self-examination and rational searching for mutual understanding that are capable of finding other forms of institutionalization than the family itself.[32]

Habermas argues for an empirical connection between the private world of the bourgeois family and the primordial forms of the literary public sphere. While the salon admittedly originates in aristocratic society, the bourgeois salon loses its representational and ritualistic functions: Its form of communication is no longer dramaturgical and rhetorical; its social structure no longer reflects the hierarchy of a society of orders.[33] Architecturally and socially linked to the private living quarters of the family, the new salon extends and enlarges the original principle of intimacy by revealing the subjectivity of each individual in the presence of the other, thus linking privacy to publicity. The ideal of seeking understanding through open-ended reasoning and mutual persuasion, without regard for prestige and status, is maintained. Somewhat more distantly, Habermas sees the institutions of club, café, and lodge as extensions of the same principle. He does explicitly note, however, the exclusion of women from these latter institutions of enlightenment, linking this exclusion to the discussion of political and economic rather than primarily literary and artistic matters.[34] Yet the connection of the first institutions of an audience for works of art, and especially of literary and reading circles, to salons dominated by women remains close, and it is through these agencies that the reasoning public modeled on the intimate family first begins to approach universal significance.[35] This connection to the reception of art also develops a dimension of the literary public that is present in the new intimate sphere only in the form of self-reflection and self-examination: the critique of all received ideas and meanings.

2. While Koselleck tends to focus on those enlightenment institutions, from the lodge to the secret society, that paradoxically seek to establish the principle of publicity by negating it, and for which critique eventually became a means rather than an end in itself, Habermas's own stress is on institutions whose road to politics, slower and less complete, implies neither a compromise of fundamental principles nor a merely hypocritical renunciation of power. The public sphere in his conception comes into being not through the politicization of small-scale face-to-face intimate interaction but through the establishment of a critical audience for literary works by means of newspapers, journals, and public performances. Only this road allows the conversion of the principles of intimacy into those of a critical publicity. But even on this longer road, the literary public grows into politics, into a political public sphere with a structure different from those of political organizations dedicated to the pursuit of power. Even if both roads were in fact divorced from the more feminine world of the salon, the political public sphere maintained something of its spirit in the idea of critique as an end in itself.

It is Habermas's thesis that the emergence of a political public sphere from the critical literary one preserves the principle of unconstrained communication originally established in the intimate sphere of the new family type. Unlike Koselleck, who points to a project of a counterpower hypocritically aiming at destroying and replacing established power, he insists that what is at stake is the transformation of the principle according to which power, old or new, is to operate.[36] Critique in this model attempts its own institutionalization rather than a conversion into a new form of power that would potentially feel itself endangered by critical reason. Even in Habermas's analysis, the modern state, in its originally absolutist form, represents the challenge motivating the establishment of a veritable countersociety, a society against the state. But this society, even when it turns political, aims neither at the utopian destruction of the state nor at becoming a new state, nor even at the unification of these aims as in the Reign of Terror, but rather at a new form of political dualism in which a political public sphere would control the public authority of the modern state.

The argument goes against the grain not only of Koselleck's Schmittian analysis but also of the Marxian conception of the bourgeois revolution. Nevertheless, Habermas hopes to save something of the latter by insisting that the bourgeoisie, whose power is by definition private, cannot rule and yet cannot accept a form of state that is potentially arbitrary and uncontrolled. A further complication: This same class, unlike the aristocratic opponents of absolutism, needs and wants a form of unified sovereign power capable of guaranteeing the political and legal preconditions of a private capitalist market economy within and even beyond a national territorial setting. The historical solution was to preserve the modern state created by absolutism, but to formalize and rationalize its operation in terms of the rule of law, to force it to establish forms of self-restraint as defined by fundamental rights, and to bring it under social scrutiny and control through the establishment of the political public sphere, itself rooted in the rights of communication and franchise. It is these normative limitations that Habermas has in mind when he refers to changing the principle of the operation of power.

3. It is not clear that the suggestive ideal type can save the thesis of a bourgeois revolution. In France, where a revolution did occur,

one that was hardly bourgeois,[37] the pattern outlined by Habermas was originally established only transitionally, during the constitutional monarchy. Moreover, given the outcome, it is not difficult to argue that the forms of public life Habermas describes as extending Koselleck's analysis into the revolutionary period (journals, pamphlets, clubs, popular assemblies) represented the projects of counterelites hoping to replace the existing elite (and, soon enough, one another). To show that an alternative principle could have been established, Habermas is forced to shift his emphasis from Koselleck's terrain of French politics, culminating in revolution and terror (the context of choice of conservative opponents of the liberal idea of politics), to the English context of the *evolutionary* transformation of parliamentary absolutism. This "model" is in turn used as the standard for evaluating the constitutional monarchies of the early liberal epoch. From its point of view, French developments in the period of high absolutism appear incredibly retarded. They seem to follow a slower but fundamentally English path during most of the eighteenth century, when politics against the absolutist regime from the points of view of the traditional estates and the new public forms were not always easily distinguishable.[38] The revolutionary period enforced this distinction dramatically in a process of tremendously accelerated creation of public political forms (the transformation of the estates assembly into a modern parliament, the creation of journals, clubs, associations, and assemblies, and, above all, the institution of formal constitutional guarantees for all of these). The revolutionary dictatorship and Napoleon destroyed the institutions of the political public sphere, however, and France paradoxically (and still inconsistently and with many reversals) reentered the basic model of liberal development only with the Restoration. Accordingly, in this depiction of French developments from the point of view of the liberal public sphere, the accelerating revolution turns out to be a parenthesis. From the same perspective, developments in the Germanies through various models of the authoritarian *Rechtsstaat* appear simply as slower and perhaps never entirely completed versions of the English model.

The choice of England to outline an actual historical path that is somehow adequate from the point of view of the normative construct of the liberal public sphere helps to dispel the doubt raised by Schmitt that the parliamentary state as a form of self-organization of society breaks down at the moment of its realization. Against this objection, Habermas is able to show the institutionalization of dualism in terms of parliament and a political public sphere. The same choice, however, is still potentially exposed to Koselleck's critique, which might focus in the English context on the hypocritically bourgeois rather than the hypocritically statist character of the liberal public sphere. In other words, in the English case the project for liberal publicity seems to have been a cover for the will to power of the propertied classes. The charge is not as strong as it might at first seem, though, because the parliamentary absolutism that emerged from the Glorious Revolution was already fully compatible with the economic interests and political representation of the propertied classes. The struggle for a political public sphere and for the rights of speech, press, assembly, association, and the franchise that would sustain it was not restricted to the owners of bourgeois property, nor did it stop with the full political victory of their program in the New Poor Law. While it is possible to argue that the outcome of these struggles helped make parliamentary rule legitimate and thus stabilized bourgeois domination, this legitimacy was nevertheless a function of new forms of protection, self-organization, and public oversight achieved by social strata whose traditional forms of life were undermined by the transition from a paternalistic, moral economy to the self-regulating system of liberal markets.[39]

English absolutism does not end in Habermas's picture with the demotion of the monarch to "King in Parliament" but with the new relation between public sphere and state expressed in the full publicity of the proceedings of Parliament.[40] However, when publicity, originally a weapon, becomes a principle linked to the normative experience of everyone capable of reasoning, it cannot be restricted either institutionally (to the press and the parties) or socially (to the middle classes).[41] The growing public thematization of fundamental political questions leads to the organization of political meetings, clubs, associations, and committees[42] that in turn provide forms for the self-organization of strata that are not formally included in the political system until the end of the century. Democratization does not in itself, as Habermas elsewhere unfortunately suggests,[43] lead to the decline of the critical capacities of the public: It is, in fact, after the First Reform Bill, when the parties must appeal to a socially much more heterogeneous electoral public than before, that they are forced to publicize their electoral programs and to discuss them in terms of arguments and principles rather than slogans, personalities, or even narrow sectoral interests.[44]

Habermas's linking of his study of the development of the liberal-bourgeois public sphere to a specific historical pattern of development should not lead us to neglect his theoretical model of this sphere, however ideal-typical or even composite it may appear. This is all the more important because he insists that it is this abstract model, rather than any particular historical version, that attained normative and even utopian status for modern society. Broadly speaking (in the tradition of Hegel), Habermas not only differentiates between civil society and state but also relativizes the traditional distinction of private and public with which the liberals and Marx identified the new polarity. He does this by dividing each sphere, public and private, into two:

private:	intimate sphere (family)	private economy
public:	public sphere	public authority (state)

We expect one specific role to correspond to each of the spheres, though Habermas makes the point clear only in the case of the private sphere:[45]

private:	human being ("*homme*")	bourgeois
public:	[citizen]	[subject]

Habermas recognizes that the relationship of this fourfold categorial framework to the concept of civil society, or *bürgerliche Gesellschaft*, is ambiguous.[46] In the narrow sense (that of Marx), *bürgerliche* society refers to the sphere of the private, bourgeois economy. When used in this sense, the public sphere is to be understood as a mediation between society and state. However, in the broader sense (that of Hegel), the term *civil society* means all the spheres of society juxtaposed to the state.[47] In that case, it will include the public sphere as well as the domestic one, and thus it will have three fundamental roles (of which Habermas stresses only the first two): human being, bourgeois, and citizen.

If Habermas does not consistently adopt this second, more Hegelian, usage, it is because he seems to be sensitive to a fictional identification criticized by the young Marx: that between "*l'homme*" and "*bourgeois*."[48] He, too, considers this identification to mask the bourgeois character of the new public sphere and an ideology that subordinates the sphere of the citizen to the imperatives of the private economy. As a result, and in order to provide an analytical contrast to liberal ideology, Habermas refuses to make the category of the public sphere simply an internal self-determination or mediation of civil society.

He does not thereby manage to find an adequate locus, even in principle, for the activity of the citizen. His desire to differentiate spheres stops short exactly at this category. He is, however, on his way to doing this when he points to a second fiction in liberal ideology: the identification of literary and political publics as a unified public opinion. Unfortunately, he tends to regard this identification only as the vehicle by which the first fiction, the identity between man and bourgeois, claims normative superiority over the citizen. Thus, he seems not to see the necessity in this case for yet another analytical differentiation of what ideology misleadingly identifies: man and citizen. This omission seems to concede the liberal point that subordinates the normative source of the status of the citizen in the modern world to the norm of the new conception of humanity, even if not in its bourgeois version.

The basic model is at times differentiated as if Habermas wanted to avoid *both* fictional identifications:[49]

private:	intimate		private economy
public:	literary	political	state

This scheme corresponds to the historical development of the political public sphere, which may have emerged from the literary public sphere but can fully replace or subsume it only at its peril. "The humanity of the literary public," he says obliquely enough, "serves as a mediation for the effectiveness of the political public."[50] On the other side, however, the argument presupposes that a literary-cultural public sphere cannot itself control or directly influence the modern state. Habermas stresses the differentiation of the two publics in terms of two audiences that draw on different sources for their members, one mainly women, the other exclusively men.[51] All this would seem to point to a differentiation in the tradition of Tocqueville between civil and political society, corresponding to Habermas's own differentiation of two publics (literary and political) and two roles (human being and citizen). It is just this differentiation, however, involving sharper boundaries between political and prepolitical public spheres, that Habermas wants to avoid. To the extent that the two publics have important continuities and even formal similarities, Habermas is right. But another motive is at work here as well, one that produces a certain overreaction. In order to preserve the modernity of his conception as against Arendt's stylization of the ancient notion of citizenship, Habermas wants to break definitively with the old meaning of *societas civilis* that contained the level of political society. Instead of choosing a strategy of differentiation, however, he abandons the latter notion. In his conception, all that is left of political society is the political public sphere as a projection of the literary public into areas dealing with questions of economic policy.

Habermas quite deliberately constructed his model of the public sphere in the structural position that Arendt considered the very negation of public life, the intermediary or mixed realm between private sphere and state, which she called "society."[52] Though he admits that the ideological inspiration of the Greek model continues into our own time, Habermas consistently disputes its institutional relevance. Unlike Arendt, he has no use for a concept of political society, admittedly still a component of the eighteenth-century conception of *societé civile* or *Zivilsozietät*, that would somehow preserve what is essential about the ancient republican idea of citizenship. This idea Habermas understands as membership in an incorporated, genuinely political body, the *res publica*, that collectively acted to guarantee justice and military security. The "political" task of the bourgeois public sphere is, on the contrary, the regulation of *bürgerliche Gesellschaft* in the sense of securing the exchange of commodities in the market.[54]

Thus, Habermas seems to make the assumption of the tasks of the *oikos* the functional definition of the new bourgeois public sphere;

this is what Arendt considered the basis of the decline of publicity as such. But it is the liberal as well as the bourgeois dimension of the modern public sphere that sets it apart from the ancient notion of citizenship. Contrary to the Greek model, the modern public sphere is juridically private. Legally separated from the state, this sphere and its members have a polemical, critical, argumentative relation to the state rather than a participatory one. They can supervise, influence, and perhaps somehow "control" power, but they cannot themselves possess a part of state power.

In spite of some serious inconsistencies, Habermas's model of the political public sphere does not refer primarily, as does Schmitt's, to the parliamentary deliberative body itself, whose members do in fact have public law status. The importance of parliamentary deliberations is established only with their publicity, and this is what makes this form of rule uniquely permeable to the gaze of a public composed of private individuals. If the parliamentary deputies are part of the political public sphere, this is because of their continuity with the society of private, reasoning individuals who compose that sphere. The point is somewhat lost when Habermas argues that public opinion came to regard itself as the only legitimate source of law.[55] But he interprets this claim in terms of the contrast between the rule of law and rule by men, with society supposedly achieving a condition beyond all domination through a transformation of the form of law (generality) and the form of lawmaking (publicity). Thus, Habermas argues that the political public sphere "puts *pouvoir* as such up for debate."[56]

This argument seems to conflict with the dualistic conception according to which the public sphere is to coexist with the modern state, whose principle of operation, but not whose existence, is to be placed in question. Habermas is, of course, well aware of the resistance of "public" administration and other organs of executive power to the principle of publicity.[57] But he follows the internal logic of the liberal conception of the public sphere to such a point that the only form of effective social control of the state that seems to be logically possible is its abolition. Rightly rejecting the ancient notion of citizenship proposed by Arendt, Habermas was not able to point, at least within the tradition he reconstructed, to a modern, intermediary model. In short, the liberal model of the literary public sphere, with its overarching norms of humanity and critical reason, tends, once "politicized," to point not to participation within, but to the abolition of, state power, indeed, of power *tout court*, and its replacement by a closed system of legal norms.

Interestingly enough, in view of Habermas's deep analysis of Hegel, he does not use the latter's conception of a plurality of associations within the private sphere that might prepare the participation of citizens. In his critique of Tocqueville, too, there is little interest in or sensitivity to the prepolitical dimension of small-scale self-organization required for the effective and democratic limitation of democratic sovereignty.[58] Undoubtedly, these levels of analysis stressing the need for intermediate powers did not appear to complement his own analysis of mediation through the public sphere. Probably they seemed to point to irrelevant atavisms or to anticipate the corporatist deformation of publicity itself. But it remains the case that his identification of the prepolitical dimension of the public sphere with a literary public, although essential as a legitimating background, involving a certain reduction vis-à-vis Hegel's classical model, renders the political public sphere much too weak in the face of state power. Habermas is aware of this weakness but not of all the causes or of the available alternatives. Thus, he is forced to register rather passively that the "person" of the political public sphere turns out after all to be the "*homme*" of the literary extension of the intimate sphere; he is able to propose no concept of the political to counteract the "characteristic erosion of the boundaries of the two publics"[59] that was the very object of Schmitt's savage criticism of liberal ideals.[60]

Habermas considers the difficulty to be a function not of the normative project but of the contradictory institutionalization of the public sphere. It is thus the specific form of the institutionalization of the new norm of "humanity" that proves to be powerless to block the triumph of the bourgeois and the official. From this critical juxtaposition of norm and institution, Habermas cannot, however, derive the philosophical foundations for an alternative institutionalization. In relation to the capitalist economy and the modern state, the value of humanity, unlike that of citizenship, is bound to remain in question.

The contradictory institutionalization of the public sphere is already apparent at the level of its original model, the intimate sphere. Habermas describes it in terms of the ambivalence of the family, which is "the representative of society, and yet is in a certain way emancipation from society and against society, held together by patriarchal domination on the one side and human intimacy on the other."[61] More precisely, the compulsion faced by the bourgeois family is a function of its specific role in the process of the "valorization" of capital and of the transmission of legal-political constraints through socialization. Habermas, still presupposing the doctrine of state and law as superstructure, unfortunately treats these two dimensions as functionally identical. In this conception, patriarchal authority, expressed in the subordination of women and children, is a transmission belt for economic and political powers that then deform the components of humanity: Autonomy, emotional community, and cultivation are subordinated to money through the instrumentalities of power.

It is an open question whether the ideals of the liberal-bourgeois public sphere are themselves deformed by patriarchal authority, or whether the deformation occurs when the state and the capitalist economy manage to impose their logic on the political public sphere. Habermas seems to choose the second of these options, though at times he also says that the ideology reflects the ambivalence. This choice may be a significant mistake, however, since the notions of "*homme*," emerging from the female-dominated salons emphasized by Habermas, and "*citoyen*," forged in the male-dominated secret societies emphasized by Koselleck, seem to represent opposite sides of the same deformation in the political realm: the powerless human being and the inhuman citizen.

The contradictory institutionalization of the public sphere, and in particular of its political dimension, parallels the ambivalence of the intimate sphere. Habermas explores the contradiction from the point of view of the bourgeois function and then from that of the liberal structure of the political public. The former is linked to the restricted or narrow concept of civil society inherited from Marx, representing the market-oriented interaction of private economic subjects freed (in two stages of development—absolutist and liberal) from estate hierarchy and state paternalism. In this materialist-functionalist train of argument, the task of the political public sphere is to mediate between civil, or rather bourgeois, society and "the state power corresponding to its needs." First and foremost, the task of this state is to work out, administer, and protect a system of private law establishing, through the laws of property, contract, employment, and inheritance, a private sphere in the strict sense.[62]

Paradoxically, then, the task of state intervention is to free civil society of this intervention, to differentiate and maintain the differentiation of state and civil society. This paradox appears on the level of the laws establishing the mediating institutions of the public sphere. The linkage of state action in the *Rechtsstaat* or state governed by law to general norms and the publicity of the making and application of law provide not only for the self-limitation of sovereign power but also for the illusion of its disappearance. This illusion, in the present argument, is traced back to the interaction of small, relatively equal owners of property who imagine that the rules of the sphere of competition make impossible the ascendancy of one owner over another. These agents desire no political rule in their affairs, exercised by a state or even by themselves, yet they require legislative provisions for their activity. The political public sphere was to be the solution of the difficulty, implying the production of measures rooted exclusively in reason rather than will.

Aside from the conflicts with arbitrary power, involving the exertion of will rather than rational persuasion and surviving in the resistance of the executive and its administration to supervision by the public sphere, the division between will and reason in the concept of law could not be removed from the political public sphere itself. On the one hand, this institution could be regarded as the foundation of the rationality of law, since it links legislatures to the ongoing critical discussion of a reasoning public. On the other hand, the laws emerging from such processes of communication had to maintain their coercive aspect in relation to those to whom they were applied.[63] The rule of law thus turns out to involve not the abolition of rule as such but the institution of rule by the legislature. The liberal bourgeois idea of abolishing the state, replacing it as the agency of rule by a system of gapless norms validated by the public sphere alone, turned out to be incoherent and impossible to realize.

Formally speaking, the liberal idea of the public sphere refers not to bourgeois society but to a wider conception of civil society that establishes, on the level of constitutional rights, not merely an economic society but the public sphere itself freed from arbitrary state intervention. Habermas presents a classical catalogue of fundamental rights to indicate the centrality of the defense of the public sphere (freedoms of speech, opinion, press, assembly, association, etc.) and the intimate sphere (inviolability of person and residence, etc.). Constitutions also guarantee the rights of individuals to engage in political activity in the public sphere (rights of petition and suffrage, etc.) and economic activity in the private sphere (equality before the law, right of property, etc.).[64] Finally, by establishing the centrality of the public sphere in political processes, constitutions go beyond the level of the rights of private individuals; in particular, constitutional guarantees of the publicity of procedures are meant to establish the "influence" of the public over parliamentary discussions and the "supervision" by the public of the courts.

According to Habermas, the model of civil society implied by this classical version of constitutionalism "does not correspond at all to the reality of civil society."[65] There are two reasons for this. First, the number of private individuals who possess the autonomy secured by property and the cultivation guaranteed by education is small. Indeed, a second minority, the traditional classes rooted in land ownership, the army, and the administration, still holds significant power. Second, bourgeois-liberal constitutions do not provide for those who do not possess the resources for participating in the literary and political public spheres, nor do they guard against those who can generate and utilize power in secret. Again, the dimension of domination reappears: that of the public sphere over those excluded from the practice of rights and that of those capable of excluding themselves from the duties required of the rest of society.

All the same, it is not Habermas's intention to interpret the liberal dimension of the public sphere as merely an instrument for exclusion. "The bourgeois public sphere stands or falls with the principle of general accessibility. A public sphere from which definable political groups are *eo ipso* excluded is not only imperfect but is not public at all."[66] Habermas does not maintain that the bourgeois public sphere was mere deception. Though it has class interest at its foundations, there is also some overlap with general interests.[67] Leaving aside this dogmatic, traditional formulation, the point seems to be that the boundaries of exclusion could not be fixed because of the norm of publicity itself. In other words, this norm, established through constitutional and legal guarantees and practiced in processes of critical discourse, made the boundaries of the public sphere permeable to themes and persons representing the interests of those excluded. The public sphere was an ideology, but because it contained a utopian promise, it was more than mere ideology.[68] This point is then reformulated in two ways. First, the idea of publicity, "in principle opposed to all domination, helped to found a political order whose social bases did not make domination after all superfluous." This formulation juxtaposes an idea linked to liberation to institutions establishing a new form of domination. Second, the ideology led, on the basis of the domination of one class over the other, nevertheless to the development of institutions "which contained, as their objective meaning, the ideal of their own abolition." This second formulation implies that something of the liberating ideal of publicity was indeed institutionalized in the bourgeois public sphere.

The notion of the contradictory institutionalization of the liberal public sphere points to a direction consistent with the second reading. But the idea that the contradiction is to be resolved, in accordance with normative requirements, by abolishing the whole institutional complex supports the first. In fact, several points remain unclear in the analysis. First, as we asked before, are the normative expressions of the principle of publicity free of the contradiction of its institutionalization? Second, what would be the form of a noncontradictory institutionalization of either the original ideal or its reconstructed version?

The difficulties Habermas encounters in answering these questions have to do with the influence of both Marxian and liberal utopias on his construction. He attempts to hold the two strands together through the notion of immanent criticism. Accordingly, he claims that Marx not only unmasked public opinion as false consciousness but did this in the name of a staunchly held ideal of a liberal public sphere.[69] Habermas's argument cannot succeed, however, to the extent that the Marxian critique always involves both immanent and transcendent elements. If Marx does indeed want to maintain in a radicalized version the ideal of politics based on democratic communication and decision making, he nonetheless rejects the ideal of differentiation between public and private, between state and civil society, that this politics presupposes.[70] One obviously cannot defend the ideal of a liberal public sphere without the model of differentiation, which has normative implications of its own expressed in catalogues of fundamental rights. Marx, however, considers differentiation to be the secret of deformation to the extent that a differentiated civil society, in the sense of the private economy, avoids thereby the possibility of public control and oversight, a process that inevitably turns the modern *citoyen* into the instrument of the *bourgeois* who disguises himself as *homme.* This line of analysis accordingly leads to the establishment of a dedifferentiated state-society by a revolutionary class that has no interest in differentiation. The strategy points to a new normative model of individuality as well: Instead of the fictional identity of man and bourgeois, Marx, according to Habermas, posits the real identity of man and citizen.[71] This goal seems to be accepted by Habermas himself.[72]

The transcendent features of the Marxian critique to the contrary, however, Habermas himself staunchly defended the liberal idea of the public sphere. Thus, while he did not reject the Marxian project of *de*differentiation, he put another, one of *re*differentiation, by its side. This he achieved through an immanent critique of his own. From the point of view of the model of differentiation, he implicitly charges the bourgeois public sphere with being insufficiently differentiated. In particular, the fictional identity of bourgeois and man expresses the very real penetration of the intimate sphere by the processes of the private economy. Hence, the true aim of the publicly controlled state-society-economy is to free the intimate sphere from economic constraint and social intervention.[73] This argument, attributed to Engels, in Habermas's version amounts to a project to establish a new form of private autonomy.[74]

What Habermas does not tell us is how such private autonomy could be institutionalized without rights, though it is certainly possible that he simply presupposes some version of the classical catalogue. But if we are to return to such a catalogue of rights, how are we to avoid reaffirming the normative model of comprehensive differentiation that these rights guarantee through their very form? Habermas could have perhaps countered this argument by referring to the need for redefining the inherited catalogues of rights, and especially their internal hierarchy. His notion, ascribed to Marx, that autonomy in the new model would be based on the public sphere rather than private property points in this direction.[75] But here the dangers of an overall model based on unification rather than differentiation show themselves; what would have been an important insight in the context of a theory of rights, undeveloped here, becomes a perilous one within the actually affirmed project of nonliberal democracy:

private autonomy is a product of an original autonomy, which is brought about by the collectivity of social-citizens exercising the functions of the public sphere expanded in a socialist manner. *It is private individuals who are regarded as the private individuals of the public, rather than the public as the public of private individuals.* In the place of the identity of *bourgeois* and *homme* . . . steps the identity of *citoyen* and *homme*. The freedom of the private individual will be defined according to the role of human beings as social citizens (*Gesellschaftsbürger*); the freedom of human beings as property owners will no longer define the role of the citizen of the state (*Staatsbürger*).[76]

It is obvious from this text that Habermas represents a position, without the slightest trace of criticism, that explicitly breaks with the bourgeois-liberal ideal of the public sphere. The point is not only that one functionalization of the intimate sphere is replaced by the project of another. More generally, the model replaces bourgeois dedifferentiation, which violates the constitutional norms of the liberal public sphere in Habermas's own argument, with a scheme of reverse dedifferentiation that would be equally incompatible with these norms if they were maintained or reestablished. Although a case could be made that the project here outlined continues the *democratic* dimension of the normative model of the public sphere, it most assuredly breaks with its equally important and constitutive *liberal* dimension. That Habermas was, in 1962 at least, insensitive to such an outcome is shown by his treatment of the "liberal" thinkers J. S. Mill and Tocqueville.[77]

Habermas is certainly right in using Marx to criticize the model of the bourgeois public sphere, its tension between norm and institutionalization. Much more questionable is his obvious preference for Marx over Mill and Tocqueville in the further development of the normative model. Arguing from the point of view of Marxian radical democracy, for example, he has no use for Mill's concern, consistently on the ground of differentiation, to defend private autonomy and the freedom of minorities from the greatest democratic power, the power of public opinion. Inexplicably, he takes this idea, in reality a precondition for the rationality of public deliberation, to be a diminution of the public sphere itself.[78] Moreover, he does not seem to understand that the idea of the public as the abolition of political power involves a renunciation of the need to limit all power through the only means possible, the establishment of counterpowers and organizations, and he is therefore powerless against the increasing power of the modern bureaucratic state. From the point of view of a strategy of democratic dedifferentiation, finally, Habermas has no sympathy for Tocqueville's stress on voluntary associations as the intermediary bodies required for the stabilization of differentiation and the establishment of democratic mediation. He does not realize that this model, required for the preparation of citizenship on levels where participation is still possible in modern societies, involves a potential relationship between *homme* and *citoyen* that escapes the invidious alternative of powerless human being and inhuman citizen. The associations of civil society in Tocqueville's theory prepare private individuals for the exercise of public power, a task that the literary public sphere is, on its own, incapable of performing. At the same time, these associations preserve the connection of citizens to the prepolitical social networks that serve as their background.[79] In place of the Marxian identity of man and citizen, Tocqueville thus proposes a differentiated and interdependent model of social being and citizen.

Admittedly, Mill and Tocqueville are only partially concerned with the dedifferentiating implications of the link of man and bourgeois. Habermas is right to appeal to Marx when he seeks to expand processes of public criticism and supervision to the economic sphere.[80] It is not clear, however, whether the ideal proposed involves an abolition of the economy in the way that the liberal utopia (judged incoherent and impossible by Habermas himself) seeks to abolish political power as such, replacing it with public discussion. An alternative would have been to affirm the differentiation of the economic realm and of its specific roles and to postulate new forms of complementarity and interdependence between economic actors, private individuals, members of associations, and participants in the public sphere.

Of course, Habermas would have considered irrelevant the combination of Marxian critique and democratic liberal norms proposed here on the basis of some strains of his early work, because he believed that neither the Marxian nor the liberal utopias were adequate guides for exploring what occurred in the liberal public sphere. In his analysis, neither option depicted here—Marxian, liberal, or even their combination—was actualized. Instead, the liberal-bourgeois public underwent a change of structure entirely incompatible with its original normative project. Tocqueville and Marx would both have understood the cause for this fundamental change, namely the dramatic expansion of the extent and power of the modern administrative state, which has continuously resisted invasion by public processes and procedures. What neither Tocqueville nor Marx could have imagined was that, apart from the socialist state-society that one feared and the other fervently desired, a comprehensive repoliticization of society could occur, supposedly removing the field of force in which the bourgeois public sphere was constituted and apparently abolishing the differentiation of civil society and state for which publicity served as a stabilizing mediation. It was Carl Schmitt who was the first to work out a comprehensive theory of the decline of the public sphere in terms of the alleged fusion of society and state.

The Fusion of Civil Society and State: Carl Schmitt

The shift of the locus of genuine publicity from the state (the model of antiquity) to an independently organized and juridically private societal sphere does not in itself avoid the thesis of fusion and decline. As already indicated, Carl Schmitt developed his interpretation of parliamentarism around this transmutation of the concept of publicity. It is thus all the more striking that he was the first important thinker to link the end of the liberal era to the refusion of society and the state—a process that supposedly eliminated the only sphere capable of sustaining the claims of publicity under modern conditions. Accordingly, parliamentary discussion, and with it the "whole system" of the protection of social communication, has become today an empty formality.[81] Parliament is now nothing but an antechamber to the real loci of power: the bureaus or committees of invisible rulers.[82] The parliamentary stage has been transformed from a *Schauplatz* for "the free deliberation of independent representatives seeking unity" into an arena where the "plurality of divided yet highly organized social forces" meet and clash.[83] In the process, all the old claims for publicity have collapsed.

For a complex set of reasons, it is democracy, or rather democratization, which Schmitt takes to be the fundamental tendency of the modern era, that is responsible for the crisis of parliament and its legitimacy. To begin with, he argues that democracy and liberal parliamentarism have entirely different principles. Democracy is a form of rule resting on social (in modernity: national) homogeneity and "if the need arises the elimination and eradication of heterogeneity." Given the actual and structural difference between rulers and ruled, democracy is possible only when, on the ground of homogeneity, the ruled can "identify" with the rulers. Starting with the Rousseauian idea according to which democracy is the *actual* identity of those who command and those who obey,[84] Schmitt winds up reducing this to a string of identifications that rest on no "palpable reality . . . something actually equal legally, politically, sociologically" but only the "recognition of identity."[85] Moreover, given sufficient identification, dictatorship, especially if supported by pedagogic claims, is compatible with democracy in this view; indeed, Schmitt believes that radical democracy must lead to dictatorship because of the inevitable lack of preparation of the masses for self-rule.

Schmitt argues that liberalism is quite different from democracy. Above all, it is a deeply unpolitical model in that it rests on discussion rather than identification, presupposing a corresponding plurality of opinions rather than their homogeneity. Schmitt does not consider for a moment the possibility that the structural connection of public opinion and parliamentary publicity establishes a medium of genuine if incomplete identity between rulers and ruled. Democracy for him is based not on actual though incomplete institutional identity but on complete though necessarily mythological identification. Thus, the two principles, liberal parliamentarism and democracy, are contrary and incompatible.

There is one historical context in which liberalism and democracy appeared as allies. In Schmitt's difficult and impressionistic line of argument, what was required for this alliance was the "identification" of the extraparliamentary "people" with the parliamentary public as its representative. Given the very real differences of parliamentary notables and outside constituencies, and of the latter among themselves, the illusion of necessary homogeneity and unity within society and of society with parliament could arise only in the face of an enemy: untamed state power. It is this friend-foe relation, rather than any Hegelian integrating activity of the state, that achieved the temporary unity of society responsible for the illusory identity of liberalism and democracy.

The problem, however, is not that this identification is illusory but that it is temporary. Although the existence of an undemocratic and illiberal state is necessary for the alliance of liberalism and democracy, both ideologies, albeit for different reasons, push toward its abolition or its transformation into a state as the self-organization of society. The military-administrative state is unacceptable to liberal principles, for these recognize the legitimacy of decisions only if they have been arrived at through the apolitical principle of discussion. To be sure, liberalism is skeptical toward any state and seeks a reduced "night watchman" variant. It does not attempt to abolish fully or to replace the military-administrative state. The latter, however, insofar as it is the remnant of a hierarchical and authoritarian era, is far more unacceptable to democracy. Moreover, once democratic forces identify with the liberal parliament, they, unlike liberal forces, cannot tolerate the fact that the state is not identical with this parliament.

Paradoxically, as the triumph of the alliance of liberalism and democracy nears its goal, with the creation of a state that represents the self-organization of society (through extension of the franchise, which is a precondition of the alliance), a state toward which a polemical attitude is necessary and possible is no longer a possibility. Along with its (supposed) disappearance, the conditions of social unity also disappear, putting liberalism, democracy, and the state itself into crisis.[86] Schmitt explores the nature of this crisis by analyzing two developments linked to the process of democratization: the emergence of a new type of mass-bureaucratic party, and the advent of state interventionism. The first leads to a fundamental transformation of the institutions and processes that the liberal model of discussion presupposed, even if counterfactually. The second represents a change with even more radical ramifications: the "functional dedifferentiation" of society and state. This "fusion" of the political and the social eliminates the space for a public discursive form of intermediation, transforming—indeed dissolving, as it were—the public spaces in both society and state.

According to Schmitt (who obviously takes England as his model), the liberal party system was originally based on free competition, through the means of discussion and persuasion, for the votes of an educated and independent (elite) public. Indeed, liberal parties were to take shape in the sphere of public opinion, that is, in parliament. This principle found its sociological correlate in relatively small, collegial parties of notables. Because of a lack of attachment to both fixed interests and organizational structures, the representatives elected by parties were supposedly capable of freedom of action and deliberation in parliament; hence the assumption that they were, as a body, in the position to generate a unified will of the state through discussion and mutual persuasion.[87] Democratization, however, has led to the emergence of an entirely new type of competitive party based on mass membership, sociologically linked to a specific constellation of interests, and heavily bureaucratized with numerous paid functionaries.[88] Such a party does not value neutrality vis-à-vis its members and tends to be deeply involved in the social, economic, and cultural life of its "clientele" in all stages of the human life cycle. Nor is it tolerant of the forms of life represented by its competitors. Each "democratic" party is tendentially totalistic insofar as it seeks full possession of the state apparatus, which is seen as the instrument for carrying out its *social* goals. The multiplicity of such parties does keep each one in check; together, they constitute a pluralistic party state (as against a single-party state), a "labile coalition state." Schmitt pointedly maintains that this type of state has itself attained a total character with respect to its predecessor, representing in effect a fragmented or parceled-out totality in which every organized complex of power seeks to actualize a totality "in itself and for itself" (*in sich selbst und für sich selbst*).

Schmitt's explanation for the changing character of political parties in the context of political democratization differs from conservative and socialist analyses of these phenomena. While conservatives stressed the supposedly inevitable bureaucratization of politics, given the problems of organizing uneducated and atomized "masses," socialists focused on the tendency to create new mechanisms of exclusion and depoliticization reconciling the "participation" of the exploited with the imperatives of maintaining the existing, exploitative socioeconomic system. Schmitt, in spite of his bizarre set of affinities with strains within conservatism as well as with authoritarian versions of Marxism, bypasses both of these explanations, focusing instead on the end of the polemical relation of state and society under the impact of democratic parliamentarism. The unity of the diverse sociological formations of a depoliticized society depended on the survival of the authoritarian state form. The emergence of the state as the self-organization of society and the weakening of the executive fragment society along lines of a plurality of interests and beliefs. Political appeal across the sociological dividing lines becomes impossible, and political parties must now organize within rigidified categories. Furthermore, successful electoral appeal now depends on satisfying sectoral economic, cultural, and ideological demands. Accordingly, the parliamentary field once again mirrors society at large. This time, however, the society it mirrors is pluralistically organized, and each segment demands specific performances in economic, social, and cultural policy. Just as the state becomes the *parliamentary state,* parliament itself becomes the expression of mutually hostile societal pluralities capable of strategic compromise but not genuine agreement.

Moreover, compromise can no longer be achieved through discussion of the truth and justice of a given policy, nor can it be openly and publicly arrived at, for compromise and open discussion violate the principles of the new type of totalizing political party. The parliamentary discussion that does take place is an empty formality, a mere facade, located "in a gigantic antechamber in front of the bureaus or committees of invisible rulers. . . . Small and exclusive committees of parties and party coalitions make their decisions behind closed doors, and what representatives of the big capitalist interest groups agree to in the small committees is more important for the fate of millions of people, perhaps, than any political decision."[89]

Schmitt's concern, unlike that of Marxian critics of pluralism, is not that the same interests always dominate through extraparliamentary pressure and deal making. Because party committees must work through an elected parliament, rule by them creates inconsistent outcomes, depending on results of elections and coalitions that strengthen one or another faction. The real danger he fears is not oligarchy but what was later called "ungovernability," since he is convinced that the pluralistic party state fragments the two conceivable sources of unity: state and society.

This fragmentation is in fact simultaneous as state and society become one. However, Schmitt's fusion thesis is not based simply on the actualization of the program of the state as the self-organization of society. Indeed this idea, based on facile generalization from the case of Weimar, is not convincing despite the dialectical virtuosity involved in the reversal of the Hegelian argument. The reality of the modern state does not in fact disappear when the democratic transformation of parliamentary democracy is complete. This is certainly not the case in presidential systems, but even in parliamentary systems a growth of the power of the executive has historically accompanied democratization. This growth of the executive is both a condition of the constitution of civil society and a threat to its independence and differentiation.[90] Thus, if the fusion of state and society is the presupposition for the decline of the parliamentary public sphere, this fusion must have foundations in addition to formal democratization processes, ones linked to the expansion rather than the weakening of the modern state.

Schmitt does provide a second train of argument for the fusion of state and society, one whose consequences are far more general with respect to the roots of independent social life. This argument, focusing on the mutual interpenetration of state and society, is difficult to disentangle from the primary emphasis on the socialization of the state, but upon closer examination it turns out that here the issue is specifically that of a two-directional functional dedifferentiation. Accordingly, the nineteenth-century liberal state was differentiated from society not only in the sense of being independent of *segmental* constellations of fixed social interests but also in the sense of being neutral with respect to the great *functional* spheres of society that are thereby depoliticized: religion, culture, economics, law, science.[91] Here Schmitt's model is above all that of the laissez-faire economic order and a state that intervenes at most to restore the disturbed conditions of economic competition. From this point of view, we get an altered catalogue of liberal fundamental rights and freedoms (personal freedom, freedoms of expression of opinion, of contract, of enterprise, of property) that does not even include the key freedoms of communication (assembly and association).[92] Here the function of rights is to maintain differentiation and depoliticization, rather than to guarantee the preconditions of public communication.

According to Schmitt, the liberal model of functional differentiation is assailed from two directions. The postliberal state is a "total state which potentially embraces every domain."[93] This statement has a double meaning. First, the new type of state is no longer neutral with respect to the various spheres of society and becomes in effect an economic, welfare, cultural, educational, scientific, even "religious" state—in a word that Schmitt does not seem to use in this context, it is a *Sozialstaat* or social state.[94] Second, the new type of state intervenes in and politicizes all spheres of society. The implication here is that the society-state distinction is abolished with such radicality that the private sphere itself, stabilized by rights modeled on that of property, is penetrated, politicized, and abolished as an independent sphere. While the model of the rise of pluralist segmental differentiation seems to make only some rights— the ones linked to communication—politically irrelevant, the model of functional dedifferentiation actually supports Schmitt's statement that liberal rights as such have become obsolete.

The relationship of these two models in Schmitt's argument is complex. The only "explanation" he provides for functional dedifferentiation is, once again, democratization, which for rather unclear reasons "must do away with . . . the forms of depoliticization characteristic of the liberal nineteenth century."[95] In fact, the argument again seems to rest on the extent to which the program of "liberal democracy" can establish the state as the self-organization of society. Here Schmitt would have us think that the idea of a *Sozialstaat*, in the sense of an economic, welfare, cultural, etc., state, and that of society becoming the state (*zum Staat gewordene Gesellschaft*) are the same. But in his own argument the culmination of the state as the self-organization of society only leads to the fragmentation—that is, the segmentation along lines of interest and ideology—of the society that takes over the state. The outcome, as we have shown, is a fragmented pluralistic party state whose sovereignty is parceled out among the units. Schmitt's never clarified argument seems to hinge again on the type of the democratic-mass-ideological party that involves itself in all aspects of the social life of its members. Such a party would presumably seek a state modeled on itself, intervening in society on behalf of the economic, cultural, and other interests it represents. Unless Schmitt has in mind the specific examples of the relationship of the Social Democrats to the economy, or of the Catholic Center party to religion, it is entirely unclear why the new party system should lead to a wholesale process of functional dedifferentiation of state and society. Indeed, even Mussolini's single-party state could coexist for a time with a liberal economic order.

Once again, we believe, the source of the confusion is Schmitt's unwillingness to concede that, whereas in the case of segmentation the source lies in social complexes seeking to capture or at least parcel out the state, in the case of functional dedifferentiation we are dealing with a powerful administrative-bureaucratic state seeking to penetrate society. From his highly committed Weimar perspective, Schmitt saw "social-democratization" but not state interventionism as a dynamic force leading to political crisis. Nevertheless, he is aware of two possible outcomes that are in line with the two tendencies we were forced to separate in his thought. Of the two versions of the "total" state he outlines, the fragmented pluralist variety is the product of the tendency toward segmentation; the authoritarian variety is the product of functional dedifferentiation driven by the logic of the state itself.[96]

Schmitt seems to have some idea that the two versions of the total state flow from different meanings of the term "social-state" or "state-society," one implying the primacy of the social, the other that of the political. He states that the "pluralistic party state becomes 'total' not out of strength but weakness; it intervenes in all areas of life because it must satisfy the claims of all those interested."[97] Nevertheless, he also believes that the fragmented variety of the total state is not so much an alternative outcome of the repoliticization of society as an artificial product, by definition almost always in crisis, a result of the survival of obsolete legal and parliamentary institutions. In particular, he believes that the culmination of the trend against the liberal neutralization of the state and the depoliticization of society has already produced the foundations of another authoritarian form of power resting on democratic-plebiscitary legitimacy. Indeed, it is an unstated consequence of his argument that such an outcome could even converge with the logical self-abolition of the party system, with the rule of many parties being replaced by that of a single, monopolistic party. Thus, the two tendencies toward fusion, segmentation and functional dedifferentiation, could converge in a new type of "democratic" dictatorship.

On the basis of his interpretation of the experience of Weimar, however, Schmitt is convinced that the operation of parliamentary legality, even if it is no longer in a position to produce a legislative state, is nevertheless capable of checkmating the emergence of a genuinely political—that is, authoritarian—state form.[98] A parliament guaranteeing the political rights of a plurality of parties is capable of checkmating decisions of the executive that arise outside the given conditions of coalition formation. And one might add that the survival of the liberal framework of legal protection outside of parliament makes the replacement of a system of a plurality of parties by that of a single party nearly impossible.[99]

According to Schmitt, the alliance of liberalism and democracy is (for the present) beyond repair. The instrument of majority rule in parliament loses its chances of popular acceptance when highly organized political groupings predetermine all possible outcomes, establish an irreversible advantage of incumbency, and rigidify a given structure of majorities and minorities and even of complete political exclusion. Thus, each partner of the former marriage of liberalism and democracy is now in crisis: democratic legitimacy along with the parliamentary principle. Their crises produce a third one, that of the state itself, to the extent that solutions beyond liberalism and the existing form of democracy are successfully blocked and the possibilities of decision are continually stymied. To Schmitt, there seem to be two choices inherent in this situation: the continuation of an antipolitical, pluralistic party-state in permanent crisis but protected and disguised by liberal principles, or the creation of a genuinely political, no longer pluralistic, authoritarian state legitimated by a new, plebiscitary version of "democracy." It is useless to deny that it is this second option that Schmitt chooses. Indeed, it was this choice that allowed Schmitt to be enthusiastic about Italian Fascism and that made his turn to National Socialism intellectually *authentic*, if not *inevitable*. For Schmitt, no return to a conservative, nonplebiscitary authoritarian regime could provide a solution for the crisis of the state, since such an alternative, by reconstituting their earlier polemical adversary, would lead to a reconstitution of the alliance of liberalism and democracy and again undermine the state. Like the leftists and rightists he admired, Schmitt proposed an alternative marriage: that of democracy and authoritarianism.

In any case, with the coming of the total state, neither of the two options (pluralistic or authoritarian) is consistent with a dualism of state and society, or with the operation of a parliamentary mediation between them. What does not occur to Schmitt is the possibility, so obvious in the American context, that the two principles, statist and pluralistic, stabilized in a framework of liberal rights, could combine to constitute a new version of the state–civil society dualism. Three features of his thought were responsible for this myopia: an unwillingness to recognize the continued existence of a tendentially authoritarian state in the pluralistic era; an inability to see the whole gamut of reasons, including especially the economic ones, for state interventionism in society; and a failure to note the emergence of yet another new type of political party, the catch-all party, based on a mixed constituency, interested neither in totally dominating nor in parceling out the political system, capable of greater fluidity in the parliamentary arena and of more than merely strategic compromise with its adversaries.

The disappearance of the state in Schmitt's picture of liberal democracy was hardly innocent: He sought to reinforce an authoritarian administration that he presented as weakened, and to do this he had to disguise its role in the crisis of the political order of Weimar. The pretense that the authoritarian element of the state was moribund, despite the power of the army, the administration, and the legal system allied to the administration, not to speak of the presidential prerogatives of the constitutional system, helped him to attack the pluralistic party system that produced new links as well as tensions between democracy and liberalism.

The Fusion Argument in Habermas's *Strukturwandel*

Given its thinly disguised authoritarian intentions, it is all the more striking that the fusion argument Schmitt worked out was adopted, and indeed dramatically refurbished, by the writers of the Frankfurt school. Their attitude to liberalism, democracy, and authoritarianism was the opposite of Schmitt's, yet the fusion argument became for all of them a significant feature of the "critique of the authoritarian state."

Consistently enough, neither the alliance of liberalism and democracy, nor the supposed decline of their adversary, authoritarian executive power, plays a role in the Frankfurt analyses. This structure of the argument is replaced by a new one: the great transformation of the capitalist economic order from liberal to monopoly and finally to state-organized capitalism. The argument, although first developed in relation to the rise of authoritarian states, also proved applicable in the postwar period, when liberal democracy was reconstructed.[100] Habermas's theory of the decline of the public sphere, however much influenced by the earlier theses of Schmitt and Arendt, derives first and foremost from the various strands of the Frankfurt school analysis of the 1930s. Indeed, Habermas ultimately managed to recast almost all of these strands in a new theoretical framework, where they became quite useful for a democratic theory oriented to practice. But in 1962, at the time of writing of *Strukturwandel der Öffentlichkeit*, Habermas had not yet achieved this position. As a result, unfortunately, he linked the notion of the transformation of the public sphere to the negative philosophy of history of Adorno and Horkheimer, and consequently he was unable to see much beyond a thesis of decline, except to the limited extent that he, unlike his teachers, still harbored some classical Marxian assumptions. The application of the theory of the public sphere to contemporary politics had to wait.

Here we need only summarize Habermas's multidimensional synthesis. The argument is composed of six levels:

1. The thesis of state interventionism in the capitalist economy. This argument, almost entirely missing in Schmitt, involves something qualitatively different from the expansion of state administration and political bureaucracy during the absolutist and even liberal epochs stressed by Marx, Tocqueville, and, in her own way, Arendt. The modern state intervenes in the liberal capitalist economy, at the price of its liberal character, to protect the capitalist structure endangered by endogenous crisis tendencies and processes of impaired self-regulation. The state seeks to correct disequilibria produced both by self- regulating market processes and by phenomena of imperfect, oligopolistic competition (fiscal and monetary regulation of the business cycle), to underwrite processes of investment, accumulation, and technical innovation, and to support aggregate demand through welfare-state expenditures. This thesis, rather undeveloped in *Strukturwandel*, was fully integrated in the Frankfurt tradition by F. Pollock and his colleagues (1932–1941) in relation to "the authoritarian state." It was powerfully extended in the writings of Habermas and Claus Offe after 1968 in the form of a critique of welfare-state crisis management.[101]

2. The thesis of the assumption of public powers by private associations (new corporatism). This thesis, first introduced into Frankfurt discussion by O. Kirchheimer,[102] derives from Schmitt's critique of Weimar pluralism. In Habermas's 1962 argument, the critique is extended to the prepolitical level. In processes of oligopolistic competition, private organizations are capable, as

against liberal capitalism, of formulating what is in effect public economic policy.[103] The collective agreements among private associations—in particular, employment associations and unions—lose their private law status in favor of a form of rule creation that was previously reserved for public law entities. While important areas of administration now fall to private law entities, the state itself increasingly uses private legal contractual devices to regulate its relations with its social partners. This argument, albeit deemphasized by Habermas in his subsequent work, was powerfully extended by Offe in the 1980s.[104] It is worth stressing, however, that he did so not only to indicate a component of overall welfare state structure (in any case, a component not equally important under all welfare states) but, under the impact of the neoconservative challenge, to stress one potential, albeit internally problematic (and normatively unattractive!), avenue for reducing the administrative and legitimating burdens of the interventionist state.

3. The thesis of the decline of the intimate sphere of the family. This thesis, an important component of Arendt's analysis whose very formulation is taken over by Habermas ("the polarization of the social and intimate spheres"), was a key contribution of Horkheimer and his colleagues in the 1930s to social theory. Habermas's 1962 analysis, drawing on new literature, stresses the destruction of the private shell of bourgeois property around intimacy, caused by the loss of the family's economic functions and the growth of client relations to a state in its capacity of providing social insurance. The family increasingly loses its functions of "education, defense, caring and direction, and even of providing traditions and orientations . . . its conduct forming power in areas that counted as the most internal spheres of the members of bourgeois families."[105] The decline of the authority of the father is, from this point of view, ambiguous: The family loses not only its repressive but also its defensive functions. The new forms of even more intensive intimacy are seen as hopelessly defensive, in the manner of Arendt; private life becomes more and more open to the gaze of outsiders, down to the very level of architecture. The fake intimacy of public communication, stressed by both Adorno and Arendt, represents to Habermas both a form of the subsumption of the intimate sphere and the degradation of public into mass.[106]

4. The thesis of the decline of the literary public sphere and the rise of mass culture. This complex of arguments represents the most successful and best-known dimension of the theory of the early Frankfurt school, above all of Adorno. The stress in Habermas's version is on the growth of the literary public into the sphere of consumption and manipulated leisure. This is linked to the decline of family-based institutions of cultural reception and criticism as well as to the industrial-commercial transformation of the media of communication. A market is no longer the precondition of autonomous art; marketability becomes a principle of the industrial production of art. The "democratization" of culture is a pseudo-democratization; what is democratized is no longer culture. The dramatic expansion of the literary public sphere is simultaneous with the decline of its critical character.[107] The new media foster a merely passive form of participation. The survival of avant-garde art and culture only splits the classical literary public sphere into "a minority of reasoning, no longer public, experts and the great mass of public consumers."[108]

The erosion of the intimate sphere and of a genuine literary public leads to the loss of the tension between *homme* and bourgeois, abolishing the private foundation of autonomy without providing a new public one. Here the theses of the decline of the family and the rise of mass culture are linked to the classical Frankfurt thesis of the decline of the individual.

5. The thesis of the transformation of the political public sphere represents a selective extension of arguments developed in relation to the prepolitical dimensions of publicity. Interestingly enough, statist-bureaucratic intervention into the economy, for Arendt the replacement par excellence of egalitarian public interaction by paternalism, is somewhat deemphasized in the analysis, although Habermas does mention the growth and increasing independence of an administration that successfully resisted, even in the liberal era, the demands of publicity. All the more important is the Schmittian argument, stressed also by Kirchheimer, according to which the assumption of public powers by private associations leads to the emergence of corporatist processes of negotiation, bargaining, and compromise that bypass public processes of scrutiny[109] and reduce parliamentary discussion and debate to a *post hoc* process of

legitimating decisions arrived at under the protection of a new "arcanum." No longer attempts by representatives to convince one another, speeches in parliament now seek to mobilize a plebiscitary opinion outside parliament. As Schmitt argued, representatives bound by party discipline lose their independence as something resembling the bound mandate is revived. Habermas recognizes that Schmitt's conception of the transformation of the party system from loose collegial groupings bound by common opinion to parties as rigid sociological groupings no longer corresponds to reality. The new type of "catch-all party" stressed by Kirchheimer among others, a further stage in the "democratization" and "massification" of the political system, only increases depoliticization by further reducing the level of political discourse and argument.[110] Of course, the new type of party is no longer associated here with the parceling out of sovereign power. Its most important result, the "vanishing of the political opposition," to use Kirchheimer's phrase, has the effect of reducing public controls upon the administration, as stressed by Max Weber, thereby strengthening authoritarian power without authoritarian means.

6. Habermas extended Schmitt's thesis that the role of parliament as sphere of mediation between a strengthened bureaucracy and private associations must decline. Equally important, however, was his use of the Frankfurt school thesis on mass culture to demystify the allegedly "democratic" character of the plebiscitary components of the new situation, stressed by Schmitt. In the tradition of Adorno and Lowenthal, who emphasized the authoritarian political potential of the new mass culture and its media, Habermas points to the place of propaganda in contemporary political discourse. Modern political manipulation presupposes the forms of commercial advertisement that become dominant as price competition ceases to be the mechanism coordinating oligopolistic groupings in their struggle for market shares. As Adorno and his colleagues well knew, propaganda—the advertising and selling of political leaders, parties, and policies—presupposes already formed, passive, uncritical, yet mobilizable audiences. While advertising as such turns to individuals in their private capacities, thus helping to decompose the intimate sphere, the intermediary form of "public relations" turns to and deforms

"public opinion" through "the engineering of consent."[111] It is this task that becomes central for political parties of the contemporary type, in parliament and especially in the electoral process. Such parties do not need continuous mass membership as much as an apparatus capable at periodic intervals of mobilizing electoral support in the manner of an advertising agency. Although the reconstitution of some kind of political public sphere in electoral campaigns is unavoidable,[112] the preferred targets of parties are those individuals, generally not members of associations or higher status groups, who have no access to what are depicted here as residual forms of a reasoning public. The targeted voters are approached not through enlightenment but through appeals to consumerist behavior, and not by agitators or even "propagandists" of the old type but by advertising experts.[113] To be successful, "the organizers of elections must not only recognize the disappearance of a genuine political public sphere, but fully consciously must help produce this outcome."[114] The result is not understanding or agreement with policies but a "symbolic identification" with leaders that is measurable, and further opened to manipulation, through popularity indices and "public" opinion polls that refer exclusively to nonpublic and atomized opinion. Even if parties and governments were actually responsive to "nonpublic opinion," the result would still be more like enlightened absolutism than a genuine democratic will formation based on the transformation of personal opinion through processes of rational deliberation into a genuine public opinion.[115]

Habermas's aim on all these levels of analysis is not only to demonstrate the deformation and deterioration of the principle of free public communication. Even more important for us is his complementary thesis: that of the destruction of the model of differentiation between civil society and state through a fusion of levels. If the deformation of mediating institutions itself promotes dedifferentiation, it can be also be argued that the tendencies toward fusion of state and society remove the social space in which the liberal public sphere could function. On one level, the difference between the two processes is only one of emphasis: Habermas is interested in the decline and revival of the public sphere, which in 1962 he still imagined to be possible *without* a model that differentiated between state and civil society. We, on the other hand, are interested in reconstructing the differentiated model, which we do not think possible or normatively desirable without a renewal of the liberal and democratic project of the public sphere.

But there is also a systematic difference between our two approaches, to the extent that the model of the decline of the public sphere refers to a much more complete process of fusion and even "one-dimensionality" than that of the new relation of state and society. This can be seen in the structure of Habermas's argument. He tells us, rightly, that the model of the repoliticization of society through state intervention in the economy cannot, on its own, establish a fusion argument, since private economic activity could be limited in important ways without such intervention affecting the private nature of large areas of personal interaction. But he is wrong to suggest that the case can be completed by referring to the complementary assumption of public powers by private associations. Even if the two processes do produce an intermediary sphere to which the distinctions of private and public, society and state, no longer apply, they do not in themselves make the distinction disappear, as the terms "statizing society" and "socializing the state" seem to imply. In particular, the spheres of intimacy and publicity proper are not directly decomposed by the two processes; for this to happen, a reification and instrumentalization of these two ultimately cultural spheres is necessary. If the two complementary processes leading to fusion are to reach their goal, the reification of the space between them, that of culture, must become more or less total. The thesis first introduced by Schmitt can be saved only with the help of the cultural theory of the Frankfurt school, especially in the version of Adorno. But this choice would lead, in the case of Habermas's own thesis as well, to a manipulated public whose agents are entirely passive and whose present dynamic could in no way point to the revival of its original promise.[116]

Such a constellation could still be open to revolutionary ruptures, in Arendt's sense. And it is in fact fair to ask at the end of Habermas's book to what extent he has escaped the ancient republican model of the public sphere he criticized in Arendt's work. In working out the consequences of the fusion argument, he suddenly tells us that "the model of the bourgeois public was based on the rigid separation of public and private spheres, since the public sphere of private individuals organized as publics counted as private."[117] While juridically correct, this argument breaks with Habermas's earlier, more Hegelian, argument according to which it was precisely the rigid distinction of public and private that was relativized by the various levels of mediation.

We should note, moreover, that the utopia Habermas derived from Marx, involving the duality of a public state-society and the intimate sphere, along with the primacy of the former, coincides with Arendt's republican model. Habermas's theory of decline also postulates the emergence of a mixed realm that is neither public nor private, leading to the collapse of genuine publicity. For Arendt, the model of the liberal public sphere worked out by Habermas, concerned as it was with mediating between state and society through regulation of the preconditions of the market economy, *already was* this mixed sphere and could involve no genuine public life and action. The idea of a public realm controlling and influencing the state without sharing in power would have appeared senseless to her. All the same, it could be argued that the only real difference between their analyses is that Habermas gives Arendt's model of decline a historically distinct starting point from which a decline could take place. And indeed, however inconsistently, the emergence of a mixed realm also seemed to Habermas to deprive "the public sphere of its old basis without giving it a new one."[118] Of course, this was a function not of the rise of the modern state as such but of the postliberal relations of state and economy. Obviously, Habermas and Arendt share an interest in working out anew such a basis. In this context, however, we should also recall that Habermas repeatedly asserts that he seeks to reinstitutionalize the liberal rather than the ancient model of the public sphere.

The ideal of the liberal public sphere contains for Habermas that of democratization. Paradoxically, the historical processes of democratization, whether of politics as in the party system or of culture as in mass culture, contributed to the decline of the institutions that sustained this ideal, in however contradictory a fashion, reducing it to an abstract principle of legitimation. The decline of liberal institutions could, however, be seen from two points of view: that of differentiation of state and civil society as expressed by the principle of rights, and that of the public sphere as expressed by the principle of rational communication. It is therefore ambiguous to argue for a reinstitutionalization of liberal principles unless one specifically refers to both or only one of these. Habermas's obvious inclination was to defend the principle of communication primarily. To be sure, the classical catalogues of rights posited this principle in terms of a series of well-known rights (freedoms of speech, assembly, suffrage, etc.). But the very meaning of "rights" in this case, as in others, involved something more: Rights as liberties differentiated between the private sphere and public authority, and they implied the protection not only of the mediating public sphere from state power but also of the private sphere from both publics.

Since Habermas does not want to abandon such catalogues, he argues for their redefinition and reconstruction. In this context, he maintains not only that the actual trend of welfare-state jurisprudence is in a direction that transforms the merely defensive, negative structure of inherited constitutional rights but also that this development represents what is in effect the only immanent tendency in our societies toward a reinstitutionalization of the public sphere.[119] Not only, then, does he speak about the survival of the principle of the liberal public sphere on the normative level, but he also claims that both the letter and the spirit of constitutional norms seeking to regulate the transition from liberal *Rechtsstaat* to the welfare state anticipate the new forms of reinstitutionalization of this principle, thereby contradicting the institutional practices of existing welfare states.[120] It is at this point that an argument that previously treated the modern public and intimate spheres as passive objects for economic and political processes leading to their disorganization suddenly discovers that the norms originating in these spheres are possible points of orientation for an alternative strategy. Accordingly, Habermas proposes a model of reconstruction. It should not come as a great surprise that we get a new version of the antinomy we found in both Hegel and Gramsci, involving two opposed orientations, one statist and one oriented toward civil society.

We should note that the argument dealing with legal developments in the welfare state suddenly breaks with the general trend of Habermas's analysis that aligns it with the negative philosophy of history and social theory of the late Frankfurt school, and with the school's legal theory as well. Habermas does refer to Franz Neumann in suggesting that, with the fusion of state and society, the generality of legal norms cannot be maintained; rather, law and administration are increasingly dedifferentiated.[121] Neumann would argue, however, that without the generality of norms it would be impossible to sustain the principle of fundamental rights, which would be incoherent without any limitations and impossible if the limitations were not defined according to rigorously general standards. Habermas, on the other hand, maintains that only the negative and defensive aspects of rights vis-à-vis the state are challenged under welfare-state constitutionalism.[122]

The motivations of the state in this context are clear: With its intervention into society, self-limitation with respect to social autonomy may seem obsolete, and, more important, new justifications are needed that can validate the new forms of state action as just. Given the survival of liberal norms as legitimations, such validation can be developed by relying on the internal logic of liberal rights. And given the decline of the competitive economic system in the context of an interventionist and redistributive state, the "positive fulfillment" of the negative, defensive rights in terms of an actual ability to practice the freedoms of speech, assembly, and association as well as those of political participation no longer follows more or less automatically. The state must therefore provide the positive and, indeed, the material guarantees for participation in terms of new social rights. From the point of view of liberal rights themselves, if these are "to remain faithful to their original intentions," their "normative interpretation must be changed." While negative rights as "liberties" (*Freiheitsrechte*) are preserved in welfare-state constitutions, they must now be seen as rights of participation (*Teilnehmerrechte*), which will be interpreted in terms of positive social rights (*Sozialrechte*) to state activities rather than forms of self-defense and self-differentiation with respect to the state.[123]

To be sure, there is sleight of hand involved here. Even the constitutions Habermas considers the most advanced contain, he admits, negative rights, rights of participation, and social rights alongside one another. This raises the question of whether Habermas himself means to affirm the need for both negative and positive rights, or whether he is arguing for a transition from the first to the second. While the issue is ambiguous in his presentation, he seems to consider the survival of negative rights to be a mark of an insufficient overcoming of the bourgeois "tax-state" (*Steuerstaat*) character of the welfare state, the incompleteness of its realization of the goal of a unified state-society subordinating economic processes to its direction.[124] In light of this goal, even rights of the intimate sphere, no longer protected by the outer shell of property, need to be redefined, according to him, as functions of or derivations from the public processes of democratic participation.[125] In this context, Habermas seems to fully affirm W. Abendroth's claim that the supposedly authoritarian implications of such a model actually involve for most individuals only a transition from dependence on the private power of particular interests to dependence on processes of collective control "whose highest unit of decision is the state itself." The only thing Habermas adds to this clearly statist and authoritarian model is the desideratum that the state as the unified planning and control organ of all social processes is itself to be subordinated in the unified state-society to processes of the "public opinion and will formation of the citizens."[126] This democratic statism is then supposed to make negative rights of individuals and groups superfluous.

Habermas does also note and affirm a competing model within jurisprudence oriented toward the welfare state. In this model, the function of mediation between social interests and state decisions does not disappear in the welfare state; only its public character is abandoned. The private-public organizations that assume this role, arising in part from the private sphere (social associations and organizations) and in part from the public sphere (parties), cooperate with the administration of the state and attempt to secure "public" acceptance through manipulative, hierarchical procedures.[127] What is left of a political public sphere is dominated by these entities, one of whose tasks is to influence the redistributive activities that represent the positive guarantees behind "social rights." The real bargaining processes in which this occurs are not public, and the demands of publicity aimed at state agencies bypass the juridically private structure of the negotiations. In this context, Habermas stresses the trend in welfare-state constitutionalism toward extending the demands of publicity from the state to the relevant social associations and political parties, and to the processes of their interaction with the state. Only such legislation could revive public discussion in the sphere that really matters, by substituting "in place of the no longer intact public of private persons interacting only as individuals, a public of organized private individuals." It is this trend that Habermas considers identical to the project of establishing a critical public sphere under contemporary conditions, in deep and not yet decided conflict with the now apparently dominant trend of the manipulation of publicity.[128]

Habermas does not seem to realize that this pluralistic model of the critical public sphere is in conflict with the ideal of a unified state-society as well. Undoubtedly, he identified both the agent (state legislative activity) and the end result (a fully public process of decision concerning all socially relevant questions) of the two processes. All the same, the project of establishing a unified state-society, expressed in the transition from negative rights restricting the state to positive rights implying state action, points toward a monolithic democratic society with a single collective actor, promoting the participation of individuals in a single, unified societal public sphere. In such a context, minorities as groups and even associations with particular interests and identities would not be protected; only their individual members would be protected as citizens of the whole. Even if such a model does not become the mask of statist authoritarian rule, it has no safeguards against a totalitarian democracy.

In comparison, the project of democratizing existing associations and parties is pluralist rather than collectivist. While its aim is to reestablish the public sphere, this is to be done in terms of establishing small publics in each association, linked together in terms of more general and, again, public processes of interaction. Even if state legislation is to play a role in establishing this model, the old polemical attitude to the authoritarian dimensions of state administration would inevitably return, and the state would be pressed not only to guarantee the new publics materially but to limit itself as well. Unless we believe that the administration of the state could altogether disappear, this double relation of publics to state would have to be institutionalized, a requirement reflected precisely in the ambiguity of the overall structure of rights found in modern constitutions. The new forms of publicity obviously require not only material inputs from the state but also forms of protection from state interference. The small publics of associations and parties, which must be autonomous even vis-à-vis the larger public process regulating their interaction, cannot do without both negative and positive rights. However, this requirement reestablishes the two normative foundations of the liberal public sphere: differentiation and communication. The point does not apply only to the rights of communication, though. The members of democratized associations need the same double protection. To be able to participate at all, they need positive supports and guarantees; to be able to function freely, they need negative rights and liberties.[129]

Habermas undoubtedly believed that his two models were competitive only to the extent that they aimed at democratizing the two separate processes leading to fusion: "the statization of society" (state interventionism) and "the socialization of the state" (neocorporatism). In assuming ultimate fusion, he assumed the convergence of the two democratizing processes as well. What he does not realize is that his first democratizing process produces only the social conditions necessary for the exercise of public freedom, in the form of "social rights," which in themselves are quite compatible with an enlightened and paternalistic absolutism. Only the second process revitalizes the constitutive interaction of the public sphere itself, in the form of genuine "rights of participation." The two processes do not fully converge, and in fact they reproduce the differentiation that state interventionism and corporatism together endangered. Moreover, they flow from two distinct theoretical traditions: the Marxian utopia of state-society, and the Tocquevillian project of reestablishing the intermediary associations of civil and political society in a democratic form.

The second reason why the two models may seem to converge is the common process by which they are to be instituted: welfare-state legislative action. Habermas does postulate the survival of the liberal value of publicity, which serves as the normative background for state actors seeking legitimacy in the context of increasing interventionism. But the norms are not linked to other actors on their behalf, for this is next to impossible in the context of the deformed and manipulated public sphere.

Logically, at least, state action can aim at its own self-limitation. All the same, there is reason to believe that models of differentiation based on rights have never been established without actors outside of and even antagonistic to the state. The model of the deformed public sphere, however, implies a society without opposition and the passivity of potential social actors. Habermas's choice follows from his analysis. The implied identification of the two models for restoring public life is a result not only of his socialist convictions but also of his diagnosis of an irreversible statist turn in the organization of modern societies. Thus, the choice between two models of the statization of society—one public-democratic and one manipulative-democratic—turns out to be no choice at all. Paradoxically, the analyst who has done most to identify the normative ideal of the modern public sphere with the differentiation of state and civil society came to the conclusion that this ideal could be saved only by accepting what has already occurred: dedifferentiation and the abolition of an independent civil society.

6
The Genealogical Critique:
Michel Foucault

One could interpret Foucault's work as another critique of the welfare state parallel to that of Arendt, Schmitt, and Habermas, albeit one that derives from a different theoretical tradition and uses different means. Of greater importance for us is the fact that Foucault presents a far more relentless critique of modern civil society than any of his predecessors or contemporaries. While he shares with Arendt her suspicions regarding the genesis and functions of the social, while his genealogical account of modern power relations has the same target as Schmitt's historicist critique (the liberal-democratic model of law and the normative conception of civil society), the thrust of his analysis is neither anti- nor prostatist. Its target comprises, rather, the categories of civil society. These move to center stage and play key parts in the story of the birth, growth, and dynamics of modern power relations. To be sure, the contemporary welfare state plays a role in the globalization and deepening of modern forms of domination, but it is neither their source nor the main actor in the drama.

Indeed, while Foucault would certainly agree with Habermas's account of the ways in which the deformed public sphere functions, as well as with the thesis of an interpenetration of societal and state power relations, he would reject the very notion of deformity to which Habermas counterposed the continued relevance of the norms of civil society. In this respect, at least, Foucault's analysis parallels that of Niklas Luhmann. Both argue that the normative conception of legitimation, law, publicity, and rights is an obsolete remnant of the aristocratic-monarchic system. Although both are aware that these concepts (along with democracy) were taken up by reformers and revolutionaries in the late eighteenth and early nineteenth centuries, they insist that they are irrelevant to modern decentered societies. However, Luhmann and Foucault give rather different reasons for this thesis. As we shall see in chapter 7, Luhmann locates his explanation in the modification of the primary principle of societal differentiation—i.e., in the reorganization of the social system of stratification into functional differentiation. In modern, differentiated social systems, it is no longer possible to represent the unity of society; representation and the normative categories of civil society have become hopelessly romantic. For Foucault, however, it is not functional differentiation but the emergence of a new form of stratification and new power relations that renders the normative juridical model anachronistic. While the problem of domination recedes into the background in Luhmann's work, it is central to Foucault's. Accordingly, and in contradistinction to Habermas, Foucault's version of the rise and development of modern civil society is unambiguously negative from the start. Moreover, since they are conceived as the product of modern technologies of power, none of the categories of civil society can provide a reference point for any project to challenge the structures of domination pervading our societies. It is to this rather alarming conception of civil society that we now turn.

Marx, Generalized

In many respects, the most important touchstone for understanding Foucault's critique of civil society is the work of Karl Marx, rather than that of his own contemporaries. If Marx was the peerless nineteenth-century critic of modern civil society,[1] surely Michel Foucault deserves to inherit that title for the twentieth. Like Marx, his purpose is to analyze the forms and techniques of a modality of power that is uniquely modern. His analysis, again reminiscent of Marx, takes up the core categories of civil society— law, rights, autonomy, subjectivity, publicity, plurality, the social— in order to show that, far from articulating the limits to domination, they are instead its supports. Although we intend to show that this analysis is one-sided, indeed, that Foucault is caught up in the very standpoint of the modality of power that he analyzes (strategic reason), it is nevertheless clear that no theory of civil society can ignore his contribution if it is to avoid apology.

Despite important differences, Foucault's analysis of the specificity of modern society builds on a core insight of Marx: Modernity involves the emergence of a new and pervasive form of domination and stratification. This is not to suggest that Foucault operates within the Marxist universe of discourse; indeed, the dialectic, economic determinism, historical materialism, the base/superstructure model, the concern with ideology, the strategy of immanent critique, and the focus on class struggle are all absent from his work.[2] He explicitly abandons this discourse for several reasons. First, the Marxian focus on the economy yields an inadequate account of power relations—neither the forms, the strategies, nor the actual functioning of power can be located in the economy or placed in a subordinate position relative to it.[3] Second, the dialectical theory of history that postulates the emancipatory potential of a macrosubject capable of totalizing local resistances into a revolutionary political movement that could end societal domination once and for all is deeply misguided and dangerously utopian.[4] Moreover, totalizing theory in any of its guises is both a hindrance to research and politically disadvantageous. According to Foucault, global, systematizing theory tends to gloss over the details, local forms, and specificity of the mechanisms of power, while at the same time holding everything in its place instead of loosening the tight grip of unitary discourses on our thinking.[5] Foucault does not reject Marxism for the sake of emphasizing the positive achievements of modern civil society. On the contrary, he does so in order to provide a superior account of the new kinds of power relations that pervade social life far more thoroughly and extensively than Marx imagined possible.

Foucault does not use the term "civil society," but he does presuppose the differentiation between state and society that, according to Marx, was the hallmark of modernity.[6] Moreover, like Marx, he argues that the locus of modern power relations is society, independent of and distinct from the sovereign state. Foucault does not reduce society to its economic substructure, nor does he see class relations as the paradigmatic form of power relations or struggle in modern society. Instead, he takes the Marxian insight into the "anatomy" of civil society a step further;[7] just as Marx discovered power relations in the factory, constituted and concealed by the juridical niceties of the labor contract, Foucault uncovers asymmetric relations of power in the other key institutions of modern society: hospitals, schools, prisons, asylums, armies, the family, and so on. Indeed, what Marx claims regarding exchange relations and contract law is, according to Foucault, true of all juridical forms and all the major institutions of modern society: Norm, legality, and rights go together with discipline, power relations, and subjugation:

Historically the process by which the bourgeoisie became in the course of the eighteenth century the politically dominant class was masked by the establishment of an explicit, coded, and formally egalitarian juridical framework, made possible by the organization of a parliamentary, representative regime. But the development and generalization of disciplinary mechanisms constituted the other, dark side of these processes. The general juridical form that guaranteed a system of rights that were egalitarian in principle was supported by these tiny, everyday, physical mechanisms, by all those systems of micropower that are essentially nonegalitarian, and asymmetric that we call the disciplines. And although . . . the representative regime makes it possible . . . for the will of all to form the fundamental authority of sovereignty, the disciplines provide, at the base, a guarantee of the submission of forces and bodies. *The real, corporeal disciplines constituted the foundation of the formal, juridical liberties.*[8] (Our emphasis)

Thus, Foucault also looks behind the juridical relations of liberal democratic regimes and an apparently egalitarian market society to the systematic (nonaccidental) forms of domination within society. Indeed, a central concern of Foucault's project is to dispose once and for all with what he calls "the juridical model of power" that still dominates our thinking, in order to direct our attention (and resistance) to the subtle yet pervasive form of power typical of modern societies that escapes articulation in juridical terms.[9] Since the fate of the categories of civil society is bound up with the contrast he sets up between the two models of power, it is well worth looking into them.

According to Foucault, the juridical model of power and the legal edifice of our own society are inherited from the ancien régime. The revitalization of Roman law begun in the twelfth century, together with the discourses of sovereignty, legitimacy, and rights, played a constitutive role in establishing the absolute power and authority of the monarchy. Right, according to Foucault, is, in the West, the king's right. Even when the juridical discourse turns against the monarch's control (in the name, for example, of preserving feudal rights or of establishing individual rights against the state), it is always the limits of this sovereign power that are put in question, its prerogatives that are challenged. Whether the juridical discourse of right was aimed at limiting or assuring the absolute character of the king's power, its aim was to constitute power as his right. "The essential role of the theory of right, from medieval times onwards, was to fix the legitimacy of power; that is the major problem around which the whole theory of right and sovereignty is organized."[10] Sovereignty, in short, is defined in juridical terms, while law constitutes power as the legitimate right of sovereignty.

In part, of course, this juridical construction served to efface the domination intrinsic to power, making the latter appear as the legitimate right of the sovereign and involving the legal obligation to obey it. In part, it also served as the instrument and justification for constructing large-scale administrative monarchies. Accordingly, the juridical does articulate the form in which power was exercised under absolute monarchies, that is, the relationship between sovereign and subject.[11] Indeed, the juridical model articulates a specific conception of the ways in which power is exercised: It is based on a model of power that operates through the mechanisms of law, taboo and censorship, limits, obedience and transgression.

Whether one attributes to it the form of the prince who formulates rights, of the father who forbids, of the censor who enforces silence, or of the master who states the law, in any case one schematizes power in a juridical form, and one defines its effects as obedience. Confronted by a power that is law, the subject who is constituted as subject—who is "subjected"— is he who obeys. . . . A legislative power on the one side, an obedient subject on the other.[12]

In short, the model of power corresponding to the juridical is repressive. Accordingly, power appears to be "strangely restrictive": It is poor in resources, sparing of its methods, monotonous in the tactics it utilizes. The only force it has is the force of the negative, a power to say no—it posits limits, it does not produce. This power is incapable of doing anything except preventing what it dominates from doing anything but what it is permitted to do. As such, sovereign power is indeed limited, insofar as it involves the right over life and death only vis-à-vis the exercise of the right to kill or refrain from killing, to let live or to take life. It is no accident that the symbol of such power is the sword, for the juridico-political model of power was indeed exercised as a means of deduction, a subtraction mechanism, as a right to appropriate a portion of wealth, a tax on products, goods, services, labor, and blood levied on the subjects. Such a form of power silences, represses, forbids, takes, seizes, but that is all.[13]

Needless to say, it is Foucault's central thesis that the new type of power that began to develop in the seventeenth and eighteenth centuries and became globalized and perfected in the nineteenth and twentieth is incompatible with the relations of sovereignty and is in every aspect the antithesis of the mechanism of power described by the theory of sovereignty. The new type of disciplinary power, one of the great inventions of bourgeois society (sic),[14] is irreducible to the representation of law: The juridical cannot serve as its system of representation.[15] Nor can the model of repression account for the mode, techniques, or exercise of this form of power. Nevertheless, this model continues to hold sway today, in part as an ideology of right, in part as the organizing principle of the legal codes Europe acquired in the nineteenth century.[16] It remains hegemonic in the field of political theory, informing both the liberal and the radical democratic versions of contractarianism.

Indeed, in a way quite reminiscent of Marx (and Carl Schmitt), Foucault scoffs at liberal political theory that sees in the universal legalisms of society (in formal equality, rights, and parliamentary democracy) limits imposed by a free societal community (composed of sovereign individuals) on the exercise of power. The contractarian illusion that power can be made visible, localized, and restricted to the political state whose boundaries are clearly delimited by the rights of juridical subject, of course had a role to play in the construction of the model of parliamentary democracy in opposition to the administrative, authoritarian, absolutist monarchies. But it remains prisoner of the juridical model of power first erected by these monarchies: Eighteenth-century contractarian criticism of the monarchy was not aimed against the juridical system but rather spoke in the name of a purer and more rigorous legality to which all the mechanisms of power would conform. "Political criticism availed itself, therefore, of all the juridical thinking that had accompanied the development of the monarchy, in order to condemn the latter; but it did not challenge the principle which held that law had to be the very form of power, and that power always had to be exercised in the form of law."[17] Neither the Rousseauian, radical democratic transposition of sovereignty from the king to the people nor the liberal idea of rights antecedent to government transcends the juridical conception of power, the doctrine of sovereignty, or the concern with legitimacy—both assume that the rule of law and the codification of rights render power legitimate and controllable. Both discuss power in terms of the state, sovereignty, consent, contract, and rights, implying that power is visible, localizable in one place, limitable, and to be exercised in accordance with a fundamental lawfulness.

The very idea of a contract among individuals that establishes legitimate power by limiting it through law and rights construes power as an original right of sovereignty that is given up, when political society is established, to the artificial sovereign. This model construes oppression as the transgression of the limits of the terms of the contract. The right to rebel against power that has transgressed its limits, thereby violating the rights of another, is the right to reestablish legitimate, juridically bound power. Accordingly,

the representation of power has remained under the spell of monarchy. In political thought and analysis, we still have not cut off the head of the king. Hence the importance that the theory of power gives to the problem of right and violence, law and illegality, freedom and will, and especially the state and sovereignty (even if the latter is questioned insofar as it is personified in a collective being and no longer a sovereign individual). To conceive of power on the basis of these problems is to conceive of it in terms of a historical form that is characteristic of our societies: the juridical monarchy. Characteristic yet transitory. For while many of its forms have persisted to the present, it has gradually been penetrated by quite new mechanisms of power that are probably irreducible to the representation of law.[18]

Foucault's point is, of course, that this model of power is anachronistic. But why is it still accepted? Apart from the historical reasons mentioned above, Foucault mentions three other roles that the juridical plays in modern society. The first is clearly ideological, despite Foucault's rejection of the notion of ideology. For he states many times that the discourse of law and rights masks the operations of power by diverting us from attending to the newly emerging discourses of the disciplines themselves, and by concealing the mechanisms of disciplinary power that operate outside, underneath, and through the law. It orients us, in other words, to questions of legitimacy and illegitimacy rather than issues of struggle and submission, to relations of sovereignty rather than domination:

The theory of sovereignty, and the organization of a legal code centered upon it, have allowed a system of right to be superimposed upon the mechanisms of discipline in such a way as to conceal its actual procedures, the element of domination inherent in its techniques, and to guarantee to everyone, by virtue of the sovereignty of the State, the exercise of his proper sovereign rights.[19]

In reality, the disciplines have their own discourse, which is not that of norms but of normalization. The discourse of rights conceals the far more important disciplinary discursivity. Here, the relation of the discourse of right to actual power relations is one of form and content. Modern society, then, from the nineteenth century up to our own day, has been characterized, on the one hand, by a legislation, a discourse, and an organization based on public right, whose principle of articulation is the social body and the delegative status of each citizen; and, on the other hand, by a closely linked grid of disciplinary coercions whose purpose is in fact to assure the cohesion of this same social body. The former anachronistic yet useful normative discourse of right and sovereignty disguises the new power relations of modernity.[20]

Foucault does, of course, discuss a new, modern development of the discourse and organization of law and right. But, as Habermas has pointed out, the reorganization of right that Foucault stresses has nothing to do with normative developments internal to law since the eighteenth century or with the explosion of civil rights in our century.[21] Not only does Foucault entirely neglect the development of normative structures in connection with the modern formation of power, but his discussion of "the juridical" as integral to "feudal monarchic" power misses the differences between the old conception of privileges and the modern conception of rights. Indeed, he seems to believe that the modern structures of right that are constitutive of the various domains of civil society and of the new relation between citizens and the public sphere are essentially the same as under absolutist regimes. Apparently, we are to conclude from his analysis that concern with the procedural principles of democratic legitimacy—with civil, political, and social rights—in short, with constitutionalism, is a relic from the period of absolutism:[22]

We have entered a phase of juridical regression in comparison with the pre-seventeenth century societies we are acquainted with; we should not be deceived by all the Constitutions framed throughout the world since the French Revolution, the Codes written and revised, a whole continual and clamorous legislative activity: These were the forms that made an essentially normalizing power acceptable.[23]

If right serves solely to establish the legitimacy of sovereign power, simultaneously concealing domination, then Foucault's strategy seems to be the demystification of former in order to make the latter visible.

But the discourse of rights and the juridical conception of power have another function. It is not only the ideological cover for a new form of domination, but is constitutive of the latter: "The system of right, the domain of the law, are permanent agents of these relations of domination, these polymorphous techniques of subjugation. Right should be viewed, I believe, not in terms of a legitimacy to be established, but in terms of the methods of subjugation that it instigates."[24] As indicated earlier, the real, corporeal disciplines constitute the foundation of the formal, juridical liberties.

Indeed, what the new, nonanachronistic (nonnormative) development of the juridical discourse and form entails is its "colonization" by the procedures of normalization, by the empirical disciplines from sociology and medicine to psychology. Individual rights, individualizing law, and the penetration of the old normative structure of law by the disciplines turn law itself into an effective medium of, and a partner in, the disciplining, normalizing techniques of domination, despite the ultimate heterogeneity of the levels of discipline and sovereignty.[25] Moreover, it is precisely these nonnormative developments within law and legal discourses that implicate it in the modern structure of power. The use of medical, psychological, sociological expertise, of statistical data, in short, of empirical information and nonlegal languages within legal discourse to make one's case, is proof that the disciplines have penetrated the juridical structures and rendered them positive, empirical, functional, and quasi-disciplinary themselves. Thus, law does not necessarily fade into the background in the nineteenth and twentieth centuries, but it now *operates more and more in the service of normalization* as the juridical institution is incorporated into a continuum of apparatuses (medical, administrative, etc.) whose functions are for the most part *regulatory*.[26]

The idea of the constitutive role of law vis-à-vis subjugation is evocative of the old Marxian-functionalist critique of rights and juridical forms. Here, too, the juridical structures are constitutive of the modern modality of power, and the juridical subject appears not as the limit to, but as the effect of, power. The analogy with the labor contract as the legal form that encodes, conceals, and constitutes the asymmetric power relations in the sphere of production is strong indeed. However, for Foucault, the modern forms of power do not contradict or violate the egalitarian norms of civil society but are, rather, their foundation. This normalizing function of an increasingly positivist and empirical conception of colonized law is quite absent in Marx. Hence, unlike some versions of Marxism, Foucault argues that the normative principles of civil society cannot serve as the referent for a critique of domination or provide valid orientations for social movements that might seek to realize them more fully. Insofar as they remain normative, the principles of right, the rule of law, legitimacy, etc., are anachronistic; insofar as law becomes colonized by the disciplines and, as it were, empirical, it serves domination. In short, Foucault explicitly rejects the path of immanent critique.

The third reason for the persistence of the juridical model of power given by Foucault is quasi-psychological. The contract model construes power as a mere limit on one's desires or freedom— legitimate power is itself limited vis-à-vis rights and freedoms that are reserved to the people. On this model, we remain free to do what the law does not proscribe. Power as a pure limit on freedom implies that a measure of freedom (negative liberty) remains intact. Indeed, this is the general form of its acceptability in our society. Thus, the social-psychological explanation of the seductiveness of the juridical model of power is predicated on the fact that "power is tolerable only on condition that it mask a substantial part of itself. Its success is proportional to its ability to hide its own mechanisms. Would power be accepted if it were entirely cynical?"[27]

While this explanation sounds suspiciously like a theory of legitimation, Foucault would reject such an interpretation. The juridical model of power is not the legitimating discourse of disciplinary power but a diversionary tactic; the discourses of the disciplines are quite different. While we shall show that, despite his disclaimers, Foucault needs a theory of legitimation and in statements like the one above does indeed bring the concept back into his framework, this is hardly the way he would wish to be interpreted. Far from leading us to analyze questions of legitimacy, consent, sovereignty, and obedience, he wants to steer us in the opposite direction, to make us look directly at domination/subjugation in its material instances, in its positive real forms and techniques. Indeed, the entire preoccupation with the normative distinction between legitimate and illegitimate power, questions of justice, the discourse of rights, and so on, must be abandoned and replaced with a reverse mode of analysis, one that starts with the microtechniques of domination in the local disparate regions of society rather than a conception of sovereign power, the state, and legitimacy.[28]

For this, however, a different concept of power is needed. If the juridical model was useful for representing a power centered around deduction and death, it is "utterly incongruous with the new methods of power whose operation is not ensured by right but by technique, not by law but by normalization, not by punishment but by control, methods that are employed on all levels and in forms that go beyond the state and its apparatus."[29] We are offered an analysis of this new modern type of power in *Discipline and Punish*, then in the series of essays collected in *Power/Knowledge*, and finally in the first volume of *The History of Sexuality*. Unlike the juridical model, which conceives of power as something that is possessed by an individual or a group, that is exchangeable and recoverable, subject to legal limits and dissolved by knowledge, truth, and authentic discourse, this disciplinary, normalizing power is conceived of above all as a relation of forces: It is exercised, not exchanged, and it operates through an intimate association with discourses of truth and the production of truth. Accordingly,

Power must be analyzed as something which circulates, or rather as something which only functions in the form of a chain. It is never localized here or there, never in anybody's hands, never appropriated as a commodity or a piece of wealth. Power is employed and exercised through a net-like organization. And not only do individuals circulate between its threads; they are always in the position of simultaneously undergoing and exercising this power.[30]

Moreover, far from being localized in one macroinstitution such as the state, power is coextensive with the social body—there are no spaces of primal liberty between its meshes. Rather, the relations of power are interwoven with other kinds of relations, including production, kinship, family, knowledge relations, sexuality, and the like. Power relations are, as it were, the immediate effects of the divisions, inequalities, and disequilibria that occur in the latter, and, conversely, they are the internal conditions of these differentiations. While power relations are sui generis,[31] emerging in dispersed, heterogeneous, localized arenas and exercised through a range of "microtechniques," they can be integrated into more global strategies and serve, for example, economic or state goals.

In short, Foucault replaces the juridical conception of power with a strategic model of a hostile asymmetric relation of forces.[32] Power is everywhere, not because it embraces everything, but because it comes from everywhere.[33] In addition, modern power is not exercised through prohibition and negation. Rather, it operates through a multiplicity of technologies of control, sorting, surveillance, and interrogation that are *productive*—of new discourses, knowledge, and truths, of new kinds of individuals or subjects, of required behaviors and functional results. Power relations are both intentional and nonsubjective, based on calculation and clearly decipherable logic and aims that are nonetheless anonymous.[34] Finally, there are no relations of power without resistances formed at the point where relations of power are exercised.

While this conception is certainly more profound than that of the liberal-legalistic model, Foucault is not the only one to view power in this way. One can find a not dissimilar positive-sum conception of power in the work of both Talcott Parsons and Niklas Luhmann.[35] However, Foucault does provide a compelling and detailed analysis of the two main forms in which this model of power came to be exercised, as well as a unique thesis regarding the relationship among knowledge, power, and truth that these entail. Disciplinary-normalizing power, geared to the subjugation of bodies and exercised through an "anatomo-politics of the human body," is analyzed in depth in *Discipline and Punish. The History of Sexuality,* on the other hand, focuses on regulatory-productive biopower, oriented to the control of populations—their health, life expectancy, and longevity—exercised through a "biopolitics of the population." While not identical, these two forms of power, emerging in the seventeenth and eighteenth centuries respectively, constituted the two poles around which the productive organization of power over life was deployed.[36] Each one developed a specific range of techniques, type of discursivity, and knowledge, and each resulted in a specific product: the soul, the docile body, and man in the first case; the desiring individual and sexuality in the second.

The new human sciences of criminology, medicine, psychology, education, sociology, education, etc., come together with the new techniques of surveillance, examination, sorting, individualizing, and normalizing to constitute discipline. It is through disciplines/disciplining that the body is diminished as a political force at the least cost and maximized as a useful force.[37] These forms of knowledge and power techniques also constitute the soul as the product of the judgmental gaze of teachers, doctors, educators, prison guards, and social workers. The effect of disciplinary power/ knowledge is thus man as knowable, calculable, normal, useful.

Biopower also operates through discursivity, produces new types of individuals, and results in knowledge that is linked to a regime of power. The discursive explosion with regard to sexuality that erupted in the eighteenth century and constituted individuals as desiring subjects also made use of techniques that emerged in disparate settings. Foucault cites the confessional techniques developed within monasteries and perfected by psychology and the gathering of statistical information by the police on the wealth, manpower, productive capacity, and health of the population. He also discusses the corresponding human sciences—especially demography, medicine, biology, psychiatry, psychology, ethics, pedagogy, and urbanology—that focused on birth and death rates, life expectancy, fertility, and patterns of diet and habitation and instigated a ceaseless discussion about the details of sexual behavior. These new forms of knowledge constitute the people as a population to be regulated and controlled in the name of increasing its life, productivity, wealth, and utility. They also constitute the individual as a desiring sexual being whose secret longings must be ferreted out, made to speak, and channeled in the proper (useful) direction through processes of self-interrogation aided, of course, by experts. Thus, sex stands at the center of the new techniques of life. Here, too, what is at issue "is the type of power it brought to bear on the body and sex. In point of fact, this power had neither the form of the law nor the effects of the taboo. On the contrary, it acted by multiplication of singular sexualities . . . it extended the various forms of sexuality."[38] The new sexualities that appear—infantile sexuality, the perversions, the hysterical woman—and that haunt the spaces of the home, the school, the prison, "all form the correlate of exact procedures of power."[39] In the process sex itself becomes constituted as a problem for truth and the target of an immense (medical/psychological) apparatus for producing the truth about ourselves.

These analyses of the forms of modern power relations are both instructive and compelling. What is questionable, however, is the theoretical presuppositions of the genealogical method of analyzing power and its implications for a theory of modernization and of modern civil society. Since our main interest is the latter, we shall only briefly touch on the former.

The Genealogy of Modern Civil Society

The Philosophical and Normative Ambiguities of Genealogy

The philosophical presuppositions of what Foucault calls humanism serve as the main contrast to his own genealogical approach. The idea that there is a human soul or self, subjectivity, an inner human nature (either as a desiring sexual being or as an autonomous sovereign subject), or an essence of man that is universal, that can serve as the ground of the basic values of autonomy, equality, freedom, and life, and that disinterested knowledge can express and liberate is rejected by Foucault in his masterful critique of the very concept of man in *The Order of Things*. Both the subject/object duality and foundationalist assumptions at the core of humanism lead to unresolvable antinomies. But this is not all. The genealogy of the modern soul presented in *Discipline and Punish* goes beyond the philosophical critique to reveal that the very notions of subjectivity, the soul, the self, autonomy, and normativity (always interpreted as normalization) are the products of disciplinary power/knowledge.[40] Accordingly, Foucault warns us against the misconception that knowledge can exist independently of the interests of power, or only where power relations are suspended. There is, on the genealogical analysis, no knowledge that does not presuppose and at the same time constitute power relations.[41] The human sciences, the disciplines, yield the objective knowledge of man, the soul, the subject, and the individual required by disciplinary power.

The same holds true for the subject side of the equation and for discursivity. The idea that intensive self-interrogation and speaking or communicating the truth that we have discovered about ourselves to others is the road to self-mastery, authenticity, and liberation from repression is as naive as the idea of disinterested objective knowledge. Far from dissolving the effects of power, the authentic individual who speaks the truth about herself, her desires, needs, identity, innermost concerns, is the product of confessional power techniques. The genealogical account of sexuality aims to show that the hermeneutic subject is the historical product of a power/knowledge regime that functions in and through discourse. Genealogy analyzes the discursive techniques of the constitution of subject-selves who probe their own depth (through self-interrogation) and speak/confess the truths discovered thereby. The rituals of confessional discourse involve the actual or virtual presence of a partner who stands as the authority prescribing and appreciating the confession, judging, punishing or forgiving, and consoling the person who articulates it.[42] Thus, not only the objectifying discourses of the social sciences, but also the subjectifying discourses by and about ourselves, are, on the genealogical analysis, deeply connected to power. Far from having an affinity with freedom, or with universality, reason, and truth, they are imbued with relations of power and are always historically specific. Accordingly, Foucault sees his genealogical investigations as part of a "political history of truth."[43] Knowledge, truth, reason, and power are intertwined and context-relative; genealogical investigations into fields of knowledge, types of normativity, forms of subjectivity, individual and collective identities reveal the technologies of power whereby truth, knowledge, and identity are produced.

The problems with this Nietzschean stance vis-à-vis norms, reason, and truth have been pointed out many times. We shall mention only a few of the most frequent objections that bear on the normative dimensions of our concept of civil society.

First, there is the problem of the normative ambiguity of Foucault's genealogical account of normativity. Are we to take this to be one among many critiques of the foundationalist metainterpretation of humanist values, or is it aimed at the substantive core of these values themselves? If the latter is the case, and the other aspects of genealogy to be explored below indicate that it is, then Foucault is left in the paradoxical position of having to deny any normative status for his own critical analyses or of being unable to justify the normative political implications of his work.[44]

Second, if one takes Foucault at his word regarding the power-relatedness of truth, then the obvious question arises: What is the status of the "truths" revealed by Foucault's own genealogical investigations? Which interests, what strategies, what form of power relations does Foucault stand for?[45]

Third, isn't the claim that all knowledge and rationality itself derive from the practices of power based on an undifferentiated concept of power? Are all power relations the same? What exactly is the difference between power and domination, if there is any?[46] The obfuscation in Foucault's concept of power lies, according to Habermas, in its concealed derivation from the concept of the will to knowledge.[47] And this, in turn, rests on an ambiguous *use* of the category "power." As Habermas points out, Foucault's use of the concept of power reproduces the "transcendental-empirical ambiguity" that he relentlessly uncovers in the humanist conception of man: On the one hand, it is used descriptively in the empirical analyses of power technologies; on the other, it is a basic concept within a theory of constitution.[48] The first explains the functional social context of the sciences of man; the second, the condition of possibility of scientific discourse about man. But doesn't the genealogical approach that claims to do both of these at once simply replace the objectivism of the human sciences with a radically historicist subjectivism?[49] And doesn't the transcendental-empirical ambiguity in his concept of power lead Foucault to overgeneralize and even ontologize power relations?[50] Moreover, doesn't the equation of reason, knowledge, and discourse with the rationality of domination derive from this ontologizing of power and involve a reductionist, one-sided, strategic-instrumental conception of reason itself?[51]

A fourth objection to genealogical assumptions is that the concept of the relativity of truth to a (power) regime is ultimately incoherent. On the relativity thesis, the transformation from one regime to another cannot yield a gain in truth, nor can there be liberating transformations within a regime. There is no such thing as truth independent of its regime, since each regime produces its own truth. But what, then, is the meaning of Foucault's claim that the truth manufactured by power is its mask, disguise, that is, untruth?[52] Does one untruth simply cover over another? Or is the discourse of the disciplines truer than the juridical discourse?

Fifth, and finally, doesn't the very notion of power relations as Foucault uses it, namely, always with the qualification "inegalitarian," imply domination, and isn't this concept meaningless without its opposite, freedom?[53] Moreover, even if we grant the idea of power without a (global) subject, even if we recognize that there is always a strategic context in which power relations are embedded and which is not under the control of the actors, does it make sense to speak of strategies of power without projects, or of society in terms of anonymous relations of forces?[54] Foucault's insistence that power relations are inegalitarian and intentional, that there is no power without resistance, implies at least that there are specific interests involved in exercising and maintaining power, and specific victims whose interests lie in overturning power relations. But whose interests are involved in the development and maintenance of disciplinary-regulatory modern power relations? Once these are in place, how is resistance possible in the carceral civil society, and in the name of what does one resist? It is time to turn to these questions.

The Genealogical Account of Modernization

According to Foucault, the historical processes that constituted the social sphere in which the modern individual lives have deprived the ideal of the autonomous sovereign subject of any progressive content[55] and have denuded social institutions of any autonomous solidarity or horizontal relations. Neither the concept of the individual nor the norms, structure, or dynamics of civil society can be understood as a gain in freedom or serve as a referent for emancipatory politics. We shall return to this theory of modern individuality and sociality, but first it is worth looking briefly at the historical "genealogy" of modern society that is clearly meant to replace the materialist theory of history and deprive critics of its reassuring dialectic.

Discipline and Punish, the first book in which Foucault presents his theory of power, also provides the clearest statement of his genealogical theory of modernization, that is, of the transformation involved in shaping our contemporary "carceral," "disciplinary" society.[56] Although the book focuses on the genealogy of the modern prison, it is clearly meant to be taken as exemplary for a wide range of homologous changes that characterize the transition from the "classical age" (the age of absolutism or, more generally, the ancien régime) to modern society (late eighteenth century to the present).[57] For it is Foucault's thesis that the asymmetric power relations and the techniques of learning about and disciplining bodies that were perfected in the prison now pervade an ever broader range of contemporary societal institutions and affect everyone. Indeed, "the carceral archipelago transported this technique from the penal institution to the entire social body."[58] Thus, the genealogy of the modern prison reveals a modality of power that is all-pervasive in modern civil society.

The innovations in Foucault's genealogical account of modernity do not lie in the specific epochs outlined in the historical trajectory he traces.[59] These epochs are quite standard in modernization theory. We are, in short, presented with descriptions of two societal types and a transitional period between them: traditional society or the "ancien régime," composed of the society of orders and the absolutist state[60] (seventeenth to nineteenth centuries), and modern society, emerging in the eighteenth century and developed throughout the twentieth. The transitional period is dealt with by analyzing the theories of the Enlightenment and the reformers' discourse preceding and during the French revolution.

Nor is Foucault's assessment of these changes in terms of a replacement of one form of domination with another particularly new or shocking, despite the challenge it poses to standard liberal accounts (contractarian or enlightenment theories). Indeed, at first sight, the similarities of Foucault's approach with at least one important stream within sociological theories of modernization are striking.[61] The red thread of Foucault's text is the theme of the emergence of the modern individual as the story of a new and pervasive form of domination evolving through two interrelated processes: the destruction of traditional group solidarities and the fragmentation or leveling of peoples, orders, and coherent social groups; and the consolidation of disciplinary techniques of surveillance and control of bodies that fabricate a new form of individuality whose illusion of sovereignty is the counterpart to the absence of any autonomous group life or group identity, meaningful traditions, forms of association, or power resources. The only serious difference on the level of content between this version of modernization and that of Tocqueville or Nisbet, for example, is that the latter attribute the leveling, individualizing form of power primarily to the emergence of the modern state, while Foucault sees it as the result of a multiplicity of institutional forces or developments in society, economy, and polity. For both (as well as for Marx), however, modern civil society is nevertheless that colonized terrain where solidarity, association, group autonomy, and spontaneity have been replaced by a new form of social control.

To be sure, Foucault does not describe the contrast between the old regime and modern society in order to idealize the intermediary political bodies of the *Ständestaat*, which represented, for Tocqueville, at least, the crucial loci of political life that limited the administrative power of the state.[62] Indeed, there is no systematic distinction in Foucault's work between the type of political action within the framework of assemblies and the state action typical of administrative power relations.[63] It was precisely this sort of distinction, however, that led Tocqueville to seek modern equivalents for the old forms of association, autonomy, and counterpower—a search that is doomed to failure on Foucault's theory.[64]

Nor does Foucault assign positive value to the cultural traditions or the integrative functions ensured by the old intermediary bodies (as Nisbet did).[65] On the contrary, it is the opportunities for disorder in the interstices of the society of orders, during the absolutist period, for which Foucault seems to be nostalgic. Thus, what is pinpointed (and somewhat idealized) in Foucault's contrast between traditional and modern society is neither the political life of the aristocracy nor the richly textured and communally integrated traditions of the social orders or semiautonomous regions, but the incomplete control, regulation, organization, and disciplining of society in the premodern period and the spaces for solidarity and spontaneous rebellion that this created. It is this relative absence of efficient control that contrasts so sharply with the inexorable organization, discipline, and surveillance techniques of modernity. And it is here that the originality of Foucault's treatment lies.[66]

Foucault's thesis is that the specific nature of the exercise and modality of absolutist power encouraged the emergence of popular revolts. This thesis is demonstrated through an analysis of the form and meaning of punishment in absolutist regimes. On the one hand, the "supplice" or public torture and execution of the criminal symbolize the absolute power of the sovereign to codify the lack of power of his subjects.[67] Publicity, visibility, and the light of appearance are all the exclusive attributes of the sovereign—the means to express and represent his personal power and his monopolization and control of the public space. Sovereign power, as indicated above, is a mixture of repression and juridical control— the sovereign is he who makes, and therefore is above, the law.[68] The discourse of rights here is the discourse of this power—of jurisdiction and immunity.[69] The power of the sovereign is the power to silence, banish, punish, and annihilate those who transgress his law. Crime is seen as an attack on the will and body of the omnipresent sovereign, that is, as an act of war or treason.[70] Punishment, as the ceremony of sovereign power that marks the body of the offender, restores and reconstitutes sovereignty. It reveals the force, terror, and vengeance of a power that is personal and arbitrary, that is made public through its periodic expenditure, yet—and this is the key—is discontinuous in time and space.

Discontinuous in two senses. First, within the framework of the society of orders, the phenomena of rights and immunities (in Foucault's terminology, illegalities) constitute a source of counterpower and autonomous group solidarity for the privileged, signifying the nonpervasiveness and incompleteness of sovereign power. But Foucault is far more interested in another type of discontinuity or "illegality," namely, that of the least favored stratum—the people. The lower orders had no positive privileges, but they benefited from a space of toleration gained "by force or cunning" in which illegality, or the possibility of acting outside of, or of ignoring, law and custom was regularly practiced: "Roughly speaking, one might say that, under the ancien régime, each of the different social strata had its margin of tolerated illegality: the nonapplication of the rule, the nonobservance of the innumerable edicts or ordinances were a condition of the political and economic functioning of society."[71] This tolerance of illegality was a sign not of sovereign beneficence but of the discontinuity of monarchic power. It was tied to the relatively weak penetration of the social body by this power and, correspondingly, to the existence of spaces within society for the emergence of autonomous solidarities and revolts.

Indeed, next to the monopoly of publicity and action by the only real individual, the sovereign, there was another form of action and publicity available to the people, namely, the riot and the revolt. This is the other side of the supplice. The necessary presence of the people at public executions provided the occasion for constituting centers of illegality in the very exercise of sovereign vengeance. The spectator, the guarantor of punishment, could, in other words, turn rebel and challenge punitive power.[72] It is here, in the carnival-like inversion of rules, in the mockery of authority, and in the transformation of the criminal into a hero,[73] that Foucault situates the link between illegality, the spontaneous solidarity of a whole segment of the population (vagrants, the poor, beggars, etc.), and revolt. This spontaneity of the assembled populace is the uncontrolled and unmastered referent of the very exercise of sovereign power. Their resistance to central control is indicative of still intact local autonomy, cultural traditions, and moral resources for constituting collective identities and solidarities opposed to the sovereign's project of monopolizing power. These popular solidarities were glorified in the broadsheets and pamphlets meant to degrade them;[74] as spaces for popular illegalities left open by the discontinuous form of sovereign power, they became the target of the new, modern modality of discipline and surveillance.

Foucault's description of sovereign power is strikingly similar to Habermas's analysis of prebourgeois *repräsentative Öffentlichkeit*. Both focus on the public display of magnificence and might, on the demonstrative dimension of the excesses of sovereignty, on the show of force as representative of power, and on the codification of its monopoly by the sovereign. But an analysis of the other side of "public power" in the old regime, of the "illegalities" and broadsheets of the popular classes, of the interrelation between representative publicity and the publicity available to the people, is not to be found in Habermas's study. This is a major omission. Habermas, conversely, analyzes two additional dimensions of publicity within absolutist society that are strangely underemphasized in Foucault's account: the emerging administrative apparatus of the state characterized by the term "public office," and the development of the "bourgeois public sphere" in the cafés, salons, literary clubs, newspapers, and so on, of the eighteenth century.[75] In Habermas's study, as we have seen, these prefigure important dimensions of public freedom in modern society insofar as the modern principle of democratic legitimacy and the conception of public office as public service, implying accountability, have their origins here.

Foucault is certainly aware of the state-making processes under the old regime, but his emphasis is quite different from Habermas's.[76] Foucault points out that it was the emerging centralized apparatus of public administration that began gathering "useful" information—demographic data on births, deaths, health, crime, poverty, welfare and so on—on an increasingly leveled (from the state's point of view) population, turning the sovereign's subjects into objects of knowledge and power. This knowledge was intimately connected with a new form of disciplinary power ("biopower") emerging within the administrative agencies of the state alongside the juridical discourses of sovereignty and legitimacy.

Nevertheless, Foucault insists repeatedly that the new technologies of power cannot be comprehended either through juridical concepts, as a relation between sovereign and subjects, or in terms of the opposition between state and society. For the state is not their sole or even primary source; rather, they emerged slowly in a wide range of institutions (the convent, the army, the clinic, the school, the factory, the prison) alongside the visible play of sovereignties in the absolutist period. These processes constitute for Foucault the birth of the modern within the womb of the old society. Accordingly, there is no need to emphasize the new form of the state as a hierarchy of *public* offices, nor to mention its counterpart—the new forms of bourgeois publicity that emerge within civil society, with their specific projects of liberalization and democratization. The public, impersonal, rule-bound character of state bureaucracies does nothing to diminish or restrict the reach or scope of administrative power; on the contrary, it makes it more efficient. And presumably the claims made for the bourgeois public sphere are sufficiently dealt with as part of the reformer's discourse. In our view, this is an error fraught with consequences, for it is precisely the new forms of publicity, association, and rights emerging on the terrain of modern civil society that will become the key weapons in the hands of collective actors seeking to limit the reach of state and other societal forms of disciplinary power.

As a consequence of the theoretical decision to restrict the concept of sovereignty as a form of power to the old regime, Foucault in effect agrees with those reformers who focus exclusively on its juridical dimensions (on the proper locus of power and on its legality and legitimacy), only to declare the entire discourse to be anachronistic. The discussion of rights, contract, popular sovereignty, and similar topics is, accordingly, nothing more than a facile inversion or imputation of the king's attributes to "the people." Instead of the representative publicity of the king's power, publicity, as claimed by reformers for the people, is to be the expression of their newly acquired sovereignty and their mode of limiting state power (i.e., the law). This discourse is epiphenomenal, however, insofar as it occurs above the real loci of modern power relations.[77] The reformers' discussion of power in terms of the state, sovereignty, consent, contract, and rights implies that power is still public, localizable in one place, and limitable. The liberal juridical concept of power, in other words, misses the essence of the new mode of domination. To focus on the edifice of rights and publicity embodied in constitutions and parliaments, to stress the development and democratization of the state, is to be deceived regarding the real dynamics of power in modern societies.

Accordingly, Foucault argues that the discourse of reform in the transitional period—the conception of a transparent power that finds its legal limit in the notion of human dignity, that punishes humanely with a view toward restoring rather than destroying the integrity of the criminal, together with the themes of sovereignty, consent, and legitimacy—constitutes a utopian model of society that is never, nor could ever be, institutionalized. This discourse has, nonetheless, certain not so unintended consequences. The most important of these is the shift in the "right" to punish from the sovereign monarch to "society." Leniency of punishment is indeed accomplished, but with the corollary that crime is seen no longer as an attack on the sovereignty of the monarch (i.e., the other) but rather as an attack on society as a whole (us), turning the offender into a "public enemy" or monster who must be rehabilitated in order to reemerge as a juridical and moral subject. "The society that has rediscovered its laws has lost the citizen who violated them."[78] In other words, once crime is seen as the violation of society's own laws, the solidarity between the popular illegalities and the criminal is severed. Indeed, the destruction of solidarity between the offender, the rebel, the criminal who refuses the law, and the population turns out to be the real target of the reformers' projects.[79] "The true objective of the reform movement, even in its most general formulations, was not so much to establish a new right to punish based on equitable principles, as to set up a new economy of the power to punish . . . so that it could be distributed in homogeneous circuits capable of operating everywhere, in a continuous way, down to the finest grain of the social body."[80]

Inserting the power to punish more deeply within the social body could accomplish two things: control of the popular illegalities, which had become too costly, and development of a more efficient economy of power. The dimension of the reformers' projects that suited this goal most admirably was, of course, the discovery of the advantages of disciplinary technologies. Bentham's panopticon speaks more loudly for Foucault than all the theories of legality, popular sovereignty, rights, and legitimacy. "The 'Enlightenment' which discovered the liberties also invented the disciplines."[81] Thus, on the one side, the reformers' discourse operates with representation, visibility, publicity (of trial and sentencing), and transparency of the power to punish and of the laws that define crimes and punishments appropriate to them. On the other side, a disciplinary technology is discovered that involves secret, continuous, and autonomous punishment processes—in short, a power that operates on the other side of legality, isolated from both the social body and juridical power. The juridical model reintegrates the juridical subject into society; the technological practice creates obedient subjects and docile bodies. For Foucault, then, it is not to a new form of publicity, legislation, and legality that we must look to find the seed of the modern in the transition from the old to the new regime. Rather, we should look to the new technologies of power developing in societal institutions and articulated in reform projects. The discourses worth attending to are those of the human sciences, which, together with the new disciplinary techniques, provide the means for constituting, learning about, and controlling the modern individual. There is one important new form of "publicity" worth noting, but it is not that of elections, legislation, rights, courts, and the like. Rather, it is the visibility of subjugated, individuated individuals before the eye of a now invisible power—a visibility at first of the inmate to the supervisors of closed institutions, but ultimately of the deviant before society at large.

The genealogical approach to "modernization" thus discounts as hopelessly naive any interpretation of the principles of civil society—legality, rights, plurality, publicity—as a basis for the emergence of spaces within modern society for new forms of autonomous association and solidarity. Foucault's vision of modern disciplinary power as complete and continuous and his (at times functionalist, at times constitutive) interpretation of rights as the anchors of this power keep him from recognizing that, like the immunities in an earlier period, modern civil and political liberties also secure spaces for autonomy, for association, for solidarities, and for the self-constitution of group life, new identities, and the development of counterpowers—the sine qua non for the resistance to biopower that he nevertheless believes is still possible. Moreover, Foucault's positivist attitude and his emphasis on the strategic dimension of the reformers' projects predispose him to view the new disciplinary technologies as the "real" innovation next to which the normative and symbolic principles of modern civil society appear as secondary—at best functional to, but ultimately irrelevant appurtenances of, disciplinary power.[82]

The above notwithstanding, Foucault's analysis of the emergence of modern society does not quite negate the thesis of differentiation as a key element of modernization. Indeed, his discussion of the genesis of the technologies of power and their globalization within contemporary society presupposes differentiation. As is well known, Foucault insists that a multiplicity of projects and interests came together to produce a new political economy of punishment, discipline, and control. He argues that Enlightenment philosophers and associated social groups contributed to this transformation but that "it was not they alone; in this overall project of a new distribution of the power to punish, and of a new distribution of its effects, many different interests came together."[83] Following Weber, Foucault argues that the specific disciplinary techniques were discovered independently and locally in distinct institutions such as the monastery, the army, the factory, and the prison. Of course, multiplicity is not the same as differentiation: Some of these are state institutions, others are societal. However, Foucault does differentiate between state and society when it comes to identifying the interests behind the globalization, if not the genesis, of the modern techniques of power. Indeed, despite disclaimers with regard to Marxian class theory and theories of state power, the two sets of interests involved in the globalization of disciplinary-regulatory power turn out to be those of the bourgeoisie and the administrative state. Let us consider each of these in turn.

Within the modernizing society of the old regime, there is one major set of interests behind the struggle against the arbitrary monarchic power and the society of orders: the concern of the bourgeoisie to abolish popular illegalities, especially vis-à-vis property rights.[84] According to Foucault, it was the need to protect accumulations of mercantile and industrial capital more than anything else that necessitated a severe repression of popular illegality.[85]

There emerged the need for a constant policing concerned essentially with this illegality of property. It became necessary to get rid of the old economy of the power to punish, based on the confused and inadequate multiplicity of authorities.... It became necessary to define a strategy and techniques of punishment in which an economy of continuity and permanence would replace that of expenditure and excess.[86]

In short, penal reform was essential for a capitalist market economy to emerge and to function; hence the struggle against the "superpower" of the sovereign, with its incalculabilities, and against the "infrapower" of acquired privileges and tolerated illegalities. Accordingly, within the confused sets of interests and goals involved in the transition from absolutism to modernity, Foucault stresses the importance of that new, differentiated structure, the capitalist market system, and its specific requirements.

The class interests of the bourgeoisie are also at stake in the development of the second dimension of the modern form of power: regulatory biopower. Here Foucault explicitly rejects the neo-Marxian thesis that the sexuality of the middle and especially lower classes had to be repressed because it was incompatible with a general and intensive work ethic.[87] "The primary concern was not repression of the sex of the classes to be exploited, but rather the body, vigor, longevity, progeniture, and descent of the classes that 'ruled.'"[88] Self-affirmation and the need to differentiate itself as a class from the unhealthy lower orders and the degenerate nobility are the interests at work in the investment of its own sex with a technology of power and knowledge that the bourgeoisie had itself invented. In part, this involved a transposition of caste manners of the nobility, based on blood, to the bourgeoisie in the guise of biological, medical, or eugenic precepts focused on bodily health, the indefinite extension of strength, vigor, and so on. Only later, in the second half of the nineteenth century, were the techniques of regulatory biopower generalized to the rest of the population. That is, only after the need developed for a stable and competent labor force and a secure technology of control was in place (through schooling, the politics of housing, public hygiene, institutions of relief and insurance, the general medicalization of the population), was the proletariat granted a body and a sexuality and were middle-class values imposed upon them. This does not challenge the main claim, however, "that *sexuality is originally, historically bourgeois.*"[89]

The place of the state and its interests is somewhat more ambiguous in Foucault's analysis. On the one hand, the critique of the sovereignty model was meant to steer us away from the state as a central locus of power or the key force in creating disciplinary techniques. On the other hand, most of the loci in which the technologies of disciplinary power did develop were (in France, Foucault's referent) state institutions: armies, schools, clinics, prisons, etc. Moreover, Foucault grants the immense importance of the development of a centralized organization of the police, "the most direct expression of royal absolutism."[90] For it is the state police who take over the previously fragmented functions of surveillance of criminality and economic and political supervision and unify these into a single administrative machine, assuring continuity of control. And this dimension of state sovereignty, at least, endures with the transition to modernity. While Foucault insists that the state is not the sole origin of disciplinary power, he grants that "the organization of the police apparatus in the eighteenth century sanctioned a generalization of the disciplines that became coextensive with the state itself."[91] In fact, the major function of the state apparatus was to ensure that discipline reigns over society as a whole.[92] This breadth of discipline along with the continuity of its exercise, potential or actual, are specific to modern domination. What has been said of the bourgeoisie can thus also be said of the state: The newly differentiated, centralized administrative state apparatuses also had an interest in abolishing the old, incalculable, and expensive personal forms of power and substituting its new techniques for them. The state, then, as a key actor in generalizing disciplinary power, does play a major role in Foucault's account of the transition to modernity.

The state's interests also play a central part in the globalization of biopower. The beginning of the eighteenth century saw a demographic upswing accompanied by an increase in wealth and an end to the great ravages of plagues and starvation; as a result, the societal preoccupation with death is replaced by a concern with managing life and accumulating people. Accordingly, the state becomes interested in gathering information about and controlling the health, wealth, manpower, resources, reproduction, and welfare of that new entity, "the population," as a means to increasing state power. Information gathering and supervision, involving a maximizing of collective and individual forces rather than a repression of disorder, was, it now turned out, a natural function for the police:

We must consolidate and augment, through the wisdom of its regulations, the internal power of the state; and since this power consists not only in the Republic in general, and in each of the members who constitute it, but also in the faculties and talents of those belonging to it, it follows that the police must concern themselves with these means and make them serve the public welfare. And they can only obtain this result through the knowledge they have of those different assets.[93]

The state's interest in the power-knowledge generated by the emerging disciplines for the purpose of administering and optimizing the life and utility of the populations under its control is thus paramount in the globalization of biopower.[94] Sex was at the heart of this political economy of population: "It was essential that the state know what was happening with its citizens' sex, and the use they made of it,"[95] because power is situated and exercised at the level of life, the species, the race, and the large-scale phenomena of population. Indeed, it is the new concern on the part of the state with life and population that marks a society's "threshold of modernity," according to Foucault.[96]

It seems to be Foucault's thesis, moreover, that by the late nineteenth century, the two forms of power—discipline and the regulation of populations—and the two great interests behind their globalization came together. These techniques came "to reveal their political usefulness and to lend themselves to economic profit . . . . All of a sudden, they came to be colonized and maintained by global mechanisms and the entire State system."[97] The apogee of this development is, obviously, the contemporary welfare state. Through its regulatory controls, the welfare state constitutes the social as a distinct object-domain of great "public" interest while simultaneously making use of the disciplinary, confessional techniques already perfected by societal disciplines and institutions to control it. On Foucault's account, however, it is not the logic of the economy or the state that penetrates and colonizes civil society. Functional reason, for Foucault, works the other way around: The institutions and practices of civil society generate the technologies of power that are then taken up and globalized by the state and the bourgeoisie.

This should provide a clue to resolving the ambiguity we have noted concerning the place of the state in Foucault's analysis of power relations. Because he insists on the decentralization and deinstitutionalization of power, yet identifies state apparatuses as key loci of disciplinary-regulatory power, commentators have come up with diametrically opposed interpretations of the place of the state in his overall analysis. Axel Honneth, among others, accuses Foucault of ignoring the state altogether by virtue of his decentralized concept of power.[98] Peter Dewes, however, asserts that, in analyzing the various disciplinary institutions of the asylum, clinic, and prison, "Foucault wishes to show that from the beginning intervention and administrative control have defined the modern state."[99] According to Dewes, Foucault is concerned to show that intervention in a societal domain by state agencies is a more fundamental characteristic of modern societies than an economy released from directly political relations of domination.[100] For one interpreter, the state plays no role at all in modern power relations; for the other, it is everything.

Foucault was questioned directly about this ambiguity. His response implied that the state, the economy, and society are three distinct elements within modern social systems, each of which has its power relations, disciplinary technologies, and modes of functioning.[101] Although the state (governmental administration)[102] does become a coordinating center for societal disciplinary power, although its administrative agencies do penetrate social institutions, these nevertheless retain specific internal power relations that have their own configuration and "relative autonomy."[103] The state, not qua sovereign but qua government,[104] does penetrate society, yet "it would be wrong to believe that the disciplinary functions were confiscated and absorbed once and for all by a state apparatus."[105] In short, Foucault maintains that the state cannot occupy the whole field of power relations and can operate only on the basis of already existing power relations connecting the family, knowledge, technology, the factory, sexuality, etc., to which the state relates as a superstructure. The state is one locus of disciplinary technology among many.

We might note that, like the modality of power he describes, Foucault's goal is to make visible not the state but society. And of course he is right in insisting that power relations are not exclusively located in, nor do they emanate from, any one place in modern society. Nevertheless, despite the elegance of some of his formulations, he does not resolve the dilemma articulated by his interpreters; he seems, rather, to validate both antinomic positions. But if the state is simply one locus of disciplinary power among others, then the very meaning of the modern state is lost, for the term refers to the differentiated entity that succeeds in monopolizing the (legitimate) means of war and violence and, in nonfederal polities, of administration as well. Such an "order" is hardly "one" among many. By using the thesis of decentralized power to deny state sovereignty, Foucault reproduces the position of the philosophical pluralists (although for opposite reasons) and opens himself to Carl Schmitt's objection that a state that is like any other association or organization of power in society is no state at all. If, conversely, the state is the coordinating mechanism of disciplinary power, if social institutions are the necessary supports and complements of state administration, if within societal institutions one finds homologous forms of domination, if, in short, "society" is equivalent to the field where administrative apparatuses have their play, then indeed the state, or at least its "logic" or modus operandi, is everywhere. But this is a convincing idea only with respect to the symbolic meaning of "totalitarian" regimes.[106]

Foucault is able to hold both positions because he sees state and society only from the point of view of strategic power relations.[107] Indeed, state, society, and economy are presented as three strategic fields with essentially the same internal dynamics and, as stated above, homologous technologies of power. Modernity is not characterized by a state that penetrates society or by socioeconomic powers that penetrate and control the state. Rather, it is constructed in terms of the penetration of each distinct realm by disciplinary technologies of power and strategic power relations. What this means is that state, economy, and society are differentiated from one another not in terms of any specific rationality of action, mode of integration, or forms of interaction but only, somehow, as separate sites of power. This is a differentiation that seems to make no difference.[108]

The Negativity of Civil Society and the Loss of the Social

Foucault presents us with a deeply disturbing analysis of the dark side of modern civil society. As indicated above, far from constituting an "increment in freedom" (Marx), the development of the components of civil society in modernity—a new form of individuality, subjectivity, rights, plurality, publicity, legality, and sociality— now appears as nothing but an effect of power relations. Civil society, in short, is equivalent to its negativity.

What is lost in this conception is a distinct concept of the social.[109] This is the real reason why Foucault gives us such an exceedingly one-dimensional discussion of rights and democracy.[110] We need to look again at Foucault's assessment of each of these key components of modern civil society to make our point.

We have already seen that for Foucault, the juridical subject is merely the support of disciplinary power. The modern legal *person* endowed with *rights* is a dimension of modern individuality that, far from indicating autonomy, is functional to, even the product of, disciplinary control. Through observation, continual surveillance, sorting, partitioning, ranking, examining, training, and judging, discipline creates the material counterpart of the juridical subject by investing the body with power relations.

But Foucault's genealogy of the modern individual does not restrict itself to revealing the underside of the "legal fiction" of the juridical subject; it extends to an attack on modern self-reflexive subjectivity as such.[111] Disciplinary practices objectify the subject and create sets of dichotomies, each side of which is an effect of power: mad/sane, sick/healthy, criminal/good citizen, abnormal/normal. What Hegel saw as the two key achievements of modern civil society—the abstract right of the legal person and the principle of subjective freedom of the moral subject whose intentions and will must be considered in any judgment of an act[112]— become in Foucault's hands the products of power relations. The moral subject is the result of the normalizing judgment that is exercised through surveillance, examination, and with the help of the objectifying sciences of man: criminology, sociology, medicine, psychology, psychiatry, statistics, demography, etc. Moreover, it is not through the "internalization" of values and norms that the "false consciousness" of the moral subject is created, nor can this subject be emancipated through the development of a "true" consciousness. Power does not stop where knowledge and self-reflection begin. Rather, knowledge, truth, subjectivity, and reflective consciousness are the coproducer and product of the objectifying disciplines. They constitute, together with the normalizing gaze of the guard, the doctor, and the teacher, a subject (subjected) object of power/knowledge.

The same holds true, of course, for the soul or psyche. These are not the products of an emancipatory process of self-understanding but of a "pastoral power" whose techniques of self-surveillance, self-interrogation, confession, and thereby self-constitution and self-discipline, initiated by the church, have become secularized and generalized in modern culture and society. Thus, the political axis of individualization has been reversed with the shift from feudal to modern society. Ascending individualization reflecting the power, privilege, and status of a family or group is replaced by a descending individualization that increases the visibility and singularity of those subjugated by and subjected to disciplinary techniques. In other words, as power becomes more anonymous and more functional, those on whom it is exercised tend to be more strongly individualized and made visible.[113] The modern individual is the combined effect of disciplinary and pastoral power—a self-monitoring subject who functions as his own soldier-priest.

This theory of individualization has clear consequences for the meaning and role of the new form of publicity specific to modern civil society. As the disciplines become deinstitutionalized and circulate freely in society,[114] "it is the dust of events, actions, behavior, opinions—'everything that happens'" that becomes visible, public to omnipresent surveillance by the faceless gaze of power.[115] Indeed, like the process of individualization, relations of public and private become inverted with the development of modern society. Instead of the spectacle of public representation of sovereign power, it is now the population who become visible to the "public" gaze, while power recedes into the background. This is, of course, the point of the panoptic metaphor. The shift in publicity from the punishment to the trial does not mean that the principles of dignity and moral freedom are respected, but rather that justice no longer takes public responsibility for the violence bound up with its practice. It also means that all of society, vicariously (through publicity) or directly, takes on the role of judge and engages in normalizing judgments. Even after the prison and punishment have been open to public scrutiny, the public remains complicitous with a technology of punishment that by definition yields visibility and control to the observer. For "discipline makes possible the operation of a relational power that sustains itself by its own mechanism and which for the spectacle of public events, substitutes the uninterrupted play of calculated gazes."[116] In place of the sovereign who displays his power, we have the carceral society displaying its disciplined subjects to the anonymous viewer. Thus, if the individual produced by disciplinary pastoral power approximates the soldier-priest, the public before whom the exercise of power is made visible is hardly distinguishable from the police.[117]

Accordingly, democratization, or the control by the public of administrative functioning, in no way limits power, as the liberal would have it, or generates a kind of power different from administrative control: It simply ensures its proper functioning. Democratic "control" of the disciplinary mechanisms through publicity entails accessibility to the great tribunal committees of the world. For Foucault, this simply means that anyone can come and see with her own eyes how schools, hospitals, factories, and prisons function.[118] Modern publicity provides no alternative, limit, or challenge to disciplinary and pastoral power.

Plurality, the third element in modern civil society hailed by its partisans, fares no better in Foucault's hands. It is simply reduced to the many loci of power relations and strategies, and the multiplicity of atomized individuals who are already products of knowledge-power relations. The discourse of these individuals, their "consensus," is as much an instrument of power relations as is the discourse of the modern sciences: It normalizes, and normatizes, while maintaining the object of power in subjection and as a potential actor only in the purely strategic sense. Thus, neither publicity nor plurality constitutes a check to power.

But what about the final term in our equation, the social? We said earlier that Foucault loses the concept of the social in his analysis of modern society. This is not, strictly speaking, correct. Rather, he presents us with a concept of the social that is identical with the network of strategic power relations described above. As already indicated, society is the terrain of apparatuses and institutions with multiple forms of subjugation. For Foucault, its "normative" dimension, so crucial to Durkheim's and Parsons's understanding of social integration, is, as we know, simply normalization. The social bond, far from being a moral commitment or a normative consensus constructed through the medium of language, tradition, and/or a reflective, discursive relation to parts of tradition, is the network of interwoven and mutually reinforcing strategies.[119] Indeed, Foucault is able to view plurality, publicity, and individuality in purely strategic and functional terms because his very concept of modern society is that of a strategic field pervaded by administrative technologies. These technologies level, individualize, and normalize, but they also rank and sort individuals and populations in a hierarchical manner that permits communication only through a third element—unequal power relations. This is the new mode of stratification that substitutes for horizontal and autonomous social interaction.

We have already seen that popular solidarities were the target of disciplinary power. The modern society that succeeds in destroying them is one "in which the principal elements are no longer the community and public life, but, on the one hand, private individuals, and on the other, the state."[120] Such an image of modern society precludes any meaning of sociality other than coordination "from above" (through administrative techniques) and/or strategic interaction. It also denies the existence of any spaces within modernity for the emergence of new forms of solidarity and association. Indeed, since Foucault maintains that disciplinary/pastoral power extends beyond the enclosed institution to become complete, consistent, and total, for the purpose of efficient and economical production of wealth, knowledge, and useful individuals, nothing else seems to be possible. The disciplinary organization of societal space multiplies communications and contacts, but only within the frame of strategies and apparatuses that have already reconnoitered and controlled the terrain. Reminiscent of Marx's notion of cooperation within a capitalist factory, Foucault's modern society is preschematized by the strategist's gaze: "The classical age saw the birth of the great political and military strategy by which nations confronted each other's economic and demographic forces; but it also saw the birth of meticulous military and political tactics by which the control of bodies and individual forces was exercised within states."[121] Accordingly, modern civil society is composed only of individualized strategists engaged in a struggle of each against all, pervaded by power and politics understood as war carried on by other means.[122]

As we stated at the outset, an analysis of the negative side of civil society and of the specifically modern forms of domination and stratification is an important component of any critical theory. One might, in fact, argue that this is all that Foucault intended to do and that it is unfair to accuse him of presenting a general model of society. One could, in short, claim that he has analyzed the logic and project of contemporary forms of power relations—the negative side, not the whole, of civil society. Perhaps. Yet it remains the case that Foucault's critique is itself caught in the strategic reason he exposes.[123] For, on the basis of his theoretical framework, he cannot point to any other category of action, any other mode of integration and interaction, that would be a basis for analyzing the struggles against disciplinary power, or the "positive side" of modernity, if there is one.

Foucault does insist that "there are no relations of power without resistances; the latter are all the more real and effective because they are formed right at the point where relations of power are exercised."[124] But, having equated legality and normativity with normalization, subjectivity with subjugation, self-reflection, morality, self-consciousness, and the soul with the products of disciplinary pastoral power, discourse and truth with administrative strategies of control, and the human sciences with the disciplines that serve or, rather, are part of power, Foucault is left with no conceptual means for describing resistances as anything other than counterstrategies of power. We are accordingly left in the dark regarding the practical thrust of the genealogical strategy of analysis, which Foucault nevertheless posits as a form of political engagement.

One thing, however, is clear: Foucault is not a partisan of a simplistic reversal of values. Genealogical analyses reveal the power strategies involved in constituting new objects and identities (the homosexual, the hysterical woman, the pervert, delinquency, insanity, sexuality) and the pejorative connotations attached to them. But the purpose of such analyses is not to encourage a revaluation in which homosexuality, the perversions, crime, insanity, sexuality are liberated, deemed natural, freed to speak out in their own voice. Such a strategy would do nothing to question the categorization in the first place or to undermine the agencies and mechanisms that perpetuate the grips of power on bodies, pleasures, and forms of knowledge. Instead, genealogy is meant to challenge not only the moral valuations of the normal and the perverse, for example, but also the very normalizing tendency associated with the demand that we understand ourselves through our sexuality, as if this says who we are.

Perhaps the critical thrust of genealogy is simply to uncover power strategies involved in the genesis of power/knowledge regimes in order to disturb the unitary, global form these take and to reveal their historical and hence contingent character. Such a project would place Foucault close to the critical theory of the Frankfurt school.[125] Presumably, this strategy would reveal the battle lines and create the possibility for a counteroffensive. Indeed, one could even interpret the focus on the societal genesis and multiple loci of domination as an attempt to invoke a civil-society-oriented strategy of resistance against both the local power structures within civil society and their globalization/colonization by the state.

Such an interpretation, however, does not resolve the difficulties created by Foucault's relentless critique of power, for he is still unable to articulate "otherness" or the forms of action that escape the logic of inegalitarian strategic power relations. On the one side, he disempowers critique, including his own, by an analysis that equates discourse, reflection, and truth with power strategies. On the other side, he cannot speak for the victim, as Walter Benjamin did, or offer a naturalistic notion of what is repressed by disciplinary power, as Herbert Marcuse did,[126] because the victim as well as her psyche are already products of power and because Foucault has rejected the "repressive" thesis regarding power relations. Indeed, if resistance is just the counterstrategy of that very product of power, the modern individual, then why support it? Why is it even interesting? What difference would it make?[127] Apparently, all that successful resistance can produce is a substitution of one strategy of power for another.

There is, in short, no basis within Foucault's work for distinguishing resistance from other strategic forms of action or strategies of control. He cannot appeal to the norms articulated by collective actors, for any appeal to norms either reproduces the discourse of power (and locks the resisters into normalization) or constitutes simply another strategy of power. Indeed, Foucault sees the coordination of action through norms as, in essence, strategic. Nor can he follow the path taken by Habermas, identifying communicative interaction as the core of an emancipatory practice that involves a reflection on and challenge to norms, institutions, and practices in the name of alternative (more just, more democratic, more liberal) norms and institutions, because, for Foucault, communication is only a means of transmitting information and (through the making of truth claims) controlling and disempowering opponents. The theoretical strategy of opening norms to reflection is closed to the theorist who views reflection as mere strategy. In other words, on the basis of Foucault's categorial framework, it is utterly unclear what goals or principles those who resist disciplinary power might invoke that could have a claim on our solidarity. The only clue he gives us is a few elliptical statements to the effect that "The rallying point for the counterattack against the deployment of sexuality ought not to be sex-desire, but bodies and pleasures."[128] However, as Foucault himself showed in the second and third volumes of his history of sexuality, neither bodies nor their pleasures are matters of sheer facticity: Both are constructed symbolically, as objects of knowledge and identity, albeit in different ways in different types of societies. Thus, to evoke the body and its pleasures as a way to break with the sex-desire regime is ambiguous, to say the least. Without this referent, however, Foucault is left with the simple fact of resistance to power, but this simple fact has no normative weight, for it would also be prey to the genealogist's cynical gaze and be revealed as another strategy for power.

But there is a prior question to that raised above regarding the reasons for partisanship with resistance. How, on the basis of Foucault's analysis, is resistance on the collective level even possible? Such resistance would have to be understood either as the defensive action of groups whose identities and solidarities have *not yet* been penetrated by disciplinary apparatuses, or as the counterstrategies on local levels of individuals who are *already* their products and hence are self-monitoring, purely strategic actors. In the first case, we would be seeing premodern solidarities in a purely defensive posture; in the second, modern rebels without any norms, institutions, principles, or discourses to appeal to, for these are already mechanisms of cooptation. The latter could only appeal to or gesture toward abstract otherness or difference per se. Indeed, it is unclear how, on the basis of Foucault's theory, individuals who wish to resist could come together to form the solidary and autonomous groups, associations, and collective identities that are the sine qua non for collective action in the first place. The body might put up some resistance to the drill, the "subject" might shy away from surveillance, and the individual might struggle against the manipulations of biopower, but even if Foucault were willing to postulate the other of reason and discourse in its primordial vitality (which he explicitly is unwilling to do), this would hardly suffice for an explanation of the emergence, solidarity, resources, collective identities, and projects of *collective actors* who challenge modern forms of domination. Foucault's analysis has deprived the modern rebel of any institutional, normative, or personal resources for constituting herself in terms other than those made available by the forces that already control her. The traditions, solidarities, and spaces for autonomous action left open by the inefficient, discontinuous modality of power in the ancien régime find, in Foucault's work, no modern equivalents. This is not because he was intent on analyzing something else but, rather, because the genealogical account of modern power relations turns the very concept of autonomous voluntary association into an anachronism in the carceral society. *Autonomy* is the illusion of the philosophy of the subject, *voluntary* consent is part of the deceptive juridical discourse, *association* (in our view, the truly modern dimension of sociality) is simply impossible in a society conceived of as a strategic field constituted by a kind of *Gleichschaltung* of all organizations by disciplinary administrative apparatuses. We are thus left with a critique of power that insists that resistance exists but cannot tells how it is possible, what it is for, or why it merits our support.

But isn't it obvious that disciplinary power in modern society is aimed against the *new* solidarities, associations, and movements that emerge on the terrain of modern civil society itself? And isn't it clear that collective actors must articulate distinct projects, new collective identities, and speak in the name of specific values and norms if they are to become collective actors and act at all? Moreover, in so doing, they appeal to precisely those new traditions (or discourses), norms, and institutions, stemming from the democratic revolutions of the eighteenth and nineteenth centuries, that Foucault has so cleverly disempowered: freedom, justice, solidarity, democracy, and, more concretely, parliaments, elections, associations, rights, and so on. Without an analysis of the *two-sidedness* of these institutions,[129] not to mention modern forms of individuation and self-reflection, the idea that modern social movements continuously emerge and challenge disciplinary power would be incomprehensible. Charles Taylor makes a similar point with respect to the tradition of civic humanism, the movements inspired by it, and the free institutions created in its name. He correctly points out that collective disciplines can function in two different ways: as structures of domination, and as bases for equal collective action. Such disciplines can, of course, undergo a change in function, sliding as it were from founding egalitarian politics into serving domination. But Foucault's analysis of modern power blurs over these processes, revealing only the negative side of modernity. He thus serves as a "terrible simplificateur."[130]

It is our thesis that the condition of possibility for the emergence of modern social movements, with their autonomous solidarities, newly created identities, and strategic resources, is precisely the differentiated structure of modern civil society:[131] legality, publicity, rights (to assemble, associate, and communicate free from external regulation), and the principles of democratic legitimacy. Indeed, we contend that the modern conception of fundamental rights is at least as important, in this regard, as the tradition of civic humanism cited by Taylor. How else can one account for the workers' movement, civil rights movements, the women's movement, the ecology movement, regionalist struggles for autonomy, or any modern social movement or, for that matter, the forces arrayed against them? Unless one sees at least the doubleness of rights and of legality, one would be forced to conclude that collective actors who do appeal to rights, and who reinterpret the key norms of modern civil society with their demands for more autonomy, more democracy, for public recognition as individuals and as group members different from one another yet meriting equal concern and respect, are somehow all mistaken, somehow articulating irrelevant, anachronistic principles and ridiculous projects.[132] Since Foucault rejects the only conceivable alternative, the project of total revolution, he has worked himself into a vicious circle: Either the norms and projects articulated by social movements are strategies of counterpower and as such have no greater normative claim than those of other power seekers, or they simply reproduce the existing discourses of power. For a critical theory with a partisan intent, as Foucault's surely is, this is indeed a serious flaw.

It is telling that Foucault cannot consistently maintain this stance, at least with respect to norms and rights. Although he reduces normativity to normalization, he nonetheless always speaks of modern power relations as inegalitarian, implying that egalitarian relations would be preferable. He always describes the latter with the imagery of a leveled strategic field of power, but it is obvious that his entire analysis is parasitic on the norm of equality, however much he may disparage norms. Similarly, he insists that rights should be viewed not in terms of legitimacies to be established but in terms of the methods of subjugation they instigate.[133] In part, this is because rights have been reorganized in our time, insofar as they have been invaded by the procedures of normalization that colonize law, thus making the legitimacy question irrelevant.[134] He even notes the tendency, on the part of those seeking to resist the disciplines and all the effects of power and knowledge that are linked to them, to resurrect the discourse of rights and legitimacy. But he sees this as a blind alley, for "it is not through recourse to sovereignty against discipline that the effects of disciplinary power can be limited."[135] The new twentieth-century discourses of social rights operate on the terrain of normalized, colonized law, while the older discourses of civil and political rights are anachronistic.

Nevertheless, even Foucault is forced to return to the language of rights when he tries to articulate struggles against disciplinary power:

If one wants to look for a nondisciplinary form of power or, rather, to struggle against disciplines and disciplinary power, it is not toward the ancient right of sovereignty that one should turn, but toward the possibility of *a new form of right*, one that must indeed be antidisciplinarian but at the same time liberated from the principle of sovereignty.[136] (Our emphasis)

That this is where he leaves the matter is not surprising. Foucault can say nothing positive about this "new form of right" because he has denuded the very category of rights and/or law of its multidimensionality. Certainly law can function as a medium of domination and control, and some rights do seem to disempower the rights-bearers. But surely this is not the whole story, or even the main part of it. As we noted earlier, Foucault misses the normative and empowering dimensions of law and rights because he, like Marx, takes the liberal ideology of rights at face value, only to reject it. On this account, the discourse of rights means the discourse of sovereignty-contract-legitimacy transposed from the king to the people, and construed this time as the polar opposite of the political, the state, and power. This form of the discourse of rights is, of course, ideological and unacceptable. But there is another meaning to the conception and effect of rights claims: In modern civil society, rights are not only moral oughts, they also empower. Rights do not only individualize, they are also a medium of communication, association, and solidarity. They do not necessarily depoliticize; they can also constitute a vital connection between private individuals and the new public and political spheres in society and state. Nor is it the case that questions of justice and legitimacy are somehow anachronistic in modern disciplinary society: These remain important to any society, no matter what form power takes.

Foucault is right in arguing that modern civil society is not equivalent to its principles of freedom, equality, democracy, justice, rights, autonomy, and solidarity. But it is also not equivalent to its strategies of domination and control. Dr. Mengele is not the truth of medical knowledge and practice but only their perversion; the use of mental institutions to punish political dissenters is not the truth of psychiatry or psychoanalysis but its abuse. Institutionalized norms (in the form of law, rights, and customs) do not only normalize, they also empower and provide a standpoint and a space for criticizing and challenging specific institutional arrangements and creating new collective and individual identities. Indeed, the symbolic dimension of discourse cannot be reduced to its "real" functions. The institutional articulation of civil society provides for a modern form of the social that is more than and other than the disciplinary apparatuses analyzed by Foucault. The two go together; both are modern, but they are neither identical nor of the same cloth. Only an analytical framework broad enough to encompass the dark and light sides of modernity can account for the conditions of possibility of the numerous and important social movements or "resistances" that animate and dynamize modern civil society. And only within such a framework can one place the fruitful yet dangerously one-sided work of Foucault in its proper perspective.

The Systems-Theoretic Critique:
Niklas Luhmann

We inherit the concept of civil society from two sources: the history of concepts and theories, and the self-understanding of social movements. The ideologists of social movements seem to confirm that a rich tradition of interpretation has not been exhausted, that it remains an adequate basis for the symbolic orientation of contemporary social actors. This argument could easily be mobilized against the historicist theses of Riedel, Koselleck, Arendt, and the early Habermas, according to which the relevance of the early modern concept of civil society, for better or worse, is to be confined to its eighteenth- and nineteenth-century origins. Indeed, their own intense interest helps to negate their claims and has itself contributed to the revival of the concept. And yet the case of the critics cannot be so easily disposed of, for their claim that the very concept of civil society is anachronistic is linked to an analysis of contemporary society as involving a fusion of realms—in particular, those of state and society—that were differentiated in the earlier liberal epoch. To respond to them one must go beyond the effort of hermeneutic recovery.

Deeply convinced of the limitations of even a critical hermeneutics,[1] we believe that it is essential to examine the concept of civil society also in light of a social-scientifically elaborated theory that at the very least incorporates an objectivating perspective. The link between the history of concepts and the self-understanding of movements may be based on a questionable double projection: The very same categories that inform the self-understanding of contemporary social actors may be projected backward by historians, who are never free of contemporary concerns, and then projected forward by movement ideologists to prove the depth and historicity of their projects.[2] While social theory also has internalized structures of interpretation and commitment, on the whole these include precisely that objectification of modern, global societal contexts that neither historians nor movement theorists are willing and able to accomplish. Thus, identity-forming narratives can be confronted with descriptive and explanatory materials.

Even more important, since modern social science has adopted a polemical attitude toward the categories of traditional political philosophy, it is in this context that we find some of the best arguments *against* contemporary applications of the concept of civil society. Thus, a confrontation with the results of social science represents an important test for those seeking to save or revive the classical concept. It is our belief that this test can be sustained only if the confrontation involves a theoretical reconstruction in light of contemporary developments addressed by systematic social theory.

Because of the normatively marked heritage of the concept, it is difficult to find systematic social theorists who take up the issue of civil society. In Max Weber's many great works, for example, there is hardly a mention of the term or of any obvious substitute. Talcott Parsons and Niklas Luhmann represent important exceptions to this trend.[3] We have already presented Parsons's concept of societal community as an attempt to translate the Hegelian category of civil society, enriched by Durkheim's concept of "the social," into contemporary terms. Luhmann, however, is right to note that this move by Parsons involves a break with the systems-theoretic assumptions of his own work, without any general theoretical justification. Here is a clue to Luhmann's surprising preoccupation with the problem of civil society.[4] Undoubtedly, his interest stems from a conviction that sociologists such as Durkheim, Parsons (his major forerunner),[5] and Habermas (his most important rival) are still under the sway of this major concept of "old European" practical philosophy. Luhmann's strategy against the concept of civil society and its social-scientific precipitates is to identify them with the traditional *societas civilis* and show the resulting inadequacies for the study of modern conditions.

Paradoxically, Luhmann's own sophisticated theory of differentiation, developed in an entirely different context, replaces Carl

Schmitt's notion of fusion between previously differentiated spheres with one of increasingly complex input-output relations among them. In this respect, he is highly important for us because he potentially resuscitates one aspect of the concept of civil society. However, he emphatically rejects the notion that one of the differentiated spheres should be understood as any kind of replacement for civil society, or the social, or normative integration. Not even law, the last significant repository of a "normative style of expectation," plays such a role in his theory. Society, in his analysis, stands only for the whole, and in some versions even for a "world society."[6]

Of course, Luhmann "reconstructs" many of the early modern subcategories of civil society on the terrain of systems theory. In each case, however, the reconstruction involves a decisive break with early modern intentions: Positive law is seen as normless in its deepest foundations, association is understood as bureaucratic organization, and public opinion is reduced to the manipulation of the themes of communication. It is characteristic that democracy is identified with the general social-cybernetic function of "meaning," that is, with the maintenance of reduced complexity. On the basis of systems theory, all that remains of the modern concept of civil society is the bare fact of differentiation itself.[7] Thus, Luhmann is also important for us, because, on the level of systematic social science, he works out a highly comprehensive challenge to the whole tradition of the concept of civil society.

Luhmann's preoccupation with the problem of civil society is indeed surprising, given his own theoretical assumptions and interests. His exercises in a sociological version of conceptual history rank with the best in this field. According to him, *politike koinonia*, translated as "political society," was first used as a concept to describe and elaborate upon the emergence of an evolutionary stage of human development, namely, the constitution of political rule that suppressed or greatly reduced the importance of archaic, kinship-based associations and the power of religion in the immediate relations of sub- and superordination.[8] The institutions of political office and political procedure were the means by which the reordering of society was accomplished, the major result being "the possibility of resolving conflicts through binding decisions."

Political rule, to be sure, meant the emancipation of human beings qua individuals. But it also meant their seamless integration into a politically defined societal framework.

Luhmann is somewhat unclear on why the "self-thematization" of this development occurred only in the Greek city-state, in particular the democratic *polis* of Athens.[9] More revealing than his actual explanation is his somewhat underemphasized addition of the principle of citizenship when speaking of the *polis* as a version of politically constituted rule.[10] He does not notice that political rule needs to be and can be thematized as such only when the wielders of the instruments of domination (here the *oikos* patriarch-despots) constitute a public. His own stress is on the dimension of domination rather than on public action. The actual rule in any political society is that of a part (in the Greek republics, citizens) over the whole. To Luhmann, several logical paradoxes associated with the concept of *politike koinonia* are to be traced to this state of affairs. Through its linguistic form and its opposition to the *oikos*, *politike koinonia* is understandable as only one type of *koinonia* among others. Yet it is also *the* all-encompassing social system, the *polis*. Thus, it is a whole that is paradoxically conceived as its own part.[11] Or: it is a whole that has parts outside itself, in particular the *oikos*.[12] The lesson is clear to Luhmann: The society that thematized itself as political society misunderstood itself. It was only a social system in which a newly differentiated political subsystem had functional primacy.[13]

For Luhmann, a second, related difficulty of the classical conception of *politike koinonia* lies in the attempt to view society as action. This was possible, according to him, because the political system, supposedly oriented toward right, just, and virtuous action was identified with the whole of society. Equally important was the understanding of political society as a body, as a corporate unity capable of action.[14] In this context, the relatively exceptional existence of differentiated, specialized organizations and their slight impact on society permitted a conception of political society as a whole as itself an organization, an organized body. Of course, the action and the goals of this supposed body were actually the actions and the goals of its ruling part; only this part constituted an organization.

According to Luhmann, the concepts of *politike koinonia* and, later, civil society in all its variants thematized the integration of this organization of rulers and the orientation of its individual actors in terms of the normative categories of morality and law (in the latter case, moralized law). Political society was stabilized through the institutionalization of "relatively universal . . . rules for interpersonal respect and mutual esteem."[15] In other words, the "generalized morality" of political societies thus served as the basic legitimation of political authority. Nevertheless, Luhmann claims that it was only functionally (and not logically) necessary to understand political society in normative terms.[16] Perhaps what he has in mind is that, although the medium of power has already replaced ordinary language communication as a means of transferring decisions, its lack of full development or the absence of other "media of generalized communication" has made a continued reliance on earlier forms of direct, linguistic models of command and obedience unavoidable. The latter, however, cannot operate without normative forms of justification. More likely, the point may be linked to his notion that the medium of power requires a normatively constructed linguistic code for its operation.[17] The binary code of right and wrong, allowing in principle the schematization of all decisions does not represent power as it actually operates; hence, normative language is actually not indispensable to the description of politically organized society. Nor would its actors need it to orient themselves within a system of power. But as long as law is not yet made positive, this moralistic-legal language is required to represent the operation of power and the workings of political society to its social environment, which is not yet linked to the political subsystem by other, functionally interchangeable, media.

Thus, in Luhmann's terminology, the institutionalization of the medium of power allows an important but incomplete replacement of *normative* styles of expectation by *cognitive* ones. Nevertheless, while on the level of social self-reflection a secular morality has now taken on the central role in social integration, in reality the emergence of power as the first "symbolically generalized medium of communication"[18] granted immense importance, and indeed functional primacy, for the first time to a subsystem relying on a cognitive rather than a normative attitude to social norms themselves. This subsystem remains linked to a structure of rules that, even if no longer tied to immediate interaction, is capable of reducing the contingency of action only by generalizing, universalistic orientations and mutual expectations that remain normative in the sense of being "counterfactually" maintained even in the face of empirical "disappointments." This linkage is functionally necessary, at least until it is replaced by functional equivalents, in order to unburden the power system of some of the needs of integration and thereby protect it (and society?) from its potentially vast overextension or "inflation."

Ancient practical philosophy, our first source for the concept of civil society, was in this context the theoretical thematization of both the primacy of the political and the moralization of politics. According to Luhmann, its errors involved a confusion of the part (politics) with the whole (society), of action with system, of power (as a medium) with morality (tied to ordinary language interaction), and of morality as a social reality with the morality of the moralists.[19]

The theory of bourgeois society is convicted of analogous if fewer errors. *Bürgerliche Gesellschaft* represents to Luhmann only superficially a revamping of the old *societas civilis*, in spite of the etymological derivation of the first category from the second. Actually, as the suggested alternative term, "economic society," indicates, *bürgerliche Gesellschaft* refers to a *topos* that is not identical with but parallel to "political society." The two also turn out to be structurally different.[20] Again, Luhmann begins with the self-thematization of economic society, which is classically represented by Marxian social theory. Here *economic* society is understood as a new type of society in which production, and even more "a metabolically founded system of needs," replaces politics as the central social process.[21] From a different point of view, also characteristic of Marxism, *bourgeois* society means that a politically defined ruling "part" (e.g., *Bürger* in the sense of *citoyen*) is now replaced as the dominant stratum by the owners of property (*Bürger* in the sense of *bourgeois*). Luhmann's reservations concerning the Marxian (as well as bourgeois) theory of economic society parallel his criticisms of Aristotelian political philosophy as a theory of political society. Both make the understandable error of taking the part for the whole, of identifying a societal subsystem with the whole of society. The error is understandable because of the dramatic nature of the emergence of each of the subsystems and their functional primacy (for a time) in relation to the other spheres of society.[22] Nevertheless, only this functional primacy should have been asserted in the case of the economy, and not the reduction of all spheres of life to economics. Only the notion of the functional primacy of the economy is compatible with the empirical fact that the extent and internal complexity of the political subsystem continued to grow in the whole capitalist epoch.[23] For functional primacy need only imply that the leading subsystem has the greatest internal complexity and that the new developmental stage of society is characterized by tasks and problems that originate primarily in this sphere.

Thus, "political" and "economic" society represent not only parallel processes of differentiation, along with parallel forms of self-thematization, but also successive evolutionary stages. Different levels of complexity indicate for Luhmann three structural differences between the earlier political society and the later, more complex, economic society: (1) transformation of the meaning of primacy; (2) replacement of a (mainly or partially) normative by a cognitive style of expectation; and (3) loss of the capacity for action on the part of the leading subsystem as a whole (not to mention the social system). Let us take each of these in turn.

First, in discussing the relation of the economic to the other subsystems, primacy can no longer be even approximately represented in terms of authority or domination, but only by the preeminence of the problem the economy deals with. The difference flows from Luhmann's distinction between the structures of power and money as communications media, with money being the medium around which the differentiated economic subsystem is organized. In the case of power, a selective decision is made for someone else who is motivated to accept or "to make" this specific decision through a particular code, and in view of negative sanctions. In the case of money, a decision is made for oneself, and the other is motivated to carry out his own complementary but generally different decision in view of possible rewards, or positive sanctions.[24] In the first case, decisions are transferred; in the second, only problems that must be dealt with. For this reason, the level of social differentiation allowed by the functional primacy of the economic subsystem is far greater than the level possible in "political society." This capacity is first thematized in terms of the "false dichotomy" of state and society, an issue to which we shall return.

Second, the primacy of the economic subsystem no longer requires a generalized morality for the integration of society. "It seems that the constancy of morality over time, which is supported by all of society, can be replaced by the constancy over time of purely economic opportunities."[25] Whereas politics still required (in the epoch of its primacy only?) "a kind of moral 'cover' or legitimation,"[26] the economic subsystem requires it neither "functionally" nor "logically," neither on the level of its representation nor for its operation. This is true because the emergence of the economic subsystem implies "a switch from a normative to a cognitive attitude. Expectations that are normative—i.e., counterfactual and incapable of adapting to changed conditions—are replaced by expectations that can learn and adapt to change."[27] The moral integration of economic life and the need of society in general for this type of integration recede with the differentiation of the economic subsystem. The society in which this subsystem has become primary can therefore (contrary to the opinion of Durkheim and Parsons) gradually dispense with normativity or confine it to the single subsystem of law, whose own foundations also become cognitive.

Finally, the disappearance of a generalized morality as a form of social integration signals (and is in part caused by) the loss of society's capacity for action. With the dominance of the market economy, it is impossible to understand the social whole as a body. "No one can claim to be the plenipotentiary representative of the economy."[28] The economic system is not a collectivity. Nor can one so represent the society in which it is primary. Any attempt to discover unified agency or subjectivity representing this society is merely an illegitimate transposition of a partially genuine possibility of political society and leads inevitably to conceptual mythology. Equally important is the stimulus given in economic society to the differentiation of organizations from the rest of society and from one another. The result of this process is that society itself can no longer even appear to fulfill the requirements of an organization, of an organized body. A plurality of the organizations in society are integrated not by means of a superordinate organization but instead by the workings of the systemic media of power and money. Thus (leaving aside the notion of interaction or intersubjectivity), the transition to the functional primacy of the economic subsystem means, for Luhmann, the necessary replacement of social integration by system integration, of action as a theoretical paradigm by system. Concepts such as "civil society" and "societal community" are the obvious theoretical victims of this shift. To this issue, too, we shall return.

Luhmann sees as obsolete not only the concept of political or civil society but also the one that replaced it. Economic society, or even the primacy of the economic subsystem, is now a thing of the past. This primacy has led to dysfunctional side effects for its various "environments," which may not have strictly economic solutions.[29] In one version of his argument, when the primacy of the economy is at an end, no subsystem is capable of dominating or even representing the whole. In an earlier version, the possible subordination of the economy and of politics to conscious, scientific control or coordination is left open. But such subordination could represent a developmental stage only if the integrity of the economic subsystem were preserved, as earlier that of the political subsystem was preserved, and if, along with this, the differentiation of society were increased. The primacy at this stage would belong to the subsystem of science[30] and not that of politics, as in Soviet-type societies. For such a society, a conception of *societas scientifica* would represent an appropriate form of false consciousness, although the level of reflection characteristic of the subsystem of science can also lead to a more appropriate (i.e., systems-theoretic) thematization of the new form of functional primacy, this time avoiding the fallacious hypostatization of *pars pro toto*.[31]

Whichever version we choose (and the recent conception of autopoietic systems clearly indicates the first), the three consequences of the primacy of the economic subsystem will continue to apply to Luhmann's understanding of modern society. For him, greater differentiation, the decline of normative integration, and the end of the capacity of society (or even a representative part) for action preclude any justifiable conception of modern society, or even one of its differentiated subsystems, as political or civil society. However, from the point of view of the concept developed in this book, which is not linked to any utopia of society as a unified agent, subject, or organization, it seems that, with respect to the fusion argument developed by thinkers from Schmitt and Arendt to Habermas and Offe, the Luhmannian theory of differentiation refurbishes an important aspect of the concept that is under threat. And yet, while on the most abstract level he does offer an alternative to the fusion thesis, this cannot benefit any conception of civil society, at least in his model. The reasons for this seem to be that he considers the state–civil society dichotomy to be false, and he replaces it by a model that draws the lines of differentiation quite differently, and that, even in an expanded model of differentiation, he sees no need to include a sphere whose focus is social integration through both norms and participation in associations.

The argument for fusion of state and society has always been plagued by a key contradiction: Many (especially the neo-Marxist) proponents of this thesis invoke it when they alternately depict the same epoch as that of the repoliticization of economy and society and that of the transition of the state from full dependence on or "positive subordination" to the (capitalist) economy to "relative autonomy" and "negative subordination."[32] Thus, they must assert dedifferentiation and differentiation at the same time. This puzzle disappears in the earlier, technocratic version of Luhmann's argument as well as in the later, liberal version. In the one case, he would speak of a movement from one functional primacy to another, from that of the economy to that of scientific planning, expanding the differentiation among spheres or, rather, subsystems. In the other, he would speak of increasing differentiation, permitting and permitted by increasingly complex subsystems whose network of mutual input-output relations could grow correspondingly more dense, giving the appearance of fusion. As he notes, the autonomy of the political system never meant its isolation. Events in the economy, for example, can help constitute problems and motivations in politics, although an autonomous political system will have to produce relevant decisions *according to its own criteria*. Thus, intersystemic communication is intensified, not reduced. "With the independence of politics, its dependence on society also increases."[33] Instead of fusion, Luhmann provides us with a persuasive model of the growth of both differentiation and interdependence, of both systemic self-closure and openness to other systems. "Reciprocal dependencies and independencies among subsystems increase simultaneously. In principle, this is possible because there is an increase of circumstances in which one can be dependent and independent."[34]

According to Luhmann, the whole discussion concerning the separation of state and society has misunderstood this phenomenon of increasing differentiation *and* interdependence. In the spirit of his thesis, one might say that the fusion argument amounts only to a partially false self-thematization of greater intersocial complexity characterizing the evolutionary stage succeeding that of the primacy of the economic subsystem. Unfortunately for the standard dichotomous conception of the opposition of state and civil society, however, this criticism of the fusion argument cannot alter Luhmann's view that it, too, represented a form of "false consciousness," this time of the historically new level of differentiation characteristic of economic society.[35] The critique of one form of false consciousness cannot refurbish an earlier form.

But what is Luhmann's case for claiming that the dichotomy of state and society is false? First, and least importantly perhaps, he thinks that the category of the state is too diffuse: It means everything from government to bureaucracy, from a part of the political system to its whole.[36] It is not obvious, however, how this criticism applies to such relatively rigorous definitions of the state as Max Weber's,[37] which could be and have often been used in political science to reformulate the opposition of state and society. Perhaps Luhmann would answer that the all-inclusive concept of the state as a political organization that monopolizes, through its administrative staff, the legitimate use of the instruments of violence in a given territory violates the internal and organizational differentiation of the political system, or reduces the political system to merely one of its aspects.[38]

Second, and next in order of importance, Luhmann rejects the supposed implication of the dichotomy—that state and society (or civil society) each consists of sets of concrete human individuals separated from one another in terms of their whole lives.[39] While this objection applies to many versions (prevalent especially in movements) of the polemical juxtaposition of society and state, even a cursory study of the more sophisticated conceptions treated here should dispose of it. For Hegel, for example, members of "estates" and "civil servants" are to be found in both civil society and the state, albeit in different "roles" and "functional" relationships. Luhmann might respond, however, that differentiated political roles should be contrasted with the multiplicity of social roles, a contrast that is still occluded by the splitting of human beings into merely two roles, whether public and private, *citoyen* and *bourgeois*, or citizen and man.

This argument is based on Luhmann's final and most important objection. He points to a characteristic diffuseness in the concept of society when juxtaposed to that of the state. Assuming that we know what "state" means (and, at best, for Luhmann it means "political system"!), the term "society" is a loose one describing its whole environment.[40] While ancient political society, understanding itself as the whole, did not recognize its environment at all, the notion of the state expresses the point of view of the political system when it is capable of seeing itself as part of a differentiated whole, a development that presupposes the political neutralization of religious, cultural, and kinship roles and meaning complexes.[41] This level of self-thematization in turn presupposes, at least in the main version of the argument, an institutionalization of the functional primacy of the economic, allowing a new level of societal differentiation. Nevertheless, even the economic subsystem does not represent the whole social environment of the political subsystem. Indeed, the differentiation of a legal subsystem allowed the differentiation of the "state" from religion (through constitutional law) and the economy (through private law).[42] Only slightly less important for the differentiation of the political system, one could speak of an institutionalization of the subsystems of family, science, and culture or art in the same historical context. All these subsystems, which cannot be reduced to a single "organization" or "collectivity" or "sphere" or "logic" or, least of all, "system," constitute the internally dynamic and differentiated social environment of the political system, which has separate input-output relations with each. Moreover, they have input-output relations with each other. They do not constitute any coherent entity (for Luhmann, a system) in relation to the political system. The notion of civil society is thus decomposed rather than saved by the model of differentiation.[43]

But which conception of civil society is thereby decomposed? Certainly the liberal or Marxist dichotomous models do not stand up to Luhmann's criticism. The Hegelian theory, on the other hand, while it does not include art or science or family, was highly differentiated internally. To the objection that this model no more differentiated the economic subsystem from law, associations, etc., than did its Marxian heir, Gramsci's response, differentiating economy and civil society, might seem sufficient. The potential outcome becomes clearest in Parsons, who differentiates the cultural and economic systems from both the political system and the societal community, the latter understood as the integration subsystem of society. It is this last sphere of society, composed of normative-legal and associational components, that we consider the most advanced reconstruction of the concept of civil society within academic social science. Luhmann shares this interpretation of Parsons but does his best to eliminate any such a sphere in whatever guise from the systems theory of society.

Here Luhmann's strategy is twofold. First, he draws the line defining the polity in such a way as to include within it all politically relevant associations and publics. Accordingly, institutions that other theorists rooted in civil society and that served as mediations with the state are now located within the political system proper. In the process, however, Luhmann severs the connection of these institutions with rational communication and even with the Parsonian "medium" of influence that is dependent on these processes. Second, he interprets the function of law and rights in the differentiation of society as pertaining only to the (self-) limitation of the political system, not to the institutionalization of any specific sphere in need of protection from administrative penetration. Explicitly rejecting the idea that rights might also protect against economic tendencies toward dedifferentiation, he emphasizes the standard liberal notion of protecting private spheres from the state. This model of law does apparently create a reservation for normativity. Unfortunately, within the terms of Luhmann's theory, the boundaries of a legal subsystem that is not stabilized by a medium on the model of power or money cannot be easily maintained against either a cognitive style of expectation or, more concretely, the administrative subsystem of the political system. In the rest of this chapter, we shall address in more detail Luhmann's analyses of the relations between, first, the political system and civil society and, second, the legal system and civil society.

1. The differentiation of the political system into administration, parties, and publics seems to be common to Parsons and Luhmann. Actually, Parsons's conception is quite different from what Luhmann makes of it. For Parsons, parties and publics as institutions can play a role in the "support system" of politics because they are rooted in the societal community. What seems to be an ambiguity among various Parsonian texts concerning the primary location of these institutions in the polity or the societal community is, rather, an example of a quasi-Hegelian theoretical move focusing on mediation, in the sense of providing both differentiation and the interpenetration needed to stabilize differentiation.[44] If, from the point of view of the political system, the function of publics and parties operating in the public sphere is to generate consent and loyalty for binding decisions, from the point of view of the societal community their role is primarily social integration and, secondarily, to establish elements of social control over the state. Located first and foremost in the societal community,[45] the public is capable of generating support for the political system only to the extent of being able to draw on the resources of solidarity generated by autonomous rather than bureaucratic associations in civil society.[46] While Parsons recognizes the possibility of manipulation and opinion creation by the mass media, he believes that even stronger trends toward autonomous expression and discussion counteract this possibility.[47] In Parsons's conception, the internal differentiation of the political system into leadership, administrative, integrative, and legitimating subsystems[48] (or government, bureaucracy, legislature and parties, and the judiciary) gives the latter two the role of generating legitimacy and motivational commitment for

decisions produced and executed by the first two. But he does not share what he sees as the *illusion* of the elite theory of democracy, namely, that these resources can be generated entirely from above. Nor does he accept the view of legal positivism that legislative enactment is the only source of law, or even of its validity. The very idea of seeing the "support system" in terms of a double interchange between polity and societal community presupposes important trade-offs: Political power is increased and exposed to genuine social control through the same institutions.[49]

Thus, it is fair to conclude that, like Hegel but less consistently, Parsons presents the institutions of political association and publicity in terms of a double location that both differentiates and interconnects state and civil society. To Luhmann, however, the supposed double role of political institutions on which Parsons bases his dualistic topological conception reflects only the difference between the official, textbook version of politics and the reality accessible to social science. Moreover, an internal differentiation of the political system reflecting term by term the differentiation of its environment (Parsons, Hegel) would seriously endanger the autonomy of this system.[50] In order to be autonomous, the political system must have time, which in turn presupposes an internal structure that need not immediately react to inputs from its various environments. But this could not be avoided if the structures of the environment were reproduced within the political system, or even directly linked as constituencies to the subsystems of the polity. "If all subsystems would have their legitimate spokesmen in the political system, politics would be continually confronted with an overproduction of the possible."[51] This is Luhmann's shorthand for the Schmittian *topos* of a decisionless, ungovernable form of democracy. In his conception, however, this is not necessarily the implication of contemporary political party and parliamentary institutions. On the contrary, when they function properly, they operate neither in terms of the traditional bridging function between society and state nor in terms of the fusion of these two domains, but as autonomous forms within a political system uncoupled from just those types of inputs that lead to problems of governability.

The autonomy of the political system also depends on its "acceptance" by its various environments. This acceptance, however, is favored by the differentiation of the environment, which fragments the various possible sources of demands. Therefore, it can be a function primarily of the internal processes of the political system, and only secondarily of exchanges with the various environments. Indeed, the internal differentiation of the political system into public, politics, and administration favors the crystallization of certain roles whose function is to link the environments in a desirable way but also to limit this linkage to forms that are separated from other roles and are internally fragmented. Thus, the client, the voter, and the participant of the public are divorced from the family member, the worker, and the professional, on the one side, and do not add up to a comprehensive citizen role, on the other. It is above all this specialization into separate political roles that produces a form of acceptance of political decisions that Luhmann repeatedly describes as quasi-automatic and almost without motivation. This thesis requires a redefinition of the meanings of publicity, party politics, elections, and parliamentary representation (here a part of administration), all of which were once linked to the category of civil society but are now placed within the political system. Is this a redifferentiation without a difference? Luhmann's redefinition of democracy is our first sign that it is not.

According to Luhmann (here squarely in the tradition of Schumpeter), any normative definition of democracy—whether based on participation, representation, or pluralistic competition—should be abandoned. One reason is that each one seeks to make sense of the idea of popular self-government or self-rule, which is in fact incompatible with the logic of an autonomous political system differentiated from the other spheres of society. Moreover, any scheme to extend participation in the business of rule, in terms of either a direct role in the production of decisions or a control and monitoring of those who actually decide, can only raise perpetual frustration to a principle because of the scarcity of time to participate in relation to the quantity and complexity of what must be decided.[52]

The second reason is even more revealing. Any normative definition threatens to prejudice one's own political system (in this case, Western multiparty systems) against "functional equivalents" (in particular, single-party regimes of the Soviet type). For Luhmann, even the Schumpeterian residue of democratic theory—namely, the existence of competitive parties and contested elections—represents a merely secondary consideration in analyzing the democratic character of a society. One ought, instead, to turn to more abstract matters and develop a concept of democracy that can apply to a variety of systems, as long as they are sufficiently complex.[53] Luhmann produces such a definition. As processes of decision imply the reduction of complexity, a selection of a relatively small segment from the realm of possible events and the elimination of the rest, "democracy means the maintenance of complexity in spite of the ongoing work of decision, the maintenance again and again of a sphere of selectivity as wide as possible for future and different decisions."[54]

Luhmann realizes that this definition associates democracy with his *differentia specifica* of social systems as such, namely, "meaning" itself, understood as a form of reduction of complexity that maintains the eliminated options within the horizon of possibilities.[55] He does not notice, however, that this move tends toward the definition of all societies as democratic; at most, there can be differences of degree that seem to correspond primarily to the level of complexity. Indeed, Soviet-type single-party, ideologically steered societies are repeatedly pronounced democratic, indeed as democratic as multiparty systems as long as ideology is "preserved from dogmatism and is practiced opportunistically," which means the continual possibility of changing relations of priority among a high number of core values.[56] Luhmann does recognize that single-party rule threatens to restrict consequential social communication to a small politocratic group and to turn other spheres of society to secondary functions of the political system that instrumentalize them. This trend is one of dedifferentiation and is contrary to the increase of complexity. Characteristically for that time (1968), Luhmann proposes that the recovery of the primacy of a differentiated economy represents, in context of a single-party regime, the major dimension of the work of democratization.[57] Indeed, he considers the freeing of social expectations and demands as well as "public opinion" from ideology and the radical expansion of elements of dependent pluralism incompatible with the nature of such a system.[58] While representing some ideal limit on the level of attainable complexity, these restrictions are not such as to place Soviet-type societies out of the range that defines them as democratic. It is in this sense, too, that they are the functional equivalents of today's liberal democracies. The reader has a hard time avoiding the suspicion that this is the case only because Luhmann has adopted the most "disenchanted" and "realistic" view possible of Western multiparty democracies.[59]

Luhmann's realism is in many respects welcome. It is helpful, for example, to see that, from the point of view of maintaining structurally permissible complexity, the assimilation of party programs to one another and the systematic elimination of many intelligent options from political discussion diminish the range of democratic options. It is even more important to admit the tension between the open horizons of possibility for action and experience and the realistic recognition by individuals that they can actually "change nothing."[60] It is, however, both premature and dogmatic to *define* this paradox as democracy and to declare the goal of institutionalizing the ability to change something as by definition irrelevant and obsolete. It is, moreover, unconvincing to dismiss all reform attempts based on the extension of politically consequential communication with a simple reference to the scarcity of time. Once this is done, one gets the strongest impression that, in Luhmann's view, *both* Soviet-type societies, at least those with reformed economies, and Western multiparty regimes in their present forms are in principle impervious to attempts at structural transformation of their political systems, in the sense of democratization.[61] Thus, in the case of Western societies, forms of social-political interaction that others have strongly criticized—in particular, a public sphere assimilated to mass culture, depoliticized parties, plebiscitary elections, and parliamentary theatrics—turn out to be elements of the mature organization of a genuinely autonomous, differentiated political system.

Luhmann, like Habermas, presents the liberal model of the public sphere as historically confined to a single epoch, as indicated by its linkage to the polemical, enlightenment notion of "society"—yet another version of the pre-systems-theoretic fallacy of *pars pro toto*. All publics—ancient, liberal, and modern—represent, according to Luhmann, a neutralization of role demands from differentiated social spheres. The liberal version involved the differentiation of a sphere of small circles of communication integrated through public discussion from already modern, functionally differentiated subsystems of society: economics, politics, science, religion, family. The internal differentiation of this new public sphere was anachronistically segmental; externally, it was a differentiated sphere without a specific function. Without a function, the new public (a part) could (mis)understand itself as society (the whole), but only for a transitional moment because of its built-in instability. Its role structure not only was not in a position to control the other spheres of society, but was completely at the mercy of functional roles, with their access to money, power, etc.[62] Against Habermas, Luhmann therefore denies that a structure of rational communication, inherited from a functionally undifferentiated public, could today be revived (as part of a program of democratization) within functionally differentiated organizations themselves necessarily based on the "parcelization of consciousness." Thus, he asserts not only the structural transformation of the public sphere but the obsolescence of its normative assumptions as well.

Luhmann does seek to save something of the liberal notion, but only in the context of transposing the public sphere into the political system as one of its subsystems. Now neutralization becomes the specific integration function of the political system as a whole; its role is to establish a form of communication not determined by the nonpolitical roles of society (familial, commercial, scientific, religious) or even by partial political interests (party political or bureaucratic).[63] This may sound like a repackaging of the liberal norm in a functionalist wrapping, but there are two major differences. First, the purpose of neutralization is now the uncoupling of politics, and in particular the processes of decision, from society, not the creation of a new form of social control over the state. Second, the process of neutralization lies not on the level of the open interaction of participants but on that of the formation of the implicit themes of their various forms of political communication.

Indeed, *public opinion* is here defined not in terms of the "unattainable publicity" of all political communication but as the structuring of even nonpublic communication by institutionalized themes. It is the *themes*, defined phenomenologically as "pre-understandings hardened during the course of communication into more or less firm systemic boundaries in a commonly accepted lifeworld, presupposed in an inarticulate manner" that structure political communication, not the *opinions* articulated and expressed.[64] Public opinion thus not only refers to but also derives its relative unity from institutionalized themes, that is, subtexts of communication, rather than from the generalization of articulated opinions. These themes contribute to decision making by limiting the arbitrary nature of what is politically possible. But they also contribute to democracy as defined here by keeping alive possibilities according to a different logic than that of decision making itself. They are not parts of the mechanism of democracy in any other definition, however; public opinion "takes over the function of a steering mechanism that, while not determining the exercise of rule and the generation of opinion, lays down the boundaries of the possible at any given time."[65]

Referring to such subjects as priorities among various values, the meaning and perception of crisis, the status of various individuals who play important communication roles, the (relative) newness of events, and the definition of socially relevant pain or pain substitutes (threat, stress, loss), the key themes of public opinion are ultimately understood as rules that determine, in the context of the scarcity of the resources of attention, that to which attention can and even must be paid at a given time. These themes or attention rules are seen as contingent and variable, in line with the steering requirements of complex systems. Their origin and logic of development are left in some doubt. On the one side, the institutionalization of themes is said to depend on the structure of the political system, which regulates public opinion without rigidly determining it.[66] This view, consistent with the aim of presenting the political system as fully autonomous, seems to imply mainly that the structure of the political system determines which institutionalization of themes is possible, not what is actually institutionalized. Given the stated function of public opinion, however, this ultimately means that the structure of the political system determines what themes are possible, which in turn determines what decisions are possible. In effect, then, the structure of the political system determines what is politically possible, with public opinion representing only the dependent process by which this is accomplished.

On the other hand, Luhmann also wants to suggest that public opinion has important reciprocal effects or feedbacks (*Rückwirkungen*) on the structure of the political system. But this takes the particular form of developing modes of organization and processes that would not be affected by the variability of themes—in particular, proceduralism and neutrality toward values. In other words, the response to public opinion is to generate and maintain forms that allow the political system not to respond to public opinion.

Such a revealing way of speaking is also important in the present context, because it implies that shielding the political system from publicity is part of preserving its autonomy, as if public opinion had, after all, something to do with the nonpolitical environment of the political. And Luhmann does in fact call it an overhasty judgment that public opinion has now been reduced to the inner medium of the political system without any overall social function, the language only of the interaction of politicians within a political system totally differentiated from the social, everyday, diffuse lifeworld.[67] In this context, he is forced to restate and, in effect, partially abandon his hypothesis on neutralization. If it is still true that unpolitical roles are neutralized in the political system by the public sphere, the same is not true for political communication outside the political system.[68]

But can there be political communication at all outside the political system, which is itself defined in terms of specific communication processes? Luhmann insists that differentiation does not represent a tearing out of the social fabric of communication and the establishment of self-referentially closed subsystems. Thus, the communication of public opinion cannot be exclusively assigned to the political subsystem; its themes have a relatively context-free character that can structure communication in contexts whose nonpolitical nature is self-conscious.[69] But now neutralization of nonpolitical inputs cannot be defined as the function of the public sphere. Instead, and rather surprisingly, Luhmann returns to the classical function of "mediation" (*Vermittlung*), defined in terms of both differentiation and integration between political and unpolitical contexts. The presentation of mediation is, however, astonishingly impoverished: The possibility of transposing themes from a political to a nonpolitical context and the activation of different roles of the same person, political and nonpolitical, are said to help stabilize the difference between the political and the nonpolitical. The aim remains the differentiation and autonomy of the political system; mediation accomplishes this not by neutralization but by forcing the processes of intersystemic communication into narrow and politically manageable channels.[70]

Despite these efforts, Luhmann does not manage to present a concept of the public sphere that completely shields the political from the nonpolitical. His second, life-cycle, model of the origin and logic of public opinion is a clue to this failure. According to the life-cycle model, themes that can be articulated in their "latent phase" by anyone become political themes only when they get into the hands of those who make politics with changing themes, namely, the politicians. But whether they do so (and with what force) depends on the energy of their generally nonpolitical suppliers and on the success of these suppliers in making a theme "popular" and "fashionable." After this happens, powerholders are no longer in a position to censor themes. Now, politicians can compete only in getting themes into the decision processes of the administration or in delaying this as long as possible. Either way, the importance of themes tied to their novelty will diminish, and new ones will take their place.[71] This whole train of argument indicates that Luhmann's linkage of the model of public opinion to a prepolitical setting does not restore the liberal meaning behind what is in effect a "liberal" *topos*, but rather ties the nonpolitical dimensions of publicity to the mechanisms of commercial, indeed manipulated, communication. Here, too, he is in the Schumpeterian tradition.

Luhmann seems to deny the necessary role of manipulation, defined in contrast to interaction as a form of unanswerable communication.[72] But when admitting the possibility of going around public opinion or using it tactically, his analysis is far more detailed and convincing than that of "mediation."[73] Technically, only methods of going around public opinion are manipulative according to his definition. Moreover, both these forms and those of instrumentalizing public opinion are presented as ways of regulating the internal processes of the political system. Nevertheless, the techniques he mentions, such as the production of pseudo-crises, pseudo-novelties, or pseudo-expressions of the will of the electorate, represent direct utilizations in the political system of methods of manipulative, commercial advertisement that, in effect, dedifferentiate the political system by turning one of its subsystems into commercialized entertainment.[74]

Undoubtedly, Luhmann does not believe that manipulative mechanisms of either type exhaust the possibilities of public opinion formation. Nevertheless, it is precisely in this context that he draws the following conclusion: "Under the described conditions, in the realm of politics we can count on the multiplication of the possibilities of behavior and at the same time on the restriction of the possibilities of active participation." Because of the specialized technical skills required for the tactical use of public opinion, what starts out as "management by participation" invariably winds up as "participation by management."[75]

The model of differentiation and manipulative linkage runs through Luhmann's discussion of elections and legislatures, moving the analysis to the interior of the political system, whose relation to its public subsystem duplicates the latter's relation to the nonpolitical spheres of society. More exactly, electoral politics and political party structures are understood to constitute the "political" subsystem proper of the political system, while legislatures are put within the administrative subsystem. The function of the former is to build political support, to provide a mechanism for recruiting officials, and to manage and absorb conflict and protest. Only the latter is to have any role in decision making, which is understood as a particular combination, uncoupling, and reconnecting of actual processes of decision making with that of the "presentation" of its production. By putting the legislature into the realm of administration "broadly understood," Luhmann makes a shift within the political system that parallels his shifting the public into the political system. In each case, he moves a structure classically understood as an element of the public mediation between society and state closer to the interior of the political system itself, understood as administrative decision making.

It is striking that in these shifts Luhmann cannot fully eliminate the element of publicness that seems to be attached to elections and parliaments. The specifically political role of the voter is linked to participation in the public[76] up to the point of actually voting; the working out of themes capable of consensus is said to be among the tasks of party politics;[77] the maintenance of the image of politicians is among the tasks of parliament; and finally, the public presentation of grounds and arguments in parliamentary sessions is said to seriously reduce the choice of representable positions.[78] In all this, more seems to be involved than merely the usefulness of being able to represent the process of decision making by two stories: an "official," civics textbook story that is important for building support and shielding the actual, nonpublic process of decision making, and a "realistic" story (Luhmann's own) that is important for the self-reflection (or at least the proper scientific understanding) of the political system. Characteristically, the democratic function of maintaining reduced complexity in the realm of the possible is assigned not only to the public but to politics[79] and parliaments[80] as well, linked in particular to the institution of the opposition, whose alternatives survive even electoral or parliamentary defeat.

With this said, the essential function of both politics and legislature remains, from the point of view of the social system as a whole, differentiating the political system and ensuring its autonomy by uncoupling political decision making from social inputs. This problem is solved not through total separation but by processes of filtering and selection that manage society and build political support (a "permanent problem" with the passing of premodern forms of legitimation) at the same time. Electoral procedures convert the problem of support from relying on the nonpolitical roles of the (premodern) ruler to drawing on the strictly differentiated political roles of voters.[81] In their roles as voters, individuals are guaranteed access to the political system independently of other social roles or statuses (universal suffrage, equality of votes), and the influence of social ties and pressures is minimized (secret ballot).[82] Indeed the particular, atomized choice of the voter, having almost no consequences for other aspects of the individual's life, including other politically relevant roles, involves no social responsibility and cannot be the source of any social conflicts.[83] This point has several consequences, all strengthening the autonomy of the political system. Not being open to "social" influence, the voter is all the more exposed to immanent political influence, presumably by the mechanisms of public opinion. In seeking to influence political processes, the voter has a choice of a small degree of influence at minimum cost (voting) or more influence at great cost (voluntary associations, petitions, letters to newspapers, etc.). Given the separation of either form of influence from decision making, Luhmann has no doubt that the first option will be chosen, although the continued presence of the second contributes to democracy, at least in the sense of "everything is possible, but I can do nothing." But even the restricted and minimized influence of the voter role distinguishes the individual from a subject (*Untertan*) of rule who receives but never sends political communications, thereby contributing to legitimation through procedure.[84]

The situation is analogous for conflict-oriented collective actors with specific interests. Luhmann adheres to the view that elections are not suited to the expression of particular interests. Because those elected receive generalized support and are not bound to any constellation of interests, electoral processes cannot easily produce decisions for concrete conflicts. Nevertheless, they do allow the political system not to suppress conflicts but to channel them, including even radical protests, into the interior of the political party subsystem in a manageable form. Here the advantage of competitive elections over single-party uncontested elections shows itself. Unfortunately, multiparty systems with conflicting lists do not solve the problem automatically because of the tendency to undifferentiated programs. The continuing dilemma of political party subsystems is to avoid both reproducing too much social conflict (which would threaten the differentiation and stability of the political system) and absorbing too much conflict (which could mean the reappearance of unmanageable conflict outside the political system).[85]

Characteristically, Luhmann tells us next to nothing about what happens in the context of being caught on either of the horns of the dilemma of too much or too little conflict in the political system. It would appear that the legislature plays a role in the resolution of too much political conflict. Here, Luhmann runs into Carl Schmitt's thesis of the fragmentation of sovereignty and the reduction of parliament to mere show. To Luhmann, the thesis is based on the false assumption that open sessions of parliament ever were or should be at the center of actual decision making. Parliament, especially its plenary session, is and should be "mere show," in the sense of symbolically presenting the production of decisions in accordance with our official script of politics. Such a show (with its important functions for democracy, in Luhmann's sense) can have relatively large room for plural interests, open conflict, and the self-presentation of political personalities.[86] It is, however, the informal mechanisms, shielded and veiled by the formal procedure, that are the stuff of the realistic script of decision making. While the parliamentary process as a whole, as even the classical theory of free representation realized, should not mirror social conflicts, the appearance of the party system, at least in the version analyzed by Schmitt, threatens to do just this. Luhmann implicitly accepts here the decline of the classical principle of representation, and he admits some dangers for the autonomy of the process of decision making. In his own terms, there is a danger of a bottleneck between the political and the administrative subsystems of politics.[87] Models of endless discussion or conflict indicate only the problem rather than the solution in this context. Instead, the separation of decision making from formal parliamentary procedure implied by reliance on informal and even deviant mechanisms[88] clears the potential bottleneck and reduces the influence of politics to its proper measure. The real decision making occurs elsewhere than in parliamentary procedure, although the conversion of political power into a zero-sum game by the formal mechanisms of majority rule considerably simplifies the interactions and bargaining processes of those who actually decide.

Thus, the old thesis concerning the crisis of parliamentarism is resolved by Luhmann in a way that points to something like the neocorporatist duality between public and secret, formal and informal, parliamentary and functionalist processes of interest aggregation. He is, however, perceptive enough to realize that today there is a new threat to parliamentarism. A crisis of parliamentary legitimacy can result not only from too many societal inputs and too much party conflict, but also from too much social apathy and too much absorption of conflict. The method of shielding the mechanisms of decision making can be overly successful; the number of logically possible social alternatives loses its link to the actually possible if the feeling that "I can do nothing" becomes generally and publicly thematized.

In this context, Luhmann passes up the chance to build on the one element of genuine democratic legitimacy that appears in his presentation. In his conception, it is above all the dramaturgical elements of elections and parliaments that have the function of "informing" the uninformed, of energizing the apathetic, of symbolizing democracy as an open horizon of possibility somehow present and charged with meaning, even if detached from the possibilities of action. But this argument, as he elsewhere notes, threatens to dedifferentiate politics, this time in relation to art or mass culture and entertainment. The citizen is said to participate in politics to the extent of being able to identify with some of the actors of the drama, becoming part of the public in the sense of audience (*Publikum*).[89] It is hard, though, to keep the show good or even entertaining when people begin to notice that there is nothing at stake. This train of argument soon leads us back toward Luhmann's concept of public opinion, involving the compulsion to produce novelty in the face of the predictable obsolescence of fashionable themes and even the manipulative use of this opinion to produce pseudo-events, pseudo-crises, and pseudo-personalities.

At one point, however, Luhmann points to another type of phenomenon, and implicitly to a model of the public elsewhere denounced as obsolete. During plenary sessions of parliament, "one's grounds, unlike motivations and backers, have to be publicly presented and exposed to the criticism of opponents. This restricts the choice of representable positions."[90] Luhmann does not, and we believe cannot, tell us where this compulsion to defend positions "with the help of arguments and reasons for decisions (*Argumenten und Entscheidungsgründen*)" originates. Some candidates for a possible answer, such as a political culture with built-in standards of rationality, or a lifeworld that has undergone normative as well as cognitive learning, or a public sphere organized according to the possibility of rational discourse rather than merely dramaturgically or as an organ of mass culture, are in principle excluded from his theory.

Our point is not to deny the empirical importance of Luhmann's description of the political system, based on the primacy of a core administrative system capable of shielding its autonomy and internal selection processes by the outer rings of politics and publics. Rather, it is to register an uneasy relationship between the two scenarios Luhmann associates with the political system, the "realistic" one and the "official" one. The latter, in order to play its role, cannot confine itself to a dramaturgical status. But to eliminate its discursive or rational components, which represent, in Luhmann's oft-stated opinion, undesirable (societal) restrictions on the freedom, variability, and pragmatic case-by-case nature of decisions, would put the procedural legitimacy of the political order into jeopardy.[91]

2. Luhmann is fully aware that an overextension of the logic of the political system would be harmful for this system itself. His theory of the autonomy of the political system from societal inputs is not automatically a theory of the freedom of the various social spheres from political penetration. A differentiated political system is indeed far more powerful than its predecessors and has both greater possibilities and greater interest in intervention. Luhmann undoubtedly accepts Schumpeter's insight that if the realistic model of democracy is to work at all, care must be taken that political mechanisms not be extended to too much of society.[92] He also agrees that such limitation must be primarily a self-limitation of the political system. In contrast to Schumpeter's version of legal positivism, however, he claims that the mechanism can be that of legal enactment, which is necessarily the product of political decision. In fact, he develops a functional theory of fundamental rights as forms of protection against the overextension of the political. Such a move, if justifiable, could help to diminish qualms such as Schumpeter's that positive enactment is not in itself sufficient to limit political power. Unlike Parsons, however, Luhmann does not locate a societal center of normative integration and associational life as the core of what is to be protected by the self-limitation of the political system.

It is instructive to compare the conceptions of fundamental rights in Parsons and Luhmann. Derived from equality, one of the core values of the "democratic revolution," rights in Parsons's theory seem to have more to do with the internal structure of the "societal community" than with its differentiation from polity, economy, or culture. Following a famous and influential text of T. H. Marshall,[93] Parsons decomposes citizenship into *civil* and *political* rights and their *social* prerequisites.[94] Equal participation in these three components defines full admission to or membership in—that is, citizenship in—the modern, democratic societal community.[95] Of course, Parsons understands the democratic revolution and especially its other core values, liberty and fraternity, in terms of a large-scale process of differentiation between societal community and polity. Moreover, the prehistory of the democratic revolution, especially English legal developments, already involved a transformation of law from an "instrument of government" to a "mediating interface" between state and society. In particular, the establishment of "the rights of Englishmen" (such as habeas corpus, fair trial, and protection against arbitrary searches) is said to play an important role in this development.[96] Thus, while Parsons never brought together the strands of his argument about rights, it is fair to say that, aside from the fundamental problem of inclusion to which he links his whole citizenship complex, his conception stresses both differentiation and integration, with civil rights playing a more obvious role in differentiation and political rights providing for new forms of integration ("mediation") between the spheres of state and society (polity and societal community).

It is striking that Luhmann makes a determined attempt to reduce the function of fundamental rights to the single dimension of differentiation.[97] His stark, "realistic" conception of the modern political system and of political power as potentially "totalitarian," aiming at the politicization of all spheres of life, underlies this thesis.[98] And yet the modern political system is born of social differentiation. Its modernity presupposes differentiation, and its performance for other societal subsystems requires economy of power resources.[99] The establishment and self-establishment of limits to state power is thus a positive-sum game. Whatever the actual historical origins of basic rights,[100] neither the state nor a purely social sphere produces them alone; they represent gains in the autonomy of the nonpolitical and the power of the political.[101]

The logical paradox of legal positivism with respect to rights—the supposed impossibility of the self-limitation of political power through political enactment—is thus sociologically resolvable. Fundamental or constitutional rights are not rooted in an extrapolitical or extralegal order but are presuppositions and products of the differentiation of society. While they are not the only institutions that stabilize this differentiation, today at least they are indispensable for this purpose.[102]

Accordingly, the structure of rights cannot be deduced from a single principle such as "individual freedom" or "society against the state." Nor can they be arranged according to a hierarchy.[103] The reason is that fundamental rights consist of several complexes, each of which regulates the relationship of the political system to one or another subsystem according to different and unique structural requirements. To begin with, liberties or freedoms (*Freiheitsrechte*) have to do not with the autonomy of the individual in the strong sense, but with the protection of the individual personality (itself a subsystem presupposed by the other subsystems), which in turn is highly dependent on the maintenance of conditions for adequate self-presentation. These depend on the freedom of the actor from visible and open constraint, in particular from binding decisions, and on a basic consistency of self-presentation, here defined as the essence of dignity. Within what are ordinarily considered freedoms, Luhmann distinguishes between rights of freedom and of dignity, respectively related to the external and internal preconditions of the presentation of the self.[104] As goods that exist prior to the state, they are not products of rights and are only protected by them with respect to the political system. Rights of freedom, strictly speaking, protect the space of individual action and expression; freedom of speech in all its forms seems central in this context. Luhmann considers the "rights of dignity" to be more difficult to define and to establish, and he notes a certain tendency in many (especially liberal) legal systems to subsume them under *Freiheitsrechte*. Nevertheless, he considers them in principle quite distinct, to be connected with the protection of an intimate sphere that should be separated from that of public action.[105] So-called freedom of conscience is the best contemporary illustration of this requirement.[106] Without it, the individual loses the responsibility to work out for herself a consistent and convincing self-presentation.

As in the case of freedom, Luhmann considers the protection of dignity by fundamental rights to be relevant only when the threat comes from the state.[107] Yet he believes that the false dichotomization of state and society leads only to the mistaken liberal attempt to derive all fundamental rights from freedoms.[108] He nevertheless feels compelled to note the importance of *Freiheitsrechte* in stabilizing the other complexes of rights, relevant to other spheres of society, all of which presuppose the possibility of the free self-presentation of individual personality. This seems to be the case especially for the so-called freedoms of communication. Let us note, in passing, that Luhmann also considers the rights of personality to be linked to a type of communication, namely, self-expression in a form recognizable to others as free and dignified.

In the case of the rights of assembly, association, press, and opinion, however, the context changes from personality to culture, from subjectivity to intersubjectivity and its presuppositions. As before, Luhmann considers fundamental rights to be relevant protections of communication only as long these are potentially threatened by the state.[109] He is not particularly successful in connecting in a clear-cut way a set of communication functions (culture and its internalization, the specification of the need for consensus, the mobility of contacts, and the determination of the themes of public opinion) with a series of rights (of religion and belief, of association and assembly, of the press, of art, of scientific research and teaching, and many others in an eclectic list). The point is nevertheless clear enough: In different ways, the modern state needs, yet potentially threatens, a many-leveled framework of societal communication that can be stabilized, in part, through fundamental rights.

The threat is statization and not politicization as such. For Luhmann, the state/society dichotomy is a misleading basis on which to construe the rights of communication, because it supposedly implies the political neutralization of nonstate spheres. Political problems and political power arise not only in the political system but also in frameworks of protected social communication. This societal power should be absorbed and processed by the political system rather than eliminated through statization. The unburdening of the state is essential, even at the cost of political threats arising from other social spheres.[110]

As in the case of rights relevant to personality, here, too, Luhmann claims a preeminent status for rights of communication. All social systems and identities, including personality, presuppose processes of social communication and require their protection vis-à-vis a dynamic modern political system. Economic rights do not seem to have the same fundamental importance in this presentation. While they themselves presuppose free personality and communication, the reverse is not argued (in contradistinction to liberal and neoliberal claims). To be sure, Luhmann does also oppose the derivation of the right of property and the "freedom" of profession from *Freiheitsrechte*.[111] It is not persons but roles and functions that must be protected in the case of the economy. Once again, despite the possibility of other social spheres (family, religion, science, etc.) inhibiting economic processes, Luhmann maintains that fundamental rights are relevant only when the state is the source of the threat. While the modern state and a differentiated economic order have long been presuppositions for each other,[112] the state as the source of binding decisions nevertheless has a tendency to intervene directly in economic processes. Rights of property and the freedoms of contract and profession protect the differentiation of economic processes and roles. They block some interventions not in the name of justice and injustice but in order to protect the economy from uncertainty and disorganization.[113] For this reason, these rights can be and are generally made compatible with forms of intervention that increase interdependence without dedifferentiation and with interventions that increase economic efficiency.[114]

Luhmann stands apart from the classical liberal and neoliberal notion of rights, based on a polemical rejection of state intervention in society, yet he stays within this tradition to the extent that he repeatedly claims that fundamental rights by their nature, and not only historically, represent forms of protection in the face of the state or, in other words, forms of self-limitation of the state. One reason for this preference lies in his definition of rights as forms of self-limitation by means of legal enactment. For the legal positivist, the only source of such enactment is the state. In the present context, however, this position leads to the paradoxical consequence that, although the primacy of the economy has replaced that of the political system,[115] and in principle the highly precarious economization of other spheres of society, including politics, is seen as a genuine danger,[116] self-limitation in the form of economic "constitutionalism" cannot and should not be introduced.[117] In Luhmann's framework, there are no rights against the economy. This prejudice leads him to rely even more on interventions from the political system to manage the risks of a highly dynamic economic subsystem, a position not really compatible with his intention to limit political intervention to acts designed to improve internal functioning. Indeed, as we now know, political interventions of the type he readily affirmed as late as the early 1970s could become dysfunctional from the long-term economic point of view, in the process producing additional negative side effects.

This partially self-contradictory outcome is all the more paradoxical because Luhmann cannot consistently restrict the notion of fundamental rights to self-limitations of the state in contexts where the political system represents the major source of risks for other subsystems. A case in point is political rights, which for Parsons represented mediating and integrating principles primarily. Eschewing this interpretation, Luhmann saves his general conception based on differentiation by reversing his perspective. Political rights such as suffrage, the secret ballot, as well as the rights of political associations (parties) and of elected officials represent for Luhmann, however paradoxically, forms of protection of the political subsystem against external (including economic!) pressures. They are ultimately mechanisms of selectivity uncoupling and insulating the highest instance of producing binding decisions, namely, the administration.[118] We have already seen this train of thought in Luhmann's political sociology. His stress is on preserving elections as the narrowest possible channel through which societal conflict, communication, and influence can enter the political system from outside and enter the administrative subsystem from the public and political subsystems of the political system. While, in comparison to Soviet-type systems,[119] he seems to note the role of political rights in protecting society from over-

politicization and the political subsystem from overbureau-
cratization, his emphasis in relation to the Western liberal democracies is entirely on shielding the political and the administrative.
Indeed, in this context the protection of electoral and public-
political procedure has its point only in the legitimation of the
decisions of an administration, which are arrived at through wholly
internal and uncontrolled procedures.[120]

Luhmann's affirmation of political rights as the self-protection of
the political sphere rather than its self-limitation with respect to
other social spheres is not only inconsistent with his conception as
a whole but also a statist aspect of his doctrine of rights. This stress
is only partially explained by the legal-positivist search to find
adequate political motivation for the self-limitation of the political
system through legal (including constitutional) enactments. The
idea that political rights are the self-protection of the political once
again helps Luhmann demonstrate the inadequacy of a model of
rights derived from the idea of defending society against the state.
For each complex of rights, he has used both the idea of the
differentiation of the spheres to be protected and the idea of
"interdependent independence" to criticize the rigidly dualistic
model of society and state. Differentiation in his model of rights
works initially through political-legal enactment, itself a form of
interdependence. Nor does differentiation, as we have seen in the
case of economic rights, exclude the possibility of new interrela-
tionships. Here, however, these considerations do not lead Luhmann
to claim the complete obsolescence of the state/society dichotomy.
Instead, he argues for its preservation through generalization in a
conception of systems communicating with one another.[121]

This new model is not designed to save the conception of civil
society. On the contrary. Luhmann seeks in particular to decompose the idea of a sphere in which mutually reinforcing and
stabilizing normative structures, forms of association, and public
communication confront the modern state and the modern
economy. To be sure, his hint that the rights of personality and of
communication represent each other's presuppositions on the
deepest level cuts through his framework of rigid differentiation.
Personality and communication are presented in some contexts
(even if vaguely) as each other's foundation, not as logically

separate albeit interdependent systems. But Luhmann does not develop this insight, although it could have served as the foundation for a deeper theory of rights. For him, fundamental rights differentiate and protect differentiated systems; they do not have their ground and justification in a single unified framework that, together, they help to establish as well as differentiate.

An exception, perhaps, is the legal system itself. Whatever else rights help to differentiate, their ability to function at all seems to depend on the differentiation of a system of procedures in which they can be autonomously interpreted and applied, and perhaps even enacted.[122] If rights are to defend differentiation from the political system, it would seem that they themselves must be differentiated from this system. And Luhmann does in fact attempt to treat (increasingly, as his legal sociology is developed) the legal system as a differentiated subsystem of society. Rights, which for him are legal institutions like any other, albeit with specific functions, belong to this subsystem. Since Luhmann considers law to be fundamentally linked to a normative style of expectation, we might assume that the legal subsystem itself represents a differentiated residue of the conception of civil society constructed in part around shared fundamental normative structures. In our view, however, and probably in his own, Luhmann's intended break with the concept of civil society is too radical to allow such an interpretation. The question is whether he can work out an adequate and consistent theory of the legal system, as differentiated from the political, in the context of his radical campaign against civil society.

The reevaluation of the problem of norms in Luhmann's legal sociology, and the restoration of a central place for norms in his sociological analysis, is striking, given his previous polemic against the theory of normative integration in Durkheim and Parsons. This polemic is now only partially mitigated. He argues that norms are important in the social structure, but to construe them as identical to that structure is to misunderstand their place.[123] Nor should norm and institution be considered synonymous: Not all institutions embody norms, and not all norms are institutionalized. Finally, it is wrong to assume that the normative integration of society is based on common and shared norms. In all differentiated societies, norms are contested and represent important stakes of conflict.[124] In this theory, legal norms, representing only a small portion of normative phenomena,[125] play a crucial role in managing and stabilizing normative conflict rather than expressing, symbolizing, and reaffirming normative order.

According to Luhmann, norms are "counterfactually stabilized behavioral expectations."[126] Laws are *institutionalized* norms, stabilized in terms of *procedures,* whose structure of expectations is guarded from and restored after disappointments by *sanctions.*[127] These definitions rest on detailed theoretical considerations that can only be outlined here. In the context of complexity and contingency, social action can be coordinated only through structures of complementary expectations and mechanisms capable of dealing with disappointment.[128] For Luhmann, "internal" expectations by individuals about the actions of others generally replace coordination through actual communication, which is understood as a time-intensive and therefore scarce resource, one best reserved for a few open, unsettled contexts, generally conflicts.[129] Expectation, however, as a response to the contingency of the other's actions, is put at risk by the fact that the other is the same as the self and has its own expectations. This leads potentially to double contingency: Each can be disappointed by the other. The coordination of social action is therefore possible only if the *expectations of expectations* are stabilized.[130]

In Luhmann's largely silent society, there are two and only two basic styles of expectation: the cognitive style, which is capable of learning and altering expectations in the face of disappointments, and the normative style, which involves inability or, rather, unwillingness to learn. What is typically considered to be a necessary yet very precarious form for projecting self-identity in the case of the individual psyche (not learning as involving immune reactions bordering on the pathological) becomes, in the case of normative expectations, a socially stabilized and guaranteed structure.[131] For both psychological projection and social norm, the main goal is to stabilize an identity-related structure of expectation rather than to secure empirical compliance. But while the origin and operation of psychical projection can be entirely internal to the individual, Luhmann is able to point to genuinely external, social mechanisms for stabilizing and reproducing norms.

Luhmann's treatment of the problem of origins is inadequate. The only social process of norm creation to which he can point—actual communication and coming to an understanding to create or alter rules and define deviance—he considers exceptional, characteristic only of small-scale social systems. Indeed, the validity of norms supposedly depends on the impossibility of actual communication concerning them, or at least concerning all of them within the same time horizon.[132]

The differentiation of society involves an increasing differentiation of the normative and cognitive styles of expectation. In their pure form, each is open to new risks: the risk of a hardening of social identities in one case, those of a completely contingent, and therefore unbearable, future in the other. The main response in modern society is not dedifferentiation but combinations involving "contrary ordering," as allowed by the reflexive structure of the expectation of expectations. In particular, one can cognitively expect a normative expectation and normatively expect a cognitive expectation.[133] The former combination, the cognitive expectation of the normative, has key importance for Luhmann's legal theory.

Norms become laws only if institutionalized in terms of sanctions and procedures. Institution building plays a crucial role in managing normative conflict. Luhmann defines institutionalization by the possibility of basing expectations on "the presupposed expectations of expectations on the part of a third party."[134] Different from external observers, third parties are potentially coexperiencing and coexpecting, albeit unknown and anonymous, members of the same fabric of interaction. The role of the judge crystallizes historically around the figure of the third party. For Luhmann, institutions, like norms, do not depend on actual communication or consensus. Actual consensus being scarce, institutionalization uses it economically. Instead of creating or presupposing consensus, institutions involve a better use of the small amount available, distributing it to relevant areas. For their own functioning, institutions only need an anticipation of consensus, with relevant third parties, in the expectation of expectations, a presumption that is rarely tested.[135] While empirically there is little to object to in this conception, we again note Luhmann's repeated inability to link the mechanisms of real communication and consensus building, which he cannot totally neglect, to his other mechanisms of stabilization, or even to assign any other reason for their existence than the implicit one that some actual consensus is needed to make plausible the anticipation, or "successful overestimation," of consensus.

In the case of legal norms as institutions, the actual mechanisms needed to stabilize expectations are sanctions and procedures. The importance of sanctions lies not in their secondary task of motivating compliance but in the possibility of relief from disappointment through a symbolic restitution of the norm. In developed societies, according to Luhmann, sanctions are the only way of demonstrating "the presumed consensus of third parties." Occasional coercion thus symbolizes anticipated consensus and can therefore replace factual consensus in Luhmann's model of law. In this model, though, the continuous functioning of law is not based primarily on coercion, an instrument that would become blunted by its very use. There is a need to represent continuity through a mechanism that is entirely present and yet can be presumed to exist beyond the current community of participants. Differentiated procedures play this role and thus have priority in the institutionalization of law.[136] Procedures are better than sanctions for symbolizing continuity because they can refocus concern from (increasingly less likely) agreements about outcomes to mutual, if only implicit, acceptance of an abstract framework for determining possible outcomes.[137]

Procedures are the central presupposition for the emergence of positive law. Not only are they the only mechanism available for the operation of the new level of reflexivity involved in the "normative regulation of the creation of norms,"[138] they are the (quasi-) medium[139] around which the differentiation of law from religion, morality, and scientific truth becomes possible. According to Luhmann, the central premise of positive law is production and alterability through enactment, that is, through procedurally correct decision. This can be put two ways—one legal, the other political—that indicate reflexivity: Norms regulate the making of norms, and decisions regulate the making of decisions. The norms that guide the making of norms, such as the constitution, are a set of norms like any other. So are the decisions that regulate decision making. Positive law means rejecting the possibility of extralegal sources of law and even of a hierarchy of legal levels. Nevertheless, it would be a mistake to interpret the positivity of law as meaning that normatively valid decisions are the only source of law. Norms, even potentially legal norms, emerge from all spheres of society. Legislation involves a process of making a selection from what is projected from elsewhere as potential law and then validating that selection as law. Only what passes through the procedural filter of legislation becomes valid law in this model.[140]

Luhmann's treatment, unlike some other versions of legal positivism, leaves room for sources of law creation other than legislative enactment. While he thereby prepares the way for reconciling historical and positive jurisprudence, he does so in an undifferentiated way at both poles. First, he does not distinguish between active and passive societal sources of law creation. This is connected with his focus on isolated subsystems and a theoretically anchorless, nondescript everyday life rather than, in the manner of Parsons, an organized social sphere in which culture and associations intersect. While he notes that patterns or institutions in any sphere of society can be turned into legal norms, he does not note the difference between social norms and social facts raised to the level of legal validity. Thus, he bypasses the question of whether normative as against legal *validity* can be produced apart from legislation and whether, therefore, the legislative process in the case of valid norms is a source of a higher validity or only of a form of binding and possibly universalization. Most importantly, he does not raise the question of whether or not a special role is played, as a source of norms for the legal system, by the processes of norm creation through coming to an understanding that he has described.

Second, his framework expresses uncertainty, similar to that of the tradition of legal positivism taken as a whole, concerning the legal as against the political character of positive law. The issue is whether or not the making and operation of positive law are functions of the political subsystem, in a way recalling the incorporation of other dimensions and mediations of civil society into this subsystem. In early writings on this topic (1967), Luhmann tended simply to affirm that the political subsystem supports and administers the mechanisms of positive law.[141] Later (1976), with the differentiation and autonomy of the legal subsystem already affirmed, Luhmann was still constrained to point to the overlap of the institutions and events of the two subsystems and to note the difficulties for law making inherent in legislation by a political body, the parliament.[142] Indeed, this overlap goes so far that the institutions of making, applying, and executing law turn out to be the three branches (legislative, executive, and judicial) of the central, administrative, decision-making subsystem of politics.[143] Thus, his assertion of the autonomy of the legal system has some difficulty in overcoming his other, earlier depiction according to which positive law is "state" law whose "destiny is bound up with that of the political system of society."[144]

Luhmann does speak of different selectivity[145] and, later, of different connections, linkages, and exclusions[146] of the two systems, legal and political, even in the case of shared institutions and events. One might argue, although he does not, that legislative decision making selects norms for legalization, whereas legislative procedures endow laws with the structure of validity. Finally, as in Luhmann's recent conception of law as an autopoietic system, one might consider law to be normatively closed while cognitively open. The first of these dimensions would yield legal autonomy and self-reproduction, while the second would provide for openness to the political system in which learning takes place.[147] The reason why none of these strategies will succeed in providing for the differentiation and autonomy of the legal system lies deep in Luhmann's conception of positive law and the shift contained therein toward a cognitive style of expectation.

> Positive law is here understood as a system of norms that comes into being through decision and can be changed through decision. We find in the processes of law positing decisions primarily a cognitive learning, determined by goals, one hardly structured by norms. . . . Correspondingly those affected by law must constantly learn the changes in the law, whether or not they are disappointed. They will have to take a primarily cognitive attitude to law.[148]

What is involved here is not a simple shift from a normative to a cognitive style of expectation but a shift to a combination ("contrary ordering") in which we cognitively expect a normative style of expectation. Positive law can adopt this structure because of the differentiation of legal procedures and roles. In the context of the general alterability of all legal norms, including constitutional ones, the natural attitude is that of learning. But positive law, in order to remain law at all, must preserve its normative function within alterability. In principle, this is possible as long as structures are not problematized in the situations they structure and as long as these situations are differentiated from others in which the same structures are questioned and perhaps changed.[149] It is judicial procedure and the role of the judge that institutionalizes a normative attitude to structures within a system of positive law. Of course, given the obvious alterability of law, even judges must "learn not to learn." While it is the task of the legislator to process disappointments, to correct expectations, and to take responsibility for failure to learn, the judge is ordinarily determined not to learn from the lawbreaker and learns how not to learn in the face of infringed norms.[150] One mechanism for this in the courtroom, paradoxically, is the technique of converting conflicts about norms into conflicts about facts, normative stakes into cognitive ones. In this way, judges need never expose their own norms to critical questioning and need not learn from those who have disappointed their expectations because of alternative normative expectations.[151]

Can a system that combines normative and cognitive expectations still be described as primarily normative? Luhmann does not ask this question, but he does indirectly answer it. He introduces the problem of legitimacy as a way of dealing with the binding character of the legal system as a whole. Here, too, the issue is the combination of learning and nonlearning, of cognitive and normative expectation. Both those who make and those who are affected by decisions avoid learning in the context of legal contingency only at their peril. Legitimacy in this context is defined by the possibility of assuming "that any third parties expect normatively that the directly affected persons cognitively prepare themselves for what the decision makers communicate as normative expectations."[152] An assumption is a cognitive expectation. Legitimacy is a circle of cognitive expectations in which only third parties—judges—are expected to expect normatively, and even their normative expectation of others is only that they will cognitively adapt to the judges' normative expectation. No wonder that Luhmann, almost uniquely in the sociological literature, considers physical force to be an essential legitimating factor,[153] most likely because it is the basis of the judges' often mistaken but not therefore abandoned expectation that potential lawbreakers will cognitively adapt. The structure of the law in this conception rests only on attitudes of cognitive expectation and the learned false consciousness of judges.

With all this said, the idea of law as an autopoietic, normatively closed, and cognitively open system seems to be merely a verbal solution to the problem, or at best a normative desideratum for the reconstruction of law. It is hard to see how Luhmann actually conjoins the two premises that "there may be political control of legislation, but only the law can change law."[154] Even if it is insertion into the legal system, with its own internal requirements, that turns legislation into law, a normative attitude of expectation would be saved only as a characteristic of a purely intellectual system incapable of performing functions for the rest of society, aside from motivating the functionally necessary false consciousness of judges. Because he has never found an integrating medium for law comparable to money or power, Luhmann's claims for boundary-maintaining, self-productive autonomy sound rather hollow. Thus, while the cognitively open dimension of law would remain rooted in the political system, which in turn is not opened up to the normative inputs of law, its normatively closed dimension would be suspended without social foundations, or at best become one of the closed rule systems established and institutionalized in the cultural sphere alone. Such are the consequences of abandoning the constitutive links of law to a framework of societal action, association, and communication and of the one-sided acceptance of the privileged relation of law to the political system, a deficiency balanced only partially by the affirmation of the heterogeneous societal sources of norm creation.

Despite Luhmann's self-understanding, the idea of law as an autopoietic system may be a normative desideratum born in a context characterized by increasing doubts about welfare-state interventions into society, which seems to involve a loss of legal formality and autonomy. But even as a project of reconstruction, the idea of the autonomy of law from politics requires an independent institutional context on which law can rely, without the dangers of an alternative (e.g., economic) instrumentalization.

This insight calls not only for a notion of civil society but also for its reconstruction in terms other than that of a subsystem of society in the manner of the Parsonian societal community. It is in the context of such a reconstruction that Luhmann's notion of autopoiesis first becomes serviceable for a postinterventionist model of the relations of the political system to the other spheres of society.

III

The Reconstruction of Civil Society

8

Discourse Ethics and Civil Society

We have before us two theoretical *topoi*: modern civil society and discourse ethics. The first evokes the theme of classical liberalism: The term "civil society" today calls to mind rights to privacy, property, publicity (free speech and association), and equality before the law. The second, with its emphasis on the equal participation of everyone concerned in public discussions of contested political norms, obviously refers to the principles of democracy. The current vogue in political theory is (once again) to view liberalism and democracy as fundamentally antithetical. Defenders of the core tenets of classical liberalism tend to see democracy, with its emphasis on majority rule and participation, as either illusory or, even worse, dangerous to existing liberties, unless suitably controlled or restricted.[1] Advocates of direct or radical democracy, on the other hand, have come to stigmatize the liberal tradition itself as the main impediment to achieving a participatory democratic society.[2] Nevertheless, we contend that the plausibility of each depends on its intimate conceptual and normative relation with the other. Even more, we assume that the defense and expansion of acquired liberties rests on the further democratization of the institutions of modern civil society and on their achievement of greater influence over the polity. We shall demonstrate this thesis by exploring the concepts of democratic legitimacy and basic rights in the framework of the theory of discourse ethics and by establishing the connection of both to a coherent conception of a modern, and potentially democratic, civil society.

Fortunately, we are not speaking in a void. The connection between the two principles has been made by many contemporary collective actors in the West and in the East who have put the project of the defense and/or democratization of civil society on their political agendas.[3] By "civil society," these actors have in mind a normative model of a societal realm different from the state and the economy and having the following components: (1) *Plurality*: families, informal groups, and voluntary associations whose plurality and autonomy allow for a variety of forms of life; (2) *Publicity*: institutions of culture and communication; (3) *Privacy*: a domain of individual self-development and moral choice; and (4) *Legality*: structures of general laws and basic rights needed to demarcate plurality, privacy, and publicity from at least the state and, tendentially, the economy. Together, these structures secure the institutional existence of a modern differentiated civil society.

The rediscovery of the key components of civil society by contemporary collective actors, however, does not in itself imply its normative justification. The projects of social movements are hardly self-validating. Furthermore, the normative ideals of civil society are not without their critics. As we have seen, Hannah Arendt and Michel Foucault have each made powerful arguments attacking these claims.[4] For Arendt, the differentiation of a social realm distinct from the state was the beginning of a fateful depoliticization of society, leading to the collapse of the boundary between public and private and the emergence of both mass society and totalitarianism. For Foucault, the very norms of civil society constituted only the visible support of less obvious social disciplines and microtechnologies that combine into a new and seamless system of bondage. We should remember, too, that the young Marx, the forerunner of these views, produced powerful arguments for equating civil with bourgeois society and the separation of state and society with political alienation.[5] If these and other critics of the norms of civil society are to be answered, it must be on the basis of a new, comprehensive, and justifiable practical political philosophy. It is our contention that discourse ethics, suitably reinterpreted, is the best candidate to accomplish this task.

Admittedly, the theory of discourse ethics also has its difficulties. First, there is some question whether its domain of application is morality, politics, or both. Second, it has been argued that the theory has authoritarian implications. Third, it is uncertain whether discourse ethics can make genuine universal claims without prescribing a particular form of life. Finally, the relation of discourse ethics to democratic and liberal institutions has never been satisfactorily elaborated.

We hope to show that it is possible to articulate plausible responses to all of these issues. We shall do so in five steps. Beginning with a discussion of Habermas's most detailed version of discourse ethics, we first consider the proper object domain of the theory. We then argue that, when suitably reinterpreted, discourse ethics avoids authoritarian implications. In order to make this point, we replace "generalizable interests" with "rational collective identity" as the legitimate substantive referent of formal discursive procedures. Next, we focus on the relationship of discourse ethics to concrete forms of life (*Sittlichkeit*). We go on to argue that while no single model of the good life follows from discourse ethics, this need not mean an insoluble institutional defect for the theory. It is in this context that the category of civil society allows us to bring together a plurality of forms of life with a political model that implies the institutionalization of discourses. Specifically, we link discourse ethics and modern civil society through the categories of democratic legitimacy and basic rights. Finally, we shall try to show that our reinterpretation of discourse ethics has the utopian horizon of what we shall call a "plurality of democracies."

The Object Domain of Discourse Ethics

The basic framework of discourse ethics consists of two dimensions.[6] The first specifies the conditions of possibility for coming to legitimate rational agreement; the second specifies the possible contents (on a formal level) of such an agreement.[7] A legitimate or rational procedure for coming to an agreement has been defined by Habermas as the *metanorm* that prescribes the only valid procedure for grounding or justifying norms of action.[8] No norm is assumed from the outset to be valid—only the procedure for validating norms can make such a claim legitimate. According to Habermas, a norm of action has validity only if all those possibly affected by it (and by the side effects of its application) would, as participants in a practical discourse, arrive at a (rationally motivated) agreement that such a norm should come into or remain in force.[9] What is to be understood as rationally motivated agreement, however, has rather demanding preconditions. In order that all those affected have an "effective equality of chances to assume dialogue roles," there must be a mutual and reciprocal recognition, without constraint, of each by all as autonomous, rational subjects whose claims will be acknowledged if supported by valid arguments.[10] But, in order that the dialogue be capable of producing valid results, it must be a fully public communicative process unconstrained by political or economic force. It must also be public in terms of access: Anyone capable of speech and action, who is potentially affected by the norms under dispute, must be able to participate in the discussion on equal terms. Furthermore, the participants must be capable of altering the level of discourse in order to be in a position to challenge traditional norms that may be tacitly presupposed.[11] In other words, nothing can or should be taboo for rational discourse— not the preserves of power, wealth, tradition, or authority. In short, the procedural principles underlying the possibility of arriving at a rational consensus on the validity of a norm involve *symmetry, reciprocity,* and *reflexivity.*[12]

These features constitute an "ideal speech situation," in which the validity claims implicitly raised in any act of communication can be discursively redeemed. It should be stated at the outset, however, that a theory of legitimacy should not be confused with a theory of organization. If we view the much-disputed concept of "ideal speech situation" as a set of criteria (metanorms) that enable one to distinguish between legitimate and illegitimate norms, we can avoid the confusion caused by interpretations that identify the formal rules of argumentive speech or discourse as a concrete utopia. The "ideal speech situation" refers solely to the rules participants would have to follow if they were to strive for an agreement motivated by the force of the better argument alone. If these conditions are not met—if, for example, actors in a debate do not have equal chances to speak or to challenge assumptions; if they are subject to force or manipulation—then participants are not taking all other arguments seriously as arguments and hence they are not really engaging in argumentative speech.

Clearly, not all processes of coming to an agreement satisfy such conditions. Habermas (and Karl-Otto Apel) repeatedly distinguish between "rational" and "empirical" consensus. Most processes of consensus formation are "only empirical."[13] The norms of discourse that are the source of validity are not produced by agreements; rather, they are the conditions of possibility of valid agreements. The results of actual agreements carry normative validity only to the extent that they are consistent with the metanorms. On the other hand, and some think paradoxically, Habermas insists on an *actual* rather than a virtual dialogue because only an actually carried out discourse allows an exchange of roles of each with every actor and hence a genuine universalization of perspective that excludes no one.[14] He thereby distinguishes himself from all approaches that assume agreement to follow from monologically attainable truth as well as from most traditions of contract theory (which postulate a discursive model only in terms of a myth of origins). Only an actual, practical discourse cooperatively engaged in by all participants potentially affected by the norm under discussion can lead to a rational consensus on its validity, for only under such conditions can we know that we, together, and not privately, are convinced about something. The metanorms of discourse ethics are thus peculiar in the sense that their normative implications are available only in contexts of actual dialogue.

Accordingly, Habermas has reformulated the Kantian categorical imperative along lines compatible with the procedural rules of argument: "Instead of prescribing to all others as valid a maxim that I will to be general law, I have to offer my maxim to everyone with the aim of discursively testing its claim to universalizability. The emphasis shifts from what each can will without contradiction to be a general law, to what all can will in agreement to be a universal norm."[15]

The idea of a rational consensus, however, involves more than the actual participation of every affected person in the relevant discussion. In addition to a process of consensual will formation, our assertion that a norm is legitimate means that we hold it to be *right* and not merely conformable to our collective will. Habermas insists that discourse ethics, like all cognitivist ethics, assumes that claims to normative validity have cognitive meaning and can be handled, with certain adjustments, like cognitive truth-claims.[16] The factual recognition of a norm by a community merely indicates that the norm could be valid. Its validity can be ascertained only if we make use of a "bridge principle" that establishes a connection between the process of will formation and the criteria for judging the acceptability of a particular norm. The *Unparteilichkeit* of judgment must complement the *Unbeinflussbarkeit* of collective will formation.[17]

In elaborating this second aspect of discourse ethics, Habermas addresses the dimension of content alluded to above. This brings us to the second aspect of discourse ethics: the formal content of agreements. Habermas maintains that in order to be objective (*unparteilich*), rational, and legitimate, norms of action upon which we agree must express a generalizable interest:[18] Every valid norm must satisfy the following condition; "All affected can accept the consequences and the side effects that its *general* observance can be anticipated to have for the satisfaction of *everyone's* interests (and these consequences are preferred to those of alternative possibilities for regulation)."[19] This "principle of universalization" requires actual discourses if those affected are to be able to discern what all can agree to recognize as a universal norm.

Thus far we have simply summarized Habermas's formulation of discourse ethics. As several critics have recently pointed out, however, the status or object domain of the theory is unclear.[20] On the one hand, Habermas clearly considers it to be a universalistic moral theory in the Kantian tradition. On the other hand, he also presents discourse ethics as the heart of a theory of democratic legitimacy and the core of a universalist conception of human rights that provide alternatives to traditional and neocontractarian theories. To make matters even more complicated, Habermas has argued that, as a principle of legitimacy, discourse ethics can resolve the apparent rift between legality and morality by revealing the political ethic underlying law.[21] His purpose is to account for the link between morality and legality in a way that—unlike Marxist approaches, which seek to abolish the distinction between the two—presupposes their difference but nevertheless adjusts formal law to moral principles. The first question to address, then, is what exactly is the object domain of discourse ethics? Is it a theory of morality, or a theory of political legitimacy? Can it be both?

We intend to defend discourse ethics as a *political ethics* and as a *theory of democratic legitimacy and basic rights.* We hold that it provides a standard with which we can test the legitimacy of sociopolitical norms. Terms such as "public dialogue," "general interests," "all those affected," and "social norms" do in fact evoke the categories of political philosophy. The theory becomes unnecessarily overburdened when presented as more than this. Indeed, the two most significant objections that have been raised against the ability of discourse ethics to serve as a moral theory focus on those dimensions that make it a plausible candidate for a theory of democratic legitimacy, namely, the reformulated principle of universalization and the requirement of an actual dialogue.[22] We want to bracket the question of which general theory works best in the realm of autonomous moral judgment. We believe it is none-theless possible to defend discourse ethics as a political ethic without committing oneself to a specific moral philosophy.

This means that we construe the project of discourse ethics as an attempt to employ the insights of deontological ethical theory primarily against legal positivism and legal realism as well as against systems theory of the Luhmann type. The task, in short, is to show that there is a normative and rationally defensible component of legality and politics that, independent of sanctions or empirical motives, accounts for the obligatory dimension of legal norms and the legitimacy of a sociopolitical system.

Differentiating between a general moral theory and a theory of political legitimacy, however, leaves us with a key question: How does one draw the boundary between the two? It is not sufficient to state that morality entails the individual reflections of a moral conscience whereas justice concerns social norms and requires a real dialogue, for both morality and legality relate to societal norms, and the issue at hand is precisely the reach of law with respect to these norms. Nor are those attempts convincing that try to draw the boundary between the two by designating certain spheres of life as private by definition and off-limits to law and others as public and thus open to legal-normative regulation. In our view, this approach cannot work, for a society's understanding of the institutional arrangements and relations that should be set beyond justice and left to individual judgment changes over time. Moreover, the designation "private" with regard to institutions and relations does not exempt them from satisfying the demands of justice but, rather, implies a different form of legal-normative regulation.[23] One cannot reason from a spatial metaphor or division among institutions to designate the boundary between private and public, between what should be left to the moral choice or personal judgment of individuals and what should be legally regulated. Instead, we must start from the assumption that privacy attaches to the individual in certain capacities (as an autonomous moral subject), regarding certain choices (those impinging on identity needs), and within the framework of certain relations (friendship, intimacy) that we must be ready to analyze and give arguments for. Indeed, the private and even the intimate "spheres" have always been constituted and regulated by law, even if what is constituted includes a domain of autonomous judgment that can come into conflict with law. Thus, we insist on retaining the analytic distinction between between a domain of autonomous moral reflection or judgment and a domain of legal norms, but we reject any attempt to set up a one-to-one correspondence between this distinction and spheres of life or sets of institutions. Rather, law must be self-limiting with respect to the autonomous judgment of individuals, provided that this does not entail the violation of basic principles of justice. Privacy rights operate precisely in this manner, although just what content falls within the protection of a right to privacy is, of course, open to debate and revision.

From the other side, our interpretation of discourse ethics as a theory of democratic legitimacy and basic rights presupposes the sociological insight concerning the positivization of law and the corresponding separation between the spheres of legality and morality. Yet our version of the theory rejects the view that the total denormatization of politics or law and the depoliticization of morality are the inevitable consequences of this process. How can this apparent paradox be resolved?

It is clearly Habermas's view (and ours) that the development of autonomous universalist morality as well as the emergence of a formal, differentiated system of positive law must be seen as immense historical achievements. These developments, moreover, are linked to the emergence of specifically modern conceptions of democracy and rights, representing the constitutive conditions of a modern version of civil society. There is, however, another side to this process: The uncoupling of positive legal norms from the body of private morality based on principles that accompanied the emergence of constitutional states and capitalist market economies entails a potential conflict between the loyalty of the citizen to the abstract rules of the legal system (which are valid only for the area "pacified" by a particular state) and the "cosmopolitanism of the human being" whose personal morality makes general claims.[24] Even more important, ever since the decline of modern natural law theories and the rise of legal positivism, the claim that laws have normative content beyond the correctness of the appropriate legislative and legal procedures, that they are binding independently of relevant sanctions, has been repeatedly disputed. The differentiation between legality and morality has involved both the separation of politics from the everyday life of citizens and the denormatization of legality itself, at least according to a good deal of legal theory since the nineteenth century.[25]

Moreover, when law is understood as the will or command of the sovereign (Hobbes, Austin), and when constitutions and fundamental rights are declared to be only special instances of positive law, the results go beyond the separation of morality and law. In effect, legal positivism announces the denormatization of law, its transformation into a class of empirical facts. Obligation is turned into prudent behavior in the face of possible sanctions. Even within legal positivism (H. L. A. Hart), such extreme results are often rejected and the ideas of law as command and obligation as calculation have been decisively refuted. Nevertheless, it is hard to see how a conception of law as a system whose purely legal terms need be related only to one another and satisfy only demands of consistency (Kelsen) or validity in terms of a "secondary" legal order (Hart) can lead to anything like a genuine political ethics capable of grounding legal or political legitimacy. This is even harder to see in the case of the view that reduces law to sociological predictions about what courts, legislatures, communities, and political officials or other holders of power will wish to enforce with sanctions (legal realism; some versions of critical legal studies).

In his debate with Weber and Luhmann concerning the foundation of legal-rational domination, Habermas has repeatedly pointed to the impossibility of deriving the legitimacy of a modern legal system as a whole solely from the formality and systematic nature of legal procedures.[26] Law as legitimate authority rests on extralegal sources of justification. References to constitutions as the ultimate source of authority, at least on the part of formally democratic states, implies that the legitimacy of law is ultimately *parasitic* on the principles of democracy and basic rights—embodied in constitutions and in the democratic process allegedly behind the development of constitutions. The principles of democratic legitimacy and basic rights underlie the authority of law. These principles, however, can no longer be defended as sacred, "self-evident truths," as they were both in theories of natural law and in republican theories of civic virtue. The task of discourse ethics is to provide a contemporary equivalent of such theories while avoiding their presuppositions. Thus, the principles of democracy it justifies must not be seen as given, once and for all, but as the outcomes of an original and repeatable communicative process that ascertains the generality of admissible norms and the discursive redeemability of the validity claims with which they appear.

We propose to define legality in terms of the old reference to formal sanctions that potentially invoke the executive and judicial powers of the modern state on behalf of valid norms. Moral rules cannot call upon such enforcement. Accordingly, discourse ethics as we see it would apply to the legal and political system as a whole, as well as to particular complexes of legal norms that depend both on sanctions and on the interpretation and compliance of those concerned. In the first instance, we reinterpret discourse ethics as a principle of democratic legitimacy; in the second, as part of a theory of basic rights that can be institutionalized. As we shall show, these two dimensions of discourse ethics imply a province of autonomous moral judgment that is beyond its reach but nonetheless is its presupposition and must be guaranteed by basic rights. Let us first address this latter issue.

We are assuming that discourse ethics pertains to the sphere of legality in two interdependent yet distinct dimensions: democratic legitimacy and basic rights. Each of these dimensions touches on morality. However, even if we can say empirically where legality begins and autonomous judgment ends by referring to formal sanctions, we have not yet touched on the normative question of where these boundaries ought to be. Of course, all modern civil societies draw a boundary between a realm of autonomous judgment and what can be legally regulated, but they draw these boundaries at different places. In case of disputes, the issue is inevitably whether the boundaries should be drawn from the point of view of legality or individual judgment, public discourse or private moral reflection. In our opinion, in such cases discourse ethics must be considered superior to any monologically attained moral standpoint, at least in the first instance. This is so because only in an actual discussion with everyone potentially affected by a legal norm can *we* find out what, if anything, is common to us all, what should be the domain of legal regulation, what forms of political decision making are legitimate, what should be left to the autonomous subject's personal judgment, and what must be compromised with. In other words, it is only after debatable issues have been publicly discussed that we can decide which must be considered "private," that is, left to the autonomous judgment of the individual to determine with respect to a personal ideal of the good life.[27]

Discourse ethics thus has a double status: Its specific object domain comprises institutionalized social relations, the legal and political system as a whole, and particular laws and rights. It also provides a way to decide the boundary question between autonomous individual judgment and justice. To be sure, the boundaries drawn from the point of view of actual discursive processes may not be acceptable from the standpoint of the moral convictions or identity needs of individuals or groups. A majority might seek to legally regulate areas of decision making that have previously been construed as private and that a minority does not want to deliver to such regulation. Conscientious objection and civil disobedience are legitimate options from the moral point of view. They should be respected as efforts to acknowledge publicly drawn boundaries while attempting to circumvent or change them from the point of view of an unusually intense concern. However, in these cases, the claims of justice have priority in the following sense: One cannot be compelled to renounce one's way of life, identity, or moral convictions, and yet the moral consciousness that doesn't want to be unjust must be self-limiting in that it must accept the principle of democratic legitimacy and basic rights provided that these are self-limiting in turn. In other words, they must protect the space for articulating difference. This means that, in the case of conflict between conceptions of the good life and legality, it should not be deemed unethical for the individual to follow his or her moral conscience or judgment and to act accordingly. But one must, nonetheless, act under the dictates of self-limitation. Within the framework of a democratic constitutional polity, a morally legitimate violation of law presupposes the acknowledgment of constitutional principles, acceptance of the democratic order, and a symbolic orientation of the action toward influencing public opinion and developing a new normative consensus.[28] The legal response to such action ought to be able to distinguish it from common criminality and thus avoid being overly harsh.[29] All principled acts of disobedience, from individual acts of conscience to tactics of social movements, rest on these ideas.

Thus, our interpretation does not collapse the boundary between morality and legality. On the contrary, it preserves a realm of autonomous judgment for the individual. At the same time, it protects positive law from the potentially incapacitating interference of absolute moral judgments without thereby delivering it into the hands of legal positivists. Indeed, once we restrict the relevance of discourse ethics to questions of democratic legitimacy and rights, it leaves room for a variety of moral principles, cultural values, and ways of life. Without having to judge the internal adequacy of any of these, discourse ethics adjudicates between them only in cases of conflict over general societal norms. Thus, the autonomy of conscience and the plurality of ways of life are respected by the principles of democratic legitimacy and basic rights, even though the latter bring principles to bear on the domains of law and politics. Although in this case, too, processes of discursive will formation decide the boundary between "private" and "public," they cannot entirely abolish the private (understood here as the domain of autonomous individual moral choice or judgment).

The metanorms of discourse themselves presuppose, even if they cannot ground, the autonomy of the individual moral conscience.

If all persons affected have the chance to assume dialogue roles, if the dialogue must be unconstrained, if each individual can shift the level of discourse, and if everyone can articulate their need interpretations, then practical discourse presupposes autonomous individuals with the capacity not only to be self-reflective regarding their own values but also to challenge any given norm from a principled standpoint. The processes necessary for the requisite socialization of individuals would be impossible without institutionalizing moral autonomy and the mutual recognition of difference secured by rights.

Thus, the very rules that underlie argument and the cooperative search for consensus imply the distinction between morality and legality. By articulating the metanorms of the principle of democratic legitimacy and some key rights, discourse ethics presupposes the justification for the autonomy of the moral sphere and, as it were, its own self-limitation. There is yet another reason for this. No consensus, no matter how unanimous or long-lasting, can know itself to be permanent, for there is no automatic coincidence between the just and the moral, between what is deemed normatively right at any given time for a solidary community and what is always morally acceptable to each individual. Even if the legal norm has survived the most ideal process of discursive testing, it may yet conflict with the particular values or identity requirements of an individual. Neither moral autonomy nor individual identity can be sacrificed to the collective identity or consensus of a group, because this would violate the very raison d'être of discourse ethics: to provide a formal principle for the legitimacy of norms in a society that is plural and composed of individuals with distinct and different conceptions of the good life. Even in a situation that closely approximates the requirements of symmetric reciprocity, there is no basis for assuming either the absence of difference or the absence of change. Every consensus is, after all, only empirical and must be open to challenge and revision.[30] From the standpoint of justice, we cannot know that today's value change on the part of a minority of individuals might not become tomorrow's general will. Thus, individual judgment, differing ways of life, and experiments with new ways must be granted autonomy from the current consensus on what is just.

One might nonetheless object, from the point of view of a moral consciousness, that a separate theory of ethics for the realm of law and politics is unnecessary. As a moral subject, I obey the law because it is right, and when it becomes morally wrong to do so, I would have to disobey the law, whatever the consequences to myself. Morality is certainly wider than legality—from both objective and subjective points of view. Formal law cannot regulate every domain of action, whereas, from the subjective point of view, morality ought to. The moral consciousness could grant the necessity of law and sanctions because we are not gods, not always moral, and thus need external constraint in certain cases. But if the moral component of law is equivalent to what the moral reflections of an individual actor could arrive at, then there is no need for a separate ethical theory for politics. Why develop a discourse ethics at all?

There are, in the modern context, two reasons why we cannot move directly from morality to legality or resynthesize them, as it were. First, as is well known, we moderns live in a plural moral universe—the plurality of value systems, modes of life, and identities would be violated if laws or political decisions were made from the point of view of any of them. Every good liberal thus can argue against making any single moral standpoint absolute for the whole of society. To do so would lead either to subjugating individual dignity and rights to the concerns of general welfare or to violating the integrity of those who do not share the particular concept of the good life that has become dominant. Not all action, not even all moral action, can or ought to be institutionally regulated.

The second and more compelling reason why we cannot equate the obligatory dimension of social/political norms with what motivates even the postconventional moral actor is that the genesis of legality, unlike morality, can and must involve in principle actual discourse. To be sure, Habermas himself tends to conflate morality and legality because he rightly sees that moral testing involves an inner dialogue to which the rules of argument apply.[31] It would thus seem possible, if one followed these rules and considered the potential side effects of a maxim on all others, that one could arrive at the same judgment that an actual discourse would yield. The core difference between virtual and actual dialogue would, nonetheless, remain: Only an actual dialogue in which all concerned can participate on equal terms of mutual recognition would involve a reversal of perspectives and yield or reaffirm a *we*, a solidary collectivity, having a collective identity and the capacity for articulating a general or common interest. As Hannah Arendt pointed out long ago, only in a public space can a public opinion merge. Even if one imagined an ideal moral subject, able to consider all the possible arguments of everyone involved, the outcome would not automatically converge with the political judgment of a duly constituted public, because the relevant, emergent collective identity would be missing. At best, an idealized, self-reflective moral judgment could imply tolerance of others and of different arguments, but it could not yield or reaffirm the solidarity of a collectivity or an understanding of what our collective identity is and, flowing from this, what our general interests might be. This, however, is the object domain of institutionalized norms. Nor would it yield insight into perspectives entirely different from our own, and thus the possibility of solidarity with difference—and the limits this implies on normative regulation—would be missing. Indeed, it is quite possible that a judgment could be moral and yet not be just. On our interpretation, discourse ethics implies that the justice of justice, the legitimacy and normative force of law, derives in principle from democratic will formation and the articulation of a general interest in the norm. From the point of view of morality, a law imposed by an enlightened despot might be moral according to everyone's personal point of view, and it might even articulate a general interest (the common good). Yet—and this is the limit to the standpoint of the moral consciousness—even if it were moral, even if it were to coincide with what a community would have agreed upon as its interest, it would not be just, for justice requires that those affected determine this for themselves, in a discursive process of collective will formation.

Let us summarize the argument thus far. (1) The division between morality and legality is a major and characteristic achievement of modernity. (2) Discourse ethics provides the core of a normative theory of political legitimacy and of a theory of rights, but it cannot serve as a moral theory informing the choices of individuals in all areas of life. (3) We interpret the meaning of justice along the lines of a concept of democratic legitimacy and basic rights. Accordingly, the object domain of discourse ethics comprises institutionalized norms with legal sanctions attached. (4) Discourse ethics grants autonomy to other modes of moral reasoning. (5) Based on the theory of communicative action, discourse ethics is able to account for the obligatory aspect of social norms that is distinct from the attached sanctions. (6) Political and legal institutions can be made responsible to moral insight without involving the collapse of legality and morality. Indeed, in constitutional democracies with civil societies, the principles of democratic legitimacy and basic rights already are the ultimate source for justifying political norms and processes.

The Charge of Authoritarianism

The charge of authoritarianism, leveled specifically against Habermas's version of discourse ethics, contends that the focus on rational consensus implies a Jacobin-Bolshevik suppression of independent ways of life and, hence, of civil society. We shall start by refuting this charge and developing a version of discourse ethics immune to it. Our next step will be to deny an intrinsic connection between discourse ethics and any specific concrete ethos or *Sittlichkeit*, while demonstrating that this does not leave it merely formalistic or empty. Indeed, we shall argue that discourse ethics has an elective affinity for a societal arrangement that permits a plurality of ways of life to coexist. In this way we hope to show that, among the versions of civil society, only the modern ones are relevant to discourse ethics.

It seems that two apparently contradictory charges have been made against Habermas's discourse ethics: authoritarianism on the one side, and excessive formalism on the other. Presumably the two charges could be combined: Either discourse ethics is so formalistic as to have no institutional consequences, or, if it has, they inevitably have authoritarian implications. We prefer to deal with these charges separately, since the issues involved are completely different.

The charge of authoritarianism has several variants. The first involves a blanket application of Hegel's critique of Kant, linking abstract morality and terror to discourse ethics as a whole. On this level, the objection has been successfully dispatched by Albrecht Wellmer.[32] More specific objections discover an authoritarian potential in two particular sets of distinctions made by Habermas: (1) between "empirical" and "rational" consensus, and (2) between "particular" and "universal" or "general" interests. According to Robert Spaeman, for example, with these distinctions "the utopian goal for the abolition of domination serves precisely the legitimation of the domination of self-appointed enlighteners."[33]

1. It is certainly very wrong to apply this objection to Habermas, as if he merely belonged to the romantic, anticapitalist generation of Marxists of the early twentieth century. Yet the distinction between "empirical" and "rational" consensus, if interpreted as calling for the abolition of one for the sake of the other, indeed recalls the classical Jacobin-Bolshevik contempt for the merely empirical people or working class.

Habermas, however, has been careful to avoid this implication. Even after rejecting the full applicability of a psychoanalytic model of reflection to a critique of society, he holds on to the assumption that "only the techniques of discourse (should be used) to establish the conditions for beginning possible discourses."[34] He goes beyond that model by insisting that, in the discourse whose function is to establish or reestablish discourse, "there can be only participants," because no one can have "a privileged access to truth."[35] The implication of Habermas's argument, in other words, is not to forcibly replace the conditions of one type of discourse with those of another but to establish new forms side by side with the old ones and perhaps to revitalize existing forms of public life. Indeed, Habermas explicitly denies a privileged discourse of intellectuals or political organizations that would play a "leading role" with respect to empirical processes of communication.[36]

It is Albrecht Wellmer, however, who goes the furthest in an antiauthoritarian direction by frankly announcing that *actual* consensus necessarily means *factual* consensus.[37] How, then, can we tell when an empirical consensus is rational? To doubt the rationality of an empirical consensus means either to propose specific counterarguments or to doubt the rationality of the participants. The latter, however, cannot be grasped with the help of the structural conditions of the ideal speech situation. The doubt remains an hypothesis that can be sustained only by carrying out a new discourse and arriving at a new agreement: The participants must recognize their previous unreason. As Agnes Heller aptly puts it, the norms of argument, together with the insistence on a real dialogue open to all, imply a democratic process of will formation such that the general will can, after all, only be the will of all.[38] Even if a consensus is the product of a "rationally organized society" that allows for both discourse and dissent in its public spaces, we may not assume that the rationality of the procedure guarantees the absolute truth or rightness of the result. The truth of norms cannot be established once and for all. The content of a rational consensus is not necessarily true—we consider it to be rational because of procedural norms, true because of good grounds that we offer in the discussion and that are accepted as such.[39] But we could be mistaken or, to put it better, the kinds of reasons we are willing to accept can change over time. At best, we can arrive at a rational grounding of the conviction of truth that we must treat as true but that nonetheless we, as reflective moderns, must consider to be fallible and open to new arguments. Thus, the idea of a rational consensus does not mean the attainment of absolute truth. The possibility of agreeing on norms involves the possibility of *rational* disagreement! In short, a rational empirical consensus, the product of discourse, is open to learning and, of course, to dissent.

2. If the distinction between rational and empirical consensus (linked to the procedural dimensions of collective will formation) can thus be protected against authoritarian implications, the distinction between particular and general interests (tied to the principle of universalization) exposes Habermas once more to these charges, this time with regard to issues of content rather than form. As already indicated, discourse ethics tests the validity of norms according to whether they articulate generalizable interests. In both early and recent formulations, Habermas maintains that discourse ethics brings need-interpretations into discussions of norms, so that a constraint-free consensus permits only what all can want.[40] Only if norms express generalizable interests, in addition to being the product of a general will or agreement, are they based on a rational and true consensus. However, given the thesis that, in formally democratic, capitalist, class-based societies, the results of

empirical discursive processes suppress "generalizable interests," Habermas has repeatedly resorted to the conditional language of ascription: "would agree" "were [they] to enter into an unconstrained discourse," etc.[41] The status he gives to such ascription is only that of a social-scientific hypothesis that requires testing and confirmation in actual processes of practical discussion. Nevertheless, the theory is ambiguous at this level. While "discursively redeemable norms" or universalizable general interests must be "both formed and discovered in processes of practical discourse,"[42] Habermas also seems to imply that, strictly speaking, only from the "perspective of the third person, say of the social scientist" could the model of generalizable interests be applied critically. In earlier texts, Habermas has spoken of "suppressed generalizable interests" in order to relate the theory critically to those social systems that prevent the conditions necessary for practical discourse from emerging. The apparently objective vantage point he postulates for social science (that of the nonparticipant "monologically" arriving at true general interests) seems to correspond to the old Leninist or Lukácsian point of view for distinguishing between "real" "universal" vs. "false" "empirical" particular interests. The ambiguous status of the concept of suppressed generalizable interests thus opens Habermas to the charge of authoritarianism.

One way to avoid this charge would be to argue that the model of generalizable interests is not as central to discourse ethics as some interpreters, including Habermas himself, have maintained. To be sure, Habermas insists that the satisfaction of interests need not be a zero-sum game, and that some interests in all societies are, in fact, generalizable. Yet one could argue that discourse ethics could survive an empirical situation largely to the contrary. Assuming only particular interests, the discourse that is needed for agreement on the rules of their coordination could still be seen as an expression of the general. Even a stable compromise needs *normative* grounding and rests on a consensus as to its binding character, whether traditional or discursive. Habermas has had a tendency to interpret plurality in individualistic terms, group forms of plurality as particularistic, and compromise as strategic.[43] Nevertheless, he now insists on the need to discursively map out the boundaries between generality and plurality, consensus and compromise, giving all of these terms a communicative foundation.[44]

In his most recent text on the topic,[45] Habermas has corrected his earlier formulation in which compromise appeared to correspond to the failure of communicative action. He still distinguishes between the attempt by all concerned to clarify what is a common interest and the effort of those seeking compromise to strike a balance between particular, conflicting interests. But he has come to see that binding compromise also requires specific conditions. Participants in a binding compromise assume that a fair balance can be achieved only if all concerned can participate equally. "But these principles of compromise formation in turn require actual practical discourses for justification."[46] A nonstrategic relation to the structure of compromise that involves accepting its underlying normativity is the sine qua non for stable compromises to occur. The rules of the game must be taken seriously. If the structure of compromise itself has the capacity to obligate, it is the common concern of all.

The communicative foundations of compromise among a plurality of particular interests could be made stronger if the typical case of a "rational coming to an agreement" were interpreted as that of a rational argument for a plurality of points of view, forms of life, or interests that could lead to compromise. According to Wellmer, the index of particularity that attaches to all human situations should be thought of not as a "possible *limitation* to rational self-determination and communication" but as "moments of situatedness" to be brought into the concept of reason. "Exactly where unification cannot be attained, there at least all must have the same right to get a hearing for their arguments and to participate in decisions."[47] Thus, generality is attached not to the content of interests but to the structure that allows all to articulate their particular interests, and this is what leads to valid and binding compromise.

As seductive as this solution to the problems raised by the conception of general interest is, it is not entirely compelling. Indeed, Habermas has explicitly addressed a version of this argument, that of Ernst Tugendhat, and rejected it. Tugendhat attempted to equate argumentation with processes of collective will formation and to excise the cognitive dimension from the theory of communicative ethics.[48] On the basis of the position that every "rational agreement" is in fact an empirical one, he argues that the issue is solely one of elaborating principles for equal, symmetric participation in acts of collective choice. Questions of justification are not relevant here—acts of collective choice are acts of will, not of reason.

Against this position, Habermas points out that the price of excising the cognitive dimension of discourse ethics is that we are no longer able to distinguish the de facto social acceptance of a norm from its validity.[49] If we replace the "*Unparteilichkeit*" of judgment with the "*Unbeinflussbarkeit*" of will formation, we cannot say why even the product of a unanimous collective choice would be binding, if no principle besides a momentary agreement underlies it. This is the classic objection against theories of democratic will formation and majority rule. A mere empirical consensus does not in itself produce legitimate obligation. Nor, for that matter, is it stable. Moreover, it has no authoritative character if it can be changed at will and if it depends only on our momentary agreement. Habermas thus repeats his stress on the centrality of the idea of general interest to discourse ethics.

The insistence on the cognitive component of norms is also meant as the basis for a reply to the inevitable decisionism that generally accompanies the Weberian thesis of the war of the gods, that is, of the irreducible plurality and even irreconcilability of values in modern societies. Habermas maintains that we can give rational grounds for the intersubjective recognition of validity claims without resorting to metaphysics or dogmatism. The validity claims of norms are not, accordingly, located in the irrational volitional acts of the contracting parties but in a "rationally motivated recognition of norms, which can be questioned at any time."[50] The fact of pluralism need not mean that it is impossible to separate, by arguments, generalizable interests from those that are and remain particular. Yet he insists that "the cognitive component of norms is not limited to the propositional content of the normed behavioral expectations. The normative validity claim is itself cognitive in the sense of the supposition, however counterfactual, that it could be discursively redeemed through the giving of reasons and the gaining of insight—that is, grounded in consensus of the participants through argumentation."[51]

Habermas confuses several distinct issues. To insist that the cognitive character of a general interest yields the validity of a norm confuses several meanings of the term "cognitive." It is one thing to argue that the principles of argumentation can provide a metanorm to which participants can appeal in testing the outcomes (norms) of an existing empirical consensus. It is quite another to locate the standard for the validity of norms in a concept of general interest that is, by its very nature, ascertainable from the social-scientific or observer's point of view. The latter strategy revives the naturalistic fallacy that equates the objective generality of interests with the universality of norms. Indeed, Habermas seems to be confusing two meanings of "rationality" that he has elsewhere painstakingly differentiated. The rational process of coming to an agreement involves principles of argumentation that are cognitive in the sense that we can test them in discourse. Nevertheless, the processes of raising and arguing validity claims with respect to the rightness of a norm is distinct from the rationality or cognitive character of truth claims involved in statements of fact. To treat normative validity claims like cognitive truth claims would be to confuse the object domains explored by practical and by theoretical discourse, respectively. Practical discourse refers to a world (the "social world") experienced and even reconstructed in the performative attitude, that is, the attitude of participants. It is implicated in a double hermeneutic and always depends on the validity claims made by the relevant social actors. Theoretical discourse, even about society, requires objectifying the social actors and their actions. The language of general or generalizable interests is theoretical in this sense. It replaces the opinions of participants about what they need, want, and desire with an objective judgment (based on an analysis) about their interests. Thus, Habermas's stress on the criterion of general interests, in response to Tugendhat's renunciation of the rationality claims embodied in the metanorms of argumentation, relies on the wrong discursive test. The generality of the interests does not yield the validity of the norm. Indeed, the idea that the legitimacy of a norm rests on the fact that it reflects a general interest makes consensus superfluous, for it implies that because the norm reflects such an interest (however this is ascertained), consensus on its validity should follow. In short, consensus would follow validity rather than the other way around.[52]

Tugendhat's denial that the metatheoretical foundations of discourse have any relevance and Habermas's insistence on the concept of general interest as a standard for testing the validity of norms represent two mistaken solutions to the problem of obligation. The former involves arbitrariness; the latter, objectivism. To his credit, Habermas is aware of the embarrassment faced by a reflective mode of justification in the context of value pluralism, posttraditional law, and postconventional moral reasoning. The viable part of his response is his insistence that the objectivity (*Unparteilichkeit*) of judgment is rooted in the structure of argumentation itself—it is not brought in as a value from the outside because we happen to choose it.[53] Although every consensus can be only empirical, this does not mean that we are left with an arbitrary collective will. Rational grounds can be given not for the truth of values per se, but for their incorporation into sociopolitical norms. The principles of argumentation can provide a metanorm (symmetric reciprocity) to which participants can appeal in testing the outcomes (norms) of an empirical dialogue. The rationality of a consensus can be tested by referring validity claims back to those metaprinciples that alone can make it valid and obligatory. Thus, the principles of discourse that imply both the consideration of every rational argument and the respect of everyone capable of arguing allow us to arrive at what is normatively right. This is the convincing part of Habermas's position.

But this still leaves unclear the role of the concept of "general interest" and what the "principle of universalization" adds to the principles of argumentative procedure of discourse ethics. If "generalizable interests" refers to "raw" need-interpretations, then the objection first articulated by Hume and repeated by Agnes Heller that a discussion around interests and needs can only be inconclusive would be legitimate.[54] On the other side, we have already shown that if the concept of general interest refers to the objective interests of a group, then this cannot be used as the criterion for the rightness of norms without authoritarian implications.

Nevertheless, the concept of interest is important to our interpretation of discourse ethics. We suggest that the term "general interest" must give way, or rather priority, to the idea of "common identity." In societies characterized by a plurality of value systems, modes of life, and individual identities, discourse ethics provides a way of discovering or reaffirming what, if anything, we who come into contact with one another and who are affected by the same political decisions and laws have in common. As stated earlier, we affirm and in part constitute through discourse who we are, and under which rules we wish to live together, apart from our personal or particular identities and differences—that is, what our *collective identity* as members of the same civil society is. Interpreted in this way, the discovery of generalizable interests in discussion implies something prior, namely that, despite our differences, we have discovered, reaffirmed, or created something in common that corresponds to a general social identity (which is itself open to change). A public discussion can show us that, after all, we do have something in common, that we are a *we*, and that we agree on or presuppose certain principles that constitute our collective identity. These become dimensions of the content of legitimate legal norms and the foundation of social solidarity. The collective identity of a community can then provide the minimum criterion, with respect to content, of the legitimacy of norms in the negative sense as *that which cannot be violated.*

In his writings on legitimation problems, Habermas has explicitly stated that the claim to legitimacy is related to the social-integrative preservation of a normatively-determined social identity. "*Legitimations* serve to make good this claim, that is, to show how and why existing (or recommended) institutions are fit to employ political power in such a way that the values constitutive for the identity of a society will be realized."[55] Social integration, social solidarity, and collective identity are the "societal" (in Habermas's terms, the lifeworld) referents of normative claims to political legitimacy on the part of polities. While the political-administrative system cannot create identity (or meaning), its claim to legitimacy involves the nonviolation of collective identity and the reinforcement of social solidarity and social integration.[56]

One could object that resorting to the concept of collective identity merely transposes to another level the problems mentioned earlier involving the concept of general interests. What precludes a given collective identity from being authoritarian? Whose interpretation of group identity is to prevail? How could it be anything other than particular, and why make universalist claims for its defense? The answer lies in the peculiarities of a collective identity that has, as a core component, the principles of democratic legitimacy and rights. The principle of democratic legitimacy implies that the conditions of justification—the procedures and presuppositions of rational agreement themselves—obtain legitimating force and become the legitimating grounds (metanorms), replacing such material principles of justification as nature or god.[57] The principle of democratic legitimacy involves a level of justification that has become reflexive and a procedural principle that is universalizable. This means that the modern procedural principle of democratic legitimacy presupposes a postconventional, posttraditional orientation to our own traditions, or at least to those aspects of our tradition and collective identity that have become problematic. Moreover, it implies that only those aspects of our collective identity and common tradition that are compatible with the principles of democratic legitimacy and basic rights can provide the content of valid political norms. The fact that discussion and democratic principles constitute a part of our tradition militates against the authoritarian thrust of the concept of collective identity, because it means that we can accept as valid inputs into sociopolitical norms only those dimensions of our political culture that do not violate the metanorms of discursive conflict resolution.

Let us try to clarify our argument for replacing "general interest" with "collective identity" as the substantive referent of a procedurally defined discourse ethics and then return to this issue. We propose our interpretation as an alternative to three positions that are unacceptable for different reasons. First, there is Habermas's own position that makes generalizable interests the centerpiece of a new principle of universalization. This necessarily makes an objective category—one that is open to analysis from the third-person point of view—the core of discursive will formation, but it has unavoidable authoritarian consequences that Habermas himself does not want. Second, there is the opposite position that bypasses the issue of generalizable interests by identifying all consensus as merely empirical and by making empirical agreement itself the goal of discursive procedures. The results of empirical consensus then become, by definition, justice in the political sense. We believe that Habermas's objections to this position (instability and an extreme variability of results that could lead to moral skepticism similar to that of legal positivism and, especially, legal realism) are correct. A third position (such as that of Karl-Otto Apel) seeks to bypass the issue of generalizable interests by insisting on rational (rather than empirical) consensus as an end in itself. Those who engage in argument, according to this interpretation, must seek to institutionalize and spread the institutionalization of rational discourse in order to avoid performative contradictions. But this approach tends to devalue all actual or empirical discourse in the name of an ever-vanishing counterfactual, and therefore it cannot even begin to specify its own conditions of institutionalization.

Our position involves two interrelated steps. First, we start with empirical norms, traditions, and consensuses that claim to be democratic, but we hold that they can be evaluated (by participants) in terms of their possible degree of rationality and democratization, that is, in light of the metanorms provided by discourse ethics. Second, we remain, nonetheless, aware of the instability of the results of even rationally debated empirical consensus, and we seek to remedy this by an argument based on collective identity in the first instance, and on general interests and social solidarity in the second. We focus on actual processes of public discourse that can, if rationalized or democratized, constitute or reaffirm a rational, democratic collective identity or political culture. In such contexts, discourse ethics provides the standards with which to select those aspects of our tradition, collective identity, and political culture that we wish to maintain and develop and that can provide the content for legitimate norms. Processes of public communication constitute the *we* of collective action, certainly before it can be asked (formally speaking) what the interests of a society or group may be and before the conditions of solidarity of its members with one another can be explored.

Of course, no collective identity is simply or exclusively self-reflective, nor can any collective identity be universal in all of its aspects. The universalizable principles of democratic legitimacy and basic rights can be only components, not the totality of a common identity. Their reproduction on the symbolic level presupposes the discovery or reappropriation of the traditions, collective memories, preexisting patterns of interaction, established values, and relevant practices (lifeworld) that are the sources of solidarities that can sustain the rational core of a political collective identity. From the point of view of a discursive, postconventional collective identity, this reappropriation must be posttraditional, that is, critical in relation to tradition. It must select out traditions of discourse and of empirical solidarity that are not compatible with a postconventional collective identity and must establish a highly critical relationship to them. The latter cannot serve as the content of political norms. Thus, while every collective identity is by definition particular, those that are able to have a critical relation to their own traditions can develop content that is not incompatible with the principles of discursive conflict resolution. Whatever we have been, *we* as members of modern civil societies now partake in a political culture predicated on the principle that we ought to resolve conflicts discursively. In other words, we have more than the mere temporally bound and limited discursive procedure itself to validate our decisions and to comprise our collective identity (which otherwise would be paper-thin), and we do not have to rely on objective interpreted interests for this "more." The free public discourse that affirms our identity has itself a tradition that gives this identity substance over time. Thus, the level of generality sought by Habermas can, in the first instance, be derived from participation in discourse. But it can more solidly be based on discourses aimed at renewing the traditions of discourse that underlie the principle of democratic legitimacy in modern civil societies.

In our definition, common identity is not equivalent to general interest. Yet once a common identity is established or reaffirmed, it is then possible to arrive at an understanding of what constitutes the general interests of a community. These would entail those institutions or arrangements that are needed to reproduce "materially" (as distinct from normatively) the relevant collective identity of the community. Here the social-scientific standpoint has a place. It is possible to argue, for example, as Habermas does, that differentiating between system and lifeworld and reproducing some kind of modern economy and political state are in the general interest of all those who participate in a modern lifeworld and have the corresponding postconventional moral and cultural collective identity that it presupposes. It is possible, in short, to specify the necessary structural preconditions for reproducing a common identity whose principles have received discursive validation. We would still have to argue for generalizing these interests by raising cognitive validity claims as to their truth. Moreover, we must be open to debate on whether specific institutional arrangements are needed for our common identity or whether a variety of institutional arrangements might serve this purpose, some of them possibly better than the existing ones. Indeed, there is an important distinction to be kept in mind between the institutional requirements (general interests) that are necessary for reproducing a postconventional collective identity and those that are contingent. Neither adds up to a way of life, and even the former may have functional equivalents. We must also be careful to avoid confusing the principles of democratic legitimacy and basic rights or justice with any specific organizational arrangement. With these provisos, we can accommodate the criterion offered by the principle of universalization, namely, that the interests justified by valid norms must be general. This does not involve deriving the legitimacy of the norm objectively.

The concept of collective identity also helps resolve the problem of the stability or authority of a consensus. Even if one grants that the metatheoretical principles of argumentative discourse yield metanorms, could one still maintain that these are applied only in empirical contexts and then ask what gives these applications their stability or authority? There is no single correct application of the metanorms. This means that applications can vary from day to day, from tradition to tradition, from way of life to way of life. In short, one could still maintain that nothing really follows from the metanorms after all. Our answer is that "common identity" mediates between the metaprinciples and interests (which can also vary) of a group, thereby providing the stability and authority of the applications agreed upon, although they also remain open to change. In the case of a modern lifeworld and political orders making democratic claims, the group's common identity has two components that allow it to play this mediating role: (1) the postconventional universal dimension, which implies self-reflection and a nontraditional attitude to problematic norms; (2) the dimension of a particular tradition, the source of content, which, however, involves (among other elements) specific modes of institutionalizing discourses, basic rights, and particular traditions for applying metanorms. When questioned, these can be opened up to discussion on the basis of the former attitude without thereby bursting the framework of the common identity.

Relying on this tradition does not take us from one authoritarianism to another, from that of objectively conceived general interests to that of a hermeneutically accessible tradition that is treated as sacred. Because the tradition of discourse allows, even requires, a nontraditional relationship to itself (attainable only in genuine discursive procedures), the possibility of rejecting or renewing its institutions and concrete procedures—and even of creating entirely new ones in the context of a renewed collective identity—becomes available. The only really general interests in modern society are based on this collective identity, itself rooted in traditions that have become self-reflective and self-critical.

Even modern societies characterized by value pluralism and a plurality of groups with distinct collective identities would not be societies if there were no shared principles regulating their interaction, and if there were no common (political) identity shared by their members, however different from one another they may otherwise be. Radical pluralism, the war of the gods discovered by philosophy and sociology in the heart of modern society, cannot be so radical as to exclude meaningful normative coordination and commonality, however minimal, that is recognized, at least implicitly, by all of us insofar as we communicate and act together.

In distinction from Durkheim's mechanical solidarity based on the homogeneity of a single group integrated through a single collective identity, in modern civil societies a minimal or "weak" collective political identity can be shared by a plurality of groups, each with its own particular version of "the good life." With discourse ethics (restricted to the domain of legality) as its foundation, such a collective identity is capable of expressing commonality. It can be a source of solidarity precisely because it can be a component of the identities of quite different social groups.

This is the real meaning of Habermas's insistence that the principle of universalization is also a metanorm implicit in all communicative interaction. Interpreted in this way, this principle can have no authoritarian implications.

Discourse Ethics and the Good Life

Our interpretation of discourse ethics introduces a substantive dimension into the discussion that has bearing on the charges of formalism mentioned above. Indeed, it might be objected that, given the procedural and formal character of discourse ethics, introducing considerations of identity violates its status as a deontological theory. The concept of identity does seem to involve substantive assumptions about what constitutes the "good life," implying judgments on the validity of particular ways of life.[58] This issue is especially pertinent to our interpretation of discourse ethics as a *political principle* of (democratic) legitimacy and basic rights, for the standards of legitimacy as well as the laws of any polity can be seen as part of its overall concrete way of life (as articulations of its ethos or *Sittlichkeit*) and hence as particular. Deontological ethical theories, however, dissociate questions of "justice" from evaluative judgments about what constitutes the good life. In the spirit of such an ethic, Habermas has disqualified discourse ethics from providing judgments about the validity or quality of a form of life or of a particular life history.[59] Accordingly, rational consensus about the validity of a norm does not supply criteria for choosing between different forms of life or for developing a hierarchy of need-interpretations.

On the other hand, Habermas's principle of universalization claims to be able to handle content insofar as it brings into consideration the need-interpretations of all those who might be affected by a norm. Practical discourses find their content given in the horizon of a social group's lifeworld—this is where norms come from in the first place. The concept of collective identity seems to have a place here, after all. We thus confront a paradox: Discourse ethics apparently insists both that we judge and that we refrain from judging forms of life.[60]

From the point of view of democratic theory, this paradox seems disturbing. It resolves into the following problem: How can the claims of solidarity of particular social groups be reconciled with the more general demands of justice both within pluralistic societies comprised of many groups and among such societies? Two issues are involved here: The deontological character of discourse ethics and the problem of motivation. If discourse ethics addresses need-interpretations, how can one exclude judgments concerning values (which underlie need-interpretations) or forms of life from its purview? Are not the critics right in claiming that, without such judgments, without the integration of substantive concerns into discourse ethics, it becomes formalistic, empty, and "*lebensweltlich* irrelevant"? Yet, if discourse ethics does imply a specific way of life, if it presupposes a set of values and thus a "hidden concept of the good" (Charles Taylor), how can it claim to be either universal or neutral with respect to competing models of the good life? Doesn't it represent just one more model among many?[61] On the other hand, the motivational question that arises is why actors with conflicting value systems should be willing to enter into a dialogue or to entertain the points of view of others as valid or worth hearing at all. Let us take up these issues in turn.

Excessive Formalism

Discourse ethics, like all procedural theories, seems vulnerable to the charge of excessive formalism.[62] It appears to exclude a concern for the welfare of fellow human beings and to bracket considerations that pertain to "the good." Questions such as what constitutes a harmonious form of social life or the successful conduct of an individual life are avoided. In response to these objections, Habermas's most sympathetic critics have introduced an additional principle into the overall framework of discourse ethics. They postulate a criterion under the heading of an ethics of benevolence, empathy, intuition, or caring as an autonomous legitimate moral standpoint that complements considerations of justice.[63]

The main problem with these approaches is that they involve an alternative to the discourse-ethical conception of justice in whose name it can be suspended or disregarded, rather than a bridge principle capable of mediating between justice and the good. What is usually assumed here is an extremely narrow interpretation of the meaning of justice as simply involving fair or equal treatment of persons. Justice, in short, is downgraded to the status of a principle (equal rights) and then supplemented by a second principle, benevolence, and both are thought to be derivable from a higher principle: equal respect for the integrity or dignity of each person. But as Habermas has correctly pointed out in his response to a similar attempt by Lawrence Kohlberg, this approach cannot succeed, in part because it equivocates on the concept of the person.

Equal respect for each person *in general* as a subject capable of autonomous action means equal treatment; however, equal respect for each person *as an individual* subject individuated through a life history can mean something rather different from equal treatment: instead of protection of the person as a self-determining being, it can mean support for the person as a self-realizing being.[64]

Respect for integrity does not involve caring for another's well being. Moreover, a principle of benevolence derived from the principle of equal respect refers only to individuals and not to the common welfare or the sense of community. Thus, on the narrow conception of justice assumed by Habermas's most sympathetic critics, questions of the good must appear as external. As such, justice excludes sensitivity to the particularity of each individual, to considerations of the welfare of the community, and to the concerns of the "concrete other." Justice translates into negative freedoms and subjective rights of persons, and that is all.

These interpretations lose sight of the richness of the communicative and intersubjective presuppositions of discourse ethics. Discourse is a reflexive form of communicative interaction that involves more than the equal treatment of those affected. The analytic starting point of discourse ethics is not a conception of sovereign, disconnected, disembodied individuality but rather the intersubjective communicative infrastructure of everyday social life. Individuals act within relationships of mutual recognition in which they acquire and assert their individuality and their freedom intersubjectively. In the dialogue process, every participant articulates his or her views or need-interpretations and takes on ideal roles in a public, practical discussion. This provides the framework in which the understanding of others' need-interpretations is made possible through moral insight and not only through empathy. It is here that the presence of commonalities is tested and respect for difference is potentially affirmed.

Habermas develops these themes in two recent essays in which he uses the concepts of identity and solidarity systematically for the first time.[65] He is able to show that there is no need for an additional ethical theory to supplement the theory of justice because a "substantive" dimension has been "formally" present all along. In sum, Habermas insists that the proper complementary concept for justice is not benevolence, empathy, intuition, or caring but *solidarity*, and that justice and solidarity do not represent two distinct moral principles but are two sides of the same principle.

The argument works as follows. Human beings are individuated through communicative processes of socialization (*Vergesellschaftung*) in the context of a speech community and in an intersubjectively shared lifeworld. They acquire an individual identity only as members of a collective, and simultaneously, as it were, they acquire a group identity. The further individuation proceeds, the more the lifeworld is differentiated and the more the individual is involved in a thick and subtle network of multiple and reciprocal interdependencies. Indeed, the extreme vulnerability of individual and collective identities derives from the fact that "the person forms an inner core only to the extent to which she simultaneously externalizes herself in communicatively produced interpersonal relationships."[66] Moralities are designed to shelter vulnerable identities.

The increases in reflexivity, universalism, and individuation that accompany the differentiation processes involved in the modernization of the lifeworld do, of course, reinforce our awareness of the chronic vulnerability of individual and collective identity.[67] But it is precisely through the "discontinuous" means of discursive redemption of claims that the continuity of meaning and solidarity is maintained in such situations.

Because discourses are a reflective form of understanding-oriented action that, so to speak, sit on top of the latter, their central perspective on moral compensation for the deep-seated weakness of vulnerable individuals can be derived from the very medium of linguistically mediated interactions to which socialized individuals owe that vulnerability. The pragmatic features of discourse make possible a discerning will formation whereby the interests of each individual can be taken into account without destroying the social bonds that link each individual with all others.[68]

To be sure, both collective and individual identities established through socialization processes need to be reaffirmed, since they require ongoing mutual recognition and are continuously open to challenge and change. Individuals can never maintain their identity in isolation. The integrity of the individual cannot be secured without the integrity of the intersubjectively shared lifeworld that makes possible their shared interpersonal relations and relations of mutual recognition.

Habermas calls this "the double aspect of the moral phenomenon": Moral provisions for the protection of individual identity cannot safeguard the integrity of individual persons without at the same time safeguarding the vitally necessary web of relationships of mutual recognition in which individuals can stabilize their fragile identities only mutually and simultaneously with the identity of their group.[69] Indeed Habermas insists that every ethics has two tasks: it must ensure the inviolability of socialized individuals by requiring equal treatment and respect for the dignity of each, and it must protect the intersubjective relations of reciprocal recognition by requiring solidarity among individuals as members of a community in which they are socialized. Solidarity is thus rooted in the experience that each must take responsibility for the other, because as consociates they all share an interest in the integrity of their common life context—in short, a collective identity. From the perspective of communication theory, then, concerns for the welfare of others and for the general welfare are closely connected through the concept of identity. The identity of the group and of unique individuals is reproduced through intact relations of mutual recognition. The complementary concept to justice, then, must be solidarity and not some vague notion of empathy or benevolence. The procedural principles of justice, understood in the deontological sense of respect for persons and equal treatment of dialogue partners, requires solidarity as its other—they are two aspects of the same thing. [70]

To be sure, Habermas does not, as we do, distinguish between morality and the principles of justice. For him, discourse ethics serves for both. Yet the above discussion clearly applies most appropriately to the concerns of a political principle of legitimacy. On this view, justice refers to the equal freedoms of unique and self-determining individuals—legitimate norms are those that are accepted by all potentially affected *participants* in a discursive process. Solidarity thus refers to both the concern of consociates, linked together in a lifeworld, for the integrity of a shared common identity as well as for individual and even subgroup identities. Thus, legitimate norms "cannot protect one without the other: They cannot protect the equal rights and freedoms of the individual without protecting the welfare of one's fellow man and of the community to which individuals belong."[71] Discourse ethics thus presupposes both the autonomy and integrity of individuals and their prior embeddedness in an intersubjective way of life. The very content of reflections on the justice of norms derives from shared or overlapping forms of life. This is the source of the hidden link between justice and the common good. Consideration of interests as to their generalizability/compromisability thus involves consideration of the "structural" aspects of the "good life" that can be generalized from the standpoint of communicative socialization and that are characteristic of all ways of life—that is, the requirements of respect for and protection of the integrity of individual and collective identities.[72]

This structural dimension of the good internal to discourse ethics provides the standard by which the principle of universalization must operate, namely, articulating and considering identity-requirements of all individuals and groups affected by a norm. In addition to articulating standards of fairness and respect for abstract rights of abstract persons, discourses reflexively reproduce those intersubjective communicative accomplishments (reciprocal recognition) that reaffirm and reproduce core components of individual and group identities. "Even those interpretations in which the individual identifies needs that are most peculiarly her own are open to a revision process in which *all* participate. . . [and which] adds the reciprocity of mutual recognition to the sum of individual voices."[73] The structural concept of the good that is operative here can thus be formulated as follows: The institution-alization of any norm that might cause irreparable damage to the integrity of the identities of individuals and groups who are willing to discuss and abide by the procedural principles of symmetric reciprocity is proscribed. This, of course, is another way of saying that discourses cannot legislate or judge forms of life. Yet some-thing more is involved here. Since need-interpretations and iden-tity concerns are brought into the discussion, the dialogue itself is guided by the principles of respect for the abstract and situated dimensions of personality, on the one hand, and for the minimum solidarity required for the maintenance of individual and group identity, on the other.

This concept of the good lays to rest the charge of empty formalism without thereby violating the deontological status of discourse ethics. Respect for the ability of each to formulate a coherent model of the good life and solidarity among those who have differing ways of life yet share a common lifeworld, or overlap-ping lifeworlds, and at least key aspects of a political collective identity do not unfairly favor any particular model of the good. Yet they are "*lebensweltliche*" relevant! Nor do they amount to a hidden, concrete concept of the good that undermines the deontological character of discourse ethics (Taylor's charge). The practice of discourse respects both individuation and intersubjectively shared ways of life. Each individual must be able to participate in the solidary process of dialogue that presupposes and potentially reaffirms solidarity since it involves considering the position of the other and openness to the other's identity needs. Indeed, the quality of a "*Zusammenleben*" ought to be measured both by the degree of solidarity and well-being it ensures and by how far the interests (identity requirements) of each individual are considered within the common interest.[74]

This discussion of the structural aspects of the good internal to discourse ethics rests nonetheless on a differentiation between the right and the good, between the universal(izable) and the particu-lar, between matters of justice and matters involving the self-realization of individuals, that is, their particular life histories, identity requirements, and forms of life. Individual need-interpre-tations can, of course, be brought into discourses so that we can discover which dimensions of these could become the content of a generalizable norm. But after such a discourse, there remain dimensions of individual life histories, conceptions of the good, forms of life that cannot be generalized and hence remain particular. Even if we draw the boundary line between the right and the good after discourse, the latter by definition raise evaluative issues that escape the demanding logic of discourse, because they involve differences about which we cannot reach a consensus and that we cannot judge through a discourse. Those necessarily particular components of individual and group identity constitute the limit to the reach of discourse ethics. From what has been said above regarding the structures of mutual recognition within which individual and group identities are formed, it is clear that Habermas believes that the principles of justice must not violate—indeed, must protect—the intersubjectively shared form of life from which both solidarity and individual autonomy draw their resources. However, since the structural aspects of the good life are distinguishable from the concrete totalities of particular forms of life (and life histories), the question remains as to the relation between discourse ethics with its "structural conception of the good" and the particular identity needs, values, etc., of individuals or groups.

To the extent that such issues do not impinge upon matters of justice—that is, to the extent that they involve forms of conduct that we neither wish to see generalized beyond a specific context nor see as conflicting with any principle of justice, these fit the standard of "that which ought not to be violated" by or even subjected to claims of justice that are in principle irrelevant. What is involved here are standards of action, values, and components of the identities of individuals or groups that deserve (mutual) recognition as a domain of difference, of personal choice, distinct from the domain to which legal norms must apply. Legal recognition of such a domain that is beyond justice, as it were, could take the form of fundamental rights that secure the autonomy of individual judgment and the self-limitation of legal regulation. Discourse ethics is self-limiting precisely with respect to this domain; it "refers negatively to the damaged life instead of pointing affirmatively to the good life."[75]

But it is clear that what appears to the individual or to a group as the constitutive components of one's form of life, of one's identity, can come into conflict with the demands of justice. In cases of conflict between demands for self-realization and demands for justice, our immediate impulse is to say that those needs or components of identities that violate the principles of symmetric reciprocity and have become controversial must give way. There remains, however, the option of conscientious objection and civil disobedience when the conception of justice itself is under dispute.

Universality?

Although the requirements of reciprocal recognition can be traced back to the conditions of communicative action and identified as the common root of both justice and solidarity, these duties do not reach beyond the concrete world of a particular group—be it a family, a tribe, a city, or a state.[76] If we interpret discourse ethics as an ethic of citizenship, as a principle of democratic legitimacy and basic rights, how can we make universal claims for it? Don't ethics and citizenship vary with the particular form of the polity to which they relate? How can we arrive at that universal stance that alone would be able to ground not only tolerance but also solidarity with a plurality of group identities, without reverting to a Kantian formalism?[77] Habermas's answer is that discourses constitute more demanding forms of communication than everyday communicative practice. They are reflexive, governed by the principles of argumentative speech, and they reach beyond the particularity of a community's mores without thereby breaking the social bond. *The principle of solidarity loses its ethnocentric character when it becomes part of a universal theory of justice and is constructed in light of the idea of discursive will formation.* Arguments transcend particular lifeworlds. "Discourse generalizes, abstracts, stretches the presuppositions of context-bound communicative actions by expanding their range to include competent subjects beyond the provincial limits of their own particular form of life."[78] The limits of the lifeworld of a family, tribe, or state can be transcended in a context where discourses are institutionalized and the structural principle of the good is respected.[79] Moreover, moral argumentation can involve an invocation of principles that differ from the norms of a community, and the community must then respond with good and convincing arguments or else acquiesce to the compelling argument of the one who thinks differently. Far from repressing particularity or "community," the universalizing thrust of discourse ethics, by virtue of its very abstractness, is the only basis on which to grant legitimacy to difference and to require solidarity with it. "As interests and value orientations become more differentiated in modern societies, the morally justified norms that control the individual's scope of action in the interest of the whole become ever more general and abstract."[80]

Habermas justifies this claim to universality in his analysis of the pragmatic presuppositions of communicative action that are formalized in discourse. In our opinion, however, this argument is not entirely satisfactory, because it implies an abstract and hence incomplete form of universalism. While it is quite probable that other cultures besides ours could make the transitions from normative to communicative action, and from the latter to discourse, it is also certain that such steps are impossible and irrelevant for many cultures, especially those that are not modern and not self-reflective. It would be preposterous for us to require that such a culture surrender its identity for ideals externally imposed on it. Respect for the collective identity of the other must obtain in these cases, perhaps in the form of toleration. But such respect cannot be equated with the solidarity one feels for those with whom one has at least some components of a collective identity or some principles in common.

Let us be clear here. There are two contexts in which solidarity becomes problematic: within plural civil societies and between different societies. The modern concept of solidarity that we have in mind does not require empathy or sameness with the other with whom we are solidary. The solidarity complementary to discourse ethics does, however, involve an ability to identify with the nonidentical. In other words, it involves the acceptance of the other as an other, as one who must be accorded the same chance to articulate identity needs and arguments as one would like oneself. Discursive situations within a single society, in which conflicts over norms are adjudicated, establish the possibility of such solidarity, because here one can put oneself in the place of the other, grasp what his or her needs and interests are, and discover, constitute, or reaffirm commonalities and a collective identity. Such processes should enrich the self-understanding of all the actors involved. On the other side, solidarity makes discourse meaningful and reaffirms the logic of reciprocal recognition at its heart. In other words, we can have solidarity with others with whom we share a collective identity without sharing or even necessarily liking their personal needs and values (assuming that they are not incompatible with the preconditions of discursive conflict resolution or compromise). But we do have to accept these differences, to the extent that they are constituted in discourse as private.

The issue of solidarity between collectivities that do not share a common political identity is more complex. The easiest case concerns interactions between two societies that are rooted in different cultural traditions but have both institutionalized discourses and the principles of democratic legitimacy and basic rights. We have already seen that solidarity reinforces the collective political identity of members of a modern civil society, integrating those who differ from each other yet share in the political culture of the society at large. This kind of collective identity is capable of asserting a *we* while fostering solidarity among the many group identities that compose a modern civil society. It is this version of a modern collective identity and a modern form of social solidarity that can be expanded in a universal direction to include solidarity with those who are not members of the same civil society but who are members of other civil societies. For cultures that have not institutionalized discourse or rights, we must still show respect if not solidarity.

There are, however, two points at which the universal implications of discourse ethics apply to *all* cultures. First, when the demands for democratic participation and basic rights are raised within a given culture, we cannot avoid solidarity with those who articulate them. The minimum meaning of human rights is that those who claim them have them against any state. Such rights can be secured only within the context of citizenship in a particular polity. But their referent (universal human rights) points beyond any given polity. Second, to the extent that various cultures meet one another in peace and potential war (and today hardly any cultures are excluded from such a possibility), discourse ethics implies that the principles of rational dialogue among equals represent the only normatively acceptable form of conflict resolution. This version of universalism is, moreover, the only basis on which solidarity with those who are truly different is conceivable, since it opens the possibility of arriving at common norms or principles and mutual recognition.

The Habermasian idea that those who act communicatively can, in principle, raise themselves to the level of discourse does not have to imply a universal yardstick that lets us judge (and even less, interfere with) forms of life radically different from our own. But it does give us a way to address the two cases in which radically different cultures meet. The existence of different forms of life within modern civil societies allows us to think that internalizing such a relationship of mutual recognition and respect for individuality and difference is not in principle impossible. This would entail neither the bad faith of pretending to place all forms of life on an equal footing with our own (relativism) nor an abstract universalist stance that is incapable of according each particularity its own dignity.

The universal referent, in the last instance of discourses in the above sense, is, of course, the "ideal speech community." The identity to which this refers is our identity as human beings; the formal concept of the good it implies is solidarity with all humanity capable of speech.[81] This is a regulative, practical ideal in the domain of a political ethic. Discourse ethics thus preserves the eighteenth-century insight that justice without solidarity is untenable. Indeed, this is the principle behind the idea of human rights. Yet it presupposes difference, not sameness, within the general and basically empty rubric of humanity. Thus, when interpreted in terms of the concepts of collective identity and solidarity, the structural understanding of the good can indeed operate as the other side of the theory of justice: "Without unrestricted individual freedom to take a position on normative validity claims, the agreement that is actually reached could not be truly universal; but without the empathy of each person in the situation for everyone else, which is derived from solidarity, no resolution capable of consensus could be found."[82]

Identities arrived at (or reaffirmed) in a discursive process of self-constitution involving a postconventional testing of candidates for political norms leave room for transcultural solidarities that have universal implications in a deeper sense than any supposed universal interest. In order to feel solidarity with the other, we must have potential access to a nonviolent form of conflict resolution when we encounter one another. A *we* constituted in part through discourse has ready access to the only possible medium for such conflict resolution: cross-culturally relevant communication. To possess the capacity for solidarity at all, we must have access to a cultural tradition; but to be able to feel solidarity with an other (with whom we have little in common), we must be able to criticize our own political tradition. The two steps taken together imply the possibility of a broadening of collective identities in a universal direction without breaking substantive links to a plurality of different traditions and, hence, identities.

This does not amount to a synthesis of Kant and Aristotle, for the restrictions with respect to value judgment about the worthiness of individual and group identities still hold. Discourse ethics does not force us to judge past ways of life that have never developed discursive forms of grounding norms. But it does imply that, in the case of contact between pluralities (nationally or internationally), the only acceptable form of conflict resolution is discourse. Let us repeat: *Instead of supplying a substantive standard of the good with which to judge particular ways of life, the structural concept of the good proscribes norms that might cause damage to the integrity of individual and group identities.* Components of identities that either resist processes of discursive conflict resolution, in the case of contested societal norms, or violate the metanorms of discourse ethics (those based on forms of domination, exclusion, inequality, etc.) would have to either yield to a political ethic that provides for moral autonomy and solidarity with difference.

Motivation

The previous point raises the problem of motivation. As stated earlier, deontological procedural judgments seem to offer demotivated answers to decontextualized questions. Indeed, the metanorms of discourse apply only to the dialogue situation itself and can neither motivate participation nor provide criteria for applying results. Nor does the principle of solidarity that is the flip side of discourse ethics provide a ready answer to this problem. It has its limits precisely at the point at which one is unwilling to engage in discursive communicative processes that involve altering one's perspective and possibly even aspects of one's way of life. Why should anyone participate in discourse?

There are all sorts of pragmatic or strategic reasons for participating in dialogue. One might, for example, come to the conclusion that peaceful, dialogic forms of conflict resolution are better than the use of force and violence, given the existing constellations of interests and balance of power. But there would be nothing intrinsic to the dialogue itself that would automatically yield obligation. Indeed, dialogue is not equivalent to discourse.

Habermas's answer to the problem of motivation that faces all deontological moral theories is twofold. First, he insists that the presuppositions of discourse are really a reflective form of communicative action, and thus the reciprocities undergirding the mutual recognition of competent subjects are already built into action oriented toward reaching an understanding, the action in which argumentation is rooted. In reply to the stance of the radical skeptic who refuses to argue, thereby rejecting the moral point of view, Habermas thus insists that one cannot drop out of the communicative practice of everyday life. Since the presuppositions of communicative interaction are at least partly identical with the presuppositions of argumentation as such, the option of opting out is really no option at all.

In reaching an understanding about something in the world, subjects engaged in communicative action orient themselves to validity claims, including . . . normative validity claims. This is why there is no form of sociocultural life that is not at least implicitly geared to maintaining communicative action by means of argument, be the actual form of argumentation ever so rudimentary and the institutionalization of discursive consensus building ever so inchoate.[83]

Second, Habermas acknowledges the fact that practical discourse does disengage problematic actions and norms from the substantive ethics of their lived contexts, subjecting them to hypothetical reasoning. He grants that unless discourse ethics is undergirded by the thrust of motives and by socially accepted institutions, the moral insights it offers will be ineffective in practice. Discourse cannot by itself ensure that the conditions necessary for the actual participation of all concerned are met. Discourse ethics is dependent upon a form of life that "meets it halfway."

There has to be a modicum of congruence between morality and the practices of socialization and education. The latter must promote the requisite internalization of superego control and the abstractness of ego identities. In addition, there must be a modicum of fit between morality and sociopolitical institutions.[84]

In other words, what Rawls calls the "circumstances of justice" have to obtain for discourse ethics to be complemented by the appropriate motivational complex. For Habermas, this means that what is required is at least the beginnings of the institutionalization of discourses, the articulation of the principle of basic rights, the requisite socialization processes such that dispositions and abilities necessary for taking part in moral argumentation can be learned, and material living conditions that are not so desperately impoverished and degrading as to render universalistic moral strictures irrelevant. It is Habermas's view that in modern civil societies the principles of basic rights and public discourses have been, albeit selectively and haltingly, institutionalized in the public spaces of civil and political society. This means that discursive testing of normative validity already is part of our intuitions about the legitimacy of institutions. Thus, the subjection of controversial norms to discourse can be understood on the model of Rawl's "reflective equilibrium," as a reconstruction of everyday intuitions underlying the impartial judgment of social and political institutions in modern civil societies.

But even if participation in discourses concerning norms implicitly commits the participant to the metanorms of symmetric reciprocity, it remains possible to maintain an overall strategic relationship to one's participation in specific discourses. Yet participation can have socializing effects on its own, and the relevant principles are such that we all can come to embrace them. It is in such a process that discursive conflict resolution could itself acquire normative power. While *phronesis* (good judgment) is necessary for the application of the principles of discourse ethics, the normative learning that is necessary to resolve the motivational problem from the input side is in principle possible in societies with modernizing lifeworlds, since such societies provide at least for the possibility of internalizing a few highly abstract and universal principles that follow from practical argumentation. In discussing the postconventional level of moral consciousness necessary for discourse ethics, Habermas insists that the gap between moral insights and culturally habituated empirical motives needs to be compensated for

by a system of internal behavior controls that is triggered by principled moral judgments (convictions that form the basis for motivations). This system must function autonomously. It must be independent of the external pressure of an existing recognized legitimate order, no matter how small that pressure may be. These conditions are satisfied only by the complete internalization of a few highly abstract and universal principles that, as discourse ethics shows, follow logically from the procedure of norm justification.[85]

Beyond this, no deontological theory can or should say more. The question of the generation of empirical motives for participation in discursive conflict resolution then belongs to the domains of social theory or social psychology.

An Institutional Deficit?

Discourse ethics does not prescribe a particular form of life. A great variety of forms may be compatible with it, yet no modern form of life (including the one that made it historically possible) can escape its critical potential. The concept of "life form" includes the cultural, institutional, and socialization patterns of a society. Such a broad concept could easily lead to misjudgments about the implications of discourse ethics. It is thus worth noting that the critique can be restricted to specific social spheres without leading to an evaluation of whole social formations or civilizations. Interpreting discourse ethics as a theory of justice could, nevertheless, imply that, without determining entire forms of life, the conception leads to a specific model of *political* practice.[86] It is indeed difficult to conceive of democratic legitimacy without democratic

institutions. Nevertheless, we insist that no single model of democratic institutions follows from discourse ethics. Moreover, none
should be derived from it, if democratic theory is to avoid an
authoritarian turn vis-à-vis existing (even if deficient) patterns of
democracy. Nevertheless, we shall argue in this section and the
next that (1) discourse ethics does have a link to an institutional
level of analysis, and (2) the principles of democratic legitimacy
and basic rights that it grounds imply an open-ended plurality of
democracies and hence projects of democratization that presuppose both modern civil societies and a critical relation to them.

The cornerstone of our argument is the distinction between
principles of legitimation, on the one hand, and the institutionalization (or organization) of domination (or rule) on the other.[87]
Habermas uses this distinction to show the shortcomings of both
realistic and normative theories of democracy. From Weber to
Schumpeter and beyond, "realist" theories of "elite democracy"
identify as democratic a procedure (of elite competition) that has
at best a minimal connection to democratic norms. It is not based
on presuppositions of arriving at a free agreement or public
discursive will formation or on an orientation to general interests.
The problem of legitimation is either reduced to the empirical
question of acceptance of the rules of such procedures or disregarded altogether. Conversely, the theorists of direct democracy,
from Rousseau to Arendt, derive a set of idealized practices from a
genuine democratic principle of legitimacy. Yet their arguments
place in doubt the very possibility of genuine democracy.

The strict separation of legitimacy and the institutionalization of
rule points beyond both of these alternatives. Nevertheless, it is easy
to suppose from Habermas's own train of thought that he is merely
combining the two types of theory, deriving his stress on democratic legitimacy from the normativists and his acceptance of
empirical procedures of organization from the realists. He rightly
abandons Arendt's illusions concerning the desirability and possibility of the absence of rule in democratic public life.[88] Yet, at the
same time, he seems to leave behind a somewhat Weberian impression that democratic organization is merely one form of domination among others.

The apparent concessions to the realistic theory are due to a
combination of agnosticism vis-à-vis democratic utopias and pessi-

mism vis-à-vis the current stage of parliamentary democracy. We would like to develop our own conception in relation to these two postures. Habermas defines democracy as all political orders that satisfy a procedural type of legitimacy, in the sense of the procedures validated by discourse ethics: "Democracies are distinguished from other systems of domination by a rational principle of legitimation."[89] There are, in principle, many forms of organization that can qualify under this definition. We are told that a choice among them "depends on concrete social and political conditions, on scopes of disposition, on information." However, democracy on the organizational level should be understood in terms of democratization, defined in terms of a "self-controlled learning process" that is capable of allowing and even generating institutional change.[90]

Habermas claims that, in the modern procedural type of democratic legitimacy first worked out by Rousseau, the formal conditions of possible consensus formation, rather than ultimate grounds, obtain legitimating force. This means that the level of justification itself has become reflexive. Accordingly, any given consensus, including the one on organizational structures for arriving at a consensus, is, in principle, open to learning and revision, guided by the criteria articulated by discourse ethics and presupposed by it as the constitutive conditions of discourse. Democratization understood as a self-controlled learning process means precisely this.

We have no quarrel with this train of thought, as far as it goes. We, too, think of democratic legitimacy as prior to the inevitably plural forms of democratic organization. We, too, see democratization as an open-ended process. But we believe that, while rightly denying that any particular form of organization (e.g., council democracy) can be derived from the principle of democratic legitimacy, Habermas has omitted to give the minimum conditions necessary for organizing democratic institutions. The statement about historical preconditions in this context says much too little. Beyond this, Habermas can only reiterate that "It is a question of finding arrangements which could ground the presumption that the basic institutions of the society and the basic political decisions could meet with the unforced agreement of all those involved, if they could participate, as free and equal, in discursive will formation."[91]

Characteristically, this statement draws us back from the question of institutions. Habermas is here describing, in the sense of discourse ethics, the procedures that can provide legitimating grounds for accepting any arrangement as democratic. We should notice, however, that the restatement of discourse ethics is itself affected by avoiding the institutional issue. There is a noticeable shift in the passage from *actual* to *virtual* discourse. A "presumption" that certain institutions and decisions "would" generate "consent" if those involved "could participate" requires either interpreting mental states, in the sense of Weber's concept of *verstehen*, or the social-scientific analysis of constellations of interests, in the sense of the Marxist tradition. Neither approach is consistent with the deeper thrust of discourse ethics that implies that the formation of identity and the analysis of interests depend on public communication and dialogue. Thus, democratic legitimacy requires at the minimum establishing actual processes of discourse on the level of organization. Without this minimum, the illusion could arise that we can speak about democratic legitimacy without insisting on the presence of institutions having some internal relationship (even if not that of a simple derivation of one from the other) to the procedures of discursive validation and justification. While the requirements of valid discourse are not generally or fully satisfied by actual, empirical, institutionalized discourse, there is nevertheless an intrinsic connection between the counterfactual norms and actual processes of discourse. We have argued that discourse is always actual discourse, and the norms of discourse are available only to participants in empirical, institutionalized discourse.

The idea of institutionalizing discourse is hardly absent from Habermas's overall conception, and it is useful to examine the place of modern formal democracy in this context. The institutionalization of discourse refers to the existence of a "generalized and obligatory expectation that under definite conditions, a discourse can be carried out."[92] Actual historical examples of social embodiments of discursive norms are understood to be variable, contingent, and precarious.[93] Habermas includes three such examples: the beginning of philosophy in Athens, the rise of early modern experimental science, and the creation of a political public sphere in the Enlightenment and the revolutions of the seventeenth and eighteenth centuries.[94] Here we are interested only in the meaning and fate of the last example.

According to Habermas, "bourgeois" democracy claimed to link "all politically consequential processes of decision to legally guaranteed discursive will formation of the citizen public."[95] This claim indicates that the idea of a valid consensus penetrates the structure of rule itself in "the form of democratization."[96] Thus, at least for the moment of genesis of modern parliamentary democracy, Habermas recognizes the internal link between legitimation and rule that we have postulated. But he has also argued that, in the course of development, legitimation and rule became uncoupled. The claims of bourgeois democracy have remained (or become) a fiction (however effective for legitimation, in Weber's sense). Consequently, a deep split has developed between those who are increasingly cynical about the substance of democratic claims and normative theorists of democracy.[97] Habermas has always been critical not only of "elitism" and "realism" but also of their two antagonists: Marxist critiques of formal democracy, and normative theories of democracy. He rejects the council model as an alternative to representative democracy because it is based on a category mistake. It is worth noting, however, that, as organizational mechanisms, he by no means considers the devices of either form of democracy incompatible with the discursive model. Formal mechanisms, such as majority rule, protection of minorities, or parliamentary immunity, are potentially important political devices delimiting yet preserving discursive procedures in the face of material and temporal scarcities and a multitude of interests and identities.[98] On the other hand, direct democratic forms have a potential for increasing the participatory features of representative democracy; they need not imply a serious restriction of complexity.[99] Nevertheless, with the development of modernity, each of these models of democracy, representative and direct, enters into crisis. The extension of direct democracy runs into the "structural violence" built into those institutions that seem to exclude the introduction of genuine forms of participation. But if one may proceed to a full participatory model only discursively, the latter runs into the intractable problem of finding the means for first establishing discourse where it is excluded or deformed.

Habermas's position remains somewhat ambiguous with respect to formal, representative democracy. On the one hand (from his early work to the present), he has presented the history of this model as a process of decline variously conceived. On the other hand, he is uncomfortable with a mere replay of the neo-Kantian dichotomy between *Sollen* (legitimacy) and *Sein* (institutions) on the level of democratic theory. He warns that a necessarily counterfactual ethical theory should not imply "radically ignoring . . . the *already operative* ideas of justice, the orientations of *already present* social movements, the *existing* forms of freedom."[100] While the target of this remark is the interpretation of the political implications of discourse ethics in terms of revolutionary rupture, the exact referents for the terms *justice* and *freedom* are hard to locate. It is also difficult to specify precisely how already existing social movements fit into this class of terms. Justice and freedom seem to refer to the institutions of democratic politics and to established rights. But even the latest version of Habermas's theory puts into doubt the possibility that the increase in freedom and justice in these contexts can be a matter of further institutionalization. Here Habermas depicts the great historical stages of state formation leading to the development of the modern democratic welfare state as epochs of juridification.[101] Of these, the nineteenth-century *Rechtsstaat* and its younger contemporary, the democratic constitutional state, are initially presented as guaranteeing freedoms (or rights) in the face of the modern state, while their common successor, the twentieth-century democratic welfare state, is presented as ambiguous from the point of view of freedom, because its "very means of guaranteeing freedom . . . endangers the freedom of the beneficiaries."[102] Habermas has in mind the negative features of the welfare state that involve surveillance, control, and the bureaucratization of everyday life. From this point of view, however, the nineteenth-century democratic constitutional state becomes ambiguous as well. While Habermas insists that the principles of participatory rights remain (unlike the very principles of the welfare state) "unambiguously freedom-guaranteeing," the organization (institutionalization) of these rights is seen as already bureaucratic. Thus, "the possibility of spontaneous opinion formation and discursive will formation" are considerably restricted "through segmentation of the voter's role, through competition of leadership elites, through vertical opinion formation in bureaucratically encrusted party apparatuses, through autonomized parliamentary bodies, through powerful communication networks, and the like."[103]

To proceed from the side of contemporary political institutions to locate the necessary minimum for democratic legitimacy thus seems quixotic. Rather than appearing as instances of actual discourses, these institutions seem to reduce the principles of democratic legitimacy to their counterfactual status. The standards of discourse ethics seem to lift the democratic veil off the political practices of mass democracies, rather than finding institutional supports in them.

It might be objected that the civil and political rights established outside the state sphere do represent institutionalizations of freedom and justice. Indeed, if one proceeds from the standpoint of civil society rather than that of the political system, a way beyond the antinomy of normative development and institutional decline opens up.[104] More specifically, the conception of rights could lead to a theory of civil society as the minimum framework for institutionalizing discourse ethics.

We claimed earlier that both the principle of democratic legitimacy and the principle of rights can be justified by discourse ethics. In the first place, it should be clear that public, democratic discourse has a role to play in generating and maintaining rights. We have already shown that, as a principle of democratic legitimacy, discourse ethics implies that the generation of law and power must be referred back to the democratic participation of all concerned in order to be considered legitimate. In the case of basic rights, to the extent that they are to be institutionalized, our thesis is that they require enactment through discursive processes as well as opportunities for participation in public discourses. The discursive process is, in other words, duplicated on the level of the constitutional origin of rights and on the level of the renewed argumentation and participation necessary for their sustenance. We shall argue that this second dimension depends on the chances to assemble, associate, and articulate positions publicly on the terrain of civil society.

At issue is the relationship between asserting rights and legalizing rights. While rights in the modern sense presuppose the positivization of law, they cannot be reduced to positive law. The rights that we have can become effective and stable only when embodied in constitutions and legal codes. But such rights are necessarily paradoxical: Formally they represent a voluntary self-limitation of state power that could be annulled by a legislative act (in England, for example, 51 percent of parliament could abolish any right). But rights do not simply emerge, nor are they sustained or expanded as mere acts of positive legislation. What the state could take back on the legal-constitutional level, it ought not take back from a normative point of view, and it cannot take back if certain social-historical conditions are fulfilled.

Discourse ethics points to the conditions of possibility of this *cannot* on the sociological side and to the ground of this *ought* on the philosophical side. First, the survival and expansion of basic rights depend very much on vital political cultures that allow for and even promote the mobilization of concerned constituencies on behalf of rights. The claims of individuals to protections by basic rights would be hollow if they could not be backed up by public discussion, assembly, and, in many cases, social movements practicing civil disobedience. The principle of rights thus requires the possibility of participation in societal public spaces. Discourse ethics has obvious relevance here, for it implies an institutionalization of discourses in civil society that is crucial for positing and defending rights.

Second, discourse ethics not only points to the sociological process of creating and expanding rights but also provides part of the basis for a theory of rights. It gives us arguments for having fundamental rights, and it helps us isolate the central clusters of rights among them. Indeed, the core of the very meaning of basic rights entails the "right" to assert rights on the part of the citizenry. This "right" is, of course, neither a particular positive right nor a negative liberty, but rather a *political* principle involving a new and active relation on the part of citizens to a public sphere that is itself located within civil society.[105] We believe that the metanorms of discourse ethics can justify the principle of the right to assert rights, and hence the idea of rights itself.

This claim rests on a crucial set of distinctions that we can only summarize here. What relationship, if any, exists between the metaprinciples of discourse ethics and fundamental rights? There are three possible ways of conceptualizing such a relationship: (a) fundamental universal rights could be presupposed by discourse ethics, but the metanorms of rational discourse would not be able on their own to supply the "ground" or principle for such rights; (b) fundamental rights could enter in as the content of a possible rational consensus; or (c) fundamental rights could be implied by the metaprinciples of discourse ethics. We shall argue that all three ways of relating discourse ethics and basic rights obtain, depending on which classes of rights one is considering. We shall take up each position in turn.

(a) Let us assume that the principles of constitutionalism include the idea that during the course of writing and amending constitutions, we arrive at (constitutional) rights by coming to agreement. Nevertheless the idea of rights in the strong sense cannot be reduced to constitutional legal positivity.[106] They are in a crucial sense always antecedent to positive law, even to positive higher law (constitutions). Yet we need not fall back into natural rights dogma to account for the antecedent character of rights. Instead, we can link the idea of rights to the metaconditions of discourse: Without individuals whose autonomy is guaranteed by rights, the demanding preconditions of rational discourse (against which any empirical agreement can be measured) cannot in principle be met. Accordingly, rights can be interpreted as normative requirements for participation in practical discourses about society.[107] If our individual and collective autonomy were not secured by rights, our participation in discourses could not be protected from constraints whose absence can never be taken for granted by the individual, even if these constraints are arrived at democratically. Civil and political rights constitute the preconditions for an institutionalized discourse claiming to be democratic. In other words, both rights and democratic discussion presuppose autonomous individuals able to assert moral norms or values as possible candidates for a rational consensus. In this sense, the metaprinciples of rational discourse "demand" the principle of basic rights.

This argument needs to be unpacked, however. We are assuming that behind the idea of basic rights is a "substantive moral principle," the principle of autonomy.[108] On the one side, there is a conception of autonomy that flows directly from discourse ethics (grounded in the theory of universal pragmatics). In this context, autonomy means the ability to take on dialogue roles, to engage reciprocally in ideal role taking, to achieve reflexivity vis-à-vis these roles, and to articulate one's own needs, interests, and values in order to determine their universalizability and arrive at a common agreement on general norms.[109] But this conception of autonomy is not enough to encompass what comes to mind when one speaks of the antecedent character of basic rights or the autonomous individual as the subject of basic rights. The communications-theoretic conception of autonomy establishes a link between the metaprinciples of discourse (symmetric reciprocity) and a conception of the individual who is to participate in such a discourse. But this conception is nonetheless parasitic on a more complex principle of autonomy that is not derivable from the metaprinciples of rational discourse. The concept of autonomy we have in mind here has two components that attach to the abstract and situated dimensions of personality, respectively. The first can be construed as the principle of self-determination and individual choice along Kantian lines that is presupposed by the abstract and general conception of the rights-bearing person. The second refers to the ability to construct, revise, and pursue one's own life plan (Mill, Rawls); this component attaches to the idea of unique personality and to the dynamics of individual identity formation. One or the other aspect of this dualistic conception of autonomy has always been invoked as the core principle of liberty or inviolate personality underlying the liberal idea of basic individual rights. It constitutes a moral principle irreducible to the metanorms of rational discourse that underlie the idea of democratic legitimacy, although, as indicated above, discourse ethics always has a role to play in the process of asserting rights. In our view, the dualistic conception of autonomy comprises the "truth content" of liberal arguments for fundamental rights based on a conception of freedom as negative liberty or the free self-development of unique, inviolate personalities.

It is not necessary, however, to saddle the ideas of negative liberty and inviolate personality with atomistic, asocial conceptions of the individual or to establish the paradigm of property rights as the conceptual heart of the rights that protect individual autonomy. We have already noted the fragility of individual identity due to the fact that individuation occurs in complex, intersubjective, communicative processes of interaction. Individual identities are vulnerable because they are never set once and for all. One develops one's identity throughout one's life, and it is dependent on the dynamics of mutual recognition for its stability and self-esteem. Thus, the set of rights that articulate respect for the dignity, uniqueness, and inviolability of socialized individuals (liberty, personality, and privacy rights) are indispensable guarantees of autonomy in both of the above senses. While we may need some form of property rights (to our homes, personal possessions, etc.) in order to be able to concretize our negative liberty and to express our personality, it is only on the untenable assumption of possessive individualism that negative liberty, inviolate personality, and property in the economic sense become equated. In short, property rights, suitably reduced, may be one among many sets of rights we may need, but they are not the conceptual core of the idea of autonomy.

Thus, the principles of symmetric reciprocity comprise the metanorms of practical dialogue, while core aspects of the principle of autonomy constitute the metanorm underlying the conception of the individual who is to participate in such a dialogue. Accordingly, there is a sense in which an important dimension of rights involves negative liberties and personality rights that do not flow directly from discourse ethics.

(b) As Albrecht Wellmer has noted, the dimension of negative liberty that *is* bound up with determinations of the type and structure of property rights, and with market relations, can be linked to discourse ethics on the second model mentioned above, that is, on the level of content. In other words, "the delegation of steering functions to the market—as a sphere of negative freedom—can be seen as at least potentially resulting from—and being limited by—a democratic process of decision making. This kind of legitimation of a sphere of "strategic" economic action is the one which is built into Habermas's theory of communicative action."[110] The same holds true for what have come to be called "social rights" or matters of redistributive justice. Here, too, the precise range and variety of social rights we want to accord one another would have to enter into a discourse on the level of content, although we could of course agree to construe these as basic liberties. As such, property rights and social rights can be the content of a democratic discussion. They do not stand as external limits to it.

(c) There is a third class of rights that mediates between autonomy and democratic legitimacy: the rights of communication (speech, assembly, association, expression, and all citizenship rights). It is our contention that this class of rights is implied by discourse ethics; that is, they have the structure of basic rights (they can be conceived of as antecedent to and inviolable by any democratic consensus), but insofar as they are the conditions of possibility of any consensus claiming to be legitimate, they can be read off directly from the principles of symmetric reciprocity underlying the idea of discourse ethics itself. This class of rights is constitutive of discourse. These rights enter in neither as possible contents of a discussion (they could not be rejected without violating the procedural principles of discourse) nor as limits to the reach of a possible discussion, but rather as the constitutive principles of discussion itself. Needless to say, we argue that these rights institutionalize the public spaces within civil society in which democratic legitimacy is generated.

We can now make sense of the possible opposition between rights and democracy that haunts liberal and democratic political theory. Even if rights are required for the very conception of democratic discourse, it is nonetheless possible for there to be conflict between democratic decisions and rights of communication and between democracy and rights of autonomy. Are these conflicts on the level of principle, or are they conflicts between the ways two different but interdependent principles are institutionalized? We believe that the latter, not the former, is the case. This claim is based on our attempt to reinterpret the core idea of basic rights in terms of the idea of autonomy and the democratic principle of the "right to have rights." This reinterpretation involves the following steps. First, we sever the idea of autonomy from the unnecessary baggage of anthropological assumptions of atomistic, asocial individuals. Second, we free it from the ideology of possessive individualism in which property appears as the paradigm of all rights and of negative liberty itself. Certainly the "communitarian" insight that individuation occurs through socialization and participation in the culture, traditions, and institutions of society and that individual and collective identities emerge together through complex processes of communicative interaction does nothing to diminish the claims of individual autonomy, the principle of negative liberty, or the idea of fundamental rights. Third, we explain a key complex of rights in terms of the metanorms of discourse ethics itself, namely the rights to communication that are the sine qua non for the principle of democratic legitimacy to find an institutional locus. Fourth, we argue that civil and political society are constituted by these basic sets of rights and provide for their institutionalization. Finally, we argue that the idea of the right to have rights is a democratic political principle involving the active participation of individuals in the institutionalized public spheres of civil and political society and also in noninstitutionalized public spheres that emerge in the milieux of social movements. The assertion of rights is thus seen as a political act, even if its thrust is, in part, to establish a terrain of individual autonomy with respect to which democratic decision making must be self-limiting. These steps greatly diminish the distance between rights-oriented liberal theories and participatory democratic theories.

Empirical discourse can violate both the communicative preconditions of discourse and its preconditions on the level of autonomy. From the point of view of the claims of autonomous individuals, every discourse is only empirical and always stands to be corrected. This is the most obvious case and easiest to handle theoretically. But even from the point of view of an ideal rational communication, conflict between democracy and autonomy is conceivable. We are not trying to deny this. Indeed, we began this discussion by restricting the object domain of discourse ethics to legal norms and to the legal system as a whole, insisting that a realm of autonomous judgment for the individual beyond the purview of law must be respected. Obviously an individual's judgment can come into conflict with a given political norm even when it is democratically arrived at. As Wellmer has pointed out, the demands of communicative rationality in any specific historical context will have some kind of public definition in terms of institutions, moral beliefs, public opinion, or societal norms, and these must be open to critique and revision and must leave room for dissent.[111] However, it is a mistake to construe this as an opposition between the principles of rights *tout court* and democracy.

Certain rights institutionalize the positions of moral conscience and individual judgment as a legitimate, principled standpoint from which one can challenge any empirical norm. The right to dissent, the right to be different, the right to act on one's judgment, and privacy rights protect negative liberty and inviolate personality. Yet what is involved here is not, as Wellmer believes, a right to be irrational, but rather a right, metapolitically grounded, to be autonomous and different. Freedom of conscience and the right to particularity follow from this, but these are still rational rights. Moral conscience can then exercise these rights according to its own standards, rational or irrational. Individual autonomy would be lost in fact if we insisted on a specific way of exercising freedom of conscience or of pursuing one's particular conception of the good. But it would also be lost if in our own sphere we violated the autonomy of others.

The principles of rights and democracy, each in its own way, define the limiting conditions of what the legitimate content of an empirical consensus might be. Each provides for dissent, the first by delimiting the reach of such a consensus (to which those involved must nonetheless agree), the second by delimiting the procedural principles through which a valid consensus can be reached. Both, in other words, provide a principled reference point from which one can challenge the legitimacy of an empirical agreement.

It should be clear from what we have said so far that only some rights involve negative liberty and that the principle of rights itself is a profoundly political one. Nonetheless, there is a boundary question about the limits to the reach of democratic decision making. The specific content of rights, the norms agreed upon within a dialogue, and the ways in which one acts out one's negative liberty and identity goals within generally agreed-upon constraints, all impinge on this boundary question. The concepts of negative liberty, inviolate personality, and privacy set limits to the reach of democratic decision making in the name of particularity and individual autonomy and draw upon a foundation independent from that of consensus itself. While the boundary line between basic autonomy rights and democratic decision making cannot be drawn in advance of a discussion of content, it nevertheless has to be drawn in principle. There is no way in advance of a practical discourse to settle controversies over what constitutes issues of the good life and what belongs to the domain of generalizable "interests. "[112] But we insist that once such a boundary line is drawn, those matters that are particular (my determination of and pursuit of my life plan, my identity) are then off limits to democratic decision making yet retain a moral worth—they cannot be reduced to error, egoism, interest compromise, or matters of taste—for what is at stake is the individual's identity, moral autonomy, or way of life (as a member of a particular group within a larger social whole or simply as an individual with a unique identity). Controversial identity needs can be brought into a general discussion when they impinge upon general norms of action. The first set of rights protects this domain. One can gain a certain reflexivity regarding one's projects, but it would be too much to demand that, for the sake of justice, one give up one's identity, for that would surely not be just. In other words, here the standard of "the least disruptive impact" on identity needs discussed in the previous section with respect to collective identity enters in with respect to individual identity—and provides a limit to the democratic determination of what is just—with one proviso: Those dimensions of particularity that violate either the autonomy of others or the metanorms of discourse (symmetric reciprocity) have no claim to legitimacy. In this sense, the right and the good, autonomy rights and democratic legitimacy, must be *mutually* self-limiting.

Accordingly, the two sets of rights most fundamental to the institutional existence of a fully developed civil society are those that secure the integrity, autonomy, and personality of the person and those having to do with free communication . However, all rights, including those securing moral autonomy, require discursive validation. From this point of view, it might appear that the rights of communication are the most fundamental, since they are constitutive of discourse itself and hence of the key institution of modern civil society: the public sphere. This appearance is due in part to the sociological primacy of the rights of communication.

In fact, discourse ethics logically presupposes both classes of rights. By basing rights not on an individualist ontology, as classical liberals have done, but on the theory of communicative interaction, we have strong reason to emphasize the cluster of rights of communication. It would certainly be possible to argue that other clusters of rights, such as those of privacy and suffrage, are required to maintain this key complex. The rights to privacy and autonomy would be affirmed because of the need to produce the autonomous person without whom rational discourse would be impossible. Such would be the result of a purely Habermasian deduction of rights from discourse ethics understood as the sum total of practical philosophy.[113] In our argument, however, the two sets of rights represent two pillars of ethical life that are irreducible to each other. From one we can reason to the principle of unconstrained communicative interaction; from the other, to the principle of the autonomous and unique person. Both are preconditions of actual discourse that seeks to be rational. Thus, both are required as preconditions of democratic legitimacy, even if not in the same way. From this point of view, the rights of communication point us to the legitimate domain of formulating and defending rights. The rights of personality identify the subjects who have the right to have rights.

This catalogue of rights constitutive of the public and intimate spheres of civil society is crucial for any version of rational communication, in the sense of discourse ethics. Political and socioeconomic rights are also important, if less directly so. Some version of these represents the precondition for stabilizing the public and private spheres and hence for institutionalized discourse by "mediating" between them and modern states and economies.

Habermas has recently argued that fundamental rights are realizations of the universal content of norms that are not only legitimate, in the sense of discourse ethics, but also central to the moral substance (*Sittlichkeit*) of our legal system. [114] In the West, there has in fact been a decreasingly selective realization of the norms of such an ethics precisely to the extent that here has been an expansion of rights.[115] Nevertheless, selectivity and one-sidedness have been the rule in exercising and interpreting rights in the modern capitalist economy and the modern state. Dividing rights somewhat roughly into liberties (*Freiheitsrechte*) and membership rights (*Teilhaberrechte*), Habermas suggests that the latter are organized today in such a way that bureaucracies restrict actual participation and spontaneous public will formation.[116] The former are construed, in capitalist societies, on the basis of individualistic premises. Foreshortened in these two ways, rights appear as the prerogative of the private individual, severed from the principles of solidarity and citizenship that, on the basis of communicative interpretation, they should ideally entail. Thus, once again on the level of norms and principles, we can speak of the expansion of "justice" and "freedom," but the institutional embodiment is presented as either primarily negative or highly selective.[117]

There is a crucial difference between these two options. Indeed, Habermas has actually taken an important step away from a thesis of institutional decline and toward a thesis of selective institutionalization. His stress on legal institutions (counterposed to legal media that have steering functions and can be disconnected from the normative substance of everyday interaction) and on selective institutionalization of the emancipatory potentials of modernity points beyond the antinomy of normative development and institutional decline. Accordingly, we argue that, even if rights and liberties are institutionalized selectively in contemporary capitalist mass democracies (i.e., if they are limited to individualistically conceived rights), they are nonetheless institutionalized. Moreover, the right to have rights has come to be recognized as a core component of democratic political culture. As Claude Lefort has shown, the symbolic significance of rights is the open possibility of fighting for the fuller realization, expansion, reinterpretation, and creation of new rights.[118] Even if the normative development that represents the positive side of modernity is only selectively established in stable institutions, such partial achievements create the space for social movements to renew and reestablish the relevant principles in less selective ways.

Habermas has argued that social movements are the dynamic factor behind the expansion of rights. The practice of movements can culminate in the alteration "of interpretations given to publicly recognized needs or wants" and the thematization of the normative contents of everyday life institutions, making them "accessible to communication." As far as the present is concerned, though, Habermas maintains that "the concept of 'democratization' is not adequate to what is at issue here, because, except in some cases, the initiatives and movements . . . are not likely to enlarge the scope for effective participation in political decisions."[119] It is fair to say that Habermas's stress remains on the contribution of social movements to a new political culture or new cultural hegemony, which is only connected indirectly, in the long run, and in an indeterminate fashion to democratic institutions.[120] The reason for this foreshortened assessment of the effects of social movements is that Habermas does not connect the principle of democratic legitimacy (as he does the concept of basic rights) to institutions that actually express democratic processes. Thus, he has to limit the consequences of movements to the transformation of political culture—a process that could affect the viability of rights but not lead to their expansion. The paradox of this position is that the nonselective institutionalization of basic rights required by discourse ethics is inconceivable without the generation of new democratic institutions, and this requires the contribution of social movements. The transition from a purely individualistic to a communicatively organized structure of rights is impossible on the basis of a democratized political culture alone. A new definition of rights needs new types of legislative activity. But the exclusionary mechanisms and selectivity of contemporary representative systems set key limits to the requisite broadening of basic rights. Quasi-legislation through courts can supply some of the missing elements for the democratization of rights, but, without a democratized political system, such activism has serious limits. Habermas's attachment to the thesis of the decline of mass democracy, however, opens up very little perspective for the institutionalization of democratic legitimacy. Thus, the relationship of discourse ethics to institutional analysis remains deeply antinomic in his work.

It would be unfair not to stress those dimensions of his social theory that, in some respects, point beyond the antinomy. Habermas's recent discussions of system and lifeworld point in a direction that views institutions as dualistic.[121] Instead of locating normative development exclusively on the levels of personality and culture, while construing social institutions to be one-dimensional, the recent theoretical construction recognizes the dualistic features of a variety of institutions ranging from law, mass communications, and the family to the political structures of compromise. This approach makes the rigid juxtaposition of democratic legitimacy and pseudo-democratic forms of domination untenable. Rather, on this model, it becomes clear that contemporary democratic institutional forms are two-sided, that they *internalize* the antinomy as a set of dual possibilities of development, a conclusion that in any case follows from the idea of democratic legitimacy itself. We have already argued as much in the case of basic rights. What remains at issue is how, on the level of a theory of democratic legitimacy, discourse ethics can throw light on the dual possibilities of existing democratic institutions, instead of emphasizing only their distance from the normative claims of this form of legitimacy. Our reformulation of democratic legitimacy severs discourse ethics from a form of life and even from a specific set of political institutions supposedly derivable from it. It thus breaks with any utopia of a fully transparent discourse as a form of life as well as with the corresponding disregard of all dimensions of human existence that give it its index of particularity.[122] But we have not yet moved beyond a conception that focuses on the counterfactual character of this principle. The most paradoxical conclusion of this analysis would be to deny any possibility of deriving institutional consequences from the principle of democratic legitimacy while diagnosing existing societies as entirely undemocratic. Such a conception would amount to a discourse-theoretic reformulation of the *dialectic of enlightenment.* Our point is not that Habermas's social theory is nothing more than such a reformulation; this was true (partially) only for *Strukturwandel der Öffentlichkeit.* Rather, we are proposing that discourse ethics needs to be refined further if it is to be related adequately to the dualistic social theory emerging from *The Theory of Communicative Action.*

At issue is the notion of rational consensus. We maintain that it is the extreme formulation of this notion that leads either to an untenable utopia based on the ideal speech situation or to a restatement of the neo-Kantian dualism of *Sein* and *Sollen* in terms of ethics and institutions. We do not, however, propose to replace rational consensus with the liberal democratic notion of empirical or factual consensus. The objection that such a replacement would be impotent in the face of manipulated or enforced consensus is well taken. Nevertheless, we believe, with Wellmer, that all consensus is empirical. The parameters of discourse ethics can exist only in empirical contexts. Rationality in such contexts can be only a matter of degree. Furthermore, it is always a matter of a *process* of rationalization, in the sense of the development of the potentiality for the communicative coordination of action. Accordingly, any doubt as to the rationality of a consensus must be regarded as a hypothesis that can be sustained only by carrying out another discourse, culminating in a "more rational" consensus, in the sense that participants recognize their previous unreason.[123]

With this reformulation, do we commit ourselves to an overly minimalist interpretation of discourse ethics? We would, if we were to assert with Wellmer that no evaluation of the legitimacy of concrete institutions can be derived from the principle of discourse because "it can never be derived from principles what is possible in concrete historical situations."[124] This statement brings the reformulated version of the notion of consensus back into the antinomic straightjacket we have already analyzed. But Wellmer also tells us that (1) a negative procedure for criticizing existing institutions can be based on Merleau-Ponty's principle that "we cannot intend the realization of sense, only the elimination of nonsense,"[125] and (2) "the principle of discourse can give us a *direction* . . . that demands the expansion of the realm of discursive rationality till that limit which we . . . can find only in historical practice."[126] Thus, we might say in the spirit of this conception that a more minimal statement of discourse ethics actually opens up the field for its institutional implications: We can criticize existing institutions and plan new ones if we take into account both what the principle requires and what is possible in concrete historical situations. Not only the development of moral consciousness and ego identity but "the history of institutions and revolutions" belongs to the history of the unfolding of universal principles.[127]

But how is concrete history to be taken into account? The Western Marxist tradition from Lukács to Adorno tended to postulate a rupture with history, implicitly assuming that emancipation has no historical basis. Yet Habermas and Wellmer have explicitly repostulated historical *continuity* without using the orthodox Marxist productivist basis to which their theoretical forebears objected.[128] In the new argument, emancipation has normative preconditions that, according to Wellmer and Habermas, exist in formally democratic societies in the form of the principles of democratic legitimacy and basic rights, which have been established since the seventeenth or eighteenth centuries. But the implications of this position in relation to inherited institutions remain unclear. Indeed, Wellmer finds two strands in Habermas's work that do not coexist very well—one stressing continuity, the other discontinuity; one linked to a revised Hegelian tradition, the other to a politically interpreted Marxian tradition.[129]

The Hegelian tradition implies the theory of civil society. To adhere to it critically means to accept neither Hegel's vision of the modern state nor an unchanging view of the capitalist economic system. Nonetheless, it does mean that differentiation of a sphere of negative freedoms along with the steering mechanism of the market cannot be overcome without the massive regression of totalitarianism. The same is true for the related issue of legal universalism and formalism: In the Hegelian model, this cannot be overcome in the form of an allegedly higher, substantive form of social freedom. Preserving the autonomy of law is not possible without culturally differentiating the sphere of legality from morality, art, and science and distinguishing all of these from everyday life practice. Even a rationally organized society in such a revised Hegelian model would involve contingency, particularity, and hence the continued existence of conflict-filled social relations. Finally, emancipation would have the meaning of realizing the full potential of already institutionalized structures of universal law and morality.

But Wellmer insists that another Marxist utopia is also present in Habermas's work, involving a communication-theoretic translation of the project of a direct democratic republic of councils: "A society free of domination would be one in which collective processes of will formation have taken on the form of discursively achieved associations, without compulsion."[130] We have already accepted Wellmer's criticism of the use of the theory of communication as the constitutive framework for an anticipated utopia of this sort, and Habermas himself had abandoned such a conception by the mid-1970s. Indeed, the model cannot possibly withstand Hegel's critique of a rationalist-enlightenment concept of freedom. Yet Wellmer is equally uncomfortable with the model of civil society derived from Hegel,[131] because it no longer seems to allow a clear, sharp conceptualization of the idea of a rational society and therefore of emancipation. We want to contest this last idea.

Wellmer notes the internal relationship between discourse ethics and the concept of civil society and, even more important, the link between civil society and the institutionalization of discourses in political public spheres and parliaments. He speaks of democratic legitimacy as itself institutionalized; capitalist private property now appears as *its* limitation rather than as the fetter of the forces of production. However, the formulation of this point is somewhat ambiguous: Capitalist relations of production "block the real institutional carrying out of this organizational principle of democratic legitimacy."[132] In the context of this metaphor, the Marxian and Hegelian alternatives appear as restatements of the old "revolution or reform" option, and Wellmer, after all our experience with these processes, can work up little enthusiasm for either. No wonder that the Habermasian antinomy of democratic legitimacy (whose unfolding is assigned to the development of new identities and political culture) and pseudo-democratic institutions periodically returns in his work.[133]

Our own conception of civil society, in the tradition of Tocqueville, Gramsci, Parsons, and (as we shall show) the new dualistic social theory of Habermas himself, has a chance of linking up with discourse ethics in a way that avoids an ultimately negative outcome involving the trilemma of reform, revolution, or resignation. By using a three-part model of economy, civil society, and state, we remove the almost definitional connection (in Hegel, and even more in Marx) between capitalist economy and modern civil society. By focusing on the antinomies of the institutions and the contradictory institutional development of civil society, we avoid the model of decline derived from the older Frankfurt school, the womb metaphor of Marx, and also all pluralist apologies for existing societies. By linking the notions of differentiation and democracy, we derive a model of the plurality of democracies that restores the utopian thinking that Wellmer feared lost with the Hegelian model without buying into fundamentalisms that imply either dedifferentiation or the total replacement of steering mechanisms by the communicative coordination of action.

Discourse Ethics and Civil Society

The concept of civil society we defend differs from Hegel's model in three essential respects. First, it presupposes a more differentiated social structure. Taking our cue from Gramsci and Parsons, we postulate the differentiation of civil society not only from the state but also from the economy.[134] Our concept is neither state-centered, as was Hegel's, however ambiguously, nor economy-centered, as was Marx's. Ours is a society-centered model.[135] Second, following Tocqueville and the early Habermas, we make the public spheres of societal communication and voluntary association the central institutions of civil society. Of course, the *private*, understood as the domain of autonomous individual judgment, is also crucial to a modern civil society. Third, we conceive the institutionalization of civil society as a process that always (as in Hegel) involves a stabilization of societal institutions on the basis of rights ("abstract right"), but also one that has the immanent possibility of becoming more democratic and whose norms call for democratization.

Civil society in the historical sense is the ground of possibility of all modern political ethics, from secular natural law to discourse ethics. The latter in particular (whose forerunners reach back to the nineteenth century) would not have been possible without the institutionalization of discourse in the modern liberal public sphere. However, discourse ethics differs from all other modern political ethics (natural rights, utilitarianism, Kantian political philosophy, and even the recent neocontractarianism and neo-Aristotelianism) in that its political implications center on the normative necessity and empirical possibility of democratization in civil society. Thus, it is the only ethics that reconciles the claims of classical liberalism with radical democracy.

We accept the argument that different models of democratic organization are compatible with the discourse-ethical principle of democratic legitimacy. This compatibility need not be viewed only in terms of an opposition between direct and representative democracy. The requirements of the principle of democratic legitimacy may be fulfilled, in principle at least, by a direct democracy of councils pyramidally organized, as well as by a representative type of democracy whose delegated authorities are controlled by viable public spheres with general access and real power. But, on another axis, the principle is compatible with a federalist polity as well as one organized on centralist lines. Finally, it may even be compatible with spheres of life that are not discursively or democratically organized, as long as the need for nondiscursive organizational principles and the boundaries between them and democratic organizations are established and confirmed in discursive processes. We claim, though, that discourse ethics is not easily made compatible with the suppression of already existing forms of democracy. This claim implies that total revolution is not legitimate in democratic contexts. We do not mean thereby to deny either the legitimacy of revolutions under authoritarianism or the right of excluded people or groups to revolt against even "democratic" conditions that exclude them.[136] We do mean, however, to question attempts to overturn the formally democratic institutions of contemporary civil societies by people who, in principle, have access to them (with the unlikely exception of cases in which discursive procedures have allowed everyone concerned a direct access to this decision). We take this position because frameworks of representative democracy provide the only access for large numbers of people to global processes of democratic will formation. As Hannah Arendt frankly admitted, direct democracy involving constant high levels of political participation is inevitably aristocratic. Thus, new forms of democracy meant to replace the old ones can never in principle replace them for all people. This does not deny that many of those whose access was previously weak would not, with the introduction of new forms, find more meaningfully participatory frameworks. For this reason, we argue that existing forms of democracy can be supplemented, complemented, or democratized according to the requirements of discourse ethics, but they cannot be replaced.

The affinity of discourse ethics with a plurality of forms of democracy and its implication that existing forms not be suppressed link us to civil society in two ways. First, civil society and the existing forms of representative democracy politically and juridically presuppose one another. Second, only on the ground of civil society can an institutionalized plurality of democracies be conceived. Let us examine these two claims in turn.

First, political society organized in the form of representative democracy and modern civil society share two key institutions that "mediate" between them: the public sphere and voluntary associations. The frameworks of politically relevant public discussion (the media, political clubs and associations, party caucuses, etc.) and parliamentary discussion and debate are continuous. As even Marx noted, it is inconsistent (even if temporarily possible) for a parliament, formally a body of discussion and debate, to try to eliminate or even to severely limit political discussion or voluntary association in society.[137] But equally important, existing forms of the politically relevant publics in society, through their built-in logic, must imply the eventual establishment of such a public sphere within the institutional network of the state itself, or rather within political society.[138] Furthermore, a plural, dynamic civil society finds in a parliamentary structure (together with other structures of compromise, including political parties) the most plausible general framework in which the conflicts of member groups and individuals can be politically mediated, rival interests can be aggregated, and the possibility of reaching a consensus can be explored. Parliamentary structures of interest aggregation and conflict mediation, on the other hand, work well only if there is a more or less open articulation of these on the social level. In short, in representative democracies, political society both presupposes and must be open to the influence of civil society.[139]

On a juridical level, the concept of rights indicates a similar relationship. Representative democracy and modern civil society share rights as common presuppositions: political, communication rights are presuppositions of parliamentary democracy, while communication and private rights make modern civil society possible. Political rights permit and regulate the access of citizens to parliamentary (and local) representation, while private and communication rights guarantee the autonomy of the persons and associations of civil society. Thus, communication rights have a double function. The freedoms of expression, association, and so on extend the autonomy of civil society, but without them the parliamentary public sphere is also not possible. However, the relationship of representative democracy and civil society on the level of rights goes even deeper. Rights, as against privileges, immunities, or estate-type liberties, begin and are reaffirmed when asserted by individuals, groups, or movements in the public spaces of civil society. They can and must be guaranteed by positive law, but as *rights*, that is, as limits on the state itself, they are not logically derivable from it. In the domain of rights, law secures and stabilizes what has been achieved by social actors in civil society. Positive law in this context, however, is civil society being constituted and reconstituted by its own actors through a political-legislative or political-judicial mediation.

For several reasons, modern civil society cannot be institutionalized without the political reaffirmation of rights through positive law. First, the complexity of modern civil society (and probably of any postprimitive society) requires legal-juridical regulation in all spheres of life. Even the private, intimate spheres are protected as such by legal dispensations. In other words, morality and *Sittlichkeit* cannot and must not, as Hegel knew, fully substitute for law, for any sphere of a modern society, or make law entirely superfluous. This point holds for fundamental rights as well: Social conflicts over these and their interpretation and enforcement require a high degree of legal regulation. Second, the very power of the modern state to intervene in society cannot be contained without self-imposed legal limits on such intervention. The legalization of fundamental rights has this meaning of self-imposed limits on the state. In other words, rights become limits in this sense only through being legally posited.

It is at this point that there is an "elective affinity" between fundamental rights and the modern representative, democratic politics. While historically many individual rights could be legislated by authoritarian or merely liberal constitutional states, the catalogue of rights we have indicated as constitutive of modern civil society can be established and defended in a convincing manner only by representative democracies. Even if we exclude political rights that tautologically imply such a polity, many of the communication rights (as against private ones) of our catalogue would in themselves severely threaten all other political systems that we know of. Thus, their acceptance of these rights can be only a tactical concession. Differentiating modern civil society from the state through rights strongly implies representative democracy.

Second, we contend that modern civil society not only logically presupposes and (historically) facilitates the emergence of representative democracy but also makes historically possible the democratization of representative democracy. This is in line with the tendency of discourse ethics to defend existing forms of democracy while simultaneously demanding further democratization. Both the complexity of and the diversity within contemporary civil societies call for the posing of the issue of democratization in terms of a variety of differentiated processes, forms, and loci, depending on the axis of division considered. Indeed, modern civil society is the terrain on which an institutionalized plurality of democracies can emerge. We can identify two sets of distinctions as most relevant in this regard. The first has to do with the structural possibilities and limits to democratization specific to each differentiated sphere: political, economic, and civil society. The second concerns pluralization of democratic forms within each sphere.

Marx made the point long ago that, if democracy is restricted to one sphere (the state) while despotic forms of rule prevail in the economy or in civil associations, then the democratic forms of the first sphere become undermined. On the other side, all our historical experience after Marx indicates that differentiation poses limits to democratization. The need for steering mechanisms for the state and the economy must be respected if we expect them to function efficiently. This, as is well known, militates against total democratization along the lines of direct participatory models. Yet it would be fallacious to conclude that no democratization is possible in these domains. On the contrary, once one takes into account the different logics of the coordinating mechanisms of each sphere, it becomes evident that there are forms of democracy adequate to each, even if they need to vary according to the relevant structural conditions. This point is clarified if we focus on the spheres of political and economic society, as the institutional levels in which the mechanisms of state and economy are anchored.

Representative democracy on the level of political society articulates the minimum degree of democratic participation required by modern interpretations of the citizenship principle. At the same time, the limits posed to direct participation by the very existence of a state, whose functions are coordinated through power relations and which is defined by its monopoly on the legitimate use of force, are obvious. The separation of powers, the rule of law, and requirements of efficient bureaucratic functioning guided by the principle of due process preclude the direct participation of everyone in policy making at the state level. At most, participants can work at this level indirectly through party and parliamentary supervision, control, and publicity—in other words, through the institutions of political society. Further democratization of a formally democratic polity must respect these limits.

Political society is not limited to global or national structures. These can be complemented by local and regional structures that could allow for more direct participation than is usually the case today. In addition, the procedures for revising constitutional principles or norms could be made more open. Moreover, in some countries, structures of functional representation, albeit in undemocratic, corporatist forms, complement territorially based representative structures. These are, in principle at least, open to more democracy and participation, the old dream of Durkheim and the philosophical pluralists.[140] What seems to be missing everywhere is the institutionalization of total social input by local and functional bodies in global, open, public procedures that share legitimacy with already established representative bodies. The recurring call for a second parliamentary chamber by the guild socialists, Austro-Marxists, and other democratic socialists all the way down to some contemporary social movements points in this direction. Of course, the exact device for democratization in this area cannot be at issue in our more abstract context.

The notion of functional representation already touches on questions of economic democracy. It is clear, however, that, insofar as the economy or, rather, economic society is concerned, the requirements of efficiency and market rationality can be disregarded in the name of democracy only at the cost of both. Here the levels of representation and participation need to be reconciled with the social needs of production and consumption. Forms of economic democracy need not be as inclusive as those of the polity. Yet, as indicated by the institutionalization of mechanisms of collective bargaining, codetermination, and representative workers' councils, democratization is not per se incompatible with efficient functioning.

The plurality of democratic forms that are possible and desirable with respect to economic society could include, among others, consumer and producer cooperatives, employer and union representation within corporate bodies, councils with various powers, grievance committees, and, as we now see in Eastern Europe, new forms of ownership. Each of these could in principle be made compatible with efficiency requirements and with one another (or at least the loss of efficiency implied by them could be kept within acceptable limits). The further democratization of economic society would involve institutionalizing these various forms of participation up to the point at which efficient steering is threatened, and this can be done without dedifferentiating the economy, society, and the state. The intermediary realms of political and economic society thus have a double role: They stabilize differentiation while acting as receptors to the influence of civil society aimed at the economy and the polity.

It is our central thesis that democracy can go much further on the level of civil society than on the level of political or economic society, because here the coordinating mechanism of communicative interaction has fundamental priority. Leaving aside the systematic aspects of this claim, to which we shall return in the next chapter, it is inductively certain that the functioning of societal associations, public communication, cultural institutions, and families allows for potentially high degrees of egalitarian, direct participation and collegial decision making—higher than is possible for political parties or labor unions, for example. Of course, experimentation with levels of participation can only occur where a wide range of associations, publics, and informal groups already exists and is guaranteed by rights. Where such plurality exists, small-scale participation may become, as Tocqueville hoped, not only the real substance of democratic local government but a basis for processes of self-education that can lead to a democratic political culture. Many contemporary civil societies are linked to what are, in effect, quasi-oligarchic political practices, yet the foundations for plurality, in voluntary associations, universities, and even churches, are well established. These structures are not always democratic and rarely involve genuine participation, but in the context of democratic norms they are constant targets for democratization.

In *Strukturwandel der Öffentlichkeit*, Habermas also argued for the democratization of existing corporate entities as one possible solution to the decline of the public sphere.[141] We believe that the principle of democratic legitimacy, when linked to the theory of civil society, leads to a revitalization and extension of this kind of alternative, for three reasons. First, participation in modern societies is ultimately only illusory if there is no small-scale participation in addition to representative parliaments. Second, discourse ethics in this context cannot be used to validate the suppression of existing pluralities in the name of one all-inclusive discursive process. Third, the democratization of existing pluralities is more compatible with the preservation of modern structures than their "totalization" by some kind of council model. The latter would imply the reembedding of steering mechanisms (administrations, markets) in directly social relations, and this would conflict with the presupposition of a modern civil society, namely, differentiation. Nevertheless, the limits to democratization on the level of the steering mechanism would be partly compensated for by the democratization of societal associations that can indirectly influence the state and economy as well.

The norms of the public sphere in civil society, even if distorted, reflect a constant demand for the overseeing, control, and democratization of existing forms of association. Originally a form of society-generated discursive control over state-bureaucratic power, the liberal public sphere has declined to the extent that private associations have been transformed into large-scale organizations with a quasi-political character that are partially responsible for tasks of economic and political steering. The normative demands of publicity in the new situation inherently imply the public exposure and the democratization of these private associations, even if to differing extents in civil, political, and economic society. Historically, just such developments, along with the renewal of alternative, public, formal organizations, have complemented processes that defend the liberal public sphere. The renewal of political public life is an ever-present potentiality of this aspect of the overall process.

Beyond the norms of publicity itself, two components of discourse ethics militate for the plurality of democracies: the critique of the exclusion of anyone who is at all concerned, and the stress on actual participation. In fact, all existing forms of democracy have built-in processes of exclusion. Liberal representative democracy in the nineteenth-century model excluded passive citizens. Modern representative democracy diminishes the relevance of (if it does not formally exclude) those who are not members of strong voluntary associations or party organizations. Direct democracy excludes those who do not seek public happiness first and foremost (i.e., the politically inactive). Territorial democracy discriminates against producers, industrial democracy against consumers. Federalism can reduce the importance of large national majorities as well as of dissenting individuals and groups within each member unit. Centralizing democracy provides no incentive for potentially important self-governing units. While no combination of these principles would exclude exclusion altogether, fostering a plurality of forms of democracy offers the promise of meaningful participation on several levels that are otherwise reduced in importance.

Let us sum up. Democratic legitimacy and basic rights interpreted in the sense of discourse ethics strongly imply a plurality of democracies for which modern civil society represents an institutional terrain of potentiality in two ways: (1) The differentiation of state, society, and economy as institutional spheres—and of political and economic society between them—allows democracy and democratization to be defined according to the different logics of these spheres. (2) The structures of plurality—actual and potential—in civil society itself allow for the possibility of democratizing the social sphere in terms of *participation* and *publicity*. Today the question of democracy has migrated back to the sphere in which it first emerged—that of civil society. The further democratization of formally democratic polities must be posed with reference to civil society and not simply to the state or the economy. Discourse ethics as we have interpreted it, together with a revised theory of civil society, not only allows for such an approach but, as an ethics of democratization, demands it as well. If the principle of rights based on discourse ethics implies the protection of modern civil society, the principle of democratic legitimacy implies its democratization beyond the liberal-democratic model.

The plurality of democracies as conceived here is utopian. The meaning of this utopia, however, is open to two very different interpretations. The first would presuppose continuity with the existing institutional framework of modern civil society. This would involve an institutional project in part articulated on the basis of a philosophical ethics that would, of course, require dynamic agencies of all kinds for its realization. Wellmer rightly points out that historical probability cannot be derived from a philosophical ethics. However, an existing institutional framework can mediate between *ought* and *is*, between philosophy and existing society.

If the institutional framework of civil society turns out to be anachronistic in light of what we know about contemporary states and economies, we would indeed be dealing with a utopia in a second sense of a pure *ought* that should not be imposed on a recalcitrant reality. In this case, discourse ethics should certainly be freed from the useless weight of the concept of the plurality of democracies. What is at issue, then, is the viability of a reformulated concept of civil society in relation to contemporary conditions. This reformulation—using the language and arguments of modern social theory, which we feel still provide our best access to contemporary society—is our next goal.

9

Social Theory and Civil Society

Reconstructing Civil Society

Perhaps because it has become so fashionable, the idea of civil society is increasingly ambiguous today. When articulated by social actors, the notion of rebuilding or defending civil society certainly tends to increase mobilization. But their imagery is not really adequate as a foundation for critical self-reflection or even for orientation in relation to the most important constraints on collective action. It is equally easy for such actors to slip into fundamentalist postures or to identify the project of civil society with the goals of economic and party-political elites, thereby renouncing their own autonomy and originality. What is needed is a conception of civil society that can reflect on the core of new collective identities and articulate the terms within which projects based on such identities can contribute to the emergence of freer, more democratic societies.

Even the best theories of civil society inherited from the past cannot accomplish these tasks today. The contemporary weakness of projects directly based on the conceptions of Hegel, Tocqueville, Gramsci, or Parsons derives not only from their very real internal antinomies, which we have explored, but also from their relative vulnerability in the face of critics such as Arendt, Schmitt, the young Habermas, and Foucault. Without a doubt, the theses concerning the decline of the public sphere and the transformation of the social into new forms of manipulation, control, and domination correspond at least as well to the experience of the advanced capitalist countries as do the optimistic views of the theoretical defenders of civil society who see democratic publics, intact solidarities, and forms of autonomy everywhere. But when the views of a staunchly realistic analyst of existing society like Luhmann start to match those of the most radical critics,[1] the defenders of civil society, whose eyes are often closed to negative phenomena, start to fall under the suspicion of ideology.

To be usable today, the category of civil society must be reconstructed. We define "reconstruction," in the nonsystematic sense, as "taking a theory apart and putting it back together again in a new form in order to attain more fully the goal it has set itself."[2] This is the normal way of "dealing with a theory that needs revision in many respects but whose potential for stimulation has still not been exhausted."[3] In our reconstruction of the category of civil society, we shall rely, albeit critically, on the second step of Habermas's own two-step theoretical strategy, namely, the development of a dualistic social theory that differentiates and links the equally necessary methodologies dealing with "lifeworld" and "system."[4]

We proceed in the following steps. (1) Using a three-part model of lifeworld and political and economic subsystems,[5] we deepen the paradigm inherited from Gramsci and Parsons, and we also develop it to reflect the more advanced theory of differentiation available in Luhmann, to help relativize and limit the fusion argument of Schmitt and the others. (2) In the face of Luhmann's system-theoretic objections, we try to demonstrate the modernity of civil society, understood in terms of a lifeworld capable of rationalization. In particular, we show the role of normative learning and of fundamental rights in stabilizing modern civil societies. (3) To deal with the genealogical and ideological attacks on civil society, we use the notions of reification and colonization of the lifeworld to show that all the negative phenomena stressed by critics can be accommodated in our conception, unlike earlier versions of the three-part model. In particular, we demonstrate the historical link between one-sided struggles of emancipation and the emergence of state-society-economy relations burdened by new forms of heteronomy, culminating in the forms of colonization characteristic of welfare states. Nevertheless, (4) we insist, against those who doubt the critical implications of the concept of civil society and accuse us of "soulless reformism," that the model of a differentiated civil society retains its utopian promise in welfare states as well as in states formerly governed by state socialism, a promise that points to the reconstruction and defense of publicity and intimacy in a new model of rights. (5) We try to show that the utopia of civil society is not merely an abstract "ought" in relation to existing heteronomous versions. In the face of various Frankfurt-type theories of one-dimensionality and total administration, we outline a conception showing that the negative phenomena we have insisted on represent only one side of an institutional fabric of the capitalist democracies. Finally, in the longest section of this chapter, we present a detailed political project for democratizing existing civil societies, in terms of the reflexive continuation of both the democratic revolution and the welfare state. We believe that such a project would also allow a reorientation of political strategies in Eastern Europe away from the probably unfeasible (and, in our opinion, undesirable) alternative of the West's past and present toward a model based on a possible (and, in our opinion, normatively desirable) common future.

Civil Society, Lifeworld, and the Differentiation of Society

The superiority of a three-part framework for the understanding of civil society is fundamental for our conception.[6] The dichotomous model of state and society, still used by some Marxists and particularly by neoliberals, neoconservatives, and present-day heirs of utopian socialism,[7] represents a quintessentially nineteenth-century figure of thought. Both of its social historical foundations are included in the ambiguous term "liberal": the antiabsolutist struggle presupposing and temporarily cementing the "polemical" unity of all social forces (Schmitt), and the emergence for the first and probably last time in history of an "economic society" dominated by a self-regulating market mechanism (Polànyi).

As Luhmann has shown, the inconsistent ideas of an all-inclusive economic society and of a dichotomy between state and society represent characteristic forms of consciousness (for him, "false consciousness") of the liberal epoch.[8] Both sophisticated Marxists and liberals, especially when dealing with politics, preferred the dichotomous conception of *bürgerliche Gesellschaft* to the purely economic one. From our review, the reason seems obvious. Whether we accept Polànyi's argument for a tendency toward a reduction of all social relations (habitat, status, culture) to market economic ones or Luhmann's thesis of the emergence of a new functional primacy of the economy, we cannot avoid observing that the growth of a self-regulating economy did not negate but occurred alongside the emergence of the increasingly differentiated apparatus of the modern state. In terms of Polànyi's concepts, this can be explained by the political demands involved in maintaining the negatively "utopian" preconditions of reducing land, labor, and productive enterprise to "fictitious" commodities.[9] As he says, unlike the beginning of planning, "laissez-faire was planned."[10] For Luhmann, the primacy of the economy allows, for structural reasons, greater differentiation than the earlier primacy of the political, and it furthers the transformation of a diffuse structure of political-religious-social-economic domination into a modern state that is more powerful than its predecessor.

Although less reductionist than the idea of economic society, the dichotomous model of state and (economic = civil) society is still reductionist. In Luhmann's terms, the economy is never the only social environment of the state; the differentiation of the economy assumes and promotes the differentiation of other spheres: law, science, art, and family.[11] Even in Polànyi's more dynamic model (which was far more sensitive to the dangers of our civilization), the utopia of the self-regulating market and the creation of a "market society" was never, nor could ever be, completely successful in its efforts at self-closure, as shown by the "countermovement of society." Accordingly, the "society" of the nineteenth century contained two very distinct "organizing principles" in deep potential conflict: economic self-regulation and societal self-protection.[12] We would add that the conflict between the two principles (economic-liberal and democratic) increases and becomes open, especially as the old enemy of societal forces, the bureaucratic-authoritarian state in its inherited form, is abolished or decisively weakened. The dichotomous model, whatever its relative merits in describing the classical liberal epoch, could not describe either the forces behind its transformation or the new structure of society.

Such is the matrix of the origins of the three-part model of civil society–economy–state relations. Polànyi's discovery was vitiated by his own ultimate identification of state regulation and even the statization of the economy with the self-defense of society. Battling against Marxist and liberal versions of reductionism, respectively, Gramsci and Parsons were the first to see that contemporary society is reproduced not only through economic and political processes, or even their new or renewed fusion, but through the interaction of legal structures, social associations, institutions of communication, and cultural forms, all of which have a significant degree of autonomy. Both writers were influenced by Hegel. Both understood the revival of associational life not as the fusion of the logics of private and public, economy and state, but as the re-creation of a fabric of societal intermediations older than the industrial and French revolutions, *in a new and posttraditional form.*

It is doubtful that the models of Gramsci or of Parsons could be sustained against the fusion argument we have seen in Schmitt, in Habermas's *Strukturwandel,* and even in Arendt, which is the alternative way of conceiving the "great transformation" of liberal society. Gramsci was notoriously unable to distinguish clearly between state and civil society, domination and hegemony, and he was able (or willing) to thematize the independent institutions of civil society most of the time only in terms of their function for reproducing the existing state and economy. In this picture, civil society could still be seen as the extension of a state itself serving the reproduction of the given economic order. Hegemony would thus remain the continuation of domination by other means. Parsons, having made the societal community the normative center of society, could declare its independence, but his treatment of societal community, state, and economy as entirely analogous subsystems, each regulated by a discrete medium of exchange, implies that he has replaced substantive with methodological reductionism. For this reason, among others, he is totally insensitive to the phenomena of statization and economization emphasized by the fusion theorists. As indicated by his one-sided adoption of Polànyi's argument, which allows him to see only the differentiation but not the (transitional) dominance of the self-regulating market, he is unable to conceive the threat to civil society from the logic of the large, expanding structures of the modern state and the capitalist economy. Thus, Gramsci's and Parsons's different forms of functionalism have opposite, yet equally undesirable, consequences for a theory of civil society. The former yields a picture overly integrated in the given structure of domination, and the latter leads to a model of self-regulation and boundary maintenance that is unrealistically immune to heteronomy.

We need a theory capable of thematizing both the threat and the promise. Habermas's "critique of functionalist reason"[13] provides the best available conceptual framework for reconstructing the three-part model of civil society. At first glance, the methodologically dualistic distinction between system and lifeworld appears to be Habermas's version of the state/civil-society duality that has informed the liberal and standard Marxian models. Upon closer examination, however, the thesis that *two* subsystems are differentiated both from each other and from the lifeworld implies a model that corresponds more closely to a tripartite framework of the Gramscian type. In this theory, the media of money and power, integrating economy and state respectively, are seen as less analogous in their operation than Parsons proposes. Their "standard situations" involve a fundamentally different structure: exchange linked to gain and ultimately to a "positive sanction" in the case of money; sub- and superordination in the case of power, linked ultimately to a "negative sanction" exercised from a hierarchically differentiated position preserving an element of direct command. This difference leads not only to conditions of weaker symbolization in a far more heterogeneous system of codes, less fluid circulation, less stable accumulation, greater difficulties in measurement, and greater dependence on organization but also to a need to compensate for asymmetries in ruling and being ruled by direct legitimation linked to tradition or agreement.[14] The structure of institutionalization via civil and public law reflects this difference: Only the latter is linked to "obligation."[15] Unlike money, furthermore, generating and even preserving power presuppose regeneration in the world of communicative action.[16] Yet power, like money, is linked to a reference to empirical motivations, namely interests, and provides a "certain automatism" in interaction based on a capability of dramatic substitution for ordinary language communication. It is, accordingly, institutionalized as the constitutive steering medium of the modern state, albeit on a lower level of formalization than money.[17]

Thus, methodological dualism is preserved with respect to the "logic" of the three institutional spheres. The two media/subsystems participate in the same fundamental social function, that of *system integration,* which refers to the unintended functional interdependencies of the effects of action coordinated without reference to actors' orientations or norms.[18] Yet methodological dualism leads to a three-part framework. The differences and similarities in the forms of institutionalization of the modern state and the capitalist economy, while distinguishing them from the lifeworld, are sufficient to indicate three different patterns within a "twostep" theory of society. The two types of differentiation, between logics in one case and forms of institutionalization in the other, also affect the meaning of the interaction of these three spheres. While the direction of influence and the degree of interpenetration between lifeworld and system involve issues of normative principle, the degree of the inter-penetration of state and economy (their "double interchange") and its directionality now become "merely" technical problems.

The concept of the lifeworld, socially integrated through interpretations of a normatively secured or communicatively created consensus, occupies a theoretical space similar to that of civil society in the three-part model. Indeed, Habermas often introduces the lifeworld as a translation of Parsons's notion of societal community, although in a wider synthesis that sometimes includes culture and at other times personality as well.[19] With this said, it is not at all self-evident, even on a superficial level, that the concept of the lifeworld can be translated without distortion into that of civil society. On the contrary, these concepts seem to operate on very different categorical levels, especially if one thinks of the phenomenological tradition of conceptualizing the lifeworld.[20]

It is our thesis nonetheless that the concept of the lifeworld, as Habermas advances it, has two distinct levels that, if adequately differentiated and clarified, will allow us to pinpoint the exact locus of civil society within the overall framework (figure 1).[21] On the one hand, the lifeworld refers to the reservoir of implicitly known

Subsystem:	Economy		State	
Lifeworld institution:	personality	social integration		culture
Symbolic resource:	competence	solidarity		meaning
Structural background:		linguistic-cultural lifeworld		

figure 1

traditions, the background assumptions that are embedded in language and culture and drawn upon by individuals in everyday life. The linguistically structured stock of knowledge, the reservoir of unshaken convictions, and the forms of solidarity and competence that are used and relied upon are given to actors without question. Thus, individuals can neither step out of their lifeworld nor bring it into question as a whole. It is on this level especially that Habermas integrated the deeper levels of the Parsonian concept of culture, giving it, however, the structure of interpenetrating linguistic meanings and resources rather than that of a boundary-maintaining system.

According to Habermas, the lifeworld has three structural components—culture, society, and personality—and these can be differentiated from one another.[22] To the extent that actors mutually understand and agree on their situation, they share a cultural tradition. Insofar as they coordinate their action through intersubjectively recognized norms, they act as members of a solidary social group. As individuals grow up within a cultural tradition and participate in group life, they internalize value orientations, acquire generalized action competences, and develop individual and social identities.[23] Reproduction of not only the cultural-linguistic background but also the second dimension of the lifeworld—its "institutional" or "sociological" components— occurs in the medium of communication.[24] This involves the reproductive processes of cultural transmission, social integration, and socialization. But, and this is the main point for us, the structural differentiation of the lifeworld, which is part of the modernization process, occurs through the emergence of *institutions* specialized in the reproduction of traditions, solidarities, and identities.

Habermas's discussion of the structural components of the lifeworld focuses on reconstructing the form of the stock of knowledge, the relied-upon solidarities, and the abstract competences of personalities that our culture makes available to us. But this reconstruction involves a range of institutions that can be equated neither with the cultural background knowledge on which they draw nor with the steering mechanisms that coordinate action in the economy (money) or in formally organized, bureaucratically structured organizations (power).[25] It is here, on the institutional level of the lifeworld, that one can root a hermeneutically accessible, because socially integrated, concept of civil society. This concept would include all of the institutions and associational forms that require communicative interaction for their reproduction and that rely primarily on processes of social integration for coordinating action within their boundaries.

Identifying civil society, a category of political theory and political sociology, with the terms of a general sociology would lead to an overly politicized understanding of the social structure. Neither Parsons's societal community nor Habermas's lifeworld is intended so narrowly. It helps, therefore, to restrict the effort of translating these concepts to political and economic sociology to the study of institutions and processes that are directly relevant politically and economically and are also rooted in the general social structure. Habermas himself helps us in this effort and, interestingly enough, in the process links his dualistic social theory to his earlier understanding of public and private. He posits that money and political power require, for their establishment and anchoring as media, an institutionalization in the very lifeworld from which they are differentiated. This is accomplished by the mechanisms of civil (or private) and public law, respectively.[26] These mechanisms constitute and are rooted in two distinct complexes of institutions: the private and the public. Thus, looked at from the point of view of the steering systems, the three-part model becomes articulated as a four-part model understood in terms of the redoubling not only of the public sphere (as in the *Strukturwandel*) but of the private sphere as well.[27]

Unlike the model of *Strukturwandel*, in the present context the public and private spheres are seen not as mediations but as spheres within the lifeworld with which economy and state can have input-output relations structured exclusively in terms of interchanges of money and power, which also structure state-economy relations. This systems-theoretic point of view, whose deficiencies will later occupy us, has some important advantages. The first and most obvious is that we can follow Luhmann in replacing the notion of fusion with that of increasingly complex input-output relations, simultaneously increasing autonomy and interdependence. This may seem to carry the liability of buying into a framework of differentiation in which civil society and its various replacements disappear or are absorbed by the political system—an argument that involves, as we have seen, a systems-theoretic restatement of the fusion thesis—but Luhmann's own efforts to work out the function of the public sphere and of the legal system also lead to a characteristic doubling, inside and outside the political subsystem. Habermas's scheme (figure 2), which retains systems-theoretic terms of exchange, is in fact identical to this outcome of Luhmann's partially failed attempt to eradicate the category of civil society. Unlike the point of view of the lifeworld, this scheme does without structures of integration between public and private spheres. Instead of destroying civil society by absorption, here the danger is destruction through fragmentation. We shall return to this point.

The second advantage of this framework over dualistic models of state and civil society is that it allows a clarification of the structural interrelations among civil society, economy, and state by severing the ideological, one-to-one correlation of civil society with the private sphere and of the state with the public sphere. The two sets of public and private dichotomies, one at the level of subsystems (state/economy) and one at the level of civil society (public sphere/family), allow a distinction between two meanings of privatization and "publicization." As a result, state intervention into the economy is not automatically equivalent to state penetration of the private sphere, any more than economic liberalization must logically mean the erosion of public and private spheres. Conversely, given the two meanings of "private," unlike the case of

	Public	Private
System	political subsystem or "state"	economic subsystem
Lifeworld	public sphere	private sphere

figure 2

the dichotomous model of state and society, the withdrawal of the state here need not be to the benefit of the expansion of the private economy, and the limitation of the private economy need not be seen merely as the other side of the growth of state intervention.[28]

Here, too, there is a corresponding disadvantage to this model, though not to the benefit of its simpler dichotomous competitor. From the standpoint of exchange relations between the two subsystems and civil society, the framework is too symmetrical. It is in this context that the systems-theoretic schematizing of the lifeworld from the point of view of spheres that can enter into monetary and power input-output relations again shows its limits. Of the three institutional dimensions of the lifeworld, the notions of public and private as used here activate only those of the reproduction of culture and personality. The institutions of social integration, institutionalized groups, collectives, and associations are omitted from this treatment, despite their obvious political and economic relevance. In their absence, the possibility that lifeworld institutions can influence "the formally organized domains of action"[29] is not really thematized; the idea that communication between lifeworld and system could use channels other than the media of money and power is not even raised. We shall also return to these issues, which again reproduce in Habermas's scheme some of the limitations of Luhmann's model.

The theory we adopt responds to the fusion argument on two levels: by reconceptualizing differentiation in a manner similar to Luhmann's, and by differentiating the spheres (economy, private sphere, etc.) traditionally grouped as the presumed targets of dedifferentiation. From the empirical point of view, both of these theoretical choices can be important; moreover, in any given context, it is possible that neither version nor even their combination can eliminate the possibility of "dedifferentiation." Unlike

Parsons, we do not wish to replace what was always intended as an "empirical diagnosis" (i.e., fusion) with a "prior analytical distinction" (i.e., differentiation).[30] Even Luhmann considers dedifferentiation with the political system as its center as a genuine possibility in modern societies. Polànyi's treatment of the self-regulating market had analogous consequences with respect to the dynamism of the economic system. The model we have adopted is empirically open to both of these forms of fusion or dedifferentiation.[31]

In the twentieth century, the mirror of "totalitarian" politicization shows the absurdity of applying the fusion argument literally to democratic welfare states.[32] As the experience of Soviet-type societies indicates, it is possible to completely politicize "from above" for relatively long periods all four spheres we have isolated: the economy, the realms of culture, personality, and associational life. Yet our two-level conception of the lifeworld allows us to say even here that the linguistic-cultural substratum of civil society was not destroyed, thus preserving the constituent conditions (meanings, solidarities, competences) for later efforts at reconstitution.

The situation is more complex for interventionism and corporatism under capitalist democracies. Even if we considered these to be quasi-totalitarian, in the tradition of the older Frankfurt school, and even if we thought that the tendencies toward politicization from above and corporatism from below fully complemented each other, we would still have to admit the possibility available under totalitarianism—namely, the reconstitution of civil society outside of official institutions on the basis of the cultural potentials of the lifeworld.[33] On closer examination, the problem turns out to be more an artifact of an unacceptable overextension of a model of totalitarianism than derivative from a two-part model. This is clear from the work of Claus Offe, who has noted two separable problems: maintaining (liberal) democratic bridges or mediations between citizen and state,[34] and the compatibility of democracy and capitalism.[35] In this context, corporatism, implying fusion and the shrinking of mediation, and welfare-state interventionism, implying only the growth of complex input-output relations with the economy, do not attack and endanger the same societal structures. Their functional complementarity for the reproduction of "democratic capitalism" need not be seen as part of the single process of fusion. Corporatism never eliminates or replaces a comprehensive network of voluntary associations; state interventionism leaves in place large competitive and market-oriented sectors of capitalist economies. The threat to social integration represented by both processes—the first directly, the second indirectly through the extension of the money medium—is real. But so are the institutionalized and cultural resources of a civil society potentially countering them: legal rights, associations, and autonomous institutions of culture on one level; shared meanings, solidarities and personal competences on the other.

Beyond Traditional Civil Society

A theory of differentiation cannot in itself reconstruct the concept of civil society. We have seen how a theory such as that developed by Luhmann tends to lead either to the absorption or the fragmentation of the *topos*. And while Luhmann cannot avoid redifferentiating legality and publicity, he resists their relocation into a single network of institutional life, which, in his opinion, was possible only in the form of a traditional, corporate organization of civil-political society. On the other side, while recognizing the internal connection of personality and communication under the conditions of modernity, he refuses to consider the possibility that this internal connection has a substratum, namely, the lifeworld. Although a lifeworld linked to actual processes of coming to an understanding appears in his conception, it does so only under premodern conditions, before the emergence of generalized media, when tradition yielded the foundations of a consensus that could be immune to discursive thematization and could eliminate the need for much time-consuming discussion.[36] While reconstructing the concept of civil society in terms of the lifeworld might be logically possible in Luhmann's framework, the synthesis as a whole would be consigned to traditional society. He would thus contest not the possibility but the modernity of the model of civil society that we propose.

We believe that our reconstruction responds to the problem of modernity far better than any previous theory of civil society. The differentiation between the two dimensions of the lifeworld not only indicates the locus of civil society within a general systematic conception but also allows us to develop, on all relevant levels, the important distinction between a *traditional* and a *modern* civil society. To put it another way, the analytic distinctions between system and lifeworld and between the two levels of the lifeworld itself point a way beyond the choice, insisted on by Luhmann, between a traditional, corporately organized, civil society dependent on an *ethos* or *Sittlichkeit* and a modern framework of differentiation that has no place for civil society even in the guise of societal community or communicatively reproduced lifeworld.

To begin with, the two-level conception of the lifeworld allows us to conceive the unity of a civil society not on the level of institution, organization, or even a shared, fundamentally unquestioned normative order. The cultural-linguistic background, the source of the underlying unity of the whole lifeworld complex, is neither an institution nor an organization but a network of resources for institutions and organizations. Moreover, it can have a shared, unquestioned normative content only in traditional society, and even then this is not necessary. Traditional society is in fact defined here not in terms of a common tradition but by its traditional relation to traditions and ultimately to the lifeworld itself. The idea of the modernization of the lifeworld, on the other hand, implies two interlocking processes: a differentiation, on the sociological level, of the structural and institutional components of the lifeworld, and their resulting internal rationalization; and the rationalization of the cultural-linguistic substratum of the lifeworld.

It is difficult to separate these two processes and impossible to prioritize them. To some extent, each presupposes and fosters the other. The differentiation on the sociological level precludes the already somewhat illusive possibility of treating society as a single organized network of institutions (of kinship or of civil-political society). What is involved is the differentiation not only of institutions of socialization (family, education), social integration (groups, collectives, and associations), and cultural reproduction (religious, artistic, scientific) but also of the constituents of the spheres of personality, "society," and culture. In the process, social institutions gradually become uncoupled from worldviews and concrete persons, the scope of contingency for forming personal identities and interpersonal relations is freed from traditional values and institutions, and the renewal and creation of culture is freed from the dominance of social institutions with other than cultural purposes; the result is the emergence of a critical and reflective relation to tradition.[37]

The process of differentiation continues within each institutional complex. In this context, so-called cultural rationalization represents the bridge to the modernization of the deeper, linguistic-cultural substratum of the lifeworld. The rationalization of culture involves the differentiation of the cultural spheres into sets of institutions grouped around the cognitive-instrumental, aesthetic-expressive, and moral-practical values or forms of validity first called to attention by Nietzsche, Weber, and the neo-Kantians. For Habermas, it is this modernization of the cultural spheres of the lifeworld that makes possible (but not necessary) the development of posttraditional, communicatively coordinated, and reflexive forms of association, publicity, solidarity, and identity. Only on such a new cultural basis is the replacement of a traditional by a posttraditional civil society conceivable. This cultural modernization, as its results feed back from specialized institutions into everyday communication, powerfully fosters the transformation of the cultural-linguistic assumptions of the lifeworld and their mode of operation in relation to action.[38]

A modernized, rationalized lifeworld involves a communicative opening-up of the sacred core of traditions, norms, and authority to processes of questioning and the replacement of a conventionally based normative consensus by one that is "communicatively" grounded. The concept of communicative action is thus central to that of the rationalization of the lifeworld and to our concept of a posttraditional civil society. Communicative action involves a linguistically mediated, intersubjective process through which actors establish their interpersonal relations, question and reinterpret norms, and coordinate their interaction by negotiating definitions of the situation and coming to an agreement. By analytically distinguishing this model of rational action from the rationalities of four other types of action, Habermas provides the theoretical tools to show that the dissolution of traditional forms of solidarity and authority need not, by definition, result in the emergence of a one-dimensional society composed solely of strategically or instrumentally acting individuals lacking the resources for autonomous solidarity. The action theory, in short, implies that a *gemeinschaftliche* coordination of social action (normative action based on unquestioned standards) can have modern replacements.[39] In other words, on the basis of Habermas's concept of communicative action, the analysis of the rationalization of the lifeworld, as distinct from that of economy or state, allows us to turn the Parsonian concept of "societal community" (or civil society) away from its strategic pole of interpretation, while its traditionalist pole is put into the context of the possible modernization of tradition itself, meaning not its abolition but a new and reflexive relation, *a nontraditional relation to tradition.*

As we have already noted, the rationalization of the lifeworld is also a presupposition and stimulus for the further modernization of its structural components and institutional spheres. In particular, it allows the emergence of a new form of voluntary association with equal rights of membership, freed from kinship, patriarchal, or other ascriptive restrictions on belonging and holding office, and renewing its forms of solidarity primarily in the free interaction of its present members. Equally important are the emergence and stabilization of postconventional types of personality and critical forms of culture (postauratic art, postconventional morality, science), both of which presuppose a changed relation of action to its lifeworld backdrop and an ability to thematize and criticize any of its components, including normative structures. While the stages of normative orientation were first discovered in the context of the development of personality, the presuppositions for acquiring competences remain rooted in the structures of the lifeworld into which individuals must grow.[40] The modernization of the lifeworld is thus the foundation for the parallelism between individual, social, and cultural forms of moral consciousness.

Most important for a theory of civil society is the penetration of the modern structure of the lifeworld into legal institutions and legal practice, via the forms of a differentiated moral-legal cultural value sphere gradually freed from all remnants of a sacred order. The result is the institutionalization of positive law. Luhmann interpreted this process to mean that the foundations of positive law are primarily cognitive rather than normative. He also defined the normative attitude of expectation as one that is resistant to learning, thereby weakening one of the key institutional components of a civil society differentiated from the success-oriented spheres of politics and economics. We should also recall that Luhmann understands legal development as a two-step process involving the differentiation of normative and cognitive attitudes of expectation and their relinking, without dedifferentiation, in new reflexive combinations, expectations of expectations. Throughout these developmental steps, the counterfactual structure of expectations is supposedly embodied in the unchanging norms, hardened against learning.

As distinct from Luhmann's train of argumentation, the idea of the modernization of the lifeworld involves the foundation of normative learning in two senses, one documented by cognitive developmental psychology[41] and the other by the possibility of transposing its results into a theory of social evolution.[42] Accordingly, the well-known preconventional, conventional, and postconventional stages of moral and legal consciousness represent the actual development of normative structures not only in the sense of the differentiation of norm from fact (including sanction), which actually explains only the emergence of the conventional stage, but also in the development of forms of argumentation to which we resort when we seek to reestablish, in the case of disappointed expectations (Luhmann), the foundations of endangered intersubjectivity (Habermas).

At the *preconventional stage*, at which actions, motives, and acting subjects are still perceived on the same plane of reality, only the consequences of action are evaluated in cases of conflict. At the *conventional stage*, motives can be assessed independently of concrete action consequences; conformity with a certain social role or with an existing system of norms is the standard. At the *postconventional stage*, these systems of norms lose their quasi-natural validity; they require justification from universal points of view.[43]

The stage of postconventional structures of moral argumentation implies learning both with respect to earlier evolutionary stages and within this stage itself. Indeed, postconventional structures can be said to institutionalize ongoing normative learning, without surrendering a normative style of expectation.

The duplication of the legal sphere, in the context of postconventional structures of moral consciousness and argumentation, in terms of the two levels of norms and principles (Kohlberg) or of rules and principles (Dworkin) is crucial.[44] While in "easy cases" it may be possible to apply norms dogmatically and even to convert normative conflicts into cognitive questions, "hard cases" represent either difficulties of interpretation or deep normative conflicts that cannot be resolved without turning to a higher normative level of valid principles.[45] It would be futile to treat rules and principles as fundamentally functions of the same types of enactment and application (Luhmann) or as mere examples of the distinction between primary and secondary rules (H. L. A. Hart).[46] The reason is that turning to principles, in defense of rights or democratic participation, involves an entirely different and structurally more demanding form of argumentation, a normative discourse that cannot be kept within the institutional or time frame of legal enactment and application. In such cases, it is simply false to say, as Luhmann does, that the judge, especially of the highest courts (as against parliamentary majorities), may not learn from the lawbreaker; the case of civil disobedience is a counterexample.[47] Of course, such learning can occur and yet avoid a cognitive-pragmatic turn only if the counterfactual constituents of a discursive procedure continue to apply, that is, if the conditions of empirical discourse are continually corrected in terms of these principles.[48]

Thus, it would be a mistake to consider the positivization of law to lead to a weakening of normative structures or even to maintain, as Habermas seems to at times, that enactment is forced to rely on normative justifications of a new type *only* on the level of the legitimation of the legal system as a whole.[49] Nevertheless, this aspect of the legitimation of the legal system as a whole in terms of normative structures capable of withstanding the test of postconventional argumentation—above all, fundamental rights and democratic procedures—is an important dimension of the institutionalization of positive law. Modern positive law is in an especially favorable position to produce the detailed regulation of

modern economic and administrative systems. The norms of civil
law thereby become direct constituents and regulators of economic processes, which in turn produce, indirectly, much of their
own legal regulation. The same could probably be said of the
development of public law as administrative law and regulation. As
Habermas puts it (in relation to civil law and the bourgeois
economy), law thereby loses its earlier status as a metainstitution,
available for the resolution of conflict and insuring against the
possibilities of the breakdown of integration.[50] The duplication of
rule and principle, or of law and constitutional law, is made
possible by, and in turn stabilizes, the emerging subsystems of
modern state and capitalist economy.

Accordingly, the two overall processes constitutive of the modernization of society as a whole—the emergence of the economic
and administrative subsystems, and the rationalization of the linguistic-cultural and societal levels of the lifeworld—presuppose
each other. The lifeworld could not be modernized without the
strategic unburdening of communicative action coordination by
the development of the two subsystems. They, in turn, require
institutional anchoring in a lifeworld that remains symbolically
structured, linguistically coordinated, and yet, to a certain extent at
least, modernized. This need is not restricted to the existence of
metainstitutions of conflict regulation. The subject of private law is
needed by an economy coordinated through monetary exchange
(based on contractual relations) just as a subject capable of political
obligation (and later the rights of citizens) is needed by a state
administration organized through bureaucratically structured
power relations. These "subjects" can emerge only if the requisite
cognitive and moral competences and institutional structures are
available in the lifeworld. Such a precondition involves changes
within the institutions of civil society that are responsible for
cultural reproduction, social integration, and personality development, in the relation of these institutions to one another, and in the
relation of lifeworld institutions to their modernized linguistic-
cultural substratum.

It is important to keep the complementarity of the two dimensions of modernization in mind, if one is committed to either.
Communication can play a posttraditional and potentially demo-

cratic role in social integration because, as Luhmann has maintained, other forms of social coordination—the media of money and power, in particular—relieve communication of many of its time constraints. At the same time, since there is no natural limit to the "mediatization" of the lifeworld, the expansion of subsystems coordinated by money and power represents a possible replacement to communicative action coordination in any given area.[51] The same processes that are among the constitutive conditions of a modern lifeworld also represent the greatest potential threats to that lifeworld.

This circumstance forces us to redefine our concept of civil society as the institutional framework of a modern lifeworld *stabilized by fundamental rights*, which will include within their scope the spheres of the public and the private, this time from a lifeworld point of view. The institution of fundamental rights represents an essential component of the modernization of the lifeworld because their postconventional structure is linked to legal principles rather than normative rules and also because rights contribute to modernization in the sense of differentiation.

A civil society in formation, being molded by movements and other civic initiatives (as in Eastern Europe recently), may for a time have to do without a settled structure of rights. We would argue, though, that the index of their success in institutionalizing civil society is the establishment of rights, not just on paper but as working propositions. The reason for this rests on the underside of modernity: the power and expansion of the media-coordinated spheres or subsystems that make the structures of this modern lifeworld singularly precarious. In the face of the possible penetration and distortion of the internal processes and the reproduction of cultural, social, and socializing institutions, these can be stabilized only on the basis of the historically new form of juridification represented by rights. Indeed, one can actually map out the terrain and even determine the type of a modern civil society in terms of the universal and subjective fundamental rights of the modern period. Of course, this terrain can be defended only in the context of an appropriately modern form of political culture that values societal self-organization and publicity. The practice of rights and the corresponding forms of social learning help, in turn, to establish just such a political culture.

Focusing on the institutional spheres of civil society, we can isolate three complexes of rights: those concerning cultural reproduction (freedoms of thought, press, speech, and communication); those ensuring social integration (freedom of association and assembly); and those securing socialization (protection of privacy, intimacy, and the inviolability of the person). Two other complexes of rights mediate between civil society and either the market economy (rights of property, contract, and labor) or the modern bureaucratic state (political rights of citizens and welfare rights of clients). The internal relationships of these complexes of rights determine the type of civil society that is institutionalized. We shall return to this issue when we consider the negative dimensions and the utopia of modern civil society.

The discourse of rights has been accused of being purely ideological and, even worse, the carrier of statist penetration and control of populations. The classical Marxian objection is that formal rights are merely the ideological reflex of capitalist property and exchange relations. Clearly, however, only some rights have an individualist structure, and not all of them can be reduced to property rights.[52] The typical anarchist position (exemplified by Foucault) is that rights are simply the product of the will of the sovereign state, articulated through the medium of positive law and facilitating the surveillance of all aspects of society.[53] No one can bind the state to respect its own legality; it does so only when its own interests lead it to do so. This can be seen, for example, in the focusing of protest within narrow and manageable channels, as in the case of the right to strike, which is coupled with an obligation to avoid illegal forms of labor conflict.

While the state is the agency of the legalization of rights, it is neither their source nor the basis of their validity. Rights begin as claims asserted by groups and individuals in the public spaces of an emerging civil society. They can be guaranteed by positive law but are not equivalent to law or derivable from it; in the domain of rights, law secures and stabilizes what has been achieved autonomously by social actors. Nevertheless, rights should not be understood as products of a zero-sum conflict. The tendencies to dedifferentiation of the modern economy (Polànyi) and the modern state (Luhmann) represent threats to the modernity and the institutionalization of these spheres. If from the actors' point of view rights tend to be created and defended from below, from the point of view of social systems they represent, as Luhmann has shown, the principle of differentiation. This, of course, is a project of increasing power, but it occurs through limiting power rather than extending and inflating it (through networks of surveillance, for example). This convergence of the two methodological points of view points to one of our key theses: Fundamental rights must be seen as the *organizing principle* of a modern civil society.[54]

The Negative Dimensions of Civil Society

The forms of cultural modernity have played an important role in the emergence of civil societies. Nevertheless, we shall argue that the full potential of these forms has never been realized anywhere. On the contrary, modernization in the West has proceeded according to patterns that have distorted the institutions of civil society and the potentials of a modernized lifeworld. Habermas offers a historical typology that shows how the processes of differentiation between system and lifeworld have yielded a modernity burdened by its negative dimensions.[55] In our view, this typology becomes especially useful if critically revised and reconstructed.

In Habermas's discussion, the main stages of juridification (*Verrechtlichung*) turn out to be a veritable set of state–civil society–economy relations.[56] The analysis partially parallels arguments to be found in works such as Polànyi's *The Great Transformation* and Nisbet's *In Search of Community*, but it avoids the naive expectations of the former vis-à-vis the state and the innocence of the latter vis-à-vis the capitalist market economy. Indeed, the historical typology reveals the virtues of a three-part model against a more simplistic, polemical conception of society against the state. It does this by avoiding the identification of economy and society, economic and state power, or social and state interests. All of these identifications turn out to reflect transitional historical constellations. The autonomy of civil society in particular depends on its ability to protect itself against both subsystems.

Habermas marks out four stages in the development of the relation between the lifeworld and the modern state and economy:

the bourgeois state; the bourgeois-constitutional state (*bürgerliche Rechtsstaat*); the democratic constitutional state; and the social (welfare) and democratic constitutional state.[57] The first is a misleading term for the absolutist state, which is apparently misunderstood in this analysis, representing a rather ahistorical projection of the Hobbesian model of politics to this era.[58] Concerned with "waves of juridification," Habermas defines the absolutist state in terms of its establishment of legal orders guaranteeing private property, security, and equality before the law, all in the form of objective law rather than actionable subjective rights. The aim is the institutionalization of the new media, without any concern for the lifeworld, considered only as a source of a still traditional resistance. At best, however, this projection represents a stylized starting point for the analysis, focusing on developmental trends in which the modern sovereign state and the capitalist economy symbiotically support each other's freedom of motion while depriving the (traditional) lifeworld of all protection. Even in England, such was not the case in the era of (parliamentary) absolutism, which was characterized by many structures of paternalistic protection and "moral economy." The model is even less applicable to continental absolutism proper, a new historical creation combining the elements of a partially modern and bureaucratic state with a society of orders (the depoliticized orders of the *Ständestaat*). Until the projects of enlightened despotism and especially late eighteenth- and early nineteenth-century legal codifications, this double system was rooted also in the structure of law. While indeed rightless, as in Habermas's conception, absolutist legal systems protected a traditional lifeworld by hierarchically ordered privilege.[59]

The problem with this erroneous model of the absolutist state is that it prepares the evaluation of the next stages in a misleading way. While Habermas expresses various degrees of doubt about the freedom-guaranteeing character of most of his stages, he omits doing so in the case of the constitutional state. Nor does he present its liberal and bureaucratic-authoritarian variants. Habermas is entirely right in stressing the first institutionalization of subjective civil (vs. political) rights or freedoms (*Freiheitsrechte*) as actionable claims. However, he is not in a good position to evaluate the lifeworld-threatening character of this stage. Having located under absolutism the establishment of the subsystems of the modern state and economy, with all the devastating consequences for cultural and social relations, he sees the work of the *Rechtsstaat* only in terms of limiting the threat of one of these subsystems: the state. What was actually involved was a trade-off from the point of view of the lifeworld: The limitation of the state was bought at the cost of establishing an economic society for the first time in history. Only reformist and revolutionary ("from above") opposition to both the absolutist state and the society of orders can explain this outcome. But the establishment of the *Rechtsstaat* along with the capitalist economy should certainly be described as highly ambiguous from the point of view of "securing freedom." The ambiguity is evident in the particular model of subjective rights that is established, involving everywhere the centrality and the model character of property rights.

The same point is more or less valid for the other path of development beyond absolutism: the revolutionary path of democratic movements leading to the establishment (rapid or eventual) of the democratic constitutional state. Here a wider set of rights, civil and political, protect the (modernizing) lifeworld against the state, limiting it but also attempting to bring it under a measure of social control. If the *Rechtsstaat* protected only the private and intimate spheres against the modern state, the democratic constitutional state added the institutionalized protection of the public sphere as well. However, here it should also be said, as against Habermas, that the strengthening of the economy at the expense of the societal lifeworld occurs precisely in this phase (and not in the previous absolutist one), as Polànyi has convincingly shown. Thus, protecting the lifeworld or civil society from the state is again accomplished at the cost of strengthening the other, equally threatening, subsystem, an outcome again documented by the primacy of property rights in the catalogue of rights, even if it is less central than under the conditions of the predemocratic *Rechtsstaat*.

In the case of the democratic constitutional state, Habermas does note an ambiguity in the structure of juridification from the point of view of the lifeworld. He seeks to explain this by the partially false contrast of civil rights (*Freiheitsrechte*) and political rights under-

stood as membership rights (*Teilhaberrechte*). The latter are organized in such a way as to restrict "the possibilities of spontaneous
opinion formation and discursive will-formation."[60] The rights
themselves (suffrage, assembly, association, press, etc.) are not to
blame, but rather the elite democratic, bureaucratized political
party and the culturally manipulative forms of their organization.
Unlike Luhmann's narrower conceptualization of political rights,
which lead to an autonomous political system, here the rights of
membership intrinsically point to forms of control over political
bureaucracy, to rights of participation (*Teilnehmerrechte*). As a
result, it remains unclear why Luhmann's description turns out to
be right after all, in that political rights are, despite their own
teleology, organized bureaucratically rather than autonomously. It
is misleading, if not entirely incorrect, to explain this anomaly by
pointing to the establishment of rights in bourgeois formal law.
Formal laws are in fact better for negatively demarcating private
autonomy than for positively *guaranteeing* inclusion in the sense of
participation in the public sphere.[61] But this is only part of the story.
In addition, we must stress that, precisely under this stage of
juridification, a civil society organized as an economic society is
comparatively weak in its ability to utilize the positive channels
opened up by formal, political rights.[62]

Civil society and a modern lifeworld were strengthened by the
countermovement to the self-regulated market spearheaded by the
movements of the industrial working class that established democratic welfare states. But the gain is again ambiguous. This situation
is, in a sense, the reverse of the previous two stages: The subsystem
brought under new forms of limitation is that of the economy, and
the trade-off strengthens the interventionist administrative state.[63]
Again, Habermas tries to indicate the difference in terms of social
rights conceived on the model of freedoms and on the model of
membership rights (*Teilhaberrechte*). Labor legislation unambiguously protects the lifeworld against uncontrolled economic forces,
but comprehensive sets of welfare-state entitlements, while they
may intend to promote autonomy and rebuild social integration,
have the opposite effect because of the bureaucratic, statist manner
of their implementation. And yet, as T. H. Marshall recognized
(although with an opposing conclusion), these rather than the

rights of labor represent the classical social "rights" of the welfare state. From another point of view, one has good reason to doubt whether benefits whose exercise does not depend primarily on the free activity of their beneficiaries are rights at all.[64] The structure of benefits, unlike that of political rights of participation, has an elective affinity with bureaucratic implementation. Contrary to Marshall, social rights of the entitlement type achieve the benefits of membership for individuals as clients rather than as citizens. Thus, unlike the rights of work, in their present form they strengthen the administrative state and not civil society.[65]

Social "rights" in the sense of entitlements are possible and do actually exist in societies without a structure of rights at all. In this context, we should add authoritarian state socialism to our typology. This is a peculiar formation that combines features of a revolutionary successor to absolutism and the statist response to the capitalist market economy, yet cannot be identified with either form. From the point of view of juridification, this society, in line with its state-socialist ideology, seeks protection from only one of the two subsystems, the economic one. In this respect, state socialism is unlike the democratic welfare state, whose legal structure preserves liberal and democratic limitations on the state as well. The lifeworld under authoritarian socialism is supposedly protected not by a structure of rights but by a comprehensive system of state paternalism. Thus, the party-state drapes itself in the familial, associational, and even movement character of the lifeworld, which in fact is totally unprotected from an interventionism that contains no self-limitation. The juridical character of this formation is that of the primacy of the prerogative state, in a dual legal structure in which the ever-changing boundaries of discretionary and normative practice are determined by discretion itself.[66] Authoritarian state socialism, a formation without rights or constitutionalism, is a response to the economic threats to the lifeworld, but it takes the form of suppressing civil society along with bourgeois society (with which civil society is identified). As such, it represents a great danger to the modernity of the lifeworld, to the functioning of the politicized economy, and to the rationality of the political system itself.

Habermas may have omitted state socialism from his typology because of the difficulties of fitting it into any theory of modernization and because of his unwillingness to declare—as Parsons did—that the Soviet model constitutes a dead end of modernization. Yet the whole discussion concerning the waves of juridification falls into a tradition of open-ended modernization theory. The differences with Parsons's late treatment of the differentiation and modernization of the "societal community" are instructive. First, Habermas treats the contemporary period as highly ambiguous from the point of view of the autonomy of the lifeworld (i.e., the societal community/civil society), as evidenced by his critique of the welfare state from *Legitimation Crisis* onward. Second, while Parsons considered social movements to be the ineffectual fundamentalisms of each epoch corresponding to new stages in the development of the societal community, Habermas treats both "bourgeois" emancipation movements and working-class movements as the key dynamic promoting relevant institutional transformation while defending the lifeworld. These movements thus play a major role in realizing the potentials of cultural modernity. The ambiguity of the last stage of development (and in our view of the last four stages, including the unambiguously negative experience of state socialism) is, however, an unintended consequence of the actions of the defenders of society (irrespective of Habermas's linkage only of the freedom-guaranteeing part of the outcomes with the action of movements). We might say that the absence of reflection in each case about *both* of the lifeworld-threatening subsystems leads to a strengthening of one or the other in the name of the defense of the lifeworld.

The stage model just described indicates that the reconstruction of the theory of civil society in terms of the system/lifeworld duality aims to accommodate the negative side of civil society accentuated by Foucault and others. However, in the stage model, negative dimensions appear primarily as threats posed to civil society from the outside. Habermas's complex discussion of Weber's theses of the "loss of meaning" and the "loss of freedom" involved in modernization (in his terms, the cultural impoverishment and the colonization of the lifeworld) indicate that these dimensions are to be found *within* modern civil society itself.

The conceptual contrast between the potentially nonselective and the actual selective patterns of modernization allows Habermas to combine the diametrically opposed assessments of contemporary civil society, here stylized as the positions of Parsons and Foucault, as alternatives *within* modernity. Moreover, our concept of civil society, reconstructed on the basis of Habermas's concept of the lifeworld, has the advantage of pinpointing the negative side of modernity without equating all of the institutions of civil society with its one-sided development. In short, the existing model of civil society that has selectively institutionalized the potentials of cultural modernity is only one of its logically possible paths.[67] It is not completely negative, but the negative side must be accounted for. In more concrete terms, Habermas maintains that the rationalization of the lifeworld with respect to the realization of cultural potentials embodied in the aesthetic and moral/practical domains has been blocked to a significant extent. The rationalization of the economic and administrative subsystems and the preponderant weight given to their reproductive imperatives has proceeded at the expense of the rationalization of civil society. The resulting gap between expert cultures involved in the differentiation of the value spheres of scientific knowledge, art, and morality and that of the general public leads to the cultural impoverishment of a lifeworld whose traditional substance has been eroded. However, contrary to the Weberian thesis,[68] it is not cultural modernity itself but its selective institutionalization that results in cultural impoverishment.

Furthermore, the one-sided institutionalization of the cognitive-instrumental potentials of cultural rationalization (in the institution of science and in the two subsystems) prepares the ground for a penetration by the media of money and power into the spheres of the reproduction of civil society, which require integration through communicative processes. Acting subjects become subordinated to the imperatives of apparatuses that have become autonomous and substitutes for communicative interaction. But the distinction between system and lifeworld, between state, economy, and civil society, allows us to show that *it is not the emergence of the differentiated political and economic subsystems and their internal coordination through system integration that produces the "loss of freedom," but rather the penetration of an already modernized lifeworld by their logic, prompted by the selective pattern of institutionalization.* Habermas calls this penetration the reification or colonization of the lifeworld, thereby both retaining and revising Lukács's key category.

The discussion of the negative side of a selectively rationalized, partly colonized, and hence insufficiently modern civil society implies that the existing version of civil society is only one logically possible path of institutionalizing the potentials of cultural modernity. At issue is the fact of differentiation and also the relation between terms of the system/lifeworld model. Societal modernization always involves the replacement of some aspect of social by system integration.[69] But one should distinguish between the effects of the differentiation of the subsystems out of a traditionally structured lifeworld and those resulting from the penetration of steering mechanisms into a lifeworld that has begun to modernize. In the first case, the cost is the destruction of traditional forms of life and the development of political and economic institutions pervaded by domination. But the gain, in addition to relative economic and administrative efficiency, is the opening of the lifeworld to modernization and the creation of potentials of a postconventional culture of civil society. In the second case (colonization), the cost is the undermining of the communicative practice of an already (partly) modernized lifeworld and the blocking of the further modernization of civil society. It is a real question whether one can continue to count gains (such as state-guaranteed security) as unambiguous in such a context. As the institutions specialized in socialization, social integration, and cultural transmission are increasingly functionalized to serve the imperatives of uncontrolled and ever-expanding subsystems and as communicative coordination of action in the relevant areas is replaced by the media of money and power, there will be more and more pathological consequences.[70]

This can be clarified with respect to the relation between the public and private spheres of civil society and the economy and state in welfare state systems. When the subsystems penetrate the private sphere of the family and subordinate it to their imperatives, then the role of consumer (with respect to economic requirements) comes to predominate over the roles of worker and autonomous solidary family member. The one-sidedness of life-styles focused on consumerism was a major theme of cultural criticism in the 1960s. If system imperatives penetrate the public sphere (with respect to administrative requirements of loyalty), then the citizen role becomes fragmented and neutralized, with the result that the burden of depoliticization must be borne by an overinflated client role rooted in the private sphere.

Habermas interprets these transformations in the public and private spheres of civil society and the reifying and pathological side effects that accompany them in terms of the colonization thesis. He is thus able to account for the negative dimensions of modern civil society without confusing the negative side for the whole. He concretizes his analysis of this side of contemporary developments in his discussion of welfare-state social policy that involves the administrative penetration (through juridification) of areas of civil society previously free of such forms of interference.[71] As noted above, the monetarization and bureaucratization of the social relations of civil society are highly ambivalent processes that create a set of social benefits and securities at the cost of creating a new range of dependencies and destroying both existing solidarities and the actors' capacities for self-help and for communicatively resolving problems. For example, the administrative handling of care for the aged, of interfamilial relations, and of conflicts around schooling involves processes of *bureaucratization* and *individualization* that define the client as a strategic actor with specific private interests that can be dealt with on a one-to-one basis. But this involves a violent and painful abstraction of individuals from an existing social situation and damage to their self-esteem and to the interpersonal relations that make up the relevant institution. *Monetarization* of these areas of life also has negative consequences. Retirement payments cannot compensate for the loss of a sense of purpose and self-esteem of an elderly individual who has been forced out of a job because of age. Finally, the "therapeutization" of everyday life fostered by social service agencies contradicts the very goal of therapy—to achieve the autonomy and empowerment of the patient. When administratively based professionals claim expertise and have the legal power to back up their claims, a cycle of dependency is created between a patient who has become a client and the therapeutic apparatus.

The dilemma in each case consists of the fact that welfare-state intervention in the name of serving the needs of civil society fosters its disintegration and blocks further rationalization. Foucault's description of the techniques of surveillance, individualism, discipline, and control is thus explicitly accommodated in Habermas's analysis.

Nevertheless, despite appearances, Habermas does not join in the Foucaultian (or, for that matter, the neoconservative) critique of the welfare state. For him, legality, normativity, publicity, and legitimacy are not just carriers of or veils for disciplinary mechanisms. Even in this age of the supposed end of utopia, Habermas challenges us not to lose sight of the utopian promise of the liberal and democratic norms of civil society, which for him do not reduce to a mere "legitimation" of the contrary state of affairs.

The Utopia of Civil Society

In an age when totalizing revolutionary utopias have been discredited, the dualistic model of civil society we have reconstructed avoids "soulless" reformism by allowing us to thematize a self-reflective and self-limiting utopia of civil society. We can thereby link the project of radical democracy, reinterpreted in terms of our notion of "the plurality of democracies,"[72] to some key institutional premises of modernity.

The slogan "society against the state" has often been understood as a fundamentalist call for generalizing participatory democratic decision making, as a coordinating principle, to all spheres of social life, including the state and the economy. Indeed, the ideal of free voluntary association, democratically structured and communicatively coordinated, has always informed the utopia of civil (political) society, from Aristotle to the young Marx in 1843. But such a "democratic" utopia, if totally generalized, threatens the differentiation of society that forms the basis of modernity. Moreover, from a normative point of view, any project of dedifferentiation is contradictory, because it would involve such an overburdening of the democratic process that it would discredit democracy by associating it with political disintegration or by opening it to subversion through covert, unregulated strategic action.

As opposed to this, the self-limiting utopia of radical democracy based on the dualistic model of civil society would open up "the utopian horizon of a civil society." To quote Habermas: "The rationalization of the lifeworld allows, on the one hand, the differentiation of independent subsystems and opens up, on the other hand, the utopian horizon of a civil society in which the formally organized spheres of action of the bourgeois (economy and state apparatus) constitute the foundations for the posttraditional lifeworld of *l'homme* (private sphere) and *citoyen* (public sphere)."[73]

This utopia is one of differentiation rather than unification. Of course, the idea of differentiation is in itself not utopian. It involves a normatively desirable model of an alternative society, one that is "regulative" for critical thought (and thus a "utopia") only through its link with another idea: the creation of institutions capable of fully realizing the potentials of the communicative reproduction of a modern lifeworld.[74] In particular, the development of postconventional structures of culture would allow the projection of interconnected institutions of intimacy and publicity, which would replace unexamined traditional relations of domination with unconstrained forms of solidarity produced and reproduced through free, voluntary interaction. This second, genuinely utopian idea is linked to a theory of differentiation involving processes of self-reflection and self-limitation.

Given the experience of the liberal utopia of the self-regulating market, on the one hand, and of socialism, with its synthetic utopia of a rationally organized (planned) society of free producers (or creative, working individuals), on the other, it is clear that utopian thought can be saved only if critical self-reflection can be built into it. One element the two failed utopias have in common is their attempt to totalize a single model of a "rational" society, rooted in one or both of the subsystems, each linked to a single value: negative freedom in one case, substantive equality in the other. Today we know that the very plausibility of these utopias, and what linked them with the logic of history itself, lay in the dynamism of an economy-centered instrumental reason in one case and of state-centered functional reason in the other.[75] We should now be aware of the negative consequences of either type of subsumption. While each of these utopias made greater or lesser concessions to democratic models of social organization, the stress on a fully autonomous market rationality or on a form of power capable of coordinating a nonmarket but nevertheless modern economy was incompatible with the reproduction of the lifeworld substratum of democratic coordination of action. That this was not a fundamental internal dilemma for either model is shown by the existence of authoritarian versions of the utopias of both market and planning.[76] From the point of view of democratic politics, both utopias had to and did become suspect even before the disastrous consequences were manifested in practice.

Since its emergence around 1919, the tradition of Western Marxism has always been aware of the dangers of the productivist utopias of classical socialism: The alternatives of Lukács, Bloch, and Marcuse had little to do with a laboring society. Instead, these thinkers developed some of the inherent teleologies of the modern spheres of aesthetic culture (the young Lukács, Bloch) and personality (the later Marcuse) in utopian and totalizing directions. Their affinities with Leninist avant-gardism—explicit for Lukács and Bloch, implicit for Marcuse—indicate, however, that they could not really free themselves from the utopia of power. It certainly seems to be the case that primarily cultural utopias, to the extent that they are fundamentalist and revolutionary, implicitly base their promise of social transformation on the dynamic potential of the medium of power. Within the Marxist tradition, only Adorno and Horkheimer were able to escape the charms of power, at the price, however, of developing a utopia of solidarity whose terms could not be linked to any politics or even explicitly articulated.[77]

Admittedly, democratic utopias drawing on the resource of solidarity and projecting the vast expansion of communicative processes of will formation can also be, and have often been, totalizing. This feature of democratic fundamentalism, whenever present, has tended to make anarchist utopias either transparent covers for projects of power or projects for the primitivist dedifferentiation of society. While totalization led to the destruction of democracy in the case of utopias of market and power, in early versions of the utopia of communication the result was self-destruction. The reason for this difference is that, in the case of the utopia of communication, totalization represents a contradiction in principle. The lifeworld is dissimilar to money and power; even its associationally organized institutions cannot easily or spontaneously invade and subsume the differentiated subsystems. Even more important, its own modernization depends on the differentiation of modern economy and state; their dedifferentiation would deprive civil society of time resources for democratic deliberation and decision making. Thus, the totalization of the (communicative) logic of democratic association is not only conducive to short- and long-term dysfunctional side effects and pathologies; it is in principle self-contradictory. It is evident, therefore, that the self-reflection of utopian thought leads both to the idea of the limitation of the logics of power and money, "pulling the emergency break" with respect to their dynamism, and to the idea of the self-limitation of radical democracy. This double setting of limits requires differentiation.

There is yet another reason for the self-limitation of democratic utopianism, and this is the link, admittedly contingent, between many historical utopias and the idea of revolutionary rupture. Irrespective of their projects, revolutions in the modern sense are carried out, or at least won, by organizations of power that, in a genuine rupture with the old society and in the inevitable chaos and power vacuum that follow, are driven to increase rather than limit sovereign power.[78] It is this constellation, for example, that led to the difference in spirit between the American constitution and Bill of Rights and the French Declaration of the Rights of Man.[79] While the utopias of power have an elective affinity with total rupture, the utopia of democratic communication is threatened by revolution despite its own revolutionary origins.[80] Obviously, the issue of the desirability of revolution in a given context cannot be decided from the point of view of utopian projects alone, especially when the overthrow of an oppressive system is involved. But it is important to note the dangers of revolutionary rupture for democracy, and also to note an indispensable precondition for its legitimacy: Democracy's only possible legitimation lies in a principle contrary to revolutionary logic, namely, the lasting institutionalization of a new power accompanied by limits to even the new forms of power in terms of rights.[81]

Even a democratic revolution must be limited by rights. Such is the consequence of the utopia of differentiation. This is equivalent to saying that democratic revolutions can remain democratic in the modern world only if they institutionalize civil society. This is in fact never possible on the basis of abolishing even imperfect models of civil society. And yet the utopia of communication, the plurality of democracies, cannot simply be a project of establishing *any* kind of civil society or any model of rights. The utopia of civil society that we have in mind is not identical to the models of civil society discussed so far, and the structure of rights implied is not equivalent to any found in today's constitutions. The legitimating principles of democracy and rights are compatible only with a model of civil society that institutionalizes democratic communication in a multiplicity of publics and defends the conditions of individual autonomy by liberating the intimate sphere from all traditional as well as modern forms of inequality and unfreedom.[82] The model of rights we require would put the rights of communication (the public sphere) and the rights of the intimate (or "private") sphere into the center of the catalogue of constitutional freedoms. These would have priority over all political, economic, and social rights, which would constitute only their prerequisites. The establishment of such a catalogue would indeed signify the institutionalization of a new model of civil society.

We are aware of the link in all utopian thought between moral-practical justification and affect-oriented motivation. To some, the utopia of civil society developed here may appear, because of its remoteness from substantive cultural objectives and concrete forms of life, to be deficient in its motivational ability. But despite its legal-political emphasis, the utopia of civil society understood in terms of the differentiation of a modern lifeworld need not break with all conceptions of cultural transformation. There is a fundamental link in our analysis between the colonization of the lifeworld ("loss of freedom") and the selective institutionalization of the potentials of a modern, differentiated culture ("loss of meaning"). The project of a democratic civil society, its model of differentiation, is obviously one of decolonizing the lifeworld. It is precisely colonization, or the penetration of the lifeworld by the logics of money and power, that today promotes a pattern of selective, primarily cognitive-instrumental, feedbacks of cultural potentials. The organization of democratic institutions and new types of interpersonal relations within civil society would make the enrichment of every-day communicative practice through moral as well as aesthetic cultural resources both desirable and possible. Of course, a new relation between expert cultures in these spheres and everyday communication would have to be established for such feedback to occur on a significant scale. If successful, this transformation would affect the deepest level of the lifeworld itself. At the same time, cultural transformation could in this utopian model shed its total-izing potential by shifting its contribution to the micro level, to the lives of associations and groups that have built the idea of self-limitation into their daily practice.

To sum up: The "utopian horizon of civil society" as conceived here is based on preserving the boundaries between the different subsystems and the lifeworld (and, as we shall see, also on the influence of normative considerations, based on the imperatives of the reproduction of the lifeworld, over the formally organized spheres of action). Lifeworld contexts, freed from system impera-tives, could then be opened up to allow for the replacement, when relevant, of traditionally secured norms by communicatively achieved ones—process already begun but not by any means completed, as the situation of women and children in the "mod-ern" family demonstrates. The self-limiting aspect of the utopia refers to the restriction of the communicative coordination of action to the institutional core of civil society itself, in place of imposing this organizing principle on all of society and thus dedifferentiating the steering mechanisms and thereby society as a whole.

The Institutional Two-Dimensionality of Existing Civil Society

Totalizing utopias, especially those linked to the idea of revolution-ary rupture, aim for a constitutive rather than a regulative relation to politics. The rationally constructed model is to be actualized in practice. Such utopias can rely entirely on a transcendent critique of existing reality, with a revolutionary movement as a kind of deus ex machina obliterating existing structures and creating entirely new ones. Revolutionary utopias can use versions of genuine immanent criticism, relying on the contradictions between counterfactual norms and actual institutions, only inconsistently, since the idea of rupture excludes the notion that something is intrinsically worth saving.[83] From such a point of view, however, the norms of a society become nothing but a transparent subterfuge for strategic action, and this is an attitude incompatible with immanent criticism.

The proper relationship of self-limiting utopias to reality should be a regulative one. Projects of reconstruction ought to be guided by normative principles that determine only the legitimate procedures but not the actual contents of new institutional life. Above all, such utopias do not aim at imposing a single form of life beyond all conflict. Like all utopias, the one we have in mind has an element of transcendence with respect to existing reality. But self-limiting utopianism has an intrinsic relation with immanent criticism, since it cannot and ought not construct the new society, even ideally, from its own substance. Thus, the utopia we advocate must combine, as Adorno foresaw, transcendent and immanent forms of social criticism.

All the more serious, then, is Adorno's own suspicion, echoed by Marcuse, that in both the West and the East, one-dimensional and totally administered societies, characterized by the reification of all spheres of life, have become dominant. In such societies, ideologies in the true sense disappear, carrying with them the only possible object of immanent criticism.[84] This radical judgment, seemingly resting on an implausible identification of capitalist liberal democracies with totalitarian societies, was in fact backed up by the whole tradition of Frankfurt School analyses of economy, politics, culture, family, and personality.

The utopia of civil society starts out from the obviously plausible counterthesis according to which the Western liberal democracies, unlike Soviet-type societies, are civil societies, however imperfect. If true, this claim would validate the self-limiting and regulative status of this utopia and give it a potential link to politics by a refurbished immanent critique. Unlike the one-dimensionality thesis, which was supported by interdisciplinary research, the idea of the immanent critique of civil society has at this time relatively little critical social science behind it. Even worse, some of the most rigorous models in established sociology—Luhmann's systems theory in particular—lend support to the idea of the end of civil society as well as to many of the particulars of the one-dimensionality thesis, especially in political sociology.

Nevertheless, we believe that our reconstructed concept of civil society allows us to take the phenomena of reification seriously without forcing us to construe the whole of existing society in this way. Reification and the formation of the media of money and power (implicitly identified by Lukács) can now be distinguished. The replacement of ordinary language by media in the coordination of everyday interaction is not equivalent to the replacement of traditional forms of heteronomy by modern forms of unfreedom linked to the rise of new, impersonal, formal systems. The development of media-steered interaction allows a tremendous widening of the possibilities of communication, thus constituting a positive-sum game, as it were, involving the simultaneous development of the media and of new, modern forms of communicative action coordination. Reification is thus equivalent neither to the emergence of the subsystems nor to the replacement of traditional structures of the lifeworld by modern ones; it is, rather, the subsumption and erosion of the latter by money and power. From this theoretical point of view, the modernization of lifeworld institutions can be explored in terms of a double aspect, as reification and as communicative rationalization.

This double aspect represents the best point of view from which to explore the institutional domains of family, culture, and associations, as well as the domain of legality that is so important for the modern subsystems. Those aspects of contemporary institutions that contribute to the autonomy and further rationalization of civil society constitute the positive side; the reified structures that promote colonization, the negative. Here we can only indicate the outlines of the conception that would have to be developed for a theory of the institutional dynamics of contemporary civil society. Our evidence is constituted at this stage only by the tradition of social and political theory that seeks to contest the opposing theses of one-dimensionality and system integration. Even from such a preliminary point of view, we believe that it is possible to claim that the institutional developments of the modern family, of political and cultural public spheres, and of associations are all similarly dualistic.

1. With respect to the family, we support Habermas's challenge to the old Frankfurt thesis (which he used to share) that the assumption of socialization by the schools and the mass media and the loss of the property base of the middle-class patriarchal family entails, along with the abolition of the father's authority, the end of ego autonomy. From the standpoint of the system/lifeworld distinction, the picture looks rather different. The freeing of the family from many economic functions and the diversification of the agencies of socialization create a potential for egalitarian interfamilial relations and liberalized socialization processes. The rationality potential of communicative interaction in this sphere is thereby released. Of course, new types of conflicts and even pathologies appear when these potentials are blocked and when the demands of the formally organized subsystems in which the adult must participate conflict with the capacities and expectations of those who have experienced these emancipatory socialization processes.[85]

2. The principles of democratic legitimacy and representation imply the free discussion of all interests within institutionalized public spheres (parliaments) and the primacy of the lifeworld with respect to the two subsystems. As we have seen in Luhmann, however, uncoupling the centralized public sphere from genuine participation leads to a screening out of a wide range of interests and issues from general discussion. The role of political parties and the electoral process is to aggregate certain important social constellations of interest and to limit, in time and space, more general societal inputs to politics to the narrowest channels of privatized, depoliticized individuals. The political organizations that are to mediate between civil society and politics become bureaucratic organizations of the political system itself, and they defuse rather than actualize democratic participation. Parliaments in this view specialize in the show of decision making; they are smokescreens for decisions made outside all pubic discussion. Finally, the political public sphere is merely the extension of a commercialized mass culture and is equally manipulated.

But this is not the whole story. Luhmann, for example, is never able to show how elite democracy can avoid both the repoliticization and republicization of spheres outside the political system and the spread of dysfunctional forms of apathy with respect to politics. Nor does he satisfactorily explain why elite democracies are forced not only to propagate the official conception of the classical theory of democracy but also to structure important parts of the dramaturgy of political process accordingly. He does not consider the reversal of power relations made possible by this dramaturgy that can easily be played out "for real." The empirical case for the predominant, almost exclusive, process of political communication filtering downward is not convincing. Large structural shifts such as the creation of welfare states, but also the current neoliberal turn, seem to respond to many grass-roots initiatives. Moreover, the bureaucratic catch-all party form presupposed by elite theorists does not seem to provide sufficient centers of social identification, nor is it able to respond well to the emergence of new issues of great urgency. Thus, some countries have experienced the emergence of extraparliamentary oppositions or parties with a new type of relation to movements. These phenomena have affected the structure of the political public sphere as well. While the central political public sphere, constituted by parliaments and the major media, remains rather (but not everywhere equally!) closed and inaccessible, a plurality of alternative publics, differentiated but interrelated, time and again revives the processes and the quality of political communication. With the emergence of new types of political organizations, even the public discussion in parliaments and party conventions tends to be affected, as has been the case in West Germany. It seems, therefore, that along with the elite democratic, oligarchic tendencies toward the drying up of political public life, we should postulate a contrary, if weaker, trend of redemocratization, based on the new cultural (practical, aesthetic, and cognitive) potentials of the lifeworld.

3. Nor can one construe the development of the mass media as a purely negative sign of the commodification or administrative distortion of communication. This point is especially important because, in Habermas's early thesis on the public sphere, the fusion argument, implying the obliteration of the bridges between state and civil society, works only if the cultural substance of mediation is "commodified" and "industrialized." There is little reason to deny the immense role in our societies of a top-to-bottom, center-

to-periphery model of mass communications. Yet generalized forms of communication also deprovincialize, expand, and create new publics. In the area of general communications, what we said about the differentiation and pluralization of political publics is even more true. From subcultures to great educational institutions, from political to scientific publics, from social movements to microinstitutions, the spaces for consequential, critical communication have immensely expanded along with the growth of the commercialized and manipulated frameworks of public relations, advertising, and industrial culture. Since the project of an enlightened public sphere was first articulated, we have had neither a single history of decline (the rise of mass culture) nor a process of "democratization," but two simultaneous histories made possible by democratization: one of the penetration of culture through money and power, and another of the renewal of a more universal, inclusive, and pluralistic public life made possible by the modernization of the lifeworld. While the first of these processes often seems to be dominant, this is not due to an inevitability latent in the technical means of communication. The technical development of the electronic media does not necessarily lead to centralization; it can involve horizontal, creative, autonomous forms of media pluralism.[86]

4. The problem of associations, which is excluded from Habermas's analysis,[87] is parallel to that of culture, to which it is linked through the structures of the public sphere. As Durkheim and Gramsci realized, the hostility of the modern state and economy to corporate bodies and associations could not block their reemergence and modernization. In this context, the bureaucratization of associations and the emergence of pseudo-pluralist and corporatist forms of interest representation and aggregation, a key dimension of the fusion argument, cannot be considered the only tendency in contemporary associational life. The existence of an immense number of voluntary associations in all liberal democracies,[88] the emergence of new ones in the context of corporatist bargaining, and their role in citizen initiatives and social movements[89] may not demonstrate the somewhat one-sided Parsonian point that ours is the age of association and not bureaucracy; but it is clear that legitimate left criticisms of a pluralist thesis that occludes the highly

differential access of various types of associations to the political system should not close our eyes to the validity of this thesis against all claims of atomization and massification in our societies. The resilience of associations and the periodic revival of their dynamism can be explained through the modernization of the lifeworld and its normative contribution to the scarce resource of solidarity.

5. Finally, the development of legality up to the contemporary democratic welfare state involves both the modernization of civil society and its penetration by administrative agencies. It is, moreover, in the double nature of law itself that one must locate the ambiguous character of the contemporary juridification of society. According to Habermas, as a "medium," law functions as an organizational means together with money and/or power to *constitute* the structure of economy and administration in such a way that they can be coordinated independently of direct communication. As an "institution," on the other hand, law is "a societal component of the lifeworld . . . embedded in a broader political, cultural, and social context . . . in a continuum with moral norms and superimposed communicatively structured areas of action."[90] Juridification in this sense plays a regulative rather than a constitutive role, expanding and giving a binding form to (the ethical principles of) communicatively coordinated areas of action. This empowering dimension of at least some types of legal regulation is fostered by juridification itself. Foucault's error in this regard, typical of all anarchist postures, is to have focused exclusively on the role of law as medium, while dismissing the freedom-securing, empowering institutional moment as mere show. Both dimensions are present in Luhmann, but by definition they are always present, and thus the tension between the two options and the possibility of choosing between them cannot arise. The distinction between system and lifeworld allows us to contrast and choose (in some areas of life at least) between two forms of legal regulation, only one of which is compatible with the autonomy of the institutional life of civil society.[91]

At first sight, law as institution seems like a weak competitor for law as medium, with the latter expressing the extension of the purposive-regulative activity of welfare-state administrations primarily. The fact that this activity interferes with the reproduction of the lifeworld may appear as an irrelevant externality. However, the reduction of law entirely to a medium, most complete in the political instrumentalization of modern law, is not only an inefficient form of intervention in many life spheres, including the economy, but also leads to that weakening of the normative in law that Luhmann at one time considered to be the function of the positivization of law.[92] This outcome would affect the binary code of right–wrong through which law must operate and would weaken the legitimacy of the legal system as a whole. Law as medium, despite its tendency to replace law as institution, is possible only if law is also an institution. At least a partial choice for law as institution is necessary if the steering functions of law are to be protected.

The choice between law as medium and law as institution does not help with another pressing problem: the legal regulation of the subsystems themselves. Like Habermas's analysis in *The Theory of Communicative Action* of the other alternatives within the structures of existing civil societies, the idea of law as institution tells us only what we should defend against colonization. Hence his inclination, later reversed, to see new social movements as primarily defensive reactions to colonization, hardly constitutive of a politics. It may very well be that the absence of the concept of association, both within the institutional analysis of civil society and with respect to the dynamics of social movements, led Habermas to revive the classical breakdown thesis that understands movements merely as reactions to normative disintegration or other types of dislocations accompanying modernization.[93] Our task is to prove that the recovery of the concept of association, when linked to new ideas of publics and legal regulation, allows the formulation of a new politics of civil society.

The Politics of Civil Society

We have reconstructed the concept of civil society in terms of the categories of system and lifeworld in order to develop a political theory that might contribute to contemporary democratic projects in both the West and the East. We are concerned, to say the least, about the emergence of three, increasingly dominant, interpretations of the reconstruction of civil society: a neoliberal model that identifies the civil with the bourgeois; an antipolitical model that rigidly juxtaposes society to the state; and an antimodern interpretation that seeks to absorb the modern economy in a less differentiated society. These approaches all have in common a dichotomous model of civil society and state, albeit in different forms. In opposition to state socialism in the East and the welfare state in the West, the neoliberals, the antipoliticians, and the antimoderns variously seek to rebuild a market society, a society animated by cultural or social movements yet free of interest-group and party politics, or a nondifferentiated, socially embedded economy.

Only a model that differentiates civil society from both state and economy, and analyzes the mediations among them, can avoid such misinterpretations of the projects of its reconstruction. Moreover, we believe that our particular interpretation of such a three-part model accommodates a critical assessment of the welfare state that avoids both neoliberal and neoconservative traps, without adopting the illusions of an antipolitical or antieconomic fundamentalism.[94] The political project developed from this critique should be significant not only in the West but also in the East, where democratic forces seeking "to rejoin Europe" are suddenly on the horns of a dilemma constituted by the two models of Western Europe's past (economic liberalism) and its present (welfare-state interventionism).

Critique of the Welfare State

The traditional left critique of the welfare state, based on a rejection of "class compromise," is now irrelevant. Without some meaningful notion of a socialist society achieved through a radical break with the present one and a revolutionary agency constituted by the working class, there is no reason why workers and others should not try to represent their interests through compromise as well as through strategies based on economic and political pressure.[95] Today a newer leftist criticism focuses on the destructive side effects of administrative intervention (cutting across class boundaries) on personality, social solidarity, culture, and ecology as well as on the role of the citizen (now reduced to that of client). We appreciate this line of criticism and have dealt with it by appropriating the perspectives of the French second left and the German "realist" Greens[96] and by exploring the "negative side" of civil society as a colonized lifeworld, as described by Foucault and Habermas.[97]

We must still address the neoliberal (and neoconservative) criticisms. These were anticipated and in part reappropriated by leftist critics, who were in fact the first to interpret the rationality deficits of welfare-state interventionism as a "crisis of crisis management."[98] According to this line of analysis, interventionist and redistributive policies have the following drawbacks: They put unacceptable burdens on public finance, disorganize administration by generating excessive and conflicting demands on the part of different constituencies (including the bureaucracies themselves), and inhibit investment and accumulation under the weight of taxation and regulation; they reduce the mobility and the motivation of labor and capital, favor increases in wages in excess of increases of productivity, and make sustaining current levels of social spending dependent on implausible and undesirable levels of growth; in the absence of such growth, they produce unacceptable levels of inflation. Indeed, the policy of welfare-state compensations depended for its success on solid and continuous growth, but through its very activities this state interfered with the possibility of just such growth. Directly or indirectly, the forms of economic dysfunction of the welfare state not only interfere with the mechanisms of the capitalist economy but are harmful to many of the strata that redistributive policies are designed to support. This is true because the expansion of the unproductive public sector becomes a drag on capital accumulation, which in turn restricts the fiscal resources available for public spending.

It is possible to accept much of the neoconservative description without buying into its normative premises or political conclusions. Claus Offe has argued convincingly that right-wing diagnoses retain their empirical validity even though it is impossible in liberal democracies to create political coalitions to institute radical versions of the neoliberal market-oriented scenario, which in any case could leave most capitalist societies "in a state of exploding conflict and anarchy."[99] However, if we combine the left and right critiques of the welfare state, we would certainly come to realize that not only a set of particular strategies associated with a few advanced capitalist democracies but a whole model of directed social change associated with the term "socialism" has become obsolete.[100]

Habermas has seen the stakes clearly. He has argued that the establishment of the welfare state represented both a defense of the lifeworld against the capitalist economy and a penetration of the lifeworld by the administrative state. This second consequence was unintended. The aim of the welfare state was to promote and develop solidarity, not to disorganize it. The root of its failure in this respect lies in a particular model of democracy, one identified with "socialism," implying the possibility of "society," globally speaking, acting upon itself through the supposedly neutral medium of political power.[101] However, global societal action upon society itself in the paradoxical presence, however weak, of societal self-knowledge (based on interlocking public spheres drawing upon the common background knowledge of the lifeworld) but also in the inevitable absence of a global subject capable of collective action turned out to be impossible; hence the dysfunctions and destructive side effects produced by welfare-state intervention. As Luhmann has seen, neither the body of citizens nor the state can act for society as a whole. Citizens can participate at best in collective reflection, but not collective action; the political system is organizationally only a subsystem of society, one exposed to internal conflicts and tensions despite its selectivity. Worse still, the state that *is* capable of action is in fact (as Luhmann and others have shown) largely uncoupled, despite or even because of the procedures of electoral democracy, from the public processes of reflection about society. Furthermore, as the doubleness of juridification (*Verrechtlichung*) phenomena demonstrates (the atomization, control, normalization, bureaucratization, disciplining, and surveillance of everyday life), power is not a neutral medium; state penetration saves the lifeworld and solidarity from the medium of money only at the cost of further "colonization."[102] Power, as Habermas aptly puts it, is incapable of creating meaning or solidarity, of replacing these resources once they are dissipated by administration.

it turns out, the action of society as a whole on the modern
c subsystem is also a statist illusion that leads to serious

consequences. Converging with Luhmann's conception of autopoietic systems, we can now provide a general interpretation of what went wrong with state intervention into the economy, supposedly on behalf of the lifeworld. The introduction of the medium of power into economic relations on a wholesale basis, as we know from the experience of state socialism, replaces the hard budgetary constraint needed for economic self-regulation with mechanisms of bureaucratic decision making and bargaining.[103] Outcomes in such a setting have a system logic that never in fact corresponds either with the intentions of actors or with an economic logic that would reward those who are efficient, innovative, and productive and punish those who are not.[104] In capitalist welfare states, significant internal and international competition and the existence of capital markets, however imperfect, continue to keep budgetary constraints relatively hard. Nevertheless, among other factors, oligopolistic "mark-up" price setting, the "cost-plus" principle of state (especially military) procurements, state protection of (at times obsolete) domestic industries, state guarantees for institutions of credit, the softening of credit requirements to stimulate production, corporatist bargaining and lobbying, and policies of taxation and subsidies directed at maintaining full employment and social services do manage to soften these to a varying, but at times considerable, extent.[105]

Of course, the sources and justifications of these phenomena ought to be differentiated. Some of them are due primarily to oligopolistic concentration and "imperfect competition," or to military rather than welfare spending. But the welfare state greatly exacerbates the budget-softening tendencies of advanced capitalism, and it has had for a long time a popular mandate to do so. Because of social pressures and the paternalistic ideology of the welfare state, it seems to be difficult, moreover, to disentangle interventions that soften budgetary constraints from those that do not. It is equally difficult to differentiate areas of life that should be removed from the influence of markets from those whose economic self-regulation is the guarantee for commercial dynamism and technical innovation.[106] Under these conditions, we have a paradoxical situation in which the lifeworld is insufficiently protected against penetration by economic rationality while economic self-regulation does not function adequately. At the same time, external regulation itself functions less and less well with the passing of time, as routine state intervention and support become predictable by firms, who will now invest only when guarantees (tax exemptions, depreciation allowances, etc.) are available.[107] In order to promote investment, the volume of regulative intervention increases beyond the technical requirements of effective fiscal and monetary policy. Such a context produces a form of specifically noneconomic expectation that links success not to sensitivity to market signals, to cutting of costs, or to innovation but to lobbying, bargaining, and involvement in networks of political power.

On a macro level, Kornai's distinction between hard and soft budgetary constraints indicates two relations of the economy to its environment: in one, this environment refuses to compensate for economic failure; in the other, it does so for extraeconomic reasons. For our purposes, it is even more important that the hard budgetary constraint indicates a high level of differentiation, based on a structure of expectation in which success and failure depend on *economic* forms of competition with other *economic* units. The soft budgetary constraint implies a lower level of differentiation between politics and economics in which economic units rely on hierarchical relations to extraeconomic, political institutions and success depends on the power these units can generate and/or on the degree of state paternalism. Relying on power, one's own or the state's, means that a specifically economic rationality will suffer, even if in the West the degree of budgetary softness that produces phenomena of shortage is nowhere reached.[108] As opposed to this, the idea of the hard budgetary constraint, even if interpreted in terms of a relatively high degree rather than absolute hardness, calls to our attention the need to maintain a differentiated economy with a considerable level of self-regulation.

Reflexive Continuation of the Welfare State and Liberal
    Democracy

    of the welfare state presents us with difficult political
        ough we agree with some aspects of neoconservative
            economic diagnoses, we cannot accept the strategy

of privatization and deregulation or the neoconservative emphasis on tradition and authority. Systematically speaking, these recipes call for the reeconomization of society and the destruction through monetary relations (and at times through political repression) of many of the institutions and cultural potentials of a modern civil society. But neither can we identify with the loyalist (generally, social democratic) defenders of the welfare state in Europe, or their counterparts in the United States, because of their insensitivity to the phenomena of colonization by power and to the long-term economic failure of state interventionism. Social democracy has been historically concerned with extending the realms of freedom and solidarity, but Adam Przeworski is right in arguing that the Keynesian welfare state was the only genuinely political project produced by social democratic reformism, the only successful democratic strategy of the left. With that model now in crisis, reformism has declined to a form of crisis management, a basically conservative strategy unable to thematize its own ambiguity with respect to freedom and solidarity.[109]

Finally, we believe that programs of "the great refusal," whether directed against the state in the name of a civil society suspicious of all politics or against the modern economy in the name of some kind of socially reembedded nonmarket economy based on mutuality, reciprocity, and direct cooperation, are incompatible with modernity and with the presuppositions of modern democracy, despite the self-understanding of many of their proponents.[110] From the point of view of our three-part model, great and justified sensitivity to colonization by money and/or power has driven movement fundamentalists to dedifferentiate civil society with respect to the economy and/or the state. The problems here go beyond the self-understanding of movement activists and affect some theories of civil society as well. Those who work with a two-part state–civil society model, for example, may be able to see the demerits of fundamentalist opposition to the state, but they are unable to see the parallel problem with respect to the economy. Hence, to avoid neoconservatism, they wind up adopting a species of utopian socialism.[111]

We believe that fundamentalism represents only one side of th new social movements. Indeed, the remarkable characteristic many contemporary radical movements, from the Greens to Solidarity, is their principled self-limitation. Moreover, affirming the necessity of a renewed reformism that relies on institutionalized political actors, we have long argued for a dualistic political strategy combining differentiated movement and party forms as the best hope for democratizing civil society.[112] The framework introduced here allows us to develop this position beyond its earlier versions.

Habermas's idea of the reflexive continuation of the welfare state[113] is an important, though one-sided and still undeveloped, clue as to what needs to be done. The idea is important, on the most obvious level, because the welfare state represents many forms of social protection that should not be abandoned either as realities (in Western Europe) or as aspirations (in the United States and now Eastern Europe). It is true, moreover, that historically the welfare state promoted, with respect to the capitalist economy, "a highly innovative combination of power and self restraint"[114] that served solidarity without promoting dedifferentiation. This strategy failed in part because the belief in the neutrality of political power hampered development when the time came for defending society against the state as well. The idea of the "reflexive" continuation of the welfare state, in the name of its own value of solidarity, means the application of the same innovative combination of power and self-limitation that the state once applied to the market economy to the welfare state itself, this time from a vantage point equidistant from the administrative state and the capitalist economy. "The political public sphere . . . wins a similar distance from the political system as before from the economic."[115]

The project of the movement of organized workers and now of other subjects should be continued in the sense of being redirected to their own earlier achievement, the welfare state itself. But such a reflexive and self-limiting project cannot be successful unless it is implemented by another one: the application of its results to the ¬cratic revolutions that created modern civil society. A "reflex-¬nuation" of liberal democracy would then mean the ¬of the strategy of self-limiting democratization to lib-¬in the name of its own value, freedom. As we have ¬democratic movements, including those active ¬g the modern state under control, but without seeking to abolish it. Such strategies are also distinguished by innovative combinations of power and self-restraint, but they fail to include sufficient reflection on the socially destructive consequences of the other medium-steered subsystem, the economy. In order to avoid mere repetition of earlier outcomes, liberal democracy today must learn to limit its own built-in tendency to contribute to the economic colonization of the world.

The program of the defense of the lifeworld with respect to both subsystems can be reached equally well from liberal democracy as from social democracy; there is no need, for example, for a social-democratic detour where a modern welfare state is not yet established.[116] More generally, there is no need to advance projects against either the capitalist economy or the administrative state that would simply strengthen the other with respect to the lifeworld. We should instead seek innovative forms of limiting both subsystems. Our attitude to rights should reflect such a new posture. It would be wrong to think, for example, that the institutions and specifically the structure of rights of liberal democracy will be less essential for the new model than welfare-state protections or social rights. For this reason, too, it is important to identify the new project explicitly as the continuation of liberal democracy. Only then can we retain sensitivity, without paternalism, to today's democratic movements in the East and the South as well as the new social movements in the West.

Defense of the Lifeworld

The formulation of the political project of self-reflexive, self-limiting democracy is only at its beginnings.[117] But this is just part of the problem. Habermas's own preliminary statement is still weighted more toward protecting the lifeworld than toward the equally important project of controlling and redirecting the political and economic subsystems. Admittedly, he speaks not only of the need to establish "thresholds of limitation" in and by the lifeworld, in order to limit penetration by the media of money and power, but also of the need to create "sensors" that can indirectly influence the operation of the steering media themselves.[118] The two steps presuppose each other. Only an adequately defended, differentiated,

and organized civil society can monitor and influence the outcomes of steering processes, but only a civil society capable of
influencing the state and economy can help to restrain or redirect
the expansive tendencies of the media, which are, paradoxically,
strengthened rather than weakened by processes of differentiation. Nevertheless, the theory of system and lifeworld in its present
state has difficulties formulating the project of establishing sensors
within apparently closed, self-regulating, autopoietic subsystems.

Let us examine the two dimensions of establishing "thresholds"
or "barriers" of protection and "sensors" of influence. What the
barriers must above all protect is the resource of *solidarity*, which
refers to the ability of individuals to respond to and identify with
one another on the basis of mutuality and reciprocity, without
exchanging equal quantities of support, without calculating individual advantages, and above all without compulsion. Solidarity
involves a willingness to share the fate of the other, not as the
exemplar of a category to which the self belongs but as a unique and
different person. Despite this orientation to "difference," the
resource of solidarity nevertheless presupposes common membership in some actual or ideal group, and beyond this some common
norms, symbols, and memories as well. Solidary individuals are
consciously rooted in the same or significantly overlapping
lifeworlds, and this guarantees consensus about important matters,
even in a modern lifeworld where their content can be discussed
and challenged.

Solidarity is not a steering resource like money or power.[119] It
cannot accomplish its own self-closure and self-protection. Even
less is it able to bring the other media under its control. The task
of protecting solidarity falls to the interlocking institutions of civil
society, associations and publics, which in turn presuppose rights
of association and communication.[120] Associations seem to presuppose solidarity, since otherwise they are susceptible to "free rider"
problems, but they can come about through selective incentives or
constraints as well as through the motivation of public freedom.[121]
In the latter case especially, they can build, given sufficient time, a
common identity and solidarity. The small public spheres within
voluntary associations that allow for direct participation and the
relative transparency (if not elimination) of power and monetary

relations are crucial for preserving and renewing this scarce and precarious resource.

The structural transformation of the public sphere, the development of the culture industry, and the emergence of corporatist arrangements that bypass the political public sphere preclude any naive optimism regarding association and publicity today. Nevertheless, the possibility of the *renewal* of solidarity through the continual reemergence of a plurality of associations that are public and egalitarian in their structure and highly responsive to other similar publics has been documented by the pluralist tradition of political theory, albeit from a restrictive point of view. Recent research on social movements aimed at disproving the pluralist concept of mass society has confirmed this claim from another standpoint.[122] But while the effects of reconstituting the microstructures of publicity on preserving solidarity are clear, it is less obvious how the formula can imply, as Habermas suggests, *indirect* influence over the political, economic, and functional systems that are "self-referentially closed" and hence "immune to *direct* intervention." Linking publicity to associations, most of which have purposes other than fostering communication, becomes a problem precisely as the threshold of protection of the lifeworld is passed in the direction of influencing the economy and the state.

It is not evident to what extent the new forms of self-organization could be capable of action beyond these thresholds, even if one seeks to conceptualize this in terms of an influence far less direct and total than the project of (a global) society acting on itself through the allegedly neutral medium of power. The new grassroots associations capable of spreading enlightenment lose their rootedness in the lifeworld when they step over the limit to complex formal organizations capable of reducing complexity. In other words, the cost of being able to act on the political and economic systems seems to be the penetration of societal self-organization by the logic of bureaucracy, that is, the medium of power. At the same time, if societal self-organization resolutely stays on the lifeworld side of the threshold, it is hard to see how it can do more than contribute to the development of "political culture" or "new identities."

The question is how movements can resist Roberto Michels's iron law of oligarchy. Would they not themselves reproduce the organizational structures determined by power and money the moment they attempted to influence the subsystems of state and economy? Can the movement form survive the step over the boundaries of the lifeworld, and influence structures coordinated through means other than normative or communicative interaction, without succumbing to the pressure for self-instrumentalization? Can one, in short, move forward without giving up the lifeworld/system distinction, which seems to abandon the most powerful spheres to systems rationality? We shall return to these questions in the next chapter.

Dualistic Solutions?

The combination of associations, publics, and rights, when supported by a political culture in which independent initiatives and movements represent an ever-renewable, legitimate, political option, represents, in our opinion, an effective set of bulwarks around civil society within whose limits much of the program of radical democracy can be reformulated. Yet even this combination does not yield a system of effective "sensors" capable of bringing the political and economic subsystems, which are uncoupled from civil society in elite-democratic and capitalist arrangements, under social control. It would be possible to stylize this outcome in terms of a process of political change turned inward toward civil society, the lifeworld, and the "realm of freedom," leaving the "realm(s) of necessity" outside the range of free organizations. André Gorz postulated in his writings of the late 1970s a solution to the problem of economic transformation that involved the creation of two socioeconomic realms.[123] The first was defined, following the Marx of the third volume of *Das Kapital,* as a *realm of necessity* structured by work and employment, to be coordinated by state central planning of the production of necessities, which is to be achieved "with the maximum efficiency and the least expenditure of effort and resources," a realm that can be humanized only partially through workplace (rather than firm-level) democracy.[124] Gorz's project is above all to reduce the scope of this sphere and especially the time resources committed to it, to the benefit of the *realm of freedom,* defined by autonomous activity and coordinated by cooperation, reciprocity, and creativity. Gorz further insists that the realm of necessity or heteronomy must be subordinated to the realm of freedom, although he never even begins to tell us how that is possible in his rigid dualistic model.[125]

Gorz's analysis suffers from a contradiction between a three-part framework differentiating state, economy, and civil society and a two-part one that identifies the realm of necessity with the state alone. On the one side, he speaks of two types of heteronomous activity in the realm of necessity, one corresponding to the social production of necessities and the other to the (material) administration of the whole of society.[126] On the other side, the two become simply different functions of the state, in that he leaves no room in his proposal for the market coordination of social production, which he thinks leads only to inequality and class domination.[127] Pervasive state economic organization can be avoided in this two-part framework only in the direction of the realm of freedom, a civil society coordinated by neither market nor state. Astonishingly, we are not told how "maximum efficiency and the least expenditure of effort and resources" can be attained without markets operating in a mixed economy.

The problem with Gorz's overemphasis of state ownership and planning is not that "future state planning of socially necessary production could not function rationally without workplace democracy."[128] Rather, the point is that neither planning in the genuine and therefore necessarily limited economic sense nor industrial (firm-level and workplace) democracy can function rationally without markets. Thus, those who follow Gorz are left with a problem that depends in part on how much time and activity one wishes to assign to the realms of necessity and freedom, respectively. If one seeks to avoid a return of traditional socialist statism (about which Gorz is less concerned), one must propose a vast reduction of (state-controlled) labor time and an increase of autonomous activity (in civil society). In this case, however, Gorz's criticism of the identification of civil society with premodern autarchic communities comes into its play. Needless to say, this would also involve a serious and unacceptable reduction in economic complexity and efficiency. But if one takes this criticism seriously, Gorz's framework makes sense only if a much larger portion of economic activities is assigned to the realm of necessity, where criteria of efficiency must dominate; and this means, in the two-part model, recourse to the state and a vast increase (in Western societies) in its planning and coordinating activity. The only way out of the unattractive choice between statism and utopian socialism is, first, to recognize that there is a difference in principle between economically efficient, market-oriented production and distribution and the plurality of socially embedded material activities that do not have a strictly economic character and, second, to affirm some version of the former, in a new combination or interrelation with both state and civil society.

To put this another way, the need for both economic rationality and societal solidarity cannot be effectively addressed in a single program of liberating civil society from the state because they are conceptually two different issues. Even more important, economic rationality and societal solidarity represent competing claims. Thus, the liberation of each from the state can take place at the expense of the other: Solidarity could be sacrificed to a program of economic liberalism; economic rationality could be sacrificed to a utopia of a reembedded, moral economy. One program leads to an apology for the capitalist version of modernity, the other to the abandonment of an essential prerequisite of modernity itself.

An alternative project geared toward separating the realm of freedom from that of necessity starts out with this premise. Claus Offe and his colleagues start by recognizing the de facto split of the labor market today between prestigious, well-paid work in a formal sector and less prestigious, badly paid work (the lower end of the service economy) along with a range of services and material activities that are "exchanged" but not through the medium of money.[129] They then propose a form of dualization that would equalize participation as well the economic and status outcomes in both market-oriented and nonmarket-oriented forms of productive activity. Unlike Gorz's model, this approach relies on the productivity of a less regulated market economy that has the potential of releasing labor time, which in turn could be used in part to replace, on an informal but socially organized basis, some of the now unaffordable welfare-state services. Like Gorz's model, however, this approach offers little concerning the establishment of some forms of indirect control over the realm of necessity; in this case, the problem is the steering mechanisms of the market economy, whose logic is today certainly incompatible with the establishment and survival of an informal "economy" of free activity, however attractively conceived.[130]

Offe also mentions the possibility of a "constitutionalization" of employment in the first economy in terms of the extension of labor rights ("industrial citizen rights"). Interpreting this "highly ambivalent" strategy in terms of welfare-state interventionism and juridification, he comes up with the following dilemma: Either the hierarchically inferior, market-dependent positions of workers will not be affected by merely formal rights, or they will be affected but at the cost of serious interference with the propensity to investment. Thus, the workers lose either way, despite their new rights.[131] This analysis, while undoubtedly right as far as it goes, underestimates the real importance of establishing such rights, for these would become all the more significant in frameworks beyond welfare-state legal instrumentalism, within new and different models of postregulatory regulation.

The Return of Mediations

The category of "rights," albeit on an abstract level, goes beyond programs of dualistic reorganization. We have already stressed that rights are crucial for establishing thresholds for defending the lifeworld against the media. Thus, for movements, they represent important targets that can be achieved without self-bureaucratization.[132] But rights also represent the institutionalization of forms of self-reflection and self-limitation, until now primarily in and of the political subsystem. Even if we look at rights from the point of view of social norm creation and institutional pressure, it remains remarkable that their legal enactment, application, and enforcement are left to the organs of the state whose disabilities are established by constitutional rights. The motivations of state actors are not hard to understand: They could be acting under pressure or under the impact of recognizing that a positive-sum game is being established in which the state also gains. It is, rather, the process by which rights work in a relatively continuous manner without being constantly reinstrumentalized (on a retail rather than wholesale basis) that is remarkable. The phenomenon is explainable only through the institutionalization of a higher level of learning and reflection within state institutions. Furthermore, to the extent that rights represent a regulation of the state by institutions of civil society, this regulation is a form of autoregulation. Rights are the examples par excellence of law as institution, but they are also examples of postregulatory legal regulation in a more general sense.

Rights, however, represent a form of self-regulation of the political system whose consequence is *only* the strengthening of the barriers defending the lifeworld. They do not in themselves go beyond the first phase of the program of "barriers" and "sensors." Nevertheless, their particular double status, as institution of civil society and as self-limitation of the state, recalls the original mediating role of a whole series of institutions in the classical theory of civil society.

Societal self-organization, associations, and the public sphere are, of course, the categories of civil society that we have inherited and developed. Initially, it seemed fully acceptable for Habermas to link these categories to each other (and, presumably, to legal institutions) only on the horizontal level, and even then on the basis of an explicit theory not of civil society but of the dimension of the lifeworld that institutionalizes stored-up meanings, solidarities, and competences. However, the concept of civil society, unlike that of lifeworld, also involves *vertical* linkages, which can be conceived either as mediations, between individuals and groups, between groups and social institutions, and between social institutions and global political (and presumably economic) institutions, or, in the case of the latter set, as an analytically separate but complementary political (and economic) society. In the Hegelian system, this role is played by family, corporation, estates, and estate parliaments; in Habermas's book on the public sphere, it is played by the family, the literary public sphere, and the political public sphere. In Tocqueville's analysis, many of these mediations are located on the separate analytical level of political society, which in the three-part model must be logically supplemented by economic society.

Whichever of the two basic variants we choose, Hegelian or Tocquevillian, it seems to us that Habermas's current theory of system and lifeworld, which we want to defend on the most abstract level, does not easily allow for either mediations between society and the subsystems or for analytically separated spheres of political and economic society playing analogous roles. Nevertheless, one can use Habermas's analytical framework in a different way than he himself has done.[133]

The abstract categories of system and lifeworld indicate only where the *weight of coordination* lies in a given institutional framework. Cultural, social, and personality-reproducing institutions have their center of gravity in communicative/normative forms of action coordination. Nevertheless, it becomes possible to locate strategic dimensions as well as forms of administration and monetarization in lifeworld institutions (a point that has unduly disturbed critics such as Axel Honneth and Nancy Fraser) without pathological consequences, as long as they remain subordinated to communicative coordination and goal definition and as long as they are not allowed to develop their own logics—the proper meaning of colonization. Whenever pertinent, normatively speaking, this framework allows us (as well as Habermas) to speak of decolonization on the basis of the immanent possibilities within such lifeworld institutions. But we go further, insisting on the possibility of democratizing political and economic institutions. Here, the center of gravity of the coordinating mechanisms (in a modern society) is and must be on the level of *steering performance* through the media of money and power, that is, through system rationality. But that does not preclude the possibility of introducing institutionalized forms of communicative action into state or economic institutions. All types of action can and do occur in societal institutions; not even the market economy can be understood exclusively in terms of instrumental or strategic calculations. The normatively desirable project of introducing economic democracy (involving different possible forms of participation on the various levels of workshop and firm) must be tempered by the necessity of keeping intact the self-regulation of steering systems. But the mere existence (however inadequate) of parliaments and of forms of workshop self-management, codetermination, and collective bargaining indicates that publics can be constructed even within institutions that are primarily system-steered. These would and in some cases do constitute receptors for societal influence within the belly of the whale, as it were. In figure 3, then, institutions that must be *coordinated* communicatively appear under the heading of "civil society," whereas those that must be *steered* by money and/or power appear under the institutional level of system. Neither dimension ought to be conceived as "self-referentially closed," for both are open to democratization (albeit to different extents).

This rough diagram shows that the political issue is how to introduce public spaces into state and economic institutions (without abolishing mechanisms of steering or strategic/instrumental action) by establishing continuity with a network of societal communication consisting of public spheres, associations, and movements. Here one could debate, for example, the determination of preferences among economic and political choices, keeping in mind the needs articulated in societal publics. However, self-limitation would mean that the debate over how much and which forms of democratization are desirable in economic and state institutions must grant in each case the necessities of system maintenance. Such is the meaning of a democratization that complements Habermas's idea of decolonization. Correspondingly, the elimination or pure instrumentalization of political and economic participation constitutes a form of unfreedom that is a counterpart to the colonization of any institution.[134]

Reflexive Law and Postregulatory Regulation

The proposal to extend the theory of lifeworld and system in the direction of institutions penetrating the subsystems—"political" and "economic" society, as it were—is exclusively from the point of view of the lifeworld. Unfortunately, the compatibility of such a scheme with system functioning is not thereby assured, even if the viability of steering performances is conceived as the limit beyond which democratization ought not, and actually cannot, go. It may be the case, for example, that introducing democratic processes into state and economy either will not limit them in any significant way or will do so only at the cost of seriously damaging self-regulation. At issue, then, is the possibility of postregulatory regulation from a systems point of view.

Lifeworld

Lifeworld Institutions–Civil Society

Political and Economic Society
(political and economic institutions of mediation)

Political and Economic Steering Mechanisms

---

figure 3

Just this issue is addressed by legal scholars who seek to extend the theory of autopoietic systems in a social-critical direction. While sympathetic to the idea of promoting "law as institution," G. Teubner considers a strategy focusing on the defense of the lifeworld insufficient.[135] As the crisis of the welfare state shows, media-steered subsystems can themselves suffer from overregulation, and overregulation could prove harmful to the legal medium used for regulation. The idea of law as institution, guaranteeing the autonomy of a given sphere, indicates the necessary but not the sufficient condition for a new, more successful form of subsystem regulation. In particular, Teubner notes the dangers to the social environment of unregulated political and economic subsystems, dangers that can be defused only if their autonomy is channeled by a form of self-regulation that implies self-limitation.[136]

Following Luhmann, this argument insists on the impossibility of steering society from a single center of control without regressive dedifferentiation, mainly because of the absence of adequate knowledge about subsystems outside of these.[137] The only alternative is to rely on the self-regulation of subsystems, or rather to legally regulate processes of self-regulation. The aim of this regulation of self-regulation is to promote forms of reflexivity that produce self-limitation in order to counter both negative side effects and internal contradictions in steering.

Interestingly, the new form of indirect legal regulation that promotes reflexivity in subsystems is said to actualize the reflexive structure of law itself. Law can take account of its own limits in regulating subsystems to the extent that a new, more abstract, less direct, indeed self-limiting form of regulatory law guided by social purposes but preserving the autonomy of the regulated social spheres comes into being. In the former respect, reflexive law is like substantive, interventionist law; in the latter respect, however, it resembles formal law.

Today, the program of reflexive law seems to be just a program, albeit a highly ingenious one. Its potential is indicated, however, by existing legal forms and practices that now seem to represent inconsistent elements within formal, or especially substantive, systems of law. Reflexive law restores the rule of law as opposed to political discretion by relying on what Habermas calls "external constitution," which restricts direct intervention to the enforcement of a limited number of predefined general legal principles whenever these are violated.[138] But reflexive law, unlike law as institution, cannot stop with this dimension. Instead of directly insisting on and enforcing particular goals to be achieved in a regulated area, reflexive law tries to establish norms of procedure, organization, membership, and competence that can alter decision making, change the weights of different parties and members, and make overall processes of decision sensitive to side effects and externalities.[139] Common to all of these devices is the desire to achieve new effects through an alteration of procedures, that is, through procedural rather than formal or substantive law.[140]

According to Teubner, collective bargaining and codetermination are examples of reflexivity in existing labor law.[141] His goal is to generalize their lesson through a program of introducing constitutional principles into economic and administrative institutions. Speaking generally, this program, derived from the earlier writings of Habermas (among other sources), corresponds to the project of democratization argued for in this book. Unlike the early Habermas, though, Teubner gives a new sense to democratization in relation to the subsystems. The aim is not to increase participation as an end in itself, nor should the results be judged by this standard. Instead, reflexive law aims at a level and a specific type of participation that would make institutions "sensitive to the outside effects of their internal attempts to maximize internal rationality."[142] It is because of this self-limitation of the participatory project that reflexive law has a chance to mediate the requirements of two types of rationality, practical and functional.

It is important to stress that the establishment of sensors in the subsystems in terms of discursive forms must be compatible with internal rationality. In the case of the economic system, for example, the establishment of new decision-making procedures must observe the limits of economic rationality—profitability, in particular—by producing profit and investment levels within the range of functionally equivalent organizational solutions. Teubner's confidence that this is possible in principle is based on the assumption that, if unregulated and unlimited, the pursuit of internal rationality is itself paradoxical from the organizations' own point of view. The pursuit of profit, as the leaders of an organization may define it, is often incompatible with long-term investment and accumulation goals. Similarly, in the case of the political system, the function of producing binding decisions and the performance aspect of generating and preserving power enter into conflict because the almost unavoidable tendency toward overextending political decision making tends to dissipate power. Reflexivity leading to self-limitation helps to reconcile these two dimensions.[143] In summary, then, reflexive law aims at establishing organizational structures geared to optimal balancing of performance and function by taking into account the requirements of the external environment.[144]

There is a certain asymmetry in this analysis between the political and other subsystems. Since the reflexive self-limitation of all subsystems is insisted on, the political system cannot be an exception. If Teubner does not thematize the relevant features of constitutional law that make possible the self-limitation of the political and its self-regulation in terms of external social needs (rights, discursive forms of procedure), this may be because the problem of the welfare state, which dominates the discussion of reflexive law, seems to put the primary focus on economic regulation and self-regulation. Yet it is an open question to what extent existing procedures in political systems fashioned in liberal or welfare states have already institutionalized the proper level of reflexivity. This is important because politics can promote reflexive self-control in the economy only by reflexively controlling itself. This formulation, however, already indicates the asymmetry we have in mind: Political power seems to remain a source of external pressure indispensable for the self-regulation of other systems, even if this power is to be treated more "economically" here than in systems of substantive-purposive law.[145]

The privileged position of politics is understandable but does raise some questions. The problem is not that the political system is a source of compulsion but that its special position seems to imply some coordinating role for its definition of the common needs and interests that are to be protected through the various forms of self-regulation. The only difference between instrumentalist and postregulatory regulation would then be that the political system in the latter case would have learned that regulation is more successful if it tries to stimulate self-regulation. Teubner tends to avoid this implication by denormatizing and decentering his argument. He notes, for example, that the generalization of the perspective of law as institution to that of reflexive law tends to leave behind Habermas's normative concerns, which are rooted in the lifeworld.[146] The lifeworld, moreover, is not replaced in Teubner's argument as the central point of reference; the relevant subsystems are to be fully decentralized and totally disconnected.

This strategy is paradoxical for two reasons. First, Teubner seems to indicate that self-regulation takes the form of decentralized moral self-control.[147] Second, in a "neo-Habermasian" vein, he posits (though not consistently for all areas of law) that reflexivity in subsystems is possible only through the establishment of discursive structures.[148] It seems, however, that Teubner can make no argument from a consistent systems-theoretic point of view concerning the source of the relevant morality or the universal potential of any of the partial discourses that establish reflexivity. The requirement of reconciling function, performance, and side effects does not in itself lead to an organizational procedure compatible with universal norms, or even compatibility among the functionings of different subsystems. In short, there is no guarantee that the discursive structures institutionalized in the various subsystems would actually be sensitive to environmental problems that might appear to them or to expert management as mere noise.

H. Willke's formulation of the program of reflexive law ("relational programs") addresses these deficiencies by breaking in part with the systems-theoretic framework. While he notes that law cannot come about without "legislative guidance," his emphasis displaces the state on two levels. Like Teubner, he insists that external regulation, in the form of "legislative self-restraint," must be restricted to highly indirect stimulation of self-regulation through the establishment of procedures capable of reflexive self-limitation. The state is thus dependent on using and activating the power to process information and solve the problems of relevant actors. Furthermore, more clearly than Teubner, Willke asserts that the state, itself a subsystem, cannot authoritatively set goals and purposes for the various forms of self-regulation. This problem is especially serious from the point of view of coordinating the forms of self-regulation of the different subsystems, which is Willke's primary concern. He proposes a model that breaks not only with that of Teubner but with the whole monistic paradigm of autopoietic systems. Drawing this time on somewhat later works of Habermas (especially the 1973 *Legitimationsprobleme*), he proposes a discursive framework outside all regulated systems in which "representatives of centrally affected interests are procedurally guided towards finding their common cause, their 'common sense,' their 'generalizable interests.'"[149] Whereas Teubner identifies the forms of procedural self-regulation *in* subsystems with the establishment of discursive structures and sees no role (and probably no time!) for a metasystemic discursive process, Willke does exactly the reverse. He does not identify the empirical "discourses" to be established within the subsystems in the counterfactual terms of a discourse ethics, but hopes to institutionalize the latter in a communication-theoretic supplement to the systems-theoretic framework.[150]

From a lifeworld perspective, the superiority of this version of the model of reflexive law is obvious. The alternative model, based on a consistent theory of autopoietic systems, must either assume a miraculous coordination of regulated self-regulation[151] or propose that one subsystem remain its central vantage point. In the latter case, however, it becomes difficult to thematize the possibility that this subsystem (politics or law, for example) or its medium can be self-limited in exactly the same sense as the regulated subsystems. What, for example, would be the source of the necessary external regulation? The dualistic conception that Willke implicitly adopts has the makings of a more convincing solution. The lifeworld, because of its lower level of complexity, can affect the subsystems only indirectly, with a far softer compulsion. Its superior normative position cannot develop into a superior control position—the danger with state regulation.[152]

Here it is worth considering the difference between the mechanisms of influence and those of money and power. The differences are obvious even in Parsons, who tried to treat influence as a medium.[153] Habermas is right to insist on making this difference between strategic and consensual sources of motivation a difference in principle.[154] Unlike money or power, influence acts on the intentions rather than the situation of other actors, offering the normative value of a desired action (rather than a positive or negative sanction) as its own reward. The actors in the case of influence are oriented not to success or to general consequences but to reaching an understanding with one another. Relying on persuasion in principle, the "intrinsic persuaders" behind influence are arguments (reasons and justifications) rather than facts or items of information. The type of pressure involved is thus on an entirely different level than in the case of power. This is the case even when influence cannot rely on actual, detailed processes of ordinary language communication because of time and space constraints. Both Parsons and Habermas call our attention to the possibility of generalizing influence as a medium or a quasi-medium. Habermas is right to insist, however, that this possibility does not lead to a reification of the lifeworld. Stressing the linkage of influence detached from actual argumentation to the resources of personality and culture, he attaches the potential for influence to persons and institutions capable of disposing the cultural resources of normative, cognitive, and aesthetic argumentation. Somewhat more useful for our purposes is Parsons's insistence on his central category of integration through associations, according to which the generalization of influence is based on a background of diffuse solidarity that depends on and at the same time reinforces the constitution of a collective identity.[155] Influential persons can influence only those with whom they constitute a "we," in the sense of people who belong together by virtue of common opinions, norms, or forms of participation—all possible bases of group formation and solidarity. Having influence is thus not restricted to members of cultural elites. Those who articulate the opinions and projects of groups and associations can also be influential, but they can influence through arguments only those who are open to being influenced.

Our use of the category of influence is meant to indicate that the theory we are outlining is sensitive to the concerns of both Teubner and Willke. We agree with Willke that the problem of setting goals and purposes cannot be solved within a systems-theoretic framework and that only the idea of institutionalizing discourse can help us in this context. The category of influence then indicates the type of pressure institutionalized discourses can exert on subsystems without damaging their self-regulation. But we also agree with Teubner's implicit argument that the idea of the one central discursive public sphere cannot be revived to solve the problem of coordination among subsystems. We agree, moreover, because of the scarcity of time and information among other reasons, that discourses, involving more restricted forms of participation, must be established as parts of the self-regulatory procedures of the subsystems themselves. Moreover, we believe that, without such sensors in the economy and the state, the discursive processes outside of them cannot influence the subsystems at all. In this sense, the point of discursive forms in the subsystems is not to increase participation per se but to constitute structures of sensitivity to the results of participation. It is therefore important that the plurality of democracies be articulated in terms of both types of discursive forms, in institutions linked to the subsystems and in the institutions of civil society.[156]

Another Glance to the East

Is our reconstruction of the category of civil society, and the politics of civil society derived from it, relevant only to late capitalist welfare states, as the ideas of the reflexive continuation of the welfare state and reflexive law seem to suggest? This would be paradoxical since the world-historical impetus to revive the category, in theory and action, comes first and foremost from the state-socialist countries. Indeed, the more common suspicion (of Timothy Garton-Ash for example) is that the politics of civil society is irrelevant to the politics of the contemporary West. With a little lack of phronesis, one might reduce this point to absurdity by adding that, now that the East is about to "join the West," the category of civil society and all politics of self-limitation will be everywhere irrelevant.[157]

It helps in this context to distinguish between constituent and constituted phases of the creation of free institutions, corresponding to Alain Touraine's distinction between historical and social movements.[158] The reconstitution of civil society is a hallmark of the great transition process we have witnessed from the rise of Solidarity to the present, including today's projects of democratization in the Soviet Union. The dramatic forms of self-limitation and self-discipline that distinguish primarily democratic from primarily national movements are rooted in learning experiences whose loci are the publics, associations, and cultural norms of civil society.

In the constitutive phase, the process of transition can be centered in civil society (Poland) or political society (Hungary). It is important not to see this as an either/or proposition. Aside from a dualistic defensive phase, no transition can be completed without at least a partial turn to political society, as signified, for example, by the ubiquity of round-table negotiations everywhere in the East. Even a process of evident collapse of the ruling regime requires alternative political actors, which could come from the transformation of movements into political actors (Civic Forum) or from external sources (as in the movement of West German government parties into the GDR). But without the participation of civil society, whether in a highly mobilized noninstitutional form (as in the GDR) or in a more institutionalized form (as in the case of the Hungarian referendum of November 1989), the process must fall back on elite democratic transitions from above, which would seriously endanger the legitimacy of the whole process.[159]

The situation is somewhat different with respect to the relations between economic and civil society. Neoliberals tend to identify, even for the process of transition, the liberation of the economic and the civil. This is less harmful if actors behind the dynamism of the process are civil rather than political, since the necessary project of liberating the economy in this case must occur side by side with the self-organization of noneconomic domains. That this is possible, that democratic actors are compatible with the establishment of markets, is shown by the first phase of Polish economic restructuring. But these actors will not be able to accept liberal economic policy as anything but transitional, since a fully automatic market would become destructive for the social fabric, for social solidarity. Karl Polànyi's lesson should not be forgotten, particularly in his native country, and indeed the actors of civil society will certainly relearn it.

When political actors are in charge, however, the possibility persists that elites will seek to limit the reconstruction of civil society to the dimension of a suitable environment for market economic self-regulation, given that the creation of such an environment will be a serious problem for a period well beyond the political transition. While this program of "minimal civil society" has already failed in the form of "reform dictatorship," it may remain an option for some time to come in its elite democratic form.

It is in this context that our proposal for reconstructing the politics of civil society as a reflexive continuation of both the democratic revolution and the welfare state becomes important for East and West, especially for actors hoping to save something of "the spirit" of the democratic transition.[160] Our first thesis is that the political culture needed to sustain the new democracies and to avoid destructive cycles between authoritarianism and populism cannot be developed without institutionalizing civil society in the widest possible sense. This institutionalization belongs to the constituent phase and requires conscious institution building even where social mobilizations played a major role in the transitions.

Our second thesis is derived from our normatively based analysis of the politics of civil society in the West and refers to the "constituted" phase of the new democracies. The civil society needed to reproduce democratic political culture can be developed and defended only through a double process of limiting the colonizing tendencies of the administrative state and market economy and establishing new forms of social control over these subsystems. We admit the necessity of first building differentiated subsystems: an expert administration and a self-regulating market economy. In this sense, there is no substitute for establishing an economic system of hard budgetary constraints based on free prices, demonopolization, and abolishing the paternalistic patronage system of subsidies and bargaining.[161] But raising a liberal transitional program to the status of a long-term model can have negative economic consequences, such as the destruction of potentially productive along with inefficient forms of enterprise, and also dramatically negative social consequences. While resource-constrained economies of the Soviet type are far more destructive of the environment than market economies, radical market-oriented strategies offer no cure for devastated environments. While paternalism in its state-socialist form has led to the collapse of welfare and social protections, it will take more than the magic of the marketplace to restore the living minimum for marginalized segments of the population. Finally, while only democratic movements and actors can today legitimately institute market economies that, initially at least, ask for great sacrifices from those who have been victims of the last phase of state socialism, their legitimacy can be maintained only if their goals include tangible economic improvements and political trade-offs that the combination of liberal economy and elite democracy cannot provide. Those who push this latter combination for the long term run the risk of social conflict and, as we know from Latin American experience, a destructive cycle between populism and authoritarianism.

Unfortunately, the creation of a Western-type welfare state is not an option either, except perhaps for the special case of East Germany. Such a strategy could reinforce existing forms of paternalism and soft budgetary constraints in the period of transition (which could be an extended one in the area of economic life); moreover, it is unclear on what financial basis today's bankrupt state-socialist or tomorrow's dependent capitalist economies might finance such arrangements when they are increasingly unaffordable in the West itself. Still, we cannot accept Kornai's claim that even those who want to establish mixed capitalist economies today must for an extended period promote yesterday's unregulated version.[162] First, there is no guarantee that a classical liberal economic system will lead to a welfare state of the traditional type. Second, it is not at all certain that it will actually work, in either the economic or the social and political sense, as a model of development. Instead of copying solutions from the West's past or present, the new democracies would do well to understand the reasons why both liberal and welfare-state models are experiencing new problems today. This does not mean that one should look for a mythical third way between capitalism and socialism, West and East, in the manner of either market socialism or the various neopopulisms. If there are any solutions here, they lie in the experience of the West, pointing not to the West's past or present but to its future. To join the West, in other words, should not mean the West as it was, or even is, but as it should and could become in response to present challenges.

Our analysis of the politics of civil society focuses, however tentatively, on at least one possible future of the West. Its combination of differentiated subsystems and a well-defended civil society, in which the latter is to have primacy, involves neither the economic costs nor the social side effects of the models involving social domination of one or the other subsystem, which have been hitherto prevalent in modern European history. It promises both economic self-regulation and the removal of important spheres of life from the economy, and it poses the question of how this self-regulation might be regulated without statism and paternalism. The politics of the influence of civil on economic and political society moves to the fore here. Despite its programmatic nature and utopian elements, this proposal may represent a more realistic path of reconstruction in the West and the East than the well-known and well-tried programs that have shown their underside elsewhere and will not simultaneously satisfy the criteria of efficiency and popular acceptance in today's more or less mobilized new democracies.

10

Social Movements and Civil Society

It is our thesis that social movements constitute the dynamic element in processes that might realize the positive potentials of modern civil societies. We also hold that our reconstructed theory of civil society is indispensable to an adequate understanding of the logic, stakes, and potentials of contemporary social movements. As indicated in chapter 1, the theme of the self-defense of "society against the state" (and the unregulated capitalist market economy) has been raised by a number of contemporary collective actors struggling for an autonomous and democratic civil society. We have also demonstrated the continuing relevance of the key categories of modern civil society and the two-dimensional character of its core institutions. What remains to be shown are (1) the systematic relation between the potentials of an already (albeit incompletely) modern civil society and the projects of contempo-rary collective actors and (2) the importance of our reconstruction of the categories of civil society in terms of the system/lifeworld distinction for an (admittedly partisan) interpretation of these projects. We address the first issue by demonstrating the centrality of the key features of modern civil society to the two main theoretical paradigms in the study of social movements. Using the example of the feminist movement, we then try to show that the dualistic strategy of contemporary movements aimed at political and societal democratization can be best understood in light of the structural analysis of contemporary civil society outlined in chapter 9.

New Theoretical Paradigms and Contemporary Social Movements

The term "new social movements" has gained wide currency among theorists sympathetic to the peace, feminist, ecology, and local-autonomy movements that have proliferated in the West since the mid-1970s. But it remains unclear whether there really is something significantly new about these movements and what the theoretical or political import of the innovations is. Indeed, there is little agreement among theorists as to just what a movement is, what would qualify as a new type of movement, and what the meaning of a *social* movement as distinct from a political party or interest group might be.

We have taken up many of these issues elsewhere.[1] What concerns us here is neither the definition nor the "newness" of social movements per se, but rather the relation between contemporary collective action and civil society. We shall approach this topic by looking at the way it is addressed in the two competing paradigms in the field: the "resource-mobilization" paradigm and the "identity-oriented" paradigm.[2] Each approach involves a theoretical framework that excludes the main focus of the other. We shall try to show that the approaches are not necessarily incompatible, in part because both rely on key features of modern civil society to pinpoint what is specific to modern social movements. Neither paradigm directly addresses the theoretical import of the odyssey of civil society for the emergence and transformation of modern movements, but a look at the analyses developed within each perspective reveals the centrality of the concept of civil society to each of them.

Our presupposition is that the contemporary movements are in some significant respects "new." What we have in mind, above all, is a self-understanding that abandons revolutionary dreams in favor of radical reform that is not necessarily and primarily oriented to the state. We shall label as "self-limiting radicalism" projects for the defense and democratization of civil society that accept structural differentiation and acknowledge the integrity of political and economic systems. We do not believe that it is possible to justify this claim about what is new in movements on the basis of a philosophy of history that links the "true essence" of what the movements "really are" (however heterogeneous their practices and forms of consciousness) to an allegedly new stage of history (postindustrial society). Nor does the theme "society against the state," which is shared by all contemporary movements (including some on the right), in itself imply something new in the sense of a radical break with the past. On the contrary, it implies continuity with what is worth preserving (even if this is hotly contested) in the institutions, norms, and political cultures of contemporary civil societies. The question, then, is whether and in what way this theme has been connected to new identities, forms of organization, and scenarios of conflict.

There are two possible ways to answer these questions. One involves a hermeneutic approach to the self-understanding of contemporary collective actors vis-à-vis their identity, goals, targets, and strategies.[3] But the interrogation of the identity of contemporary movements based on interpretations of theoretical forms of self-expression should not be methodologically absolutized. In particular, confronting this method with systematic social science should be quite fruitful. It will be important, for example, when judging the contribution of competing social-scientific paradigms, to determine the extent to which each is capable of accounting for the experiences articulated by theories for and within movements. If we are to avoid the objectivist fallacy that defines "truth" as the sole possession of the system of science, we shall have to insist on learning not only about but also from movements. But we must also take care to avoid the hermeneuticist fallacy. The hermeneutic inquiry must be complemented by an approach that involves taking the point of view of the observer rather than that of the participants. This will enable us to assess the ways in which the context and transformations of civil society are related to the appearance and logic of collective action. Here, a different analytic level is involved— that of objectivating social science. Theories of contemporary movements must thus pose the following questions: In what societal types do the movements occur? What continuities or discontinuities exist with respect to the past? Which institutions are at issue? What are the general political stakes of the conflicts? And what are the developmental possibilities available to collective actors? We shall show that the categories of civil society provide clues to answers in both paradigms. They also structure the "classical" approach to the study of social movements against which the newer paradigms explicitly distinguish themselves. We shall summarize this approach in order to highlight the changes in assessing the interrelation between civil society and social movements that serves as the starting point of both contemporary paradigms.

The classical theoretical paradigm, dominant until the early 1970s, was the social-psychology tradition of the Chicago school.[4] The variants that have received the most attention and criticism from contemporary theorists have been mass-society theories (Kornhauser, Arendt, etc.) and Smelser's structural-functionalist model of collective behavior.[5] There are important differences among these versions of collective-behavior theory, but they all share the following assumptions:

1. There are two distinct kinds of action: institutional-conventional and noninstitutional-collective.

2. Noninstitutional-collective action is action that is not guided by existing social norms but is formed to meet undefined or unstructured situations.

3. These situations are understood in terms of a breakdown, due to structural changes, either in the organs of social control or in the adequacy of normative integration.

4. The resulting strains, discontent, frustration, and aggression lead individuals to participate in collective behavior.

5. Noninstitutional-collective behavior follows a "life cycle," open to causal analysis, that moves from spontaneous crowd action to the formation of publics and social movements.

6. The emergence and growth of movements within this cycle occurs through crude processes of communication: contagion, rumor, circular reaction, diffusion, etc.

Collective-behavior theorists have focused on explaining individual participation in social movements, looking at grievances and values as responses to rapid social change (strain) and social disorganization. Of course, not every theorist in this tradition deems collective behavior to be an abnormal or irrational response of unconnected individuals to change. Nevertheless, they all view the *crowd* as the simplest atom in the anatomy of collective behavior. All collective-behavior theorists stress psychological reactions to breakdown, crude modes of communication, and volatile goals. This indicates an implicit bias toward regarding collective behavior as a nonrational or irrational response to change. It is this bias, most explicit in the mass-society and Smelserian approaches, that has triggered the criticism of contemporary theorists. It is also this bias that precludes any examination of the relation between collective action and the modernization of civil society, for it presupposes from the outset that collective action derives from the breakdown (normative and institutional) of civil society.

The inadequacies of the classical tradition became obvious in the 1960s and 1970s when large-scale social movements emerged in the United States and Europe. The development of movements in polities characterized by pluralists as democratic and in civil societies with a multiplicity of voluntary associations and vital public and private spheres belied the mass-society version of the collective-behavior paradigm. So, too, did the fact that actors in the New Left, civil rights, and feminist movements hardly conformed to the image of anomic, fragmented, irrational deviants. Nor was the Smelserian model (structural strain/generalized belief/short circuiting) adequate to explain the timing, cognitive character, organizational forms, conduct, or goals of movement actors. The movements of the 1960s and 1970s were not responses to economic crises or normative breakdown. They involved concrete goals, clearly articulated general values and interests, and rational calculations of strategies. Clearly, they required a new theoretical approach. In the United States, the response was the "resource-mobilization" paradigm; in Western Europe, it was the "new social movements" paradigm.

Despite crucial differences, both paradigms assume that social movements are based on conflicts between organized groups with autonomous associations and sophisticated forms of communication (networks, publics). Both argue that conflictual collective action is normal and that participants are usually rational, well-integrated members of organizations. In short, collective action involves forms of association and strategies specific to the context of a modern pluralist civil society. This context includes public spaces, social institutions (mass media, the press), rights (to associate, to speak, to assemble), representative political institutions, and an autonomous legal system, all of which are targets for social movements seeking to influence policy or initiate change. Both approaches also distinguish between two levels of collective action: the manifest dimension of large-scale mobilizations (strikes, rallies, demonstrations, sit-ins, boycotts) and the less visible, latent level of forms of organization and communication among groups that account for the everyday life and continuity of actor participation. It is the insistence of these approaches on the prior organization of social actors and on the *rationality* of collective conflict that directly challenges the classical theories of social movements, for it implies that characteristics previously deemed unique to "conventional" collective action are true for nonconventional forms of collective behavior as well. In other words, it is civil society, with its intermediary and autonomous associations so dear to the pluralists, and not their nightmare image of mass society that forms the terrain on which the anathematized social movements appear!

The Resource-Mobilization Paradigm

Resource-mobilization theorists began by rejecting the emphasis on feelings and grievances, the use of psychologizing categories, and the focus on breakdown characteristic of the collective-behavior approach. Moreover, they marshaled a wealth of empirical evidence to disprove the notion that unconnected individuals, motivated by social strain, are the main actors in social movements.[6] Most significant from their own point of view, resource-mobilization theorists demonstrated that sophisticated organizational forms and modes of communication going well beyond the crude mechanisms described in the classical literature are needed to mobilize collective action.

Drawing on the work of economists (Olson), political scientists (Salisbury), and historians (Rudé, Hobsbawm, Soboul, Wolff), resource-mobilization theorists stress such "objective" variables as organization, interests, resources, opportunities, and strategies to account for large-scale mobilizations. These variables are addressed from the standpoint of a neoutilitarian logic imputed to collective actors. The "rational actor" (individual and group), employing strategic and instrumental reasoning, replaces the crowd as the central referent for the analysis of collective action. Of course, there are different orientations within this paradigm, ranging from the strictly individualist, utilitarian logic of the pure rational-actor approaches pioneered by Olson to the organizational-entrepre-neurial approach of McCarthy and Zald and the political-process model of the Tillys, Oberschall, Gamson, Klandermans, and Tarrow.[7] Most of the latter group relax the strict individualist calculus of interest typical of Olson by positing solidary groups with collective interests as the protagonists of collective action. Despite their differences, all versions of the resource-mobilization approach analyze collective action in terms of the logic of strategic interaction and cost-benefit calculations.[8]

Resource-mobilization theorists share the following assumptions:

1. Social movements must be understood in terms of a conflict theory of collective action.

2. There is no fundamental difference between institutional and noninstitutional collective action.

3. Both entail conflicts of interest built into institutionalized power relations.

4. Collective action involves the rational pursuit of interests by groups.

5. Goals and grievances are permanent products of power relations and cannot account for the formation of movements.

6. Movements form because of changes in resources, organization, and opportunities for collective action.

7. Success involves the recognition of the group as a political actor or increased material benefits.

8.Mobilization involves large-scale, special-purpose, bureaucratic, formal organizations.[9]

Organization and rationality are the catchwords of this approach. Analysis does not proceed from a hermeneutic relation to the ideology or self-understanding of collective actors. Of course, from a hermeneutic standpoint, it might be retorted that the point of view of the analysis does approximate that of a movement organizer concerned with the imperatives of mobilization, but it is fairer to say that what dominates here is an observer's overview of the political environment that could be useful to organizers.

Nevertheless, we find it striking that references to "still viable or partially viable communities" or "associational groups organized for purposes other than opposition" (Oberschall), to the existence of "collective interests" (Tilly), "social incentives" (Fireman, Gamson), or "conscience constituencies" who donate resources (McCarthy, Zald) abound in the literature, implying cognizance of the "civil" rather than "mass" societal basis of rational, organized, modern collective action.[10] What remains problematic in the whole approach is giving an adequate account of the organizational forms it presupposes. Such an account would require exploration of the social and political terrain that forms the condition of possibility for the emergence and success of modern movements.

Charles Tilly's reconstruction of the impact of the shift from local to national structures of power on organizational forms and types of collective action takes an important step in this direction. Moreover, his version of modernization theory describes the emergence of the action repertoire and the types of associations presupposed by resource-mobilization theory. Thus, his comparative-historical analysis both situates and transcends his framework, and many of his most significant findings regarding new forms of group life have implications for the development of key dimensions of civil society that are not reducible to the analytic categories of his resource-mobilization approach.[11] Nor does he offer adequate means to account for the new forms of organization or the projects of those contemporary movements that do not simply target the economy or the state for inclusion and material benefits. Indeed, the limit to Tilly's corrective to the resource-mobilization model is that it allows civil society (differentiated from the state and the economy) to appear as the terrain but not the target of collective action. Nonetheless, because it makes the strongest case for the importance of civil society to the understanding of modern movements, it is worth examining Tilly's model more closely.

Despite his explicit polemic against the Smelserian and Durkheimian versions of the "breakdown" model of collective behavior, Tilly retains the thesis that large-scale structural change ("modernization") affects collective action.[12] He disproves standard breakdown theories by showing that the timing and pace of urbanization and industrialization do not govern the tempo of collective action and that it is not possible to link hardship, anomie, crises, and conflict directly. But his analysis of structural change does not challenge the fact of differentiation in the transition from "community" to "society." Instead, he shows how economic transformation, urbanization, and state making produce a long-term shift in the character and personnel of collective action. These processes (along with the development of the mass media) facilitate the emergence of new types of mobilizations and organizations while undermining others. What is new in Tilly's version of modernization theory is the linkage between a specific action repertoire and structural changes that have an impact on the everyday life of the relevant actors: "The reorganization of everyday life transformed the character of conflict . . . long-run reshaping of *solidarities*, rather than the immediate production of stress and strain, constituted the most important impact of structural change on political conflict."[13]

Through analysis of the changes in the daily routines of populations—their locus and mode of work, the structure of life in neighborhoods, population shifts from countryside to city, and changes in the sites of power—Tilly shows how the action repertoires developed by collective actors interrelate with their forms of association and why new forms emerge. The long-term development involves the replacement of communal solidarities by voluntary associations. This entails a shift of collective action away from routine assemblies by communal groups and local markets, festivals, and officially sanctioned gatherings toward deliberately called meetings by formally organized groups.[14] The major forms of collective action thus change: The food riots, tax rebellions, and appeals to paternalistic authorities typical of the "eighteenth-century action repertoire" are replaced by the demonstrations and strikes typical of the "nineteenth-century action repertoire."

Tilly's analytic categories of types of collective action capture this overall shift. The eighteenth-century action repertoire involves "competitive" and "reactive" claims. The former entails conflict among existing communal groups on the local level over resources claimed by rivals. "Reactive" collective action involves communal groups threatened by efforts of state makers to gain control over the general population and its resources. It also involves resistance to the growth of the national market and insistence on the priority of local needs and traditions. In this case, a group reacts to the claims of another group over a resource currently under its control. In both cases, collective action is carried out by preexisting solidary communities. It involves richly symbolic and expressive action, admirably described by Tilly despite his overall stress on the strategic rationality even of these types of conflicts.[15]

"Proactive" collective actions, on the other hand, assert group claims to power, privileges, or resources that have not previously existed. Here, attempts to control rather than resist elements of national structures lead to the formation of complex special-purpose organizations in place of communal groups.

The types of mobilization that correspond to the latter two types of claims are "defensive" and "offensive," respectively. Reactive struggles involve defensive mobilizations in the face of a threat from the outside. Clearly, what is at stake is the defense of a traditional, communally structured lifeworld against "modernization." The offensive mobilizations typical of proactive claimants involve a pooling of resources for the sake of recognition or a larger share of power.

Tilly continually warns against viewing competitive, reactive, and proactive collective actions as stages in an evolutionary process. Moreover, he argues that elements of an action repertoire can be used to make a variety of claims: A demonstration is not by definition proactive or offensive. Nevertheless, he traces a long-term shift, with the first two dominating until the midnineteenth century and the third dominating thereafter. The shift occurred because the "big structures" won control over the resources formerly wielded by households, communities, and other small groups. In addition, urbanization and the mass media reduced the costs of large-scale mobilization for formally organized associations. The new loci of power and the new structures of everyday life fostered the selection of a new action repertoire and the emergence of new associational forms. Social conflict increasingly took the form of proactive, offensive struggles for inclusion in the structures that control national-level resources. Last but hardly least, the development of mass electoral politics created an environment amenable to voluntary association and large-scale mobilization.

Indeed, Tilly argues that the growth of elections and the beginning of popular participation in national politics promoted the spread of the demonstration as a key form of collective action, because it involved a legal umbrella that could be extended to more and more groups and types of gatherings: "The grant of legality to an electoral association or an electoral assembly provides a claim to legality for associations and assemblies that are not quite electoral, not *only* electoral, or not *now* electoral."[16] The rights to organize, recruit, speak publicly, assemble, solicit, publicize, and demonstrate (the key institutional components of modern civil society) are, of course, essential to a multiparty system operating in a context of universal suffrage. The presence of elites with a strong interest in a broad definition of acceptable political activity makes it hard, over time, for governments to withhold these rights from other social actors. Electoral politics thus offers an incentive to social actors to select the demonstration, public meeting, and strike as modes of collective action, since "those groups are more successful, on the whole, which can produce the highest multiple of numbers, commitment, and articulation of claims."[17]

This means that *civil society* has become the indispensable terrain on which social actors assemble, organize, and mobilize, even if their targets are the economy and the state. Tilly's work thus challenges the conclusions of Foucault, who holds that all means of achieving effective, autonomous solidarity have been abolished by the "individualizing" and "normalizing" techniques ushered in with modern forms of power. Tilly does show that the communal solidarities of the famous intermediary bodies of the ancien régime, along with the sites and types of contentious gatherings specific to the structures of everyday life in "premodern" (eighteenth-century) conditions, did eventually disappear. But his point is that they were replaced by new forms of solidarity, association, power resources, and modes of conflict on the terrain of modern civil society. Indeed, Tilly views these forms of organization and protest as *more autonomous* than the "spontaneous" gatherings typical of the eighteenth-century action repertoire so lovingly described by Foucault!

From our point of view, Tilly's work shows that modern collective action presupposes the development of autonomous social and political spaces within civil and political society that are guaranteed by rights and supported by the democratic political culture underlying "formal" representative political institutions. But he stresses primarily the political opportunities and strategic implications these have for the emergence of the nineteenth-century action repertoire. In short, he looks only at those dimensions of these processes that are relevant for the mobilization of organized groups competing for power. Tilly's historical work does imply that the transformation of the loci of power and the corresponding changes in form of collective action presuppose the creation of new meanings, new organizations, new identities, and a social space (namely, civil society) in which these can appear. But the resource-mobilization perspective he embraces leads him to treat the latter merely as obvious preconditions for effective collective action. The combined polity and mobilization models[18] focus attention on the interplay of repression/facilitation, power, and opportunity/threat on one side, and interests, organization, and the mobilization of capacities on the other. It is presupposed that collective action involves costs and brings benefits in the form of collective goods (including inclusion). The struggle is construed as between members and contenders for inclusion in the polity (access to power) and the material rewards this can bring. In short, social conflicts in and over institutions of civil society and the form of the political public sphere are viewed from only one side—as defensive or offensive reactions to changing power relations.

There are several drawbacks to this narrow focus. First, it presupposes what has, with the transition from the communal to the associational basis of group identity, become problematic and needs to be explained. In other words, Tilly's own historical work suggests that the construction of group identity, the recognition of shared interests, and the creation of solidarity within and between groups can, with the emergence of modern civil society, no longer be treated as givens. These are achievements that have increasingly come to be treated as such by the actors involved in these processes. Increased self-reflection regarding the social construction of identity and reality involves learning along nonstrategic dimensions.

These questions become even more pressing if we consider those contemporary collective actors that do not simply target the state or the economy for inclusion or increased benefits and whose identities cannot be deduced from these subsystems. In short, Tilly's approach excludes the possibility of analyzing the "politics of identity" of contemporary collective actors.

Second, while Tilly provides tools for analyzing how the institutions of civil and political society offer a means for excluded and relatively powerless groups to exert pressure on those with power (and money) in order to gain entry into the polity, his focus on the goal of inclusion and on the acquisition of power leads him to obscure the implications of the "politics of influence" aimed at political society. Influence, as we have already seen, is a peculiar "medium" that is specifically suited to modern civil societies whose public spheres, rights, and representative democratic institutions are, in principle at least, open to discursive processes that inform, thematize, and potentially alter social norms and political cultures. It is possible for collective actors in civil society to exercise influence on actors in political society, to make use of public speech not only to gain power or money but to restrict the role of the media of power and money in the lifeworld in order to secure autonomy and to modernize (democratize and liberalize) the institutions and social relations of civil society. By implicitly collapsing "power" and "influence," Tilly is blinded to the logic of collective action that seeks to apply the principles of civil society to civil society itself and to realize them more fully within social institutions. It is our thesis that in contemporary social movements, a dualistic politics of identity and influence, aimed at both civil society and the polity (or political society), replaces the monist logic of collective action stressed by Tilly.

Moreover, Tilly has explicitly rejected the idea that changes in the tactics (sit-down strikes, mass picketing, sit-ins), issues (local autonomy, gender equality, ecology, right to a distinct life-style), or actors (prevalence of the new middle classes) engaged in contemporary collective action amount to a new action repertoire. "Looked at closely, however, almost all of these cases in point involve forms of action that already have their own histories."[19] Despite some innovation, contemporary collective actors continue to use the routines of meeting, demonstrating, striking, etc. To Tilly, then, although issues and alignments have changed, the fundamental fact is continuity—the means of action have remained the same. But do they have the same meaning? Are the demonstrations, meetings, etc., of the new movements really only proactive and offensive? Clearly, in the case of the new dimensions of the feminist, gay, ecology, peace, and local-autonomy movements, this is not so. And Tilly himself has argued that no action is in itself proactive or reactive, offensive or defensive. Indeed, contemporary movements combine features of both of Tilly's main types. They are often defensive and reactive but do not protect preexisting traditional communities from outside incursions. Rather, they defend spaces for the creation of new identities and solidarities and seek to make social relations within the institutions of civil society more egalitarian and democratic. While they are associationally organized, the associations are treated not as interest groups but as ends in themselves. Nor are the expanded public spaces, literary and media-based counterpublic spheres, forms of discursive conflict resolution, and democratic participation construed solely as means to the end of attaining increased material benefits or inclusion as an interest group in the access to and exercise of power. Finally, the new movements also have an "offensive" side, not only in the sense of struggles for inclusion and power in the polity but also insofar as they involve efforts to influence actors in political society to make policy and initiate reforms appropriate to new collective identities.

Many resource-mobilization theorists have recognized the unique aspects of contemporary movements. Indeed, the paradigm was initially elaborated by theorists involved in or directly affected by the New Left. These theorists explicitly addressed innovations in the organizations, mobilization processes, strategies, and targets of the movements of the 1960s and early 1970s.[20] According to one of the most significant analyses, these movements were new precisely to the extent that they were mobilized by "professional social movement organizations" or SMOs (outside rather than indigenous leaders), who carefully calculated and steered collective action to gain media coverage and public sympathy for movement goals and thereby influence elite conscience constituencies to provide funding and advocacy that would lead to the further professionalization (bureaucratization) of social discontent and success in the sense of ensuring the representation of the unrepresented through viable interest groups.[21] Clearly, the goal of this theory is to account for the possibility and success of collective action on the part of those excluded from direct representation within the political system by either parties or entrenched interest groups. The analysis of this particular strategy of influence on the part of professional SMOs shows that contemporary collective action does not simply involve direct power struggles between "contenders" and authorities. Instead, the decentralized, public, pluralist structure of civil society encourages efforts to influence sectors of public opinion, in this case the opinion of external "conscience constituencies," that is, social elites.

This analysis is quite convincing with respect to disorganized and powerless groups that would otherwise be unrepresented, such as children, the poor, or consumers. As with Tilly, however, the exclusive focus here on strategies to attain political representation and benefits leaves us with a one-sided understanding of the peculiar "power" of influence and obscures the distinction between social movements and interest groups. Movements are reduced to professional organizations that mobilize mass collective actions for political-instrumental reasons. On this analysis, collective actors could neither be mobilized nor be influential without money and power, and attaining influence amounts to the same thing as gaining money and power (and organizational resources). Yet the politics of influence is the recourse par excellence of those who are relatively powerless, political outsiders, and those without economic clout. Hence the importance of "professional SMOs." However convincing this logic may be in the abstract, in the case of McCarthy and Zald's theory it turns out that collapsing influence into the media of money and power has the unfortunate result that the dynamics and logic of the most significant contemporary social movements are misconstrued.

As Jenkins and Eckert, among others, demonstrate, the new social movements were indigenous challenges organized by local leaders who emerged from the "aggrieved" populations and drew on autonomous networks of local associations, grass-roots groups, social clubs, churches (for the civil rights movement), etc., to mobilize collective action.[22] They were organized into "classical SMOs," associations dependent on the volunteer labor of direct beneficiaries, employing innovative tactics that registered striking successes well before professionalization occurred. Their strategies aimed at influencing public opinion and thereby, indirectly, elites, not in order to gain patronage or, in the first instance, even political power, but to convince others of the justice of their cause.[23] Indeed, once professional SMOs became primary, as they did in the 1980s, they signaled (although they did not cause, *pace* Piven and Cloward) the decline of the cycle of protest and of the movement character of collective action. We are thus confirmed in our thesis that autonomous, voluntary, and indigenous associations within civil society using and expanding public discourse and public spaces for discourse are the *differentia specifica* of contemporary social movements.

Even when "success" is defined in the standard terms of resource-mobilization theory, as political inclusion of formerly excluded groups or as increased material benefits, it would be impossible to understand the successes of the civil rights movement if influence were confused with power and if the targets of influence were reduced to potential patrons or political adversaries. The sit-ins, boycotts, and freedom rides were aimed at influencing public opinion and thereby the courts (federal and Supreme) to enforce federal laws and to invalidate, as unconstitutional, local ordinances institutionalizing segregation. It was influence, not money or power, that was operative here. To be sure, the strategy of influence was also directed at persuading political elites in Congress to pass legislation. In the context of a favorable "political opportunity structure," these influence-oriented strategies of collective action led to the civil rights acts of 1964 and 1965 and the institutionalization of significant gains during the early 1970s.[24] These were all successes of indigenous organizing and a mass movement.[25]

Patronage and professionalization did indeed occur in the civil rights and other new movements, but this process did not initiate, control, quell, or coopt the movements. Rather, they played an important role in following up on their victories. "As the women's and environmental movements have demonstrated, litigation, close monitoring of government agencies, and professionalized lobbying can be quite effective if allied with an indigenous movement and if there is a clear statutory and administrative basis for implementation."[26] Moreover, the decline of the movements was due not to cooptation or professionalization, as some critics of McCarthy and Zald have claimed, but to movement successes and their internal logic of development, neither of which involved the transformation of goals and tactics in exchange for political incorporation.[27]

The analysis of Jenkins and Eckert must be taken as a corrective rather than an alternative to the resource-mobilization paradigm. While they demonstrate that successful collective action must now involve both indigenous mass movements (based on autonomous and local associations) and professional interest groups, they still define success as "bringing an excluded group into the polity." Although they expand the targets of influence to include not only political adversaries or potential patrons but also public opinion in general, there is still an overly strong political bias to the discussion that leads to a one-sided interpretation of contemporary movements. Accordingly, the dualistic character of contemporary collective action is recognized only with respect to organization (grass-roots associations plus interest groups); the ultimate target of these organizations and of collective action in general remains monistically construed. Full recognition and inclusion within the polity, and not the defense and transformation of civil society, is at issue on this interpretation. The goal of the civil rights movement, however, was not only acquiring civil rights but also modernizing civil society in the sense of undoing traditional structures of domination, exclusion, and inequality rooted in social institutions, norms, collective identities, and cultural values based on racial and class prejudice. And the feminist movement, to take another example, takes clear aim at patriarchal institutions in civil society and works for cultural and normative change as much as for political and economic power. Indeed, the pervasive concern on the part of all contemporary collective actors with autonomy, identity, discourses, social norms, and cultural significations remains unexplained by this theory.[28]

Resource-mobilization theory in general is limited by its focus on power to thematizing the strategic uses of influence. In other words, the approach focuses on the expansion of "political society" to include new actors or to increase the power of old ones. Certainly this is an important dimension of contemporary collective action, as is success defined in terms of inclusion in the polity and increased benefits. But this is hardly the whole story. A civil-society-oriented approach could highlight two additional dimensions of contemporary collective action: the politics of influence (of civil on political society) and the politics of identity (the focus on autonomy, identity, and the democratization of social relations outside the polity).

With these limits in mind, it would nonetheless be possible to apply some of the core concepts of the resource-mobilization approach to contemporary movements. Within the spirit of Tilly's work, we could ask whether a new twentieth-century action repertoire is in the making. We could attempt to correlate changes in the organizational forms, targets, and tactics of collective action (internal resource-mobilization concerns) with changes in the locus and technology of power, resources, and political opportunity ("external" polity model issues), alterations in the relations among state, economy, and society, and transformations in the experiences and structures of everyday life. In other words, the abstract elements of the resource-mobilization approach could be used to develop a theoretical account of changes recognized by everyone in aspects of contemporary collective actions. Tilly himself grants the legitimacy of such an inquiry.[29]

This inquiry, however, would need to transcend the narrow framework and focus of resource-mobilization theory. Contemporary collective actors consciously struggle over the power to construct new identities, to create democratic spaces within both civil society and the polity for autonomous social action, and to reinterpret norms and reshape institutions. It is therefore incumbent on the theorist to view civil society as the target as well as the terrain of collective action, to look into the processes by which collective actors create the identities and solidarities they defend, to assess the relations between social adversaries and the stakes of their conflicts, to analyze the politics of influence exercised by actors in civil society on those in political society, and to analyze the structural and cultural developments that contribute to the heightened self-reflection of actors.

The New Social Movements Paradigm

The new social movements paradigm purports to do all this. European theorists of contemporary movements turned to the dimension of social integration in collective action without, however, reproducing the Durkheimian thrust of the breakdown thesis or Smelserian models of collective behavior. These theorists are also aware of the inadequacies of Marxist analyses of social movements, despite their sympathy with those dimensions of neo-Marxism that stress the importance of consciousness, ideology, social struggle, and solidarity to collective action. These "post-Marxist" thinkers argue that theories stressing the primacy of structural contradictions, economic classes, and crises in determining collective identity are inappropriate to contemporary collective actors. They also maintain that one cannot rest content with applying neoutilitarian, rational-actor models to contemporary conflict (in the manner of resource-mobilization theory) because collective action is not restricted to political exchanges, negotiations, and strategic calculations between adversaries. Today, collective actors focus primarily on issues of social norms and collective identity. This means that the logic of collective interaction entails more than strategic or instrumental rationality.

It would be misleading to imply, however, that a new paradigm has been formed around a *pure* identity model such as the one proposed by Pizzorno.[30] Indeed, this model has serious difficulties and has been criticized in the more complex theoretical approach articulated by Alain Touraine and his school.[31]

Touraine defines social movements as normatively oriented interactions between adversaries with conflicting interpretations and opposed societal models of a shared cultural field.[32] Yet he explicitly rejects a purely identity-oriented analysis of social movements, arguing that such analyses tend either to reproduce the ideological self-understanding of actors or to slip into a social-psychological account of interaction at the expense of a truly sociological analysis of struggle. This is especially risky in the case of contemporary collective actors. Their quests for personal and communal identity, their advocacy of expressive as opposed to strategic action, and their focus on direct participation involve a tendency to "retreat to autonomy"—to abandon the field of social-political struggle and turn in on themselves in the fashion of communitarian or sectarian groups. Thus, an exclusive theoretical focus on the creation of identity would only parallel the tendency of some contemporary actors to construe their own ideological representation of social relations (direct, democratic, communal) as a utopian organizing principle for all of society and to equate their expressive development of identity with the cultural stakes of the struggle. Although Touraine maintains that cultural orientation cannot be separated from social conflict, he nevertheless insists on the objectivity of a common cultural field shared by opponents. The various *institutional potentials* of the shared cultural field, and not simply the particular identity of a particular group, comprise the stakes of struggle. Actors and analysts who focus exclusively on the dynamics of identity formation therefore tend to veer off the map of social movements.

Yet, one might argue, the salient feature of the new social movements is not that they engage in expressive action or assert their identities but that they involve actors who have become aware of their capacity to create identities and of the power relations involved in the social construction of those identities. Contemporary actors are concerned not only with affirming the content of a specific identity but also with the formal elements involved in identity formation. They have articulated the formal principle of an equal chance for all to participate in group processes through which identities are formed, and they have become self-reflective regarding the social processes of identity formation.[33] This increased self-reflection is also applied to existing societal norms and to the structures of domination involved in their maintenance. In other words, contemporary collective actors see that the creation of identity involves social conflict around the reinterpretation of norms, the creation of new meanings, and a challenge to the social construction of the very boundaries between public, private, and political domains of action.

On this basis, one might say that collective actors strive to create a group identity within a general social identity whose interpretation they contest. However, even a stress on the new self-reflection of social movements concerning identity problems does not on its own introduce the dimension of conflict-laden social relations between adversaries. Not even the self-reflective defense of an existing or newly created identity involves a generalizable political aim. Thus, what is needed is an approach that looks at the political aspects of conflict and can say why identity has become a major focus today.

Nevertheless, analyses focusing exclusively on strategies also tend to veer off the map of social movements. Strategic action is only barely social and relational. Of course, it involves taking into account others' likely calculations within the rules of the game, and it entails interaction in this minimal sense. But strategic calculations exclude explicit reference to a common cultural field or to structured social relations between actors:

A strategic concept of change entails the reduction of society to relations between the actors and particularly to power relations, detached from any reference to a social system. . . . There are no stakes in the social relation and there is no field other than the relation itself.[34]

Accordingly, an analytical framework that focuses exclusively on strategic interaction misses both the cultural orientations and the structural dimension of conflict and thus bypasses what is specific to social movements.

Touraine sees exclusive orientations to identity and to strategy as opposite sides of the same coin. Both look at social conflicts in terms of a response to long-term change (modernization) rather than in relational terms of social structure.[35] Moreover, both correspond to an image of contemporary society as a loose ensemble subject to a permanent spiral of technological innovation and structural change led either by managerial-entrepreneurial elites or by the state. From this standpoint, "society" is stratified in terms of the actors' ability to adapt successfully to change (elites), their success in securing protection from change (operatives), or their victimization by change (marginalized masses).[36]

Both of the "nonsocial" accounts of collective action theorize about the conflict behavior of "actors" conceived in one of these three terms. The pure identity model corresponds to the *defensive* behavior of actors who resist their reduction to the status of powerless dependent consumers of change by withdrawing into countercultures or refusing innovations that threaten existing privileges or the cultural integrity of groups. Conversely, the purely strategic analysis corresponds to the standpoint of managerial or state elites, even when it is meant to take the part of "ordinary people" and offer the view from below.[37] When the stake of collective action is construed as membership in elites that control developmental resources, collective actions appear as *offensive*, proactive struggles of interest groups competing for power and privilege in areas opened up by development or modernization. Here the effort is not to resist change but to adapt to it. The problem with this approach is that neither the direction of the change nor the structural relations of domination it involves appear open to contestation because actors relate to a changing environment rather than to one another. In short, these theories of collective action articulate only those dimensions of conflict behavior that correspond to organizational developments or structural crises of the state and the political system.[38]

Touraine's own approach starts from a hermeneutic relation to the self-understanding and ideologies of contemporary movements. But he moves beyond this level of identity formation to account for the historical and structural context of social conflict and for the new stakes and features of struggle—self-reflection regarding the creation of identity and norms, emphasis on the democratization of civil society, self-limitation, and a focus on cultural issues. His work moves on two analytical levels: the elaboration of a theory of the structural and cultural dimensions of contemporary society, and an action-theoretic analysis of the conflict-laden processes of identity construction and the formation of political projects by collective actors. In addition, he focuses on the social dimension of collective action, in part by reviving the concept of civil society. In fact, his theoretical framework allows one to see why civil society is both the locus and the target of contemporary social movements and why this is the case above all in countries that already have vital civil societies.

In order to clarify the difference between the modes of conflict behavior described above and the concept of a social movement, Touraine introduces an analytical distinction between the "pattern of development" of a society (diachronic axis) and its mode of functioning (synchronic axis). The state, system crises, change, and conflict behavior opposing elites to masses are situated on the diachronic axis. Social relations and the "system of historical action"—that is, the conflict-laden processes by which norms, institutions, and cultural patterns are created and contested by social actors—are situated on the synchronic axis. The collective actions in which Touraine is interested and for which he reserves the term "social movement" are struggles around the institutional potentials of cultural patterns of a given societal type.

Touraine thus reintroduces many of the dimensions of collective action that are stressed by collective behaviorists, since he argues that social conflicts between actors must be understood in cultural and normative terms. But there are three differences between Touraine's approach and the classical tradition. First, Touraine rejects all versions of the breakdown thesis; in his model, breakdown and development govern conflict behavior on the diachronic axis of change. Second, he sees social movements not as abnormal occurrences but as creators of social life through their production and contestation of social practices, norms, and institutions. Third, unlike Parsons, he does not see the cultural orientations of a given society (its pattern of knowledge, type of investment, and image of the relation of humans to nature) as incontestable givens, seamlessly transposed into social norms and institutions. Instead, he argues that the way a society institutionalizes its cultural orientations involves both social conflict and social relations of domination. Society itself is understood as "the changing, unstable, loosely coherent product of social relations, cultural innovation, and political processes."[39] Unlike the societal model of strategic-action theorists, however, this fluid view involves a conception of society as a set of systems of action or structured social relations among actors. Consequently, dimensions of social action ignored by resource-mobilization theory move to the center of analysis. The focus turns to fields of alterable but nonetheless structured social relations rather than development, the state, or the market. Here, civil rather than political society moves to the fore, while the cultural dimensions of civil society assume major importance.

The meaning of collective action is thus redefined. Action now refers to the capacity of human societies to develop and alter their own orientations—that is, to generate their normativity and objectives.[40] An action is *social* only if it is normatively oriented and situated in a field of relations that includes power and shared cultural orientations. A social *movement* involves a double reference to cultural orientations and social relations, opposed social projects and contested structures of domination. Therefore, the social field that is contested by movements cannot be conceived as a battlefield for which a military model of action (strategy) is appropriate.

But what is this contested social terrain that is neither the state nor the market mechanism? It is, of course, civil society. According to Touraine, civil society is the locus of the "light side" of collective action—of social movements. Indeed, they rise and fall together: Both require a certain autonomy from the state to exist, and both can be crushed by a total state. Yet social movements do not target the state; they involve confrontations between social, civil adversaries within and over the institutions of civil society. Civil society, then, is seen in action terms as the domain of struggles, public spaces, and political processes. It comprises the social realm in which the creation of norms, identities, institutions, and social relations of domination and resistance are located.

Touraine is aware of those theories that implicitly or explicitly deny the relevance of "civil society" to contemporary social systems. Indeed, he grants that the increased capacity of contemporary society to act on itself at the expense of absolute state power and the metasocial guarantees of social order also opens the way for enlarging the state's role in social and cultural life.[41] He nevertheless maintains that increased societal self-reflection involves the expansion of civil society and the public realm. This double vision reveals, at least on a descriptive level, the new stakes for contemporary movements. Touraine's idea of the "expansion" of civil society is directly related to contemporary movements contesting the control of an increasing range of social activities formerly shielded from public scrutiny by tradition, a rigidly defined private sphere, or metasocial guarantees:

The public space—*Öffentlichkeit*—strictly limited in a bourgeois society, was extended to labor problems in an industrial society and now spreads over all fields of experience . . . the main political problems today deal directly with private life: fecundation and birth, reproduction and sexuality, illness and death, and, in a different way, home-consumed mass media. . . . The distance between civil society and the state is increasing while the separation between private and public life is fading away.[42]

The issues raised by the feminist, ecology, peace, and local-autonomy movements are thus all connected to the shifting boundaries between public, private, and social life and involve struggles against old and new forms of domination in these areas.

In countries that have already secured vital institutions of civil society through rights, the newly opened terrain is vulnerable to state penetration and control. This is why the modernizing state that imposes economic regulations and the administrative state that intervenes in social and cultural organization as much as it does in the economic order have become the targets of the revived liberal current that stresses the expansion of human rights and the autonomy of society against the state. And yet, in one of his most important insights, Touraine insists that, qua social movements, contemporary conflicts do not have as their stakes simply the defense and autonomy of civil society against the state. Rather, the issue is, above all, *which kind* of civil society is to be defended. It is not enough to secure the autonomy or even primacy of civil society against the state, for, as the example of liberal capitalism in England and the United States shows, this might simply mean the primacy of socioeconomic over administrative elites.[43] Rather, social movements must strive to defend *and* democratize all those institutions of civil society in which discrimination, inequality, and domination have become visible and contested. If we remain on the diachronic axis alone, then the liberal project of defending society against the state would indeed appear anachronistic or, at best, a holding action serving primarily the interest of elites dominant in nonstate institutions. But if we remain focused exclusively on the synchronic axis, we can lose sight of the fact that the modern state is always capable of intervening in the field of social movements, decisively modifying or even abolishing the conditions that make social movements and their struggle possible. The double perspective that Touraine offers is thus crucial for an understanding of why in the most civil of societies, in the West, the autonomy and democratization of the institutions of contemporary civil society remain at the heart of contemporary social conflicts:

But since we have had the privilege of living several centuries in increasingly civil societies, is not our duty to seek the great alliance between the liberating struggle against the state and a social conflict to prevent this struggle from being waged only for the profit of the leaders of civil society?[44]

In short, it would be a great mistake to embrace only the liberal project of defending society against the state, for this would leave the relations of domination and inequality within civil society intact.

Instead of pursuing and clarifying this suggestive line of inquiry, however, Touraine turns to a different analytical level and constructs a model of our contemporary societal type, which he calls "postindustrial" or "programmed," in order to specify the stakes for contemporary movements and to ground the claim that they are radically discontinuous with previous movements. While this theoretical model can pinpoint the new arenas open to conflict, it has the disadvantage that it obscures the significance of the concept of civil society that is so central to Touraine's understanding while at the same time leading to a one-sided view of contemporary social movements.

Postindustrial society is an allegedly new societal type characterized by new loci of power, new forms of domination, new modes of investment, and a "self-reflective" cultural model. Power, investment, and domination are located at the level of cultural production itself. Innovations in the production of knowledge (media, computers, data banks) transform our representation of human nature and of the external world. "For these reasons, research and development, information processing, biomedical science and techniques, and the mass media are the four main components of a postindustrial society."[45] More and more domains of social life are opened up to technocratic projects of control or alternative projects to maintain the autonomy and ensure the internal democratic structure of the newly contested terrain. In short, postindustrial society represents itself as capable of producing its own knowledge, normative guidelines, and sociocultural forms. The stakes of social conflict revolve around the institutionalization of this cultural model: autonomous, self-governed, egalitarian institutions vs. elite-controlled, technocratically managed structures permeated by relations of domination.

The increase in self-reflection entailed by these developments governs the change in the identity of collective actions and the kinds of movements they develop. The struggle for autonomous, democratic social institutions and the concern with participatory forms of association on the part of contemporary collective actors are due to a recognition that both the means and the ends of social production are social products. This is why they focus on the cultural and normative dimensions of everyday life and conceive their struggles in terms of a population's right to choose its own kind of life and identity. The new dimensions of the identity of contemporary actors, and what makes them radically discontinuous with earlier movements, are thus not their action repertoire but the level of self-reflection and the changed loci and stakes of struggles that correspond to the emergence of a new societal type.[46]

The circularity in this mode of argumentation is obvious. Contemporary collective action is new because it involves struggle around the areas opened up by postindustrial society, but postindustrial society is a new societal type because it triggers new forms of collective action. Touraine's theoretical model, however, is not meant to be neutral. Indeed, he hopes to avoid the circularity of the theoretical argument by means of his partisan method of sociological intervention. His purpose is to tease out of existing conflict behavior the dimension of a social movement (in our terms, the new self-limiting collective identity):

> What we must now discover is how, *in our kinds of countries*, defensive reactions against permanent change can be transformed into social conflicts and antitechnocratic action, and how such struggles extend the area of political activity and create what we might call a new *Öffentlichkeit*. . . . The major problem is to move from the defensive to the counteroffensive, from the quest for identity to collective action, to control the process of change.[47]

While this method does provide fascinating data on the self-interpretation of contemporary collective actors, while it does reveal, in some instances, the emergence of a new self-reflective identity, it does not extricate the theory from its circularity.

We have criticized elsewhere the dogmatic aspects of Touraine's methodology and his creation of a hierarchy of forms of social struggle to correspond to the theory of social types.[48] We have also criticized his insistence on radical discontinuity between societal types and social movements as antithetical to the use of the concept of civil society. By "our kind of countries," Touraine means countries that have had, still have, and are animated by struggles to preserve and expand civil society. But the idea that civil society existed in the West at least since the seventeenth century implies institutional and cultural continuity with our own past—an idea at odds with the thesis of radically discontinuous societal types, cultural models, and social movements. While the distinction between synchronic and diachronic axes renders the innovations of contemporary struggles visible, while it provides room for institutional analysis of civil society, the implicit evolutionary theory of societal types conceals the continuity between past and present. It thus becomes impossible to account for the learning processes on the part of collective actors with regard to past movements, institutional forms, and societal projects. The concept of "societal type" is too abstract for the institutional analysis of civil society. Moreover, the rather streamlined concept of postindustrial society forces one to construe those aspects of struggle that do not involve the new self-reflective collective identity as regressive or anachronistic.

At the same time, the thesis of the new loci of domination, investment, power, and protest does seem to offer an account of the dual character—defensive and offensive—of the new dimensions in contemporary collective actions. The former includes the defensive preoccupation with identity and autonomy; the latter, a tendency to take the counteroffensive and engage in struggles for the control and democratization of social institutions. For Touraine, unlike Tilly, "offensive" action refers not to a competitive, strategically oriented battle for inclusion and power in a polity but to the struggle to extend the field of political activity and to democratize new and existing public spaces at the expense of state control and the technocratic model of society. Both defensive reactions to permanent change and offensive struggles against technocratic projects to monopolize and reprivatize the control of social institutions and cultural innovation are elements of contemporary collective action. Nevertheless, the distinction between the synchronic and diachronic axes of action does have one major drawback: It blinds Touraine to an important dimension of collective action, namely, the struggles on the part of social actors to ensure the *influence* of democratic institutions in and over the political system and the economy. Without this dimension, civil society would remain vulnerable to political and economic power, and the focus of collective action would be reduced to a single dimension. Touraine's theoretical framework is not complex enough to allow him to construct a model that integrates the best parts of resource-mobilization theory.

Moreover, although Touraine offers an action sociology of the new features of contemporary movements, he does not develop a theory of the type of action presupposed by the thesis of increased self-reflection. Of course, he does analyze the processes of communication engaged in by contemporary collective actors as they articulate new identities and societal projects. But only a theoretical self-reflection of communicative action of the type offered by Habermas could articulate the specificity of these processes, pinpoint their limits, and open the way toward understanding the relations among all types of actions in collective conflicts. Because this level of analysis is missing in his theory, Touraine takes the false step of excluding strategic interaction from the concept of a social movement and from his vague image of civil society. He is correct in asserting that a one-sided focus on strategy misses the social and norm-oriented dimensions of contemporary struggles that are central to the emergence of new collective identities. But he is wrong to restrict strategic interaction to lower levels of conflict or to the diachronic axis of change because, as resource-mobilization theory clearly demonstrates, both social movements and civil society involve strategic interaction.

Habermas's recent reformulation of the theory of communicative action allows us to see how the paradigms of collective action discussed above can be complementary. His action typology corresponds quite well to the various logics of collective action.[49] The concept of "teleological action" presupposes an actor who chooses between alternative courses of action (means) with a view to realizing an end. This involves relations between an actor and a world of existing states of affairs that obtain or can be brought about by purposeful intervention. The degree of rationality of the action can be assessed by a third person with respect to success and "truth"—that is, the fit between the actor's perceptions and the actual case.[50] Teleological action thus corresponds to the concept of rational action at the heart of resource-mobilization theory.

The "political-process model" of Tilly, Tarrow, and others involves a switch from theories of rational action to theories of rational interaction, corresponding to an expansion of the teleological model to a strategic one in which calculations of success involve the anticipation of decisions on the part of at least one other actor. This type of action still presupposes only the "objective world" but now includes within it decision making by others. Other actors are treated as external factors to be reckoned with, not as subjects with whom one shares an understanding.

The pure identity model argues for a rationality of action specific to new social movements that fits the Habermasian concept of dramaturgical action. This action type involves the purposeful and expressive fabrication and disclosure of one's subjectivity (feelings, desires, experiences, identity) to a set of others who constitute a public. Here, at least two "world relations" are presupposed: an orientation to the subjective world of the actor and one to the external world. The "presentation of self" entails an effort to get one's subjectivity and identity recognized. But from the standpoint of the actor, normatively regulated interpersonal relations are considered only as social facts. Thus, dramaturgical action can take on latently strategic qualities and become cynical impression management. The dimension of collective action that encompasses the expressive assertion of an identity is, accordingly, not a matter of spontaneous expressiveness but involves a stylized and planned staging of one's identity for the purpose of gaining recognition or influence.

Smelser's concept of a normatively oriented social movement corresponds to the concept of normative action. According to Habermas, the concept of normatively regulated action refers to members of a group who orient their actions to common (institutionalized) values that have a general binding force for interpersonal relations. Each is entitled to expect that all others will comply with shared norms. Thus, in addition to presupposing the external world, normative action involves a relation to a social world and a social identity—that is, a normative context that designates the totality of legitimate interpersonal relations. This means that cognitive and motivational dimensions are relevant to the assessment of the validity of normative action and that learning can occur on both of these levels. Action can be evaluated in terms of its conformity with a given norm; norms can be assessed in terms of whether or not they deserve to be recognized on the basis of an accepted standard. It should be noted that, to Smelser, movements that do not act in the name of an ultimately valid order of norms become irrational.

Communicative interaction takes the second level of questioning of norms a step further. This concept goes beyond the limits of the action theory of Parsons and Smelser. It refers to the linguistically mediated, intersubjective process by which actors establish their interpersonal relations and coordinate their actions, involving negotiating definitions of the situation (norms) and coming to an agreement. Whereas normative action presupposes a consensus that is merely reproduced with each interpretive act, communicative action involves uncurtailed communication among actors who must first create a consensus. This involves a self-reflective relation to dimensions of all three "worlds"—the objective, the subjective, and the social. Here, any aspect of our culturally ingrained knowledge that has become problematic can be thematized and tested through an interrogation of validity claims. Touraine's concept of a social movement utilizes this conception of communicative action.

If we apply this abstract analysis of action to the conceptual strategies described above, it becomes clear that, although each tends to screen out the forms of action analyzed by the others, they can all inform the study of collective action. For it is perfectly conceivable that a concrete social movement can involve all the forms of action. This is obvious in the case of contemporary collective actions. Key sectors of the new movements, from feminism to ecology, have a self-reflective relation to the objective, subjective, and social worlds insofar as they thematize issues of personal and social identity, defend existing norms, contest the social interpretation of norms, communicatively create new norms, and propose alternative ways of relating to the environment. As indicated above, all collective action also involves strategic, instrumental, and norm-oriented activity. There is thus no reason why the analysis of the various logics of collective action should be seen as incompatible, so long as they are not construed as the sole form of rationality of collective action to the exclusion of others. Moreover, on the basis of this analysis, one can see that movements can struggle simultaneously for the defense and democratization of civil society and for inclusion within and the expansion of political society.

While the analysis of action types accommodates the various logics of collective action, it can neither explain a particular configuration within a given movement nor unite the types in a coherent theoretical framework. For this, one must turn to an analysis of civil society. Touraine's work points us in the right direction, but he does not offer a *theory* of civil society. Instead, he makes use of the category without explaining its internal articulation. Nor does he explain what mechanisms connect the various spheres to one another and to the state and the economy. Consequently, the dualistic logic of contemporary movements is misconstrued as alternatives addressed to civil society alone. The resource-mobilization approach suffers from the opposite blindness, highlighting only strategies aimed at political and economic structures. The competing paradigms of the study of social movements thus leave us with an unsatisfactory choice: Either one interprets the movements in terms of the strategic logic of organization involved in pressuring the "big structures" of state and economy, or one opts for a stress on identity, norms, cultural models, and associational forms articulated by the most innovative actors themselves, targeting the institutions of civil society. What we need is a theoretical framework that can accommodate both approaches and account for the dual logic of contemporary movements.

Dualistic Social Theory and Contemporary Social Movements

We began with the claim that the new social movements construe the cultural models, norms, and institutions of civil society as the main stakes of social conflict. Clearly, attempts to influence economic structures and state policy also play an important role in these movements. For example, ecologists have turned to the state to restrict economic actors from plundering the environment, while civil rights activists and feminists have, through various organizational strategies, sought to pressure the state to enact and enforce laws securing the rights of minorities and women in the economy, civil society, and the polity. Some components of the new movements have organized political parties (the most famous example being the West German Greens), while others have sought to work within existing parties or to exert pressure on political society through lobbying efforts, all without relinquishing their links with movement activists and associations outside the political system. Thus, contemporary movements have a dual face and a dual organizational logic. In chapter 9, we reviewed the social-theoretic presuppositions of this claim, reformulating the categories of civil society in terms of the system/lifeworld distinction developed by Habermas. Now we want to make the link between dualistic social theory and social movements more explicit. We shall argue that the reconstruction of the system/lifeworld distinction in terms of the categories of civil and political society yields the tools we need to account for both the defensive and offensive aspects of contemporary movements.

Habermas's most significant contributions to the theory of contemporary movements are three theses that, taken together, offer insight into the stakes of contemporary collective action.[51] The first states that the emergence of cultural modernity—of differentiated spheres of science, art, and morality, organized around their own internal validity claims—carries with it a potential for increased self-reflection (and decentered subjectivity) regarding all dimensions of action and world relations. This opens up the possibility of a posttraditional, postconventional relation to key dimensions of social, political, and cultural life and of their coordination through autonomous processes of communicative interaction. This would form a basis for further modernization of the lifeworld through an incorporation of the achieved potentials of cultural modernity into everyday life, involving the replacement of *gemeinschaftliche* coordination by potentially self-reflective forms.

The second thesis involves the "selective institutionalization" of the potentials of modernity (self-reflection, autonomy, freedom, equality, meaning). A dualistic model of society, one that distinguishes between system and lifeworld, lies at the heart of the thesis. In this model, the processes involved in the modernization of the economy and the state are distinct from those involved in the "rationalization" of the lifeworld. On the one hand, we have the development of media-steered structures in which strategic and instrumental rationality are unleashed and expanded; on the other, the development of communicatively coordinated and egalitarian cultural, social, and socializing institutions appropriate to the new forms of decentered subjectivity made possible by cultural modernization. Societal rationalization has been dominated, however, by the imperatives of the subsystems; that is, the requirements of capitalist growth and administrative steering have predominated over lifeworld concerns. The "selective institutionalization" of the potentials of modernity has thus produced overcomplexity and new forms of power on the system side and the impoverishment and underdevelopment of the institutional promise of the lifeworld. The "colonization of the lifeworld" related to capitalist development and to technocratic projects of administrative elites has blocked and continues to block these potentials.

The third thesis insists on the two-sided character of the institutions of our contemporary lifeworld, that is, the idea that societal rationalization has entailed institutional developments in civil society involving not only domination but also the basis for emancipation. The dualistic theory of society thus places the core elements of civil society—legality, publicity, civil associations, mass culture, the family—at the heart of the discussion. Here is the dimension of institutional analysis missing in Touraine's theory of societal types. The important point for us is that Habermas's sketch of developments *within an already (albeit incompletely) modern civil society* provides a way to understand the double character of contemporary movements and also their continuities or discontinuities with the past. The idea of the double character of the institutional makeup of civil society is a real gain because it goes beyond a one-sided stress on alienation or domination (Marx, Foucault) and an equally one-sided focus on integration (Durkheim, Parsons). We are thereby afforded a theoretical means of avoiding the stark alternative between apologetics and total revolution. If modern civil societies are not entirely reified, if our institutions are not thoroughly pervaded by inegalitarian power relations, then it becomes possible to think in terms of the positive potentials of modernity that are worth defending and expanding through a radical but self-limiting politics. Considered together with the colonization thesis, this allows us to explain why civil society is the target as well as the terrain of contemporary collective action.

Taken together, these theses reveal the stakes of contemporary movements in the struggle over the detraditionalization and democratization of social relations in civil society. The redefining of cultural norms, individual and collective identities, appropriate social roles, modes of interpretation, and the form and content of discourses (which we have called the "politics of identity") is part of this project. However, since authoritarian institutions are often reinforced by unequal control of money and power, and since the colonization of the institutions of civil society by these media prevents their further modernization, contemporary collective actors must also address political society. A "politics of inclusion" targets political institutions to gain recognition for new political actors as members of political society and to achieve benefits for those whom they "represent." A "politics of influence," aimed at altering the universe of political discourse to accommodate new need-interpretations, new identities, and new norms, is also indispensable. Only with such a combination of efforts can the administrative and economic colonization of civil society, which tends to freeze social relations of domination and create new dependencies, be restricted and controlled. Finally, the further democratization of political and economic institutions (a "politics of reform") is also central to this project. Without this effort, any gains within civil society would be tenuous indeed. While the democratization of civil society and the defense of its autonomy from economic or administrative "colonization" can be seen as the goal of the new movements, the creation of "sensors" within political and economic institutions (institutional reform) and the democratization of political society (the politics of influence and inclusion), which would open these institutions to the new identities and egalitarian norms articulated on the terrain of civil society, are the means to securing this goal.[52]

We are not arguing that Habermas himself has provided the synthetic theoretical paradigm of social movements that his framework makes possible. While available movement theories have much to learn from that framework, Habermas's own social theory could also benefit from integrating the results of other contemporary analyses. Indeed, his most recent discussion of the new social movements is misleading because it is based on a one-sided interpretation of the dualistic conception of society that he himself introduced.

Habermas's approach to social movements has evolved over time. His earlier analysis was close to that of Alain Touraine.[53] Like Touraine, he saw the New Left and especially the student movement as potential agents of societal democratization against technocratic projects to functionalize social institutions and the existing public sphere. These movements seemed to hold a promise of new, rational social identities and a revived democratic political culture to the extent that they sought to expand and democratize public spaces from the university to the polity.

In more theoretical terms, Habermas ascribed two interrelated roles to social movements. First, movements were seen as the dynamic element in social learning processes and identity formation. Drawing on potentials embedded in cultural traditions and new forms of socialization, social movements transpose latently available structures of rationality into social practice so that they can find embodiments in new identities and norms. Second, movements with democratic projects have the potential to initiate processes by which the public sphere might be revived and discourses institutionalized, within a wide range of social institutions. These roles were only very abstractly situated in contemporary institutional developments, however, because the old Frankfurt School thesis of "one-dimensionality" still haunted Habermas's assessment of existing social, economic, and political institutions. Thus, while he (like Touraine) criticized the revolutionary rhetoric of the sixties movements for diverting attention from the project of democratizing political and social institutions in favor of their total overthrow, he could provide no alternative to their totalizing critique of modern society.[54] We have criticized the earlier version of Habermas's theory for its "institutional deficit," that is, for locating emancipatory potentials on the abstract level of cultural modernity and in socialization processes and not in the institutional articulation of civil society.[55]

Habermas resolved this difficulty by introducing the dualistic conception of society as a basis for analyzing the two-sided character of contemporary institutions.[56] He interprets the ambivalent potentials of our social institutions in terms of a clash among system imperatives with independent communication structures. By implication, these institutions are open to both defensive struggles to protect and democratize the communicative infrastructure of everyday life and offensive projects of radical institutional reform. It is all the more ironic that this recent work has also yielded what we consider to be an extremely one-sided interpretation of the new social movements, for in this conception, these movements appear primarily as defensive reactions against the colonization of the lifeworld.[57]

Habermas maintains that what is at stake in the new forms of resistance and conflict is the defense not of a traditional (communal, ascriptive, diffuse) sociocultural lifeworld but of one that is already partly modernized. He also distinguishes between defenses of property and status acquired on the terrain of a modernized lifeworld and "defensive" action involving experiments in new forms of cooperation and community. The latter form the core of the new conflict potential. Nevertheless, the new movements are seen only as forms of resistance and retreat seeking to stem the tide of the formally organized systems of action in favor of communicative structures. Although they signify the continued capacity of the lifeworld to resist reification, and thus take on positive meaning, Habermas is skeptical of their "emancipatory potential" and suspicious of their apparently anti-institutional, defensive, antireformist nature. In short, he does not see the new movements as carriers of new (rational) social identities but as mired in particularism. Nor does he see them as oriented toward or capable of fostering the institutionalization of the positive potentials of modernity or of transcending an expressive politics of withdrawal.

Nevertheless, Habermas is on to something when he argues that the new conflicts arise at the "seam between system and lifeworld"— over precisely those roles that institutionalize the media of money and power and mediate between the public and private spheres and the economic and administrative subsystems. Resistance to the functionalized roles of employee and consumer, citizen and client, surely characterizes much of contemporary collective action:

It is just these roles that are the targets of protest. Alternative practice is directed against the . . . market-dependent mobilization of labor power, against the extension of pressures of competition and performance all the way down into elementary school. It also takes aim at the monetarization of services, relationships, and time, at the consumerist redefinition of private spheres of life and personal life-styles. Furthermore the relation of clients to public service agencies is to be opened up and reorganized in a participatory mode. . . . Finally, certain forms of protest negate the definitions of the role of citizen.[58]

In Habermas's view, however, the movement challenges to these roles are purely defensive. He construes the attempts of collective actors to come up with counterinstitutions within the lifeworld to limit the inner dynamics of the economic and political-administrative systems not only as "reactive" but as tendentially antimodern communalist projects of dedifferentiation and withdrawal.[59] The only exception he sees is the feminist movement. It alone has a dual logic and a clear emancipatory potential: an offensive, universalist side concerned with political inclusion and equal rights, along with a defensive, particularist side focusing on identity, alternative values, and the overturning of concrete forms of life marked by male monopolies and a one-sidedly rationalized everyday practice.[60] The first dimension links feminism to the tradition of bourgeois-socialist liberation movements and to universalist moral principles. The second links it to the new social movements. As indicated above, however, the new resistance movements, including the second dimension of feminism, involve exclusively defensive re-actions to colonization. Hence the label "particularist" for the concern with identities, norms, and alternative values, and hence the charge of a "retreat" into ascriptive or biologistic categories of gender. According to Habermas, the emancipatory dimension of feminism therefore involves nothing new, while the new dimension of feminism suffers from the same drawbacks as the other new movements.

We believe that this analysis of the new movements in general and of feminism in particular is misleading. Indeed, Habermas's interpretation of what is new in these movements as particularist and defensive reactions to the penetration of social life by the media of money and power involves a revival of the classical breakdown thesis.[61] This, in turn, derives from a one-sided interpretation of his own dualistic social theory. Thus, Habermas's analysis of movements does not do justice to the potential of his theory, for two reasons. The first has to do with the failure to translate the categories of the lifeworld into a full-fledged conceptualization of civil and political society. The suggestive passages on the public and private institutions of the lifeworld neglect the one key dimension that would have enabled him to avoid the breakdown thesis, namely, that of associations. Despite his acknowledgment that contemporary struggles are situated around the dimensions of cultural reproduction, social integration, and socialization, he fails to link these to the positive side of the institutions within civil and political society.[62] Instead of recognizing that the new movements have a role to play in the further modernization of these spheres, he perceives only their defensiveness vis-à-vis the expansion of steering mechanisms. At best, he sees the new movements as having the potential to contribute to learning along the dimensions of cultural transmission and socialization but not to institutional change within civil society.

Habermas is wrong to conclude from their focus on reinterpreting traditions and identities that what is involved in the new movements is only an anti-institutional, cultural politics. The movements also generate new solidarities, alter the associational structure of civil society, and create a plurality of new public spaces while expanding and revitalizing spaces that are already institutionalized. This involves challenging the roles that mediate between system and lifeworld. The other side of contemporary collective action, however, entails institutional change along the dimension of social integration. It involves conflict over social relations in civil institutions ranging from the family to the public spheres.

Habermas's tendency to view the subsystems as "self-referentially closed" screens out from view the possibility of institutional reform in these domains as well. His overly rigid separation of the domains of system and lifeworld blinds him to the offensive strategies of contemporary movements aimed at creating or democratizing receptors within the subsystems, for it makes success tautologically impossible. Consequently, his account of movements does not do justice to the thesis of institutional doubleness alluded to above, to which the dual logic of the movements is addressed. He is thus led to a reductive analysis of the ecology, citizen initiative, green, and youth movements and to misconstrue the dual logic when he does perceive it, as in the case of feminism.

Our reconstruction of the system/lifeworld distinction along the lines of a theory of civil society corrects these two blind spots. On the one hand, we translate the concept of the lifeworld into the institutional articulation of a civil society secured by rights. On the other hand, we argue that there are receptors for the influence of civil society within political (and economic) society and that these can, within limits, be added to and democratized. Consequently, on our version of the dualistic conception of society, the dual logic of all the new movements can come into view. Our approach enables us to see that movements operate on both sides of the system/lifeworld divide, and we are thus able to accommodate the contributions of both paradigms of collective action.

Our framework also yields a more synthetic interpretation of the meaning of "defensive" and "offensive" collective action than can be found in any of the approaches discussed above. On this account, the "defensive" aspect of the movements involves preserving *and developing* the communicative infrastructure of the lifeworld. This formulation captures the dual aspect of movements discussed by Touraine as well as Habermas's insight that movements can be the carriers of the potentials of cultural modernity. This is the sine qua non for successful efforts to redefine identities, to reinterpret norms, and to develop egalitarian, democratic associational forms. The expressive, normative, and communicative modes of collective action have their proper place here; but this dimension of collective action also involves efforts to secure *institutional* changes within civil society that correspond to the new meanings, identities, and norms that are created.

The "offensive" aspect of collective action targets political and economic society—the realms of "mediation" between civil society and the subsystems of the administrative state and the economy. Certainly, this involves the development of organizations that can exert pressure for inclusion within these domains and extract benefits from them. The strategic/instrumental modes of collective action are indispensable for such projects. But the offensive politics of the new movements involve not only struggles for money or political recognition but also a politics of influence targeting political (and perhaps economic) insiders and (self-limiting) projects of institutional reform. How else are we to understand attempts to make the subsystems more receptive to new issues and concerns, more responsive to the needs and self-understanding of actors in civil society, and more internally democratic than they are now? In other words, those elements of the new movements that target political society (and will one day perhaps target economic society as well) articulate a project of self-limiting, democratic institutional reform aimed at broadening and democratizing the structures of discourse and compromise that already exist in these domains.

A Feminist Critique of Dualistic Social Theory

While we believe that all contemporary social movements are amenable to analysis in these terms, we are going to focus on the feminist movement to make our point. Several interesting discussions of the relevance of Habermas's dualistic social theory to the contemporary women's movement have already appeared.[63] In the most comprehensive article on the subject, Nancy Fraser argues that, far from facilitating an understanding of feminism, Habermas's dualistic social theory, and especially his distinction between system and lifeworld, is not only "gender-blind" but also "in important respects androcentric and ideological."[64] Fraser proposes a far more radical critique of dualistic social theory than the one we have adumbrated above. Because this critique aims at the very conceptual apparatus of the dualistic social theory that we have appropriated and revised, we shall consider it in some detail. It involves five key claims:

1. Fraser maintains that the system/lifeworld distinction leads one to construe the family as a socially integrated institution having

only an extrinsic, incidental relation to money and power.[65] To place the modern family and the official capitalist economy on opposite sides of the system/lifeworld divide is to occlude the fact that contemporary families are economic systems and sites of labor, coercion, exchange, exploitation, and violence. Moreover, this legitimates the modern institutional separation of family and official economy, childrearing and paid work, and public and private spheres that has been anathema to contemporary feminism.[66] Habermas is thus allegedly blinded to the fact that childrearing is the unpaid work of overseeing production of the appropriately socialized labor power that the family exchanges for wages.[67]

2. A slightly different argument is made with respect to Habermas's distinction between normatively secured, conventional forms of social integration and communicatively established, self-reflective, postconventional ones. Fraser concedes that this distinction provides critical resources for analyzing interfamilial relations by rendering the "consensus" on family norms and roles suspect to the degree that they are prereflective or achieved through dialogue vitiated by unfairness, coercion, or inequality. Yet she claims that an insufficient stress is placed on the fact that actions coordinated by normatively secured consensus in the patriarchal nuclear family are actions regulated by power. The fault here lies in Habermas's apparent restriction of the use of the term "power" to bureaucratic contexts. By implication, power relations within the family are construed as being the result of external pressures upon it (economic pressures in the case of classical capitalism; bureaucratic pressures in the case of the welfare state).[68]

3. This approach has the implication, according to Fraser, that male dominance is a sign of the insufficient modernity of social relations. The fact that patriarchy is intrinsic to rather than an accidental byproduct of capitalism is thereby obscured.[69]

4. Although Fraser (somewhat inconsistently) praises Habermas's expansion of the classic public/private distinction into a four-part scheme of family, public sphere, economy, and state (clearly based on the system/lifeworld distinction), she argues that the critical potential of this model is blocked by the gender blindness of the overall approach. Habermas misleadingly conceptualizes the roles around which the interchange relations between the four terms of

the model take shape (worker, consumer, client, citizen) in gender-neutral terms. Moreover, he makes no mention of the fact that these roles are complemented by the crucial fifth role of childrearer.[70] Fraser's point here is that the links among the two sets of public and private spheres are adumbrated as much through the medium of gender as through the media of money and power.[71]

5. Finally, Fraser argues that the colonization thesis leads Habermas to misrepresent the causes and to misconstrue the scope of the feminist challenge to welfare state capitalism. According to this thesis, the private and public spheres of civil society cease to subordinate the economic and administrative systems to the norms and values of everyday life but are instead increasingly subordinated to the imperatives of those systems. Fraser points out, however, that patriarchal norms continue to structure the state-regulated capitalist economy and the state administration, as indicated by the continued segmentation of the labor force and the structure of social welfare systems. Thus, the channels of influence between system and lifeworld are *multidirectional.* Habermas's analysis of the ambivalences of welfare state reforms, however, fails to note the gendered subtext of these developments. That women are overwhelmingly the new clients of precisely those "ambivalent" reforms of the welfare system goes unnoticed. The colonization thesis for the welfare state thus compounds the errors and lacunae deriving from the original theoretical conceptualization of the system/lifeworld divide. It is both gender-blind and androcentric.

This critique raises issues that cannot be disregarded, especially if one wants to argue that dualistic social theory as we have reconstructed it contributes to the understanding of contemporary movements. It is certainly the case that Habermas has not paid much attention to gender, and the gender blindness of the model does indeed occlude important features of the institutional arrangements he wants to understand. Nevertheless, the claim that the system/lifeworld distinction and the colonization thesis are antithetical to such concerns is unconvincing. We believe that the critical potential of the theory and its relevance for feminist movements can be demonstrated. In fact, most of the difficulties cited by Fraser lie not in the overall theoretical model but in Habermas's interpretation of it.[72] Thus, we shall show that the bulk of the valid part of her criticism can be accommodated in our revised version of the model, which can in turn shed light on some of the forms of domination and conflict specific to contemporary feminism.[73]

1. As we have seen, Fraser rejects the system/lifeworld distinction, arguing that there is no meaningful way to differentiate categorially between the spheres of paid and unpaid labor, between the family and the "official" economy.[74] Indeed, she argues that there is no warrant for assuming that a system-integrated organization of childrearing would be any more pathological than that of other work. This response, however, misses the real thrust of the distinction between system and social integration and is itself unconvincing.

While Habermas, in his more Marxist moments, does try to distinguish between symbolic and material reproductive processes, the heart of the theory rests on the far more important distinction between modes of action coordination and not on the substantive elements of action itself. The claim, in short, which Fraser has not at all disproved, is that there is a fundamental difference between processes (cultural reproduction, social integration, socialization), social relations, and institutions in which the weight of coordination must be communicative and those that can be "media-steered" without distortion, such as markets or bureaucracies. This is not because labor or creative/productive activity takes place only in the second domain but because meaning, norms, and identities cannot be maintained, reinterpreted, or created through functional substitutes for the coordinating accomplishments of communicative interaction. The heart of the difference between formally organized sets of social relations (subsystems) and others lies in the tendency of the former to neutralize the normative background of informal, customary, or morally regulated contexts of action that are tied to validity claims and to substitute for these contexts of interaction that are generated by positive law and "media-steered."[75] The latter are coordinated by media that operate through linguistic codes; these codes, however, relieve actors of the necessity of mutually agreeing on the definition of the situation involved in every relevant interaction, thereby bypassing (or rendering impossible) the reference to normative validity claims. Meanings, norms, and identities are not created in such contexts but are used (or reinforced) for systemic purposes.

Viewing the family as an economic system would thus entail either a wholesale embrace of systems theory[76] (thereby rendering it immune to the kind of normative critique Fraser wants to make) or a misunderstanding of what a system is in Habermas's theory: a formally organized, media-steered set of social relations. If one intends to challenge the meanings, norms, and identities that are constitutive of gender inequality, then this is the wrong tack to take. The systems-theoretic approach obliterates the very dimension in which these are created and reproduced. Although families do perform economic functions, although they can be and are functionalized by the imperatives of the economic or the administrative subsystem, although there are strategic interactions within them as well as exchanges of services and labor for money or support, and although these are distributed along gender lines, families are not thereby economic systems. They are neither formally organized nor media-steered. By the same token, they cannot be described as administrative systems although they are certainly imbued with power relations.[77]

The work performed by women within the family is unrecognized, unremunerated, and uncompensated, and it therefore disadvantages women even in the "official" labor market (reinforcing the image of dependency on a male "breadwinner"). Nevertheless it is unhelpful to describe childrearing as being just like the rest of social labor. The fact that it can and has been partially transferred to day-care centers or nurseries and remunerated does not mean that it can be formally organized in the way that other work can be or that it is either desirable or possible to transfer childrearing in its entirety to system-integrated institutional settings. Communicative coordination of interaction remains at the heart of childrearing and nurturing, as any parent, child-care worker, or nursery school teacher knows. Unless one is advocating the total institutionalization of preschool children and the total commodification of childrearing as the sole alternative to being raised by full-time mothers, then one must assume that children come home at some time of day—at which point they require attention and nurturing. Moreover, nurseries, day-care centers, and schools are themselves institutions within civil society. They have their economic and bureaucratic side, of course, but when

organizational or economic requirements outweigh the communicative tasks of nurturing and teaching, they subvert the raison
d'être of the institutions and have pathological consequences
(unnurtured and untaught children).

While it is certainly conceivable that more household tasks can
migrate from the home to the market, surely there is and ought to
be a limit to this. We do not agree with the notion that all creative,
productive, or reproductive activities should necessarily take the
form of wage labor. Even when they do, this does not mean that the
institutional frameworks in which these activities occur can be
analyzed as economic systems. Only on the misleading assumption
that all "social labor" is equivalent and thus equally amenable to or
distorted by system integration could one consider primary socialization and nurturing in the same light as all other work. Only,
in short, if one construes families simply as sites of unpaid socially
necessary labor time could the differences between interfamilial
relations and social relations of production disappear from view.
But this sort of assumption has been criticized by many feminists for
overextending the categories of the Marxian critique of capitalism
to issues they were not constructed to address.[78]

If one is willing to grant that a modern economy requires that
some forms of labor be commodified and formally organized, the
central question for critical theory is to how to distinguish the sorts
of activities that should be left to the market mechanism or formally
organized from those that should not be. There are two distinct
issues here. For example, feminist critiques of "surrogacy contracts"
challenge the appropriateness of exchanging babies for money
(commodification) and treating pregnancy and childbirth on the
model of a labor contract. Marketization in such cases does seem
to distort the woman's relation to her body, herself, and her child,
and it is not necessary to explicate this intuition on the basis of
naturalist or essentialist arguments.[79] The idea of the communicative infrastructure of the social relations of civil society suffices to
account for the distortions that arise from delivering these relations over to the market. And while day care and schooling involve
paid labor (marketization of teachers' or child-care workers' services), this does not mean that these activities can or ought to be
formally organized. They do not have the same form, purpose, or

meaning as other wage labor. The public and private institutions in which child care and teaching take place are core components of civil society, despite the fact that the professional services involved are remunerated. In short, some criterion is necessary for assessing whether or not commodification or formal organization would have implications with respect to certain forms of activity or interactions that are unacceptable and unnecessary in a modern society. Our theory of civil society offers a good start in this direction.

Instead of attempting to render the roles of worker and childrearer compatible by assimilating the latter to the former, an analysis that proceeds from the system/lifeworld distinction would lead one to challenge the gender subtext of both roles while insisting on their difference. Modernization has already involved the migration of work (including education) from the home to the market. But surely a large part of a specifically feminist solution to the double burden of the working mother, to the subordination and insecurity attached to the homemaker role, and to labor market inequities must entail the degendering of the childrearing, nurturing, and homemaker roles along with a fight against the gendered division of labor in the workplace. Wages for housework and child care would only reinforce its gendered character and lock women even more strongly into low-paid service jobs. The domestic "division of labor" clearly entails a power relation based in part on women's economic dependency that deprives women of real choice and of equal voice in the distribution of such tasks; it both derives from and reinforces their inferior position in the labor market.[80] It is this relation that must be challenged.

But this approach does not rest on the strained analogy between families and economic systems and between childrearing and other productive labor. Instead, it involves a challenge to the patriarchal norms that define families and attach genders to household and other roles. Indeed, the very possibility of articulating and challenging the ways in which the modern capitalist economy and the equally modern nuclear family intersect (through gendered roles) presupposes their differentiation. Changes in the identity, normative conception, and internal role structure of families would not alter the fact that interfamilial relations including childrearing must be communicatively coordinated. Quite the contrary. One could not even criticize the contemporary family as unjust, as deformed by the unequal distribution of money, power, and asymmetric gender relations, if one did not presuppose its communicative infrastructure.[81]

2. The distinction between conventional and postconventional orientations captures a key dimension of power in existing gender norms. The forms that male dominance takes in the patriarchal nuclear family and the ways in which it structures job categories (and client relations in the welfare state) and the corresponding gender identities are modern in the descriptive, historical sense.[82] But they are neither rational nor modern in the normative sense, that is, in the way Habermas uses these words. The norms underpinning male dominance are an example of traditionalism par excellence; that is, they are based on a conventional normative "consensus" frozen and perpetuated by relations of power and inequality that lead to all sorts of pathologies in the lifeworld. The traditionalist attitude toward de facto norms based on such a consensus does not mean that the relevant norms are lingering forms of premodern status inequalities. It does mean that they are sealed off from critique and traditionalized, as it were. Indeed, they are based on a selectively rationalized civil society, and it is precisely the blockages to its further modernization in the normative sense that Habermas's theory tries to articulate. Moreover, as indicated in chapter 9, the differentiation of the subsystems of economy and state from the lifeworld is a precondition for releasing the cultural potentials of modernity and for freeing communicative interaction from ritualistically reproducing sacralized, conventional norms. The lifeworld cannot be internally differentiated, the institutions of civil society cannot be modernized, subjectivity cannot be decentered, and roles cannot be challenged unless communicative interaction is unburdened from the task of coordinating all areas of life.

3. Nevertheless, there is more to male dominance than even a modern brand of traditionalism, and Fraser does a real service by signaling a missing dimension in Habermas's analysis of power, although she does not attempt to fill the gap. It *is* misleading to restrict the term "power" to hierarchically structured relations in

bureaucratic settings without providing another term to articulate asymmetric social relations in other institutions. One would do better to distinguish among different kinds of power or, rather, among various *codes* of power and modes of the *operation* of power. Otherwise, one is left without the means to conceptualize the differential ability to impose norms, define identities, and silence alternative interpretations of femininity, masculinity, and needs. Traditionalism results from this ability but does not account for it. It is important that we know how the various forms of power operate in the construction of gender, how they permeate socialization processes, and how the norms and identities generated in civil society intersect with functioning of power as a medium in bureaucratic settings.

This would involve an analysis of power relations that is supplemental rather than antithetical to the conception of power as a coordinating medium. We have argued that formal organization is a precondition (and hence a mark of identification) of the construction of the autonomous subsystem of power.[83] It is a necessary prerequisite for power to function as a steering medium (and to be institutionalized as such). But it is neither the only mode in which power operates nor its only code. As many have pointed out, power generated outside of formal rules exists within organizations; power relations exist before the historical emergence of the medium of power, and power relations are operative in contexts that are not formally organized.[84]

Let us define power generally as the transfer of selectivity (the ability to determine what can be done and said). Power operates through the conditioning of expectations (and of expectations of expectations), linking relatively preferred and relatively rejected combinations of alternatives of at least two persons.[85] This transfer presupposes both the availability of negative sanctions and a code (or several codes) of power. Many but not all codes of power incorporate forms of inequality that distinguish among individuals as higher and lower, superior and inferior.

In one of its guises, within formally organized contexts, power operates as a steering medium that can then be extended outward to functionalize relations and institutions of civil society that are not themselves formally organized and thereby achieve administrative goals.[86] As such, the medium of power uncouples the coordination of action from consensus formation in language and neutralizes the responsibility of participants in the interaction.[87] What counts here is not the presence of a rigid bureaucratic hierarchy or structure of domination in the sense of a clear chain of command[88] but the formalization of the action context such that abstract rules and impersonal roles (be they offices or functions) become at least the official channel (one among several) through which power (selection of what can or cannot be said or done) flows. Thus, the binary schematization of interactions in sets of formal codes (especially legal/illegal) produces an objectivating attitude toward the action situation, an abstraction from concrete persons, and a certain automatic quality to the continuation of the interaction.[89]

Power does not operate only as a steering medium.[90] There are, of course, power relations within institutional settings that are not formally organized and thus lack a necessary condition for the anchoring of the medium of power. Here, too, power operates through "binary codes" that transfer selectivity, expedite communication, and avoid the risks of dissensus so long as they are not challenged. But these "codes" have a different structure from those attached to steering media in formally organized contexts. Most important, they do not fully replace ordinary language in its coordinating function; instead, they involve second-order processes of consensus formation in language. Nor do they involve depersonalized social relations. Habermas has analyzed prestige and moral authority in this way, distinguishing these "generalized forms of communication" from steering media. Prestige and moral authority can motivate action or compliance, but the validity claims underlying them can also be challenged; and if these do not survive critique, their normative basis and their power to motivate collapse. Moreover, moral authority and prestige remain strongly attached to particular persons and contexts.[91]

It is reasonable to assume that the list of "generalized forms of communication" could be expanded to include status, authority, and gender.[92] Moreover, in line with Habermas's distinction between normative and communicative action, we should distinguish between forms that allow communicative thematization and questioning up to a fixed point (such as traditional authority) and forms that are so constructed as to allow in principle for unrestricted thematization, questioning, and even criticism. It is also possible for the structure of a generalized form of communication to change, for example, from traditional to democratic authority, from status to merit, or from one conception of gender to another.

We maintain that *gender is a generalized form of communication* or, rather, the code of such communication. Existing gender codes, even if historically changing and in this sense hardly traditional, are so constructed as to stop questioning at a supposedly unchallengeable meaning complex that is defined as "natural." That power operates through gender codes, reducing the free selectivity of some and expanding that of others, is the most important and paradigmatic core of any theory that might be labeled feminist. Gender is not another steering medium but rather the set of codes in and through which power operates. Outside formal organizations (where it can serve as a secondary code of the power medium), gender continues to displace ordinary language communication and facilitate the operation of power. However, the codification of gender does not fully uncouple interaction from the lifeworld context of shared cultural knowledge, valid norms, and responsible motivations. Gender norms and identities are based ultimately on the intersubjective recognition of cognitive and normative validity claims. While conventional understandings of gender also reduce the expenditure of interpretive energy and the risks attending mutual understanding, their ability to motivate action and compliance is still linked to the alternatives of agreement or failed consensus.[93] This "relief effect" is not neutral in relation to the intersubjective recognition of norms, identities, or meanings.

Of course, the peculiar power of conventional interpretations in this domain lies in the fact that the meanings and norms at stake are bound up with identities that are transmitted through primary socialization and reinforced in secondary socialization processes throughout one's adult life. Power operating in the code of gender delimits not only what one understands as natural/unnatural, natural/cultural, male/female, feminine/masculine, attractive/ unattractive, and appropriate/inappropriate sexual objects and aims, but also constructs the meaning of bodies and operates upon them. Gender norms and identities are, in addition, reinforced by direct or indirect, positive or negative sanctions that can (but need not) be linked to unequal access to money and power in the form of media. They must therefore be challenged on two fronts: The conventional gender codes of power must be dissolved by actors who take the responsibility for creating new meanings and new interpretations into their own hands, while inequities in the distribution of money and power must be contested.

4. It is in this sense that gender identity links the public and private domains of civil society to each other and to the economy and the state administration.[94] Viewing gender as a generalized form of communication, a power code distinct from but reinforced by the media of money and power generated in the subsystems, gives us a rich theoretical framework for articulating the public/private distinction in gender terms.

The largest gap in Habermas work is his failure to consider the gendered character of roles of worker and citizen that emerged along with the differentiation of the market economy and the modern state from the lifeworld. Feminist historians have documented the parallel construction of the roles of housewife and mother and the restriction of women to these roles (as nurturer), as the flip side of the transition from the family economy to the capitalist mode of production and the replacement of autocratic/monarchic with republican/liberal forms of constitutionalism.[95] As wage labor became dominant, the role of wage worker came to be understood as a gendered, male role, while the family was constructed to be a private sphere, the domain of women, in which no "real" work was done. The same holds true for the republican conception of the citizen-soldier, which by definition excluded women.[96] It is no accident that as the roles of male breadwinner and male citizen crystalized, a cult of domesticity emerged to provide the ideological components of the new wife and mother role. Of course, a father role also developed, but this was an empty role, another name for the breadwinner. Thus, as a generalized medium of communication, gendered power relations have been built into all of the roles developed in (a selectively rationalized) modern society.[97]

It should be obvious that this reconstruction of the gender subtext of the institutional articulation of modern capitalist societies into sets of public and private relations does not undermine the dualistic social theory we have been defending. Rather, it presupposes the argument that the lifeworld "reacts in a characteristic way" to the emergence of the economic and state subsystems by internally differentiating itself into the public and private spheres of civil society, into sets of institutions oriented to cultural transmission, social integration, socialization, and individuation.[98] In our analysis of civil society, the acquisition of actionable civil rights, however selective and problematic these may be, institutionalizes the public and private spheres of civil society and subjects the economy and the state to its norms. The norms at issue here are, of course, not the ones Fraser has in mind when she appropriates the conception of the multidirectional character of influence among the various public and private spheres of classical capitalism. Patriarchal gender norms are hardly "freedom-guaranteeing," and they have justified the exclusion of women from those rights and norms that were. By implication, the gender norms that shape the key social roles mediating among institutions must be subject to critique and replaced by nonpatriarchal identities and roles.

5. The same holds true, of course, for welfare state systems. We have argued that the norms of civil and political society continue to exert influence on the economy and state through the mediating institutions of political and economic society. The "receptors" for societal influence in these spheres are, however, restricted in scope and highly selective with respect to which norms they mobilize or reinforce. Patriarchal gender norms are certainly among the latter, and they structure the roles and policies put in place by many welfare reforms. Since these norms (already backed up by inequalities in money and power) constitute women as dependents, it is not surprising that they comprise the bulk of those who become clients. The key question today is not whether but which lifeworld norms will be decisive.[99]

The colonization thesis highlights the problems associated with the opposite direction of interchange: the penetration by the media of money and power (and formal organization) into the communicative infrastructure of everyday life. This tends to reify and deplete nonrenewable cultural resources that are needed to maintain and create personal and collective identities. This includes the resources that are needed to create nonpatriarchal norms in the lifeworld and to develop the solidary associations and active participation that would help them assert their influence on the subsystems.

Habermas's sketchy but extremely suggestive analysis of the new forms of juridification utilized by welfare states highlights the ambiguities involved in the double process of interchange between system and lifeworld. On the one hand, juridification in the domain of the family involves the extension of basic legal principles to women and children who were formerly denied legal personhood by law under the doctrine of couverture (in Anglo-American countries at least). In other words, egalitarian principles replace patriarchal norms in the form of rights—of child against parents, of wife against husband, etc. Such new rights tend to dismantle the position of the paterfamilias in favor of a more equal distribution of competences and entitlements among family members. The direction of influence here clearly flows from civil society to the state, involving a choice of norms. It is these norms that are reinforced in civil society by the state as the end result of law making.

On the other hand, if the structure of juridification involves administrative and judicial controls that do not merely supplement socially integrated contexts with legal institutions but replace these by the operation of the medium of law, as is often the case under welfare law, then emancipation in the family is achieved at the cost of a new type of possible bond.[100] Experts (judges or therapists) become the adjudicators of the new rights and the conflicts around them. They intervene with their juridical or administrative means into social relations that become formalized, dissociated, and reconstructed as individualized cases to be handled administratively or juridically like any other set of adversary relations. Formal, individualizing, and hence universalizing judgments that cannot deal with contextual complexities disempower clients by preempting their capacities to participate actively in finding solutions to their problems. It is thus the medium of law itself that violates the communicative structures of the sphere that has been juridified in this way. This form of juridification goes beyond the external legal codification of rights. The administrative penetration of civil society it entails preempts the development of procedures for settling conflicts that are appropriate to structures of action oriented by mutual understanding. It blocks the emergence of discursive processes of will formation and consensus-oriented procedures of negotiation and decision making. It also necessarily abstracts away from the specific context, conditions, relations, and needs of each individual "case." It is precisely the disempowering effects of this sort of decontextualized, individualizing, and formalistic decision making that feminist analysts of recent reforms in family law have described and criticized in some detail.[101]

Debate and confusion over the meaning and desirability of seeking rights in this domain have permeated the feminist discussion. We believe that the distinction between law as institution and law as medium and the colonization thesis are helpful here. A theory of civil society constructed along these lines allows one to conceptualize an important aspect of what it is that makes the new "rights" so ambiguous. On this approach, it becomes clear that the ambivalence of feminists vis-à-vis "equal rights" legislation in this domain is based on a real dilemma: The acquisition of formal equality through means and techniques that abstract away from particular contexts, level differences, and block the creation of egalitarian social relations within civil society is an ambiguous gain indeed. In a context not only of substantive inequality (the old Marxist insight) but also of contested and fragile identities, such means will either generate new dependencies or foster the resuscitation of the old patriarchal norms as a defence against the disintegrative side effects of state penetration. Traditional patriarchal forms of life have become formally delegitimated by the new rights for women and children, but the client/expert relations that proliferate in civil society via the medium of law neither abolish substantive inequalities in power or voice nor facilitate the creation of new meanings, identities, and norms. In effect, the new vertical relations between the legal subject and the judge or social worker substitute for the horizontal communicative interaction needed to generate new solidarities, egalitarian norms, and ways of life to replace the old ones. Consequently, autonomous processes of collective empowerment and the creation of nonpatriarchal identities in civil society are blocked.[102]

It would be extremely misleading, however, to assume that all welfare state reforms have the same structure or logic. Surely legal reforms that secure the freedom of wage workers to organize unions and bargain collectively, that protect them from being fired for such collective action, and that secure worker representation on company boards differ in kind from means-tested grants to single parent households and from social services that "instruct" clients on how to function properly as childrearers and responsible providers according to some preconceived model.[103] The difference between these types of reforms is not fully captured by reference to the genders (or, for that matter, to the race) of the people they target. In addition to stating that women are the objects of one type of reform, men of the other, one ought to be able to say what it is about the reforms themselves that make some enabling and others debilitating.

Dualistic social theory allows one to do just this. The former set of reforms, unlike the latter, do not create isolated clients of a state bureaucracy but rather empower individuals to act together collectively, to develop new solidarities, and to achieve a greater balance of power relations because they are addressed to an area that is *already* formally organized.[104] Such reforms create "receptors" in the economic subsystem for the influence of the norms and modes of action of civil society by putting procedures for discursive conflict resolution into place, thereby asserting control of the latter over the former without dedifferentiating them. The second type of reform does the reverse: It brings the full force of administrative agencies into areas that are not and should not be formally organized. This threatens the communicative infrastructure and autonomy of civil society and undermines the capacities of "beneficiaries" to act for themselves or to settle conflicts discursively. And yet one certainly would not want to argue that juridification, regulation, or monetary benefits in civil society by definition humiliate or disempower those whom they are meant to benefit. The question that arises is not whether juridification (the creation of new rights) or state intervention (the granting of new benefits) should occur in civil society, but which kind of legal rights, administrative relations, or monetary benefits ought to be established. Considering that women are the prime targets/beneficiaries of welfare in this domain, surely such a question is not "askew" of feminist concerns.[105]

A feminist version of the critique of the welfare state must involve its reflexive continuation.[106] Thus, the decolonization of civil society and its modernization (in the sense of replacing conventionally held patriarchal norms with communicatively achieved norms) are both feminist projects. So, too, is the development of egalitarian institutions that can influence the administrative and economic systems. The first project would permit juridification only in forms that empower actors in civil society without subjecting them to administrative control. The second would dissolve male domination in both public and private institutions. The third would entail structural reforms in economic and political society to make them receptive and complementary to the new identities and the newly democratized, egalitarian institutions of civil society.[107]

Dual Politics: The Example of the Feminist Movement

We are now in a position to present our alternative to Habermas's interpretation of the dualistic logic of contemporary feminist movements. We have argued that the primary targets of the new social movements are the institutions of civil society. These movements create new associations and new publics, try to render existing institutions more egalitarian, enrich and expand public discussion in civil society, and influence the existing public spaces of political society, potentially expanding these and supplementing them with additional forms of citizen participation. In the case of feminism, the focus on overturning concrete forms of life based on male dominance and reinterpreting gender identities complements attempts to secure the influence of new, more egalitarian gender identities within the public spaces of civil and political society and to attain political inclusion on these terms.[108]

Given the dualistic institutional structure of the public and private spheres of modern civil society, there is no reason to view the first orientation as a retreat. To construe the defensive politics of feminism simply as a reaction to colonization, aimed only at stemming the tide of the formally organized systems of action, is quite misleading. So, too, is the pejorative tone of the label "particularist" for the concern with identities, conceptions of gender, new need-interpretations, and the like. These ought not be taken as a sign of a withdrawal into communities organized around naturalistic categories of biology and sex. Quite the contrary. Nor are they simply reactive. Rather, these concerns focus on the normative presuppositions and institutional articulation of civil society. The feminist intervention constitutes a challenge to the particularist sexist norms and practices that dominate in both public and private spheres. It attempts to initiate and influence discourses on norms and identities throughout society. Such projects are universalist insofar as they challenge restrictions and inequalities in the communicative processes (in public and in private) that generate norms, interpret traditions, and construct identities. To be sure, the content of new identities that emerge from such challenges are particular. As Touraine has clearly shown, no identity, collective or individual, can be universal. But some identities involve a greater degree of self-reflection and ego autonomy than others, and it is this that distinguishes those particular gender identities that are based on hierarchical sexist norms from those that are not.

Given the obvious permeability of political and economic institutions to societal norms, there is also no reason to foreclose the possibility of the development of egalitarian and democratic institutions capable of influencing and controlling the polity and the economy. Feminist movements contest the norms and structures of male dominance pervading civil society, but they also challenge the ways in which these inform the structuration of the subsystems in general and social policy in particular. The "offensive" dimension of feminist politics does indeed target the state and the economy, pressuring for inclusion on equal terms.[109] It is "emancipatory and universalist" as Habermas rightly argues, but universalism and the egalitarian inclusion of women in the world of work and politics involve a challenge to the male standards behind the allegedly neutral structures of these domains. Once the "typical worker" is no longer construed as the male breadwinner, the structure of labor time, the length of the working day, the nature of benefits, and the worth of jobs must be suitably revised. And once the "responsible citizen" is no longer construed as the male soldier, the inclusion of women in the political and state spheres must entail significant changes in these domains as well. In short, the offensive politics of "inclusion," if it is really to be universalist, entails institutional reform. The dual logic of feminist politics thus involves a communicative, discursive politics of identity and influence that targets civil and political society and an organized, strategically rational politics of inclusion and reform that is aimed at political and economic institutions.

Indeed, almost all major analyses of the feminist movement (in the United States and Europe) have shown the existence and importance of dualistic politics.[110] A brief look at the trajectory of the American movement will make our point.

Resource mobilization and political opportunity theorists argue that organization, networks, allies, the presence of a cycle of protest, and a reform atmosphere are central to the emergence and success of movements. The availability of these factors in the late 1960s and early 1970s has been well documented by analysts of the "second wave" of feminism.[111] So, too, has the impact on women of structural changes that facilitated their massive entry into the paid work force, the university, and the polity.[112] But neither structural change nor the growth in the membership and political expertise of women's organizations nor the existence of powerful allies sufficed to further women's rights or feminist agendas.[113] The resources, organization, and leadership for a women's movement had existed since the turn of the century; what had been missing was a mass constituency willing to support demands for women's rights, that is, a feminist consciousness.[114]

Movement analysts also include the emergence of group consciousness, solidarity, and a sense of unjust discrimination among the preconditions to collective political action, although the form that such action takes varies with the structure of the state and the political institutions (unions, parties) in the country.[115] In the case of women, attaining group consciousness involved an explicit challenge to traditional norms that identified women primarily in terms of the roles of mother and wife and justified inequalities, exclusion, and discrimination. In short, the traditional understanding of women's place and identity had to be changed, and new identities constructed, before challenges to sex discrimination could appear as a legitimate issue and women could be mobilized around them. Indeed, it quickly became evident to key sectors of the women's movement that there was a deeper problem underlying the otherwise inexplicable resistance to equal rights: Socially constructed conventional gender identities preserved male privilege and worked against women's autonomy and women's self-determination. Thus, before any standard offensive politics of reform and inclusion could be fruitful, a feminist consciousness and ideology had to be developed on the part of movement women and then communicated to others through a different politics of identity, one aimed at the public and private spheres of civil society.[116] Hence the focus on precisely those institutional arrangements and processes involved in the construction of gender identity and the slogan that "the personal is political."

It should come as no surprise, then, that the feminist movement adopted a dualistic strategy targeting both the state (and economy) and civil society. Nor is it surprising that this duality found organizational expression in two distinct, unconnected branches of the movement. The "older" branch (older in terms of median age of activists and also temporally first) included a range of interest groups focusing on political and economic inclusion and attempting to exercise influence throughout the legal and political system to fight discrimination and attain equal rights.[117] The "younger" branch, emerging from the New Left and the civil rights movement, formed into loosely connected autonomous grass-roots groups targeting the forms of male dominance within the private and public spheres of civil society. These were the groups that articulated the great mobilizing "gender" issues of abortion, contraception, rape, violence against women, and the like. Their focus on identity, self-help, consciousness raising, and proselytizing through the underground press, their own alternative publications, and the universities was aimed at spreading feminist consciousness and achieving institutional changes in social relations based on traditionalist, inegalitarian gender norms in civil society.[118] By the end of the 1960s, the two branches of the movement started moving closer together. Political "insiders" took up many of the issues articulated by "grass-roots" feminists, while the latter began to enter en masse into the local chapters of the national political organizations.[119] By the mid-1970s, "women's movement organizations took up every political avenue to change policy. They approached political parties, Congress, the courts and the executive branch; they used constitutional amendment, legislative lobbying, and political protest."[120] At the same time, the organizations that had originally restricted their activity to standard tactics of political pressure began to take up the methods of protest and persuasion initiated by the more radical groups.[121] As a result, despite its organizational diversity, one may speak of the contemporary feminist movement in the singular, composed of various associations and organizations engaged in a wide range of strategies yet sharing a feminist consciousness.[122]

There can be no question that the dualistic strategy of the contemporary women's movement has had successes in political, cultural, and institutional terms. In 1972 alone, the U.S. Congress passed more legislation to further women's rights then had the previous ten legislatures combined.[123] Women's movement organizations helped trigger a wave of legislative action on feminist issues unequaled in U.S. history.[124] Between 1970 and 1980, women's access to and influence on political elites increased dramatically, and more women were elected and appointed to public office than ever before in American history.[125] In addition, the courts became an important and productive target of the movement in both of its forms and on both of its fronts. The landmark decision in *Reed* v. *Reed* in 1971 initiated a line of cases using the equal-protection clause of the constitution to knock down sexually discriminatory statutes in the labor market. The decision in *Roe* v. *Wade* in 1973 used the right of privacy to make abortion legal, thereby registering and furthering changes in gender relations in general and in a key institution of civil society, the family, in particular.[126] As most analysts stress, however, these political and legal successes had as their prerequisite and precondition success in the cultural sense—in the prior spread of feminist consciousness.[127] The point here is not the obvious one that a mass movement can be strategically helpful to new groups seeking power and influence but, rather, that without a politics of identity aimed at the norms, social relations, institutional arrangements, and practices constructed in civil society, and without a politics of influence aimed at political society, success in the first respect would be unlikely and limited.[128]

The spread of feminist consciousness has been documented. The 1980 Virginia Slims Poll found that 64% of women favored efforts to change and strengthen the status of women, in contrast to 40% in 1970.[129] Moreover, by 1980 60% of the population believed that society, not nature, taught women to prefer homemaking to work outside the home.[130] In addition, 51% preferred a marriage in which husband and wife shared home responsibilities, and 56% favored shared responsibility for child care.[131] These statistics indicate cultural changes that go well beyond the acceptance of equal rights and inclusion of women in the political public sphere, although the latter is also accepted, at least in principle, by the majority of the population.[132]

A politics of influence informed by new conceptions of gender identity thus made it possible to turn access to political elites into the measures necessary to achieve feminist goals. And what was true for the United States has been true of Italy, Germany, England, and France as well.[133] To cite one example, Jane Jenson has shown that the insertion of the needs and interests of women onto the policy agenda in France became possible only after the women's movement took as its fundamental goal the specification of a new collective identity. She argues that "the fundamental contribution of the modern women's movement was its ability to alter the 'universe of political discourse' and thus to press its goals in ways quite different from those of earlier mobilizations of women."[134]

According to Jenson, the feminist movement changed the universe of political discourse that had excluded them by creating a new collective identity for women and by getting the political elites to accept this identity. Jenson also shows that reforms from above that extend women's rights do not, in the absence of a feminist movement, entail a change in the universe of political discourse or a change in the identity of women. After World War II, women in France acquired the right to vote and more liberal access to contraception, but the traditional universe of political discourse that defined women as wives, as appendages of men, and as mothers was not altered by these reforms.[135] It was not until the feminist movement stepped into the cultural space opened up by the New Left in 1968, began to apply to women themes such as the critique of everyday life and the right to equality and autonomy, and redefined women's collective identity in feminist terms that the traditional universe of political discourse began to alter and reforms that were feminist in both intent and impact occurred.

It is telling that Jenson focuses on the debate around the legalization of abortion to demonstrate the impact of the women's movement on the universe of discourse. Indeed most analysts of feminism agree that what is new and specific to the contemporary women's movement throughout the West, and what brought women into the public arena en masse, were the great mobilizing themes of abortion, violence against women (rape, wife-battering), sexual coercion, sexual harassment, and stereotyping.[136] Feminists demanded that the standards of justice be applied to *all* spheres of civil society, including the family. After formal citizenship rights had been granted to women, and alongside efforts to gain equal political rights, to end economic discrimination in pay and opportunity, and to fight sexual discrimination in and segmentation of the labor force, every modern feminist movement has mobilized primarily around these formerly "private," "nonpolitical," "civil society" issues.[137] And every modern feminist movement has explicitly attempted to reshape the universe of discourse so that women's voices could be heard, women's concerns perceived, women's identities reconstructed, and the traditional conceptions of women's roles, bodies, and identities, and the male dominance supported by it, undermined. To be feminist in character, new rights and institutional reforms had to reflect the changes in gender identity and in women's aspirations.

The abortion issue encompassed all of these concerns. It quickly became apparent that this issue threw down the gauntlet to the traditional universe of discourse because it signified a fundamental change in the definition and status of women.[138] The theme of freedom of choice and the demand for "control over our own bodies" expressed more than a desire for equal rights. They symbolized a demand for autonomy regarding self-formative processes, for self-determination, and for bodily integrity, in short, for the right for women to decide for themselves who they want to be, including whether and when they choose to become mothers. Considered together with the thematization of violence against women, the demands for laws legalizing abortion and criminalizing marital violence and marital rape targeted a sphere of civil society that, under the guise of "privacy," had previously been removed from such scrutiny. On the one side, privacy as autonomy was being claimed by and for women; on the other, the notion that a social institution could be private in the sense of being immune to the principles of justice was seriously challenged.[139]

Challenges to the traditional identity and roles assigned to women articulated in the debates around the abortion issue influenced and altered the universe of political discourse: "for the first time, women alone and outside a family frame of reference became the subject of political discourse . . . the new discourse on abortion reform came to symbolize nothing less than a change in women's status and their relation to their own bodies and the state."[140] This discourse involved a conception of women as both autonomous and gendered (that is, with their own specific situation), as both different and yet worthy of equal concern and respect.[141] This is why the abortion issue cannot be construed in terms of the politics of inclusion along the lines of "bourgeois emancipation movements" that bring the excluded into the polity or economy on equal terms. Rather, it is an issue tied to the "new" dimension of the feminist movement, for it poses a fundamental challenge to traditional gender identities, to traditional conceptions of the family, to patriarchal power, and to the standard liberal conception of the public and private spheres of civil society. It is a paradigmatic example of the dual logic of the feminist movement.

Civil Society and Dual Politics: A Theoretical Summary

We have argued that the translation of the relevant dimensions of the lifeworld as civil society allows one to make sense of the double political task of the new social movements: the acquisition of influence by publics, associations, and organizations on political society, and the institutionalization of their gains (new identities, autonomous egalitarian associational forms, democratized institutions) within the lifeworld. We have tried to explain the dual organizational logic of the new movements in these terms.

There is, however, another possible interpretation of the dual logic of contemporary collective action. One could attempt an account in terms of a stage (or life cycle) model in which all social movements move from forms of noninstitutional, mass protest action to institutionalized, routine interest group or party politics.[142] They begin in the form of broad yet loose networks of local associations and grass-roots groups, with minimal distinctions between "leaders" and followers, members and nonmembers. At this initial stage, collective actors make diffuse, value-laden, nonnegotiable demands that are articulated in mass protest actions. This type of collective action is specific to the process of identity formation of new collective actors. The first task of new movements is to form the very subject that must become the collective actor who will participate in political negotiations and exchanges and then the bearer of gains and losses. "There is a category of action which may be observed in social conflicts, that can be understood only if it is asked of them not what gains and losses they will produce for the actors, but whether they will produce solidarity or not. These are actions connoting a process of formation of an identity."[143] Thus, in the formative period of social movements, expressive action and direct participation are appropriate to the goal of articulating a new collective identity, and the politics of influence targets the public sphere for the purpose of gaining recognition of the new collective actor.

The second stage of social movement activity involves routinization, inclusion, and finally institutionalization.[144] Once the new collective actor succeeds in forming an identity and gaining political recognition, action shifts from the expressive to the instrumental/strategic. Formal organization replaces loose networks, membership roles and leaders emerge, and representation replaces direct forms of participation. The logic of collective action at this stage is structured by the politics of political inclusion; success means that outsiders have become insiders in an expanded polity. The shift in the rationality of collective action from the expressive to the instrumental and the change in organizational structure from the informal to the formal are understood as a learning process involving goal-rational adaptation to political structures. Full institutionalization would involve recognition of the (demobilized) group represented by the new political insiders as a legitimate special interest whose claims become susceptible to negotiation and political exchange. Success involves inclusion of "representatives" in normal politics involving party competition, participation in elections, parliamentary representation, the formation of lobby or interest groups, and eventually the occupation of government positions.[145]

The stage theory accounts for the dual logic of movement politics in terms of a linear model of development. Moreover, it seems to provide a reassuring answer to the Michelsian dilemma that seems to face all movements at some point—the fear that any move toward formal organization, inclusion, and institutionalization will undermine movement goals and threaten the continued existence of the movement form of collective action. To the extent that these processes involve cooptation, deradicalization, professionalization, bureaucratization, and centralization, "success" in institutional terms of inclusion signals the end of the movement and the dilution of its aims (the famous iron law of oligarchy). Since, in its original form, this dilemma flowed logically from the revolutionary rhetoric of the labor movement that has subsequently been abandoned, life cycle theorists can dismiss it as utopian, unrealistic, or dangerous. When movement fundamentalists articulate such fears today, in the absence of any claim to be engaging in revolutionary politics, they can by accused of an unwillingness or an inability to learn. In short, if the normal trajectory of collective action is a shift from expressive to instrumental action, adaptation to the constraints of the political system, and political inclusion and reform initiated by insiders, then the Michelsian dilemma disappears.

While the stage model certainly captures important aspects of the dynamics of social movement development, it is unable to account for the very features of the new movements that we find most significant. Indeed, our brief discussion of the trajectory of the American feminist movement belies many of its presuppositions. This movement had a dual organizational logic from its inception. While there has been routinization and institutionalization, these have neither excluded nor substituted for mass collective action, grass-roots associations, autonomous self-help organizations, or identity-oriented politics.[146] Instead of conforming to the linear model of development, the feminist movement has shifted back and forth between mass action and political pressure, depending on the available political opportunities and the issue at hand.

Nor has learning on the part of activists entailed a one-directional shift from expressive to instrumental rationality. Our discussion of the organizational development of the movement shows that learning has occurred on both sides and in both directions— political insiders took up the issues and methods of grass-roots activists while the many activists joined the formal organizations. This is not to say that the two faces of the movement have merged, but rather that the division of labor between the two segments of the movement shifts over time.

Finally, the notions that the target of the feminist movement is primarily the political system (and, through it, the economy) and that success can be construed in terms of inclusion, reform from above, or benefits is quite misleading. The struggle over abortion is once again a good counterexample. Interest organizations targeting the courts (in the United States) or political parties and parliaments (in Europe) were necessary to achieve major changes in abortion rights. But challenges to traditionalist definitions of women's role, place, and identity lie at the heart of the issue, as proponents and newly mobilized opponents of abortion rights both understand. Indeed, attempts to alter the norms, roles, and identities of women within the public and private spheres of civil society have generated far more resistance (and even counter-movements) than claims for formal equality in the work place or for inclusion in the political public sphere. The successes of the prolife movement in mobilizing constituencies and diluting abortion rights, together with the failure to win passage of the U.S. Equal Rights Amendment must be understood in these terms.[147] Thus, legal reform and political inclusion hardly suffice to define or secure success. Identity politics and grass-roots mobilizing remain on the agenda.[148]

It is a virtue of the stage model to have called attention to the fact that social movements target both civil and political society. The model is misleading, however, to the extent that it presents these orientations in either/or terms and describes the normal trajectory of collective action as a linear movement from civil to political society. There are two root problems with the model. First, it works with an overly simple conception of learning. Collective actors are assumed to learn only along the cognitive-instrumental dimension. That is, their learning is defined as a gradual recognition that identity-oriented, symbolic politics cannot help them to achieve their goals, and the result of this learning is a shift to a disciplined, hierarchical organization and an instrumental-strategic model of action. This point of view (which is typical of political parties) tends to disregard even the importance of maintaining identity and solidarity for long-term strategic action. It implies not only a lack of reflection concerning the rootedness of the actors of political society in civil society but also the notion that social movements cannot simultaneously concentrate on strategic requirements and identity building. The tacit assumption of this approach is that identities cannot become more rational. Consequently, identity building cannot move to a level of reflection that can incorporate the tension between identity and strategy. The history of movements that have consciously combined the politics of identity and strategy would be dismissed by the claim that in the end such combinations cannot and will not "succeed."

In opposition to this view, we believe that the empirical evidence is much more ambiguous with respect to movements past and present, and that the criterion of success itself needs to be redefined. For example, the achievements and continuity of working-class movements have been due in part to their ability to combine cultural and political concerns.[149] The newness of the new movements in this respect lies not so much in their dualism as in their more emphatic thematization of this dualism. Thus, their refusal to instrumentalize cultural politics and identity building for the sake of narrowly conceived political success ought not to be construed simply as a fundamentalist unwillingness to learn. Rather, one could interpret the resistance to "self-rationalization" on the part of many contemporary collective actors as a result of insight into a range of problems specific to contemporary civil society that cannot be rectified by "normal" political means. If conventional tools of government intervention are not adequate to problems arising in such areas as gender and family relations, socialization and education practices, and biotechnology, then autonomous collective action focusing on consciousness raising, self-help, and local empowerment do involve learning after all. In areas where identities, conventional meanings, institutionalized norms, life-style patterns of consumption, and socialization practices must be altered to produce solutions to social problems, learning along the moral-practical dimension is required. A self-reflective politics of identity has its proper place here.[150]

The second error has to do with a certain poverty of the model's political conception. The stage model adds the politics of identity to the politics of inclusion and reform articulated by the resource-mobilization perspective, albeit as a transitory stage. If the two major terrains for movement politics are civil and political society, then the politics of identity and inclusion can be understood analogously, since they describe the emergence of the actors in each domain. The politics of identity constitutes the actors of civil society; the politics of inclusion, after the necessary transformations in the organization and orientation of these actors, establishes them as members of political society. The politics of reform, finally, involves the strategic activity of political organizations and parties in the generation of state policy. What is missing is a conception of the relation between collective actors in civil society and those in political society. This happens because in the stage model the former effectively disappear with the emergence of the latter. It is assumed that civil society, unlike political society, can act only on itself. Following in the footsteps of the elite theory of democracy, the model thus ruptures the link between civil and political society, between civil and political actors. There is no room for a politics of influence by collective actors in civil society aimed at those in political society. But just as political society is capable of acting on the state administration, so are the actors of civil society capable of bringing the discourse and the actors of political society under their influence. This politics of influence, for which there is a great deal of empirical evidence (as we have shown in the case of the women's movement) is the key element missing in most paradigms used for the study of social movements today.

With this conception in mind, we can revisit the Michelsian dilemma that the stage model turns into its positive paradigm. For us, the traceless transformation of movements into bureaucratic political parties or lobbies remains both a negative and an avoidable model. We do recognize the tendency for movements to reproduce the organizational structures determined by power and money the moment they attempt to act directly on the subsystems of state administration and the market economy. We believe that the movement form cannot survive the step over the boundaries of the lifeworld. Movements cannot influence structures coordinated through means other than normative or communicative interaction without succumbing to the pressure for self-instrumentalization. Here, the system/lifeworld distinction continues to provide boundaries that cannot be conjured away by movement activists if they hope to be effective.

Self-bureaucratization does not follow from the politics of influence. No "iron law of oligarchy" attaches to the activity of movements aimed at the intermediate structures of political society or at the forms of the public sphere that exist on this level. Our answer to the Michelsian dilemma is to point to the potential and actual duplication of actors in civil and political society and to the possibility of a new type of relationship between them. We do recognize the tensions between grass-roots associations in the lifeworld targeting civil society and organizations capable of strategically affecting the state and economic systems, but only at the cost of bureaucratization (penetration by the medium of power). We believe nevertheless that a higher level of self-reflection, rooted in a dialogue between theory and its movement addressees, holds the possibility of diminishing these antagonisms. The program of self-limiting radical democracy involves a critique of democratic fundamentalism typical of collective actors based in civil society and a critique of democratic elitism typical of those based in political society. This theoretical critique will be impotent, however, unless civil actors move forward to a politics capable of influencing political actors instead of retreating to the other side of fundamentalism, which is passivity.

Finally, our dualistic conception offers a criterion of success for movements that differs from those of movement fundamentalists and political professionals. We consider the development of self-reflective and self-limiting actors able to influence political discussion to be highly desirable, as are political parties that maintain a high degree of openness to civil society without surrendering the prerequisites of effective strategic action. So much automatically follows from our argument. But notions of success in civil and political society should not be assimilated to each other. In political society, organizational self-maintenance is a desideratum; in civil society, it is not, and too much attention to it may in itself lead to transgressions over the boundary between system and lifeworld.

The success of social movements on the level of civil society should be conceived not in terms of the achievement of certain substantive goals or the perpetuation of the movement, but rather in terms of the democratization of values, norms, and institutions that are rooted ultimately in a political culture. Such a development cannot make a given organization or movement permanent, but it can secure the movement form as a normal component of self-democratizing civil societies. For example, if part of the achievement of movements is the institutionalization of rights, then the end of a social movement—either because of its organizational transformation or its absorption into newly created cultural identities—does not mean the end of the context of the generation and constitution of social movements. The rights achieved by movements stabilize the boundaries between lifeworld, state, and economy; but they are also the reflection of newly achieved collective identities, and they constitute the condition of possibility of the emergence of new institutional arrangements, associations, assemblies, and movements. The classical rights achieved by the democratic revolutions and workers' movements have already functioned in this way vis-à-vis the civil rights and other movements. Theorists have yet to formulate the new rights appropriate to the challenge to the state and economy by contemporary movements. Today, both prevailing models of rights—one linked to the preeminent position of property rights, the other structured around a model of state-secured benefits—have shown their underside.[151] Nevertheless, institutionalized rights are both important footholds and catalysts (precisely because of their internal contradictions) for contemporary struggles for rights. This is especially true for initiatives that "reflexively continue" the programs of the democratic revolution and welfare state by establishing the pride of place of rights of association and communication.

This program can be completed only on the basis of a dualistic strategy in which the politics of identity, influence, inclusion, and reform all have major roles to play. From the point of view of a theory of civil society, the politics of influence is the most central of these, since it is the only means of displacing movement fundamentalism and blocking the road to political elitism. Without it, the politics of civil society turns into an antipolitics. Thus, the politics of influence merits a closer look from the point of view of political theory; this is the task of chapter 11, on civil disobedience, one of the most important means through which social movements can hope to influence modern society.

Civil Disobedience and Civil Society

We have argued that the new theory of civil society allows us to reconcile the liberal and democratic traditions of normative political theory. In chapter 8 we proposed that discourse ethics implies the compatibility, indeed, the intimate interrelation, between rights and democracy and that this interrelation is not merely an instrumental one. Our point was to show that the legitimacy of modern constitutional regimes that claim to be democratic and to respect rights rests ultimately on the supralegal normative presuppositions of both democratic and liberal theory, that is, on the ideas of democratic legitimacy and moral rights.[1]

There are many regimes that are considered liberal democracies; the problem is that the prevailing models (and theories) of liberal democracy are not, in our opinion, sufficiently democratic. From the point of view of the standard liberal model of the opposition of civil society and the state, democracy is on the whole conceived instrumentally,[2] but such a view is incompatible with our conception. Instead, we conceive of civil society as the locus of both democratic legitimacy and rights, composed of private but also of politically relevant public and social spheres in which individuals speak, assemble, associate, and reason together on matters of public concern and act in concert in order to influence political society and, indirectly, decision making. This conception bursts the dichotomous public/private framework of classical liberalism and raises democracy to the level of a fundamental value while simultaneously challenging all monistic conceptions of the possible forms and loci of democracy.

Why, then, conclude a book on civil society with a discussion of civil disobedience? We have maintained that the politics of revolutionary fundamentalism is antithetical to the project of democratizing modern civil society. We have provided normative and structural arguments to support this thesis. At the same time, we have argued for the possibility and desirability of radical institutional reform and have interpreted the projects of the new social movements along these lines. Nevertheless, it might appear that we have sacrificed to realism the utopian core of the radical democratic project, namely, the goal of achieving of genuine citizen participation in public life. Realist, elite models of democracy leave politics to the professionals in political society and advocate "civil privatism" for the members of civil society. We hope that a discussion of the role of civil disobedience within modern civil societies will dispel this interpretation. Moreover, in the context of the demise of Marxism, this century's most important utopian project of emancipation, it is necessary to consider the relation between our theory of civil society and emancipatory projects. Is it possible to conceive of a radical politics of civil society? We believe that a reflection on civil disobedience can provide an answer to this question by showing that there is indeed an alternative to the choice between "soulless reformism" and revolutionary fundamentalism, between civil privatism and the total politicization of society.

Social movements are a normal, albeit extrainstitutional, dimension of political action in modern civil societies. We have interpreted their projects of self-limiting radicalism as attempts to expand rights and democratize institutions. The politics of civil society is thus both defensive and offensive: Social movements seek to democratize civil society, to protect it from economic and political "colonization," and to exert influence on political society. While this involves the politics of identity, inclusion, reform, and influence, the latter is the most central to our present concern, since it is aimed at maintaining the link between civil and political society.

Our discussion of social movements raises a new set of questions for democratic (and liberal) theory. Social movements are not always internally democratic, and they tend to bypass the existing political channels for exerting influence. Indeed, collective actors often engage in civil disobedience.[3] The questions before us, then, are the following: What claims to legitimacy can social movements that engage in civil disobedience have within a "nearly just," "nearly democratic" constitutional regime?[4] Is there any justification for violating laws duly promulgated by democratic legislatures or for political activities that bypass the existing procedures and institutions for expressing political concerns? Do not acts of civil disobedience violate the rights of the majority to make binding law,[5] thereby challenging both liberal and democratic principles? How can illegal political action, whatever its purpose, be reconciled with the principles of a liberal and democratic polity: the rule of law, majority rule, and respect for the rights of all? And why is it necessary for normative political theory to address the question of civil disobedience at all?

It is our thesis that civil disobedience, properly understood, is a key form that the utopian dimension of politics can assume in modern civil societies. We proceed from the assumption that rights and democracy, as we have interpreted them, involve, in part, utopian political principles (in the Kantian sense of regulative principles) underlying constitutional democracies. We shall argue that civil disobedience, as a form of noninstitutional political action specific to citizens of modern civil societies, is intimately related to these utopian principles.

The peculiarity of collective action involving civil disobedience is that it moves between the boundaries of insurrection and institutionalized political activity, between civil war and civil society. By definition, civil disobedience is extrainstitutional: A legal right to engage in civil disobedience is self-contradictory. But it does not thereby violate the principles of civil society. Rather, direct political action in the form of civil disobedience keeps the utopian horizon of a democratic and just civil society alive, for two reasons. First, civil disobedience is principled collective action that presupposes at least the partial institutionalization of rights and democracy; that is, it presupposes the rights that establish and protect civil society as well as a representative political system claiming democratic legitimacy (in the sense of representing and responding to citizens' opinions and interests) and providing for at least some political participation. Second, a fully democratic and just civil society is, of course, a utopia in the classical sense; it can never be fully realized or completed but operates as a regulative ideal that informs political projects. Civil societies can always become more just, more democratic. Collective actors take this utopia seriously and hope to realize it. Indeed, without this kind of powerful motivation, there would be no social movements. Nevertheless, acts of civil disobedience are examples of self-limiting radicalism par excellence. On the one hand, civil disobedients extend the range of legitimate, even if initially extralegal, citizen activity that is accepted by a given political culture. Few would be shocked today by a workers' strike, a sit-in, a boycott, or a mass demonstration. These forms of collective action have come to be considered normal, yet all of them were once illegal or extralegal and could again become illegal under some conditions. Thus, civil disobedience initiates a learning process that expands the range and forms of participation open to private citizens within a mature political culture. Moreover, it is well known that, historically, civil disobedience has been the motor to the creation and expansion of both rights and democratization. On the other hand, civil disobedience defines the outer limits of radical politics within the overall framework of civil societies. It accepts the basic principles of a constitutional government. At the same time, we shall argue that the integrity of constitutionalism hinges on the acceptance by a political culture of the normative and valuable character of illegal collective action in the form of civil disobedience. Accordingly, we assess civil disobedience not merely as a tactic but as an expression of legitimate citizen action. We view civil disobedience as one of the means available to ordinary citizens to exert influence on members of political society and to ensure that professional politicians remain responsive to public opinion. We shall thus try, on a conceptual and normative level, to vindicate the claim that "Every constitutional democracy that is sure of itself considers civil disobedience as a normalized—because necessary— component of its political culture."[6]

For the purposes of this argument, we consider the role and appropriateness of civil disobedience under somewhat ideal circumstances, within the framework of a constitutional democracy that is "nearly" just and democratic.[7] The problem of civil disobedience is indeed, as John Rawls has argued, a "crucial test case for any theory of the moral basis of democracy."[8] However, "the moral basis of democracy" does not have the same meaning in the liberal as distinct from the democratic tradition of political philosophy. For the former, the moral basis of democracy is located in the principle of rights, whereas for the latter, it derives from the principle of democratic legitimacy. Accordingly, the question of civil disobedience is posed in somewhat different ways. In the first case, the problem is addressed within the framework of a potential conflict between the decisions (laws, policies) of legitimately established democratic authority and the principle of individual rights (or autonomy). In the second case, the issue is the quality of democratic procedures. In other words, for the democrat, the question of civil disobedience is posed with respect to the degree of representativeness and inclusiveness of a given procedure, the possibilities for participation, or the proper locus of sovereignty. Each approach tends to screen out the other's point of view.

The issue before us concerns the role of the two counterfactual normative and even utopian conceptions of rights and democracy within modern civil societies governed by the principles of constitutionalism. Indeed, the idea of a civil society secured by rights and animated by citizen participation and collective action that is able to influence "representatives" in political society is itself a utopia, albeit a self-limiting one. It links continuity with the institutional and cultural achievements of the past to radical change. We shall show how the problematic of civil disobedience has been addressed within the liberal and democratic traditions of modern political theory in order to show that each, to be consistent, must include the perspective of the other and, furthermore, that this can be done on the basis of our model of civil society.[9]

Contemporary Liberal-Democratic Theory and Civil Disobedience

It should come as no surprise that two of the most influential contemporary theorists in the liberal tradition—John Rawls and Ronald Dworkin—have devoted a number of essays to the question of civil disobedience.[10] While some of these essays were written in response to political events,[11] they are nonetheless quite revealing of the strengths and limits of contemporary liberal political theory. Both Rawls and Dworkin understand civil disobedience as involving actions contrary to the law within the limits of fidelity to the law.[12] Both seek to establish the legitimacy and limits of toleration for civil disobedience within a "nearly just" (Rawls) constitutional democracy. Moreover, the essays that they have written on the topic constitute the most "democratic" moments in their overall theories. As we shall see, here, if nowhere else, the citizen replaces the legislator, the executive, and the judge as the key political actor and the final court of appeal. Yet it is not quite true that for these theorists, civil disobedience constitutes a "litmus test for democracy."[13] Rather, civil disobedience in each case tests the degree to which constitutional democracies are liberal, that is, the degree to which they take rights seriously. Civil disobedience by its very nature poses the question of the degree and kinds of legitimate citizen participation in political life—a question at the heart of democratic theory. However, neither Rawls nor Dworkin construes civil disobedience as a response to perceived deficiencies in the extent or quality of democratic procedures in the polity. If the legislature conforms to the procedures and principles of justice enshrined in the constitution, and if the political or civil rights of the citizen are not violated, then civil disobedience is not the appropriate way to address these kinds of issues; indeed, for the liberal democrat they do not even exist. Questions of democracy are translated into the language of rights. It is assumed, moreover, that the principle of democratic legitimacy is capable of full institutionalization within the political system of representative government, secured by the rights to vote, hold office, petition, assemble, speak, and associate.[14]

Instead, civil disobedience is seen as a legitimate response only to violations of justice, that is, to transgressions by the duly constituted democratic majority (in the legislature) of individual or minority rights. Of course, the principles of justice constitute for each theorist "the moral foundations of democracy." Yet these foundations turn out to be a conception of the basic liberties in conformity with which constitutional regimes and democratic procedures must be constituted and must function. It is assumed that the citizen in such societies owes loyalty to constitutionally established institutions. The duty to obey varies with the government's respect for rights, not with the degree of participation available to citizens.

In other words, the extent of an individual's obligation to obey the law is formulated in terms of what the citizen may legitimately do or refuse to do in cases of injustice, given the allegiance owed in principle to a constitutional democracy.[15] Each theorist construes the basic liberties or rights somewhat differently, but they both assume that the justice of a constitutional state can be assessed in terms of the degree to which it secures the most extensive basic liberty compatible with the liberty of others (Rawls) or equal concern and respect (Dworkin) and, hence, basic rights for all.[16] The issue of legitimate dissent or civil disobedience therefore poses the boundary question between state and civil society, establishing the point at which democratic majorities in constitutional states must be self-limiting. Legislation that violates basic rights transgresses its proper bounds. Rawls states:

The problem of civil disobedience as I shall interpret it arises only within a more or less just democratic state for those citizens who recognize and accept the legitimacy of the constitution. The difficulty is one of a conflict of duties. At what point does the duty to comply with laws enacted by a legislative majority (or with executive acts supported by such a majority) cease to be binding in view of the right to defend one's liberties and the duty to oppose injustice? This question involves the nature and limits of majority rule.[17]

Civil disobedience for both Rawls and Dworkin plays the role of protecting individual rights *against* the democratic polity.

The moral foundation of constitutional democracy is located, for the liberal, in the principle of rights.[18] Liberal political theory proceeds from the assumption of plurality. It presupposes a modern civil society comprised of groups and individuals with different and even opposed ways of life and conceptions of the good, who are able, nonetheless, to arrive at a shared conception of political justice.[19] However, neither Rawls nor Dworkin maintains the absolute primacy of the individual's moral conscience vis-à-vis public law. Indeed, this is not even the core problem of civil disobedience. On the contrary, both theorists carefully distinguish between conscientious refusal and civil disobedience in terms of the political character of the former versus the apolitical character of the latter. Rawls defines civil disobedience as "a public, nonviolent, conscientious yet political act contrary to law usually done with the aim of bringing about a change in the law or policies of the government."[20] Civil disobedience is a political act in the sense that it is an act justified by moral principles that define a conception of civil society and the public good. It is a political act not only because it is addressed to the majority that holds political power but also because it is guided and justified by the political principles of justice that regulate the constitution. "The civil disobedient addresses the sense of justice of the majority of the community and declares that in one's considered opinion the principles of social cooperation among free and equal men are not being respected."[21] What distinguishes civil disobedience from conscientious refusal is that it is public in the dual sense of not being concealed or covert and of appealing to the general political principles of justice presumably shared by everyone in a constitutional regime, rather than to one's personal morality, religion, or particular or group interests.[22] Conscientious refusal, that is, a refusal to comply with a direct legal injunction or administrative order, can be public in the sense of not being covert, but it is based on apolitical reasoning in that it neither appeals to the sense of justice of the majority nor aims by definition at convincing others or causing changes in law or policy. Indeed, Rawls insists on the primacy of the political in such cases: The degree of toleration of conscientious refusal must be worked out from the standpoint of a political theory of justice, in terms of what is necessary for preserving and strengthening just institutions, and not from the standpoint of an absolute respect by the law for the dictates of individual conscience.[23] The latter would clearly be untenable in a pluralist civil society.

If social institutions are based on a shared conception of justice, why would civil disobedience arise at all in a "nearly just" constitutional democracy? The answer given by both Rawls and Dworkin is, in the first instance, rather simple: Legislative majorities can err or, worse, be misguided by prejudice and thus violate the moral principles underlying the constitution.[24] There is, however, a significant difference in the way the two theorists understand the status of these moral principles. Since the range and even the function of tolerable civil disobedience varies accordingly, it is worth exploring this difference in some detail.

Rawls defines a just constitutional democracy as one whose constitution would be agreed upon by rational delegates in a constitutional convention who are guided by the two principles of justice. Just laws and policies are those that would be enacted by rational legislators constrained by a just constitution and, again, guided by the two principles of justice. The latter are the principles that would be chosen in an original position that is fair.[25] And indeed, in Rawls's view, these two principles of justice constitute the moral underpinnings of the principle of majority rule, without which such rule would merely be a procedural device enshrining the power of numbers. Moreover, since no political procedure can guarantee that enacted legislation is just, given the unavoidable condition of "imperfect procedural justice" obtaining in even the best of polities, it is obvious that unjust laws may be passed by those with the constitutional right to make law.[26] Some form of the majority principle is necessary, but the majority may be mistaken more or less willfully in what it legislates.[27] Thus, when the majority violates the conception of justice shared by the community at large and embodied in the constitution, it sets the stage for justifiable acts of civil disobedience.

Rawls does not maintain that the injustice of a law is sufficient justification for such action. On the contrary, he insists that we are bound to follow unjust laws if the injustice does not exceed certain limits. Under the principles of majority rule, there are bound to be results that minorities regard as unjust, but so long as these do not exceed certain limits, the duty to support just institutions includes a duty to obey unjust laws. Nor, for that matter, is conformity of the law with the two principles of justice a sufficient condition for political obligation. Indeed, the concept of political *obligation*, strictly speaking, applies only to certain categories of individuals: those who have voluntarily accepted the benefits of institutional arrangements or taken advantage of the opportunities they offer to further their interests.[28] For the rest, Rawls maintains that there is a "natural duty" to comply with the laws and policies of a nearly just polity. Natural duties, moreover, apply to us without regard to our voluntary acts: "Each is bound to these institutions independent of his voluntary acts, performative or otherwise."[29] Rawls argues that the natural duty of justice must be understood as the outcome of a hypothetical agreement or contract and, hence, implies hypothetical consent. He insists, however, that no act of consent, express or tacit, and no voluntary act is presupposed for the duty of justice—it applies unconditionally. The reason Rawls gives for rejecting voluntary action as the basis of the duty to comply with just institutions is that this would be superfluous: Given the two principles of justice and the priority of liberty, the full complement of equal liberties is already guaranteed and no further assurances are necessary. Moreover, the recognition of a natural duty of justice provides stability and ensures against free riding.[30]

Civil disobedience involves a conflict between the natural duty to comply with laws enacted by a legitimate majority and the right to defend one's liberties and to oppose injustice. But when is the duty to comply suspended? What are the limits that cannot be transgressed by legislative majorities? Rawls mentions two ways in which such injustice can arise: Laws or institutional arrangements can depart from the publicly accepted conception of justice, or the conception itself may be unreasonable or unjust.[31] He discusses civil disobedience only with respect to the first possibility, though, and only under some circumstances.[32] The natural duty to obey is suspended, and civil disobedience is justifiable, in instances of substantial and clear injustice: "There is a presumption in favor of restricting civil disobedience to serious infringements of the first principle of justice, the principle of equal liberty, and to blatant violations of the second part of the second principle, the principle of fair equality of opportunity."[33] According to Rawls, it is usually clear when political and civil rights are being violated, because they impose strict requirements visibly expressed in institutions. Infractions of the first part of the second principle of justice, of the requirement that inequalities be to the advantage of the least well-off, are much more imprecise because they involve matters of economic and social policy, speculative beliefs, statistical information, etc. Thus, the resolution of these matters is best left to the political process.

On this conception, civil disobedience is a form of public speech, addressed to the majority that holds political power, expressing the profound conscientious political conviction that, in one's considered opinion, the political majority has violated the accepted conception of justice and the moral underpinnings of social co-operation.[34] It functions as a corrective and as a stabilizing device. It brings wayward majorities to their senses and returns the legislative system to the status quo ante. On the level of political culture, the readiness to engage in justified civil disobedience serves as a prophylactic against potential departures from justice and thereby introduces stability into a well-ordered society.[35]

While Rawls thus offers an important justification for civil disobedience, he provides a relatively narrow conception of its range and legitimacy. He assumes that political society is responsive to the concerns of civil society regarding rights and that the latter can exercise some influence on the former through collective action (understood as a discursive process rather than a power play). The political thrust of civil disobedience and of the corresponding forms of collective action is restricted, however, to a purely *defensive* posture on the part of those whose rights have been violated. Moreover, the type of "mistake" the majority can make when it enacts an unjust law is restricted to a violation of aspects of the two principles of justice. Rawls assumes that a coherent conception of justice, accepted in principle by all members of the polity, exists and can be appealed to when the majority errs. Such mistakes involve only violations of individual rights and not, for example, misunderstandings of popular will, inadequate representations of public opinion, or insufficient public considerations of the relevant issues. Indeed, for Rawls, the conception of justice is, in a constitutional democracy, fixed *"once and for all"*—and this means that there is no legitimate extralegal way to test or expand this conception without challenging the whole institution of society. Thus, those whose rights are not violated but who believe, for example, that the existing institutions and procedures of the society and polity, while just and partially democratic, are not sufficiently so, are faced with a difficult choice—either they work through the very institutions they deem inadequate or they engage in acts construable only as revolt; either they accept the prevailing conception of justice and the institutions embodying it or they become militants.[36] This is a fairly static conception of the function of civil disobedience: It can correct violations of existing rights, it can stabilize majority rule, or, at most, it can expand rights by ensuring that everyone's rights are respected, that the conception of justice is applied equally and fairly to all. Questions about the conception of justice, about new kinds or new interpretations of rights, and about more and new kinds of participation have no place within a well-ordered polity; they can lead only to its replacement.

Rawls's restriction of civil disobedience to the defense of rights derives from the liberal model of civil society, the state, and their interrelation that he presupposes.[37] Within this framework, civil society is construed as the private sphere; it is the locus of individual autonomy, of a plethora of groups with distinct ways of life and conceptions of the good, of voluntary associations of such groupings with no political thrust, and of public expression secured by rights. Political life is securely located within political society; it takes place on the terrain of the state in the form of the legislature, complemented by the usual apparatus of elections, parties, interest groups, and constitutionally articulated procedures. These comprise the sole legitimate terrain for political action and the only forms of political participation open to the citizen under normal circumstances (when neither rights nor political neutrality are violated). Moreover, the purely defensive function of civil disobedience in Rawls's theory—protecting already acquired rights or extending them in the name of clearly institutionalized principles of justice—rests on a static conception of the boundary between public and private, between the state and civil society, and of political culture in general.

Even with these restrictions, Rawls's discussion of civil disobedience tends to burst this rigid dualism. On the one hand, the formulation of civil disobedience as public speech appealing to the *conception* of justice of the political majority in the *legislature* seems to reduce such action to a model of moral suasion that simply extends the classical liberal defense of the right to conscience and the plea for toleration to a set of narrowly circumscribed collective actions.[38] On the other hand, Rawls also argues that civil disobedience appeals to the *sense* of justice of the majority of the *community*, that is, to public opinion in civil society itself. This is what he has in mind when he argues that the final court of appeal is neither the legislature nor the Supreme Court nor the executive, but the electorate as a whole.[39] It is in this context that the core democratic idea of the sovereign people who have final authority makes its sole appearance in his text. Here, he argues that both democratic legitimacy and the idea of rights provide the moral underpinning of the purely legal framework of constitutional democracy.[40]

Moreover, Rawls understands legislation within the parliamentary public sphere as a discursive process, aimed at achieving the best policy or law for the community, wherein legislators vote according to personal judgment and not according to the interests of their particular constituencies. But this judgment is not simply private; it ought to be a considered interpretation of the principles and political culture of the society. By implication, public opinion ought to be able to influence the legislative majority. Actors in civil society ought to be able to influence actors in political society. Rawls believes that this is often the case.[41] If, however, it is the *sense* of justice of the *community* to which civil disobedience appeals, if the *citizenry* is the final court of appeal, if the idea of democratic legitimacy, and not only the principle of rights, provides the moral basis of constitutionalism, then the range of legitimate (albeit illegal) collective action within civil society cannot be restricted to laws that conflict with the *conception* of justice of the legislative majority, to the violation of the rights of a minority by that majority, or to the rights dimension of the moral underpinnings of democracies.[42] By implication, civil society itself would have to be understood as having an active, politically relevant dimension: Collective action within civil society, yet outside the institutionalized channels of the political system, would have to be seen as normal. In other words, the political relevance of the rights to speech, assembly, and association would have to be addressed more seriously as securing the legitimacy of citizen action aimed at influencing political society and, indirectly, political and legal decisions.[43]

Rawls, however, retreats from the implications of these ideas. He nowhere tells us what channels of influence do or should exist between the legislature and publics within civil society. Nor does he ever concede that, absent a violation of rights, a legitimate target of civil disobedience might be the creation or broadening of such channels. He assumes, moreover, that the principles of democratic legitimacy are fully institutionalized by elections, parliaments, and

other constitutional forms.[44] After a constitutional convention—
or, rather, after ratification of a constitution—the society's conception of justice is institutionalized once and for all, and the people
cease under normal circumstances to be political actors in any
guise other than that of the electorate. Apart from this, politics
remains the monopoly of political society. Armed with this theory,
Rawls is apparently able to circumscribe the extrainstitutional
"sovereignty" or authority of "the people" as expressed in acts of
civil disobedience within the narrow bounds of defending the
rights that everyone in principle already has.

But what if the society's conception of justice, allegedly enshrined
in the constitution and serving as its guide to legislation and the
standard by which its legitimacy is to be tested, is not clear and self-
evident? What if the moral principles articulated in the constitution
that are at the heart of the idea of fundamental rights are open to
different interpretations and, hence, applications? Indeed, according to Dworkin, it is because any constitution fuses moral and
legal issues by making the *validity* of a law depend on the answer to
complex moral problems that the question of what moral rights
citizens have is always open to new interpretations.[45] Moreover, even
if the majority left the constitution alone, even if it were properly
interpreted by a Supreme Court, no constitution could institutionalize all the moral rights that citizens have. There can, in other
words, be no point in time at which one could say that all fundamental
rights have been established and are protected, because the very
meaning, interpretation, and range of fundamental rights develops over time. What a constitution can establish is a recognition
that individuals do have fundamental moral rights against the state.
It can even enumerate some of these rights in broad terms, but it
cannot articulate all of these rights, not because the list would be
long but because interpretations of rights change and new rights
will be asserted that are in tune with the principle of having moral
rights against the state but hardly derivable from this idea. Thus, a
complex hermeneutic must be at work in the interpretation of
rights, involving a reflection on constitutional principles, tradition,
precedent, and contemporary political morality.

Dworkin thus offers a more complex answer than Rawls to the
questions of why, in a nearly just constitutional democracy that

recognizes rights, civil disobedience might legitimately arise, and why it should be treated differently than criminal acts or outright acts of revolt. Indeed, as we shall see, he expands liberal theory to its furthest conceivable limits—although, for reasons that will become evident, the theory remains at the threshold of the principle of democratic legitimacy and is therefore partial. Dworkin agrees with Rawls that if the government enacts a law that wrongly invades one's rights against the government, one has a moral right to break the law. This is not a separate right but a feature of having rights against government.[46] Dworkin takes a significant step beyond Rawls's position, though, by arguing that there is no general duty to obey the law in all cases, and certainly none when moral rights are violated. Indeed, the real issue is not the obvious case just mentioned but the situation in which the law is unclear, so that there can be doubt over its validity. "When the law is uncertain, in the sense that a plausible case can be made on both sides, then a citizen who follows his own judgment is not behaving unfairly."[47] This is, of course, a very open definition of unclear law: Lack of clarity does not refer to the written text of the law but rather to a situation in which a legal norm is contested.

In the United States, it is the role of the Supreme Court to settle interpretive questions about doubtful law with respect to rights. As Dworkin notes, however, the court can "change its mind." Indeed, any court can overrule itself. Thus, we cannot assume that, at any given point in time, the Constitution is what the Supreme Court says it is.[48] It cannot be argued convincingly that the citizens may, in the case of doubtful law, follow their own judgment only until the authoritative institution decides the case. On the contrary, if citizens must act as if doubtful law were valid and the highest court were the final locus of judgment, "then the chief vehicle we have for challenging the law on moral grounds would be lost, and over time the law we obeyed would certainly become less fair and just, and the liberty of our citizens would certainly be diminished."[49] If no one challenged apparently settled law in the name of fundamental rights, then we would not be able to take cognizance of changes over time in the community's morality.[50] Without the pressure of dissent, we would increase the chance of being governed by principles that offend the principles we share. Indeed, law is in part developed through experimentation by citizens and through the adversary process, and civil disobedience helps shape issues for adjudication.[51] Because law is in a constant process of adaptation and revision, civil disobedience may be the pacesetter for long overdue corrections or innovations without which a vital republic could not maintain its citizens' belief in the continued legitimacy of laws inherited from the past.

This discussion of legal validity is central to Dworkin's defense of civil disobedience and requires further elucidation. According to Dworkin, the validity of law depends on a permanently open-ended process of testing in which the courts play a role that includes consideration of morally relevant interpretations of the principles informing the constitution. Clearly, what is at stake is not only the procedural correctness of the legislative process that generated the law but also the interpretation of moral principles informing a constitutionally articulated political culture. And just as judges may reflect on these principles, so can ordinary citizens; law testing is not the monopoly of judges.

This argument is linked to H. L. A. Hart's distinction between the internal or participant's perspective and the external or observer's perspective. This distinction implicitly corresponds to the two levels of analysis regarding the validity of law: respect for established rules and procedural requirements and for moral validity. Questions of procedural correctness within the "model of rules" involve only the observer's point of view. Questions of validity are often interpreted in this way as well: A law is taken to be valid if both its creation and its applications have been judged to be procedurally correct and not to violate other valid rules. Testing validity in this sense requires that testers put themselves in the position of "objective lawyers" estimating the chances of a successful challenge. They would agree to submit unconditionally to the subsequent judicial decision as long as this in turn is procedurally correct.[52] In this model, laws that are not overturned or repealed are valid laws. Laws that are repealed or overturned on the basis of changing constitutional interpretation (though it is difficult to draw the exact boundary here) do not retroactively lose their earlier status as law.

Dworkin, thinking undoubtedly of "hard" rather than routine cases, is not satisfied with this model of validity. His understanding of validity involves both an observer's and a participant's perspective. There could be test cases in which lawbreakers see themselves as part of an objective process aimed at clarifying valid law, but insofar as a test case involves a claim that moral principles (rights) embedded in the constitution have been violated, a participant's perspective also enters into the assessment. According to Dworkin, this sort of interpretive act is performed both by the courts and by those who break a law in order to initiate a test of its validity. Test cases involving illegal actions by citizens who believe that a given law violates basic moral rights and is therefore invalid are an integral part of the process by which courts assess the constitutionality, that is, the validity, of law. In this wider model of the test case, the result of a successful challenge is that the law in question is declared invalid, that is, nonlaw, from the moment of its promulgation, irrespective of whether the grounds for overturning involve procedure, constitutional adequacy, or higher normative principle.

In this model, civil disobedience is interpreted as a type of test case, whether the disobedients are motivated by a presumption of invalidity or by a more general belief in the injustice or illegitimacy of the law or policy. Indeed, in this interpretation, if the law that has been challenged by civil disobedients turns out to be invalid, no law has been broken after all.

The interpretation is unsatisfactory, however, because it underestimates the specific tension within civil disobedience between the trauma of law breaking by individuals who otherwise presuppose and respect the legal system and obedience to higher law or normative principle. Two examples demonstrate this point. First, perhaps the majority of acts of civil disobedience, unlike all acts intentionally raising test cases, involve the breaking of laws that are not the specific laws or policies the civil disobedients seek to challenge. Indeed, the examples of civil disobedience to which Dworkin refers—the anti–Vietnam war movement (with the possible exception of draft resistance), the civil rights movement (with the exception of lunch-counter sit-ins), and the antinuclear movement—fall into this category and can therefore not be understood as test cases in the usual sense. Dworkin's entire discussion is, in fact, addressed to these sorts of illegal acts and not to standard test cases. Second, civil disobedience directed against specific policies, whose legitimacy Dworkin restricts but does not deny, does not challenge the constitutionality of laws but argues that these laws are unwise, immoral, or both. The policies involved are not invalid and so can be abolished (though not retroactively) only by legislative repeal or replacement. In these cases, the issue is really the legitimacy rather than the validity of law. This legitimacy is challenged by actors who take a purely participatory point of view, that is, who put themselves in the place of the legislature and actually enter into a process of communication with their representatives and the electorate (or public) as a whole.

We believe that it makes sense to separate civil disobedience and test cases, at least for analytical purposes.[53] In civil disobedience proper, the primary viewpoint is participatory, and what is involved is a claim regarding above all the legitimacy of law. In law testing proper, what is at issue is procedural regularity, both prior to the test and during the judicial process of testing itself, as well as the consistency of the system of legal rules. Whatever the motivation of the tester, a test presupposes only an observer's point of view.

There are, of course, cases in which law testing and civil disobedience cannot be easily separated, in which the issue is not simply correct procedure or legitimacy but validity in Dworkin's complex sense. There are obviously cases of civil disobedience, such as draft resistance and sit-ins, in which the issue of validity is not excluded and those who disobey a statute using the techniques of collective action also hope for a change in the validity status of the law. There may also be cases of law testing in which the challenger is not ready to accept the prediction of lawyers or the judgment of the court and the courtroom action itself is supposed to dramatize the injustice and indeed illegitimacy for agents and constituencies outside the legal procedure. Despite these mixed cases and in contrast to Dworkin, we believe that it is useful to distinguish between law testing and civil disobedience. Although he does not make the distinction, for the purposes of this discussion we feel justified to assume that he is concerned with civil disobedience proper. While he tends to emphasize validity rather than legitimacy and to assimilate civil disobedience to the test case, his linking of civil disobedience with the process of the defense of fundamental rights (in which even a decision of the highest court cannot be said to be the final word) involves the highest principles of our legal order *as a whole* and obviously goes beyond the test case as a general model.

What we have here, then, is a justification of civil disobedience in situations other than obvious flagrant violations of existing individual rights. Civil disobedience can be seen as a crucial component of change within a constitutional democracy. It is a major source for *creating* rights (that is, for institutionalizing moral rights that have not been previously institutionalized), and it initiates a learning process that contributes to the development of political culture and to institutional change. The referent of civil disobedience is public opinion, in the profound sense of what we take to be our politically relevant moral principles. The role of politically relevant citizen action is thus expanded beyond defensive reactions to specific violations of individual rights to include questions of what principles, which norms, should be legislated into law. For Dworkin, such questions must be translated into the language of rights, but the action involved in asserting (and not only defending existing) rights in this model is assuredly political. Dworkin thus offers a dynamic understanding of the role of civil disobedience in the process of creating rights and in the enlightenment of public opinion.

Precisely because acts of civil disobedience are interpreted in this broader sense of political action on the part of citizens oriented to the defense and creation of rights, and precisely because they involve the exercise of influence on the political process through the public spheres of civil society, such acts need a stronger justification than do acts of conscientious objection. The latter involve moral objections to specific laws and seek individual exemptions; the former are aimed at political institutions and seek to contribute to change. In a constitutional democracy, where, after all, citizen rights to participation are secured and majority rule is the key principle for legislation, it is incumbent upon the defenders of civil disobedience to show that it does not violate the principles of majority rule and that it is not antidemocratic.

This brings us to the second explanation of why, even in a nearly just constitutional democracy, civil disobedience is a likely and important dimension of a political culture. Like Rawls, Dworkin interprets the legitimacy of the principle of majority rule procedurally: Law has a binding character if the correct procedures in a representative political system have been followed. There is, however, one substantive proviso: The rights of the minority must not be violated. Since any majority consensus is always only empirical, it could err, as Rawls maintained. This is a built-in risk of the democratic political process. A majority consensus could simply be the combined prejudices, personal aversions, majority interests, and rationalizations of the legislature or of public opinion. Moreover, "The bulk of the law—that part which defines and implements social, economic, and foreign policy—cannot be neutral. It must state, in its greatest part, the majority's view of the common good."[54] In a complex, differentiated, pluralist civil society, the institution of rights restricts the range and type of decisions open to legislative majorities. Rights are not thereby antithetical to democratic principles, for the institution of rights represents the majority's promise to the minorities that their dignity and equality will be respected—more, the substantive restrictions on majority decision making represented by fundamental rights against the state are the very source of legitimacy of the principle of majority rule.[55] Indeed, the rights thesis presupposes that there is something behind the law, namely, moral principles, which serve as the basis for the legitimacy of the legal system as a whole. For the liberal, this something is the principle of individual moral rights.

But how do we know when rights are at stake? How do we distinguish between acts of civil disobedience and acts that challenge the principles of the constitutional system?[56] Dworkin answers this question by distinguishing two different kinds of public issues: those involving policy decisions with respect to a collective goal of the community as a whole, and those involving matters of principle, that is, decisions affecting some individual or group right.[57] This distinction between policy and principle enters into Dworkin's taxonomy of types of civil disobedience and into his effort to specify when civil disobedience is legitimate and when it is not. If one breaks the law in the name of the defense of the rights of a minority against the interests or goals of the majority, one is engaging in "justice-based" civil disobedience. If one breaks the law not because of a belief that a policy is immoral or unjust but because it seems unwise, stupid, or dangerous for the society, one is engaging in "policy-based" civil disobedience.[58] While both of these types of civil disobedience are "offensive" in the sense of being instrumental and strategic (the goal is a change of policy or law), we must further distinguish between two types of strategies: persuasive strategies aimed at forcing the majority to listen to counterarguments in the hope that it will then change its mind, and nonpersuasive strategies aimed at increasing the costs of pursuing a policy in the hope that the majority will find the new cost unacceptably high. In form and intent, then, civil disobedience can be discursive (a politics of influence) or nondiscursive (a strategy of power). Persuasive strategies of civil disobedience do not challenge the principle of majority rule in any fundamental way, because the logic of the illegal collective action is to get the majority's attention and make it consider arguments. It aims to influence political society. Nonpersuasive strategies, even if nonviolent, are inferior from a moral standpoint, but they can be acceptable if one believes a policy to be deeply unjust. They do not radically undermine the principles of a constitutional democracy, because the very idea of rights against the state rests on the idea that the majority must respect rights and can be forced to be just against its will.[59] Nevertheless, with respect to policy-based disobedience, where it is not a matter of minority rights and hence not a matter of principle but of conflicting preferences, nonpersuasive strategies strike at the heart of the majority principle and cannot be justified.

This distinction between persuasive and nonpersuasive strategies is illuminating and important. But it is not obvious that the distinction between justice-based and policy-based disobedience can be made in the way that Dworkin attempts, that is, with respect to substantive areas of decision making. Either the distinction between principle and policy begs the question—since rights-related arguments can be made with respect to nearly any policy issue, and in some cases it is precisely this boundary line that is at stake[60]—or it can be held to only at the price of a purely utilitarian model of the democratic political process and the common good. The latter orientation is the dominant one in Dworkin's work. In effect, Dworkin tends to revive the standard liberal distinction between politics and morality, placing majority rule, majority opinions, preferences, the common interest, and matters of policy within the normal democratic political process and matters of moral principle or rights outside this process. By implication, and despite disclaimers, rights and democracy, morals and politics, appear to be in opposition after all. On this interpretation, public opinion tends to be reduced at best to a set of preferences, at worst to sets of external preferences, and "normal democratic processes" and legislation are denuded of their normative, principled character and reduced to interest aggregation, compromise, and responses to pressure—in short, to the utilitarian model of interest-group pluralism. By the same token, civil society appears as a moral (nonpolitical) sphere in which politically oriented action to influence political society for the sake of protecting rights is the only extrainstitutional political action that is deemed legitimate. It is easy to see why rights must trump democracy so defined and why policy decisions are not seen as involving matters of principle.

This model of politics vitiates the very insights into the creative dimensions of civil disobedience that Dworkin articulates and reduces it once again to a defensive strategy. It also prevents Dworkin from recognizing that his understanding of civil disobedience as a politics of influence challenges the standard liberal dichotomy of public and private: civil society as the sphere of privacy and individual autonomy, and the state or political society as the domain of normal political action. If civil disobedience involves a learning process and has a role to play in developing our liberal democratic political culture and institutions, if the target of the relevant collective action is, first, public opinion within civil society and thereby, second, the legislature or the courts,[61] then the democratic political process must involve more than interest aggregation, and politically relevant activity in civil society must have dimensions other than the pursuit of interests and the defense of individual rights. For this is what a politics of influence, as distinct from a strategy of power, presupposes. Otherwise, extrainstitutional attempts to change political institutions, to initiate radical institutional reform within the limits of fidelity to constitutional principles, and to influence legislation through appeals to public opinion in the name of the community's morality when individual rights are not at stake would have to appear as antidemocratic demagoguery.

Dworkin, like other liberals, cannot avoid such conclusions, because he locates the legitimacy of constitutional democracy only in the individual moral rights it preserves. Citizen rights are included among the catalogue of fundamental moral rights, but liberals assume that they, and with them the principle of democracy itself, are fully institutionalized with the universalization of the right to vote and hold office.[62] The principle of democratic legitimacy is thus dissolved into the idea of individual rights and the electoral procedures that have been institutionalized for the exercise of the majority principle. If a certain category of citizens is denied full political rights, then civil disobedience would be in order, but civil disobedience for the purpose of further democratizing civil or political society, to make the latter more representative of the views of the citizenry, or expanding its influence on the state is wholly screened out from the liberal position. This is clear from Dworkin's unconvincing attempt to interpret the contemporary acts of civil disobedience he defends solely in terms of rights issues.[63] It is even clearer from his tendency to interpret civil disobedience in situations that cannot be resolved into claims for individual rights as involving policy issues and nonpersuasive strategies and hence as illegitimate.[64] In discussing the German antinuclear protest, for example, Dworkin insists that missile deployments and deterrence strategies are complex policy issues and that discussion in such circumstances cannot be illuminated by illegal acts. He charges the peace movement with engaging in a nonpersuasive strategy aimed at raising the price of a policy they oppose.[65] The weakness of the distinction between policy and principle is particularly obvious here, for one could easily argue that it is precisely this distinction that was at stake in the relevant acts of civil disobedience. Far from making the public at large pay less attention to the complex issues involved, as Dworkin charges, the purpose of the movement was precisely the opposite: to expand public discourse and debate into areas formerly left to the preserve of state bureaucracies and *raison d'état* and to challenge the state's monopoly not over the means of violence but over politics and the moral issues involved in the legitimate use of these means.[66] Individual rights were not at stake, but democratic principles were. Indeed, it is hardly reasonable to interpret the human chains and sit-downs as a show of force, as a nonpersuasive power play, rather than as a symbolic exercise aimed at initiating a debate by "forcing enough people to look who would be ashamed to turn away."[67] There were at least two normative principles at issue in this case: the morality of a particular kind of weaponry, and the democratic or representative quality of the political society that made the policy decision. The point here is not that the distinction between policy issues and rights-related issues is untenable but that both kinds of issues can involve matters of principle and that, if this is not recognized, one risks misconstruing the character of the respective acts of civil disobedience.

Rights-oriented liberalism cannot do justice to the problem of civil disobedience in nearly just constitutional democracies on the basis of the narrowly conceived principle of legitimacy with which it operates. Liberals call for decriminalizing acts of civil disobedience oriented toward rights, arguing that there is an extrainstitutional moral basis for breaking the law that, when heeded, reaffirms rather than undermines respect for the rule of law. What they do not recognize, however, is that there is a *double* extrainstitutional normative basis for the legitimacy of law in polities guided by the principles of constitutionalism. Civil disobedience itself, unlike any other moral right, cannot without contradiction be made into a legal or constitutional right. The right to assert rights is not, strictly speaking, a right at all—it does not refer back to a conception of morality *distinct* from politics but refers directly to the normative principles of politics itself, indeed to a democratic conception of the political. Disobedience in the defense of individual rights does follow from the idea of fundamental rights, but civil disobedience proper, especially if it involves the creation of new rights, follows from the second normative underpinning of constitutional democracies, the other basis of constitutionalism forgotten by the liberal, namely, the idea of democratic legitimacy.

We can now present our own working definition. Civil disobedience involves illegal acts, usually on the part of collective actors, that are public, principled, and symbolic in character, involve primarily nonviolent means of protest, and appeal to the capacity for reason and the sense of justice of the populace. The aim of civil disobedience is to persuade public opinion in civil and political society (or economic society) that a particular law or policy is illegitimate and a change is warranted. Collective actors involved in civil disobedience invoke the utopian principles of constitutional democracies, appealing to the ideas of fundamental rights or democratic legitimacy. Civil disobedience is thus a means for reasserting the link between civil and political society (or civil and economic society), when legal attempts at exerting the influence of the former on the latter have failed and other avenues have been exhausted.[68]

Civil disobedience is thus an illegal form of political participation on the part of collective actors. It is political action with a political aim that by definition activates the public spheres of civil society and involves extrainstitutional citizen activity. Its ultimate justification in a democratic polity must lie in democracy itself as well as in the idea of fundamental moral rights. But we shall never escape the vicious circle if we assume that democracy is the sum total of procedures and institutions articulated in a constitution and that these can be theoretically grasped by a utilitarian model of politics. In that case, there could be no democratic argument for civil disobedience (other than the rights argument) that would not at the same time challenge the principle of majority rule. The solution lies in a different model of the democratic process, civil society, their normative underpinnings, and their interrelation.

And indeed, in his debate with Lord Devlin, Dworkin does sketch a nonutilitarian model of the democratic political process. He maintains that when legislation cannot be neutral, when it involves issues that touch on the community's morality,[69] legislators must engage in moral hermeneutic reflection similar to that of judges. That is, the attempt to determine the community's moral position on a specific issue is not a matter of taking an opinion poll or aggregating preferences (policy) but rather one of discerning the moral principles inherent in the collective identity the community wishes to preserve. Thus, "if there has been a public debate involving the editorial columns, speeches of his colleagues, the testimony of interested groups . . . the legislator must sift these arguments and positions trying to determine which are prejudices or rationalizations, which presuppose general principles or theories."[70] In short, the legislator must refuse to take popular indignation, intolerance, and disgust as the moral conviction of the community.

If Dworkin wanted to avoid a charge of moral elitism, he would have to deal with the implications of this kind of relation between public opinion and legislation for the conception of democracy and the principle of majority rule. What is implied here is that there is more to the political process than the representation of interests, more to legislation than interest compromise, more to the common good or common interest than aggregated preferences, and more to the moral principles underlying constitutionalism and majority rule than the protection of individual rights. The idea that legislators should try to discern the community's moral principles and that an informed, and formed, public opinion ought to be able to communicate these principles to legislators and have an influence on legislation indicates that civil society has a politically relevant dimension. Indeed, they indicate that there is a dimension to legislation that involves interpretation of the political culture or collective identity of the community. These are formulated in civil society. The influence of civil on political society in this respect is a central dimension of democracy. Laws that institutionalize aspects of a community's morality (and no polity can ever be completely neutral in this regard) are reducible neither to policy decisions nor to rights. Moreover, the public discursive process requires a reflective relationship to the community's collective identity (traditions and common norms), as in the case of moral rights. Here, too, there can be no single authoritative instance, but the appeal beyond the legislative body is, in this case, not to the courts (assuming that matters of individual rights are not at stake) but to public opinion itself. The public turns out to be the final court of appeal; the ultimate locus of legitimacy of the decisions arrived at in the parliamentary public sphere is the opinion developed and articulated in the public spheres of civil society. Liberals understand that vital public spaces within civil society guaranteed by rights (speech, assembly, association) are fundamental to the defense of rights. But they are also fundamental to the principles of democracy. This conception bursts the rigid dualism of morality and politics, of civil society construed as the nonpolitical private sphere and the state construed as the sole legitimate locus of politics. It also bursts the utilitarian conception of the democratic process. Although individual rights to speak, assemble, and associate are the precondition for institutionalizing public spaces within civil society, their animating principle is deeply political: It is the principle of democratic legitimacy itself.

Democratic Theory and Civil Disobedience

Radical democratic theory proceeds from the principles of democratic legitimacy rather than the idea of individual rights against the state. This tradition refuses to abandon the utopian democratic norms of direct participation by citizens in public life in favor of more "realistic" elite models of democracy supplemented by catalogues of individual rights. It takes up the second utopian ideal of civil society: to articulate an institutional arrangement that would realize the classical principles of citizenship on modern, egalitarian grounds, namely, the participation of all in ruling and being ruled.

The questions before us are: What role, if any, would civil disobedience have in a nearly democratic constitutional democracy, and what would constitute a democratic argument for civil disobedience? Would there even be a need for civil disobedience in a radical democratic model of civil society? Isn't this just a liberal problem?

As in the case of liberal theory, we can identify two general orientations within the radical democratic tradition: the first tends to reject civil disobedience in the "nearly democratic" polity; the second justifies it on the grounds of democratic norms. Let us look at each in turn.

The most influential formulation of the radical democratic ideal of participatory democracy is that of Jean-Jacques Rousseau. The classical Rousseauian solution to the problem of the citizen's moral obligation to obey the laws has the following structure: In a democratic society, under the rule of law, citizens are not subject to an alien will but obey only themselves. As a result, every person is both citizen and subject. The conflict between the citizen, concerned with the public good, and the self, pursuing private happiness, is internalized. The citizen's moral obligation to obey the law is derived both from the assumption of consent and from the fact that the gap between ruler and ruled has been abolished. Every citizen has become a legislator through an institutional arrangement that creates an identity between ruler and ruled. Thus, a citizen who refuses to comply with the general will, with the law, is either in error or an egoist and must be forced to be free.

There has always been an ambiguity in the Rousseauian version of radical democratic theory: Is the general will binding because it is just (because it expresses the general interest or the common good) or because it is the will of the people? For our purposes, both alternatives are problematic. We shall discuss the second answer because it bears most closely on our question and has the clearest relation to the procedural model of democratic legitimacy. The Rousseauian conception of democratic legitimacy is guided by the principle that all politically consequential decision making must be linked to the discursive will formation of the citizen public. Rousseau translates this principle directly into the question of the proper organization of sovereignty. Either a democratic polity provides for the direct participation of citizens in political decision making or it is not democratic. It is assumed that the norms of democratic legitimacy can be fully institutionalized in a well-organized political community. They lose their counterfactual character insofar as an identity between ruler and ruled, between norm and organization, is posited.[71]

The Rousseauian ideal of participatory democracy is conceptualized in an institutional model that is meant to substitute for (rather than complement) the undemocratic, bourgeois institution of the representative parliament. Indeed, by insisting on an identity between ruler and ruled, one has automatically ruled out the democratic potential of any version of the principle of representation (e.g., a council of councils), for representation always involves a distance between representatives and the represented. The only exception is the mystical identification of the general will with the positions arrived at by the representatives. By implication, the structural presuppositions of parliamentary democracy—the separation of state and civil society, of public and private, and the emphasis on individual rights—are deemed the source of political alienation.[72] From this point of view, it makes no difference whether the theorist harkens back to an idealized model of the Greek *polis* (Arendt), to the late medieval republican tradition (Rousseau), or to new forms of direct democracy generated within the milieu of the workers' movement and generalized as an organizational principle for society as a whole (council communism, revolutionary syndicalism). In each case, it is assumed that just one organizing principle for all social, political, and economic institutions can deliver the democratic utopia.

It should be clear that the Rousseauian model of radical democracy (along with the neo-Aristotelian and socialist models) has a *telos* of dedifferentiation. It tends to fuse morality and politics in a conception of civic virtue that leaves no room for challenges to what has been collectively agreed that stem from a moral point of view. Civil and political society are also collapsed. Disobedience to the general will or the existing consensus would be unjust and antidemocratic because there is no moral outside to civic virtue or the common good. In other words, in a nearly democratic constitutional democracy, where the procedural principle of majority rule is grounded in full, open, nonexclusive discussion and the participation of all concerned in the relevant debates, there would be almost no place or justification for acts of civil disobedience, that is, for challenges to laws arrived at through the democratic process or for acts that bypass this process.

The only conceivable justification for civil disobedience in such a polity would be that some form of exclusion has been introduced. One could claim that the institutions are not sufficiently democratic, that a group's voice has been silenced, that insufficient attention has been paid to one's arguments, and so on. But the claim that the institutions of a radical participatory democracy are not democratic enough could always be made. To recognize this, however, would be to reintroduce a difference between the locus of legitimacy and the organization of sovereignty, between ruler and ruled, between representative and represented, and between political and civil society—precisely the gap that radical democrats seek to close.

A real democrat would have to go further and recognize that democracy *can never be fully institutionalized.*[73] There can be no point in time at which one could relax and say that we have arrived at a perfect procedural institutionalization of the principles of democratic legitimacy. Like the principle of rights, democracy must be seen as a *verité à faire*, a learning process, no matter what institutional arrangement of the polity has been achieved. Every empirical organizational form of democracy has its exclusionary mechanisms: Modern representative democracy diminishes the relevance of those who are not members of strong voluntary associations or parties; direct democracy excludes those politically inactive people who don't seek public happiness first and foremost; territorial democracy discriminates against producers; industrial democracy, against consumers. Federalism increases the importance of weak members of the federation at the cost of dissenting individuals and groups within each member unit. Centralizing democracy provides no incentive for potentially important self-governing units. Moreover, no combination of these principles would exclude exclusion altogether. We argue instead for a plurality of democratic forms as the ideal institutionalization of a modern civil society, but our point is that even if one moved in this direction, one would still have to distinguish between the normative principles of democratic legitimacy and the question of the organization of sovereignty, so that the former could function as a moral standpoint from which to criticize the latter.

The second approach is that of the two best contemporary theorists of democratic legitimacy, Hannah Arendt and Jürgen Habermas. Each has rejected the Rousseauian version of radical democratic theory without relinquishing its normative ideals.[74] Each has placed the concept of the public sphere at the center of their political theory. And, interestingly enough, each has written on the problem of civil disobedience within the framework of a democratic theory that is free from many of the drawbacks of the radical democratic approach.[75] We shall briefly summarize their positions and show that they offer the possibility of a synthesis with what is best in the liberal tradition.

We can see the theoretical and political limits of the liberal theories of civil disobedience as soon as we turn to theorists who proceed not from the point of view of law or even rights but from that of democracy. Arendt is the most explicit on this point; indeed, her main argument hinges on it. Arendt's claim is that, despite efforts to distinguish civil disobedience from conscientious objection, the liberal and primarily juridical approach cannot do this adequately.[76] When jurists try to justify the civil disobedient on moral and legal grounds, they construe the case in the image of either the conscientious objector or the individual who tests the constitutionality of a statute. "The greatest fallacy in the present debate [1969] seems to me the assumption that we are dealing with individuals, who pit themselves subjectively and conscientiously against the laws and customs of the community—an assumption that is shared by the defenders and detractors of civil disobedience."[77]

The problem is that the situation of the civil disobedient cannot be analogized to that of any isolated individual, for the simple reason that the disobedient can function and survive only as a member of a group.[78] Unlike conscientious objectors who refuse to a comply with a specific statue that violates their individual moral consciences, civil disobedients often violate laws that are in themselves unobjectionable in order to protest other unjust ordinances, policies, or executive orders. In other words, a crucial aspect of the *political* nature of acts of civil disobedience—indeed, what makes them political for Arendt—is that the actor does not act alone. We are dealing with collective action, social movements, individuals who act as parts of an organized minority bound together by a common opinion (over and above common interest). Moreover, their action springs from an agreement with one another, and it is this agreement and not the individual's subjective moral fiber that gives credence and conviction to their opinion.

What is at issue is thus not the individual's moral integrity or the rules of subjective conscience (the intent issue that motivates jurists to distinguish between such acts and criminality) but the legitimacy of illegal *political* action on the part of citizens acting in concert. Thus, while civil disobedience does involve a form of *speech*, while it is addressed to majorities with the purpose of influencing them, it is also political *action* within the public spaces of civil society aimed at influencing actors in political society. It involves more than First Amendment principles protecting the freedom of speech. According to Arendt, "Civil disobedience arises when a significant number of citizens have become convinced either that the normal channels of change no longer function, and grievances will not be heard or acted upon, or that, on the contrary, the government is about to change and has embarked upon and persists in modes of action whose legality and constitutionality are open to grave doubt."[79] This definition emphasizes the fact of change, the adequacy of the channels for the influence of civil society on political society (and thereby on the state), and the principles of legitimacy (constitutionality) that are to guide and limit all state action.

Arendt also wants to situate civil disobedience between criminality and outright revolution, but, unlike the liberal or the jurist, she neither insists on nonviolence as the distinguishing feature of civil disobedience nor stresses the violation of individual rights. Indeed, she cites the whole body of labor legislation—the right to collective bargaining, the right to organize and to strike—as examples of rights that we tend to take for granted today but were preceded by decades of violent civil disobedience challenging what ultimately proved to be obsolete laws.[80] The specificity of civil disobedience must therefore be situated elsewhere. The main issue facing constitutional democracies is whether the institutions of liberty are flexible enough to survive the onslaught of change without civil war or revolution. The relation of civil disobedience to law depends on the answer to this question. Arendt's point is not to affirm violence, for she sees violence as the opposite of political action, and civil disobedience is political action *par excellence*. But collective action is complex; it is not the violent or nonviolent character of a conflict that distinguishes civil disobedience from insurrection but rather the spirit of the action and the spirit of the laws to which it is addressed.

It is Arendt's thesis that while civil disobedience is today a worldwide phenomenon, it is American in origin and substance. She claims that no other language even has a word for it. Unlike Dworkin, however, Arendt does not locate the specificity of American constitutionalism in the principle of moral rights that it articulates or in a legalistic understanding of the separation of powers. To her mind, the unique spirit behind the American republic's peculiar conception of law, and of constitutionalism, is the principle of active consent in the sense of *active support* and *continuing participation* by the people in matters of public interest and common concern. The people, moreover, are conceived not as an undifferentiated, unified mass with one will and one opinion (Rousseau) but as duly constituted in a plurality of local, regional, and national bodies politic (the federal principle of the separation of powers) within which a plurality of different public opinions can be given voice. Arendt argues that the authority and legitimacy of the American constitution rests on the principle of the power of the people: Power granted to the authorities and to government is limited, delegated, and revocable.

Arendt's point here is to connect civil disobedience to the traditions of republican political culture underlying American constitutionalism: the tradition of voluntary association, the practice of establishing bonds and obligations through mutual promises, and the tradition of private citizens coming together and acting in concert. "It is my contention that civil disobedients are nothing but the latest form of voluntary association, and that they are quite in tune with the oldest traditions of the country."[81] Consent, the right to dissent, and the art of associating to articulate a minority opinion and thereby diminish the moral power of the majority constitute civic virtue in a modern republic. And Arendt rightly sees in the mass demonstrations of the late 1960s an important example of the continuation of old traditions. She also sees that organized minorities, through acts of civil disobedience, can have astounding influence on the opinion of majorities. This political engagement in the heart of civil society that is civil disobedience is thus the associational principle in action.

Arendt never provides us with a theory of civil society adequate to the conception of civil disobedience that she defends in her essay. Like other neo-Aristotelian communitarians, she operates with a theoretically anachronistic conception. Nevertheless, when confronted with the phenomenon of civil disobedience in the United States, she is forced to introduce some of the core dimensions of the concept of civil society that conflict with her overall theoretical framework.[82] The most striking instance is her reference to the Lockean model of the social contract, the one best suited to the American prerevolutionary experience of compacts, covenants, and agreements. While Arendt had referred to the Lockean model before,[83] her interpretation in this essay is quite new. She argues that Locke assumed that compacts lead not to government but to society (*societas*), a voluntary association among individual members who then contract for their government once they have mutually bound themselves.[84] This time, however, she interprets the "horizontal" version of the social contract as one that limits the power of each individual member but leaves intact the power of society. This power cannot revert to the individual as long as society lasts, but neither can it be appropriated by the government *in toto*— the power that the government has is limited and held at the pleasure of society. What is new here is that Arendt uses the horizontal model of compacting, of acting in concert, not to describe the revolutionary founding of new bodies politic but to explain the phenomenon of civil disobedience, in which collective actors form voluntary associations within the framework of social movements that do not aim at revolution in the sense of replacing the existing forms of political society or even creating new ones.

Arendt has not changed her assessment of modern society or the modern political system, in America or elsewhere. America is still for her primarily a mass society in which consent is entirely fictitious and representative government is in crisis "partly because it has lost in the course of time all institutions that permitted the citizens' actual participation, and partly because it is now gravely affected by the disease from which the party system suffers: bureaucratization and the two parties' tendency to represent nobody except the party machines."[85] Indeed, the standpoint from which she criticizes existing institutions is an external, idealized model of direct democracy. The norms of democratic legitimacy are transcendent with respect to modern constitutional political systems. Hence the ambiguity of her entire defense of civil disobedience. On the one hand, she seems to provide convincing arguments for the normalcy of civil disobedience when it comes to defending the political participation of private citizens in civil society and expanding their influence on economic and political society; on the other hand, on the basis of her overall theoretical framework, she seems to see the tradition of voluntary association as a potential substitute for, rather than the societal presupposition of, the representative political institutions of political parties and parliaments. After all, the tradition of compacting and associating to which she refers was, as she argued in *On Revolution*, one in which political institutions were first founded (the colonial experience) and then re-created (the revolutionary experience). For Arendt, they constituted political spaces for direct democratic participation: embryos for the future reorganization of the political system away from parties and parliaments toward some sort of council model.

Nevertheless, in her essay on civil disobedience, Arendt does rediscover some of the core dimensions of modern civil society— voluntary association and social movements—while putting her finger on the type of extrainstitutional political action and civic virtue that is specific to private citizens of a modern differentiated society. In this essay at least, she locates the principles of democratic legitimacy not in the political system or government but, implicitly at least, in civil society as differentiated from both. Moreover, her vantage point of democratic rather than liberal theory allows her to see clearly the political character of civil disobedience as well as its political function: Civil disobedience for the sake of further democratizing civil society, the polity, and the economy is legitimate political action. Arendt would defend civil disobedience that aims at either the defense or assertion of minority rights or the democratization of political society and (quite inconsistently) economic institutions.

While there can be no legal justification for the violation of law, Arendt argues that a niche for civil disobedience is conceivable within the institutions of government. It is not covered by First Amendment rights to free speech, since it involves political action, but a crucial component of civil disobedience, one at the core of American political culture, could be articulated as a constitutional right, namely, the right of association (which does not exist in the American Bill of Rights). This, she concludes, would be an amendment well worth the trouble. For if the freedom of association, along with civil disobedience, is a dangerous expedient to obviate a still more formidable danger, she argues, citing Tocqueville, "it is by the enjoyment of dangerous freedom that the Americans learn the art of rendering the dangers of freedom less formidable."[86] It is through the art of association that power (the power of those acting in concert and forming a public opinion) is created and dispersed throughout civil society. Or, to put it another way, what keeps limited government limited is the willingness of citizens to associate, form public opinions, act collectively on their own within civil society, and thereby influence government. By implication, although Arendt never quite spells this out,[87] democratic legitimacy in a constitutional democracy would have to find its locus not only in a federal model of the polity in which authority flows upwards from local political bodies,[88] but also in the public opinion of private, voluntarily associated citizens who act collectively and articulate their views in the public spaces of civil society that are distinguished from those in political society.

This is the core of Habermas's conception of the modern public sphere and the basis on which he has elaborated his own theory of democratic legitimacy. Habermas's analysis of the modern public sphere is in fact complementary to Arendt's discussion of the principles of voluntary association. It elaborates upon the other core institution of modern civil society that is central to any understanding of the kinds of political activity open to the private citizen who is not a professional politician. His theory of democratic legitimacy, however, is an important step beyond Arendt's theoretical framework in that its normative claims transcend the limits of a particular tradition or political culture (Arendt's focus on America) and provide principles that give a particular practice (the habit of voluntary association and of promising) a normative and obligatory character. It reintroduces a counterfactual normative standpoint with respect to existing institutions that is neither transcendent nor anachronistic. At the same time, it sees the public spheres of civil society not as a potential replacement or alternative, but as complementary, a precondition, for the representative and democratic institutions of political society. In this way, Habermas avoids the ambiguities of the Arendtian approach.

In chapter 8, we discussed Habermas's conception of the public sphere and theory of democratic legitimacy. Here we shall focus on their implications for a defense of civil disobedience on democratic rather than liberal grounds. Like Rawls and Dworkin (whom he cites), Habermas assumes that the modern constitutional state both requires and is capable of a moral justification. He, too, proceeds from the "unusually high claim to legitimacy of the modern constitutional state," from the fact that the democratic constitutional state, with its legitimating constitutional principles, reaches beyond their positive-legal embodiment.[89] For Habermas, however, this moral justification lies not in the principle of individual rights, as it does for Rawls and especially for Dworkin, but in the principle of democratic legitimacy according to which only those (constitutional) norms can be justified that express a generalizable interest and thus could rely on the considered agreement of all concerned—an agreement linked to a procedure of reasoned will formation.[90] Like Arendt, although on different grounds, he argues that the democratic constitutional state rests on a conditional and qualified adherence by its citizens to the law, because democracy institutionalizes "the distrust toward a fallible reason and the corruptible nature of man." Paradoxically, "it must protect and sustain the distrust of injustice that appears in legal forms, although that distrust cannot assume an institutionally secured form."[91] But fallibility refers in this case not to the possibility that a majority might violate individual rights (Rawls and Dworkin) but to the possibility that the institutionalized majority might make decisions in an insufficiently democratic way, even while respecting procedural legality. Habermas situates civil disobedience between legitimacy and legality. The plebiscitary pressure of civil disobedience, its status as an unconventional means for influencing the formation of political will, signals the fact that the democratic constitutional state is not reducible to its legal order. There are counterfactual democratic principles, upon which our political institutions nevertheless rest, that can be appealed to when the democratic character of decision making that superficially seems to respect the procedural principles of majority rule is challenged, and that can justify acts of civil disobedience aimed at further democratizing a decision-making process.

Thus, the focus of Habermas's analysis of civil disobedience as a politics of influence is its relation to the democratic principles underlying constitutionalism and the process through which such principles are realized. Instead of associating civil disobedience with the extreme case of an unjust order or even a serious crisis, Habermas assumes it to be a normal response to situations that will arise over and over again because "the realization of exacting constitutional principles with universal content is a long-term process which historically has been by no means linear."[92] Indeed, he maintains that civil disobedience is often the last chance to correct errors in the process of realizing democratic principles or to set in motion innovations for the average citizen who is not endowed with privileged opportunities for influence in the political system.[93]

Like Dworkin, Habermas reminds us of the fact that the constitutional state reckons with a high demand for revision, as indicated by the proliferation institutions for self-correction, from the threefold reading of parliamentary bills to the process of judicial review. This high demand for revision comes into play with regard not only to individual rights but also to the regulative principles of democratic legitimacy. It derives from the preconditions for majority rule, which include but go beyond respect for individual rights. Among the minimal prerequisites the majority principle must meet if it is to maintain its legitimating power are the avoidance of permanent minorities and the reversibility of its decisions. Nor is it self-evident where the proper locus of decision making lies in every case. Disputes over the proper distribution of sovereignty among local, regional, and central deliberative bodies can and do arise.[94] So do disagreements over the province of the authority of the political system vis-à-vis that of civil society. Claus Offe has argued for a reflexive use of majority rule in such situations.[95] This would involve placing the objects, modalities, and limits of the majority principle itself at the discretion of the majority—the principle would be applied reflexively to itself. Although this reflexivity itself must be placed in a majoritarian disposition, it must be guided by the following standard: "To what extent do the decisions, which the processes of majority rule make possible under conditions of limited resources of time and information, diverge from the ideal results of a discursively achieved agreement or a presumptively just compromise?"[96]

When challenges arise that touch on the interests and concerns of all citizens, Habermas states that the collectivity as well as individual citizens may assume the "original rights of the sovereign"; the democratic constitutional state must rely, in the last instance, on this guardian of legitimacy.[97] Collective action involving civil disobedience for the sake of democratization must, however, be self-limiting: The adoption of extraordinary means must be appropriate to the situation. More important than a mere tactical commitment to nonviolence, however, is an identification with the constitutional principles of a democratic republic. Civil disobedients avoid an elitist attitude when their action is based on the conviction that acts of protest have a symbolic character and appeal to the capacity for reason and sense of justice of the majority of the population.[98] Thus, civil disobedience occurs in the framework of a democratic constitutional state that remains wholly intact. While such a state is neutral with respect to the personal convictions of its citizens, it is not neutral with respect to the intersubjectively recognized moral foundations of legality. Civil disobedience is based on an appeal to these principles and not on the absolute nature of the private convictions of the individual. The self-limitation of such action as well as of the response by political elites is a sign of the maturity of a political culture.[99]

Democratic theory thus arrives at a similar point as liberal theory regarding the definition, nature, and function of civil disobedience in a constitutional democracy. Liberals and democrats disagree, though, on the kinds of reasons that can justify acts of civil disobedience and on the acts that fit the bill. The limits of liberal and radical democratic theory are symmetric. On their own, each screens out one dimension of the utopia of civil society. Liberals grant the legitimacy of illegal collective action only for the defense or creation of individual *rights*; democrats focus on the defense or expansion of *democracy*. As we have shown, the liberal idea of moral rights against the state presupposes a broader model of civil society and of citizen action than liberals are willing to recognize, for the public and private spaces secured by rights are politically relevant and the collective action that expands and defends them is deeply political.

On the other side, the principle of democratic legitimacy also has extrainstitutional moral and political implications. First, it presupposes that democratization is *always* on the agenda and that acts of civil disobedience in the name of further democratization of representative democracies take the principle of representation seriously and are legitimate. Democratization in this context means keeping the channels of communication and influence between civil and political society open. Here, too, one must presuppose a broader, more differentiated model of civil society than either Arendt or Habermas offers, for democrats must recognize and grant what the idea of moral rights secures, what liberals like to call negative liberty or individual autonomy and the dignity of particular interests. As we argued in chapter 8, the discourse ethics that grounds the principle of democratic legitimacy also implies the idea of fundamental, individual rights. It presupposes autonomous individuals equipped with postconventional moral capacities. Who else could challenge the taboos and limits that are put up for discussion? Who else could say that a traditional or past consensus is no longer valid? Who else could propose new values that might be institutionalized into political norms or basic rights? If participatory democracy is not to be traditionalist or authoritarian, it presupposes basic rights and a correspondingly differentiated model of civil and political society.

Two moral principles lend legitimacy to the procedural principle of majority rule within the legislative process: the principles of rights and of democratic legitimacy.[100] These are the two normative poles of constitutionalism. The situation of the principle of democratic legitimacy with respect to the institutionalized public spheres and the political system is parallel to that of the idea of moral rights with respect to the legal system. Just as it is impossible to claim at any point in time that all of our moral rights have been guaranteed by law, so it is inconceivable to maintain that any given set of political arrangements has fully institutionalized the principle of democratic legitimacy. Institutional spaces for expressing and forming public opinion, and mechanisms for its influence on legislation, must be provided in any democratic system. Yet, like the idea of moral rights, the principles of democratic legitimacy retain their status as counterfactual norms. This means that both rights and democracy involve learning processes that allow us to think that democratic institutions can become more democratic.[101]

Civil disobedience oriented to the further democratization of institutions within a constitutional democracy vindicates the principles of majority rule. Such action seeks to influence majority opinion outside the legislatures, within civil society, and bring it to bear upon the legislative process. It presupposes that majority rule must be measured not only against the standard of individual rights but also against the principles of democratic legitimacy. It also presupposes that, ultimately, the principles of rights and of democratic legitimacy have their locus first and last in the public and private spaces of a vital civil society. Civil disobedience is thus the litmus test of both democracy and of liberalism: of liberalism because it reveals the political dimensions of civil society and the normalcy of social movements; of democracy because it implies respect for rights and for a moral standpoint that is politically relevant outside the democratic consensus and procedures that have been institutionalized. A differentiated, pluralist, and modern civil society demands a political culture mature enough to accept the promise and the risks of liberal and democratic citizenship. Our hope is that we are moving in that direction.

Notes

Preface

1. The exception, of course, is the pluralist tradition of political theory. See the introduction for an assessment of this approach. Recent works in democratic theory include David Held, *Models of Democracy* (Stanford: Stanford University Press, 1987), Robert Dahl, *Democracy and Its Critics* (New Haven: Yale University Press, 1989), and Giovanni Sartori, *The Theory of Democracy Revisited*, 2 vols. (Chatham, NJ: Chatham House, 1987).

2. We are aware of the pitfalls of trying to define a term that is used today in many different contexts and that has a long and still evolving conceptual history. Moreover, we believe that if one must have a definition, it would be best to show its development through the stages by which we have attained it. (In the text, our concept of civil society is developed through political-hermeneutic, intellectual-historical, and systematic considerations.) But we are also aware of the danger of being misunderstood if we do not provide at least a working definition in the beginning. See, for example, A. Kuhlmann, "West-östlich. Der Begriff 'civil society,'" *Frankfurter Allgemeine,* January 9, 1991, where the author somewhat artificially contrasts the views of the East Europeans J. Szacki and M. Szabo with those of the "American sociologist" A. Arato. The author contends that the former understand "civil society" in terms of juridical protections of the private sphere that are inevitably dependent on state legislation, while the latter construes it in terms of extrapolitical movements and forms of pressure on the state itself. Actually, our conception encompasses both of these levels, and the differences among the interpreters in question have to do only with the existence and role in East Europe of a civil society that in our view has existed more in the form of movements, protomovements, and independent initiatives from below than in settled institutions protected by rights and the rule of law. The denial of the role of civil societies in the process culminating in the transitions of 1989 reflects (and in some cases also justifies) some very real oligarchic tendencies in the new political societies.

3. For these concepts, see Cornelius Castoriadis, *The Imaginary Institution of Society* (Cambridge: MIT Press, 1986).

4. And increasingly in the South; see chapter 1. For a discussion of the current debates and the relevance of the concept of civil society to them, see our introduction.

Introduction

1. Of course, Karl Polànyi's *Great Transformation* [1944] (Boston: Beacon Press, 1957), which has been a major touchstone for our work, brought the state "back in" in the mid-1940s. But see Peter Evans et al., eds., *Bringing the State Back In* (Cambridge, England: Cambridge University Press, 1985). The focus on the state has, however, occasioned an extremely interesting and important debate (and new research) around the relation of women and the welfare state. Here a new dimension has been captured that was ignored in the past. See such recent work as Gretchen Ritter and Theda Skocpol, "Gender and the Origins of Modern Social Policies in Britain and the United States," ms.; Linda Gordon, "What Does Welfare Regulate?," and Frances Fox Piven and Richard Cloward, "Welfare Doesn't Shore up Traditional Family Roles: A Reply to Linda Gordon," both in *Social Research* 55, no.4 (Winter 1988): 609–648; Cynthia Epstein, *Deceptive Distinctions: Sex, Gender and the Social Order* (New Haven: Yale University Press, 1988); Mimi Abramovitz, *Regulating the Lives of Women* (Boston: South End Press, 1988); Nancy Fraser, *Unruly Practices* (Minneapolis: University of Minnesota Press, 1989); and Helga Hernes, *Welfare State and Woman Power: Essays on State Feminism* (Oslo: Norwegian University Press, 1987).

2. See chapter 1.

3. This debate began in the mid-1950s and reemerged in the aftermath of the New Left. For a chronology, see John F. Manley, "Neo-Pluralism: A Class Analysis of Pluralism I and Pluralism II," *American Political Science Review* 77, no. 2 (June 1983): 368–383. The list of participants in this debate is long. Let us mention just a few key figures and representative works on each side. Elite theorists include Joseph Schumpeter, *Capitalism, Socialism and Democracy* (New York: Harper & Row, 1942); S. M. Lipset, *Political Man* (New York: Doubleday, 1963); Robert Dahl, *Polyarchy* (New Haven: Yale University Press, 1971); William Kornhauser, *The Politics of Mass Society* (New York: Free Press, 1959); G. Almond and S. Verba, *The Civic Culture* (Boston: Little Brown, 1963). Participatory democrats include Peter Bachrach, *The Theory of Democratic Elitism: A Critique* (Boston: Little Brown, 1967); Carole Pateman, *Participation and Democratic Theory* (Cambridge, England: Cambridge University Press, 1970); Sheldon Wolin, *Politics and Vision* (Boston: Little Brown, 1960). For an overview of the debate, see Quentin Skinner, "The Empirical Theorists of Democracy and Their Critics: A Plague on Both Their Houses," *Political Theory* 1 (1973): 287–306.

4. The list of participants in this debate is also too long to cite fully. Two of the best presentations of "rights-oriented liberalism" are John Rawls, *A Theory of Justice* (Cambridge: Harvard University Press, 1971), and Ronald Dworkin,

Taking Rights Seriously (Cambridge: Harvard University Press, 1977). For the liberal concept of neutrality, see Bruce Ackerman, *Social Justice in the Liberal State* (New Haven: Yale University Press, 1980), and Charles Larmore, *Patterns of Moral Complexity* (Cambridge, England: Cambridge University Press, 1987). The best and most original "neocommunitarian" work, predating but nevertheless informing the debate, is Hannah Arendt, *On Revolution* (New York: Penguin, 1963); see also Sheldon Wolin, *Politics and Vision* (Boston: Little Brown, 1960), and R. Unger, *Knowledge and Politics* (New York: Macmillan, 1975). Contemporary epistemological critics of liberalism include Alisdair MacIntyre, *After Virtue* (South Bend: University of Notre Dame Press, 1984), and Michael Sandel, *Liberalism and the Limits of Justice* (Cambridge, England: Cambridge University Press, 1982). Communitarian democrats include Charles Taylor, *Hegel* (Cambridge, England: Cambridge University Press, 1975) and *Philosophical Papers*, vol. 2: *Philosophy and the Human Sciences* (Cambridge, England: Cambridge University Press, 1985); Michael Walzer, *Spheres of Justice* (New York: Basic, 1983); and Carole Pateman, *The Problem of Political Obligation: A Critique of Liberal Theory* (Berkeley: University of California Press, 1985). A volume that brings together both sides of the debate is Michael Sandel, ed., *Liberalism and its Critics* (New York: New York University Press, 1984).

This debate has also given structure to some of the most important controversies within feminist political and legal theory. While there has always been a debate between radical, liberal, and Marxist/socialist feminists, today the battle is drawn along lines similar to those depicted above. Equal-rights-oriented liberal feminists who emphasize gender neutrality are pitted against communitarian feminists on one side and deconstructionist feminists on the other, both of whom emphasize difference, contextuality, and the limits of rights analyses, denying the very possibility of neutrality and universality in either law or politics. For two exemplary statements of the liberal-feminist position, see Wendy Williams, "Equality's Riddle: Pregnancy and the Equal Treatment/Special Treatment Debate," 13 N.Y.U. Rev. *Law and Social Change* 325 (1984–85), and Susan Okin, *Justice, Gender and the Family* (New York: Basic Books, 1989). Carol Gilligan, *In a Different Voice* (Cambridge: Harvard University Press, 1982), is the classic statement of the communitarian feminist position. For the deconstructionist approach, see Joan Scott, "Deconstructing Equality-versus-Difference: Of the Uses of Poststructuralist Theory for Feminism," *Feminist Studies* 14, no. 1 (Spring 1988): 33–50. For a neo-Marxist approach to the problem, see Catherine MacKinnon, *Toward A Feminist Theory of the State* (Cambridge: Harvard University Press, 1989).

5. See Michel Crozier et al., eds., *The Crisis of Democracy* (New York: New York University Press, 1975), and Claus Offe, *Contradictions of the Welfare State* (Cambridge: MIT Press, 1984).

6. Joseph Schumpeter, *Capitalism, Socialism, and Democracy* (New York: Harper & Row, 1942), 232–302.

7. Ibid., 269.

8. The model of the political party is the catch-all party. For the concept, see Otto Kirchheimer, "The Transformation of the Western European Party System," in Frederic S. Burin and Kurt L. Shell, eds., *Politics, Law, and Social Change: Selected Essays of Otto Kirchheimer* (New York: Columbia University Press, 1969), 346–371. Some elite theorists who are also pluralists include interest groups as actors in the political system (see Dahl, *Polyarchy*). However, the idea that interests emerge spontaneously and autonomously in civil society and are then aggregated by political parties has been criticized not only by Marxists but also by theorists of neocorporatism. For an excellent overview of these criticisms, see Suzanne Berger, *Organizing Interests in Western Europe* (Cambridge, England: Cambridge University Press, 1981), 1–23.

9. On this model, societal interests cannot be represented. Neither public opinion nor raw individual interests find representation in the political system; instead, interests are aggregated and given their political salience by elites.

10. According to Schumpeter, *Capitalism, Socialism, and Democracy*, 292–293, not everything in a democracy is subject to the democratic method. For example, judges, federal agencies, and bureaucracies are beyond the reach of this method but are not thereby antidemocratic. We agree with this argument but would insist that just how far or in which domains democratic principles ought to extend is not something that experts can decide; it is, rather, a normative and empirical question that must be decided upon democratically, as it were. (We should note that Schumpeter's point was aimed against "totalitarian" regimes, which so overextend the reach of the political—although hardly that of democracy—that they undermine the integrity and efficiency of political decision making.)

11. Ibid., 289–295.

12. Just what counts as too much participation is a matter of debate. While the elite-democracy school partially buys into this idea and extols a mixture of activism and apathy (see Almond and Verba, *The Civic Culture*, and Lipset, *Political Man*), along with civil privatism, Schumpeter went the furthest in this direction. In arguing against the imperative mandate, Schumpeter insists that people should accept the division of labor between leaders and followers, give up on the idea of instructing delegates, and even cease from bombarding their representatives with letters and telegrams!

13. See Bachrach, *Theory of Democratic Elitism*.

14. As theorists of neocorporatism have shown, such polities often have powerful semipublic organizations that are hierarchically organized, engage in behind-the-scenes deals with one another and with the state, are not internally democratic, and do not interact according to principles of democratic procedure. See the essays in P. Schmitter and G. Lehmbruch, eds., *Trends toward Corporatist Intermediation* (London: Sage Publications, 1979).

15. Jürgen Habermas, "Legitimation Problems in the Modern State," in *Communication and the Evolution of Society* (Boston: Beacon Press, 1979), 186–187.

16. Bachrach, *Theory of Democratic Elitism*.

17. That is, it loses a standard with which to judge whether consent, procedures, and so on are what they claim to be. See Phillippe C. Schmitter, "Democratic Theory and Neocorporatist Practice," *Social Research* 50, no. 4 (Winter 1983): 885–891.

18. See Arendt, *On Revolution*, and Wolin, *Politics and Vision*. See also Benjamin Barber, *Strong Democracy* (Berkeley: University of California Press, 1984).

19. Barber, *Strong Democracy*.

20. This is not true of Pateman, *Participation and Democratic Theory*.

21. It should not be forgotten that classical democratic theory rested on an undifferentiated conception of *Sittlichkeit*, that is, on an ethically superior consensus regarding the good to which all must adhere if they choose not to leave. In a modern world characterized by value pluralism and the war of gods, such a conception is anachronistic.

22. Both the elite and the participatory model make the mistake of collapsing the principle of democratic legitimacy into organizational principles. The first dissolves normative proceduralism into procedures for winning power, while the second tries to deduce organizational models from the democratic principle of legitimacy. See chapter 8 for a discussion of this problem. See also Habermas, "Legitimation Problems," 186–187.

23. In a way, this debate is a response to the utilitarian dimensions of the elite and pluralist models of democracy. Rawls and Dworkin both challenge utilitarianism, arguing that, without a principled conception of justice or a theory of rights, the utilitarian elite pluralist model of democracy cannot claim legitimacy. The communitarians, of course, challenge the model in toto, but the focus of their efforts is less the utilitarianism of the democratic elitists than the rights focus of contemporary liberalism.

24. See note 4.

25. Ibid.

26. What is new here vis-à-vis the early tradition of liberalism (or elite pluralism, for that matter) is that property is no longer placed at the heart of the conception of rights; it is one right among many, but open to "balancing." Rawls and Dworkin are, of course, strong defenders of the welfare state.

27. The rights thesis is predicated on the following assumptions: (1) there is no authority other than human reason for judging moral claims; (2) all individuals must be seen as equal partners in the moral dialogue when it comes to asserting and defending rights claims—moral reasons have to be given; (3) any tradition, prerogative, or claim is open to critique; (4) the values that individuals defend, including rights, are valid because they can be argued for vis-à-vis other moral systems. All values are values for individuals. If something is valuable for a community, it must be shown to be a value for the individual as well. See Janos Kis, *L'Égale dignité. Essai sur les fondements des droits de l'homme* (Paris: Seuil, 1989).

28. Hence the priority of the right or justice over the good.

29. That is, the alleged anthropological premise of the rights thesis is one of isolated, self-sufficient, atomized individuals outside society, fully endowed with instrumental reason and autonomy. These selves are independent of their ends and social context. Such "unencumbered" selves are deemed to be the originary locus of freedom of choice regarding one's ends, forms of life, projects, etc. Sandel, Taylor, and Walzer all criticize these epistemological assumptions allegedly underlying rights-oriented liberalism. Amy Gutman, "Communitarian Critics of Liberalism," *Philosophy and Public Affairs* 14, no. 4 (1985): 308–322, rejects the thesis as fallacious.

30. That is, Charles Taylor, Michael Walzer, and Benjamin Barber.

31. Since the 1970s. For the left critique of the welfare state, see Offe, *Contradictions*, chapters 1 and 6.

32. For a discussion of various defenses and criticisms of the welfare state, see Offe, *Contradictions*, 35–206, 252–302. He gives a definition on page 194.

33. Ibid., 147.

34. T. H. Marshall, *Class, Citizenship and Social Development* (New York: Doubleday, 1964).

35. Offe, *Contradictions*, 149–154.

36. Investors will postpone investment in the expectation of special tax incentives, or in the hope that the burdens of certain regulations will be lifted. As Claus Offe has convincingly argued, whether or not there are other reasons for the failure to invest, such as the inherent crisis tendencies of the capitalist economy, including overaccumulation, the business cycle, or uncontrolled technological change (none of which has anything to do with the welfare state), the point is that private investors have the power to define reality, and hence their perceptions create that reality. Whatever they perceive as an intolerable burden *is* an intolerable burden that will in fact lead to a declining propensity to invest. See Offe, *Contradictions*, 151.

37. See especially Crozier et al., eds., *The Crisis of Democracy*.

38. Huntington, "The United States," in Crozier et al., eds., *The Crisis of Democracy*, 73.

39. See James O'Connor, *The Fiscal Crisis of the State* (New York: St. Martin's Press, 1973); Habermas, *Legitimation Crisis*, Part II; and Offe, *Contradictions*, 35–64.

40. For the reasons for this claim, see Offe, *Contradictions*, 67–76.

41. Claus Offe, *Disorganized Capitalism* (Cambridge: MIT Press, 1985), 84.

42. This includes the family within civil society. See our discussion of Hegel in chapter 2.

43. These discussions have, in turn, been highly instructive for the development of our conception.

44. See note 8.

45. Although they do not use the term, pluralists include voluntary associations, interest groups, a free press, and basic rights within the societal realm that is

distinct from the economy. The most sophisticated three-part model to be found in pluralist theory is that of Talcott Parsons (see chapter 3).

46. See Kornhauser, *The Politics of Mass Society*.

47. This is very much contrary to the spirit of Alexis de Tocqueville, whom the pluralists frequently cite as one of their most important forerunners.

48. It is not a matter of concern whether the nuclear family is patriarchal or whether interest groups are in fact highly bureaucratized or hierarchically organized.

49. For an analysis of these norms, see chapter 8.

50. In this sense, we do not agree with Norberto Bobbio, who seeks to add the democratization of civil society to elite democratic structures that he takes to be given and unchangeable. We shall try to show that an inevitably defensive strategy of democratizing only civil society must fail and that complementary strategies of democratizing state, economy, and civil society, albeit to different extents, are possible. Indeed, the democratization of civil society would in itself open up the political terrain. Elite democracy, conversely, must either suppress the democratizing tendencies of civil society or become creatively responsive to them and hence change itself. See Norberto Bobbio, *The Future of Democracy* (Minneapolis: University of Minnesota Press, 1987), and our treatment of Bobbio in chapter 3.

51. Despite the differences between elite theorists like Schumpeter and pluralists like Dahl (who do not see the exercise of influence by interest groups on political parties or congressional representatives as a threat to the division of labor between citizens and politicians), they all recognize the importance to smooth functioning of a consensus regarding the basic procedures of the political system. See also Dahl, *Democracy and Its Critics*, 221.

52. See chapter 9.

53. We discuss this problem in chapter 8 with respect to the relation between moral autonomy and political norms, and in chapter 11 with respect to the question of civil disobedience in a "nearly just, nearly democratic" polity.

54. Neither Hobbes nor Locke presupposed the idea of neutrality, but they certainly based their theories on a methodological and ontological individualism. Theorists such as Rawls and Ackerman, on the other hand, embrace the principle of neutrality, as well as a version of methodological individualism, but do not presuppose an individualist ontology.

55. See chapter 8.

56. See chapter 8. It excludes only those need-interpretations and forms of life that are incompatible with the metanorms of symmetric reciprocity—that is, forms of life that deny equal concern and respect to others, that silence, dominate, denigrate, or otherwise treat people as mere means.

57. We discuss this point in detail in chapter 8, but we are not alone in arguing that one can defend the rights thesis without presupposing the theory of possessive individualism or a private, individual process of universalization. Two

defenses of a liberal theory of neutrality, predicated on a dialogical foundation for rights and a nonconsequentialist conception of neutrality, have recently been proposed. While we do not accept the kinds of prior constraints these theories seek to impose on dialogue in order to secure neutrality, what is of interest is that both rest on the idea of communicative interaction as the heart of a theory of political justice or rights. See Ackerman, *Social Justice in the Liberal State*, and Larmore, *Patterns of Moral Complexity*.

58. This is really an extreme libertarian rather than a liberal view. See Robert Nozick, *Anarchy, State and Utopia* (New York: Basic Books, 1974).

59. See chapter 8 for a different conception of autonomy.

60. See Daniel Bell, *The Cultural Contradictions of Capitalism* (New York: Basic Books, 1976). Bell is not, strictly speaking, a neoconservative, since he defends liberal democracy as well as socialism in the realm of the economy. For an overview of neoconservative cultural assumptions, see Peter Steinfels, *The Neo-Conservatives* (New York: Simon and Schuster, 1979).

61. For an argument in favor of resacralizing the political, see Edward Shils, *Tradition* (Chicago: University of Chicago Press, 1981). For arguments bewailing our hedonist culture and advocating a revived family life, see Christopher Lasch, *The Culture of Narcissism* (New York: Norton, 1979) and *Haven in a Heartless World* (New York: Basic Books, 1977). For criticisms of the modernist culture of critique, see Bell, *Cultural Contradictions of Capitalism*, and Alvin Gouldner, *The Future of Intellectuals and the Rise of the New Class* (New York: Seabury, 1979).

62. A series of books on "mediating structures" sponsored by the American Enterprise Institute offers a case in point. See John Neuhaus and Peter Berger, *To Empower People—The Role of Mediating Structures in Public Policy* (Washington: American Enterprise Institute, 1978), Michael Novak, ed., *Democracy and Mediating Structures* (Washington: American Enterprise Institute, 1990), and Nathan Glazer, *The Limits of Social Policy* (Cambridge: Harvard University Press, 1988). For an excellent discussion of the neoconservative position expressed in these works, see Robert Devigne, "Recasting Conservatism," unpublished doctoral dissertation, Columbia University, 1990.

63. Surely not all of them. We fail to see how social security, health insurance, job training programs for the unemployed, unemployment insurance, and family supports such as day care or parental leave create dependency rather than autonomy, even if the particular administrative requirements for such programs as AFDC (such as the man-in-the-house rule) do create dependency and are humiliating. But these are empirical questions. The theoretical issue behind such questions is the extent to which social services and social supports are symbolically constituted as welfare for "failures" or as supports for all members of the community.

64. This point can also be made against recent attempts to fashion a politics out of theories of postmodernism. "Postmodernism" refers to the work of French thinkers such as Jacques Derrida, Jacques Lacan, and Jean-François Lyotard. For

an excellent overview, see Peter Dewes, *Logics of Disintegration* (London: Verso, 1987). For one attempt to develop a politics out of this general approach, see Chantal Mouffe and Ernesto Laclau, *Hegemony and Socialist Strategy: Toward a Radical Democratic Politics* (London: Verso, 1985).

Postmodernism rests on a fully modern lifeworld and is anything but traditionalist. Moreover, the critical investigations of modernist "identitary" logic and the dualisms of the philosophy of the subject underlying it are extremely insightful (although critical theorists made similar investigations many years before postmodernism became chic). However, the political applications of this orientation are not very satisfying, primarily because they tend to favor one side of the dualisms against the other. Hence, the defense of difference against equality, particularity against universality, responsibility against rights, relatedness against autonomy, and concrete thinking against abstract reflection. In our view, this tends to throw out the baby with the bath water. The task, rather, is to formulate the second set of principles in ways that do not eliminate or establish hierarchies for difference, plurality, or particularity. For example, we ought to try to conceive of equality without insisting on sameness, universality without annihilating multiplicity, autonomy and rights on the basis of a philosophy of communicative interaction rather than atomistic individualism. Moreover, the cultural principles of modernity are not in themselves responsible for their one-sided application or interpretation. All of these principles are open to new interpretations. But to take the side of difference, particularity, and situatedness per se would leave one without the theoretical tools necessary to explain why one ought to tolerate, recognize, or communicate with difference or the other.

65. For a development of this conception, see chapter 9.

Chapter 1

1. Even if in an essayistic, not explicitly theoretical style. See, in particular, Adam Michnik, "A New Evolutionism," in *Letters from Prison and Other Essays* (Berkeley: University of California Press, 1985).

2. The latter are in principle also potentially unlimited because of the dramatic internal democratization of the ruling party.

3. Michnik, *Letters from Prison*, 86, 88, 95.

4. A. Arato, "The Democratic Theory of the Polish Opposition: Normative Intentions and Strategic Ambiguities," *Working Papers of the Helen Kellogg Institute* (Notre Dame, 1984).

5. Michnik, *Letters from Prison*, 111, 124.

6. Ibid., 77.

7. K. Wojcicki, "The Reconstruction of Society," *Telos*, no. 47 (Spring 1981): 98–104.

8. "Not to Lure the Wolves out of the Woods: An Interview with Jacek Kuron," *Telos*, no. 47 (Spring 1981): 93–97.

9. This is done critically by some, enthusiastically by others. Touraine's distinction between a social movement (unified) and a movement for the reconstruction of (pluralistic) society helps to depict the ambiguity involved. See A. Touraine et al., *Solidarity. Poland 1980–1981* (Cambridge, England: Cambridge University Press, 1983).

10. Compare, for example, Michnik, *Letters from Prison*, 89–90, 129, and 158.

11. See the interview with Jacek Kuron cited in note 8.

12. Michnik, *Letters from Prison*, 146–147.

13. For extensive analyses of the problems of reconstructing civil society in the first Solidarity period, 1980–1981, see A. Arato "Civil Society against the State: Poland 1980–1981," *Telos*, no. 47 (Spring 1981): 23–47, and "Empire vs. Civil Society: Poland 1981–1982," *Telos*, no. 50 (Winter 1981–1982): 19–48.

14. Michnik, *Letters from Prison*, 81.

15. Ibid., 57, 79.

16. The leadership of Solidarity entered negotiations with the goal of relegalizing the union movement. Very much in the spirit of the civil-society-oriented strategy of August 1980, it wanted to avoid all power-sharing arrangements that might lead to responsibility without genuine power. That Solidarity should accept one-third of the seats in the lower house, to be filled by means of a controlled election, was the regime's price for legalizing the union, while the formula of a freely elected upper chamber was the compromise around which the opponents agreed. The actual results were not anticipated by any of the participants. Among other things, they implied a shift of Solidarity's strategy and part of its identity toward *political society*.

17. Among the most relevant authors are Claude Lefort, André Gorz, Alain Touraine, Jacques Juilliard, Pierre Rosanvallon, and Patrick Viveret. They are all intellectuals for whom 1968 was an important turning point in Left politics, from which they drew democratic and liberal rather than authoritarian consequences. To various extents, they were associated with the CFDT trade union and the Rocardian wing of the Socialist party of the 1970s. The not particularly fortunate term "second Left" has been applied to this trend by its advocates, while their opponents referred to them at times as the "American Left," presumably because of their emphasis on the new social movements and on civil society. For a history of the CFDT, see Hervé Hamon and Patrick Rotman, *La deuxième gauche* (Paris: Editions Ramsay, 1982).

18. It may be worth a separate study to determine why. We would stress the continued importance in the 1970s of an unreconstructed Communist party and the general presence of a statist-Jacobin political culture as distinguishing France from other Western European countries. Obviously, the struggle over the heritage of May 1968 also played an important role, as did the efforts of the Socialist party to define itself against the dominant left tradition in France.

19. Pierre Rosanvallon and Patrick Viveret, *Pour une nouvelle culture politique* (Paris: Seuil, 1977), 22–24.

20. Ibid., 7, 129. The point, first argued by Tocqueville, was taken up by pluralist political theory in the 1960s to account for French exceptionalism and the existence of radical movements in France.

21. Ibid., 112.

22. Pierre Rosanvallon, *La crise de l'État-providence*, revised edition (Paris: Seuil, 1981), 117.

23. Rosanvallon and Viveret, *Pour une nouvelle culture politique*, 113ff.

24. Ibid., 103, 129.

25. Ibid., 129–130.

26. Ibid., 97–98.

27. Ibid., 112; see also Claude Lefort, "Politics and Human Rights," in *The Political Forms of Modern Society* (Cambridge: MIT Press, 1986), 266.

28. Lefort, "Politics and Human Rights."

29. Rosanvallon, *La crise de l'État providence*, 120–121, 136.

30. See André Gorz, *Farewell to the Working Class* (Boston: South End Press, 1982).

31. See chapter 9.

32. Claus Offe and Volker Gransow, "Political Culture and Social Democratic Administration," in Offe, *Contradictions of the Welfare State* (Cambridge: MIT Press, 1984).

33. In particular, James O'Connor, Jürgen Habermas, and Claus Offe.

34. Michel Crozier et al., eds., *The Crisis of Democracy* (New York: New York University Press, 1975).

35. See Offe, *Contradictions*, chapters 2, 6, and 8

36. Claus Offe, "The New Social Movements: Challenging the Boundaries of Institutional Politics," *Social Research* 52, no. 4 (1985): 819–820.

37. Offe, *Contradictions*, 289–290.

38. Ibid., 250.

39. Offe, "The New Social Movements," 820.

40. Offe, *Contradictions*, 182–183. This argument is older than the other two already quoted and preserves something of the democratic statism of Offe's earlier position. The state is regarded here as democratic to the extent that it is based on universal suffrage; and, curiously enough, *liberal* democratic institutions somehow make it less democratic. This position is identical to that of Carl Schmitt. Another version of Offe's argument that makes liberal democracy the "bridge" between citizen and state does not have this implication. See *Contradictions*, 163ff.

41. This conflict could in principle be resolved, as some distinctly antidemocratic liberals think, by reinforcing the elitist side of elite democracy to produce a "restoration of authority." Given existing democratic standards of legitimation, however, it is not at all clear that such a solution is possible without the

introduction of dictatorships capable of eliminating, for a time, an excess of parliamentary and extraparliamentary demands.

42. Claus Offe, *Disorganized Capitalism* (Cambridge: MIT Press, 1985), 224–226.

43. This is repeatedly asserted by Offe himself; see, e.g., *Contradictions*, 250.

44. See chapters 9 and 10. We believe that the significant overlap between the categories of lifeworld and civil society supplies the key to this problem, especially in a three-part model of state–economy–civil society.

45. Offe, *Contradictions*, 246.

46. See Offe, *Disorganized Capitalism*, chap. 9.

47. Guillermo O'Donnell and Philippe Schmitter, eds., *Transitions from Authoritarian Rule*, 4 volumes (Baltimore: Johns Hopkins, 1986).

48. O'Donnell and Schmitter, "Tentative Conclusions about Uncertain Democracies," in *Transitions*, vol. 4, 48ff.

49. Schmitter, "An Introduction to Southern European Transitions from Authoritarian Rule," in *Transitions*, vol. 1, 6–7.

50. Alfred Stepan, *Rethinking Military Politics: Brazil and the Southern Cone* (Princeton: Princeton University Press, 1988), 3–4.

51. O'Donnell and Schmitter, "Tentative Conclusions," 49–52.

52. Ibid., 51, 53.

53. Ibid., 48.

54. Schmitter, "Introduction to Southern European Transitions," 6–7; G. Pasquino, "The Demise of the First Fascist Regime and Italy's Transition to Democracy: 1943–1948," and N. Diamandouros, "Regime Change and the Prospects for Democracy in Greece: 1974–1983," in *Transitions*, vol. 1, 46, 58, and 154; M. A. Garreton, "The Political Evolution of the Chilean Military Regime and Problems of the Transition to Democracy" in *Transitions*, vol. 2, 116–117; O'Donnell and Schmitter, "Tentative Conclusions," 21–22. The Southern European examples do not, of course, fit the model of bureaucratic authoritarianism developed by O'Donnell.

55. O'Donnell and Schmitter, "Tentative Conclusions," 55.

56. F. Weffort, "Why Democracy?," in Alfred Stepan, ed., *Democratizing Brazil* (Princeton: Princeton University Press, 1989), 349.

57. This point is relevant to the elitist-authoritarian dreams of "Northern" neoconservatives as well, many of whom were strong supporters of the bureaucratic-authoritarian-liberal dictatorships of the "South," as, for example, in Chile.

58. G. O'Donnell, "Tensions in the Bureaucratic-Authoritarian State and the Problem of Democracy," in D. Collier, ed., *The New Authoritarianism in Latin America* (Princeton: Princeton University Press, 1979), 313ff., and F. H. Cardoso, "Associated-Dependent Development and Democratic Theory," in Stepan, ed., *Democratizing Brazil*, 312ff.

59. O'Donnell, "Tensions in the Bureaucratic-Authoritarian State," 317.

60. O'Donnell and Schmitter, "Tentative Conclusions," 48.

61. Diamandouros, "Regime Change and Prospects for Democracy in Greece," 154. Again, the Greek case involves a somewhat different type of regime.

62. O'Donnell and Schmitter, "Tentative Conclusions," 15.

63. In the same sentence, O'Donnell and Schmitter argue that "the relative absence of this upsurge reduces the likelihood of coup-induced regression" and "where 'power is with the people' or 'people are in the streets' the promoters of such coups are likely to hesitate before the prospect of provoking civil war" ("Tentative Conclusions," 55).

64. O'Donnell, "Tensions in the Bureaucratic-Authoritarian State," 287ff. In this essay, O'Donnell calls only the private sphere "civil society," using an earlier Marxian terminology that he soon abandoned. The analysis itself, stressing mediations as the voice of an otherwise silent civil society, already breaks with the Marxian conceptualization of the whole problem, turning in an implicitly Hegelian direction.

65. Cardoso, "On the Characterization of Authoritarian Regimes in Latin America," in Collier, ed., *The New Authoritarianism*, 37, 43–44.

66. O'Donnell, "Tensions in the Bureaucratic-Authoritarian State," 317.

67. Weffort, "Why Democracy?," 329.

68. Cardoso, "Associated-Dependent Development and Democratic Theory," 319. He rightly calls this a return to a different conception, although he misleadingly equates "a Latin conception of civil society" with political society.

69. Ibid., 313–314, and Stepan, *Rethinking Military Politics*, 5.

70. Stepan, *Rethinking Military Politics*.

71. This point was made by Juan Corradi in a lecture to the Democracy Seminar at the Graduate Faculty of the New School for Social Research in the spring of 1987.

72. Stepan, *Rethinking Military Politics*, 3–5.

73. Compare pages 5 and 6 of Stepan's book. Both as a target of democratization and as an agent for pushing this process forward, civil society is indispensable in a wider view that Stepan himself elsewhere presupposes. See his "Paths Toward Redemocratization: Theoretical and Comparative Considerations," in O'Donnell and Schmitter, eds., *Transitions*, vol. 3, 78–79. Compare also pages ix and xi in the introduction to *Democratizing Brazil*.

74. B. Lamounier, "Authoritarian Brazil Revisited: The Impact of Elections on the Abertura," in Stepan, ed., *Democratizing Brazil*, 55.

75. Stepan, "Paths Toward Redemocratization," 79–81; O'Donnell and Schmitter, "Tentative Conclusions," 37–39.

76. Cardoso, "Associated-Dependent Development," 45ff.; Lamounier, "Authoritarian Brazil Revisited," 63.

77. Stepan, "State Power and the Strength of Civil Society in the Southern Cone of Latin America," in Peter Evans et al., eds., *Bringing the State Back In* (Cambridge, England: Cambridge University Press, 1985).

78. Cardoso, "Associated-Dependent Development," 319–320. All interpreters of the German Greens have noticed the same problem. See chapter 10.

79. O'Donnell and Schmitter, "Tentative Conclusions," 37ff.

80. Ibid., 42.

81. Ibid., 42, 47.

82. Ibid., 57–58.

83. Lamounier, "Authoritarian Brazil Revisited," 55.

84. O'Donnell and Schmitter, "Tentative Conclusions," 58–59.

85. Ibid., 62.

86. Lamounier, "Authoritarian Brazil Revisited," 69, 71.

87. Ibid., 62–63.

88. Ibid., 58.

89. O'Donnell and Schmitter, "Tentative Conclusions," 26, 55–56.

90. Cf. A. Hirschman *Shifting Involvements* (Princeton: Princeton University Press, 1982).

91. See Garreton, "The Political Evolution of the Chilean Military Regime;" also, C. G. Gillespie, "Uruguay's Transition from Collegial Military-Technocratic Rule," in *Transitions*, vol. 2.

92. O'Donnell, "Introduction to the Latin American Cases," in *Transitions*, vol. 3, 15–17.

93. Ibid.

94. Norbert Lechner, "De la révolution à la democratie (le débat intellectuel en Amérique du Sud)," *Esprit* (July 1986): 1–13; Robert Barros "The Left and Democracy: Recent Debates in Latin America," *Telos* (Summer 1986): 49–70; José Casanova, "Never Again," unpublished ms.

95. Weffort, "Why Democracy?," 332–333, 335–337.

96. Ibid., 345.

97. Cardoso, "Associated-Dependent Development," 323–324.

98. Ibid., 319.

99. Ibid., 321.

100. We are referring here to the development of forms of political and economic society that are open to the influence of civil society. For many years, our own ideas on this topic have been close to the model worked out by Cardoso. See "Social Movements, Civil Society and the Problem of Sovereignty," *Praxis International* 4, no. 5 (October 1985): 266–283; "Civil Society and Social Theory," *Thesis Eleven*, no. 21 (1988): 40–64; "Politics and the Reconstruction of Civil

Society," in Axel Honneth et al., eds. *Zwischenbetrachtungen im Prozess der Aufklärung. Jürgen Habermas zum 60. Geburtstag* (Frankfurt: Suhrkamp, 1989). For our present conception, see chapters 9 and 10.

101. J. Staniszkis, "On Some Contradictions of Socialist Society," *Soviet Studies* (April 1979): 184–186; *Poland's Self-limiting Revolution* (Princeton: Princeton University Press, 1984), 36–67, 144–145. See also the partially overlapping criticism by A. Arato, "The Democratic Theory of the Polish Opposition: Normative Intentions and Strategic Ambiguities," *Working Papers of the Helen Kellogg Institute* (Notre Dame, 1984), which aims at the reconstruction—not, as Staniszkis, the abandonment—of the theory of civil society.

102. The Soviet Union was the ultimate guarantor of the availability of key material resources in the periphery, despite their noneconomic (irrational and wasteful) utilization. This guarantee was mutually harmful. For the basic model, see J. Kornai, *Contradictions and Dilemmas* (Cambridge: MIT Press, 1986); for analyses of the crises of the model, see G. Markus, "Planning the Crisis: Remarks on the Economic System of Soviet-type Societies," *Praxis International* 1, no. 3 (October 1981): 240–257; T. Bauer, "From Cycles to Crisis?: Recent Developments in East European Planned Economies and the Theory of Investment Crisis," in A. Arato and F. Feher, eds., *Crisis and Reform* (Transaction Books, forthcoming). On the exhaustion of the resource constraint model and its consequences, see J. Kis, "Forr a vilàg," *Beszélö*, no. 26 (1989): 5–12. The first important theoretical article that spoke of the beginning of a "general economic crisis" of the Soviet bloc was published in 1982 by T. Bauer; it was translated as "The Second Economic Reform and Ownership Relations," *Eastern European Economics* 23, nos. 1–2 (1984).

103. Lecture at the New School, February 22, 1988, reported by the *New York Times*, February 28, 1988. Also see A. Nove, "What's Happening in Moscow," *National Interest* (Summer, 1987).

104. See, above all, J. Kornai, "The Hungarian Reform Process: Visions, Hopes, and Realities," *Journal of Economic Literature* 24 (December 1986): 1687–1737.

105. T. Bauer, "A màsodik gazdasàgi reform és a tulajdonviszonyok," *Mozgó Vilàg* (November 1982): 17–42.

106. Bauer saw this issue most clearly, at least in 1982.

107. Kornai, "The Hungarian Reform Process."

108. Tamàs Sàrközy, *Gazdasàgpolitika, Szervezetrendszer, Jogpolitika* (Budapest: Kossuth könyvkiadó, 1987).

109. Worse, this could be only one of the several unmediated polarizations that can occur within Soviet society, along with those between nationalities and center, as well as nationalist and democratic forces within the Russian center itself, and perhaps elsewhere as well.

110. In particular, J. Kis and the editors of *Beszélö*. See Kis, "Gondolatok a közeljövöröl" (Thoughts about the near future), *Beszélö*, no. 3 (June 1982): 7–27.

111. J. Kis, "Korlàtainkròl és lehetöségeinkröl" (About our limits and possibilities), in *A Monori Tanàcskozàs* (an underground publication), 1985.

112. See the collective work "Fordulat és reform" (Turning point and reform) and M. Bihari, "Reform és democracia," both in *Medvetànc*, no. 2 (Budapest, 1987): 5–129, 165–225.

113. Even in Poland, where the negotiations of early 1989 achieved a compromise formula with an astonishing resemblance to that of the *Social Contract*, it cannot be said that this happened merely as a result of overwhelming grass-roots pressure, which in fact had led to stalemate earlier. While the strike movements of 1988 were important, they were far weaker than those of 1980, and yet (against the intentions of the Solidarity leadership) they achieved a much more comprehensive result. This consisted not only in a (re)legalization of the union but also in elections that were to a significant extent freely contested, opening up the way in June 1989 to a "plebescitary" defeat of the Communist party, an upper house controlled by Solidarity, and a combined legislature in which the opposition could veto all legislation as well as the ruling party's choice of a president of the republic. The result was, unexpectedly to all concerned, the formation of a Solidarity-led governmental coalition.

114. See L. Bruszt, "On the Road to a Constitutional State?," unpublished ms, 1989.

115. Kis, "Forr a vilàg," and also his "A visszaszàmlàlàs megkezdödött," *Beszélö*, no. 27 (1989). Kis argues that in Poland, where a powerful social organization already existed, its viability as a partner was not sacrificed (despite challenges from below) even if it accepted constraints on the processes of political competition. In Hungary, however, where the new organizations could become genuinely popular only in the context of open elections, all such restriction would have jeopardized the potential partners and also made them useless from the point of view of Communist reformers.

116. See Arato, "Civil Society against the State" and "Empire vs. Civil Society."

117. We would certainly hesitate to derive the actions of the reformist leaders and their group from the project of wider elites to conserve or convert their existing economic powers into new ownership and control arrangements. Compare E. Hankiss's excellent book, *Kelet-európai alternativàk* (Budapest; Közgazdasàgi és jogi kiadó, 1989), 300 and chap. 9. The relevant conversion for a small political elite is a political one: from a party state to a successful electoral and even presidential party. The failure of this conversion in Hungary does not prove that it was not the most important motivation of the leading reformers, or that other forms of (apparently) more successful economic conversion belonged to the motivation of the leadership at all. Within the context of the transition, and the anticipation of a different set of economic rules, largely unorganized economic elites had an opportunity to undertake decentralized efforts of conversion that became a reason not to resist the pattern of transition, even if they could have done so. The same criticisms apply to the somewhat different analysis of E. Szalai, "Elites and System Change in Hungary," *Praxis International* 10, nos. 1–2 (April–

July 1990): 74–79. Szalai focuses on a somewhat different elite with different political alliances and, unlike Hankiss, does not believe that a system so transformed could possibly yield a functioning market economy. See also her essay "Az uj elite" (The new elite), *Beszélö*, no. 27 (1989).

118. In some cases, some of these are combined. Many now use the term "revolution" to describe all except the first option, reform from above. While definitions are always subject to historical drift, we believe that "revolution" is not the most fortunate choice in the case of Poland, Hungary, and the Soviet Union, for at least three reasons: (1) the necessarily self-limiting, gradual nature of the process that all actors have in mind, not only for decreasingly important geopolitical reasons but for reasons of principle as well; (2) the rejection by most relevant actors of the state-strengthening logic of modern revolutions, first discovered by Tocqueville; and (3) the important continuities of East European movements with movements in the West and especially the South that seek to go beyond the alternative of reform and revolution, at least in the traditional sense of these terms. The counterargument is based on a single model: the Hungarian revolution of 1956. The differences between the democratic opposition, with its 13-year history prior to 1989, and the movement against an unreconstructed Stalinist regime are obvious, even if today, after other important changes have been achieved, many of the goals of 1956 are again on the agenda. (Not all, though. There is no talk now, for example, of radical industrial democracy.) The 1956 uprising, like all great revolutions, did not have a self-limiting character; rather, it had aspects of a civil war, precisely what today's movements desperately seek to avoid. For this reason, neither the "peaceful revolution" in East Germany nor the "velvet revolution" in Czechoslovakia should be understood as a nonviolent version of the model of 1956. Interestingly enough, it is still an open question whether these "revolutions" represent more or less radical models of democratization than the nonrevolutionary Polish and Hungarian paths. See A. Arato, "Revolution, Civil Society and Democracy," *Praxis International* 10, nos. 1–2 (April–July 1990): 24–38.

119. We have in mind the remarkable openness of its debates, on the one side, and, on the other, the continued control of the process, especially the selection of the Supreme Soviet (the actual legislature) first by the conservative apparatus and later by Gorbachev's small group of officials.

120. We consider nationalist mobilization, especially of the particularist, aggressive variety, to be a pathology of civil society. In Eastern Europe and the Soviet Union, its origins are complex and, aside from the legitimate national and ethnic grievances of minorities and colonized peoples, reflect the following elements: (1) The insufficient and superficial processes of modernization of communist regimes, which could suppress traditional practices, symbols, and ideologies but could not effectively transform them. (2) The increasing utilization, with the decline of Marxist-Leninist forms of legitimation, of nationalist and historicist forms of self-presentation and self-justification. (3) The growing insecurity and economic decline of the period of transition, which makes the defense of material interests increasingly precarious. Even those most adversely affected by

the changes find it difficult to oppose them to the extent that they are prerequisites for dismantling hated regimes. There is, as a result, a tendency to mobilize around symbolic rather than material issues, identity rather than interest. (4) The fact that an appeal to a self-organizing civil society implies the general possibility of constructing new identities, but only for those capable of intensive participation in the life of organizations and associations. For those not so involved, the reconstruction of civil society and its associations seems to be only a program of atomization, all the more precarious in the context of declining state paternalism. The appeals to national identity and nationalist mobilization compensate these strata by the hope of "illusory community."

121. When written, our text could not anticipate several important developments. Viable parliamentary mediations have now emerged in the Soviet Union, but only on the level of the republics, including astonishingly enough the Russian Federal Socialist Republic. This situation, reflecting the development of a multiplicity of civil societies, one for each republic, does not in itself solve the problem of mediation on the level of the whole society or avoid the dangers of (multiple) polarization. It only displaces it to one between republican governments supported by their own civil societies and a central government whose internal structure does not provide for sufficient mediations. Worse, the failure of agreement (hopefully temporary) concerning economic reform between central and republican governments now reproduces the same structure of conflict on the economic level as well, reinforcing the political and cultural lines of division. Unless institutions of mediation, involving genuine constitutionalism and a parliamentarism that incorporates in a convincing manner a federal or confederal structure, are created, the possible outcomes are few and all extremely precarious. (Note added fall 1991.)

122. See, e.g., Z. Bujak, "West of Centre," *East European Reporter* 4, no. 3 (Autumn/Winter 1990). This position is not uncontested. In Czechoslovakia, J. Urban has forcefully argued for the conversion of Civil Forum into a party of the West European type. See "The Crisis of Civil Forum," *Uncaptive Minds* 3, no. 4 (August–October 1990). This issue cuts across other ideological divides. In Hungary, for example, the SzDSz is more comfortable with the "modern" party form; the FIDESZ seems less so. Within the ruling MDF on the right, both positions seem to be represented.

123. Lena Kolarska-Bobinska, "The Changing Face of Civil Society in Eastern Europe," unpublished ms. (1990). For the Hungarian case, see F. Miszlivetz, "The Injuries of East Central Europe: Is the Auto-therapy of Civil Society Possible?," unpublished ms. (1990); for the Czech case, see the interview with Ladislav Hejdanek published as "Democracy without Opposition Is Nonsense," *East European Reporter* 4, no. 3 (Autumn/Winter 1990): 96. For a general theoretical assessment, see Arato "Revolution, Civil Society, and Democracy."

124. G. M. Tamas has defended this perspective in several places. See, e.g., "Glemp biboros intö szava," *Élet és irodalom* 33, no. 36 (September 1989). There are important sectors in all three leading parties as well as many economists and economic policy makers who hold the same position.

125. See the analyses of the best of these theories in the following articles by A. Arato: "Autoritärer Sozialismus und die Frankfurter Schule," in A. Honneth and A. Wellmer, eds., *Die Frankfurter Schule und die Folgen* (Berlin: de Gruyter, 1986); "Bahro's Alternative: from Western to Eastern Marxism," a review of U. Wolter, ed., *Bahro: Critical Responses, Telos*, no. 48 (Summer 1981): 153–168; "Critical Sociology and Authoritarian State Socialism," in D. Held and J. Thompson, eds., *Habermas: Critical Debates* (Cambridge: MIT Press, 1982); "Immanent Critique and Authoritarian Socialism," *Canadian Journal of Political and Social Theory* 7, nos. 1–2 (Winter–Spring 1983): 146–162; "The Budapest School and Actually Existing Socialism," *Theory and Society*, no. 16 (1987); "Facing Russia: Castoriadis and Soviet Society," *Revue européenne des sciences sociales* 37, no. 86: 269–291.

126. See A. Arato, "Marxism in East Europe," in Tom Bottomore, ed., *Dictionary of Marxism* (Oxford: Blackwell, 1983), and "Marxism," in J. Eatwell et al., eds., *The New Palgrave: A Dictionary of Economics* (London: Macmillan, 1987).

127. See Jean L. Cohen, *Class and Civil Society. The Limits of Marx's Critical Theory* (Amherst: University of Massachusetts Press, 1982).

128. See chapter 3.

129. See Evans et al., eds., *Bringing the State Back In.*

130. See Jürgen Habermas, "The New Obscurity," in *The New Conservatism* (Cambridge: MIT Press, 1989).

131. See André Gorz, *Strategy for Labor* (Boston: Beacon Press, 1967).

132. G. M. Tamas represents this perspective, albeit elaborating it in terms of the idea of a "bloodless and legal" revolution that would be combined eventually with "reform" from above after the constitution of a legitimate form of power. Opposing any idea of "social revolution," his conception deliberately leaves open the possibility that present-day power holders will convert their power into economic ownership. See "Tájkép csata elött" (Landscape before battle), *Élet és irodalom*, August 4, 1989, and his speech to a public meeting of the SzDSz reported in *Szabad Demokraták*, nos. 4–5 (1989).

133. This position has been articulated by Agnes Heller and Ferenc Feher at various meetings and conferences but, to our knowledge, not yet in published form. They define political revolution as a break in the structure of sovereignty, as the replacement either of one sovereign or one form of sovereignty by another. Even the second, more convincing, version is both too wide and too narrow to describe the changes in most of the East European countries: Too wide because it neglects the continuities in the structure of political rule that are only gradually eliminated (in particular, the rule of old parliaments and the ruling party in the *pouvoir constituant* and the continued validity of the inherited legal system); too narrow because the transformations imply a wholesale change of systems and are not at all restricted to the sphere of the political. Interestingly enough, their definition best corresponds to the most violent and least radical case, namely, Rumania.

134. In a brilliant paper, which appeared too late to be incorporated into our argument, Ulrich Preuss has shown that the East European revolutions break with Carl Schmitt's model of sovereignty, which was in his view established by the French Revolution, especially in its Rousseauian-Jacobin self-interpretation ("The Influence of Carl Schmitt on the Legal Discourse of the Federal Republic of Germany," paper presented at a conference on the "Challenge of Carl Schmitt and Democratic Theory," spring 1990, Graduate Faculty, New School for Social Research, New York).

135. Admittedly, a rather old-fashioned use of the term *revolution* has now emerged in some countries, such as Hungary. This combines elements of premodern usage (return, restoration) with elements of the revolutionary semantics first invented by the Jacobins and their allies, in order to compensate for a deficit of democratic legitimacy rooted in civil society. The movement wing of the MDF that (primarily but not exclusively) pushes this usage is unfortunately forced by the logic of the position to invent enemies as well as to seek retroactive, extralegal retribution. Fortunately, appeals based on revolutionary semantics seem to find little response in a context that is still "postrevolutionary" in the sense of our notion of self-limitation. We would be foolish, however, to deny the possible dangers in revolutionary demagogy as the economic situation worsens before it can improve. Walesa's rise as the champion of a right hoping to "accelerate" change is ample warning in this context.

136. See chapter 2. Of course, what has been added by some (including ourselves) is families and movements.

137. For the distinction, see Polànyi's great essay, "The Economy as an Instituted Process," in G. Dalton, ed., *Primitive, Archaic and Modern Economies. The Essays of Karl Polànyi* (Boston: Beacon Press, 1968).

138. Recently, defenders of civil society in Hungary have stressed the plurality of forms of property within the process of privatization as the dimension through which civil society can gain a foothold within the new economic society in formation. See the latest essays in E. Szalai, *Gazdasàg és hatalom* (Budapest: Aula Kiado, 1990), which represent the best treatment of this question from the point of view of democratic theory as well as stringent economic analysis. In our view, property may have a role to play for civil society's relation to economic society that is analogous to the role political parties play with respect to political society. Private property as well as political organizations achieve only differentiation from civil society, while genuinely pluralistic forms of property as well as democratic parties are required to gain a mediating foothold of the civil in the economic and the political. Without such mediations, civil society becomes bourgeois and atomized, while democracy becomes elite.

139. See chapter 6 and A. Arato, "Civil Society, History, and Socialism: Reply to John Keane," *Praxis International* 9, nos. 1–2 (April–July 1989): 133–152.

140. This is the point of view of J. Kis. The idea of a multilevel civil society, including its political "mediations," could in principle satisfy the intellectual needs of a period of turning to politics in the more traditional sense. While it is

true that the partisans of civil society often stress a "horizontal" model, placing all associations and organizations on the same level, the "vertical" dimension of the concept of political society is present in the old Hegelian idea of mediation. However, in principle at least, it is just as possible for a civil society divided by alternative interests and identities to be pluralistically organized as for a political society to become monolithic. To be sure, with civil society taking on the function of political society in the face of a hostile and more or less unified authoritarian state, as in Poland, the constantly predicted pluralization of civil society never really developed beyond its beginnings. But here the pluralization of political society even in its parliamentary form also seems to have been surprisingly delayed. One may see the reason for this in a political society that has developed as the political mediation of a unified civil society. On the other hand, the premature overpluralization of political society—as in Hungary, where the project of transition is more consensual than it would seem from the political conflicts—can have the unfortunate consequence of further contributing to the demobilization of a society disgusted by needless aggression and demagogy in politics.

141. Cf. G. M. Tamas's attack on independent societal self-organization in *Uncaptive Minds.* Such calls for a new statism in the form of parliamentary absolutism are heard in both of the leading Hungarian parties; the opinion of I. Csurka on the independence of the press, which he hopes to replace by party political control through de facto parliamentary power, represents the same point of view. In both cases, the argument is based on a recognition that societal organization represents power and the claim that the only legitimate power is one that is an outcome of national elections.

142. This differs from the pluralist correction of Schumpeterian elite democracy in one crucial respect. While Dahl et al. tried to include civil society and its "influence" on political society within their conception of elite democracy, they counted on a general demobilization of civil society, an absence of social movements, a syndrome of civil privatism, consensus with a minimum degree of participation within civil society, and a restriction of participation to one specific form, namely, interest group pressure.

143. See Stepan, *Rethinking Military Politics,* and the introduction to Stepan, ed., *Democratizing Brazil.* This argument is inconsistent, since even if the institutionalization of civil society represented only the results of liberalization, the movements of civil society would be important in the emergence of political society itself as well as in the overall process of democratization.

144. Tamas, "Tájkép csata elött."

145. In this context, Cardoso's stress on industrial democracy finds many parallels in East European sources, which hope furthermore to institutionalize social autonomy above all through the development of a genuinely pluralistic structure of private property, including not only private ownership in the narrow sense but also ownership by employees, nonprofit organizations, and local government as well as ordinary citizens participating in new mutual funds. Such

devices are important not only for normative reasons coming from democratic theory, but also as the best ways to achieve a necessary speeding up of the privatization and demonopolization of East European economies. See Szalai, *Gazdaság és hatalom.*

Chapter 2

1. Manfred Riedel, "Gesellschaft, bürgerliche," in O. Brunner, W. Conze, and R. Koselleck, eds., *Geschichtliche Grundbegriffe*, vol. 2 (Stuttgart: Klett, 1975).

2. Niklas Luhmann, "Gesellschaft," in *Soziologische Aufklärung*, vol. 1 (Opladen: Westdeutscher Verlag, 1970), 138.

3. K. Polànyi, "Aristotle Discovers the Economy," in G. Dalton, ed., *Primitive, Archaic and Modern Economies. Essays of Karl Polànyi* (Boston: Beacon Press, 1968).

4. It hardly needs emphasis today that the *polis* was a community with a highly restrictive notion of citizenship, excluding foreigners, women, and usually manual workers as well.

5. M. I. Finley, *Politics in the Ancient World* (Cambridge, England: Cambridge University Press, 1983).

6. Riedel, "Gesellschaft, bürgerliche."

7. O. Brunner, *Land und Herrschaft*, 5th ed. (Darmstadt: Wissenschaftliche Buchgesellschaft, 1973), pt. 2, 115.

8. In his debate with Gierke and Hintze in particular. See *Land und Herrschaft*, 156ff., 161ff.

9. G. Jellinek, *The Declaration of the Rights of Man and Citizen* (New York: Henry Holt, 1901).

10. Reinhart Koselleck, *Critique and Crisis: Enlightenment and the Pathogenesis of Modern Society* (Cambridge: MIT Press, 1988), originally published as *Kritik und Krise* (Freiburg: Karl Alber Verlag, 1959).

11. Riedel, "Gesellschaft, bürgerliche," 740.

12. Talcott Parsons, *The Structure of Social Action* (New York: Free Press, 1949), 89ff.

13. John Locke, *The Second Treatise on Government* [1690] (Indianapolis: Hackett, 1980), chap. 7.

14. Ibid., chap. 8.

15. Ibid., chap. 4.

16. Ibid., chap. 19.

17. Montesquieu, *The Spirit of the Laws* [1748] (New York: Harpers, 1949), I(3), 5.

18. Ibid., 6; Nugent's English translation is seriously misleading.

19. Ibid., II(4); V(10, 11).

20. Z. A. Pelczynski, ed., *Hegel's Political Philosophy: Problems and Perspectives* (Cambridge, England: Cambridge University Press, 1971).

21. For Rousseau, civil society is in effect citizen society; political freedom means participation of free and equal members in ruling and being ruled.

22. See Koselleck, *Critique and Crisis.*

23. This "society" was also counterposed to the family. This was unfortunate, because the opposition was a gendered one based on the location of men alone in civil society and the sequestration of women in the privatized domestic sphere. Thus, while the egalitarian norms of the new civil society were conceptualized in opposition to the principles of hierarchy, status, and caste, the entire construction was built upon the preservation, in a new and all-pervasive form, of a gendered caste system. Unlike property, which anyone could in principle acquire and which, according to Locke, everyone started out with (property in one's body), the sexual qualification for membership in civil society was antithetical to its own principles.

24. Koselleck, *Kritik und Krise*, 46; Werner Conze, "Die Spannungsfeld von Staat und Gesellschaft im Vormärz," in Conze, ed., *Staat und Gesellschaft im deutschen Vormärz 1815–1848* (Stuttgart: Klett, 1962), 208.

25. Riedel, "Gesellschaft, bürgerliche," 748–750.

26. Ibid., 740–742; W. Conze, "Sozialgeschichte," in H. U. Wehler, ed., *Moderne Deutsche Sozialgeschichte* (Königstein: Athenëum, 1981).

27. Riedel, "Gesellschaft, bürgerliche," 758–761.

28. Ibid., 764.

29. G. Heiman, "The Sources and Significance of Hegel's Corporate Doctrine," in Pelczynski, ed., *Hegel's Political Philosophy*, 111–135.

30. In perhaps his greatest work in political theory, the young Marx paid great attention to the link in Hegel between statism and system building; see his *Critique of Hegel's Philosophy of Right* (Cambridge, England: Cambridge University Press, 1970).

31. G. W. F. Hegel, *Grundlinien der Philosophie des Rechts*, in *Werke*, vol. 7 (Frankfurt: Suhrkamp, 1970; hereafter cited as *Rechtsphilosophie*), par. 255 addendum. T. M. Knox's translation in *Hegel's Philosophy of Right* (New York: Oxford University Press, 1967; hereafter *PR*) is not quite right.

32. *PR*, par. 4, 142.

33. To a certain extent, Hegel follows Aristotle in construing the family (household) as the natural background of civil society, but he has in mind a family form quite different from the "extended" household characteristic of the *oikos.* Hegel presupposes the bourgeois nuclear family, denuded of a great many of the economic functions characteristic of earlier forms, which were now being taken over by the market. Accordingly, as extrahousehold economic functions expanded, the heads of households related to each other not only in the polity but in the economy as well.

34. *PR*, par. 33.

35. Charles Taylor, *Hegel* (Cambridge, England: Cambridge University Press, 1975), 382.

36. Ibid., 376.

37. *PR*, par. 147, 151, 155.

38. He cannot, of course, accept these identities on traditional, nonreflective, grounds and warns against a merely habitual acceptance of *ethos*. Astonishingly enough, his certainty that, after reflection, the existing ethos will turn out to be rational was always unshaken. But what if, after the most thorough reflection, the opposite turned out to be the case? In this respect, the incomparably greater modernity of Kant's conception of practical philosophy is obvious.

39. *PR*, par. 213.

40. *PR*, par. 142.

41. Nor is it absent on the level of the family. The tension between the normative model of the monogamous bourgeois family as a love community, presupposing a form of mutual recognition between peers, and the patriarchal and hierarchical structure, reproduced in law, of the actual bourgeois family is implicit in Hegel's discussion.

42. The actual spirit of a family and a people; see *PR*, par. 156.

43. *PR*, par. 157.

44. *PR*, par. 181.

45. *PR*, par. 184. Indeed, the level of *Sittlichkeit* at which, in Hegel's view, there is no tension between is and ought, between common good and individual interest, between right and duty, is not that of the state, as Taylor thought, but that of the family, the "natural" level of *Sittlichkeit*.

46. Z. A. Pelczynski, "The Hegelian Conception of the State," in Pelczynski, ed., *Hegel's Political Philosophy*, 12. Pelczynski's emphasis, in this article and elsewhere, is on the reemergence of positive social integration *within* civil society.

47. *PR*, par. 255.

48. But it is also due to the illusions of system building that the family appears as a natural, immediate form of *Sittlichkeit*—one that is neither in nor of, but rather external and prior to, civil society. Hegel's idiosyncratic three-part division of ethical life requires comment. Hegel counterposes the family to both civil society and the state, but it is the first opposition that concerns us here. Now, the differentiation between the family and civil society, conceived of as the system of needs, is not particularly surprising, since the exclusive orientation to individual self-interest of actors in a market economy who are integrated through impersonal relations does seem quite distinct from the mutuality of feeling (love), the commonality of purpose (children), and the community of interests (family property) that are fundamental to Hegel's concept of the monogamous family. Unlike the Marxian conception, however, Hegel's theory of civil society does not stop at the system of needs. On the contrary, Hegel's most important insight with

regard to civil society is his recognition that it involves the principle of *voluntary association* and, with it, new forms of solidarity, egalitarian participation, membership, and ethical life. It is precisely the function of the associations of civil society (corporations, estates) to provide a context in which new forms of solidarity, collective identity, and common interest can emerge. Their most important function is to mitigate the centrifugal tendencies of the system of needs, bind individuals together in a common purpose, and temper the egoism of self-interest. This is why Hegel refers to the corporation as the "second family" (*PR*, par. 252).

Why, then, instead of seeing the family itself as the voluntary association par excellence, does Hegel exclude it from civil society altogether, while at the same time using it as the metaphor for solidarity throughout his text? (Hegel refers to civil society as the universal family, the corporation as the individual's second family [*PR*, par. 238, 239], and the state as the "self-conscious ethical substance that unifies the family principle with that of civil society. The same unity which is in the family as the feeling of love is, in its essence, receiving however . . . the form of conscious universality" [*Enzyclopädie der Philosophischen Wissenschaften* (1830) (Hamburg: Meiner Verlag, 1969), par. 595].)

We can discern two reasons for this, one logical, the other ideological. Given the systematic structure of Hegel's text, if one reasons logically from the existence of the legal person constituted by the system of abstract right—the atomized individual proprietor—then it does seem that something prior is presupposed, namely, the context in which the person is literally generated, and this context cannot be the system of needs itself. The substantial existence of the individual implies a "natural universal" (the species and its procreation), and every individual is first situated, generated, in the context of the family. Accordingly, Hegel sees the family as the logical presupposition of civil society.

However, it requires another, ideological step to construe the family as the prereflective, natural form of ethical life. Hegel recognizes that the natural factor, the sexual tie, is elevated in the monogamous family to a spiritual significance—the unanimity of love and the temper of trust—but it is so, he insists, in a prereflective form, as feeling. The family is the first form in which the unity of individuals is actualized as a love community. Through the institution of monogamous marriage, however, an indivisible personal bond is constituted, resulting in moral attachment and the community of personal and private interests. In short, the monogamous family merges the will and interests of its members, making the mutuality and merging characteristics of love permanent.

But there is nothing natural about the monogamous bourgeois family form; it is a historical, institutional, and legal construction, as Hegel undoubtedly knew. It seems that he characterizes it as a natural community because he assumes that there is no conflict or even difference of interests among family members despite the physical difference of sex, which "appears at the same time as a difference of intellectual and moral type" (*Enzyclopädie der Philosophischen Wissenschaften*, par. 519). Indeed, the family bond, its unity, is allegedly so all-encompassing that it forms a single person such that the *one* person representing the family property acquires an ethical interest.

That Hegel presupposes without question the patriarchal, bourgeois, monogamous family form is obvious here. The less obvious theoretical motivation underlying the exclusion of the family from civil society is the double assumption that the individual presupposed by the system of needs cannot be produced by it and that the only really important dynamic of conflicting, antagonistic interests is the one constituted by the system of needs between economic actors. Accordingly, it could appear that family members have no separate interests so long as they remain in the family. Hence, the *indissoluble* bond of the *monogamous* family. But the only person who never leaves the family is, of course, the wife. Children, when they become adults, leave to enter their second family, civil society, where they are free to act on their now separate interests. But new families are formed, once again removing women, it would seem, from civil society. Of course, Hegel does not explicitly say that only men are actors in the system of needs; he refers instead to heads of households. But the exclusion of the family itself from civil society and the assumption of a perfect harmony of interests within it makes sense only if it is assumed that one of the two adult members does not have separate interests and never attains the status of legal personhood, or at least relinquishes it upon marriage (which was the legal situation of married women all over Europe at the time). It must, then, be the male head of household who enters civil society and through whom the property of the family appears as an individual in the system of needs.

There may be yet a third reason for excluding the family, in the form that Hegel defends, from civil society, one never thematized by Hegel but that would make a great deal of sense. The patriarchal family is unlike any other association in civil society because it allegedly does not reconcile divergent interests of persons within it but constitutes an immediate unity of interest. But it also diverges from the two principles of integration typical of a modern civil society: contract (and system integration typical of the market mechanism) and voluntary association. Despite the metaphor of a marriage contract, the family is not a contractual arrangement in the standard sense. It may be freely "contracted" into, but it is in part indissoluble, and an important set of its members, children, do not contract into it at all. Indeed, Hegel elsewhere explicitly rejects the Kantian conception of the family as a contractual relationship.

Nor, however, is the *patriarchal* family a voluntary association like any other, because its internal structure and mode of integration conflict with the basic egalitarian and horizontal mode of social integration that is the principle of coordination of interaction in voluntary associations. A patriarchal family is, instead, integrated through the principle of hierarchy and preserves a gendered caste status predicated on the absence of equality and autonomy for its female members. In order for the family to be situated within civil society, as a particular form of voluntary association, it would have to relinquish its patriarchal form and become, at least in principle, egalitarian. Of course, as far as children are concerned, equality and autonomy form a goal rather than a starting point, but this does not affect the issue. Thus, the family in the form in which Hegel constitutes it must be excluded from civil society and deemed to be a natural, prereflective form of ethical life despite its patently social, legal, and cultural constitution.

We nevertheless believe that it would have been better to include the family within civil society, as its first association. This alternative would have been far superior to the one Hegel chose, from both theoretical and normative points of view. For then the family could have taken its place as a key institution in civil society, one that, if conceived of in egalitarian terms, could have provided an experience of horizontal solidarity, collective identity, and equal participation to the autonomous individuals comprising it—a task deemed fundamental for the other associations of civil society and for the ultimate development of civic virtue and responsibility with respect to the polity.

49. T. W. Adorno, "Cultural Criticism and Society," in *Prisms* (Cambridge: MIT Press, 1981).

50. On the historical roots of this inconsistency, and on the republican strain in Hegel's thought, see K.-H. Ilting, "The Structure of Hegel's *Philosophy of Right*," in Pelczynski, ed., *Hegel's Political Philosophy*, and "Hegel's Philosophy of the State and Marx's Early Critique," in Z. A. Pelczynski, ed., *The State and Civil Society: Studies in Hegel's Political Philosophy* (Cambridge, England: Cambridge University Press, 1984).

51. Karl Polànyi's *Great Transformation* [1944] (Boston: Beacon Press, 1957) is both an eloquent analysis and a symptom of this statist trend.

52. Jean L. Cohen, *Class and Civil Society: The Limits of Marxian Critical Theory* (Amherst: University of Massachusetts Press, 1982).

53. See, e.g., *PR*, par. 190.

54. *PR*, par. 187.

55. *PR*, par. 183.

56. *PR*, par. 182.

57. Only for the system of needs can Hegel maintain that in civil society everyone is an end for himself/herself and all others are nothing. See *PR*, par. 182, add.

58. Georg Lukács, *The Young Hegel* (Cambridge: MIT Press, 1975); Shlomo Avineri, *Hegel's Theory of the Modern State* (Cambridge, England: Cambridge University Press, 1972).

59. *PR*, par. 184.

60. Ibid.

61. This is what Habermas has called "system integration" (*PR*, par. 187, 199).

62. *PR*, par. 189 and add.

63. *PR*, par. 243.

64. *PR*, par. 195.

65. *PR*, par. 196, 198.

66. *PR*, par. 243. See Avineri, *Hegel's Theory*, 108–109, 149, and elsewhere.

67. *PR*, par. 207.

68. *PR*, par. 206, 207.

69. See Cohen, *Class and Civil Society.*

70. This anticipates and would influence Marx's formulation, according to which the proletariat is "in but not of" civil society.

71. *PR*, par. 203.

72. *PR*, par. 204.

73. *PR*, par. 205.

74. *PR*, par. 200.

75. *PR*, par. 241.

76. He did, however, note the problem of conflict management by the public authority (par. 236).

77. The point is that there are two different kinds of integration at work in Hegel's concept of civil society: system integration and social integration. See our chapter 3 on Parsons and chapter 9 on Habermas.

78. Hegel's political contradiction between statism and antistatism is revealed in the order of exposition. While the outline of the argument concerning the state in paragraph 273 moves from the legislature to the executive and finally to the crown as the highest level, the actual exposition in paragraphs 275–320 moves from crown to executive and finally to the legislature itself, culminating in the doctrine of public opinion. The legislature is, of course, civil society in the state!

79. *PR*, par. 213, 218.

80. *PR*, par. 215, 216, 224.

81. *PR*, par. 217.

82. *PR*, par. 211.

83. *PR*, par. 209.

84. *PR*, par. 211, 216.

85. This is contrary to Taylor's interpretation of the concept of *Sittlichkeit*, according to which "the end sought by the highest ethics is already realized" (*Hegel*, 383).

86. *PR*, par. 212.

87. This is true even before in the argument, although we should recognize that part of the system of needs—the section on the estates where the two logics are already visible—belongs, at least in part, to the later discussion of social rather than system integration.

88. For a discussion of the development of this model of civil society, see Cohen, *Class and Civil Society.*

89. Such is Avineri's stress in *Hegel's Theory of the Modern State.*

90. *PR*, par. 205.

91. *PR*, par. 296; Avineri, *Hegel's Theory of the Modern State*, 107-108, 158-160.

92. Which is also not always as easy as Marx thought in 1843. The author of the *18th Brumaire* can teach us this lesson as well.

93. Thus, Hegel surely does not suffer from the problem noted by Niklas Luhmann: that theorists of the state/society dichotomy are forced, in a preposterous manner, to distribute actual individuals neatly on one side or the other of the societal divide.

94. *PR*, par. 303.

95. *PR*, par. 295.

96. *PR*, par. 234.

97. *PR*, par. 236.

98. *PR*, par. 239.

99. *PR*, par. 245.

100. *PR*, par. 248.

101. *The Old Regime and the French Revolution* (1856).

102. *PR*, par. 239, 240.

103. *PR*, par. 241 and also 239.

104. *PR*, par. 249.

105. See *Rechtsphilsosphie*, par. 238. Had Hegel's primary concern been democratization rather than integration, then perhaps the family in an egalitarian form could have taken its place within civil society and served as an important model of horizontal, solidary ties for the other voluntary associations. The problem is that Hegel was reluctant to draw out the full implications of the modern concept of voluntary association. He knew, of course, that it differed from the idea of community, because it presupposed members who were individuals with particular interests as well as common group interests. He also knew that a voluntary association was more than the liberal model of an interest group, because it is capable of generating new ties, solidarities, and even collective identities. As *voluntary*, the association must allow for free entry and exit. As an *association*, presumably of peers, it should accord equal voice to its members and mutual recognition as members sharing a collective identity. Only in a democratic, egalitarian association in which entry and exit are based on universalistic criteria and in which all have equal voice could social integration be effective in the way Hegel hoped it would be. But for this, for the self-integration of civil society on a fully modern basis, the restrictions Hegel places on the number and types of voluntary associations in civil society would have to be abandoned.

106. See Heiman, "Sources and Significance of Hegel's Corporate Doctrine."

107. T. M. Knox, translator's notes to *Hegel's Philosophy of Right*, 360.

108. *PR*, par. 295.

109. *PR*, par. 289.

110. Heiman, "Sources and Significance of Hegel's Corporate Doctrine," 125ff.

111. *PR*, par. 303; see the English translation, 198.

112. *PR*, par. 311.

113. Hegel raises this issue only in his polemic against the democratic, i.e., universal, participation in politics of all members of civil society. In his own terms, he has a good argument here to the extent that he wants to include only those already organized. It is not clear why he does not recommend (and even seems to exclude) organizing all members of civil society in associations, communities, and corporations so that they could thus participate in politics and the election of deputies. Furthermore, voting by the unorganized for deputies who are themselves organized (as in the English and American political parties, even in Hegel's day) would not have the consequence that Hegel feared: the appearance of atomized opinion on the political stage. It is another matter, as the debate around the views of Carl Schmitt was to show, that the representation of a democratic electorate in the liberal nineteenth-century form could be seen as raising the problem of "indecision" or "ungovernability." For this to happen, one key component of legislation as understood by Hegel had to lose its power, namely, rational, public discussion and deliberation. See Carl Schmitt, *The Crisis of Parliamentary Democracy* [1923] (Cambridge: MIT Press, 1985).

114. *PR*, par. 308.

115. *PR*, par. 301.

116. *PR*, par. 302.

117. *PR*, par. 298.

118. *PR*, par. 309.

119. *PR*, par. 316.

120. *PR*, par. 318.

121. While Hegel rightly calls to our attention the volatility and manipulability of public opinion, he is also quite insistent that the essential truths of politics do have this medium for their vehicle. Unfortunately, he also says that interpreting these truths is the role of political leaders and theorists. He considers the following of public opinion, both in life and in science, to be the road to mediocrity. And yet he finds unproblematic the passive acceptance of the views of elites by public opinion (*PR*, par. 318).

122. *PR*, par. 319.

123. *PR*, par. 315.

124. *PR*, par. 316.

125. See Heiman, "Sources and Significance of Hegel's Corporate Doctrine," 129–135. Somewhat less clear is Ilting's essentially similar argument according to which "civil society and the state" are in Hegel "two different spheres of *public* life" ("The Structure of Hegel's *Philosophy of Right*," 107).

126. See Jürgen Habermas, *The Structural Transformation of the Public Sphere* [1962] (Cambridge: MIT Press, 1989).

127. See Jellinek, *Declaration of the Rights of Man and Citizen*, 2–3, 49.

128. Hegel's critique of Jacobinism and republicanism rests on his alternative theory of civil society. The stark opposition between private egoism and civic virtue in Jacobin and republican thought was predicated on a model of society as one divided by a rigid public/private dualism that allowed for only a moralistic overcoming of particular interests and private concerns. In the absence of mediations between the levels of the individual and the political community, the ultimate logic of such moralism was, in Hegel's view, the Terror. See the introduction to the Knox edition of *Hegel's Philosophy of Right*, 22.

129. *PR*, par. 255 add., quoted in Pelczynski, "Political Community and Individual Freedom," 72, in Knox's translation (which we have had to revise).

130. *PR*, par. 265.

131. Quoted in Pelczynski, "Political Community and Individual Freedom," 76.

132. "Hegel's Concept of the State and Marx's Early Critique," 100–103.

Chapter 3

1. For a reconstruction and critique of Marx's views on civil society, see Jean L. Cohen, *Class and Civil Society: The Limits of Marx's Critical Theory* (Amherst: University of Massachusetts Press, 1983).

2. Talcott Parsons, *The System of Modern Societies* (Englewood Cliffs, NJ: Prentice-Hall, 1971), 1.

3. Ibid., 115.

4. Ibid., 84. Parsons's great essay "Full Citizenship for the Negro American?," reprinted in *Politics and Social Structure* (New York: Free Press, 1969), represents an important exception to this thesis of the closure of the democratic revolution. But Parsons, because of a generally suspicious attitude toward social movements, never tried to generalize this model. Of course, he was also unaware of most of the areas in which the democratic revolution could and should be continued, such as women's rights.

5. See Lothar Gall, "Liberalismus und bürgerliche Gesellschaft. Zu Character und Entwicklung der liberalen Bewegung in Deutschland," in L. Gall, ed., *Liberalismus*, 2d ed. (Königstein: Verlag Anton Hain, 1980).

6. See the critiques of two members of the Polànyi school: Terence K. Hopkins, "Sociology and the Substantive View of the Economy," and Harry W. Pearson, "Parsons and Smelser on the Economy," in K. Polànyi et al., eds., *Trade and Market in the Early Empires* (New York: Free Press, 1957).

7. Cf. G. Poggi, *The Development of the Modern State* (Stanford: Stanford University Press, 1978), 13ff., who argues otherwise, leaving out of consideration Parsons's linking of differentiation with integration, leading to complexity but not dedifferentiation.

8. Parsons, *The System*, 99. The inconsistency of Parsons's analysis is pointed out by Jürgen Habermas in *Theorie des kommunikativen Handelns*, vol. 2 (Frankfurt: Suhrkamp, 1981), 423–424 and note 131.

9. Parsons, *The System*, 101.

10. Ibid., 87.

11. Parsons, we believe mistakenly, discusses social rights as well in the context of the democratic revolution, whose central line of conflict is on the state–societal community axis. The notion of equality inherent in social rights involves a defensive reaction on the economy–societal community axis instead.

12. Parsons, *The System*, 84. Compare Habermas's thesis on the public sphere, discussed below in chapter 4.

13. See his essay "On the Concept of Political Power," in *Politics and Social Structure*.

14. Parsons, *The System*, 106–107.

15. Ibid., 97.

16. Ibid., 99–100, 117–118.

17. Neil Smelser, *Theory of Collective Behavior* (New York: Free Press, 1963).

18. Smelser's analysis of even this type of movement was hardly unambiguous or wholly sympathethic. For Parsons's rather different conception, see "Full Citizenship for the Negro American?"

19. In the case of the modern state, even Niklas Luhmann, for example, sees this tendency. See his *Grundrechte als Institution* (Berlin: Duncker & Humblot, 1965). Here it is the function of fundamental rights to stabilize the differentiation of society. As Luhmann's work developed, this function was attributed to yet another subsystem: the system of law, in which rights are located along with all other instruments. What this approach cannot address, however, is how the legal system is to be protected against the dedifferentiating tendencies threatening this very subsystem. It seems that the systems-theoretic idea of the differentiation of society cannot be sustained if we stay within the limits of systems theory. See chapter 7.

20. Parsons, *The System*, 12, and "The Political Aspect of Social Structure and Process," in *Politics and Social Structure*, 345

21. Parsons, *The System*, 24; for Luhmann's critique of this conception, see chapter 7.

22. Parsons, "On the Concept of Political Power," 355.

23. Parsons, *The System*, 9–10. What he does not see is that, for a collectivity of collectivities, consensus can only be about procedures that are compatible with different sets of values but that do not themselves imply forms of life, as substantive values do.

24. Ibid., 13.

25. Ibid., 62–64.

26. Ibid., 18–19.

27. Ibid., 8–10. "The core of a society . . . is the patterned normative order through which the life of a population is collectively organized . . . [T]he enforcement of a normative system seems inherently linked to the control . . . of sanctions exercised by and against a people actually residing within a territory" (Parsons, *Societies. Evolutionary and Comparative Perspectives* [Englewood Cliffs, NJ: Prentice-Hall, 1966]).

28. See "On the Concept of Influence," 418, where he distinguishes between associational bases, inevitably particularistic, and norm reference, tending toward universality.

29. Parsons, *The System*, 93.

30. "Full Citizenship for the Negro American?," 253. The whole analysis of the citizenship complex repeatedly draws on the work of T. H. Marshall, *Class, Citizenship and Social Development* (New York: Doubleday, 1964). See also *The System*, 20–22, 82–83.

31. Parsons, *The System*, 21; see also Luhmann, *Grundrechte*, passim.

32. Cf. "Full Citizenship for the Negro American?," 260, and *The System*, 21.

33. Quite in the Hegelian sense of this term; see "Full Citizenship for the Negro American?," 260. We agree with this conception of rights as institutionalizing a differentiated civil society as well as its influence over the state (through political society), but we believe that certain kinds of social rights (such as collective bargaining) play the same role with respect to the economy.

34. Parsons, *The System*, 83.

35. Parsons, "Polity and Society: Some General Considerations," in *Politics and Social Structure*, 507.

36. Parsons, *The System*, 110.

37. Democratic participation in economic life is indeed repeatedly rejected; see *The System*, 103, and "Polity and Society," 500–502.

38. Parsons, *The System*, 24-26. For an earlier and different definition of solidarity that did not adequately distinguish it from power, see Talcott Parsons, *Economy and Society* (New York: Free Press, 1956), 49.

39. Parsons, "The Political Aspect of Social Structure and Process," 334, 340.

40. Ibid., 336.

41. Parsons, "'Voting' and the Equilibrium of the American Political System," in *Politics and Social Structure*, 214, 217–218.

42. Ibid., 220.

43. Parsons, "Polity and Society," 503.

44. Parsons, "On the Concept of Influence," 416, 418.

45. Parsons, *The System*, 14, 27; see also the three essays on power, influence, and value-commitments in *Politics and Social Structure*.

46. See Parsons, *Economy and Society*, 49, where this view is most explicitly expressed.

47. Parsons, *The System*, 14.

48. Parsons, "On the Concept of Influence," 410; "On the Concept of Value-Commitment," 363.

49. Is it backed up by an ultimate reference to "intrinsic persuaders," information capable of determining where the interest of the other lies? (See "On the Concept of Influence," 416.) This idea, later rejected (422–423), would again bring influence close to the model of money and power, which act in frameworks of objectifiable interests and the relevant sanctions. Is it backed up by the possibility of justification in terms of norms regarded as binding on "ego" and "alter" both (417)? Or is the ultimate reference point the reputation and prestige of influential people rooted in a *Gemeinschaft*-type solidarity?

50. Parsons, "The Political Aspect of Social Structure and Process," 335–336.

51. Parsons, "Full Citizenship for the Negro American?," 260; "'Voting' and the Equilibrium of the American Political System," 208–209; "The Political Aspect of Social Structure and Process," 339.

52. The problem is avoided in an illusory way when Parsons, relying on the architectonic of his system, links the economy to the "latency" subsystem represented by households rather than to the societal community represented by the public. (Why is the family not part of the societal community when elsewhere it is treated as a paradigmatic form of association?) Of course, an entirely individualistic access to the economy is a tendency of the ideal laissez-faire market, but the existence of unions, cooperatives, and professional associations, which he brings in elsewhere, speaks against this trend.

53. Parsons, "The Political Aspect of Social Structure and Process," 340.

54. Parsons, *Politics and Social Structure*, 500ff., 512.

55. Parsons, *The System*, 109–111.

56. Ibid., 114.

57. Ibid., 93.

58. Ibid., 97, 106–107.

59. See Parsons, "Full Citizenship for the Negro American?," 285–288. In this context at least, Parsons sees that the movement form in contemporary societies need not mean only fundamentalism, but can also mean the actualization of universalistic normative potentials (here the premises of the democratic revolution) in a manner capable of forming particular identities.

60. In this context, G. Almond and S. Verba go further than Parsons but not far enough. See *The Civic Culture* (Boston: Little Brown, 1965). The experience of fascist and communist mass movements was clearly formative for the whole generation of postwar pluralists.

61. See Parsons, "The Distribution of Power in American Society," in *Politics and Social Structure*.

62. Parsons, *The System*, 102.

63. See Parsons, "The Distribution of Power."

64. Ibid., 198, and "The Mass Media and the Structure of American Society," in *Politics and Social Structure*, 251.

65. Parsons, "The Mass Media," 248–250.

66. Ibid., 244.

67. Parsons, *The System*, 117.

68. Talcott Parsons, "Law as an Intellectual Stepchild," *Sociological Inquiry* 47, nos. 3–4 (1977): 11–57. See also his review of R. M. Unger, *Law in Modern Society* (New York: Free Press, 1976), in *Law and Society Review* 12, no. 1 (Fall 1978): 145–149.

69. From the point of view of his system building, he identifies four "absolutisms" threatening our understanding (and perhaps the survival) of modern law: economic absolutism in Marx and Friedman; political absolutism in Weber; moral absolutism in Bellah; and legal absolutism in Unger. Both within his systematics and in relationship to Unger's communitarian assumptions, it would have been better to speak in the last case of the absolutization of the dimension of social integration, which in turn could lead to dedifferentiation, the traditionalization of the societal community, and the disappearance of law in the modern sense. See "Law as an Intellectual Stepchild," 13–15, 16, 26, 31, 33, and 44. The theses concerning political and economic absolutism anticipate Habermas's conception of the colonization of the lifeworld, while those of moral and legal absolutism anticipate our critique of democratic fundamentalism (see chapter 8).

70. Indeed, he protests against the very possibility when, for example, he insists that Unger exaggerates the difficulties of legal autonomy in postliberal societies (ibid., 40ff.).

71. He laments that Unger uses only the dichotomous conception of state and society, without clearly noting that this position leaves him without a foothold to criticize both economic and political reduction of law, driving him to stress traditional components of society against modernity (ibid., 37).

72. Ibid., 42.

73. For an excellent comparison of the relevant views of the three, see Norberto Bobbio, "Gramsci and the Concept of Civil Society," in J. Keane, ed., *Civil Society and the State. New European Perspectives* (London: Verso, 1988). It is not implausible to argue that Gramsci derived his notion from the Marx of *The 18th Brumaire of Louis Bonaparte*, as does Perry Anderson in "The Antinomies of Antonio Gramsci," *New Left Review*, no. 100 (November 1976–January 1977): 5–78. The somewhat idiosyncratic status of this position in Marx's oeuvre and Gramsci's use of a transformed version of Hegel's corporate doctrine speak against this interpretation. But the great influence of the *18th Brumaire* on Gramsci's conception is undeniable.

74. We should perhaps note that disinterest in or skepticism concerning the transformation of existing economic relations was obviously not one of these

reasons. See A. Arato, "Civil Society, History, and Socialism: Reply to John Keane," *Praxis International* 9, nos. 1–2 (April–July 1989): 133–152.

75. Antonio Gramsci, *Prison Notebooks* (New York: International Publishers, 1971), 235–238.

76. Ibid., 160.

77. Under the influence of Sorel (via Croce), Gramsci believed that "the new" that needed to be born was, if not a myth, then a unified world view that could provide meaning and orientation to collective action. For Gramsci, this new culture was available in the theory of Marxism, but it had to be built into practice through the organization of a set of counterinstitutions, associations, cultural forms, etc., on the terrain of civil society. In other words, working-class hegemony and a socialist civil society had to be developed on the terrain of civil society to counter the dying liberal and religious models of the past and to form the masses into a class-conscious collective actor. For a discussion of the differences between Gramsci and Croce on civil society, see Walter L. Adamson, "Gramsci and the Politics of Civil Society," *Praxis International* 7, nos. 3–4 (Winter 1987–1988): 322.

78. Anderson, "The Antinomies of Antonio Gramsci," seems the most reliable guide through Gramsci's terminological shifts. An alternative approach, much less well motivated but nevertheless quite plausible, is that of Christine Buci-Glucksmann in *Gramsci and the State* (London: Lawrence and Wishart, 1980); she argues that Gramsci operated with two concepts of the state: "the state in the strict sense" and "the integral state," the latter including civil and political society, the former excluding civil society. While this suggestion would correspond to Hegel's distinction between "political state" and "state," it would not solve all terminological and theoretical problems. Terminologically, we would still have no way of accounting for the times Gramsci claims an identity between civil society and state. Theoretically, it remains difficult to fix the boundaries of "state in the integral sense." Interestingly, in an apparently later interpretation, Buci-Glucksmann seems to opt for a historicist solution, according to which the differentiation of civil society and the state corresponds to liberal capitalism (or Gramsci's depiction thereof), while the notion of the integral state depicts state-interventionist capitalism. See Christine Buci-Glucksmann, "Hegemony and Consent: a Political Strategy," in A. Showstack Sassoon, ed., *Approaches to Gramsci* (London: Writers and Readers Cooperative Society, 1982). This argument, like all consistent fusion arguments, is open to Anderson's objection that it clouds the difference between liberal democratic and authoritarian capitalist systems.

79. The issue is not only terminological, however. If civil society is understood in contrast to the state, then in Gramsci's functional scheme both hegemony and domination would appear as functions of a system of reproduction rooted in the economic base. If civil society and political society are understood as both being within the state, then hegemony and domination would be understood as functions of the state. It is this latter possibility that guides Althusser's interpretation in "Ideology and the Ideological State Apparatuses," in *Lenin and Philosophy* (New York: Monthly Review Press, 1971).

80. Walter Adamson rejects Bobbio's interpretation, arguing that Gramsci did not assign primacy to the superstructure but rather retained the idea of the primacy of the economic in the traditional Marxist way while altering its role in the theory of revolution. He insists on this, of course, to counter the charge of idealism. However, if the key to grasping revolutionary possibilities became the "essentially cultural-political analysis of hegemony and counterhegemony within the superstructures of civil society" ("Gramsci and the Politics of Civil Society," 323), then it is hard to see the primacy of the economic at work. The irrelevancy of the base/superstructure model as well as the materialist/idealist opposition is the more convincing conclusion (ibid., 320–339).

81. One might object that, even if we accept the idea that on the whole Gramsci differentiates between civil society and state, this need not imply that consent and coercion, hegemony and domination, can be strictly differentiated along the same axes. Some interpreters insist that, in general, Gramsci involves the state in the generation of hegemony. See Carl Boggs, *The Two Revolutions: Antonio Gramsci and the Dilemmas of Western Marxism* (Boston: South End Press, 1984), 191–192. Anderson refines this point by claiming that Gramsci realized (or should have) that, while (legitimate) coercion is absent from civil society, the state and, in particular, the parliament encompass both coercion and consent ("The Antinomies of Antonio Gramsci," 31–32, 41). In our view, this idea would be best articulated by stressing the Hegelian concept of mediating institutions between civil society and state. Both Boggs and Anderson seem to realize that Gramsci's theory of differentiation is too rigid and has too few terms.

82. Our concern in this chapter is not with the details or trajectory of the Marxian project but with the conception of civil society as developed within that framework, in the most open and least dogmatic form. It should be kept in mind, then, that Gramsci's main concern was proletarian revolution and the creation of a socialist society. Accordingly, his entire analysis is framed within the general paradigm of the Marxian class theory and geared to the strategic questions flowing from the revolutionary project, namely, how to develop working-class consciousness, a socialist counterhegemony, and, ultimately, working-class power. Indeed, Gramsci's Marxist orthodoxy prevented this most interesting of all the revisionists from developing the results of his double "declaration of independence" of civil society from the economy and the state. For while Gramsci discovered both the modern associational forms of civil society and the autonomy of its coordinating mechanisms (consent), thereby differentiating between what is now called social and system integration, he persisted in viewing the former as instrumental to the latter. He interprets the dynamics and logic of social integration through the theory of class struggle and the goal of working-class revolution—an approach that blinded him to the difference between the communicative and strategic coordination of interaction. Of course, Gramsci understood that the market economy and the state are integrated through mechanisms organized by money and power and that civil society, on the contrary, is coordinated through communicative means of generating consent. But he understood communicative interaction in primarily strategic terms. This

orientation enabled him to see the underside, as it were, of "mass communications" and to pinpoint the ways in which dominant or aspiring classes seek to manipulate and create opinion favorable to their projects. But, as we shall see, it locked him into a functionalist analysis of communicative interaction and of civil society, posing great difficulties for his overall theoretical analysis.

83. Another key difference between Gramsci and Hegel, linked to the former's antistatism, is that Gramsci denudes the state of the ethical substance attributed to it by Hegel. The state, for Gramsci, integrates primarily on the basis of power and domination; its weapons are above all coercive. Civil society becomes the terrain par excellence of ethical life—it is the locus of political legitimacy or, in Gramscian language, the place where the hegemony so functional to the reproduction of state power (as well as of the power of the dominant class) is generated and secured. See Adamson, "Gramsci and the Politics of Civil Society," 322.

84. Gramsci, *Prison Notebooks*, 259; here is a motivation, vis-à-vis Hegel, to separate civil society from the economy. Their relative fusion was for Gramsci a medieval remnant in Hegel, to the extent that modern associations need not be organized exclusively along economic lines.

85. Ibid., 268; cf. Alexis de Tocqueville, *The Old Regime and the French Revolution* (New York: Doubleday, 1955).

86. Ibid., 54.

87. Ibid., 245; see Bobbio, "Gramsci and the Concept of Civil Society," 95.

88. This is one of the contexts in which domination and hegemony, the forms of control characteristic of political and civil society, are both presented as instruments of the same state power. Clearly, functionalist arguments converge with the ones characterized by a residual and inverted historical materialism.

89. Gramsci, *Prison Notebooks*, 54, 265.

90. Adamson sees the central antinomy in Gramsci as being between conceptions of civil society as open-ended democratic competition and free communication and as the space within which one unitary and unified culture can be replaced by another ("Gramsci and the Politics of Civil Society," 331–332). While we are not convinced that Gramsci's work contains a communication model, we take Adamson's posing of this issue as basically sound. We divide the one antinomy into two, though: on the analytical level, between functionalist and conflict-oriented models; and on the normative level, between unitary and pluralist utopias.

91. Gramsci, *Prison Notebooks*, 265.

92. See Bobbio, "Gramsci and the Concept of Civil Society," 92. Carl Boggs, too, hopes to locate the foundations for such politics in Gramsci, but he is forced to admit ambiguities and internal contradictions all along the way. See the last two chapters in *The Two Revolutions*.

93. The first is stressed by Anderson, the second by Adamson in their cited articles. Adamson's position is supported by J. Femia, *Gramsci's Political Thought*

(New York: Oxford University Press, 1981). We believe that both positions are present in Gramsci's work and that he never noticed their incompatibility.

94. See Anderson, "The Antinomies of Gramsci," 69; and Femia, *Gramsci's Political Thought*, esp. chap. 6. Outside of Italy, few have argued that Gramsci replaced a revolutionary strategy of seizing power with one of building an alternative structure of hegemony and thus a new civil society. However, those who are interested in the radical democratic dimension of his thought are rarely conscious of the contradiction of this dimension, not only with the Leninism that they all see but with the doctrine of the revolutionary seizure of power under liberal democracies.

95. Moreover, even though Gramsci knew that "bourgeois civil society," secured by sets of rights such as free speech, assembly, and association, was the condition of possibility for the emergence of proletarian forms of organization and cultural expression, for him this simply meant a shift in the battlefield from the state to society, not that there was anything in the institutional or juridical makeup of existing versions of civil society that was worth preserving.

96. This is true only if another functionalism, reducing civil society to a function of the reproduction of the economic base, is avoided. It seems to us that Gramsci, unlike some of his followers, never fell into this version of Marxist functionalism.

97. Gramsci, *Prison Notebooks*, 242.

98. Ibid., 247.

99. Ibid., 268.

100. Ibid., 253. On this point see Anne Showstack Sassoon, *Gramsci's Politics* (Minneapolis: University of Minnesota Press, 1987), 224–225.

101. Indeed, Marx thought that the existence of civil society and of the state as differentiated entities was the cause of, or identical to, political alienation. He never articulated a project for reconstituting, democratizing, or preserving any version of civil society. See Cohen, *Class and Civil Society*.

102. Gramsci, *Prison Notebooks*, 263.

103. This criticism is developed by Cornelius Castoriadis in several important works. See, for example, *The Imaginary Institution of Society* (Cambridge: MIT Press, 1987).

104. Gramsci, *Prison Notebooks*, 263.

105. Ibid. 268.

106. Gramsci deliberately makes no concessions to liberalism with respect to this question. See *Prison Notebooks*, 263.

107. The postulate is ultimately linked to Gramsci's underlying Marxist ortho-doxy, for, while his three-part model is as heterodox as his rejection of historical materialism, he never abandons the class theory. Thus, he defends a pluralistic conception of collective action and a broad system of class alliances (and a complex model of the associational life of civil society) as the strategy to be pursued en route to socialist hegemony, but once that hegemony is achieved, he

pictures the associations, institutions, and norms of the new civil society as being as monolithic, one-dimensional, and functional as those of its bourgeois predecessor.

108. Without an expert administration relieving a society of time constraints, a society cannot be simultaneously modern and democratic. Thus, the idea of abolishing the state is incompatible with democracy for functional reasons.

109. A version of this interpretation can be found in Adamson, "Gramsci and the Politics of Civil Society," 331. Adamson argues that the main antinomy in Gramsci's thought is between (1) a conception of civil society as the public space outside the state in which organizations could be democratized and there could exist free communication among a multiplicity of social parties and (2) a totalizing, unitary cultural model or world view (Marxism as *Sittlichkeit*). The latter would supposedly solve the crisis of culture in a way that is distinctly antipluralistic and would replace the alienation and meaninglessness of bourgeois civil society with a "coherent, unitary, nationally diffused conception of life and man," a philosophy that has become a "culture." In this sense, as Adamson correctly notes, the politics of civil society would be closed. But Adamson seems to have little ground to argue that the central category of Gramsci's reconstruction of civil society is that of the public sphere, and he errs in reading Gramsci's concept of hegemony, of the organization of consent, through the lens of Habermas's concept of communicative interaction (331–333). For Gramsci, communication, culture, and intellectual life are always linked to some strategic purpose; indeed, it is precisely the norms of the public sphere and the notion of communication and discussion oriented to rational argument that Gramsci explicitly rejects. The concept of hegemony is the alternative to this "bourgeois" ideology of neutrality.

110. Althusser, "Ideology and the Ideological State Apparatuses," 142ff. and note 7.

111. He does not even bother to try to show what certainly cannot be shown— that they all represent "apparatuses" (i.e., bureaucratic, administrative mechanisms).

112. Althusser, "Ideology and the Ideological State Apparatuses," 146.

113. Ibid., 148ff. Of course, one could abandon the argument that civil society's *function* is to reproduce the power of the state (a point at least plausible for political, legal, and educational institutions) and argue that civil society belongs to the *structure* of the state (implausible for all but educational institutions) and thus maintain that its function, together with repressive institutions, is to help reproduce the whole system. Althusser never attempts this empirically questionable conceptual strategy.

114. Ibid., 149.

115. Buci-Glucksmann (*Gramsci and the State*, 66) notes an antinomy between conflict-theoretical and functionalist positions in Althusser, who in fact only rarely leaves the functionalist perspective, without seeming to notice it in Gramsci, whose whole perspective is characterized by this dualistic tension.

116. Anderson, "The Antinomies of Antonio Gramsci," 35ff.

117. Ibid., 35–36. Anderson does not notice what might have been Althusser's main motivation for the move. In all state-socialist societies, especially the Soviet Union and China, social institutions were far more consistently statized than under fascism, a state of affairs that brought on some of Gramsci's hesitant criticisms. If we pronounce social institutions to be part of the state apparatus in the West, too, a critical vantage point vis-à-vis the existing socialisms would have to be surrendered, and the politics of the French Communist party rather than the Eurocommunist parties would be confirmed. Anderson's reference in this context to the Chinese cultural revolution is incomprehensible.

118. Ibid., 31–34. Unfortunately, after having earlier distinguished between including civil society in the state and identifying the two (very rare in Gramsci), Anderson seems to go ahead and identify the two options. The harshness of his critique of Althusser is to some extent linked to this slip.

119. Ibid., 22. All the worse, in the given context, Anderson's point of reference was the Soviet Union, which he viewed as a (deformed?) workers' state.

120. Ibid., 44–46.

121. Ibid., 27–29.

122. Ibid., 28.

123. Althusser, too, thought for a moment to stress parliaments in this way, before settling on his own candidate for ideological primacy under advanced capitalism, namely, educational institutions. See "Ideology and the Ideological State Apparatuses," 152–155.

124. In the period January–April 1969 (!), Althusser was able to point only to the resistance of a few isolated, heroic teachers who in dreadful conditions managed to teach against the grain of the prevailing ideology (ibid., 157).

125. Anderson, "The Antinomies of Antonio Gramsci," 28.

126. Ibid., 71.

127. Bobbio, "Gramsci and the Concept of Civil Society," 88–90.

128. Ibid., 92–93.

129. Ibid., 94–95.

130. See especially *Which Socialism?* [1976] (Oxford: Polity Press, 1987) and *The Future of Democracy* [1984] (Oxford: Polity Press, 1987). Even here, though, we do not find a criticism of Gramsci's views of "regulated society." These are supplied by Bobbio's British editor, Richard Bellamy, in the introduction to *Which Socialism?*

131. Bobbio, *Which Socialism?*, 43. See also page 66 for a more detailed discussion of the principles of majority rule, etc. Oddly enough, in this latter essay, Bobbio drops the notion of control from below in his definition.

132. Ibid., 99.

133. Bobbio, *The Future of Democracy*, 24–25. The definition provided on pages 19–20 of this work, apparently still later in origin, is again less procedural, but it also breaks with the classical model of Bobbio's earlier writings by focusing on interest aggregation and compromise. It is not obvious, however, why this latter model needs to be connected to formally democratic institutions at all, and thus it certainly cannot be used to define these institutions.

134. Compare pages 25–26 of *The Future of Democracy* with pages 114–116.

135. Ibid., 27–36. Unfortunately, this list is rather heterogeneous. Pluralism is not so much a broken promise of individualism as an alternative theory and promise of democracy, going back to Montesquieu and especially Tocqueville. And there never was a promise in either the classical or liberal traditions of extending democracy beyond politics. This issue comes up only in the works of the critics of these democratic models, especially the utopians, the Marxists, and the anarchists.

136. Ibid., 40.

137. Ibid., 41–42.

138. Bobbio insists that the situation is even worse in existing "socialist" societies (*Which Socialism?*, 75).

139. Ibid., 101.

140. Bobbio, *The Future of Democracy*, 52–54.

141. Ibid., 50–51.

142. Even with interest group bargaining formally made public, the real decisions could occur in secret, in smoke-filled rooms as it were. Here, a second chamber would be no different than the first. But in both cases, representatives of the parties or interest groups would also be forced to articulate their positions in such a way that they could be publicly justified. We hold that this requirement alters considerably the positions and bargains that emerge. Of course, Bobbio might answer that while the representatives of the party would have to justify their views to the whole society, the representatives of interest groups would only have to do so for their own groups. But political parties also appeal to specific constituencies, while the need to justify decisions to one's own interest group could itself represent an important gain over present arrangements in many countries.

143. Bobbio, *The Future of Democracy*, 54–55.

144. Ibid., 56.

145. Ibid., 62.

146. Ibid., 57.

147. Ibid.

148. See especially ibid., page 105, where he clearly returns to a Marxian and liberal two-part model.

149. Ibid., 69, 77.

150. All that is left here of socialism in the traditional sense is a hesitant call for economic democracy and a more determined argument for a new social contract that is to solve the problem of justice along the lines suggested by Rawls. See *The Future of Democracy*, chap. 6.

Chapter 4

1. In particular in *The Origins of Totalitarianism* [1951], 2d ed. (New York: Meridian Books, 1958; hereafter cited as *OT*); *The Human Condition* (Chicago: University of Chicago Press, 1958; hereafter *HC*); *On Revolution* [1963] (New York: Penguin Books, 1977; hereafter *OR*); and the essay "The Crisis in Culture" [1960], in *Between Past and Future* (New York: Meridian, 1963; hereafter "Crisis").

2. Jürgen Habermas, "Walter Benjamin: Consciousness Raising or Redemptive Criticism," in *Philosophical-Political Profiles* (Cambridge: MIT Press, 1983).

3. It is not particularly important in the present context that Arendt has two very different conceptions of the social, the first based on that of a natural and even prehuman propensity for association (*HC*, 23–24) and the second, the dominant view, having to do with a specifically modern creation out of preexisting institutional components. While most of the time the two conceptions are reconcilable, at times a stress on the first leads to the peculiar conception of the *modern* social realm as the invasion of political life by a natural principle.

4. *HC*, 198.

5. Ibid., 50ff., 176–179.

6. Ibid., 198.

7. Ibid., 200.

8. *OR*, 75.

9. *HC*, 26 and note 9.

10. These two stresses are different in her major works; *HC* relies primarily on the rhetorical-dramaturgical model, while *OR*'s stress is on binding and promising. Unlike Habermas, Arendt never realized that two different models of action are at stake. Both models involve mutual recognition: The first entails recognition of each other's unique personality; the second, mutual recognition as equal members of a solidary political community. Indeed, both presuppose the norm of equality, albeit in different ways: The first presupposes equality in the sense of equal concern and respect for each individual's uniqueness; the second, equality in the sense of equal membership and participation in the political community. Arendt never adequately distinguished between these models of action because she located them both in a single public sphere: the Greek *polis*.

11. According to Arendt, the two are increasingly differentiated historically, yielding in effect two modalities of action (*HC*, 26–27). Once again, however, Arendt is open to the objection that she sees power as a constitutive condition of all forms of stable rule; see *On Violence* (New York: Harcourt Brace Jovanovich, 1969), 41ff. At times, this essay does seem to restrict power to one component of

rule: generating consent, or achieving legitimacy by generating consent (see Habermas, "Hannah Arendt: On the Concept of Power," in *Philosophical-Political Profiles*). But whatever the ambiguities concerning her general concepts of action and power, Arendt's theory of the public sphere is an explicitly historical one, consciously relying on the ancient republics as the original models that remain, in this respect at least, unsurpassable.

12. This is obviously not an impossible rendering of Aristotle's taking a turn between ruling and being ruled.

13. But since the public sphere is capable of processing only opinion rather than knowledge, and since the idea of an irreducible original plurality of opinions excludes the possibility of preexisting normative consensus, it is unclear on what grounds individuals could be persuaded in this model, which has difficulty going beyond the art of rhetoric. The problem is linked to another one concerning the goals of public life and deliberation.

14. *HC*, 194–195.

15. This goal has never been fulfilled, according to Arendt, not even in America. Constitutional government has at best confined the pursuit of objectives that are, in her view, apolitical or prepolitical within a framework of fundamental rights and the rule of law. It therefore remains unclear what the purpose of an already institutionalized public sphere would be, aside from the continual generation of power needed to keep it in existence. Even more unclear is how this purpose is to be fulfilled by individuals who do not have any grounds for mutual persuasion.

16. Arendt is not consistent when describing the private world in terms of uniqueness and difference, since in her model the opinion of the private realm is homogeneous and unified (*HC*, 39–40). Thus, on this model, only the male head of the household, as a product of the private sphere, is the true representative of the principle of difference vis-à-vis other heads of households. Nor is she consistent in defending intimacy as the unique achievement of the modern (bourgeois, nuclear) form of the family while remaining silent about the nonegalitarian, patriarchal relations within this form that conflict with the achievement of true intimacy. The problem lies in Arendt's uncritical adoption of the standard republican insistence on the one-to-one institutional embodiment of the principles of private and public, literally identified as the domestic vs. the political sphere. This, together with her analysis of the emergence of society in terms of an eruption of needs, interests, and "household concerns" out of the private sphere, has been rightly criticized by feminist theorists as a gendered, patriarchal set of dichotomies predicated upon the exclusion of women and "their" concerns (nature, life, needs, interests) from a public realm that would be the terrain only of civil virtue. See Jean Elshtain, *Public Man, Private Woman* (Princeton: Princeton University Press, 1981), and Joan Landes, *Women and the Public Sphere in the Age of the French Revolution* (Ithaca: Cornell University Press, 1988), on the patriarchal presuppositions of republican thought. Our point here is to claim not that the abstract distinctions between public and private, autonomy and political freedom, intimacy and publicity, are in them-

selves objectionable but rather that the more concrete institutional and normative interpretation of these institutions adopted by Arendt from republican thought rests on a gendered subtext and is at the heart of her contradictory analysis of privacy and the social and of her amazing naiveté regarding the exclusion of interests and needs from the purview of the public sphere.

17. *HC*, 30–31.

18. Ibid., 61–65, 71. Even in this text, Arendt notes the "nonprivative" aspects of privacy; yet one would be hard put to imagine anyone's unique personality (apart from potential heads of households) being nurtured in the *oikos*.

19. *OT*, 301. It is striking that, unlike Habermas, Arendt never questions whether the private sphere might not be organized on some other principle, i.e., according to egalitarian norms. This is all the more surprising since the modern family form is not based on the presence of "strangers"—servants, domestics, slaves—and hence could in principle (and indeed this is its principle, if not its practice) be organized in an egalitarian way. Nor does she ever question the specific content of the civic virtue she so praises as the specific value of the public sphere. In republican thought, however, this always translated into the concept of the citizen-soldier whose core virtues were honor, glory, and patriotism, the willingness to fight and to sacrifice private for public interests and the common good.

20. *OR*, 252.

21. *HC*, 28–29. Actually, her critique began with that of the model of the nation-state in *OT*. At that time, Arendt already saw this model as one of the decline of genuine politics, in the sense of rendering impossible the construction of equality under the rule of law. She did not, in this earlier work, criticize civil society in the form of the rise of a mixed social realm; indeed, she saw, in a way reminiscent of the young Marx, an increasing division between state and society as the other side of the absolutist state organizing itself as a tremendous business concern (*OT*, 17). The abolition of the boundary between public and private is ascribed to the spurious claims of totalitarian movements (*OT*, 336), and the preparation of atomization in mass society (and under totalitarianism) is attributed to the bourgeois instrumentalization of politics, to the depoliticization—indeed, privatization—of all classes in bourgeois society (*OT*, 275). The only anticipation of the later concept of the social comes when Arendt describes the role of social conformism for the hitherto pariah caste of the Jews, who gain equality as parvenus in the context of depoliticization (*OT*, 52–56, 64–65).

22. *HC*, 33.

23. Within the framework of *OT*, this explanation was in fact presented in terms of concepts belonging to this tradition, stressing the depoliticizing consequences of the separation rather than the fusion of public and private.

24. *OT*, 17.

25. *HC*, 28–29.

26. *OR*, 252.

27. "Crisis," 199ff.

28. *HC*, 34–35. It is quite another issue that the political life of the medieval estates could be represented in terms of another meaning of publicity, that of a "representative public." See Jürgen Habermas, *The Structural Transformation of the Public Sphere* (Cambridge: MIT Press, 1989), 5ff.

29. *OR*, 48, 90–91.

30. Ibid., 91.

31. Ibid., 105.

32. Ibid., 115, 218.

33. Ibid., 221.

34. Ibid., 252.

35. Tocqueville discovered the forms and (he thought) the roots of American mass society before the two processes stressed by Arendt, mass production and mass immigration, even began.

36. *OR*, 139.

37. She also shares some of the problematic features of their analyses. Most notably, she uses the category of "normalization" to describe a model of *social* integration and *socialization* that involves internalizing norms in such a way as to deprive the individual of all autonomous possibilities for action (*HC*, 40–41). Even if this conception does correspond to the assumptions of what used to be the dominant (but never the only available) paradigm in socialization theory, the resulting juxtaposition of political action and social integration is a highly unfortunate extension of Arendt's critique of the social. It gives the impression that public political action is not in any way oriented toward rules, and that orientation toward rules can never be autonomous or "postconventional." The resulting contrast of ancient and modern society thus yields an unacceptable reverse modernization thesis that unjustifiably disregards the role of tradition, custom, convention, and even law in the ancient world as well as the Marxian conception of the simultaneous rise and alienation of individual freedom in the modern world.

38. *HC*, 40.

39. *OT*, 43–45.

40. *On Violence*, 38–39.

41. *OR*, 269.

42. *HC*, 203; *OR*, 105.

43. Here, Arendt tends to reproduce uncritically Rousseau's critique of society and, by implication, of women. See J. J. Rousseau, *Emile* [1762] (New York: Dutton, 1974), book 5, esp. 348ff., 352ff.; and "Discourse on the Sciences and the Arts," in R. D. Masters, ed., *The First and Second Discourses* (New York: St. Martin's Press, 1964).

44. *OR*, 105.

45. "Crisis," 199; *HC*, 40–41; for a very different view, see Reinhart Koselleck, *Critique and Crisis: Enlightenment and the Pathogenesis of Modern Society* [1959] (Cambridge: MIT Press, 1988).

46. *OT*, 64–65.

47. Arendt tends to reproduce the republican critique of salon society, which was later aimed, among other things, at silencing and disempowering women.

48. *OR*, 76–78, 226–228.

49. It is worth noting that the two events Arendt seems to combine into a single logic—the revolutionary transfer of the notion of sovereignty from the king to the people and the rise of a politics of interest (i.e., the intrusion of the poor and their demands onto the political scene)—are not logically connected. Indeed, even Arendt separates them in her own narrative in *On Revolution*. The bulk of that book, including the central chapter on the social question, emphasizes the collapse of nascent republican institutions founded by the revolutionaries (the rule of law, the National Assembly) in the face of the pressure of the *sans-culottes* or *le peuple*, whose will Robespierre claimed to "represent" or, rather, embody. The people appear for the most part as a needy mob screaming for bread. In the same context, Arendt enters into a long critique of Rousseau, whose brand of republicanism based on the ideas of indivisible sovereignty, general will, and hatred of plurality (faction, federalism, corporate bodies, etc.) was inherited by the Jacobins. This is supposedly the ideological reason why the French Revolution was diverted from the task of founding political institutions and focused instead on solving the social question by whatever means necessary, in the process violating even revolutionary legality and starting the Terror. In this case, however, Arendt is too close to the standpoint of the revolutionary actors (the Jacobins), taking their ideology at face value. It should not be forgotten that for Rousseau, the sovereign people whose will and interest could not be divided or alienated were by no means the miserable or the poor or even wage laborers, but rather an idealized community of independent farmers. Thus, the unitary logic that Arendt correctly criticizes—leading from the king's sovereignty to the indivisible sovereignty of the people, which cannot be represented but only embodied, which cannot be institutionalized in one assembly because no hall will hold them all, and which leads to the logic of substitutionalism, instability, competition between contenders claiming to embody this will, manipulation, plebiscitary acclaim, and terror—is not the logic of misery gone public, but instead a dilemma inherent in any model of radical democracy that rejects representation in principle. Later in her text (240–241), Arendt corrects her own historical record and claims that in France, as in America, real republican institutions were created during the course of the revolution and by the people themselves. Here, at last, the people appear not as a mob demanding bread but as collective *actors* creating their own political institutions. She also indicates that Robespierre crushed these free spaces developed by the people—the popular societies, the sections of the Paris commune, the revolutionary municipal

council, the clubs—in the name of "the great popular Society of the whole French people." This claim is distinct from those emergency measures necessary to overcome dire misery. Perhaps the two logics came together historically, but they are nonetheless separate, and in Robespierre's hands the blur between them made for a convenient ideology. Arendt's brilliant critique of both of these logics does not lead her to reflect on the political dilemmas of direct democracy (what she calls "republicanism") because she shares some of its core premises, namely, the rejection of interest representation and parliamentarism. Her own carefully crafted pluralistic, federal, council model is thus subject to some of the same dilemmas she criticizes yet obscures by attributing them to the social-economic question.

50. The connection between the social as high society and as the problem of poverty is still not clear. Indeed, we are not convinced that there is a connection. However, on the symbolic level at least, Arendt clearly saw them as being connected. She certainly does not believe that the intrigues of a courtly society whose elite is denied real political power are unique to the absolute monarchies of the eighteenth century—the courtly life of many oriental despotisms could be similarly described. What was unique, however, and could be the missing link on a symbolic level between the two extremes of her concept of the social (high society and the poor) was the prominent and visible role of women in both. After all, women were the ones who ran the salons of high society just prior to the French revolution and who brought the concerns of the household into the public arena during that revolution. The republican hatred of the immoral, false, hypocritical, unnatural, and frivolous ways of aristocratic society came to be symbolized by the all too visible women (the *precieuses*) of the salon, against which the moralistic discourse of republicanism was explicitly aimed. This discourse was easily transformed into a condemnation of the disorderly and increasingly visible revolutionary women in the streets and in the sections when it came time to repress the voices of society in the name of republican principles (civic virtue for, and responsible public action by, men; domesticity and private virtue for women). Women were the first to be excluded from the radical clubs and sections, the first to be silenced by the Jacobin dictatorship, and the most notable exception to the universal rights of man and citizen. It is ironic that, while Arendt abhors this "republican" solution to the social question, which of course quickly moved beyond the exclusion of women from the public realm to its destruction and to the demise of republicanism itself, she shares the very categories of the republican discourse that justified the process. It is a pity that her critique of Jacobinism did not encompass this discourse; but, given her categorial framework, such a critique was impossible. See Landes, *Women and The Public Sphere.*

51. *OR*, 268–269.

52. *HC*, 59–61, 64, 67 (note 72), 70–72.

53. Ibid., 126, 133–134.

54. Ibid., 40.

55. Ibid., 38, 50.

56. Ibid., 47, 50, 70. Characteristically, the Arendtian model of intimacy does not assume the model of intersubjective relations, based on communication and solidarity, that is stressed by the Frankfurt School from Max Horkheimer to Jürgen Habermas. The private and public spheres, intimacy notwithstanding, are not organized in a structurally homologous way. Rather, they are based on competing models of organization. The public sphere is composed of peers and organized on the basis of egalitarian principles; the private sphere is composed of unequals and organized on the principles of patriarchy. As a result, Arendt has no way of postulating any continuity between the sphere of the family and the public sphere. Arendt's concept of intimacy reinforces the notion of a watertight separation between them that always remains desirable in her framework. Intimacy is important to Arendt because it creates modern individuality and modern literature. Given the patriarchal structure of the intimate sphere, however, it is clearly only males who can become *full* individuals; they are the ones who are nurtured in the private-intimate sphere to develop into autonomous individuals and then to leave it to become recognized as individuals in the public sphere. Thus, one of the main reasons why the intimacy of the private sphere cannot withstand the onslaught of "the social"—i.e., of leveling and state penetration—is that the private sphere itself is institutionalized in a contradictory way: On the one hand, the modern family is based on the norms of equality, freedom, voluntary association, subjectivity, mutual recognition, and hence intimacy; on the other, it is structured hierarchically and predicated on the subjugation of women.

57. This view does in fact appear in Arendt's later essay on civil disobedience, but it does so despite, rather than on the basis of, her categorial framework. (See chapter 11.) In other words, while Arendt is intent on the revival of political society, her very conception of modern society prevents her from developing Tocqueville's other crucial category and examining the relation between civil and political society. Civil society appears only as the private sphere preserved through individual rights or as mass society. The associational components of modern civil society are either ignored or interpreted in terms of interest groups.

58. *OR*, 169–171.

59. Ibid., 255 and passim.

60. Ibid., 168.

61. Ibid., 179. She omits restrictions based on birth in the form of gender or race.

62. Ibid., 275–279.

63. Ibid., 273.

64. Ibid., 232.

65. Ibid., 144.

66. Ibid., 182.

67. Ibid., 189–190.

68. Ibid., 147.

69. *OT*, 290–297.

70. Ibid., 252ff.

71. Ibid., 92, 115, 134, 218.

72. *OR*, 108–109.

73. Ibid., 126–127.

74. Ibid., 143.

75. Ibid., 32, 108.

76. Ibid., 217–218.

77. Ibid., 32; note the phrasing.

78. Ibid., 218.

79. *OT*, 295–297.

80. This is the position Arendt herself was to take in *Crisis in The Republic* (New York: Harcourt Brace Jovanovich, 1969) in her discussion of civil disobedience, in spite of rather than on the basis of her theoretical framework.

81. *HC*, 215.

82. Ibid., 215–220. This is a play on Marx's formula "in but not of civil society," from his "Critique of Hegel's *Philosophy of Right*: An Introduction" [1843], in Karl Marx and Friedrich Engels, *Collected Works*, vol. 2 (New York: International Publishers, 1975). This link helps to establish, philologically, Arendt's critique of the social as a critique of civil society, if such a proof were needed.

83. *OR*, 273–275.

84. *HC*, 219.

85. Indeed, it seems as if Arendt wants to replace the party-parliamentary system with a federal model of workers' councils and an efficient but greatly reduced state administration—the first being the properly political space, the second the space in which interest claims would be processed. Civil society would be protected by individual rights, but, on this model, it certainly could not protect itself against the state since it would have no political form, no public representative bodies or spokesmen, and no internal public spaces distinct from the councils that comprise political society. Civil society would, in short, be helpless not only against the state administration but also against political society itself.

86. *OR*, 270.

87. See chapter 10. The prewar "collective behavior" school of Blumer did not automatically identify social movements with mass movements and was in fact still capable of seeing their "public" dimension.

88. For a distinction between these two concepts of the political and politics, see Dick Howard, *The Marxian Legacy*, 2d ed. (Minneapolis: University of Minnesota Press, 1989). Howard convincingly demonstrates that Claude Lefort and, espe-

cially, Cornelius Castoriadis have a very different attitude to modern politics than Arendt. This is striking because of the many important parallels between their work and Arendt's.

Chapter 5

1. Jürgen Habermas, *The Structural Transformation of the Public Sphere* [1962] (Cambridge: MIT Press, 1989; hereafter cited as *Public Sphere*).

2. Nevertheless, the starting point of Schmitt's revival of the *topos* of publicity— the assertion that discussion and openness represent the principle of parliamentarism—can be interpreted in two ways that lead to each of these thinkers. One of these seems to indicate a model of the state—a parliamentary state based on public discussion—and leads to Arendt. The other, focusing on the emergence of a social and apolitical sphere in the state, leads to Habermas.

3. Carl Schmitt, *The Crisis of Parliamentary Democracy* [1923] (Cambridge: MIT Press, 1985; hereafter cited as *Crisis*), 2–5.

4. Ibid., 5, 34.

5. He does not see the fundamental difference between integration through strategic calculation and through mutual persuasion. (The same is true of liberals who talk about "the marketplace of ideas.") For an elaboration of the difference, see Jürgen Habermas, *Theory of Communicative Action*, vol. 1 (Boston: Beacon Press, 1984), chaps. 1, 4.

6. *Crisis*, 35; Carl Schmitt, *The Concept of the Political* [1932] (New Brunswick, NJ: Rutgers University Press, 1976), 71–72.

7. *Crisis*, 3. He says, moreover, "Great political decisions ... no longer result today [1923] (*if they ever did*) *from balancing opinions and counteropinions in public debate*" (49, our emphasis). The point is that Schmitt treats the idea of decision through public discussion as a normative counterfactual principle of legitimation that has, however, some institutional foundations. Thus, it makes as little sense to criticize him by contrasting the discussion principle with nineteenth-century reality as by recalling the preliberal, nondiscursive types of parliamentarism. See, for exmple, John Keane, *Democracy and Civil Society* (London: Verso, 1988), 164–170. Both of these elements represent essential contrasts for Schmitt's own thesis.

8. *Der Hüter der Verfassung*, 2d ed. (Berlin: Duncker & Humblot, 1931; hereafter cited as *Hüter*), 78. It would be futile to deny that these secondary norms following from the primary one received their institutional expression under nineteenth-century conditions. Schmitt overlooks their continued significance in the twentieth century, but he certainly has a case to the extent that only in the latter context did there develop a comprehensive practice of party politics that tended to reduce dramatically the significance of the norms linked to the metanorm of publicity. Max Weber is right to find the roots of this party politics in the nineteenth century, yet he also distinguishes democratic party politics from classical parliamentarism. See, e.g., "Parliament and Government in a

Reconstructed Germany," in *Economy and Society*, vol. 2 (Berkeley: University of California Press, 1978). Schmitt's thesis concerning a fundamental change in parliamentarism cannot be refuted around the empirical presence or absence of genuine public discourse, always a counterfactual, but only by refuting Weber's thesis on the transformation of party politics, which was in fact the primary source for *Crisis*.

9. *Crisis*, 3–4.

10. Ibid., 47.

11. *Hüter*, 73–74.

12. This analysis does not apply very well to England, whose absolutism was a parliamentary one and whose state, even in the liberal epoch, was a self-organization of a (narrowly conceived) society. See Werner Conze, "Die Spannungsfeld von Staat und Gesellschaft im Vormärz," in Werner Conze, ed., *Staat und Gesellschaft im deutschen Vormärz 1815–1848* (Stuttgart: Klett, 1962), 208–210. The polemical contrast in the English-speaking context was best developed by Thomas Paine in *Common Sense*, taking the point of view of colonial "parliaments" against the parliamentary state.

13. *Hüter*, 73–74. Note the shift from a discussion-based model of publicity to a dramaturgical one.

14. Though less clearly than the Marx of the *18th Brumaire of Louis Bonaparte* (New York: International Publishers, 1963), 65–66.

15. *Crisis*, 36, 39.

16. Ibid., 49–50.

17. Ibid., 50.

18. Ibid., 38.

19. Reinhart Koselleck, *Kritik und Krise* [1959] (Frankfurt: Suhrkamp, 1973), published in English as *Critique and Crisis: Enlightenment and the Pathogenesis of Modern Society* (Cambridge: MIT Press, 1988).

20. Koselleck does not include England in his thesis, although he does stress that Hobbes and Locke were the first to thematize the dualistic consequences of absolutism. According to him, by the time of the Enlightenment, English elite society represented in Parliament successfully avoided a polemical polarization with the royal executive (46). See also Conze, "Die Spannungsfeld," 208. Neither Conze or Koselleck notes the obvious inconsistency of this English exception with Schmitt's picture of the polemical stabilization of liberal parliamentarism.

21. *Kritik und Krise*, 46–54.

22. Ibid., 65–68.

23. Ibid., 81–97.

24. Koselleck could answer that what occurred in France in a very short period, during the rise and collapse of revolutionary parliamentarism on its road to democracy, was to occur in the German states in a much longer period, simply

because the bureaucratic-military state did not collapse until 1918. This would be convincing but would have to be extended in a way inconsistent with Schmitt's thesis. In effect, apart from a few constellations that proved to be temporary, the modern state created by absolutism did not collapse, and its parliamentary (societal-public) limitation remained extremely relevant. The decline of parliamentarism, although empirically plausible, has to be analyzed in terms other than the subsumption of the state by society.

25. This similarity to Walter Benjamin's notion of *Dialektik im Stillstand* is hardly fortuitous. See Arendt's essay introducing Benjamin's *Illuminations* (New York: Schocken, 1969).

26. We leave out of consideration the fact that at the time Habermas was a rather classical Marxist for whom the rise of the modern state was a function of the development of capitalism and the liberal moment of the early modern public sphere was subordinated to the bourgeois one. In fact, his rich analysis, focusing on the enlightenment struggle against absolutism, contradicts in many respects this simple Marxian scheme.

27. We discussed the reasons for this prejudice in chapter 2.

28. *Public Sphere*, 53–55.

29. Ibid., 46 (our translation).

30. Ibid., 55–56.

31. Including feminist critiques of the ideology of the bourgeois model of the intimate sphere of the family as well as the liberal-bourgeois public sphere.

32. One hopes that they can also be institutionalized in a nonpatriarchal form of the family.

33. For a discussion of this transition from a feminist point of view, see Joan Landes, *Women and the Public Sphere in the Age of the French Revolution* (Ithaca: Cornell University Press, 1988). Her thesis is that, along with the new forms of discourse, the very ideals of the bourgeois public sphere were permeated by a deeply patriarchal republican ideology, explicitly constructed over and against women's forms of speech and power in the prebourgeois salon society. The target of the bourgeois public sphere was the hierarchical structure, privileges, hypocrisy, corruption, and exclusionary mechanisms of the society of orders, but the salon society run by the *precieuses* came to symbolize all that was wrong with the old regime. Thus, the dissolution of the salon, together with the exclusion of women from all aspects of public life and their sequestration in the newly emerging domestic sphere, was deemed to be essential if new forms of publicity outside this sphere were to be developed. Landes argues that the very articulation of the general norm of bourgeois publicity—interaction free from domination—in terms of a set of dichotomies such as universality vs. particularity and objectivity vs. emotionality reflected a rigid, gendered separation between public and private (domestic) spheres. This only apparently universal symbolic code was in fact male: It locked women out and silenced them (in part by making their attempts to represent their interests appear as particularistic or irrational).

Overall, women had suffered a loss of power, privilege, and legal standing compared with the old regime, while the bourgeois public sphere based on republican ideology emerged as a highly gendered one—essentially, and not contingently, masculine.

34. *Public Sphere*, 33.

35. Ibid., 53, 55.

36. Ibid., 28, 82.

37. See Alfred Cobban, *The Social Interpretation of the French Revolution* (Cambridge, England: Cambridge University Press, 1964); François Furet, *Interpreting the French Revolution* (Cambridge, England: Cambridge University Press, 1982).

38. *Public Sphere*, 67ff.

39. E. P. Thompson, *The Making of the English Working Class* (New York: Random House, 1963).

40. *Public Sphere*, 59–64. In order to see the relationship between particular interests and general norms, it is worth taking a closer look at Habermas's depiction of the development of the English model of the political public sphere. According to him, this development involved, with some historical connections to "coffeehouse society," the emergence of public opinion as an institution from a context in which political journalism and the rise of an "opposition" mutually conditioned each other. The political press, first established as an organ of the government, really came into its own in the hands of the Whig and later Tory oppositions that sought, at times successfully, to influence policy from outside of parliament, by mobilizing and manipulating *public opinion*. Indeed, it is through political journalism rather than public meetings and organizations that the opposition led by Bolingbroke first institutionalized itself in the long period of Whig rule under Walpole. The emergence of the political public sphere might be depicted in instrumental terms that would apply to the journalism of Defoe, Swift, and Bolingbroke; public opinion would then be an instrument by which an opposition could exert and retain some power, an instrument reluctantly permitted by a ruling party with a doubtful electoral base in order to avoid a return of open conflict, that is, civil war. Habermas's stress is not this instrumental one, however. In order to mobilize a public opinion already formed by the critical spirit of the audiences for literature and art, even Bolingbroke is compelled to try to demonstrate the justice and rightness of the case of the opposition against the corrupt party of the government. Even more important, the institutionalization of forms of public scrutiny over the actions of government, promoted by oppositional journalism, leads to institutions that will bind this same opposition when in power. The gradual transformation of the deliberations of parliament into public ones, a development that took a century and a half, allowed the transformation of a reasoning public, originally the instrument of parties, into the main agency exercising political supervision. It seems somewhat exaggerated for Habermas to declare the parliament following the First Reform Bill an "organ of public opinion." It might be more appropriate

to describe the "critical public," socially wider than parliamentary representation even after the Reform Bill, as a constantly expanding foreground of parliamentary deliberations capable of exerting an influence upon those deliberations.

41. *Public Sphere*, 84–85.

42. Ibid., 65.

43. Ibid., 4: "Tendencies pointing to the collapse of the public sphere are unmistakable, for while its scope is expanding impressively, its function has become progressively insignificant."

44. Ibid., 66–67.

45. See Cohen, *Class and Civil Society*, 34.

46. *Public Sphere*, 30.

47. The further possibility of differentiating civil society from the bourgeois economy and the state, first suggested by Gramsci and eventually taken over by Habermas, does not yet appear in *Public Sphere*.

48. *Public Sphere*, 55–56.

49. This is a modified version of the scheme (ibid., 30).

50. Ibid., 55–56.

51. Ibid.

52. Ibid., 19.

53. Ibid., 4.

54. Ibid., 51–52.

55. Ibid., 54.

56. Ibid., 82–83 (translation modified).

57. Ibid., 84.

58. Ibid., 136–138.

59. Ibid., 55.

60. The irony of this development is striking. The ideal of humanity coming from the intimate sphere of the family and pervading the literary public sphere is of course moral, universalist, and antipolitical—a clear reflection of the position of women in bourgeois civil society. Women came to represent "morality" and the "interests of humanity" by virtue of their very powerlessness and "disinterestedness" (their supposed lack of a strong self with real particular interests), without being deemed capable of attaining a universalist, reasoned moral point of view themselves; their presence as the audience of the literary public sphere and as the symbol of moral humanity was linked to their exclusion from all the spheres of civil society and the polity, apart from the family. This is why they could symbolize rather than attain the universalist, moral point of view and why the norm of humanity itself reflected the problematic position of women: powerless humanity. Such an ideal of moralistic humanism seeking to abolish the power of

institutions—be they in civil society or the state—is ambiguous, to say the least. Accordingly, the identification of *l'homme* and *citoyen* is doubly ideological.

61. *Public Sphere*, 55–56.

62. Ibid., 74–75.

63. Ibid., 81–82.

64. Ibid., 83.

65. Ibid., 84.

66. Ibid., 85.

67. We would add gender interests also.

68. *Public Sphere*, 88.

69. Ibid., 123–124.

70. Ibid., 125.

71. Ibid., 127–128.

72. Ibid., 161.

73. Ibid., 129.

74. He does not, however, tell us what would happen to the patriarchal character of the bourgeois family. Did Habermas in 1962 simply assume that, once the family is no longer bourgeois, once economic power no longer penetrates the intimate sphere, the problem of patriarchy dissolves? This standard Marxist position is unconvincing.

75. *Public Sphere*, 129.

76. Ibid. (our translation and emphasis).

77. It is a mistake to stylize them as liberal, as Habermas does, although, unlike Marx, they do maintain the full idea of the liberal public sphere.

78. *Public Sphere*, 136.

79. For Tocqueville and Mill, participation in egalitarian and democratic voluntary associations and other types of deliberative bodies in civil society (such as juries) provides the experience of freedom to the private citizen. On such a model, the first association in which the experience of and training for the exercise of freedom could be made would, of course, be a nonbourgeois, nonpatriarchal, egalitarian form of the family. However, unlike Hegel, Tocqueville and Mill never assume that individuals abandon their particular interests within the associations to which they belong: They take on the (relatively) more general interests of the association, but without losing their own particular concerns and goals.

80. *Public Sphere*, 128–129.

81. "Today" here refers to the Weimar period.

82. *Crisis*, 6–7.

83. *Hüter*, 89. Here Schmitt assumes that this unification was, after all, real. Elsewhere he maintains that it was mere show. The ambiguity is paralleled by his two arguments maintaining, respectively, the emergence of one (mere show) vs. two (real) wills of the state under liberalism.

84. To Schmitt, this Rousseauian model is completely impossible.

85. *Crisis*, 8–9, 13–14, 26–27.

86. Ibid., 15.

87. *Hüter*, 83–88. This point is inconsistent with the idea of a polemical relation of parliament to the executive. The question is whether there are, according to Schmitt, two partially antagonistic state wills in liberal parliamentarism, a view difficult to reconcile with other assertions of his, in particular his quasi-Hegelian insistence on the state as a unified center of loyalty (see *Hüter*, 90).

88. See Weber, "Parliament and Government in a Reconstructed Germany." Weber's analysis is analogous to Schmitt's regarding the end of the liberal parliamentary model of the emergence of good leaders. Weber's normative concern, however, unlike Schmitt's, was to find a counterweight to the bureaucratic state.

89. *Crisis*, 7, 49–50.

90. See Claude Lefort, "Politics and Human Rights," in *The Political Forms of Modern Society* (Cambridge: MIT Press, 1986).

91. *Concept of the Political*, 22–23.

92. *Hüter*, 78.

93. *Concept of the Political*, 22.

94. Ibid., 23; *Hüter*, 79.

95. *Concept of the Political*, 23 (our emphasis).

96. Confusing the two forms of differentiation leads to the ambivalent attitude noted by Leo Strauss (without seeing the actual reason) toward functional differentiation. It is defended against a form of segmentation implying the primacy of the social, which is a greater threat to sovereignty, but is given up vis-à-vis functional totalization or dedifferentiation implying the primacy of the political.

97. Carl Schmitt, *Legalität und Legitimität*, 3d ed. (Berlin: Duncker & Humblot, 1932, 1980), 96.

98. Ibid., 89–90. On page 98, he argues that, in effect, the result was the existence of two constitutions in one.

99. Otto Kirchheimer claimed that the authoritarian state in Germany did not manage to overcome internal pluralization and fragmentation. See his "Changes in the Structure of Political Compromise" [1941], in Andrew Arato and Eike Gebhardt, eds., *The Essential Frankfurt School Reader* (New York: Urizen, 1978), 49–70.

100. The Frankfurt writers foresaw this possibility early, as in Friedrich Pollock's distinction between democratic and authoritarian versions of state capitalism. See his "State Capitalism" [1941], in Arato and Gebhardt, eds., *The Essential Frankfurt School Reader*, 71–94.

101. Jürgen Habermas, "Technology and Science as Ideology," in *Toward a Rational Society* (Boston: Beacon Press, 1970); *Legitimation Crisis* (Boston: Beacon Press, 1975); Claus Offe, *Strukturprobleme des kapitalistischen Staates* (Frankfurt: Suhrkamp, 1972). It is important to note that, well before the emergence of neoconservatism, Offe stressed that state interventionism produced dysfunctions in administrative rationality (the "crisis of crisis management"), while Habermas insisted on unavoidable gaps in democratic legitimacy concerning the use of public intervention for private ends, given shrinking resources in cultural motivation.

102. Otto Kirchheimer, "Changes in the Structure of Political Compromise" and "In Search of Sovereignty," in *Politics, Law and Social Change* (New York: Columbia University Press, 1969).

103. *Public Sphere*, 144.

104. See his essays in *Contradictions of the Welfare State* (Cambridge: MIT Press, 1984) and *Disorganized Capitalism* (Cambridge: MIT Press, 1985).

105. *Public Sphere*, 155.

106. Ibid., 159, 162.

107. Ibid., 169.

108. Ibid., 175.

109. Ibid., 198.

110. Ibid., 203–204.

111. Ibid., 193ff.

112. Ibid., 211, 213.

113. Ibid., 215.

114. Ibid., 216.

115. Ibid., 218–219.

116. This was especially the case because, even in the 1960s, Habermas did not make use of Walter Benjamin's arguments concerning the possibilities of emancipation inherent in the cultural situation of modernity.

117. *Public Sphere*, 176.

118. Ibid., 177.

119. This argument also breaks with Arendt, who could not see anything positive about the welfare state. Habermas criticizes its depoliticizing consequences but finds its dedifferentiation of state and civil society positive to the extent that it anticipates the unified Marxian state-society. Since he juxtaposes this projected entity to a noneconomic intimate sphere, in the end he produces a synthesis of

Marx and Arendt that is more dualistic than the utopia of Marx but, unlike that of Arendt, includes economic affairs in public deliberations.

120. *Public Sphere*, 222–225.

121. Ibid., 178–179.

122. Ibid., 224–225. This argument, too, was introduced into Frankfurt School discussions by Otto Kirchheimer; see "Weimar und was dann?," translated as "Weimar—and What Then?," in *Politics, Law and Social Change*. Kirchheimer subsequently abandoned it with the development of the authoritarian state, which suddenly made the critical dismissal of negative rights unacceptable.

123. *Public Sphere*, 226.

124. Ibid., 229.

125. Ibid., 229. Evidently Habermas interprets the ambiguous term *Teilhaberrechte* (rights of participation, or rights of membership) in the sense of active democratic "participation" rather than mere passive belonging.

126. Ibid., 229–231.

127. Ibid., 177–178.

128. Ibid., 232–233. According to Habermas, this conflict is at present undecided. We should not take too seriously his optimistic assessment according to a model of the Hegelian "List der Vernunft," which seeks to conceive "the public sphere operating under conditions of the welfare state as a process of self-realization: being able to establish itself only gradually, competing with the other tendency, which, turning against itself, reduces the critical power of the principle of the public in the tremendously expanded public sphere" (233, our translation).

129. See chapter 8.

Chapter 6

1. For a detailed analysis of the strengths and limits of the Marxian critique of civil society, see Jean L. Cohen, *Class and Civil Society: The Limits of Marxian Critical Theory* (Amherst: University of Massachusetts Press, 1982).

2. As the most important of Louis Althusser's students, Foucault, of course, is well versed in Marxism. However, he rejects both humanist and structural versions of the theory and sees Marxism not as a radical break with modern (nineteenth-century) thought but as one element within it. As he puts it in *The Order of Things* (New York: Random House, 1970), "Marxism exists in nineteenth-century thought like a fish in water: that is, it is unable to breathe anywhere else" (262).

3. Michel Foucault, *Power/Knowledge* (New York: Pantheon, 1972), 89.

4. See Foucault, *The Order of Things*, 250–263, 367–387, for the critique of utopian thought. The section on "Man and his doubles" constitutes an important critique of the philosophical tradition begun by Descartes that has come to be called "the philosophy of the subject." According to Foucault, Marxist theory does not

escane the antinomies typical of this philosophical tradition, despite its revolutionary self-understanding. Indeed, the Marxian theory of a revolutionary macrosubject (the proletariat) shares the project of mastery that is typical of all the versions of the philosophy of the subject and in this respect is quite dangerous.

5. Foucault, *Power/Knowledge*, 81, 145.

6. See Cohen, *Class and Civil Society*, 23–52.

7. For a discussion of the Marxian thesis that the anatomy of civil society is to be located in economic relations and in the category of labor, see Cohen, *Class and Civil Society*, 53–82. For an excellent critique of Marx's analysis of rights, see Claude Lefort, "Politics and Human Rights," in *The Political Forms of Modern Society* (Cambridge: MIT Press, 1986), 239–272.

8. Michel Foucault, *Discipline and Punish* (New York: Pantheon, 1977), 222.

9. Foucault, *Power/Knowledge*, 95.

10. Ibid.

11. Foucault argues that, even for absolutism, the juridical-political concept of power was by no means adequate to describe the manner in which power was exercised. Nevertheless, it is the code according to which power presents itself.

12. Michel Foucault, *The History of Sexuality*, vol. 1 (New York: Pantheon, 1978), 85.

13. Ibid., 136.

14. Foucault, *Power/Knowledge*, 104–105.

15. Foucault, *History of Sexuality*, 89.

16. Foucault, *Power/Knowledge*, 105.

17. Foucault, *History of Sexuality*, 88.

18. Ibid., 88–89.

19. Foucault, *Power/Knowledge*, 105.

20. Ibid., 106.

21. For a discussion of this point, see Jürgen Habermas, *The Philosophical Discourse of Modernity* (Cambridge: MIT Press, 1987), 286–293.

22. Ibid., 290.

23. Foucault, *History of Sexuality*, 144.

24. Foucault, *Power/Knowledge*, 96.

25. Ibid., 107.

26. Foucault, *History of Sexuality*, 144. Foucault clearly has in mind legal developments in the welfare state, geared to regulate, control, and increase welfare and the security of life.

27. Ibid., 86.

28. For a discussion of the normative ambiguities of Foucault's work, see Nancy Fraser, *Unruly Practices* (Minneapolis: University of Minnesota Press, 1989).

29. Foucault, *History of Sexuality*, 89.

30. Foucault, *Power/Knowledge*, 98.

31. For a critique of Foucault's hypostatization of the concept of power, see Bernard Flynn, "Foucault and the Body Politic," *Man and World* 20 (1987): 65–84.

32. Foucault, *Power/Knowledge*, 142, and *History of Sexuality*, 92–93.

33. Foucault, *History of Sexuality*, 93.

34. Ibid., 94–95.

35. See chapters 3 and 7.

36. Foucault, *History of Sexuality*, 139.

37. Foucault, *Discipline and Punish*, 221.

38. Foucault, *History of Sexuality*, 47.

39. Ibid., 47–48.

40. "This real, noncorporeal soul is not a substance; it is the element in which are articulated the effects of a certain type of power and the reference of a certain type of knowledge, the machinery by which power gives rise to a certain corpus of knowledge. . . . On this reality-reference, various concepts have been constructed and domains of analysis carved out: psyche, subjectivity, personality, consciousness, etc.; on it have been built scientific techniques and discourses, and the moral claims of humanism" (*Discipline and Punish*, 29–30). See also the discussion in Fraser, *Unruly Practices*, 35–53.

41. *Discipline and Punish*, 27.

42. Foucault, *History of Sexuality*, 60–61. This authority can, of course, also be ourselves.

43. Ibid., 60.

44. See Fraser, *Unruly Practices*, 42–43.

45. See Habermas, *Philosophical Discourse of Modernity*, 270.

46. Fraser, *Unruly Practices*, 17–54.

47. Habermas, *Philosophical Discourse of Modernity*, 270.

48. Ibid.

49. Ibid., 276. See also Charles Taylor, "Foucault on Freedom and Truth," in David Couzens Hoy, ed., *Foucault: A Critical Reader* (Oxford: Blackwell, 1986), 69–102, and Thomas McCarthy, "The Critique of Impure Reason: Foucault and the Frankfurt School," in *Ideals and Illusions: On Reconstruction and Deconstruction in Contemporary Critical Theory* (Cambridge: MIT Press, 1991), 43–75.

50. Flynn, "Foucault and the Body Politic," criticizes Foucault's positivist account of power relations.

51. Habermas, *Philosophical Discourse of Modernity*, 286–293. See also McCarthy, "The Critique of Impure Reason."

52. Taylor, "Foucault on Freedom and Truth," 94.

53. Ibid., 90–91.

54. Foucault, *Power/Knowledge*, 61.

55. The concept of the subject is one of the main targets of Foucault's work. The dilemmas and traps of the modern theory of subjectivity form the main focus of *The Order of Things*. For an analysis of Foucault's critique of the modern theory of the subject and a comparison with the relevant theories of Adorno and Horkheimer, see Peter Dewes, *Logics of Disintegration* (London: Verson, 1987), 144–171. See also the chapters on Foucault in Axel Honneth, *The Critique of Power* (Cambridge: MIT Press, 1991), and Habermas, *The Philosophical Discourse of Modernity*, 238–266.

56. Foucault had already analyzed the connection between discourse and practices, knowledge and power, in *Madness and Civilization* [1961] (New York: Random House, 1965). Confinement and continuous supervision, isolation, individuation, regulation, and manipulation of the inmate constituted the new social techniques (practices) that were intimately connected with the emerging disciplines of the human sciences (psychology, pedagogy, sociology, penology, etc.) that subjected the object of observation to the monitoring gaze of the specialist. The discussion of confinement, supervision, and the refined differentiation of the inmates of the new total institutions (first the asylum and clinic, but then also the barracks, the school, the prison, and the factory) from the start rested upon a conception of practices that involved the coercive disciplining of some by others. But in *The Birth of the Clinic* [1963] (New York: Random House, 1973), Foucault abandoned the hermeneutic approach and replaced it with a structuralist analysis of discourses that refrained from seeking any access to the excluded and repressed. *The Archaeology of Knowledge* [1969] (New York: Harper & Row, 1972) is Foucault's methodological statement of this switch in orientation. Yet the basic concept of power was not refined and articulated until *Discipline and Punish*. Similarly, the epochal divisions that characterize the development of the modern penal system are the same as those described in Foucault's earliest work, *Madness and Civilization*.

57. In his earlier works, especially *Madness and Civilization* and *The Order of Things*, four epochs of history were stressed: the High Middle Ages, the Renaissance, the classical age, and modernity. For our concerns, we take up the last two stages as they appear in *Discipline and Punish*.

58. Foucault, *Discipline and Punish*, 298; see also 299–308. Foucault's point here is that disciplinary power and techniques of surveillance and control have appeared in nonpenal institutions (public assistance within the orphanage, the reformatory, the school, the charitable society, the workshop, the hospital, etc.) and now constitute a continuous process of "normalization"—continuous within and across societal institutions, continuous in criteria and techniques, continu-

ous in constituting not only crime but every departure from the norm as deviance. Indeed the prison itself as a closed institution may become anachronistic as disciplinary networks throughout the social body take over judicial functions of normalizing judgment and assume ever greater shares of the powers of supervision and assessment.

59. As indicated above, these epochs correspond to standard models of cultural and social history. Of course, Foucault's very enterprise of genealogical historiography makes claims to be a new way of doing history. For our purposes, the conceptual and methodological innovations and problems involved in genealogy are not directly at issue, but they bear on our problematic and are worth a brief comment. In *The Order of Things* and the *Archaeology of Knowledge*, Foucault had already analyzed the "discursive formations" and "practices" specific to the new human sciences and the modern philosophy of consciousness initiated by Kant. He argued that the "will to truth" is typical of the inexorable striving of that modern entity, the cognitive subject, toward the impossible goal of mastery of itself and the external world. The sciences of man (criminology, pedagogy, psychiatry, medicine, psychology, etc.) enter into this project by creating and controlling the individual subject through their specific social techniques, which take shape in the relevant institutions (prisons, schools, clinics, hospitals) and construct a link between knowledge and power. The turn to genealogical historiography places power at the core not only of the modern discursive formation or the types of truth claims of the human sciences but of all discourses in every society. The term is Nietzsche's; see Michel Foucault, "Nietzsche, Genealogy, History," in *Language, Counter-Memory, Practice: Selected Essays and Interviews* (Ithaca: Cornell University Press, 1977), 139–164, and the introduction to *The Archaeology of Knowledge*, 3–17. The modern interweaving of knowledge and power is only one among many historically distinct forms of the "will to power," each of which apparently has its own type of knowledge/truth claims. Genealogy unmasks these relations, revealing the connections among the rise, shape, and displacement of discursive formations and the emergence, techniques, and shifts from one relationship of forces to another. *Discipline and Punish* is exemplary in this regard. It answers the previously unresolved question of just how scientific discourses and practices are related: Genealogical research reveals the productivity of power technologies that not only instrumentalize discourses but are their constitutive preconditions. (As Habermas points out, though, this question is resolved only at the cost of introducing another set of problems, not the least of which is Foucault's "ambiguous" use of the category of power itself.) Genealogical historiography, together with an all-encompassing but never quite defined conception of power, constitute a theoretical and methodological universe within which it is possible to articulate social relations, truth claims, forms of knowledge, and social/political projects only as forms, expressions, or strategies of power.

60. The dates differ from those of other modernization theories, and the whole emphasis differs from the Marxian approach in one crucial respect: What others call traditional society, Marx calls "feudalism," and he himself neglects the

absolutist state. For a neo-Marxian attempt to address the absolutist period head on and fit it into the Marxian trajectory, see Perry Anderson, *Lineages of the Absolutist State* (London: New Left Books, 1974), 15–59.

61. The classic work in this area is Alexis de Tocqueville's *The Old Regime and the French Revolution* (New York: Doubleday, 1955). See also Robert Nisbet, *The Quest For Community* (New York: Oxford University Press, 1953), and *Readings on Social Change* (Englewood Cliffs, NJ: Prentice-Hall, 1967), and Theodor Adorno and Max Horkheimer, *Dialectic of Enlightenment* (New York: Herder and Herder, 1972).

62. Tocqueville, *The Old Regime and the French Revolution*.

63. That is, the distinction between the discussions, deliberations, and debates characteristic of legislatures and bureaucratic/administrative forms of decision making. For an analysis of the systematic distinctions between these forms of "action," see Hannah Arendt, *The Human Condition* (Chicago: University of Chicago Press, 1958).

64. Alexis de Tocqueville, *Democracy in America* (New York: Doubleday, 1969).

65. See Nisbet, *The Quest for Community*. Foucault offers no theory of social integration. Apparently, he believes that society can be integrated solely through strategic power relations and disciplinary technologies. Since he dispenses with the various models of integration offered by sociological theory (social integration through the medium of language, values, norms, or processes of mutual understanding) without resorting to systems or exchange theories as an alternative, he is unable to account for the stabilization of forms of interaction or for the institutionalization of power. See Honneth, *The Critique of Power*, and Habermas, *The Philosophical Discourse of Modernity*, 287–288.

66. This, of course, despite the genealogical disclaimer regarding the possibility of a common measure on the basis of which two different power-truth regimes might be compared. Foucault clearly means to say that asymmetric power relations are more pervasive, more intrusive, and more controlling of people's everyday lives in modern society than in the old regime.

67. Foucault, *Discipline and Punish*, 48.

68. This was the standard definition of sovereignty in the eighteenth century. See Foucault's discussion of the historical understanding of the concept of sovereignty in *Power/Knowledge*, 92–108.

69. Only in a separate and, strangely enough, earlier lecture does Foucault argue that sovereignty and rights are the stakes in the struggle between competing camps around the general system of power (*Power/Knowledge*, 103). This is the only hint one can find of the competition between the society of orders and the state-making project of the absolute monarch.

70. Foucault, *Discipline and Punish*, 47. It is interesting to compare Foucault's account with that of Emile Durkheim, *The Division of Labor in Society* (New York: Free Press, 1933). Indeed, Foucault seems to be inverting the classical Durkheimean thesis.

71. Foucault, *Discipline and Punish*, 82.

72. Ibid., 59.

73. Ibid., 91.

74. Accordingly, the sovereign's law could appear as something imposed from above. The criminal's challenge to the law could thus activate the support and solidarity of the population. The criminal could become a hero because it is the law of the other, not of the local community, that is at issue. Punishment here strikes terror into peoples' hearts but does not create an identity of the people with the sovereign and his law. On the contrary, the identity created is between the people and the criminal, who is seen as one of their own. This is what changes when, under the claims of popular sovereignty and liberal jurisprudence, based on the idea of the law as emanating from the community as a whole and the moral subject as the counterpart of the legal person, the criminal is created as an enemy of society.

75. Foucault, *Discipline and Punish*, 27–141.

76. For a "pro-Foucaultian" analysis of this difference, see John Rajchman, "Habermas' Complaint," *New German Critique*, no. 45 (Fall 1988): 163–191. For a "pro-Habermasian" account, see Dewes, *Logics of Disintegration*, 144–245.

77. "To pose the problem in terms of the State means to continue posing it in terms of sovereign and sovereignty, that is to say in terms of law. If one describes all these phenomena of power as dependent on the State apparatus, this means grasping them as essentially repressive. . . . I don't want to say that the State isn't important; what I want to say is that relations of power, and hence the analysis that must be made of them, necessarily extend beyond the limits of the state. . . . The state is superstructural to a whole series of power networks that invest the body, sexuality, the family, kinship, knowledge, technology and so forth" (Foucault, *Power/Knowledge*, 122).

78. Foucault, *Discipline and Punish*, 110.

79. Ibid., 63.

80. Ibid., 80.

81. Ibid., 222.

82. See Flynn, "Foucault and the Body Politic," for a critique of Foucault's positivism and reductionism vis-à-vis the symbolic dimension of social life, even in his analysis of the old regime.

83. Foucault, *Discipline and Punish*, 81.

84. Ibid., 85.

85. Ibid.

86. Ibid., 87.

87. Foucault, *History of Sexuality*, 6. But see page 114 for a somewhat contradictory claim.

88. Ibid., 123.

89. Ibid., 127.

90. Foucault, *Discipline and Punish*, 213.

91. Ibid., 215.

92. Ibid., 216–217.

93. Foucault, *History of Sexuality*, 25.

94. Foucault, *Power/Knowledge*, 171.

95. Foucault, *History of Sexuality*, 26.

96. Ibid., 143.

97. Foucault, *Power/Knowledge*, 101.

98. Honneth, *The Critique of Power*, 157–175.

99. Dewes, *Logics of Disintegration*, 145–146 and passim.

100. Ibid. This is what distinguished his analysis from both classical liberal and neo-Marxist theories that see state intervention as a relatively recent phenomenon. Dewes is clearly using a three-part model, and his interpretation of Foucault surely leads to the implication that civil society is, from the start, a domain permeated by power relations and domination.

101. Foucault, *Power/Knowledge*, 188.

102. For a discussion of Foucault's theory of the "governmentalization of the state," see Barry Smart, *Foucault, Marxism, and Critique* (London: Routledge, 1983), 119–122.

103. Ibid., 188.

104. Ibid., 116–119.

105. Foucault, *Discipline and Punish*, 215.

106. Just how one would differentiate between "totalitarian" or modern "authoritarian" regimes and Western democracies from a Foucaultian point of view is unclear.

107. See Honneth, *The Critique of Power*, chap. 5, and Habermas, *The Philosophical Discourse of Modernity*, 266–294. For a neo-Marxist account, see Smart, *Foucault, Marxism, and Critique*, 120–122. Smart's short discussion presents both Foucault's analysis of the social and that of his disciple, Donzelot. According to Foucault and Donzelot, "'the social' denotes a particular historical event, namely the emergence of a network or relay of institutions and functions through which a productive or positive power is exercised over populations" (122). The emergence of the social refers to those dimensions of life that are to be "protected" from the effects of economic fluctuations and granted a certain security. Thus, the social and the associated measures and mechanisms directed toward such dimensions of population as fertility, age, health, economic activity, welfare, and education represent a shift in the way power is exercised over individuals and a particular form of cohesion within society. The former is the exercise of power connected with knowledge acquired through the administrative, technocratic

formulas of social management. The latter, solidarity, is really a code word for the aid through control that is typical of social welfare programs. In both cases, "the social" is not something autonomous but a product of power techniques and an object that is literally created through techniques of control.

108. What remains unclear in all this is just what the globalization of power relations by the state and the bourgeoisie means. Is this a theory of the dedifferentiation of state, society, and economy? Is it a theory of the late capitalist welfare state? Is the purpose to steer us away from projects of democratization of the state or society or economy and to parry questions of legitimacy with issues of the relations of forces? If power is globalized, what about resistance to global power? There seem to be no answers to these disturbing questions in Foucault's texts.

109. Foucault seems to reduce the social to the sum of sets of power relations in which action is coordinated solely through the "reciprocity" of strategic calculations. But it has been clear to sociologists, at least since Durkheim's critique of Spencer's contractual model of society, that strategic forms of interaction don't suffice for maintaining the social bond or, in more modern terms, social integration. Yet, if all old solidarities, traditions, and autonomous associations are, in effect, *gleichgestaltet*, if norms are instruments of normalization, then what is the social bond besides power? As we shall see, this one-sided conception of the social is most significant for Foucault's theory of resistance, for it leaves him without the conceptual means necessary to account for the logic or even the possibility of collective action, which presupposes forms of solidarity, association, and social bonding that cannot be reduced to the logic of strategic interaction. Paradoxically, the "loss" of the state in the analysis of the old regime is complemented by the "loss" of society in the discussion of the new.

110. On the lack of discussion of democracy in Foucault's work, see Flynn, "Foucault and the Body Politic," 65–84.

111. See the account in Dewes, *Logics of Disintegration*, 145–199. This is tied to the critique of the philosophy of the subject.

112. This is a clear reference to Hegel's discussion of these "gains" of modernity. See the Knox translation of *Hegel's Philosophy of Right* (Oxford: Oxford University Press, 1952), 75–104.

113. Foucault, *Discipline and Punish*, 193.

114. Foucault's thesis is that disciplinary techniques originate in specific closed institutions and then are deinstitutionalized and circulate freely throughout society (*Discipline and Punish*, 211).

115. Foucault, *Discipline and Punish*, 213–214.

116. Ibid., 177.

117. For Habermas, on the contrary, it is precisely the emergence within the old regime of the administrative apparatus of the modern state, alongside and in contradiction to the society of orders with its representative publicity, that is specifically modern. State sovereignty and the emergence of a new form of

bourgeois publicity (of which the reformers' discourse is a part) constitute the two key poles of modern public life. Of course, Habermas knows that power relations develop within society and economy as well as in the state. Moreover, he, like Foucault, recognizes that the Enlightenment reformers' dream of a society free of domination and a state whose power is clearly delimited and controlled by the public representatives of society is never realized. Nevertheless, the "contradictory institutionalization" of the bourgeois public sphere—the creation of parliaments, a *Rechtsstaat*, rights, and public spaces in civil society—is more than a mere veil or carrier of a new modality of domination. The differentiation of state and society initiated under the old regime through state-making processes, struggles from below, and the legal, constitutional articulation of rights established new spaces for the emergence of new and autonomous solidarities on the terrain of a now modern civil society. In short, the continued discourse of sovereignty and legitimacy in modern society is not an anachronism. It witnesses two key institutional facts: the existence of a centralized state power distinct from society, and the institutionalization of some of the key principles of the bourgeois public sphere and individual rights. These constitute the possibility for the emergence of new forms of association, publicity, plurality, solidarity, and counterpower within the framework of a modern civil society. Civil, political, and social rights are not simply the expression of individualizing power techniques; they constitute a social realm, a terrain on which private individuals can come together, associate, communicate, and publicly articulate their views in print, in art, or in discussions. The public sphere, which is later to become a terrain of contention among conflicting groups and projects, must be seen as at least dualistic.

If Habermas errs in focusing exclusively on the rise, discourse, and structure of the bourgeois public sphere, neglecting its contradictory relation to plebeian, proletarian, and women's forms of association and publicity, Foucault errs in omitting the entire category of the public sphere and, with it, all forms of autonomous voluntary association.

118. Foucault, *Discipline and Punish*, 207.

119. See Foucault, *Power/Knowledge*, 106.

120. Foucault, *Discipline and Punish*, 216.

121. Ibid., 168.

122. Ibid.; and Foucault, *Power/Knowledge*, 208.

123. For an analysis that maintains that the critique remains caught in the philosophy of the subject, see Habermas, *Philosophical Discourse of Modernity*, chaps. 9, 10.

124. Foucault, *Power/Knowledge*, 142.

125. See McCarthy, "The Critique of Impure Reason."

126. Herbert Marcuse, *Eros and Civilization* (Boston: Beacon Press, 1955). This was Foucault's earlier strategy, which he then rejected in *Madness and Civilization*.

127. Habermas has asked precisely these questions on the basis of his critique of Foucault (*Philosophical Discourse of Modernity*, 284).

128. Foucault, *History of Sexuality*, 157. Our analysis has been based on Foucault's work up through this text. Some have argued that another shift in his thinking is indicated in the second and third volumes of his history of sexuality: Michel Foucault, *The Uses of Pleasure* (New York: Random House, 1990), and *The Care of the Self* (New York: Random House, 1988). In these texts, Foucault allegedly abandoned his one-sided conception of the self and the subject, tempered his all-pervasive notion of power, and provided the rudiments of a new conception of the social. This may be the case, but it hardly affects our general analysis of his position on civil society. Neither work addresses modern times: The first is on Greece, the second on Rome. The focus of these texts is on self-formative processes and conceptions of bodily pleasures and sexuality that do not constitute the hermeneutic, desiring subject of sexuality castigated by Foucault in the first volume of the series. While there are interesting insights in these volumes, Foucault died before he had a chance to develop the new lines of thought they suggest. We believe that his assessment of civil society as a carceral society would have to be radically revised for his late insights into the self, subjectivity, and the social to bear fruit. For a critical view, see McCarthy, "The Critique of Impure Reason," and Peter Dews, "The Return of the Subject in the Late Foucault," *Radical Philosophy* 51 (Spring 1989).

129. See chapter 9.

130. Taylor, "Foucault on Freedom and Truth," 82–83.

131. It is also our thesis that social movements struggle over the power to define norms, collective identities, etc. For a discussion of this logic of collective action, see the section on Touraine in chapter 10.

132. See chapter 9 for a discussion of the two-sidedness of the institutions of civil society and the relation of social movements to this dualism.

133. Foucault, *Power/Knowledge*, 96.

134. Ibid., 107. We suspect that Foucault's entire discussion of "the juridical" makes sense only with reference to the French conception of law as it derives from Rousseau. Law articulates the general will and protects the individual against executive arbitrariness. There is little need on this view for a distinction between individual rights against the state and law. Foucault never seriously addresses this distinction.

135. Ibid., 108.

136. Ibid.

Chapter 7

1. See especially Habermas's critique of hermeneutics, "A Review of Gadamer's *Truth and Method*," in Fred Dallmayr and Thomas McCarthy, eds., *Understanding and Social Inquiry* (Notre Dame: University of Notre Dame Press, 1977), and "The

Hermeneutic Claim to Universality," in Josef Bleicher, ed., *Hermeneutics as Method, Philosophy and Critique* (London: Routledge, 1980). For a summary of the debate, see Thomas McCarthy, *The Critical Theory of Jürgen Habermas* (Cambridge: MIT Press, 1978). Recently, several authors, including Dieter Misgeld, Thomas McCarthy, Nancy Fraser, and Hans Joas, have again challenged Habermas's position in this debate, especially around the system/lifeworld distinction. See the special issue of *New German Critique*, no. 35 (Spring-Summer 1985), and Habermas's response to some of his critics in Axel Honneth and Hans Joas, eds., *Communicative Action* (Cambridge: MIT Press, 1991).

2. Carl Schmitt and some social historians have uncovered such a double projection in the case of the liberal concept of civil society. See, e.g., Otto Brunner, *Land und Herrschaft*, 5th ed. (Darmstadt: Wissenschaftliche Buchgesellschaft, 1973). But similar difficulties arise for the *polis*-oriented concepts of Arendt and Castoriadis and the medievalist concepts of Gierke, Maitland, Figgis, and Laski.

3. The use of the concept of civil society in the work of Reinhardt Bendix and S. N. Eisenstadt is intelligent and creative, but neither has examined the social-scientific validity of this essentially philosophical concept, which they take over directly from historiography and the history of political theory. See Reinhardt Bendix, *Kings and People* (Berkeley: University of California Press, 1978), 357–377, 523ff.; and S. N. Eisenstadt, *Tradition, Change and Modernity* (New York: Wiley, 1973), 231ff. Identifying civil society more or less with Montesquieu's *corps intermédiaires*, Bendix has some difficulty in differentiating between a society of orders and modern civil society. Eisenstadt, surprisingly enough in the style of the young Marx, identifies civil with class society and thus misses the dimension that Bendix insists on, along with that of a new type of public sphere. Neither reconstructs the concept along the rich trajectory that Talcott Parsons described, perhaps because only Parsons saw his conception in terms of the multilevel Hegelian model.

4. The problem comes up again and again in essays like "Interaction, Organization, and Society," "Positive Law and Ideology," "Politics as a Social System," "The Economy as a Social System," "World-time and System History," and "The Self-thematization of Society," all in Niklas Luhmann, *The Differentiation of Society* (New York: Columbia University Press, 1982; hereafter cited as *Differentiation*); "Moderne Systemtheorien als Form gesamtgesellschaftlicher Analyse," in Jürgen Habermas and Niklas Luhmann, *Theorie der Gesellschaft oder Sozialthechnologie* (Frankfurt: Suhrkamp, 1971; hereafter *Sozialtechnologie*); "Politische Planung," in Niklas Luhmann, *Politische Planung* (Opladen: Westdeutscher Verlag, 1971; hereafter *Planung*); "Gesellschaft," in Niklas Luhmann, *Soziologische Aufklärung*, vol. 1 (Opladen: Westdeutscher Verlag, 1970; hereafter *Aufklärung, 1*); and "Die Weltgesellschaft," in *Soziologische Aufklärung*, vol. 2 (Opladen: Westdeutscher Verlag, 1982; hereafter *Aufklärung 2*).

5. *Differentiation*, 73, 223.

6. See "Die Weltgesellschaft," in *Aufklärung 2*.

7. "Interaction, Organization and Society," "Positive Law and Ideology," "Politics as a Social System," "The Economy as a Social System," and "The Differentiation of Society," in *Differentiation;* "Gesellschaft," in *Aufklärung 1;* "Die Weltgesellschaft," in *Aufklärung 2;* and "Öffentliche Meinung" and "Komplexität und Demokratie," in *Planung.*

8. *Planung,* 36; *Differentiation,* 333.

9. *Differentiation,* 335–336.

10. See Hannah Arendt, *The Human Condition* (Chicago: University of Chicago Press, 1958); and Cornelius Castoriadis's article on Aristotle in *Crossroads in the Labyrinth* (Cambridge: MIT Press, 1984).

11. "Moderne Systemtheorien als Form gesamtgesellschaftlicher Analyse," in *Sozialtechnologie,* 7–8; *Aufklärung 1,* 138.

12. *Differentiation,* 161, 295.

13. *Aufklärung 1,* 138; *Differentiation,* 19.

14. *Differentiation,* 78–80, 336–337, 339. Luhmann sees this view persisting in the Parsonian attempt to view the political subsystem as a form of collective action dedicated to the attainment of common social goals. He substitutes the generation of binding decisions for various possible social uses as the function of a political subsystem organized around the medium of power.

15. Ibid., 334–335.

16. *Aufklärung 2,* 51–52.

17. *Differentiation,* 334.

18. Here he is in opposition to Parsons and Habermas, who both seem to choose money. Thus, Luhmann seems to take more at face value the self-thematization of political society in ancient political philosophy!

19. *Differentiation,* 337.

20. Ibid., 193, 338.

21. Ibid., 341–343.

22. Ibid., 191, 222, 338.

23. Ibid., 338.

24. Ibid., 205.

25. Ibid., 203–204.

26. Ibid., 340.

27. Ibid., 202.

28. Ibid., 338.

29. Ibid., 342.

30. Ibid., 225.

31. Ibid., 357ff.

32. See Claus Offe, *Contradictions of the Welfare State* (Cambridge: MIT Press, 1985), 35–64.

33. Niklas Luhmann *Legitimation als Verfahren*, 2d ed. (Darmstadt: Luchterhand Verlag, 1975; hereafter cited as *Legitimation*), 160–161.

34. Niklas Luhmann, *A Sociological Theory of Law* (London: Routledge, 1972; hereafter cited as *Sociology of Law*), 149, 283ff.

35. *Differentiation*, 340; *Aufklärung 1*, 141.

36. *Differentiation*, 138.

37. Max Weber, *Economy and Society*, vol. 1 (Berkeley: University of California Press, 1978), 54, 56.

38. *Differentiation*, 132. In later works, this reductionism identifying the political system with the state is linked to the point of view of the administration "taking itself for the whole," and even to "bureaucracy's protection and screen," just as the understanding of politics as democracy and as leadership are identified as the reductionisms of the public and party systems, respectively. See the essays collected in Niklas Luhmann, *Political Theory in the Welfare State* (Berlin: de Gruyter, 1990; hereafter cited as *Political Theory*), 55, 148. These essays also express a somewhat different, though not necessarily inconsistent, conception implying the continued possibility and even the unavoidability of speaking of the state and of the opposition of state and society (109 and note 100) on the level of political theory and not political science. The conclusion is even more explicitly drawn with respect to the concept of the state in the essay "State and Politics," in *Political Theory*, 123, 128, 134, 136, 141–146, 152–153. Crucial in this context is the distinction between two types of theory. Whereas theories of political science (or any science) are said to be research programs operating in the subsystem of science and are validated only by scientific criteria, political theory (or any other "reflection theory" of a given subsystem) is here presented as a form of intellectual activity within the subsystem, whose function is to build elements of self-reflection, self-observation, and even self-criticism into its processes, here the political process. Political theory relies on political science (it is "subsidized" by science) but need not operate within the strict limits of scientific concept formation and validation (*Political Theory*, 24–25, 54–56, 107–109). The level of complexity of reflection theories is necessarily lower than that of their subsystems as well as of "scientific theories" of these (ibid., 118–119, 152). Nevertheless, political theory, unlike political science, can play a role in the political system of which it is an element; indeed, it is crucial for the formation of self-identity through self-observation (ibid., 119–120, 136, 153). In this context, Luhmann for the first time denounces the scientistic fallacy of imagining that in all respects scientific understandings and their applications are more adequate to political reality than are the self-understandings of political actors. He owes this insight to his theory of autopoietic systems, even if he has not been moved thereby to incorporate a hermeneutic perspective into his conception. Nor has he been able to show whether and how a two-way communication between political science and political theory is possible. Our presentation and

critique of Luhmann focus on what he understands as his scientific analysis of politics. While we understand our own work as political theory very much in the sense just articulated, we agree with Luhmann that he does not succeed in producing such a theory in *Political Theory* (see page 115). At issue, however, is something more than his style of presentation, which is what he seems to imply.

39. *Differentiation*, 140, 378 note 3.

40. Ibid., 236.

41. *Planung*, 54–55.

42. *Differentiation*, 128–129.

43. In his most recent relevant statements, Luhmann is less dismissive with respect to the differentiation of state and society. We have already seen that, on the level of political theory, he considers the distinction and the concept of the state to be a (so far) irreplaceable part of the self-identification of the political subsystem, despite its scientific untenability. But even on the level of social science, or rather of its history, Luhmann now concedes that the differentiation of state and society represented an early understanding of the differentiation of the social system, both from the point of view of the development of a differentiated economy and from that of the delimitation of the political system by constitutional law. See *Political Theory*, 133 and note 28.

44. Talcott Parsons, *Politics and Social Structure* (New York: Free Press, 1969), 208–209.

45. Ibid., 209, 240.

46. Ibid., 214, 334.

47. Ibid., 248–249.

48. This is, unfortunately, ambiguously presented in "The Political Aspect of Social Structure and Process," in *Politics and Social Structure*, 339–342. It would seem, however, that the four-part scheme presented here is his final word, since it corresponds to the general architechtonic of his system. Three of the four subsystems are involved in processes of "double interchange": the bureaucracy with the economy; the legitimating or constitutional subsystem with culture; and the integrative or associational subsystem with the societal community. This symmetry is annoying because all subsystems of the polity have interchanges with the societal community, as indicated by the three-fold system of rights of membership Parsons adopts from Marshall (civil: constitutional subsystem; political: associational subsystem; social: bureaucratic subsystem).

49. Parsons, *Politics and Social Structure*, 377.

50. *Differentiation*, 144.

51. *Planung*, 40.

52. Ibid., 39, 44.

53. Ibid., 35.

54. Ibid., 40.

55. See *Sozialtechnologie*, chap. 2.

56. *Planung*, 42.

57. Ibid., 43.

58. *Differentiation*, 114–115.

59. More recently, Luhmann has redefined democracy in ways that no longer allow an understanding of politics in Soviet societies as a species of democratic government. He now understands democracy as identical either to the political (or party-political, it is not clear which) version of the general characteristic of self-observation in autopoietic systems, or as the coding of the political sub-system of the political system in terms of the party in power (or government) and the opposition. The two are connected because binary coding in terms of the concept of the opposition is seen (rightly, in our view) as the primary method of promoting self-observation in politics. See *Political Theory*, 105, as well as chaps. 5, 9. (We leave to the side that Luhmann is inconsistent, elsewhere describing democracy as the self-observation or self-reflection of the *public* subsystem of the political system [ibid., 55]. In our view, this ambiguity is in fact a concession to a broader theory of democracy than his own; indeed, in one context at least, the two conceptions, linking public and party politics, seem to be included under the heading of "democracy" [ibid., 125].)

In our view, the new conception of democracy based on the code of govern-ment-opposition remains narrow and inadequate for the purposes of political theory in Luhmann's own sense of this term. The definition of democracy in terms of government and opposition tends to lose its specificity especially when the same pair of concepts is defined as the code (somewhat implausibly, given the friend-enemy code of modern totalitarianism) of modern politics as such: See *Ecological Communication* (Chicago: University of Chicago Press, 1989), 86. Luhmann is, of course, aware of the still somewhat exceptional nature of the politics of government and opposition; in response, he is now forced to consider systems without a political opposition as reversions to a hierarchical order of government and governed and as insufficiently differentiated, therefore by implication neither modern nor democratic. Nevertheless, for modern, differ-entiated political systems, he identifies the basic constitutive code of politics with democracy. As a result, he implicitly rules out of order all questions of more or less democracy in our type of society. All projects of democratization become for him necessarily (and not just empirically, as in many relevant cases) attempts to abolish the code of government and opposition and therefore by definition undemocratic. (See "The Theory of Political Opposition" [1987], in *Political Theory*, 167, 174–175.)

This analysis is open to immanent criticism. He asserts that the older govern-ment-governed code is not replaced but only supplemented by that of govern-ment-opposition. In this case, the issue of democracy as well as that of democratization can be redefined in terms of the relation of the two codes, the type of balance that is reached between them, and the conditions under which each has primacy. Luhmann has been able to do this quite well with the competing codes of organizations (see *Macht* [Stuttgart: Enke Verlag, 1975], chap. 3) and in the case of his analysis of the official and unofficial cycles of politics in terms of normality-conflict (see *Political Theory*, 48–50). The identification of democracy merely with the presence of the code government-opposition thus shields the code of government-governed from criticism. This position, on the level of political theory, does not support a viable political opposition and is compatible with its factual if not formal "disappearance" documented by Kirchheimer, for example. Luhmann admits as much (*Political Theory*, 177).

In our view, the viability of opposition, and therefore of democracy, is due only to the superiority of the code of government-opposition to that of government-governed. This superiority, or even a genuinely balanced relation between the two codes, depends on the establishment of a third code, one Luhmann rejects from the start: that of parliamentary and nonparliamentary politics, of political and civil society. This idea does, however, sneak back into his analysis in two places. First, the image of the "parasite" points to the public as the unintended beneficiary of the conflict of government and opposition. Excluded by the "formal" or "official" system of politics, and confined only to the "illusory" politics of elections, the public "sneaks back" on the informal or unofficial level due to the opportunities presented by a government protecting its position and an opposition seeking to take over. Both implicitly appeal to the public outside the formal system of decision making (*Political Theory*, 178–179). Second, actual antagonism between opposition and government does diminish since the two elements of a bipolar rather than hierarchical system actually presuppose each other, and hypothetically can always imagine themselves in place of the other. But Luhmann points out the tendency to produce verbal and even illusory conflicts, which he interprets as "a form of openness through which societal interests can be assigned to one side or another" (*Political Theory*, 184). He does not notice that unless social interests are actually organized and articulated by associations and organizations outside the political system, and unless these—in however a complex manner—are rearticulated and aggregated in the political system, the conflicts of the latter will be perceived as mere show, as mere "politics" in the negative sense of the term, with deeply damaging consequences for the code of government and opposition.

60. *Planung*, 44.

61. See Jürgen Habermas, *Legitimation Crisis* (Boston: Beacon Press, 1975), 130. His critique focuses on the issue of democratization of planning; our problem is the democratization of civil society and its mediations.

62. *Planung*, 10–12, 21.

63. Ibid., 21.

64. Ibid., 13.

65. Ibid., 20.

66. Ibid., 17.

67. Ibid., 26.

68. Ibid., 22–23.

69. Ibid., 27.

70. Ibid., 28. In the context of his less systematic analysis (his "political theory"), Luhmann is even less restrained in his use of the categories of civil society outside the political system proper. In particular, persons, law, and public opinion (note the correspondence to Habermas's three domains of the lifeworld: personality, society, and culture) are understood as "externalizing" forms of political problem solving outside the framework of the political system proper. See *Political Theory*, 60–62.

71. Ibid., 18–19.

72. Ibid., 13.

73. Ibid., 24–25.

74. A possibility once mentioned by Luhmann in regard to elections (see *Legitimation*, 162).

75. *Planung*, 26.

76. *Legitimation*, 158.

77. Ibid., 183.

78. Ibid., 190.

79. Ibid., 154, 161.

80. Ibid., 200.

81. Ibid., 158.

82. Ibid., 159.

83. Ibid., 169.

84. Ibid., 166–167.

85. Ibid., 161–163.

86. Ibid., 174, 190.

87. Ibid., 183ff.

88. These include the implicit distinction between "friend" and "enemy" in interactions; bargaining with selected important social interests; personal and group relations; and reliance on already packaged and bureaucratically managed information.

89. *Legitimation*, 194.

90. Ibid., 190 (our emphasis).

91. In a later text (*Political Theory*, 48–50), the official and unofficial versions of modern political process are presented in terms of two alternating cyclical dynamics. In the "official" cycle, the public influences political parties through elections, the parties set the boundaries and priorities for administrative decisions through legislative and other means, the administration subjects the public to its binding decisions, and so on. In the "unofficial" or "counter" cycle, the

administration drafts bills for the parliamentary parties, the parties influence the vote of the electorate, and the public influences the administration "through various channels, like interest groups and emotional appeals." Luhmann still asserts that the unofficial model (which in this version involves "civil society" in politics, although limited to corporatist and populist forms) prevails in normal cases. But he now argues that the official model, resting on "legally regulated authority" prevails in cases of conflict. In our view, this latter eventuality would involve the public in its peculiar mediating role, as an institution of both civil and political society. According to Luhmann, there is a balance between the two cycles that is slowly displaced toward the informal or unofficial model. This thesis links Luhmann to the Schmittian critique of parliamentarism, though less strongly than in the case of his earlier conception, which tended to reduce the official version to mere show. Indeed, the emphasis on the role of this version in cases of conflict represents an ironic, Schmittian reply to Schmitt who affirmed the irrelevance of formal institutions in "emergencies."

92. J. Schumpeter, *Capitalism, Socialism and Democracy*, 3d ed. (New York: Harper & Row, 1947), 291–292.

93. T. H. Marshall, "Citizenship and Social Class," in *Class, Citizenship and Social Development* (New York: Doubleday, 1964), 71ff.

94. Parsons, unlike Marshall, does not call these social prerequisites rights.

95. Talcott Parsons, *Politics and Social Structure* (New York: Free Press, 1969), 259–260; *The System of Modern Societies* (Englewood Cliffs, NJ: Prentice-Hall, 1971), 81–83.

96. See Parsons, *The System of Modern Societies*, 62–63; see also pages 92–94 for a discussion of the civic component in terms of differentiation rather than inclusion.

97. And this at a time when he was greatly under the influence of Parsons. See Niklas Luhmann, *Grundrechte als Institution* (Berlin: Duncker & Humblot, 1965; hereafter cited as *Grundrechte*). Admittedly he did not have access to Parsons's 1965 "Full Citizenship for the Negro American?" (reprinted in *Politics and Social Structure*), in which he introduced Marshall's framework. Whether or not he knew Parsons's conception of rights, his own roots in legal positivism pointed him primarily to the problem of differentiation because of an issue that was of little concern to Parsons: the self-limitation of the political through politically enacted law. The problem of inclusion, inherited from Marshall and Parsons, does make an appearance in a later work (*Political Theory*, 34–37), but the concept is here interpreted narrowly in terms of the political system and not in terms of the societal community or its stand-ins, which would provide more general social citizenship or membership. And while Luhmann notes the transformation, in the context of the development of the welfare state, of the semantics of political inclusion from benefits to claims, even this perception does not lead him to link the problem of inclusion to that of rights. Evidently, he links only Marshall's social dimension of citizenship to inclusion, and not the civil and political dimensions.

98. *Grundrechte*, 24.

99. See Günther Teubner, "Substantive and Reflexive Elements in Modern Law," *Law and Society Review* 17, no. 2 (1983): 239–301. Teubner points to the tension between the inflationary tendencies emanating from the political system's function of producing binding decisions and the need to manage the complicated input-output relations with other subsystems. In this argument, it is reflexivity that resolves the tension and gives rise to self-limitation. Just this self-limitation, we believe, represents the political side of rights creation, a point that Luhmann did not yet make in 1965. In our view, fundamental rights are the best examples of reflexive law (Teubner) or law as institution (Habermas).

100. *Grundrechte*, 23.

101. Ibid., 43, 182–183.

102. Ibid., 24, 41.

103. Ibid., 36.

104. Ibid., 63.

105. Ibid., 73.

106. Ibid., 76.

107. Ibid., 75 and esp. note 60.

108. Ibid., 81.

109. Ibid., 96, concerning the protection of marriage based on love, threatened by the family, not the state.

110. Ibid., 95, 99.

111. Ibid., 107.

112. Ibid., 115.

113. Ibid., 126.

114. *Differentiation*, 212–213.

115. In 1965, Luhmann did not yet affirm this position as clearly (see *Grundrechte*, 113 note 13) as he did in his 1970 essay "Wirtschaft als soziales System," in *Differentiation*, 190–225.

116. *Grundrechte*, 115; *Differentiation*, 201, 210–211.

117. *Grundrechte*, 115.

118. Ibid., 138ff., 151ff.

119. Ibid., 149.

120. Ibid., 140–144.

121. Ibid., 99. Later work seems to leave open the possibility that both models of differentiation might be used, one on the level of the science of politics and the other on the level of political theory (see *Political Theory*, 109 and note 100, 133 and note 28). See also note 38 above for this distinction of two types of theory, one interrogating the relevant participants and participating in politics by

observing and criticizing it from within, the other scientifically observing this sphere from the outside (including its self-observation).

122. This argument is made for the legal system as a whole in the 1976 essay "The Autonomy of the Legal System," in *Differentiation*, 128–129. It is, moreover, strongly implied that the end of the autonomy of the legal system—with law, for example, becoming a specification of politics (127)—would have consequences of dedifferentiation for society as a whole (130).

123. *Sociology of Law*, 17.

124. Niklas Luhmann, "Normen in soziologischer Perspektive," *Soziale Welt* 8, no. 20 (1969): 40; hereafter cited as "Normen."

125. Ibid., 47-48, for example. Luhmann often uses a concept of everyday life or lifeworld to indicate the roles, in interaction, of structures not taken up in differentiated subsystems. It is on this level that he repeatedly locates the bulk of normative experience and expectation. Unfortunately, the relation of lifeworld to system is not clarified in his model, and the usage seems inconsistent with his system/environment model of social systems and subsystems. Cf. *Sociology of Law*, 47.

126. "Normen," 37; *Sociology of Law*, 33. In contradistinction to Foucault, Luhmann distinguishes between "norm" and "normalization." Normalization represents a prenormative undifferentiated structure of expectation, involving no efforts to bring back to conformity the "deviant," whose behavior is not understood as "serious," "free," or "interested." Normalization aims at conditions rather than actions, and it involves no creation of "universal" standards (*Sociology of Law*, 36–37).

127. *Sociology of Law*, 77–80. This is our interpretation, on a lower level of abstraction, of Luhmann's own definition of law as "congruently generalized normative behavioral expectations" (77).

128. "Normen," 30–31; *Sociology of Law*, 24ff.

129. "Normen," 32; *Sociology of Law*, 27.

130. *Sociology of Law*, 26.

131. "Normen," 33ff.; *Sociology of Law*, 29ff.

132. "Normen," 33; *Sociology of Law*, 30–31. It is crucial as well as possible to refute Luhmann's premise that normative learning is a contradiction in terms (see chapter 9). In particular, the notion of the communicative creation or revision of norms, marginalized by Luhmann, is a clue to the direction this demonstration might take. Linked to the idea of critical communication about norms, the notion of counterfactuality can be brought to bear in connection with learning through the Piaget-Kohlberg-Habermas model of moral development. Luhmann's own model of a normative style of expectation is identified only with a traditional or conventional attitude toward norms. Paradoxically, as the empirically based ontogenetic model of Kohlberg shows, a cognitive attitude toward norms represents the lowest level of normative development. For Luhmann, only a

retreat to exactly this attitude would represent learning. An answer to him is possible only if a postconventional relationship to norms could be shown to be compatible with a normative (counterfactual) structure. It seems that, for Habermas at least, counterfactuality persists on the level of the ideal conditions of discourse, not to be identified with the empirical processes of coming to an understanding, which nevertheless presuppose them (see chapter 8).

133. *Sociology of Law*, 38–40.

134. Ibid., 49ff.

135. Ibid., 51–52.

136. Ibid., 78–79, 84–85.

137. Ibid., 138.

138. *Differentiation*, 95.

139. Quasi-medium because in *Sociology of Law*, 167–168, Luhmann never actually assigns the role of translating selectivity or selective decisions to procedure, and he speaks only of "the selection of collectively binding decisions." Indeed, his major work in the sociology of law never treats law directly as a medium and is therefore ambiguous about the status of law as a subsystem of society. Subsequent works are clearer on this issue. In the conception of law as an autopoietic, self-referential subsystem, normatively closed and cognitively open, its full equality with other autonomous subsystems is at least asserted. See, e.g., the chapter on law in *Ecological Communication. Political Theory*, 82ff., is alone, however, in treating law as a medium, entirely parallel to money.

140. *Sociology of Law*, 160.

141. *Differentiation*, 104.

142. Ibid., 122, 132.

143. *Sociology of Law*, 188.

144. Ibid., 187.

145. *Differentiation*, 132.

146. Niklas Luhmann, "The Self-Reproduction of Law and Its Limits," in G. Teubner, ed., *Dilemmas of Law in the Welfare State* (Berlin: de Gruyter, 1986), 113.

147. Ibid., 113, 124.

148. "Normen," 47.

149. *Sociology of Law*, 161–162, 182.

150. Ibid., 182–183.

151. "Normen," 46–47. Interestingly enough, Luhmann's conception, in which the counterfactual, normative orientation of the judges represents the sole guarantee of the reproduction of law as a normative system, comes close to H. L. A. Hart's insistence that in a legal order judges (or "officials") must be able to assume an internal-evaluative (rather than merely observational) perspective with regard to the validity of laws. But the differences between Hart and

Luhmann are even more instructive, because for the former the division of the population into officials and all others represents an almost pathological limiting case of what still constitutes a legal order. In any "healthy" society, Hart tells us, many ordinary people ("normally . . . the majority of society") regularly take the internal perspective, although it must be assumed that there are some who merely wish to observe whether or not certain laws are followed and enforced, and act accordingly. See H. L. A. Hart, *The Concept of Law* (Oxford: Oxford University Press, 1961), 86–88, 113. We should note that the meaning of the internal perspective in Hart is not reduced, as it is in Luhmann, to a more or less conventional unwillingness to learn in order to maintain counterfactual norms, but is expressed in terms of a critical-evaluative attitude that involves a postconventional, reflective attitude. Undoubtedly, both of these and even their combination are possible in the case of judgments of legal validity.

152. *Sociology of Law*, 201.

153. Ibid., 202.

154. Luhmann, "The Self-Reproduction of Law," 113.

Chapter 8

1. For the best recent defense of rights-oriented liberalism, see Ronald Dworkin, *Taking Rights Seriously* (Cambridge: Harvard University Press, 1978). For a good discussion of the liberal ideal of neutrality, see Charles Larmore, *Patterns of Moral Complexity* (Cambridge, England: Cambridge University Press, 1987).

2. See Carole Pateman, *Participation and Democratic Theory* (Cambridge, England: Cambridge University Press, 1970), and *The Problem of Political Obligation: A Critical Analysis of Liberal Theory* (New York: Wiley, 1979). See also C. B. MacPherson, *The Life and Times of Liberal Democracy* (Oxford: Oxford University Press, 1977), and *Democratic Theory* (Oxford: Clarendon Press, 1973).

3. We are thinking here of key dimensions of the "new social movements" in the West, including the ecology, citizen initiative, feminist, and peace movements, and Poland's Solidarity in the East. For a discussion of these new movements, see chapter 10. See also Andrew Arato, "Civil Society vs. the State," *Telos*, no. 50 (Winter, 1981–82): 19–48: Jean L. Cohen, "Rethinking Social Movements," *Berkeley Journal of Sociology* 28 (1983): 97–113, and "Strategy or Identity: New Theoretical Paradigms and Contemporary Social Movements," *Social Research* 52, no. 4 (Winter 1985): 663–716; Andrew Arato and Jean L. Cohen, "The German Green Party," *Dissent* 8 (Summer 1984): 327–333, and "Social Movements, Civil Society and the Problem of Sovereignty," *Praxis International* 4, no. 3 (1984): 266–283.

4. Andrew Arato and Jean L. Cohen, "Civil Society and Social Theory," *Thesis Eleven*, no. 21 (1988): 40–64. See chapters 4 and 6. The same holds true for Niklas Luhmann (see chapter 7).

5. Jean L. Cohen, *Class Society and Civil Society: The Limits of Marxian Critical Theory* (Amherst: University of Massachusetts Press, 1982).

6. What follows is a restatement of the core assumptions of discourse ethics that are shared, despite different formulations, by the two main propounders of the theory: Jürgen Habermas and Karl-Otto Apel. We rely for the most part on Habermas's version. Whether discourse ethics can be given a transcendental (Apel), a universal-pragmatic (Habermas), or only a historical (Castoriadis) foundation, and whether rational argument (Habermas) or decision (Heller) is to have ultimate priority in relation to our "choice" for such an ethics remains an open question. An impressive debate between Castoriadis and Habermas in Dubrovnik, Yugoslavia, in 1982 convinced us that equally good arguments can be given for historicity and universality. It has also become clear from this debate that the common element in the two positions is the duality of levels of analysis: Stronger types of argumentation are necessary for the meta level (the procedural level of institutionalization) than for the historical level (that which is already instituted). For the work of Karl-Otto Apel, upon which we rely, see *Towards the Transformation of Philosophy* (London: Routledge and Kegan Paul, 1980), 225–285, and "Normative Ethics and Strategic Rationality: The Philosophical Problem of a Political Ethic," *The Graduate Faculty Philosophy Journal* 9, no. 1 (Winter 1982): 81–109. For Jürgen Habermas, see "Discourse Ethics: Notes on a Program of Philosophical Justification," in his book *Moral Consciousness and Communicative Action* (Cambridge: MIT Press, 1990).

7. These two dimensions are separable, with the first having priority. See Habermas, "Discourse Ethics," and also his reply to Lukes in John B. Thompson and David Held, eds., *Habermas: Critical Debates* (Cambridge: MIT Press, 1982), 254.

8. See also Apel, "Normative Ethics," 100–101.

9. Jürgen Habermas, "A Reply to My Critics," in Thompson and Held, eds., *Habermas: Critical Debates*, 257. See also Jürgen Habermas, *Legitimation Crisis* (Boston: Beacon Press, 1975), 89, and "Discourse Ethics."

10. See Thomas McCarthy, *The Critical Theory of Jürgen Habermas* (Cambridge: MIT Press, 1978), 325; Albrecht Wellmer, *Praktische Philosophie und Theorie der Gesellschaft* (Konstanz: Universitätsverlag Konstanz, 1979), 10–11; Apel, *Towards the Transformation of Philosophy*, 227, 258–259.

11. Jürgen Habermas, "Wahrheitstheorien," in *Wirklichkeit und Reflexion: Festschrift fur Walter Schulz* (Pfullingen, 1973), 251–252, quoted in McCarthy, *Critical Theory*, 316. See also Habermas, "Discourse Ethics," 99ff., for the most recent formulation of the rules of argumentation.

12. For a succinct formulation in English, see Seyla Benhabib, *Critique, Norm, and Utopia* (New York: Columbia University Press, 1986), 284–285.

13. See Apel, *Towards the Transformation of Philosophy*, 238–239, where he so characterizes the processes of bourgeois democracy.

14. Habermas, "Reply," 257. See also Wellmer, *Praktische Philosophie*, 33–34.

15. Habermas, "Discourse Ethics," 67.

16. For a good discussion of this point, see Alessandro Ferrara, "A Critique of Habermas' Discourse Ethic," *Telos*, no. 64 (Summer 1985): 45–74.

17. Habermas, "Discourse Ethics," 68–76.

18. Habermas, *Legitimation Crisis*, 108. McCarthy stresses this dimension of the theory, while Wellmer's texts attempt to residualize it.

19. Habermas, "Discourse Ethics," 65.

20. The best discussions are by Albrecht Wellmer, "Zur Kritik der Diskursethik," in *Ethik und Dialog* (Frankfurt: Suhrkamp, 1986), and Agnes Heller, "The Discourse Ethic of Habermas: Critique and Appraisal," in *Thesis Eleven*, no. 10/11 (1985): 5–17. Most discussions of the theory of discourse ethics center around its ability to serve as a general moral theory. Ours is, we believe, the first comprehensive discussion of its ability to serve as a theory of democratic legitimacy and basic rights.

21. Habermas, *Legitimation Crisis*, 88; see also Jürgen Habermas, "Legitimation Problems and the Modern State," in *Communication and the Evolution of Society* (Boston: Beacon Press, 1979). To put this another way, Habermas's discourse ethics can be seen as a "post-Hegelian" attempt to bring together the liberal principle of basic rights (and the conception of negative liberty) and the ancient republican (and early modern) conception of positive freedom within the framework of a theory that presupposes differentiation. Unlike the Hegelian model, however, the theory of discourse ethics does not lead one to construe the normative conception of politics (or the normative principles underlying law) in terms of a monistic, substantive, and ultimately nondemocratic conception of ethical life. Instead, as a theory of democratic legitimacy, discourse ethics makes it possible to conceive of a new form of public freedom appropriate to a plurality of forms of life, one that presupposes and in part justifies the principle of basic rights; see Jean L. Cohen, "Morality or *Sittlichkeit*: Towards a Post-Hegelian Solution," *Cardoso Law Review* 10, nos. 5–6 (March/April 1989): 1389–1414.

22. Heller, "The Discourse Ethic," 7; Wellmer, "Zur Kritik der Diskursethik," 51–55.

23. For a critique of the public/private dichotomy along these lines, see Susan Okin, *Justice, Gender and the Family* (New York: Basic Books, 1989). Okin challenges the assumption that because the family is a "private realm," it is "beyond justice." She convincingly argues that the "circumstances of justice" discussed by Hume and Rawls obtain in the family: Husbands, wives, and children have differing as well as common interests. Accordingly, rights can be claimed by all family members. Our inclusion of the family within civil society accords with this argument. Of course, family law differs from contract or administrative law, but this "private sphere" is nonetheless legally regulated, even if certain decisions within it are deemed private.

24. Habermas, *Legitimation Crisis*, 87–89. For a good discussion of Wellmer's critique, see Alessandro Ferrara, "Critical Theory and Its Discontents: On Wellmer's Critique of Habermas," *Praxis International* 9, no. 3 (October 1989): 305–320.

25. Habermas specifically addresses Weber's version of this thesis.

26. Habermas, *Legitimation Crisis*, 95–117; also his *The Theory of Communicative Action*, vol. 1 (Boston: Beacon Press, 1984), 254–270.

27. Some clarification is needed here. Habermas presents discourse ethics as a general moral theory. In so doing, he distinguishes between the moral point of view ("the right") and matters of individual or group identity or cultural value systems ("the good"). His own version of the public/private dichotomy thus refers to the distinction between universalistic moral principles (public) and particular values that inform a person's way of life, identity needs, life plan, etc. (private). While he argues that cultural values can become candidates for general societal norms, the distinction rests on the assumption that those cultural values, identity needs, and components of forms of life that cannot be universalized do not belong to the realm of the moral but involve aesthetic-evaluative issues instead. This type of claim causes heated debate among moral theorists. Some argue that one can never sever the right from the good. Others argue that this way of separating the two needlessly narrows the domain of the moral while unacceptably demoting questions of the good from matters of principle to matters of taste. We have attempted to circumvent the debate at this level by casting discourse ethics as a specific subset of moral theory, one that deals with the underlying principles of legitimate decision making in a constitutional democracy. But our version of the theory does presuppose a domain of autonomous moral judgment that constitutes a limit to the reach of democratic decision making. This "domain" is itself recognized by the principle of fundamental rights, which, as we shall show, stands in a complex relationship to the principles of discourse ethics. Accordingly, what we are calling "private" refers to the moral reflections and choices of individuals as well as their judgments regarding their projects and identity needs. Privacy rights, as we shall see, secure precisely this terrain. While all rights are connected to a public principle in that they must be asserted, agreed upon, and institutionalized as law, what they protect, especially in the case of privacy, becomes off-limits to public, legal, or political control. In other words, publicly articulated, legally protected privacy rights constitute a realm of autonomous judgment that is beyond political regulation. However, privacy as such is not attached to a particular institutional domain but refers to aspects of individual functioning in all domains of life. Moreover, this conception of privacy is not based on an atomistic model of the sovereign subject or asocial individual. On the contrary, precisely because individuals develop their personal and collective identities in complex interactive processes and are always embedded in a web of relations with others, and because there is a plurality of moral conceptions in any modern civil society, the capacity to make autonomous moral choices and the ability to develop personal projects require protection and recognition. On this interactive or intersubjective conception of individuality, communication with others in the form of giving reasons or explaining identity needs has, of course, a central role to play. But so does ideal as opposed to real dialogue, withdrawal from as well as participation in interaction. Moreover, communicative interaction is not the same as discourse. Indeed, we agree

with Habermas that those values, identity needs, components of forms of life, and individual projects that cannot be universalized are not subject to the strictures of discourse ethics, although we would not deny them a moral status. In short, we assume that there are two normative realms: the private and the public. The private refers to autonomous, individual moral reflection, decision, judgment, and responsibility; the public refers to the reach of legal and political norms or justice. We thus simultaneously narrow the reach of discourse ethics, unburdening it of the weight of being a general moral theory, and extend the status of the moral to what has been deemed private.

28. Jürgen Habermas, "Civil Disobedience: Litmus Test for the Democratic Constitutional State," *Berkeley Journal of Sociology* 30 (1985): 95–116. For a full discussion of these issues, see chapter 11.

29. See chapter 8 for a full discussion of this point. See also the chapter on civil disobedience in Dworkin, *Taking Rights Seriously*, 206–222.

30. Ferrara argues this point well. However, his analysis focuses primarily on discourse ethics as a general moral theory and does not clarify the issue with respect to a theory of political legitimacy. See Ferrara, "A Critique of Habermas' Discourse Ethic," 71–74. It is a common mistake of interpreters to assume that discourse ethics naively implies the possibility and validity of any consensus in practical discourse. This is not the point. Rather, discourse ethics articulates the criteria that must guide practical discussions on norms and that may or may not lead to agreement. A consensus that violates the principles of discourse ethics could not be called rational.

31. Habermas argues that the step from virtual to actual discourse must be taken in the moral domain. But we find Wellmer's critique of this claim to be strong. Wellmer denies that an actual discourse is required in the moral domain. He also argues that the presuppositions of argument do not suffice to sustain a moral principle. Since we do not want to take a stand on the question of which type of postconventional moral theory constitutes the highest stage of moral reasoning, we grant that principled postconventional moral reasoning need not involve an actual dialogue. Neither Kantian nor utilitarian moral theory requires it, yet both are postconventional on Habermas's criteria. For a discussion of this issue, see Thomas McCarthy, "Rationality and Relativism: Habermas' 'Overcoming' of Hermeneutics," in Thompson and Held, eds., *Habermas: Critical Debates*, 57–78. See also Wellmer, *Ethik und Dialog*, 102–113.

32. See Wellmer, *Praktische Philosophie*, 11, 31ff.

33. Cited in Jürgen Habermas, "Die Utopie des guten Herrschers," in *Kultur und Kritik* (Frankfurt: Suhrkamp, 1973), 386; Alvin Gouldner, *The Future of Intellectuals and the Rise of the New Class* (New York: Seabury, 1979), 38–39.

34. Habermas, "Utopie des guten Herrschers," 387.

35. Jürgen Habermas, *Theory and Practice* (Boston: Beacon Press, 1973), 37–40.

36. Apel goes even further and explicitly postulates a dialectical relation between the "real communication community" and the "ideal" one, according to which

the second is counterfactually anticipated in the first as a "real possibility" (*Towards the Transformation of Philosophy*, 280–281). Apel oscillates between two positions: one that sees existing forms of democracy as forms of "empirical consensus" and assigns the status of a "real communication community" (laden with possibility) to all communities, and another that finds the institutions of contemporary democracies to be the loci of the dialectic between real and ideal communication ("Normative Ethics," 102–103).

37. Wellmer, *Praktische Philosophie*, 46–47.

38. Heller, "The Discourse Ethic," 13–16.

39. Wellmer, "Über Vernunft, Emanzipation, und Utopie," in *Ethik und Dialog*, 208–221.

40. Habermas, *Legitimation Crisis*, 89, and "Discourse Ethics," 65–66.

41. Ibid.

42. McCarthy, *Critical Theory*, 327–328.

43. Habermas, *Legitimation Crisis*, 65–117.

44. Ibid. See also Habermas, "Reply," 257–258; McCarthy, *Critical Theory*, 331, and Habermas, "Utopie des guten Herrschers," 384.

45. Habermas, "Discourse Ethics," 72.

46. Ibid.

47. Wellmer, "Über Vernunft," 206.

48. See the excursus on Tugendhat in Habermas, "Discourse Ethics," 68-76. Seyla Benhabib, "In the Shadow of Aristotle and Hegel: Communicative Ethics and Current Controversies in Practical Philosophy," in Michael Kelly, ed., *Hermeneutics and Critical Theory in Ethics and Politics* (Cambridge: MIT Press, 1990), 1–31, also eliminates the principle of universalization but, unlike Tugendhat, insists on the cognitive character of discourse ethics.

49. Habermas, "Discourse Ethics," 74.

50. Habermas, *Legitimation Crisis*, 105.

51. Ibid.

52. We owe this insight to Alessandro Ferrara.

53. This is the position of Agnes Heller in *Beyond Justice* (Oxford: Blackwell, 1987). For a critique of Heller's decisionism, see Jean L. Cohen, "Heller, Habermas and Justice," *Praxis International* 8, no. 4 (January 1989): 491–497.

54. Heller, "The Discourse Ethic," 13–14.

55. Habermas, *Communication and the Evolution of Society*, 183.

56. On Habermas's view, lifeworld is the complementary concept to communicative action, and discourse is a reflective form of communicative action. While language and culture constitutive of identity form a background, the structural components of lifeworld—cultural models of nature and our place in it, legitimately ordered interpersonal relations, personality structures and capabilities—

also double as components of the objective, social, and subjective worlds that we can thematize and reflect upon. The decentered structure of the modern understanding of the world and the differentiation among our formal world concepts means that "the lifeworld loses its prejudgmental power over everyday communicative practice to the degree that actors owe their mutual understanding to their own interpretative performances" (Habermas, *The Theory of Communicative Action*, vol. 2 [Boston: Beacon Press, 1987], 133). In other words, once the reproduction of the structural components of the lifeworld is no longer merely routed through the medium of communicative action, but is saddled upon the interpretative accomplishments of the actors themselves, core components of individual and collective identities lose their "givenness." It becomes possible to reflect upon these identities and to assess dimensions of them critically from the moral point of view and also from the point of view of projects for self-realization. Discourses, the most demanding form of communicative action, do not create collective identities out of nothing, but collective identities can be reaffirmed, revised, or reinterpreted in the process of discourses.

57. Habermas, *Communication and the Evolution of Society*, 184. Habermas argues that this level is reached, in theory at least, with Rousseau and Kant. Unlike Weber, Habermas finds more in natural law theories of obligation than a "metaphysics of reason" that, upon its dissolution, leaves only positive laws and legal procedures as their own self-legitimation. He finds, in short, the idea of a rational agreement under conditions of symmetric reciprocity, which he reformulates as the procedural principle of democratic legitimacy.

58. For us, the concept of identity does not replace practical reason in political ethics. Rather, it links or mediates between principles of practical reason (the procedural moment) and particular interests or need-interpretations.

59. Habermas, "Discourse Ethics," 104.

60. This paradox has led to opposing interpretations of discourse ethics. For example, Alessandro Ferrara, in "Critical Theory and Its Discontents," has interpreted it quite rigorously as a deontological theory that excludes the possibility of a discourse on need-interpretations or cultural values. Conversely, Seyla Benhabib, in "In the Shadow of Aristotle and Hegel," 16, maintains that the discussion of need-interpretations has a place in discourse ethics, provided that it is given a "weak" deontological interpretation, and that such a discourse renders our conceptions of the good life accessible to moral reflection and moral transformation. There is ample evidence to argue that in his more recent work Habermas still assumes that the need-interpretations of those potentially affected by a norm are appropriate content for discourse, but this interpretation makes sense only if one takes the meaning of the term "generalizable interest" in Habermas's version of the principle of universalization to refer to those need-interpretations based on cultural values that *are* universalizable (see "Discourse Ethics," 104). The oddity of Benhabib's position is that she wants to drop Habermas's "reformulated principle of universalization" from the theory while claiming that questions of the good life are accessible to moral reflection. This

position confuses matters of self-realization with matters of (moral) self-development, under the mistaken notion that because we can communicate about, discuss, and thereby render fluid our need-interpretations, these sorts of discussions amount to a discourse. But this is not, strictly speaking, the case for Habermas. Discussion is not the same as discourse. Rather, the discourse in which need-interpretations enter is a discourse that would draw the line between the right and the good in terms of what is generalizable and what must remain particular. The principle of universalization is essential to such an endeavor. Once that line is drawn, need-interpretations can become matters of discussion and critique but not of argumentative discourse in the strict sense. While we agree with Benhabib that one cannot draw the line between the right and the good a priori, it is our position that one cannot adequately assess how dimensions of the good enter into discourse ethics unless one retains the principle of universalization and introduces an intermediary variable—the concept of identity—into the consideration of generalizable interests. Otherwise, one tends to dissolve the distinction between the right and the good that remains the rock on which Habermas's theory stands or falls.

61. Charles Taylor, "Die Motive einer Verfahrensethik," in Wolfgang Kuhlman, ed., *Moralität und Sittlichkeit* (Frankfurt: Suhrkamp, 1986), 101–134.

62. Habermas, "Discourse Ethics," 106.

63. See Benhabib, *Critique, Norm, and Utopia*, 327–353; Ferrara, "A Critique of Habermas' Discourse Ethic." Ferrara's discussion is pertinent to our concerns. His best insight is that the very principle of universalization offered by Habermas implies that considerations of identity are central to discourse ethics. He rightly notes that disputes over the legitimacy of norms involve the clash of different identities in complex societies and that Habermas presupposes a concept of autonomy quite different from that of Kant, namely, one that combines dignity with many-sided development (the capacity to live one's life to the fullest, according to one's chosen life plan). In an extremely suggestive passage, he calls for including in the proceduralist notion of justice a "formal" concept of the good, understood as respect for the identity needs of each individual. This formal concept focuses on the integrity of individual identities potentially affected by a norm under consideration. However, Ferrara does not distinguish between discourse ethics as a general moral theory and as a theory of political legitimacy. Indeed, the bulk of his argument is addressed to the theory as a moral theory. Hence, it differs fundamentally from ours. Moreover, the theoretical means Ferrara uses to make his case are unconvincing. He sees the standard of the "least disruptive impact on identity needs of all concerned" as external to the principle of justice, that is, as an additional principle meant to balance the principle of justice. Indeed, he goes so far as to say that "if, after the ideal speech situation has come to a satisfactory close, one feels the best argument fails to do complete justice to some identity needs that to one's considered judgment would best be met by a solution in favor of which one is not able to make the best argument, then one is justified in disregarding the outcome of the ideal speech situation and acting on one's best intuition" (70). Such a position is confusing

with regard to a general moral theory and dangerous with regard to the theory of political legitimacy if left unqualified. If Ferrara means that one may engage in conscientious refusal or civil disobedience over threatened identity needs, this is fine, but if he means that one can simply disregard the outcome of a democratic discussion, then the problem of maintaining commitment to democratic procedure would be overwhelming. Our analysis of the relation between morality and legality on one side, and justice and solidarity on the other, resolves the difficulties.

64. Jürgen Habermas, "Justice and Solidarity: On the Discussion Concerning Stage 6," in Thomas E. Wren, ed., *The Moral Domain: Essays in the Ongoing Debate between Philosophy and the Social Sciences* (Cambridge: MIT Press, 1990), 242.

65. Ibid.; see also Habermas's essay "Morality and Ethical Life: Does Hegel's Critique of Kant Apply to Discourse Ethics?," in *Moral Consciousness and Communicative Action.*

66. Habermas, "Justice and Solidarity," 243, and "Morality and Ethical Life," 199–202.

67. Habermas, "Justice and Solidarity," 225, and Jürgen Habermas, *The Philosophical Discourse of Modernity* (Cambridge: MIT Press, 1987), 337–366.

68. Habermas, "Justice and Solidarity," 245–246.

69. Ibid., 243.

70. Ibid., 243–244.

71. Ibid., 244.

72. Ibid. 247.

73. Ibid.

74. Habermas, "Morality and Ethical Life," 203.

75. Ibid., 205.

76. Ibid. , 202.

77. Ibid., 203–204.

78. Ibid., 202.

79. Habermas, "Justice and Solidarity," 245–246. Habermas states that these limits can be broken through if discourses have been institutionalized. By implication, discourse ethics reconstructs the moral intuitions of those living in modern civil societies. or in societies in which discourses or basic rights are in place.

80. Habermas, "Morality and Ethical Life," 205.

81. Habermas, "Justice and Solidarity," 246–247.

82. Ibid., 247.

83. Habermas, "Discourse Ethics," 100.

84. Habermas, "Morality and Ethical Life," 207.

85. Habermas, *Moral Consciousness and Communicative Action*, 183. Alessandro Ferrara has pointed out that this argument would probably satisfy neither the antimodern traditionalist, who would reject the prospect of bringing one's norm orientation to the postconventional level, given the anomie, uncertainty, and lack of social integration that are linked with modernity, nor the postmodernist, who would contend that the experience of normativity is just another expression of power. This latter objection was discussed in chapter 6; the former will be taken up in chapter 9. Here, we simply note that the theory's obvious bias in favor of modernity does not mean that it is an apologist for existing institutions or processes of modernization. Instead, discourse ethics, in conjunction with a dualistic social theory, provides a critical stance vis-à-vis the "colonization" of the lifeworld. Nor does the theory pose an abstract *ought* in favor of modernization to traditional societies. It does, however, help to unmask strategies of *retraditionalization* in already modernizing lifeworlds. These can be interpreted as power struggles in favor of hierarchical, authoritarian, and patriarchal forms of life against egalitarian, democratic, and nonsexist institutions that are at least potentially possible on the terrain of a modern lifeworld.

86. The opposite charge, that discourse ethics is so formalistic that it has no institutional consequences, has two variants: one that accepts the project of a discursive ethics but searches for institutional mediation, and one that contests the project altogether. For the first, see Jean L. Cohen, "Why More Political Theory?," *Telos*, no. 49 (Summer 1979): 70–94, and Jack Mendelson, "The Habermas–Gadamer Debate," *New German Critique*, no. 18 (1979): 44–73. For the second, see Seyla Benhabib, "Modernity and the Aporias of Critical Theory," *Telos*, no. 49 (Fall 1981): 39–59, and Steven Lukes, "Of Gods and Demons: Habermas and Practical Reason," in Thompson and Held, eds., *Habermas: Critical Debates*, 134–148.

87. Habermas, *Communication and the Evolution of Society*, 183, 186–187.

88. It is no accident that Hannah Arendt mistranslates the Aristotelian concept of *isonomia* to mean "no rule" instead of "participating in ruling and being ruled." See Hannah Arendt, *The Human Condition* (Chicago: University of Chicago Press, 1958), 22.

89. Habermas, *Communication and the Evolution of Society*, 186.

90. Ibid.

91. Ibid.

92. Habermas, "Utopie des guten Herrschers," 382. The first major discussion of the institutionalization of discourses or the creation of public spaces in Habermas's work is in *The Structural Transformation of the Public Sphere: An Inquiry into a Category of Bourgeois Society* [1962] (Cambridge: MIT Press, 1989).

93. Habermas, *Theory and Practice*, 25; McCarthy, *Critical Theory*, 324.

94. Habermas, *Theory and Practice*, 25–26; Habermas, "Utopie des guten Herrschers," 383. The thesis of the bourgeois public sphere involves the idea that the new principle of democratic legitimacy affects power through an institution-

alization of public spaces, such as parliaments, which exercise control over executive power (in principle, at least). But in his critique of Rousseau for having confused the level of the principle of legitimacy with that of organization, Habermas does not seem to realize that precisely this step allowed Rousseau to move from a virtual to an actual discourse model (*Communication and the Evolution of Society*, 185–186). Nevertheless, identifying democratic legitimacy or even actual democratic consensus with a single model of organization remains untenable. On the other hand, as merely a principle of legitimacy, democracy can easily become a source of "legitimation" for nondemocratic practices.

95. Habermas, "Utopie des guten Herrschers," 383.

96. Ibid.

97. Ibid. Another split occurs between "realistic" democratic elite theory and Marxist critiques of formal democracy. See Habermas, *Theory and Practice*, 27.

98. Habermas, "Die Utopie des guten Herrschers," 385.

99. Ibid., 383, and Habermas, *Legitimation Crisis*, 130ff.

100. Habermas, "Reply," 252.

101. Jürgen Habermas, *Theory of Communicative Action*, vol. 2, 524ff. For the most detailed but one-sided version, see Habermas, *Structural Transformation*, 181–250. See also Cohen, "Why More Political Theory?"

102. Habermas, *Theory of Communicative Action*, vol. 2, 362. We offer a more detailed discussion of this problem in chapter 9.

103. Ibid., 364. With regard to the democratic state's forerunner, the *Rechtsstaat*, which now becomes paradoxically the only unambiguous stage guaranteeing freedom, the democratic state gains on the level of the principle of legitimacy and loses on the level of actual institutional development—a strange conclusion that Habermas might not want to claim.

104. There seems to be a significant difference in the way Habermas handles the problem of institutions from the two key normative points of view established by discourse ethics: democratic legitimacy and basic rights. The former leads to a blind alley, but the latter seems promising because, once Habermas shifts the analysis of rights from the conceptual framework of normative development/institutional decline to the system/lifeworld dichotomy, rights appear to establish that basic minimum on the institutional level that is needed for discourse ethics, and the possibility of dualistic development opens up.

105. For a discussion of this idea, see Claude Lefort, "Politics and Human Rights," in *The Political Forms of Modern Society* (Cambridge: MIT Press, 1986). Lefort draws on Hannah Arendt's *On Totalitarianism* (New York, 1958), 296, for this idea.

106. For the idea of fundamental universal rights in the strong sense, see Dworkin, "Taking Rights Seriously," in *Taking Rights Seriously*.

107. See Janos Kis, *L'Egale Dignité* (Paris: Seuil, 1989).

108. Albrecht Wellmer, "Models of Freedom in the Modern World," in Kelly, ed., *Hermeneutics and Critical Theory in Ethics and Politics*, 247.

109. McCarthy, *Critical Theory*, 327–328, 352. There is no reason why aspects of the various conceptions of autonomy cannot be combined. Thus, autonomy in the sense of moral self-legislation and judgment (Kant), the ability to choose one's own plan of life and path of self-development (Mill), and the ability to take on dialogue roles and achieve reflexivity vis-à-vis these roles and also to take on the role of the other (Habermas) are all constituent components of the idea of autonomy at issue here. Needless to say, we assume that it is possible to formulate a conception of autonomy that avoids the self-monitoring, repressive tendencies associated with the idea of mastery, so relentlessly criticized by Foucault.

110. Wellmer, "Models of Freedom," 241.

111. Ibid., 227–252.

112. Benhabib, "In the Shadow of Aristotle and Hegel."

113. This would amount to a reversal of the classical liberal approach, which views the rights of communication (assembly, association, media) and political participation (suffrage, office holding) as instrumental to securing the core complex of rights: those that institute the domain of negative liberty (which may be construed in an extreme libertarian form such that private property is the core right and the core to the concept of rights, or in a less extreme liberal form that allows for welfare and other types of property ownership). In our view, though, the rights to communication do more than protect a domain of civil society from the state. They are also the political preconditions for democratic will formation. Indeed, democratic legitimacy and participation are generated on this very terrain.

114. Habermas, "Morality and Ethical Life," 205.

115. Ibid., 268.

116. Habermas, *Theory of Communicative Action*, vol. 2, 362–363. This text has no parallel reservations about institutionalizing liberties.

117. It may still be objected that norms are defensible precisely as institutions (as is done by Parsons and, at times, by Habermas). In this case, we would have to speak about institutional development vis-à-vis rights as opposed to organizational decline. We have, however, begun with a usage that juxtaposes norms (legitimacy) to institutionalization or organization.

118. Lefort also gives a convincing argument against the liberal ideology of rights that construes them as exclusively moral and apolitical guarantors of negative liberty. Marx himself was seduced by this interpretation to envision a society that did not need rights. It would be disastrous to reproduce such an interpretation because the only possible conclusions would be, once again, apology or revolution, and we seek a way beyond this unacceptable set of alternatives.

119. Jürgen Habermas, "On Social Identity," *Telos*, no. 19 (Spring 1974), 100.

120. See Jürgen Habermas, "The New Obscurity: The Crisis of the Welfare State and the Exhaustion of Utopian Energies," in *The New Conservatism: Cultural Criticism and the Historians' Debate* (Cambridge: MIT Press, 1985). See also Andrew Arato and Jean L. Cohen, "Politics and the Reconstruction of the Concept of Civil Society," in Axel Honneth et al., eds., *Zwischenbetracthungen Im Prozess der Aufklärung* (Frankfurt: Suhrkamp, 1989).

121. Habermas, *Theory of Communicative Action*, vol. 2, chaps. 6 and 8.

122. Wellmer, "Über Vernunft," 198.

123. Ibid., 214–221.

124. Ibid.

125. Ibid., 220.

126. Ibid., 198.

127. Ibid., 209.

128. Ibid., 175–181.

129. Ibid., 190–199.

130. Ibid, 216–217.

131. Ibid., 189–199.

132. Ibid, 178–179.

133. Ibid., 200–201.

134. With respect to Hegel, this involves two levels of mediation rather than one, namely, political and economic society. His theory involves the former only, in a different, more dialectical terminology.

135. Unlike Parsons's concept of societal community, however, our conception of civil society is itself "decentered." It is not construed as a collectivity (of collectivities) or as a unified social body integrating the whole of society, but as the plural, differentiated, institutional dimension of the lifeworld.

136. Guillermo O'Donnell and Philippe Schmitter, *Transitions from Authoritarian Rule* (Baltimore: Johns Hopkins, 1986). This work demonstrates that projects for total revolution do not yield political democracy. The same point has been argued in the context of "totalitarian" regimes by Kuron's theory of self-limiting revolution. See Andrew Arato, "The Democratic Theory of the Polish Opposition: Normative Intentions and Strategic Ambiguities," *Working Papers of the Helen Kellogg Institute* (Notre Dame, 1984).

137. Karl Marx, *The Eighteenth Brumaire of Louis Bonaparte* (New York: International Publishers, 1969), 66.

138. Arato and Cohen, "The Politics of Civil Society."

139. For a more detailed discussion of the influence of civil on political society, see chapters 9 and 10.

140. G. D. H. Cole, *Guild Socialism Restated* (New Brunswick, NJ: Transaction Books, 1980); Harold Laski, *Studies in the Problem of Sovereignty* (New Haven: Yale

University Press, 1917), *Authority in the Modern State* (New Haven: Yale University Press, 1919), and *The Foundations of Sovereignty and Other Essays* (New York: Harcourt Brace, 1921).

141. For a discussion of the importance of democratizing neocorporate structures of compromise, see Habermas, *Structural Transformation*, sec. 23.

Chapter 9

1. As we have seen, even Luhmann's defense of differentiation does not redound to the benefit of civil society, whose institutions his conception absorbs into the political system.

2. Habermas reintroduced the concept of civil society in his comprehensive examination of one of its basic categories: the public sphere. Under the influence of the Frankfurt School's philosophy of history and a directly or indirectly appropriated version of Carl Schmitt's work on state/society fusion, Habermas traced out a process of the decline, or even the end, of civil society. His later attempts to reconstruct key notions of the classical doctrine of politics, such as *praxis* or *techne*, stressed the metatheoretical level. For a while, only opponents like Luhmann noticed that Habermas's relation to the classical concept of civil society actually went deeper. However, as long as Habermas was engaged in a reconstruction of historical materialism, he could not free himself from the prejudices of Marx and most of Marxism in relation to civil society. We would argue that this fundamental break occurs with *The Theory of Communicative Action*, which not only reverses (for the first time) the bleak earlier verdict concerning the concept of civil society but amounts to its reconstruction.

3. Jürgen Habermas, *Communication and the Evolution of Society* (Boston: Beacon Press, 1979), 95. The new conceptual means required for the reconstruction of civil society in this sense—the development of a differentiated theory of action and a dualistic theoretical framework stressing both lifeworld and system—were developed by Habermas over a period of fifteen or so years. However, only in *The Theory of Communicative Action* is the interrelation of these two fundamental steps finally satisfactory, and only here do the potential links to a theory of civil society become clear.

4. As is now well known, the first step of this strategy is the development of a theory of communicative action that differentiates the concepts of action and transcends the limitations of all subject-philosophies along with the concept of teleological action.

5. See Agh Attila, "The Triangle Model of Society and Beyond," in V. Gathy, ed., *State and Civil Society: Relationships in Flux* (Budapest, 1989). We do not believe it is accurate to credit Polànyi with the discovery of this three-part conception. In *The Great Transformation*, for example, he did not distinguish between societal and economic attacks on early nineteenth-century paternalism or between societalist and statist forms of response to the self-regulating market later in the century. Polànyi's very real contribution to the conception in question lies in his discovery of the tension, obscured in both liberal and Marxist dichotomous

models, between economic and civil society. Our overall analysis owes much to him, even if we are less positive than he about preindustrial paternalism and more negative about all models of postliberal statism. These attitudes are supportable precisely because of the three-part model that was not yet available to him.

6. We owe the first critical stimulus in this context to György Markus, who stressed the superiority of this model for understanding Solidarity as far back as 1981.

7. See A. Arato, "Civil Society, History and Socialism: Reply to John Keane," *Praxis International* 9, nos. 1–2 (April–July 1989): 140–144

8. See chapter 4.

9. See Karl Polànyi, *The Great Transformation* (New York: Rinehart and Co., 1944), 71.

10. Ibid., 141.

11. Max Weber's theory of modernity is predicated on this assumption.

12. Polànyi, *The Great Transformation*, 130–132.

13. This critique is free from methodological reductionism; see Jürgen Habermas, *The Theory of Communicative Action*, 2 vols. [1981] (Boston: Beacon Press, 1984, 1987; hereafter cited as *TCA*).

14. *TCA*, vol. 2, 267–272.

15. Ibid., 185, 270–271.

16. Ibid., 269; see also Jürgen Habermas, "Hannah Arendt: On the Concept of Power," in *Philosophical-Political Profiles* (Cambridge: MIT Press, 1983).

17. Aside from Parsons's fundamental article, "The Concept of Power," in *Politics and Social Structure* (New York: Free Press, 1969), see also Niklas Luhmann, *Macht* (Stuttgart: Enke Verlag, 1975). The conception of the state administration as a system integrated by the medium of power has been radically challenged by Thomas McCarthy, who seems more willing than some less careful critics to concede this status to the market economy and to money. See his essay "Complexity and Democracy: The Seducements of Systems Theory," in *Ideals and Illusions: On Reconstruction and Deconstruction in Contemporary Social Theory* (Cambridge: MIT Press, 1991). Surprisingly, given his obvious desire to continue using this conception, Habermas has chosen to answer this criticism in a somewhat sketchy and tentative manner; see "A Reply," in Axel Honneth and Hans Joas, eds., *Communicative Action* (Cambridge: MIT Press, 1991). While we cannot undertake a further metatheoretical development of Habermas's position that would be needed to make this aspect of his dualistic social theory fully convincing, the centrality of a two-subsystem, two-media conception to our overall argument requires that we reply to McCarthy.

1. McCarthy more or less disregards the fact that Habermas, unlike Parsons and Luhmann, systematically stresses the difference between money and power beyond the single point that only power requires legitimation. Indeed, Habermas, in our view rightly, offers a hierarchical conception in which the medium of

money represents the most abstract and automatic form of functioning, followed by the medium of power (with its multiple codes, lower level of circulation, dependence on action, etc.) and in turn by generalized forms of communication such as influence and reputation (which still substitute for ordinary language communication). Many of the differences between money and power stressed by McCarthy can already be accommodated on this level of Habermas's original argument.

2. Following Habermas's occasional bad example, McCarthy seems to identify being "formally organized" with operating as a subsystem. Formal organization is certainly a requirement (and hence a mark of identification) of the construction of the subsystem of power, but formal organization is a necessary condition of institutionalization and not its fundamental mechanism. With Luhmann, we might say that formal and especially legal rules represent a code of power that should not be confused with its operation. Moreover, it is not (unlike money in the case of the economy) the only relevant code. (For Luhmann, symbols of power, symbolic uses of power, and status hierarchy represent some of the other possible codes of power, and we would add informal rules as well, including the code of formal-informal itself as well as rules of gender.) Finally, the category pair formal-informal should not be identified with that of system-lifeworld since there can be informal media codes, on the one hand, and formal relationships (kinship structures) in the lifeworld, on the other.

For these reasons, the evidence of modern organization theory concerning the role of the "informal" in organizations, to which McCarthy refers, does not disprove the operation of power as a medium, which consists in the transfer of selectivity—of the ability to determine what can be said and done—without ordinary language communication, relying on a conditioning of expectations (and of expectations of expectations) through inverse linkages of relatively preferred and relatively rejected combinations of alternatives of at least two persons. (Typically, and with action-theoretic simplification: Power holders prefer a combination of noncompliance and sanction to one of noncompliance and no sanction, while weaker parties prefer compliance and no sanction to noncompliance and sanction. It is important that each must be able to anticipate the preference of the other.) Such transfer can occur through command and threat, but its efficacy is greatly enhanced when it is facilitated by a reliance on binary codes. This is the crucial point. These can be formal rules coded as legal-illegal, but they can also take the form (and in actual organizations, they always do take the form) of "subsidiary codes" as well, such as informal rules coded in terms of formal-informal, superior-inferior, higher-lower, supporter-opponent relations. Undoubtedly, actual commands and agreements among equals (although agreements among unequals should be treated with care) also play a role in organizational decision making. Assuming the well-documented ability of organizations (actualized when the informal and formal reinforce rather than oppose each other!) to reduce greatly the time constraints of decision making and to produce more or less automatic forms of functioning, it remains highly plausible to stress the central role of formal and informal codes of power, as against formal and informal ordinary language communication. Given his reliance on the evidence of recent organization theory, we doubt that McCarthy would wish to explain the efficiency of organizations, and their dramatic increase of power, on the basis of a Weberian action-theoretic conception in which the organization is in effect an instrument in the hands of the formal head of the hierarchy, who is the only genuine actor. See Niklas Luhmann, "Ends, Domination and System," in *The Differentiation of Society* (New York: Columbia University Press, 1982).

3. McCarthy is right to question whether the dualistic social theory allows a political strategy based on Habermas's own normative premises, whether too many concessions to system theory produce a political conception that is unnecessarily defensive. He is close to discovering the reason for the rightness of these qualms when he points to the ambiguities of Habermas's concepts of political system, administrative system, and state apparatus. Indeed, the acceptance of the systems-theoretic linking of the whole domain of the "state," which is hardly consistent in Habermas and which converges with the old Frankfurt School notion of the full administrative reduction of the public sphere, does lead to an unnecessarily defensive conception. Our whole argument is an attempt to show that the dualistic social theory in itself does not lead to such an outcome and that Habermas's normative theory, formalized in discourse ethics, is best interpreted in terms of this social theory as leading to a program of self-limiting radical democracy. In particular, we introduce the concept of political society as a mediating level that, from the lifeworld point of view, represents an outpost of publicity and potential societal influence and, from the systems point of view, represents reflexive forms of regulation from the outside through self-regulation.

4. The alternative conception McCarthy often alludes to but does not actually adopt (or decisively reject), namely, a praxis-philosophical retranslation of the theory of communicative action, could very well involve a return to fundamentalist dreams of the conversion of all "reified" systems to regimes of direct democratic participation. We are having some difficulty in interpreting the idea of nonregressive dedifferentiation of economy and state, which McCarthy seems to advance in the form of an open question. He does not explain what would be "regressive" and "nonregressive." He does not, moreover, clarify whether by "dedifferentiation" he means merely redefining boundaries between system and lifeworld, establishing more complex input-output relations among spheres, or even introducing institutions of mediation in which both forms of coordination, communication and power, play a role (three options we also advocate), or if he believes that the whole political domain, including the state administrative system, could and should become spheres of democratic participation and communicative action coordination primarily. The assimilation of "latent functions" to the lifeworld as background speaks for this latter alternative. Our own point is not that elements of system functioning could not be taken up and thematized in communicative contexts (in a manner similar to the background elements of a lifeworld) and perhaps reabsorbed in the lifeworld, but that

(unlike the elements of the lifeworld that represent passive reservoirs of meaning on which actors can draw) media-regulated system contexts are dynamic and have an objective, self-unfolding "logic" (e.g., the proliferation of bureaucratic offices despite the intentions of all concerned).

We share the reasons for Habermas's abandoning of his earlier interpretation of democratization in terms of participatory democracy, linked to global planning—a position McCarthy restates, but without really arguing for it. Even if hostility to a systemically functioning economy cannot in general be attributed to McCarthy, and therefore his position stops short of a complete return to traditional praxis philosophy, he does avoid criticizing the latter's assumptions with respect to the state whose systemic characteristics in one context at least he is willing to attribute to commodification, that is, penetration by a foreign, economic logic. In our view, such a thoroughly Lukácsian approach, if actually developed, would have to revive old conceptions about the state as potentially a fully neutral instrument in the hands of democratic decision makers, conceptions that can only legitimate statism itself by occluding the logic of the modern state. We can be aware of this logic and learn to restrict it only if we do not treat the whole sphere of the state, and in particular the state-administrative system, as either lifeworld or a reflex of the economic system. Granted, future conceptions may give us other ways of understanding the logic of the state than that of systems theory. McCarthy in any case hardly offers us models for a desired alternative type of functional analysis aside from *Das Kapital*, which might perhaps lead to a more dynamic conception of the logic of the economy than that of Habermas, but only at the cost of reductionism with respect to the state and of illusions (as G. Markus, J. Kis, and G. Bence have shown in a still unpublished 1971 manuscript, "Is a Critique of Political Economy At All Possible?") of replacing the anarchy of production by central planning. (The above-mentioned Lukácsian theory of reification is only a derivative of Marx's model, while the Weberian conception of bureaucracy is action-theoretic and should in any case be ruled out in light of the organization-theoretic arguments used by McCarthy.) It seems to us that Habermas's normative ideals (and the political intentions we probably share with McCarthy) can be well articulated in terms of the dualistic social theory that distinguishes between subsystems of state administration and economy and that they are incompatible with both democratic fundamentalism and the statism to which it is necessarily linked.

18. *TCA*, vol. 2, chap. 6, contains a systematic analysis of the distinction between system and lifeworld.

19. See Jürgen Habermas, "Technology and Science as Ideology," in *Toward a Rational Society* (Boston: Beacon Press, 1970) ; *TCA*, vol. 2, chap. 7.

20. Habermas discusses several approaches to the lifeworld concept, including the phenomenological approach of Husserl and the sociological approach of Schutz and Luckmann, in *TCA*, vol. 2, 126ff.

21. See Habermas's charts, *TCA*, vol. 2, 142–144. In response to criticisms, Habermas was forced to articulate the fact that his lifeworld concept has two

levels: a philosophical (formal pragmatic) one and a sociological one; see "A Reply," 245.

22. Following Parsons and Weber, Habermas argues that with the onset of modernization processes, these components of the lifeworld are increasingly differentiated from one another; see *TCA*, vol. 2, 145.

23. Ibid., 137–138.

24. Identifying the sociological and institutional levels of the lifeworld involves a "sociologistic" oversimplification. The three "structural components of the lifeworld" can each be regarded from the point of view of three processes: cultural reproduction, social integration, and socialization. Strictly speaking, we get to the institutional level only by regarding the three structural components, each linked to the resources of meaning, solidarity, and personal competence, from the point of view of social integration. This perspective leads to the three institutional complexes we focus on: *institutions of socialization*; *social groups and associations*; and *institutions of culture*. The oversimplification is acceptable in our context since the problem of civil society belongs to sociology rather than to psychology or cultural theory.

25. We mean institutions such as families, schools, universities, and those involved in the production and dissemination of art, science, etc. There was never any justification for Hegel to have omitted the family from civil society or for Gramsci to have ignored it.

26. *TCA*, vol. 2, 185, 270–271.

27. Ibid., 319–320.

28. For the converse to be strictly true, there must be a solution to the time constraints on decision making that does not involve reliance on the medium whose scope is not being reduced. This difficulty arises because, in reducing the scope of a medium, it is difficult to discover a form of "decolonization" that challenges the functioning of media per se, and this violates the requirements of modernity. However, it is certainly implausible to argue that any given restriction of democratic decision making is justified because of time constraints. We shall try to show that it is in principle possible to extend the scope of democratic participation through a combination of representative institutions, movements, and initiatives that use the mechanism of influence.

29. *TCA*, vol. 2, 185.

30. Ibid., 186.

31. It cannot, however, be indiscriminately expanded to all of the media in Luhmann's general model, such as love or scientific truth.

32. Indeed, Carl Schmitt's application of the argument to the Weimar republic was intended to legitimize existing (Italian fascist) and (possibly) desired future totalitarian states.

33. Claus Offe, "New Social Movements: Challenging the Boundaries of Institutional Politics," *Social Research* 52, no. 4 (Winter 1987): 817–820.

34. Claus Offe, "The Separation of Form and Content in Liberal Democracy," in *Contradictions of the Welfare State* (Cambridge: MIT Press, 1985).

35. Offe, "Competitive Party Democracy and the Keynesian Welfare State," in *Contradictions of the Welfare State.*

36. With the supposed shrinking of this traditional lifeworld, Luhmann's repeated references to some kind of role for actual discussion in institutionalized processes remain anomalous and without foundation.

37. *TCA*, vol. 2, 145–146.

38. *TCA*, vol. 1, 340–341.

39. This is the step beyond Parsons, whose concept of societal community allows only for normative coordination of action and a conventional relation to standards.

40. Habermas, "Toward a Reconstruction of Historical Materialism," in *Communication and the Evolution of Society*, 154–155. Habermas originally rooted all moral and legal development ultimately in the succession of three models of communicative action: symbolically mediated interaction, propositionally differentiated speech, and argumentative speech, corresponding to preconventional, conventional, and postconventional moral structures, respectively. In his later writings, the idea of modernizing the lifeworld focuses on the transition from the second to the third model. Interestingly enough, normative development in Luhmann, involving the differentiation of normative and cognitive styles, focuses on the transition from the first to the second model.

41. Habermas, "Moral Development and Ego Identity," in *Communication and the Evolution of Society*, 77–90.

42. Habermas, "Historical Materialism and the Development of Normative Structures," in *Communication and the Evolution of Society*, 118.

43. Habermas, "Toward a Reconstruction of Historical Materialism," 156. Focusing on forms of argumentation does not reduce the structure of mutual expectations to actual communication, as Luhmann might charge. Indeed, even he admits to reserving the scarce resource of actual communication to cases of conflict, without, however, seeing the need to investigate the possible structures of such communication. It is precisely these structures that allow the preservation of a normative style of expectation in the case of positive law, something Luhmann desires but is unable to explain. See, e.g., "The Self-Reproduction of Law and Its Limits," in G. Teubner, ed., *Dilemmas of Law in the Welfare State* (Berlin: de Gruyter, 1986), 125.

44. Ronald Dworkin, *Taking Rights Seriously* (Cambridge: Harvard University Press, 1978), especially chaps. 2 and 3.

45. Dworkin, "Hard Cases," in *Taking Rights Seriously.*

46. H. L. A. Hart, *The Concept of Law* (Oxford: Oxford University Press, 1961).

47. See chapter 11.

48. See chapter 8.

49. *TCA*, vol. 1, 260–261. His own distinction between law as institution and as medium, yet another version of the principle/norm distinction, speaks against this interpretation.

50. *TCA*, vol. 2, 178.

51. *TCA*, vol. 1, 341.

52. See Claude Lefort, "Human Rights and Politics," in *The Political Forms of Modern Society* (Cambridge: MIT Press, 1986), and Jean L. Cohen, *Class Society and Civil Society: The Limits of Marxian Critical Theory* (Amherst: University of Massachusetts Press, 1982), chap. 1.

53. See Anthony Giddens, *The Nation State and Violence* (Berkeley: University of California Press, 1985), chap. 8. Giddens's position is internally inconsistent, seeing rights alternately as forms of surveillance that become fields of contention between surveillance and autonomy and as forms of response to types of surveillance in society. We have less objection to the second position than to the first, which would make state administrations the source of rights, with civil initiatives producing only alternative interpretations of these rights.

54. We are using this concept of organizing principle to indicate the institutional core of a society that is responsible for its *social identity*, located at the crossroads of social and system integration. See Jürgen Habermas, *Legitimation Crisis* (Boston: Beacon Press, 1975), and *Communication and the Evolution of Society*, 154ff. Moreover, we find it convincing that, for a given formation, the model of law and morality indicates the structure of its principle of organization. See *TCA*, vol. 2, 173–175. For the social formation of civil society (Habermas speaks of state/economy differentiation only in this context), we find this principle to be linked not to the institutionalization of formal law (Habermas) or of the positivity of law (Luhmann), but to that of fundamental rights. It is revealing that Habermas, too, explores the typology of modern state and society relations from this point of view.

55. In so doing, he offers the clearest connection of his analysis of the lifeworld to the concept of civil society. In particular, his reliance on a juxtaposition of economy-state-lifeworld, or of all his historical types, indicates that he should have revised his occasional treatment of the organizational principle of the modern epoch in terms of the differentiation of state and economic (or civil) society; see, e.g., *Communication and the Evolution of Society*, 154; *TCA*, vol. 2, 178.

56. *TCA*, vol. 2, 357ff.

57. Ibid.

58. Habermas's concern in creating this typology was primarily for distortions stemming from the capitalist nature of the economy and its overextension and later from the statist implications of welfare systems. We should note that this history could be rewritten from the perspective of another serious perversion of culturally available potentials, namely, the reconstruction of the family on modern terrain. Sequestering women into the roles of wife and mother deformed the function and structure of the intimate sphere with respect to the

development of its members' subjectivity and individuality and also deformed the import of domestic gender hierarchies for the systemic differentiation of work and political roles (i.e., the interpretation of these roles as as being for men only).

59. Thus, Jean Bodin rather than Thomas Hobbes should be seen as the representative theorist of this epoch.

60. *TCA*, vol. 2, 364.

61. Ibid.

62. These, of course, could not remain rights without their protective, negative character indicating disabilities of the sovereign. See H. L. A. Hart, "Rights," in *Essays on Bentham: Studies in Jurisprudence and Political Theory* (Oxford: Oxford University Press, 1982).

63. *TCA*, vol. 2, 361.

64. See Hart, "Rights." It is conceivable that some benefit could take on the structure of a right. But for a benefit to be a right, rather than the outcome of a policy, it would have to take on the structure of a *fundamental* right: It would have to be fully actionable, limitable only by another right, and universal in its application (i.e., not related to the characteristics of a particular group but pertaining to individuals as such). Such consideratio̶   ̶ Rawls to treat the so-called social rights only as preconditions of genui̶n̶   ̶or liberties. See John Rawls, *A Theory of Justice* (Cambridge: Harvard U̶ ̶   ̶ty Press, 1971), 204–205, and also Dworkin, *Taking Rights Seriously*.

65. Thus, the contrast between *Teilhaberrechte*, in the sense of rights of membership, and *Freiheitsrechte*, in the sense of freedoms or liberties, would be well taken here. But the point should not be transposed to what ought to be called *Teilnehmerrechte*, rights of participation, even if in both cases we can speak of bureaucratic implementation leading to contradiction. In the case of membership rights, the benefit structure of their formulation is predisposed to bureaucratic implementation. Rights of participation, however, incorporate a negative as well as a positive dimension and are thus true rights.

66. Andrew Arato, "Critical Sociology and Authoritarian State Socialism," in David Held and John Thompson, eds., *Habermas: Critical Debates* (Cambridge: MIT Press, 1982); E. Fraenkel, *The Dual State* (Oxford: Oxford University Press, 1941).

67. *TCA*, vol. 1, 221–223, 233.

68. Habermas's definition of cultural modernity as involving the fall of substantive reason and the differentiation of the value spheres of art, science, and morality follows Weber. Weber attributes to cultural modernity and secularization the phenomena of loss of meaning and loss of freedom. Horkheimer and Adorno reproduce this thesis. See the discussion in *TCA*, vol. 1, 346–352.

69. *TCA*, vol. 2, 153ff.

70. Ibid., 330–331.

71. Ibid., 361–364.

72. See chapter 8.

73. *TCA*, vol. 2, 328. We have translated *bürgerlichen* as "civil." It is an obvious mistake to render as "bourgeois" a society whose three levels are indicated by *bourgeois, citoyen*, and *homme*. (Of course, *l'homme* here means humanity, not men.)

74. See chapter 8 and Jürgen Habermas, "The New Obscurity: The Crisis of the Welfare State and the Exhaustion of Utopian Energies," in *The New Conservatism: Cultural Criticism and the Historians' Debate* (Cambridge: MIT Press, 1989).

75. Ibid.

76. We see little reason to describe as utopian the welfare state model of compensation for the alienation of labor, even at the height of reformism, as Habermas does in "The New Obscurity." Indeed, we do not see the rational organization of a society of laborers as a primary characteristic of the earlier, socialist utopia, especially since many versions of this utopia involved not the humanization of labor but the dramatic minimization of labor time—in fact, the abolition of labor. The socialist utopia is primarily one of power (organizing the whole of society and not just production), just as the economic liberal utopia is one of the market. It is when they incorporated liberal dreams about the growth of production that the organization of labor became a factor in socialist utopias.

77. See especially T. W. Adorno's most utopian work, *Negative Dialectics* (New York: Seabury Press, 1973).

78. Hannah Arendt's counterexample, the American revolution, is in this context a conservative revolution at best, since it could rely on existing (state) institutions as its *pouvoir constituant*. No revolutionary utopias found inspiration in this model. We should note that Arendt's own utopia, partially based on this model, is clearly a self-limiting communications model. She refuses to totalize democratic power and seeks to limit it through law and tradition. It is another matter that in *On Revolution* (New York: Penguin Books, 1977) she links the tradition of limitation of rule to the drying up of democratic participation.

79. See M. Gauchet, "The Rights of Man," in F. Furet and M. Ozouf, eds., *A Critical Dictionary of the French Revolution* (Cambridge: Harvard University Press, 1989).

80. See François Furet, *Interpreting the French Revolution* (Cambridge, England: Cambridge University Press, 1971).

81. See chapter 1.

82. See chapter 10.

83. The best discussion of the relation between immanent and transcendent criticism is still T. W. Adorno's "Cultural Criticism and Society," in *Prisms* (Cambridge: MIT Press, 1981). See also Cohen, *Class and Civil Society*, and Andrew Arato, "Introduction to Sociology of Culture," in Andrew Arato and Eike Gebhardt, eds., *The Essential Frankfurt School Reader* (New York: Urizen Press, 1979).

84. T. W. Adorno, "Ideology," in Frankfurt Institute for Social Research, *Aspects of Sociology* (Boston: Beacon Press, 1972); Herbert Marcuse, *One-Dimensional Man* (Boston: Beacon Press, 1972). In *Soviet Marxism* (New York: Vintage, 1961), Marcuse had not yet extended the claim of one-dimensionality to Soviet society, with its supposedly genuine ideology of orthodox Marxism. Within a few years, though, he abandoned this reservation.

85. For an interesting historical analysis that supports this thesis, see Carl Degler, *At Odds: Women and the Family in America from the Revolution to the Present* (Oxford: Oxford University Press, 1980). Degler argues that the development of the intimate sphere of the family, together with the doctrine of separate spheres and the new conception of childhood, opened up the terrain on which women were able to experience the beginnings of a sense of self, despite the fact that it was tied to the role of wife and mother. It was this new conception that projected them into the "public" sphere and ultimately led to claims for autonomy and individuality in all spheres of life, thus challenging the patriarchal character of the first form of the companionate family and, ultimately, the doctrine of separate spheres itself. See chapter 10.

86. Interpreters from Walter Benjamin to Hans-Magnus Enzensberger have stressed this against the contrary view of Adorno.

87. Habermas may exclude them because of an exaggerated fear of all corporatism and particularism; see "The New Obscurity." In this context, the medicine suggested—a combination of universal normative justifications and the pluralism of subcultures—is justified. The fear that these subcultures merely constitute "a mirror image of the neocorporatistic gray zone" is not justified, however, given the relation of the associations to anything but gray forms of alternative publics.

88. The discussion in Gabriel A. Almond and Sidney Verba, *Civic Culture: Political Attitudes and Democracy in Five Nations* (Princeton: Princeton University Press, 1963), is still impressive on this point, and they were proved correct by the new movements of the period that followed publication of their book.

89. See chapter 10.

90. *TCA*, vol. 2, chap. 8.

91. The idea of law as a medium does not mean that we conceive of law as a medium of communication like money and power but, rather, that we understand law in some of its capacities, the dominant ones in contemporary society, as functionalized to facilitate the operation of the media of the administrative state and the market economy. In this view, law represents the code through which the genuine medium of power would operate, to use Luhmann's term. The distinction between law as institution and law as medium, moreover, may refer to the same legal code operating in two different ways; for example, the same statute might be applied by administrative courts and also by trial (jury) courts. We might, of course, regard the complete political instrumentalization of law as its reduction to a medium, but this would be identical to the medium of power, which in order to operate must be represented in a code that is, if no longer genuinely legal, then perhaps moral or historical-philosophical or reli-

gious. There are, unfortunately, sufficient examples of each of these options today.

Our notion that there are alternatives in contemporary legal processes could be derived by means other than the distinction between law as medium and law as institution. In particular, Unger's distinction among formal, substantive, and procedural law represents a fruitful alternative starting point. Parsons was the first to note an elective affinity between formal law and economic society, between substantive law and state administration, and between procedural law and civil society. It might in fact be better to treat formal and substantive law themselves, in analogy to liberal and welfare-state juridification, as ambiguous from the point of view of civil society, as empowering groups and individuals while also promoting new forms of dependence and unfreedom. As a form of reflexive law, procedural law (i.e., procedures applied to other procedures) cannot replace the other types of modern law. The meta level presupposes levels to which it must be applied, in this case in a reflexive manner. However, the increased use of procedural law can reinforce the empowering dimension of substantive and formal law. This could, of course, also be seen as reinforcing the dimension, aspect, or application of law as an institution. While we shall argue later that reflexive law helps introduce a new form of postregulatory regulation of state and economy, it may also represent an important bulwark of the lifeworld against colonization operating through legal codes.

92. See R. M. Unger, *Law in Modern Society* (New York: Free Press, 1976), 192–200; F. Ewald, "A Concept of Social Law," and G. Teubner, "After Legal Instrumentalism? Strategic Models of Post-regulatory Law," both in Teubner, ed., *Dilemmas of Law in the Welfare State*. Even Luhmann now seems more inclined to accept this historicized position, pointing to the politicization of law in welfare states; see "The Self-Reproduction of Law and Its Limits," in *Dilemmas of Law in the Welfare State*. He makes the mistake, though, of considering the project of "reflexive law" to be even more destructive of norms than instrumentalization. At times, Unger seems to make a similar mistake, treating substantive and procedural law in an undifferentiated way as both expressive of purposive legal reasoning and destructive of the rule of law; see, e.g., *Law in Modern Society*, 195. Elsewhere, though, he rightly notes the incorporation of formality in procedural law, which thus becomes a compromise between formal and substantive law; see, e.g., *Law in Modern Society*, 212.

93. See chapter 10.

94. In our view, neoconservatism adds the defense of a traditional, authoritarian civil society to the neoliberal cult of the magic of the market. It would take us too far afield to determine which of these approaches is politically viable, especially since we believe both are plagued by internal contradictions having to do with the neoliberal attempt to imagine a society without social integration and the neoconservative desire to make tradition and authority compatible with a fully autonomous market rationality. Nevertheless, both neoliberalism and neoconservatism remain politically more viable than the fundamentalist rejection of both the modern state and the modern economy.

95. See A. Przeworski, *Capitalism and Social Democracy* (Cambridge, England: Cambridge University Press, 1985). See also Claus Offe, "Bindung, Fessel, Bremse," in Axel Honneth et al., eds., *Zwischenbetrachtungen im Prozess der Aufklärung* (Frankfurt: Suhrkamp, 1989): "We do not know what the political and economic institutions of socialism consist of; even if we knew, the road to them would be unknown; even if it were known, relevant parts of the population would not be ready to enter it; even if they were ready, there would not be any guarantee that the established condition would be capable of functioning and immune from regressions; even if all this could be guaranteed, a great part of today's politically thematized social problems would remain unsolved" (746, note 9).

96. See the introduction and chapter 1.

97. See chapter 6 on Foucault.

98. We have in mind James O'Connor, *Fiscal Crisis of the State* (New York: St. Martin's Press, 1973); Claus Offe's essays in *Strukturprobleme des kapitalistischen Staates* (Frankfurt: Suhrkamp, 1982) and later in *Contradictions of the Welfare State*, and Habermas, *Legitimation Crisis*.

99. Offe, *Contradictions of the Welfare State*, 149–154.

100. After all, aside from the disastrous experience of state socialism, the welfare state has been the only institutional realization of some of the significant hopes of socialist movements, even if it evolved within the framework of capitalist economies. As a type of socialist experiment, social-democratic reformism ends not with the various Bad Godesberg programs but with the transition from Keynesian expansionist strategies to the crisis management of established welfare states. See Przeworski, *Capitalism and Social Democracy*.

101. See Jürgen Habermas, *The Philosophical Discourse of Modernity* (Cambridge: MIT Press, 1987), 358ff.

102. Ibid.; see also Habermas, "The New Obscurity."

103. In several works, Janos Kornai develops the concept of the soft budgetary constraint, which, unlike the concepts of "shortage" or "resource constraint," is applicable to capitalist economies. See in particular *The Economics of Shortage* (Amsterdam: North-Holland, 1980), the essays "The Reproduction of Shortage," "Hard and Soft Budget Constraints," and "Degrees of Paternalism" in *Contradictions and Dilemmas* (Cambridge: MIT Press, 1986), and "A puha költségvetési korlát," *Tervgazdasági fórum*, no. 3 (Budapest, 1986).

104. This logic was reconstructed for state socialism in the theories of cycles of economists such as T. Bauer and K. A. Sós. The cycles of investment under state socialism are the best evidence for the system-constituting ability of the medium of power, since we know that the structure of expectation and bargaining that underlies these cycles is a political one in which the possession of power and not economic efficiency determines outcomes.

105. Kornai, "A puha költségvetési korlát," 11ff.

106. Some important areas are thus underregulated, while others are overregulated.

107. Offe, "Competitive Party Democracy and the Keynesian Welfare State," 200. It is an interesting aspect of Kornai's conception as well that it is not only state intervention as such but a structure of expecting routine intervention that softens budgetary constraints and orients firms to political, hierarchical rather than economic, horizontal competition; see, e.g., "The Reproduction of Shortage," 14.

108. One should distinguish the related phenomena of shortage and inflation, even if both can be due to surplus demand. Inflation, in the West at least, is a phenomenon of demand-constrained economies in which surplus demand leads to higher prices for available goods. Shortage in Soviet-type resource-constrained economies (not to be equated with the general economic category of scarcity) represents a situation in which goods are unavailable even at an inflationary price. For the distinction between demand- and resource-constrained economies, see Kornai, "The Reproduction of Shortage."

109. See Przeworski, *Capitalism and Social Democracy*. Habermas notes that, in Europe at least, it is the loyalists of the welfare state who are the conservatives; see "The New Obscurity."

110. See Habermas, "The New Obscurity," and Arato, "Civil Society, History and Socialism," 140–144.

111. See Arato, "Civil Society, History and Socialism."

112. See, e.g., Jean L. Cohen, "Rethinking Social Movements," *Berkeley Journal of Sociology* 28 (1983): 97–113; Andrew Arato and Jean L. Cohen, "Social Movements, Civil Society and the Problem of Sovereignty," *Praxis International* 4, no. 3 (1984): 266–283.

113. Habermas, "The New Obscurity," 64.

114. Ibid.

115. Habermas, *Philosophical Discourse of Modernity*, 363–364. The term "reflexive," adopted from Luhmann, means the application of a process or a strategy to itself (procedure to procedure, decision to decision, etc.). See Luhmann's "Reflexive Mechanismen," in *Soziologische Aufklärung*, vol. 1 (Opladen: Westdeutscher Verlag, 1970), 92–112.

116. The point here is not that countries like the United States with minimal protections against market forces (lacking universal health insurance and job training programs, for example) should somehow forego these, but rather that it is not necessary to tread the path marked out by European social democracies first and only then to figure out ways to undo the expensive, oppressively bureaucratic, paternalistic structures such systems have erected in the name of solidarity. One can still selectively incorporate the achievements of more advanced welfare states—for example, substituting univeralist for "means-tested" benefits in certain cases.

117. Habermas, personal correspondence, 1986.

118. Habermas, *Philosophical Discourse of Modernity*, 364. The translation here is inadequate, though; see the German edition, *Der philosophische Diskurs der Moderne* (Frankfurt: Suhrkamp, 1985), 422–433.

119. Parsons seems to argue the contrary; see especially Talcott Parsons and Neil Smelser, *Economy and Society* (New York: Free Press, 1956). Habermas for a fleeting moment seemed to fall into this position; see "The New Obscurity," 65. Just as Habermas claims that some of Luhmann's followers are forced to let the theory of communicative action in through the back door because of otherwise unsolvable problems, he himself seems at times to experience a similar temptation with regard to the theory of autopoietic systems. In this case, though, Habermas a short time later rejects the notion that a new steering medium of another new subsystem can bring autopoietic systems under self-limiting forms of control; see *Philosophical Discourse of Modernity*, 363

120. Thus, it is a serious mistake to counterpose solidarity and rights as Unger does in his otherwise sophisticated analysis of the concept of solidarity (*Law in Modern Society*, 206–213).

121. Mancur Olson, *The Logic of Collective Action* (Cambridge: Harvard University Press, 1973); Albert Hirschman, *Shifting Involvements* (Princeton: Princeton University Press, 1982), chap. 5.

122. On the latter point, see chapter 10. We should note that Habermas has now revised the pessimistic general theses of *The Structural Transformation of the Public Sphere* and returned to his originally hesitant proposal according to which the revival of the emancipating premise of the classical public sphere in the contemporary world can only be the work of a plurality of associations, internally public in their organization and aiming at reconstituting public discussion on all levels of society. With this move, Habermas puts his theory of social movements on new foundations, replacing the (empirically false) breakdown theory with a theory of associations operating on the micro level of society.

123. André Gorz, *Farewell to the Working Class* (Boston: South End Press, 1982).

124. Ibid., 97–100.

125. Ibid., 97. John Keane in *Democracy and Civil Society* (London: Verso, 1988) repeats Gorz's bias for state planning of the realm of necessity, seems to identify state-owned or nationalized property with socialized property, and hopes to save markets by sticking them into the realm of freedom or civil society along with cooperation, reciprocity, and barter. This operation dispenses with the idea that markets on the one side and associations and publics on the other represent entirely different logics and have different relations to "necessity." This sleight of hand causes theoretical impotence in face of the assimilation of the functioning of one to the other, leading either to economic primitivism or to the colonization of the lifeworld. At issue is not the possibility or even the necessity of material activity coordinated by reciprocity, cooperation, and mutuality and linked to different forms of property as the material foundations of autonomy and solidarity in civil society. There is no reason to contest the importance of "economic" activity, in Polànyi's "substantive" sense of the term, for reproducing

civil society. What we insist on, however, and Keane neglects, is the importance for any genuinely modern society, and especially for civil society, of the existence of economic mechanisms differentiated from all forms of social integration— the importance, in other words, of the economy in Polànyi's "formal" sense. This dimension cannot be accommodated in the dichotomous framework of state and civil society without falling back into the illusions of a statist coordination of the modern economy that reappear in Gorz.

126. Gorz, *Farewell to the Working Class*, 104.

127. It may be that Gorz considers the three-part framework indispensable for describing the capitalist present, involving at least the relative mutual independence of market economy and state administration, and that he proposes the two-part model involving the statization of all economic life differentiated from civil society only for the future. Even such a model would be testimony to the Marxist orthodoxy of his conception.

128. Keane, *Democracy and Civil Society*, 87

129. See, in particular, Claus Offe, *Disorganized Capitalism* (Cambridge: MIT Press, 1985), chaps. 2, 3.

130. It is not entirely convincing that the present form of the proposed arrangement, involving guaranteed incomes, is compatible with the existence of any genuine labor market and that some fine tuning of income differentials can simultaneously maintain the prestige of forms of activity in the second sector and the relative economic advantages of work in the first. We are not competent to evaluate the viability of the overall model. Under present circumstances, though, we support the political strategy of reducing formalized work time as well as initiatives toward the broader evaluation and more extensive utilization by both sexes of cooperative and reciprocal forms of activity, which today form a sphere of activity mostly of women.

131. Offe, *Disorganized Capitalism*, 70–71.

132. See chapter 11.

133. Habermas employs his own framework in a way that is at times precariously close to Gorz's dualistic schemes, which he nevertheless rejects on a more concrete political level.

134. In our conception, political associations, parties, and parliaments represent the key institutions of political society. They can all incorporate the dimension of publicity, although this must be made compatible with the demands of strategic reason. Hence, unlike the publics of civil society, those of political society cannot guarantee open-ended, fully unrestricted communication and can achieve relative equality of access and participation only by formal rules of procedure. Despite this limitation, the political public is an open structure because of its permeability to general social communication. We must admit that it is difficult to apply the same conception to economic society, where conditions of publicity and therefore the possibilities of democratization are even more restricted. We are at present inclined to stress property and participation as the

key categories of mediation of economic society. It may be that the lower degree of participation in this sphere can be compensated for by a plurality of forms of property, through which civil society and its institutions could in principle gain footholds in economic society. Indeed, the participation of communities, non-profit organizations, and even welfare agencies in the ownership of productive property could in principle replace welfare state forms of regulation. In addition, institutions such as collective bargaining, representation of workers on company boards, and grievance procedures are all part of "economic society."

135. Teubner, "After Legal Instrumentalism?," 315.

136. G. Teubner, "Corporate Fiduciary Duties and their Beneficiaries," in K. J. Hopt and G. Teubner, eds., *Corporate Governance and Directors Liabilities* (Berlin: de Gruyter, 1985), 162; "After Legal Instrumentalism?," 315–316.

137. G. Teubner, "Substantive and Reflexive Elements in Modern Law," *Law and Society Review* 17, no. 2 (1983): 272; "After Legal Instrumentalism?," 312.

138. *TCA*, vol. 2, 371; Teubner, "After Legal Instrumentalism?," 317.

139. Teubner, "Substantive and Reflexive Elements in Modern Law," 275.

140. Ibid., 257, 267, 275.

141. Teubner, "After Legal Instrumentalism?," 317. He also mentions examples, developed to different extents, in property law (ibid., 317), contract law ("Substantive and Reflexive Elements in Modern Law," 256), and company law ("Corporate Fiduciary Duties and their Beneficiaries," 166ff.).

142. Teubner, "Substantive and Reflexive Elements in Modern Law," 278.

143. Ibid., 272–273.

144. Teubner, "Corporate Fiduciary Duties and their Beneficiaries," 165.

145. Teubner, "After Legal Instrumentalism?," 316–317.

146. Ibid., 316.

147. Teubner, "Corporate Fiduciary Duties and their Beneficiaries," 159.

148. Teubner, "Substantive and Reflexive Elements in Modern Law," 273.

149. H. Willke, "Three Types of Legal Structure: The Conditional, the Purposive and the Relational Program," in Teubner, ed., *Dilemmas of Law in the Welfare State*, 290–291.

150. It need not concern us here that Willke's empirical example—the neocorporatist *Konzertierte Aktion* (Concerted Action) established by the Social Democrats of the Grand Coalition in 1967—is a fundamentally nonpublic discourse that was not open to participation by all centrally affected interests. This weakness may flow from Willke's overall conception. To the extent that he finds it difficult to conceptualize the institutional implications of the part of his analysis that relies on a discourse model, he falls back on a discourse that seems to play a coordinating role in the context chosen, that of bargaining among government, labor, and business. The neocorporatist choice, however, is no help with the second problem: the legitimate setting of goals and purposes for all relevant subsystems.

151. This problem may be less difficult for Luhmann to deal with because his proposal for restored autopoiesis is less intrusive, less interventionist. He argues only for self-regulation per se and not for the indirect regulation of self-regulation. It is the residual idea of normative regulation that exposes Teubner to the question: What is the source of this common regulation, and how can having such a common source be reconciled with self-regulation?

152. Habermas, *Philosophical Discourse of Modernity*, 364–365.

153. See Talcott Parsons, "On the Concept of Political Power" and "On the Concept of Influence," in *Politics and Social Structure*, 363ff., 410–418, 432–436.

154. *TCA*, vol. 2, 182ff., 278–282.

155. Parsons, "On the Concept of Influence," 416–418.

156. We shall explore the nature of societal discursive processes that can become relevant for steering in chapters 10 and 11.

157. See M. Gonzales (P. Piccone), "Exorcising Perestroika," *Telos*, no. 81 (Fall 1989).

158. Alain Touraine, *The Voice and the Eye* (Cambridge, England: Cambridge University Press, 1981), chaps. 5, 6.

159. Only an East Germany fully incorporated into the West could fully turn in an elite democratic direction without delegitimation. Hence the decline of the Neues Forum, an organization obviously of civil society. In other countries, similarly constituted organizations have remained important, having made a somewhat more determined turn than Neues Forum in the direction of political society.

160. This is the task presented to all political actors, constituting part of a *pouvoir constituant* according to Hannah Arendt.

161. To this extent, we go along with the "liberal conservative" program of Janos Kornai—as expressed, for example, in *Road to a Free Economy* (New York: Norton, 1990)—even if we find it hard to understand why he proposes leaving the state-owned sector in its present form (except for a highly unlikely reduction of their budgetary supports and subsidies). Perhaps he considers the other suggested solutions, in the absence of legitimate private buyers and "operative capital" (such as workers' ownership or public stock distribution schemes), to be merely novel incarnations of the illusions of market socialism that would lead to informal bureaucratization in legitimate forms. Thus, in his view, these schemes would not be as likely to lead to reductions of subsidies to the "bureaucratic sector" as would the present, discredited arrangements. In our view, the opposite is true in the context of the existing informal "clientelistic" networks to which the old managers have access while the new workers' councils or citizen owners would not.

162. He goes as far as opposing even significant income taxes for today's entrepreneurs, despite the abundant evidence from the West that such a policy does not necessarily promote either savings or investment.

Chapter 10

1. See Jean L. Cohen, "Rethinking Social Movements," *Berkeley Journal of Sociology* 28 (1983): 97–113; Andrew Arato and Jean L. Cohen, "The German Green Party," *Dissent* (Summer 1984): 327–333; Andrew Arato and Jean L. Cohen, "Social Movements, Civil Society and the Problem of Sovereignty," *Praxis International* 4 (October 1984): 266–283; and Jean L. Cohen, "Strategy or Identity: New Theoretical Paradigms and Contemporary Social Movements," *Social Research* 52, no. 4 (Winter 1985): 663–716.

There are many other kinds of contemporary movements. Some, such as the religious right and the right-to-life movement, speak in the name of the autonomy of civil society while defending a traditionalist lifeworld against its further modernization. Movements inspired by neoconservative ideology seek to defend the economy (property rights) against state intervention and egalitarian reform. And the labor movement still exists. Our focus in this chapter, however, is solely on movements oriented toward the further democratization and modernization (in the normative sense) of social, political, or economic institutions.

2. See Cohen, "Strategy or Identity"; Bert Klandermans and Sidney Tarrow, "Mobilization into Social Movements: Synthesizing European and American Approaches," *International Social Movement Research* 1 (1988): 1–38.

3. Cohen, "Strategy or Identity," 667–668.

4. Ralph H. Turner, ed., *Robert E. Park on Social Control and Collective Behavior: Selected Papers* (Chicago: University of Chicago Press, 1967); Herbert Blumer, "Collective Behavior," in Alfred McClung Lee, ed., *New Outline of the Principles of Sociology* (New York: Barnes & Noble, 1951), and "Collective Behavior," in J. B. Gittler, ed., *Review of Sociology: Analysis of a Decade* (New York: Wiley, 1957); R. G. Turner and L. M. Killian, *Collective Behavior* (Englewood Cliffs, NJ: Prentice-Hall, 1957). For a summary of collective behavior theories, see Gary T. Marx and James L. Wood, "Strands of Theory and Research in Collective Behavior," *Annual Review of Sociology* 1 (1975): 368–428.

5. W. Kornhauser, *The Politics of Mass Society* (New York: Free Press, 1959); Hannah Arendt, *The Origins of Totalitarianism* (New York: Harcourt Brace Jovanovich, 1951); Neil Smelser, *The Theory of Collective Behavior* (New York: Free Press, 1962). With the exception of Arendt's work, which we discussed in chapter 4, the theories of mass society and mass movements constitute a synthesis of elite and pluralist theories of democracy. On this account, democracy involves a political system characterized by free elections, competition, and alternation and is predicated on a model of civil society characterized by civil privatism plus participation by active minorities through interest groups and political parties. Here, "extrainstitutional" collective actions motivated by strong ideological beliefs appear to be antidemocratic and threatening to the consensus that underlies the institutions of a civil society. In other words, they seem to herald the onslaught of "mass society," which is taken to mean the kind of society created by fascist and communist movements. Ironically, the concept of mass society was used by the theorists of the Frankfurt School (Adorno, Horkheimer,

Marcuse) to analyze the model of civil society lauded by the pluralists (especially in what seemed to be its most perfect incarnation, the United States). One might be tempted to conclude that these latter theorists defended a more egalitarian and politically active model of civil society than did the elite-pluralist or collective-behavior school, but the fact is that their neo-Marxist orientation prevented them from developing an adequate theory of either civil society or social movements.

6. For a review of the evidence, see J. Craig Jenkins, "Resource Mobilization Theory and the Study of Social Movements," *Annual Review of Sociology* 9 (1983): 527–553; Anthony Oberschall, *Social Conflict and Social Movements* (Englewood Cliffs, NJ: Prentice-Hall, 1973).

7. Mancur Olson, *The Logic of Collective Action* (Cambridge: Harvard University Press, 1965); John D. McCarthy and Mayer N. Zald, "Resource Mobilization and Social Movements: A Partial Theory," *American Journal of Sociology* 82 (May 1977): 212–241; Charles Tilly, Louise Tilly, and Richard Tilly, *The Rebellious Century: 1830–1930* (Cambridge: Harvard University Press, 1975); William Gamson, *The Strategy of Social Protest* (Homewood, IL: Dorsey, 1975); Oberschall, *Social Conflict and Social Movements*; Sidney Tarrow, "Struggling to Reform: Social Movements and Policy Change during Cycles of Protest," Western Societies Paper no. 15, Cornell University, 1983; B. Klandermans, H. Kriesl, and S. Tarrow, "From Structure to Action: Comparing Social Movement Research across Cultures," *International Social Movement Research* 1 (1988).

8. Charles Perrow, "The Sixties Observed," in Mayer N. Zald and John D. McCarthy, eds., *The Dynamics of Social Movements* (Cambridge: Winthrop, 1979), 199. Perrow characterized the political-process version of resource-mobilization theory as "Clausewitzian" because it conceives of protest as the continuation of orderly politics by other (disorderly) means—as growing out of the pursuit of interests otherwise unattainable. But he errs in arguing that only the organizational-entrepreneurial model is economistic in that it attributes cost-benefit calculations to the collective actors. Tilly's model suffers from similar difficulties.

9. Some members of the resource-mobilization school acknowledge a variety of organizational forms for modern movements, but the overall emphasis is on formal organization. The school has been accused of an inability to distinguish between interest groups and social movement associations. See Jenkins, "Resource Mobilization Theory," 541–543.

10. See Bruce Fireman and W. A. Gamson, "Utilitarian Logic in the Resource Mobilization Perspective," in Zald and McCarthy, eds., *Dynamics of Social Movements*, 1–44.

11. Ibid.

12. See Tilly, Tilly, and Tilly, *The Rebellious Century*, 6.

13. Ibid., 86 (our emphasis).

14. Charles Tilly, "European Violence and Collective Action since 1700," revised

version of a paper presented at the Conference on Political Violence and Terrorism, Instituto Carlo Cattaneo, Bologna, June 1982.

15. For a discussion of these action types, see Tilly, Tilly, and Tilly, *Rebellious Century*, 48–55, 249–252, and Charles Tilly, *From Mobilization to Revolution* (Reading, MA: Addison-Wesley, 1978), 143–151.

16. Tilly, *From Mobilization to Revolution*, 167.

17. Tilly, "European Violence," 11.

18. Tilly, *From Mobilization to Revolution*, 52–97.

19. Tilly, "European Violence," 24. See also Charles Tilly, "Fights and Festivals in 20th Century Ile de France," Working Paper no. 305, Center for Research on Social Organization, University of Michigan, December 1983, 63–68.

20. Some theorists, of course, emphasized such innovations in organization and mobilization processes as the deliberate choice of decentralized structures, grass-roots participation, and federated national organizations. They also took note of the emphasis on such goals as direct personal involvement in political action, self-help, personal change, and the creation of new identities and solidarities. However, most of the analysts in the resource-mobilization tradition concluded that these "new" orientations, on their own, result in a loss of strategic effectiveness. This is true despite Zald and Ash's early argument that different organizational structures are effective for different goals: See M. N. Zald and R. Ash, "Social Movement Organizations: Growth, Decay, and Change," *Social Forces* 44, no. 3 (1966): 327–341.

21. John McCarthy and Mayer Zald, *The Trend of Social Movements* (Morristown, NJ: General Learning, 1973), "Organizational Intellectuals and the Criticism of Society," *Social Science Review* 49 (1975): 344–362, and "Resource Mobilization and Social Movements," *American Journal of Sociology* 82 (1977): 1212–1241.

22. See J. Craig Jenkins and Craig M. Eckert, "Channelling Black Insurgency: Elite Patronage and Professional Social Movement Organizations in the Development of the Black Movement," *American Sociological Review* 51 (1986): 812–829.

23. Ibid.

24. Ibid., 816. They cite increased black voter participation, the importance of blacks as a voter block, the increase in the number of black office holders, and the reduction in the most overt forms of discrimination in education and employment.

25. Ibid., 820. Although increasing political opportunities (e.g., favorable Supreme Court decisions, federal civil rights bills) did facilitate the rise of the movement, these were opportunities, not direct patronage. An excluded group cannot count on professional SMOs and elite patrons to protect and advance its interests against powerful opponents without sustained indigenous mobilization. This is not to deny the role of professional SMOs in the successes of the civil rights movement but simply to emphasize that both a grass-roots politics of identity and influence and a politics of reform and inclusion were important.

26. Ibid., 827. This holds true for the civil rights movement as well.

27. See Alessandro Pizzorno, "Political Exchange and Collective Identity in Industrial Conflict," in C. Crouch and A. Pizzorno, eds., *The Resurgence of Class Conflict in Western Europe since 1968*, vol. 2 (London: Macmillan, 1978), 277–298.

28. This political bias is especially evident in the recent expansion of resource-mobilization theory to include consideration of what Sidney Tarrow, in "Struggling to Reform," has called the "political opportunity structure." Drawing out implications of the work of Wilson, Lipsky, Tilly, and others, Tarrow uses this concept to differentiate "external" variables that are important in explaining movement success from "internal" resource mobilization. Of course, he also defines success in political terms, as the unfolding of a process of policy innovation in the political system that addresses the protesters' stated needs, but his analysis of the political opportunity structure and his concept of cycles of protest and reform expand on the narrow discussion of influence in earlier resource-mobilization theory. At the same time, his work indicates the limits of an approach focusing exclusively on the political system for the analysis of the goals and addressees of contemporary social movements.

The political opportunity structure incorporates three features of the political system that are significant for movement success: the degree of openness of formal political institutions, the degree of stability of political alignments within the political system, and the availability and strategic posture of support groups. The first reflects formal, structural, and conjunctural factors in political systems, while the second and third bring in the targets of influence of collective action. Tarrow specifies a wide range of movement addressees, including support groups within civil society but external to the movement itself; interest groups with institutional access, who can be energized and emboldened by movement activity to press for shared goals; political and administrative elites in all sectors of the political system, whose degree of unity and perception of the electoral realignments that might result from collective action affect their openness to movement goals; and political parties, who may respond to autonomous movement activity by adopting or coopting movement issues. However, neither a favorable political opportunity structure nor efficient internal organization is sufficient to explain movement success. In addition, the impact of protest on reform must be analyzed in light of "the combination of resources and constraints that are characteristic of periods of general mobilization in whole social systems." In such periods, a protest cycle emerges in which there is a high level of conflict that is diffused throughout the national territory, involving more than one social sector and entailing the appearance of new techniques of protest and new forms of organization (Tarrow, "Struggling to Reform," 37–39). Even if the causal relation between a cycle of reform and waves of social protest remains problematic (some protest cycles simply fail, while others are triggered by reforms that precede them), they do often coincide, and the success of individual movements is often contingent upon whether and when they emerge during the cycle. In other words, both the political opportunity structure and the receptivity of political elites and support groups to strategies of influence on the part of social movements depend in part on the dynamics of protest cycles. While this is convincing as far as it goes, the expanded analysis of targets of influence is still unduly constrained by the limits of the overall approach. It is striking that a theoretical framework oriented to the analysis of influence does not address, or dismisses in passing, such obviously relevant concerns as changes in public opinion, the role of the media, and transformations in the universe of political discourse. The very way in which these issues are taken up and dismissed is in itself revealing. Changes in "mass opinion," by which Tarrow understands value change, are taken up as a possible cause of social protest (39, à la Inglehart) and then discarded as being unproved. But might it not be that public opinion and cultural change form one of the goals and targets of influence of collective action? Media coverage is also taken up in a purely instrumental way, as facilitating or obstructing movement activity (following Oberschall, "Social Conflict," and Todd Gitlin, *The Whole World Is Watching* [Berkeley: University of California Press, 1980]). But aren't the initiation and expansion of public discussion on issues and norms and the democratization of the cultural public sphere also possible movement goals? Surely one of the most striking features of modern movements is their creation of alternative communication networks—newspapers, presses, bookstores, institutes, programs of study, publications of all kinds—that expand the public sphere but are aimed in the first instance at "influencing" not elites but potential participants and "conscience constituencies." The alternative public spheres "succeed" to the extent to which they trigger reflection, survive as arenas of communication, or become part of the institutionalized public sphere. Finally, although Tarrow grants that the general evolution of informed or elite opinion is relevant to movement success, he states that changes in the political "universe of discourse" comprise a "foggy" area (34) that can affect the political opportunity structure but cannot be "operationalized." Perhaps, but this foggy area happens to be one of the central targets of contemporary collective action. Indeed, the universe of political discourse, along with social norms, social roles that are regulated by norms, and the consciousness of collective actors as well as elites, are all "addressees" of the strategy of influence of contemporary social movements. But only if one sees that civil society—its institutional structure, social relations, and normative articulation—is not only the terrain but also the target of the new social movements, can one assess the significance of such a strategy.

29. Tilly, "Fights and Festivals in 20th Century Ile de France."

30. Pizzorno, "Political Exchange," 293, and "On the Rationality of Democratic Choice," *Telos*, no. 63 (Spring 1985): 41–69. See the discussion of Pizzorno's approach in Cohen, "Strategy or Identity," 691–695.

31. Here the situation is the reverse of that of the resource-mobilization paradigm. An actual school has, in this case, emerged around Touraine's expanded model rather than around the "simple identity model."

32. Alain Touraine, *The Voice and the Eye* (Cambridge, England: Cambridge University Press, 1981), 31–32.

33. Alberto Melucci, "The New Social Movements: A Theoretical Approach,"

Social Science Information 19, no. 2 (1980): 199–226.

34. Touraine, *The Voice and the Eye*, 56.

35. Alain Touraine, "An Introduction to the Study of Social Movements," *Social Research* 52, no. 4 (1985): 749–787.

36. Alain Touraine, "Triumph or Downfall of Civil Society?," in *Humanities in Review*, vol. 1 (Cambridge, England: Cambridge University Press, 1983), 223.

37. Ibid., 221–227.

38. Hence Touraine's sweeping criticism of the resource-mobilization paradigm in "Introduction to the Study of Social Movements."

39. Touraine, "Triumph or Downfall," 220. In other words, social movements struggle over the type of civil society to be institutionalized, whereas "historical movements," situated on the diachronic axis, struggle to establish civil society and a representative political society.

40. Touraine, *The Voice and the Eye*, 61.

41. Ibid., 115. By "metasocial guarantees" of the social order, Touraine means such things as religion, philosophies of history, economic laws, and evolutionary theories of progress.

42. See Touraine, "Introduction to the Study of Social Movements."

43. Touraine, "Triumph or Downfall," 106–107.

44. Ibid., 138.

45. See Touraine, "Introduction to the Study of Social Movements."

46. For a discussion of the other societal types, see Alain Touraine, *The Self-Production of Society* (Chicago: University of Chicago Press, 1977), 92–109.

47. Touraine, "Triumph or Downfall," 229, our emphasis.

48. Cohen, *Class and Civil Society*, 214–228.

49. Jürgen Habermas, *The Theory of Communicative Action*, vol. 1 (Boston: Beacon Press, 1984), 86.

50. Ibid., 85–101.

51. See Jürgen Habermas, *The Theory of Communicative Action*, vol. 2 (Boston: Beacon Press, 1985), 332–403. For a critical discussion of Habermas's approach to social movements over the years, see Cohen, "Strategy or Identity," 708–716.

52. See the concluding section of this chapter for a more complete discussion of the four components of the dual logic of contemporary movements.

53. Alain Touraine, *The May Movement* (New York: Random House, 1971); Jürgen Habermas, *Student und Politik* (Frankfurt: Suhrkamp, 1961), *Protestbewegung und Hochschulreform* (Frankfurt: Suhrkamp, 1969), and *Towards a Rational Society* (Boston: Beacon Press, 1970).

54. Jürgen Habermas, *Die neue Unübersittlichkeit* (Frankfurt: Suhrkamp, 1985), 81–82, offers a reevaluation of his earlier political assessment of the New Left.

55. See Cohen, *Class and Civil Society*, 194–228; Jean L. Cohen, "Why More

Political Theory?," *Telos*, no. 40 (Summer 1979): 70–94.

56. See the discussion in Habermas, *The Theory of Communicative Action*, vol. 2, 301–403.

57. Among the movements Habermas refers to as new are the feminist, ecology, peace, youth, minority, antinuclear, and citizen-initiative movements (*The Theory of Communicative Action*, vol. 2, 393).

58. Habermas, *The Theory of Communicative Action*, vol. 2, 395.

59. Ibid., 396.

60. Thus, he rediscovers Tilly's "reactive" and "proactive" types of collective action.

61. In this regard, his analysis is less perceptive than that of Touraine, who saw that social movements targeting the norms and identities of civil society involve a struggle with a social adversary and that the stakes of the struggle are the future shape of the institutions of civil society.

62. Habermas, *The Theory of Communicative Action*, vol. 2, 392.

63. Nancy Fraser, "What's Critical about Critical Theory? The Case of Habermas and Gender," *New German Critique*, no. 35 (Spring/Summer 1985): 97–131. For a different view, see Linda Nicholson, *Gender and History: The Limits of Social Theory in the Age of the Family* (New York: Columbia University Press, 1986).

64. Fraser, "What's Critical about Critical Theory?," 111.

65. Ibid., 107. According to Fraser, Habermas ties this distinction to that between material and symbolic reproduction.

66. Ibid., 109.

67. Ibid., 115.

68. Ibid., 109.

69. Ibid., 124.

70. Ibid., 115.

71. Ibid., 113. Fraser states: "By omitting any mention of the childrearer role, and by failing to thematize the gender subtext underlying the roles of worker and consumer, Habermas fails to understand precisely how the capitalist workplace is linked to the modern, restricted, male-headed nuclear family. Similarly, by failing to thematize the masculine subtext of the citizen role, he misses . . . the way the masculine citizen-soldier-protector role links the state and public sphere not only to one another but also to the family and to the paid workplace. . . . And he misses, finally, the way the feminine childrearer role links all four institutions to one another by overseeing the construction of the masculine and feminine gendered subjects needed to fill *every* role in classical capitalism" (117).

72. Moreover, Fraser *presupposes* key features of the Habermasian theory of modernity even when she criticizes it and even when she reconstructs its unthematized gender subtext.

73. We by no means want to argue that this theory is sufficient to address all feminist concerns. It would certainly have to be supplemented by the crucial contributions of psychoanalytic and postmodern feminist philosophy. But as far as *social theory* goes, we find the dualistic theory of civil society to be remarkably fruitful.

74. Fraser, "What's Critical about Critical Theory?," 99–103. She takes Habermas at his word that this distinction is tied to a substantive distinction between the symbolic and material reproduction of the lifeworld. She correctly argues that it is not possible to distinguish among activities on the basis of a "natural-kinds" distinction between the material and the symbolic, and she criticizes Habermas for relying on such assumptions. This criticism echoes our own; see Andrew Arato and Jean L. Cohen, "Politics and the Reconstruction of the Concept of Civil Society," in Axel Honneth et al., eds., *Zwischenbetracthungen Im Prozess der Aufklärung* (Frankfurt: Suhrkamp, 1989). It is not true, though, that dualistic social theory stands or falls with the reified distinction between the symbolic and the material.

75. Habermas, *The Theory of Communicative Action*, vol. 2, 310. For a more detailed discussion of these points, see chapter 9.

76. For an unconvincing attempt, see Niklas Luhmann, *Love as Passion: The Codification of Intimacy* (Cambridge: Harvard University Press, 1987).

77. Fraser, however, also tends to conflate the level of analysis of coordinating mechanisms with the analysis of the various types of action. She thus insists that strategic and instrumental action occur in lifeworld institutions—in families— and that communicative action (based on patriarchal norms) occurs in the subsystems. But this is not a serious argument against the system/lifeworld distinction; indeed, it is often asserted by Habermas himself. All of the action types appear in all of the institutions. The abstract categories of system and lifeworld indicate only where the weight of coordination lies in a given institutional framework. We would also reject references to the family as an economic system for another set of reasons: The psychodynamics of identity formation in general and of gender identities in particular can hardly be analyzed in such terms.

78. See Alison M. Jaggar, *Feminist Politics and Human Nature* (Totowa, NJ: Rowman and Littlefield, 1988), 51–83, 207–249. See also the classic article by Heidi Hartmann, "The Unhappy Marriage of Marxism and Feminism: Towards a More Progressive Union," in Lydia Sargent, ed., *Women and Revolution* (Boston: South End Press, 1981), 1–42.

79. See Barbara Stark, "Constitutional Analysis of the Baby M Decision," *Harvard Women's Law Journal* 11 (1988): 19–53.

80. Studies of the domestic division of labor indicate that many women want a more equitable division of domestic labor but can't achieve it because of differentials in power and in earning capacity. For a discussion of changing family patterns and the ways in which women are deprived of equal voice in the

family, see Kathleen Gerson, *Hard Choices* (Berkeley: University of California Press, 1985). See also Susan Okin, *Justice, Gender, and the Family* (New York: Basic Books, 1989), 134–170.

81. Moreover, on our view, it is precisely because the family is a core institution in and of civil society (and neither a natural presupposition of civil society nor just one more component of an economic subsystem) that egalitarian principles can be applied to it to a far greater extent than to a firm or a bureaucracy.

82. For an interesting account of the emergence of modern gender roles in the United States in the nineteenth century, see Carl Degler, *At Odds: Women and the Family in America from the Revolution to the Present* (New York: Oxford University Press, 1980). Degler also gives a good account of the debate over the impact of the companionate family form and the cult of domesticity that formed around women's relegation to the roles of wife and mother in the second half of the nineteenth century (see 210–328 especially).

83. See chapter 9, note 17.

84. See Niklas Luhmann, *Macht* (Stuttgart: Enke Verlag, 1975), 47–48. Luhmann mentions only examples preceding the institutionalization of the medium of power, but he clearly concedes the possibility of the generation and utilization of power outside the political subsystem (91ff.; he explicitly mentions power in the family). Luhmann provides no reason against the existence of non-media-regulated forms of power, despite his general identification of modernity with media-organized forms of interaction. As might be expected, Foucault's work excels in analyzing the nonsystemic, multiple forms of power.

85. Luhmann, *Macht*, 7, 11–12, 22–24.

86. In a formal organization with several operative codes, there can be different forms of inequality—which may or may not converge in the hierarchical summit—as well as nonhierarchical power relations all operating at the same time.

87. Habermas, *The Theory of Communicative Action*, vol. 2, 263. "If responsibility means that one can orient one's actions to criticizable validity claims, then action coordination that has been detached from communicatively achieved consensus no longer requires responsible participants."

88. Such would be the action-theoretic Weberian conception of domination.

89. Habermas, *The Theory of Communicative Action*, vol. 2, 268–270. Habermas explains in what ways power differs from money as a steering medium.

90. The codes responsible for the transmission of power can take the form of commands linked to threats and involve ordinary language communication. That is, power can operate as "domination" in the action-theoretic sense. It can also operate as a general form of communication; see below.

91. Habermas, *The Theory of Communicative Action*, vol. 2, 275.

92. Luhmann, for example, under the analogous heading of the generalization of influence, speaks of authority, reputation, and leadership, all located at a level of functioning between power as a medium and direct commands. See Luhmann,

Macht, 75–76. This confirms our point that generalized forms of communication can act as forms of power. We insist, however, that the codes are never entirely fixed but are open to reinterpretation, challenges, and creative appropriatiation by actors.

93. They provide relief from lifeworld complexity but, unlike steering media, do not technicize the lifeworld. See Habermas's discussion in *The Theory of Communicative Action,* vol. 2, 277.

94. Fraser suggests treating gender as a "medium of exchange" in order to account for the way in which it links the various institutional domains. Fraser, "What's Critical about Critical Theory?," 113, 117. Of course, Fraser wants to interpret gender as a medium like money and power. She misses the distinction between steering media and generalized forms of communication and is thus led to the misleading view that gender as a power code functions in the same way as these other media. But this cannot be so, for the reasons given in the text.

95. For an overview of this process in the United States, see Julie Matthaei, *An Economic History of Women in America* (New York: Schocken Books, 1982); Degler, *At Odds;* Joan B. Landes, *Women and the Public Sphere in the Age of the French Revolution* (Ithaca: Cornell University Press, 1988).

96. Landes, *Women and the Public Sphere;* Judith Shklar, *Men and Citizens* (Cambridge, England: Cambridge University Press, 1969).

97. It would, however, be misleading to deduce from the feminist perspective on differentiation discussed above that the institutional articulation of modern civil society is wholly negative. On the contrary, the cultural potentials of modernity have entered into its institutional articulation, albeit selectively. Hence the ambivalent character, reflected in the debates among feminist theorists, of the modern family. The "companionate" family composed of a male breadwinner, a female homemaker, and their children did produce intimacy, privacy, and a new focus on childhood individuality. It also constituted an ideological and institutional terrain in which women could begin to develop their own conception of self and the power to assert control over their bodies and lives. The restriction of women to the domestic sphere, however, went hand in hand with a denial of the most basic rights and of the status of autonomous individuality, personhood, and citizenship, which appeared incompatible with the role of nurturer. By the end of the nineteenth century, the development of the family wage system (fought for by organized male workers), the exclusion of women from the union movement, and the "protective labor laws" that excluded women from most jobs had locked women into a situation of dependency that has only recently begun to be seriously challenged, ideologically and structurally. The feminist perspective thus reveals the *double* character of the family that is parallel to the dualities of all the public and private institutions in modern civil society discussed in chapter 9.

98. Fraser admits as much: "A gender-sensitive reading of these arrangements . . . vindicates Habermas's claim that in classical capitalism the (official) economy is not all-powerful but is, rather, in some significant measure inscribed within

and subject to the norms and meanings of everyday life" ("What's Critical about Critical Theory?," 118).

99. Fraser, "What's Critical about Critical Theory?," 124.

100. Habermas, *The Theory of Communicative Action*, vol. 2, 369.

101. See Lenore Weitzman, *The Divorce Revolution* (New York: Free Press, 1985); Deborah L. Rhode, *Justice and Gender* (Cambridge: Harvard University Press, 1989); Martha Fineman and Nancy Thomadsen, eds., *At The Boundaries of Law* (New York: Routledge, 1991).

102. Oddly enough, it is precisely the idea of a threat to the communicative infrastructure of civil society, articulated in dualistic social theory, that Fraser objects to most. She contests the idea that there is any categorial distinction to be made between welfare reforms addressed to the paid workplace and those addressed to the internal dynamics of the family. For her, the "empirical" ambivalence of reform in the latter case stems from the patriarchal character of welfare systems and not from the inherently symbolic character of lifeworld institutions. Indeed, having rejected the very distinction between system and lifeworld as androcentric, she argues that there is no theoretical basis for differentially evaluating the two kinds of reforms; see Fraser, "What's Critical about Critical Theory?," 124. We do not agree.

103. This seems to be Fraser's own position when she points out that there are two different kinds of programs in welfare states: one "masculine," aimed at benefiting principal breadwinners, the other "feminine," oriented toward the "negatives of possessive individuals," to "domestic failures" ("What's Critical about Critical Theory?," 122–123).

104. Habermas, *The Theory of Communicative Action*, vol. 2, 35.

105. Indeed, if we ignore such issues, they will not disappear but will be (and have been) formulated in ways antithetical to feminism. We are thinking of the neoconservative critique of the welfare state, which aims at removing system-integrative mechanisms from civil society while retraditionalizing it.

106. There is already an interesting debate among feminists on this issue. The literature is vast; for an entree into the discussion, see Linda Gordon, "What Does Welfare Regulate?," *Social Research* 55, no. 4 (Winter 1988): 609–630, and Frances Fox Piven and Richard A. Cloward, "Welfare Doesn't Shore Up Traditional Family Roles: A Reply to Linda Gordon," *Social Research* 55, no. 4 (Winter 1988): 631–648.

107. For example, once the typical worker is no longer construed as a male breadwinner but as a woman or man who is also likely to be responsible at some point for the care of children or elders, the necessity of revising the structure of labor and of labor-time becomes obvious, and the argument for day-care centers at the workplace, flexible work schedules, and parental leave, for example, becomes stronger. It is surely not accidental that feminists have begun to articulate and fight for these sorts of reforms. Clearly, such efforts must comple-

ment attempts at transforming the gender hierarchies within the institutions of civil society.

108. For a recent discussion of the the need to apply norms of justice to the family in particular and to gender relations in general, see Okin, *Justice, Gender, and the Family*. Of course, there are many new movements that seek the opposite goal; the right-to-life movement, for example, has as a basic goal a retraditionalization of the core institutions of civil society.

109. This involves a wide variety of strategies ranging from lobbying Congress or the executive branch, rights-oriented politics focusing on the courts, and working in political parties, depending on the political opportunity structure.

110. For a hermeneutic, participant observation approach, see Sara Evans, *Personal Politics* (New York: Random House, 1979). For an analysis that draws on resource-mobilization theory as well as accounts of role strain and relative deprivation, see Jo Freeman, *The Politics of Women's Liberation* (New York: McKay, 1975). The essays in the volume edited by Mary Fainsod Katzenstein and Carol McClurg Mueller, eds., *Women's Movements of the United States and Europe* (Philadelphia: Temple University Press, 1987), focus on political opportunity structures and public policy; while Ethel Klein, *Gender Politics* (Cambridge: Harvard University Press, 1984), focuses on the role of consciousness in feminist movements. Despite their varied foci, all of these works confirm our thesis that a dual logic was always operative in feminist movements.

111. While their emphases vary, most of the discussions of the origin of the "second wave" of feminism stress the following "structural" changes and technological developments that transformed the role of women in the twentieth century: advances in medical science that lowered the birth rate and the time devoted to childrearing, rising marital instability, labor-saving devices that gave women more time for tasks other than housework, improvements in educational opportunity, integration of women into the workforce, formal integration of women into the polity through acquisition of the right to vote, massive entry of women into universities, displacement of female functions outside the home through urbanization and industrialization, and increased government involvement in providing social services. On their own, however, structural changes cannot account for the genesis or logic of the movement; see Klein, *Gender Politics*, 1–32.

112. Klein, *Gender Politics*, 32–81.

113. A nationwide organizational base, resources, and leadership in the form of traditional women's volunteer organizations (which were not originally feminist in ideology but focused on women's concerns) was built between 1890 and 1925, and these associations used their resources to promote women's rights up through the 1960s. As in the case of the nineteenth-century women's movement, the contemporary feminist movement emerged in the context of other vital social movements. Moreover, it took advantage of the general reform orientation of the Kennedy and Johnson years. In 1961, President Kennedy established a Presidential Commission on the Status of Women, the first of its kind, and state-

level organizations on women's status soon followed. See Evans, *Personal Politics,* and Klein, *Gender Politics.*

114. As Ethel Klein aptly puts it, "This traditional lobby could not, by itself, succeed in passing a broad spectrum of women's rights legislation. The efforts of specifically feminist organizations, such as NOW, WEAL, NWPC, and radical women's groups, were critical to rallying the troops and forming the social movement needed to turn the concern for women's issues into action" (*Gender Politics,* 5). See also Freeman, *The Politics of Women's Liberation,* 28–29; Joyce Gelb and Marian L. Palley, *Women and Public Policies* (Princeton: Princeton University Press, 1982), 18.

115. For a comparison of the forms taken by women's movements in various countries, see Joyce Gelb, "Social Movement 'Success': A Comparative Analysis of Feminism in the United States and the United Kingdom," in Katzenstein and Mueller, eds., *Women's Movements of the United States and Europe,* 267–289; "Equality and Autonomy: Feminist Politics in the United States and West Germany," ibid., 172–195; and Karen Beckwith,"Response to Feminism in the Italian Parliament: Divorce, Abortion, and Sexual Violence Legislation," ibid., 153–171.

116. The main exceptions in this regard are Sweden and Norway. Here, the existence of powerful social democratic parties constituted a different "political opportunity structure" than in the United States, France, and Italy. Many benefits for women were enacted through pressure within these parties and not through the activities of an autonomous feminist movement. However, debates have begun today in these countries as well over the desirability of a more autonomous civil society and of an autonomous feminist movement. See Sylvia Hewlett, *A Lesser Life* (New York: William Morrow, 1986), 341–383; Helga Hernes, *Welfare State and Woman Power* (Oslo: Norwegian University Press, 1987).

117. See Freeman, *The Politics of Women's Liberation,* 48–50; Klein, *Gender Politics,* 9–31; Gelb and Palley, *Women and Public Policies,* 24–61; Ann N. Costain and W. Douglas Costain, "Strategy and Tactics of the Women's Movement in the United States: The Role of Political Parties," in Katzenstein and Mueller, eds., *The Women's Movements of the United States and Western Europe,* 196–214.

118. For an account of the emergence of this branch of the feminist movement, see Evans, *Personal Politics.*

119. While the former at first eschewed the dramatic direct-action efforts of the latter groups and the latter had little interest in the lobbying efforts of insiders such as NOW, the sharp distinction betwen women's rights advocates ("liberal feminists") and women's liberation groups ("radical feminists") disappeared after 1968. NOW became involved in sponsoring mass protest actions; and when considerable numbers of militant feminists joined local chapters, it also embraced many of the issues of the early radicals (such as abortion) as well as their participatory ideology and their focus on self-determination and autonomy alongside equal rights. At the same time, by virtue of joining organizations such as NOW, movement activists learned the importance of the politics of influence.

For detailed analyses of this trajectory in American feminism, see Costain and Costain, "Strategy and Tactics of the Women's Movement in the United States," and Gelb and Palley, *Women and Public Policies.*

120. Costain and Costain, "Strategies and Tactics of the Women's Movement in the United States," 201.

121. As Wilma Scott Heide, head of NOW in 1972, put it, "NOW has worked within and outside the system to initiate change and implement women's rights and laws and executive orders on public contracts. . . . Our tactics and strategy include polite letters, interruption of conferences and Senate committees, demonstrating and consultations, calling for and coordinating the August 26 Strikes for Equality, rhetoric and positive programs, sisterly and brotherly consciousness-raising, experiments with new organizational patterns and leadership styles" (cited in Costain and Costain, "Strategy and Tactics of the Women's Movement in the United States," 200).

122. Today the feminist movement is comprised of at least five types of groups: mass-membership organizations; specialized feminist organizations including litigation and research groups; professional lobbies; single-issue groups; traditional women's groups; and an electoral campaign sector that includes PACs and groups operating within the framework of the Democratic party. Feminist associations continue to flourish in civil society and to organize myriad newspapers, magazines, newsletters, direct actions, shelters for battered women, childcare centers, consciousness-raising groups, and so on. Despite the apparent decline in spectacular mass collective actions, the feminist movement continues to target the public sphere to influence consciousness and alter gender norms. The striking spread of women's studies in the universities and in law schools is also worth noting. See Gelb and Palley, *Women and Public Policies,* 26–27; Jo Freeman,"Whom You Know vs. Whom You Represent: Feminist Influence in the Democratic and Republican Parties," in Katzenstein and Mueller, eds., *Women's Movements of the United States and Europe,* 215–246.

123. Gelb and Palley, *Women and Public Policies,* 26–27; Freeman,"Whom You Know"; Klein, *Gender Politics,* 29–33.

124. Costain and Costain, "Strategy and Tactics of the Women's Movement in the United States," 203.

125. Gelb and Palley, *Women and Public Policies,* 26–27; Freeman, "Whom You Know."

126. *Reed* v. *Reed,* 404 U.S. 71 (1971); *Roe* v. *Wade,* 410 U.S. 113 (1973). Successes have sometimes been limited or followed by significant reversals. In the case of sex discrimination, feminists have failed to get sex included as a "suspect classification" under the fourteenth amendment or to secure passage of the ERA. In the case of abortion, since *Roe* v. *Wade* courts and legislatures have been cutting back on women's right to choose, and a vocal antiabortion movement has emerged. Moreover, within the feminist movement, debates have arisen around every "success" as the limits of legal reform along the lines of equal rights have become felt. None of this obviates our more general point.

127. We are not arguing that feminists or women initiated the reforms alluded to above. In many instances, reform processes were initiated by other interest groups for reasons having nothing to do with women's interests or feminist concerns. The institution of no-fault divorce in California and even the initiation of the reform of abortion laws are cases in point. Nevertheless, the dynamics of these reforms were informed by the feminist discourse and, soon thereafter, by feminist activists. see Weitzman, *The Divorce Revolution*, and Kristin Luker, *Abortion and the Politics of Motherhood* (Berkeley: University of California Press, 1984).

128. Until women came to be perceived as individuals, the politics of equal rights had no chance of success. And until the patriarchal structure of the domestic sphere and its negative influence on other domains of society was thematized and challenged, equal or equivalent rights could never be equal for women.

129. Gelb and Palley, *Women and Public Policies*, 45.

130. Klein, *Gender Politics*, 92.

131. Ibid.

132. Things look different in practice, however. For a discussion of the gendered division of labor at home and at work and the difficulties this continues to impose on women, see Gerson, *Hard Choices*. For statistics on the continuing wage gap between women and men and the feminization of poverty in the United States, see Hewlett, *A Lesser Life*, 51–138.

133. Katzenstein and Mueller, eds., *Women's Movements of the United States and Europe*, passim.

134. Jane Jenson, "Changing Discourse, Changing Agendas: Political Rights and Reproductive Policies in France," in Katzenstein and Mueller, eds., *Women's Movements of the United States and Europe*, 64–65. By "universe of political discourse," Jenson means the set of beliefs about how politics should be conducted, the boundaries of political discussion, and the kinds of conflicts resolvable through political processes. The universe of political discourse functions as a gatekeeper to political action, selecting or inhibiting the range of actors, issues, policy alternatives, alliance strategies, and collective identities available for achieving change.

135. Ibid., 68–80. Women got the vote in France in 1945 as a reward for service in the resistance, at a time when the feminist movement was moribund. The Loi Neuwirth of 1968 legalized contraception for married women but also restricted the advertising of contraceptives and their use by single women. The primary intent of the law was to help families control their fertility to meet family goals of material well-being and emotional support for children, not to give women a choice over whether or not to have children. Women were still defined within a family frame of reference.

136. Ibid., 80–86.

137. Gelb and Palley, *Women and Public Policies*, 30. Feminists have also challenged male conceptions of the standards of justice.

138. The abortion debate has also challenged male conceptions of rights or, rather, of the person to whom rights apply. It should not come as a surprise that this debate has posed a fundamental challenge to the very conception of rights, since it has been notoriously difficult to conceive of a right to abortion along the traditional lines of a right to one's body as one's own property when in that body there is another potential person who clearly does not "belong to" one as property. But on a nonpossessive, individualist model of rights, it becomes clear that the legal personhood, moral subjectivity, and particular identity of women are at stake, and these outweigh the state's interest in fetal life in the first trimester.

139. See Anita Allen, *Uneasy Access: Privacy for Women in a Free Society* (Totowa, NJ: Rowman and Littlefield, 1988).

140. Jenson, "Changing Discourse, Changing Agendas," 82–83. For an insightful analysis of the feminist discourse on abortion and its conflict with traditionalist discourses, see Luker, *Abortion and the Politics of Motherhood.*

141. By insisting that women be recognized as individuals, persons, and citizens as well as situated women, the contemporary feminist movement brings together the values of universalism, plurality, and difference. By implication, the concept of equality before the law itself is being altered, for it can no longer mean that equal rights and nondiscrimination apply only to those who are similarly situated. This is because women and men can never be similarly situated when it comes to the question of abortion or reproductive rights generally.

142. See Jenkins and Eckert, "Channelling Black Insurgency," or Pizzorno, "Political Exchange and Collective Identity in Industrial Conflict."

143. Pizzorno, "Political Exchange and Collective Identity in Industrial Conflict," 293.

144. For a "stage model" analysis of the feminist movement, see Costain and Costain, "Strategy and Tactics of the Women's Movement in the United States." See also Claus Offe, "Reflections on the Institutional Self-Transformation of Movement Politics: A Tentative Stage Model," in Russell Dalton and Manfred Küchler, eds., *Challenging the Political Order: New Social and Political Movements in Western Democracies* (Oxford: Oxford University Press, 1990). Offe presents an interesting analysis of the contradictions facing the new social movements at the various stages of their development. He also argues, however, that even at the last stage, that of institutionalization, there will be good reasons for these movements to retain important aspects of a civil-society-oriented "defensive" politics.

145. Offe, "Reflections on the Institutional Self-Transformation of Movement Politics," 15.

146. The vast increase in electoral and lobbying politics by organized professionals in the 1980s was a sign of the institutionalization of the women's movement in the United States. However, the continuing strength of prochoice demonstrations and self-help groups indicates that identity-oriented politics is still very much on the agenda.

147. Jane Mansbridge, *Why We Lost the ERA* (Chicago: University of Chicago Press, 1986); Luker, *Abortion and the Politics of Motherhood.* The main opposition to the ERA stemmed not from economic factors but from a fear that women's role in the family would change.

148. The stakes of feminist movement lie above all in the institutionalization of a postconventional interpretation of gender identity and nonhierarchical gender relations in *civil society.* Indeed, were women to "succeed" in gaining recognition simply as another "different and particular" special interest, as another lobby or constituency of political parties, the universal and transformative thrust of "women's issues" would disappear from view. On the other side, were feminism to be construed only as a struggle for inclusion and equal rights, the issues of gender identity, bodily integrity, the nature of the family, and the structure of institutions and social relations within the public and private spheres of civil society would be obscured.

149. See E. P. Thompson, *The Making of the English Working Class* (New York: Random House, 1963).

150. See Cohen, "Rethinking Social Movements."

151. That is, vulnerability to the capitalist economy on one side and to administrative control by agencies of the welfare state on the other.

Chapter 11

1. See chapter 8.

2. See chapters 2 and 3. In other words, our argument rests on the assumption that the ideal of democracy—participating in public life and having a say in the laws and policies under which we live—is an ideal of collective autonomy that complements the idea of moral autonomy.

3. See Michael Walzer, *Obligations* (Cambridge: Harvard University Press 1970), 24–45.

4. This is a paraphrase of Rawls's formulation. See John Rawls, *A Theory of Justice* (Cambridge: Harvard University Press, 1971). Rawls speaks of a nearly just constitutional democracy in order to indicate that no political procedural rule can guarantee a just outcome in the sense that all rights will be protected and not violated. We add the notion of a nearly democratic constitutional democracy to indicate that no single procedure or combination of procedures can guarantee the full realization of democratic participation or an outcome that all can accept.

5. For an early discussion of the various arguments for and against civil disobedience, see Carl Cohen, *Civil Disobedience: Conscience, Tactics, and the Law* (New York: Columbia University Press, 1971). For an overview of what has come to be labeled the orthodox theory of civil disobedience, see G. G. James, "The Orthodox Theory of Civil Disobedience," *Social Theory and Practice* 2, no. 4 (1973), especially the references in note 2. For a recent comprehensive discussion, see Kent Greenawalt, *Conflicts of Law and Morality* (Oxford: Oxford University Press, 1987).

6. Jürgen Habermas, "Civil Disobedience: Litmus Test for the Democratic Constitutional State," *Berkeley Journal Of Sociology* 30 (1985): 99.

7. We are not addressing civil disobedience within the framework of authoritarian regimes, which seeks to institutionalize the principle of rights and representative democracy. Rather, the issue before us is the justification and role of civil disobedience in constitutional democracies with vital civil societies, wherein rights, democratic procedures, and the rule of law are already institutionalized. See Rawls, *A Theory of Justice*, 363, for a discussion of this matter.

8. Rawls, *A Theory of Justice*, 363.

9. There is an enormous literature on civil disobedience and political obligation. Most of it falls within the framework of liberal political theory based on the social contract model or on jurisprudential reflections. Serious philosophical discussion of the matter began in 1961 when the Eastern Division of the American Philosophical Association held a symposium on the topic. Something like an orthodox liberal view is shared, with minor variations, by Hugo Bedau, John Rawls, Ronald Dworkin, Christian Bay, Rudolph Weingartner, Joseph Betz, and Carl Cohen. For references, see James, "The Orthodox Theory of Civil Disobedience," 496. See also Rawls, *A Theory of Justice*, chap. 6, and Ronald Dworkin, *Taking Rights Seriously* (Cambridge: Harvard University Press, 1978), chap. 8, and *A Matter of Principle* (Cambridge: Harvard University Press, 1985), chap. 4.

For discussions of civil disobedience within the tradition of democratic political theory, see Howard Zinn, *Disobedience and Democracy* (New York: Random House, 1978); Walzer, *Obligations*; Hannah Arendt, *Crisis in the Republic* (New York: Harcourt Brace and Jovanovich, 1969), 51–102; Carole Pateman, *The Problem of Political Obligation* (Berkeley: University of California Press, 1979); Habermas, "Civil Disobedience."

For references to the jurisprudential literature, see Hannah Arendt, *Crisis in the Republic*, 51–57, notes. For a more recent view, see Greenawalt, *Conflicts of Law and Morality*.

10. According to Dworkin, "It is silly to speak of the duty to obey the law as such" (*Taking Rights Seriously*, 192–193).

11. The essays cited in note 4 were written in the aftermath of the civil rights and antiwar movements in the United States. Dworkin's second essay in *A Matter of Principle* was written in response to the 1981 German peace movement.

12. Rawls, *A Theory of Justice*, 366–367; Dworkin, *Taking Rights Seriously*, 206–222. Both also assume that actors should have already tried to make their case through ordinary legal and political channels. But there are times when this is not possible. For example, a pregnant woman who wants an abortion cannot wait for a legislative or court decision. Civil rights activists could not make use of the courts or the legislative process in the South because these institutions were precisely the ones denying blacks justice.

13. This is how Habermas interprets Rawls and Dworkin, but in fact he uses their arguments based on individual rights to make his own case for the principles of democratic legitimacy.

14. The full range of citizen rights together with certain civil rights that guarantee freedom of speech, assembly, etc., are understood as rights of the individual that allow participation in the political system through institutions such as parties, the press, elections, parliaments, and interest groups. These, together with other guarantees such as the separation of powers and publicity, protect citizens from abuses of power by their representatives while securing their participation in the representative political system. When these work well, there would seem to be no need for illegal extrainstitutional political activity other than activity aimed at the defense of individual rights.

15. For a horizontal model of obligation, see Hannah Arendt, "Civil Disobedience," in *Crisis in the Republic*, 85–86. Carole Pateman has elaborated this view; see *The Problem of Political Obligation*, 1–36. For another model of horizontal obligations based on a philosophically pluralist conception, see Walzer, *Obligations*, 1–23.

16. For both, of course, a just society must include distributive justice (consider Rawls's second principle of justice and Dworkin's discussions of welfare mechanisms based on claims to equality). But neither of them accepts civil disobedience for the sake of distributive justice.

17. Rawls, *A Theory of Justice*, 363.

18. It is also located in the procedures set down in the Constitution for the division of powers, rule of law, voting, etc. For the best discussion of the meaning of a moral right as something that implies a suprainstitutional moment, see Dworkin, *Taking Rights Seriously*. Indeed, the work of both Rawls and Dworkin reveals an important evolution within liberal theory, in that they have sought to develop a theory of rights that has at its core a concept of individual autonomy rather than a concept of private property. In this regard, Robert Nozick's *Anarchy, State, and Utopia* (New York: Basic Books, 1968) represents a step backward.

19. See Rawls, *A Theory of Justice*, 27, on plurality, and Dworkin, "Liberalism," in *A Matter of Principle*, 181–204. The main problem confronting Rawls is how we can arrive at binding principles of justice whose justification does not derive from any particular conception of the good. The rational choice argument in *A Theory of Justice*, which apparently applies to everyone everywhere, provides one answer. Rawls's essay, "The Idea of an Overlapping Consensus," *Oxford Journal of Legal Studies* 7, no. 1 (1987): 1–25, provides another. For our position on this topic, see chapter 8.

20. Rawls, *A Theory of Justice*, 364–365. Dworkin distinguishes between conscientious refusal and civil disobedience in somewhat different terms: His "integrity-based" civil disobedience is the same as Rawls's conscientious refusal, and his "justice-based" civil disobedience is similar to Rawls's general concept of civil disobedience. Dworkin also speaks of "policy-based" civil disobedience (*A Matter of Principle*, 107).

21. Rawls, *A Theory of Justice*, 365.

22. That is, neutral arguments must be given, or, rather, arguments that do not draw on any particular conception of the good but only on the shared conception of the right. Thus, civil disobedience can involve the violation of a law other than the one being protested; it is also more than a test case because the relevant actors are prepared to oppose the statute even if it is upheld. See Rawls, *A Theory of Justice*, 365.

23. Rawls, *A Theory of Justice*, 370.

24. Ibid., 356–362; Dworkin, *Taking Rights Seriously*, 211–212. Dworkin refers to legislation based on prejudice as the imposition of "external preferences" (234–235).

25. The two principles of justice are: "(1) Each person is to have an equal right to the most extensive total system of equal basic liberties compatible with a similar system of liberty for all. (2) Social and economic inequalities are to be arranged so that they are both (a) to the greatest benefit of the least advantaged, consistent with the just savings principle, and (b) attached to offices and positions open to all under conditions of fair equality of opportunity" (Rawls, *A Theory of Justice*, 302). For Rawls's original position, see ibid., 17–22. For the definition of a just constitution, just legislation, and the discussion of the status of majority rule, see ibid., 195–201 and 356–362.

26. For the definition of imperfect procedural justice, see Rawls, *A Theory of Justice*, 353–354, 356.

27. Ibid., 371–377.

28. Ibid., 111–116, 342–350. To these categories of privileged individuals the "principle of fairness" applies; that is, in addition to their natural duty to comply, those individuals who gain real advantages from a social system are even more bound to comply. Rawls's concern in adding this principle of obligation to natural duty is to avoid free riding (116). On this topic, see also Pateman, *The Problem of Political Obligation*, 118–120.

29. Rawls, *A Theory of Justice*, 115.

30. Ibid., 335–336. Many commentators have pointed out that Rawls's understanding of the contract as "hypothetical" renders it irrelevant to the problem of political obligation as it arises with respect to civil disobedience. See Dworkin, *Taking Rights Seriously*, 151. Indeed, as we have seen, Rawls makes little use of the contract idea when addressing the issue of civil disobedience.

31. Rawls, *A Theory of Justice*, 352.

32. By implication, the second case for Rawls would involve more serious acts of rebellion or resistance aimed at establishing a new society based on a different conception of justice.

33. Rawls, *A Theory of Justice*, 372.

34. Hence the three conditions that must obtain before one can engage in civil disobedience: First, it must be nonviolent, should not interfere with others' civil liberties, and should not take the form of a threat. Second, there must be grave

injustice. Third, one must have gone through the proper channels and discovered that one cannot influence the legislative majority. See Rawls, *A Theory of Justice*, 372–374.

35. It serves as a prophylactic in two ways. First, it dissuades those in power from abusing their power—a major potential source of instability—and second, it works against fundamentalism on the part of collective actors. Civil disobedience is not action on the basis of an absolute right to act on one's moral conscience. It is based instead on an appeal to the shared political conceptions of justice and constitutional principles. In this sense, it is self-limiting.

36. Rawls, *A Theory of Justice*, 367ff.

37. This restriction not only limits the range of civil disobedience with respect to policy decisions by the legislature but also excludes an entire range of activity, namely, citizen action with respect to the economy. This is grounded theoretically by Rawls's denial of the status of rights to "socioeconomic claims" based on the distinction between the worth of liberty and liberty itself. The former refers to entitlements or other means that allow our liberty to have value to us; the latter refers to rights. Rawls has in mind issues of distributive justice, but his conception misses the issue of the structure of authority and decision making within the workplace itself. There is no room in his theory for a right to collective bargaining or anything else that falls under the heading of democratization or constitutionalization of the workplace. This is a grave omission, for a case can certainly be made for the legitimacy of civil disobedience in this domain. For an excellent discussion of this issue, see Walzer, *Obligations*, chap. 2. We agree that civil disobedience for the purpose of establishing collective bargaining and similar rights is appropriate and legitimate. Civil society must be able to influence economic as well as political society. It is able to influence the polity because corresponding structures open in principle to influence (parliaments or courts, for example) are in place (political society). The same sorts of "receptors" ought to exist in the economy (economic society). See also Greenawalt, *Conflicts of Law and Morality*, 230–233.

38. For a critique of Rawls on this score, see Pateman, *The Problem of Political Obligation*, 118–129.

39. Rawls, *A Theory of Justice*, 390.

40. Ibid., 385.

41. "A community's sense of justice is more likely to be revealed in the fact that the (political) majority cannot bring itself to take the steps necessary to suppress the minority and to punish acts of civil disobedience as the law allows. . . . In spite of its superior power, the majority may abandon its position and acquiesce in the proposals of the dissenters" (*A Theory of Justice*, 387).

42. Others have argued that Rawls's conception is overly restrictive in that it omits from the range of legitimate reasons for civil disobedience moral principles that are not generally accepted in a society. Rawls does address this problem under the rubric of conscientious refusal, but he does not take up the

issue of attempts by concerned citizens to present their moral position as a candidate for inclusion in the political culture of the society through acts of civil disobedience. Because political norms are institutionalized moral values and because, over time, the repertoire of political norms changes, new values are institutionalized, and old norms are reinterpreted, this omission is serious. We believe that it can be traced back to the relatively static conception of justice in Rawls's theory. For a discussion of this problem, see Peter Singer, *Democracy and Disobedience* (Oxford: Oxford University Press, 1973), 86–92.

43. We include the courts in our conception of "political society." Courts are not open to economic pressure or political power, but judges must be open to influence in the sense of adjusting interpretations of law to principles, tradition, and the prevailing sense of justice of the community.

44. Singer, *Democracy and Disobedience*, 385.

45. Dworkin, *Taking Rights Seriously*, 185.

46. Ibid., 192. Dworkin makes an important distinction between what is right (the perspective of moral conscience) and having rights (198–199). Having moral rights against the state means that there are limits the state cannot transgress without good reason, principles it cannot violate without doing injustice. This includes a domain of individual moral judgment (negative liberty) in which each person can decide what it is right to do. Rights, however, derive not from any individual's moral judgment but from a conception of human dignity or equality that is at the heart of a community's common conception of justice. They render each person's judgment autonomous but rest on political principles that pertain to everyone. Constitutional rights are the intersection of moral rights and legal right; they consist of moral principles that have been recognized as valid norms.

47. Ibid., 215. The issue is not that the law may not be stated clearly but that there are good arguments on both sides.

48. Ibid., 211–212.

49. Ibid., 212. Since an open, postconventional society will consider both morality (principles) and precedent, there can be no authoritative instance of interpretation. Not even the highest court has privileged access to the truth.

50. Ibid., 212.

51. Ibid., 212, 214, 216–217, 219–220.

52. Greenawalt, *Conflicts of Law and Morality*, 227.

53. Ibid., 227–229. Attempts to argue that basic rights can be defended without appealing to substantive due process or fundamental values are unconvincing because procedural democratic legitimacy also rests on a fundamental value, namely, representative democracy. For the process argument, see John Hart Ely, *Democracy and Distrust* (Cambridge: Harvard University Press, 1980).

54. Dworkin, *Taking Rights Seriously*, 205.

55. Ibid. The legitimacy of majority rule requires that the basic rights of minorities not be violated and that they be given equal concern and respect.

56. Unlike most liberal theorists of civil disobedience, who try to make such distinctions on the basis of the content of the act (violent or nonviolent, use or nonuse of force), the intent of the act, or the integrity of the actors (moral probity or irresponsibility), Dworkin recognizes that such an approach is unconvincing. All acts of civil disobedience are complex, it is hard to define force, and the violence in such acts is often a response to governmental repression.

57. Dworkin, *Taking Rights Seriously*, 82.

58. Dworkin, *A Matter of Principle*, 107. A third type of civil disobedience—basically what Rawls defines as conscientious refusal—is called by Dworkin "integrity-based civil disobedience."

59. Ibid., 111.

60. Dworkin himself has made such arguments with respect to foreign policy issues. He attempted to defend the anti–Vietnam war movement on the basis of rights arguments, but ultimately his mode of arguing is unconvincing. While there were aspects of the movement that raised questions of individual rights (student exemptions), the movement was also challenging a policy decision made by government and would have done so even if constitutional technicalities had been observed. Our point is that certain acts of civil disobedience challenge a policy when no one's individual rights are directly concerned but issues of democratic decision making and political morality are at stake; and if these cannot be justified by a rights-based argument, they can nonetheless be justified ethically by arguments based on democratic principles. See below, note 63.

61. Courts ought to be immune to pressures exercised through money or power, but judges must be open to indirect influence, mediated through arguments, by contemporary political culture. As such, they are part of political society.

62. Backed up by the relevant civil rights of free speech, assembly, association, and the like.

63. Note, for example, his discussion of the anti–Vietnam war movement: He tries to translate the claims of the dissenters into the sort of rights claims a lawyer would make. This works for draft-law inequities, but it hardly convinces with respect to the moral objection that the United States was using unconscionable weapons and tactics or that the United States had no interest at stake in Vietnam that could justify forcing citizens to risk their lives there. What was at stake was clearly how war decisions should be made, the creation of a public debate, the insistence that moral and normative political issues and not just "reasons of state" were at issue, and the insistence that, in a democracy, the people should be able to influence such a decision-making process. The issue was not one of conscientious refusal, since those involved in the movement were not only those who risked being drafted. See Dworkin, *A Matter of Principle*, 208–209.

64. Despite his defense of policy-based civil disobedience, he interprets the only example he gives of it as being covertly nonpersuasive.

65. Dworkin, *A Matter of Principle*, 112.

66. See Habermas, "Civil Disobedience."

67. The phrase used by Dworkin for the American civil rights movement, which attempted to educate public opinion, create public spaces for its expression, and find ways for its influence to be felt (*A Matter of Principle*, 112). We should note that actions such as those of Operation Rescue in the United States would not qualify as justified civil disobedience on these grounds, since they involve tactics of intimidation rather than persuasion and seek to impose a particular world view on society rather than appealing to the principles of justice of the community.

68. Every element of this definition could be challenged; this is the risk faced by any attempt at definition. To help avoid the worst abuses of such exercises, we should clarify a few points. By "public," we mean that the illegal act must be made known, but not necessarily while it is being committed (although this is usually the case). Nor is it absolutely necessary that the authors of the act make themselves known, though this, too, should ordinarily be public knowledge. The pouring of blood on draft files during the Vietnam protests is an instructive example. These acts took place in secrecy and the actors retained their anonymity, but the acts were clearly symbolic and intended to become public knowledge.

By "illegal," we mean that there is an intentional violation of the law that is not meant to call into question the rule of law as a whole or the constitutional system itself. Readiness to accept the legal consequences of transgressions of legality demonstrate the actors' fidelity to a "nearly just, nearly democratic" constitution, but it is not absolutely required.

By "nonviolent," we mean that the character of the protest is symbolic and communicative or, in Dworkin's phrase, persuasive. Strategic power plays that involve violence are hard to justify as civil disobedience. Nevertheless, in concrete situations violence can occur. The assessment of the violence must be made with reference to who initiated it, the overall context, and the purpose of the act. The history of the labor movement provides many examples of violent strikes that can be seen as acts of civil disobedience. Force and violence are notoriously hard to define, and their meaning can be stretched to include all forms of coercion or narrowed down to mean only physical violence. We accept Günter Frankenberg's formulation in "Ziviler Ungehorsam und rechtsstaatliche Demokratie," *Juristenzeitung* 39 (March 1984): 266ff.: "Only those infractions are civil that do not contravene the 'proportionality of means' and, especially, that safeguard the physical and psychic integrity of the opponents of protest and of innocent bystanders."

Finally, by appeals to the capacity of reason and the sense of justice of the population, we mean to indicate that civil disobedience is a call to members of both civil and political society to reflect upon the basic principles that underlie a constitutional democracy and to change those laws, policies, and institutional arrangements that violate these principles.

69. For example, note that here "nonneutral" means that legislation involves general norms that incorporate a conception of the good, while elsewhere Dworkin interprets it to refer only to foreign, economic, and social policy decisions.

70. Dworkin, *Taking Rights Seriously*, 255.

71. For a discussion of the concept of identity in radical democratic theory, see Carl Schmitt, *The Crisis of Parliamentary Democracy* [1923] (Cambridge: MIT Press, 1985). See also the sections on Schmitt in chapter 3.

72. This position is typical of contemporary neocommunitarians of the neo-Aristotelian (MacIntyre) or neo-Republican (Sandel, Taylor, et al.) stripe.

73. This has been recognized by nondemocrats as well. Carl Schmitt proceeds from the premise that popular sovereignty cannot be institutionalized—the people's will in the form of the *pouvoir constituant* always remains above or outside the law. The conclusions he draws from this insight are, of course, hardly democratic: Since the people's will can neither be represented nor, under modern conditions, formed in one general assembly, it can only be embodied in a person who claims to do so and who is affirmed in this claim through techniques of acclamation. Accordingly, the leader reunites in his or her person legitimacy (the principles behind the law) and sovereignty (the ability to make emergency decisions). For this reason, on the basis of the model of democracy as identity, which he finds in Rousseau, in Jacobinism, and in Bolshevism, Schmitt concludes that the line between democracy and dictatorship is a thin one indeed.

74. This is less true of Arendt than of Habermas. The great flaw in Arendt's overall theory is its antipathy to modern civil society and its anachronistic, dichotomous categorial framework (see chapter 4). Her essay on civil disobedience, written in response to practical issues in the United States, tends to burst through the rigidities of her theoretical model.

75. Arendt, *Crisis in the Republic*, 51–102; Habermas, "Civil Disobedience."

76. Dworkin goes fairly far because, unlike most liberal and legalistic defenders, he does not stress that an act of civil disobedience is legitimate only if the lawbreakers are willing to accept punishment for their act. Instead, his emphasis is on decriminalization, lenient punishment, etc.

77. Arendt, *Crisis in the Republic*, 98.

78. Ibid., 55. See also Walzer, *Obligations*, 4.

79. Arendt, *Crisis in the Republic*, 74.

80. It is worth noting here that one dimension missing in liberal and most democratic discussions of civil disobedience is its role and legitimacy with regard to the economy. It is not surprising that liberals concerned with basic liberties would ignore such considerations, but it is odd that democratic theory has not addressed it directly. Arendt mentions it only in passing. Rawls explicitly rejects the legitimacy of acts of civil disobedience with respect to matters of distributive

justice. Dworkin and Habermas are silent on the issue. Walzer is one of the few radical democrats to have discussed civil disobedience with respect to economic institutions. He argues that the private economic corporation must be considered a political community within the larger community of the state. Today corporations collect taxes on behalf of the state, maintain standards required by the state, and spend state money and enforce rules and regulations with the ultimate support of the state. They carry out semiofficial functions and exercise power and authority over workers. But the authority of corporate officers is rarely legitimated in a democratic fashion. Corporate power is exercised over employee-subjects in ways not dissimilar from those of authoritarian states. Some subjects of corporate authority have, of course, managed to win rights against it that are protected by the state, specifying such matters as working hours or the right to strike. The strike, in fact, was for a long time the most common form of working-class civil disobedience. Often, violence or force was involved in the sit-ins and sit-down strategies of the workers' movement, and Walzer argues that such actions, even if they appear as revolutionary in that they aim at altering the distribution of power within the corporation, fall within the limits of civility so long as the revolution is not aimed at the state itself (*Obligations*, 31). The point he makes here is that often there are no legal channels to be gone through. Thus, these acts of limited "revolutionary" civil disobedience can be seen as efforts to extend democratic constitutional principles to a realm in which claims to absolute power by officials based on property rights are extremely unconvincing. While corporate and state officials tend to see the corporation as a piece of property rather than a political community (as economic society, in our terminology), it clearly involves both. The point at issue in these acts of civil disobedience is not who owns the corporation but what such ownership entails and what governmental powers management can legitimately claim. Walzer points out that a characteristic features of feudal regimes is that the ownership of property entails governmental powers, but no modern state and certainly no democratic-constitutional state could tolerate such a situation. Thus, he argues that the interests of a democratic state would be best served by corporate democratization. There therefore exists a type of civil disobedience that challenges not state laws and policies but only those corporate authorities that the state protects. We agree with this argument with one proviso: Economic efficiency should not be sacrificed *in toto* to democratic pressure.

81. Arendt, *Crisis in the Republic*, 96.

82. See chapter 4. We are thinking of the rigid opposition between the private and the public spheres, on the one hand, and the conception of modern society as mass society, on the other. This theoretical model excludes, by definition, the conception of civil society we have been formulating. At best, it allows for a conception of political society between the private sphere, individualistically conceived, and the state as government. But Arendt's understanding of civil disobedience implies a model of political society open to the influence of private citizens acting collectively, and it presupposes a complex model of civil society in which power is dispersed and delegated only in part and conditionally to

political society or the state. In short, the discussion of civil disobedience forces Arendt to reintroduce on the level of content, if not theoretically, some of the core components of the concept of civil society: associations and social movements, which are distinct from prototolitarian mass movements.

83. See chapter 4.

84. Note the change in Arendt's position in *The Human Condition* (Chicago: University of Chicago Press, 1958), 23, where she castigates *societas* as the loss of the political.

85. Arendt, *Crisis in the Republic,* 89, 95.

86. Ibid., 97.

87. There are theoretical reasons for Arendt's inability to spell this out, namely, her assumption of the decline of the public sphere with the onset of modernity and the emergence and expansion of that blurred realm that mixes public and private, namely, society (civil society).

88. This is the model spelled out at the end of Arendt's *On Revolution* (New York: Penguin Books, 1977).

89. Habermas, "Civil Disobedience," 101, 106.

90. Ibid., 102.

91. Ibid., 103.

92. Ibid., 104.

93. That is, those who are not members of parliaments, unions, or parties (political society), those without access to the mass media, those who cannot threaten to withhold investments during election campaigns—in short, those without much money or power. See Habermas, "Civil Disobedience," 104.

94. For example, disputes over which instance of governmental decision making should govern the siting of a nuclear power plant. For an excellent discussion of these issues, see Claus Offe, "Legitimation Through Majority Rule?," in *Disorganized Capitalism* (Cambridge: MIT Press, 1985), 259–299.

95. Ibid.

96. Habermas, "Civil Disobedience," 111.

97. Ibid., 105. Here is the proper democratic theory of the *pouvoir constituant.* Habermas draws quite different conclusions from an insight similar to Carl Schmitt's. It is true that the *pouvoir constituant* cannot be fully institutionalized in a democratic regime. The idea that elections plus a competitive party system and the rule of law could institutionalize or circumscribe popular sovereignty is quite unconvincing. Schmitt, in his argument against liberalism, turns this insight into a justification for decisionism and the arbitrary, sovereign will of the executive. But there is another way to draw out the implications of this insight into the nature of the political. In a democratic-constitutional state, one can take it to mean, as Offe and Habermas have argued, that constitutionalism, with its principles of rights and democratic legitimacy, rests on a partial institutionaliza-

tion of the *pouvoir constituant* and indeed provides institutionally for the reversion of sovereignty to the people in the ideas of constitutional conventions and constitutional amendments. The theory of civil disobedience takes this one step further. It is not possible to institutionalize civil disobedience. But while it cannot be made legal, it can enter into a political culture. Social movements operating outside the existing party-political system can recognize the need for continual revision of constitutional democracies without thereby becoming permanent revolutions or challenging the legal order as a whole. The insight that sovereignty can never be fully institutionalized thus need not play into Schmittian arguments for executive power but can reaffirm the principles of democratic legitimacy.

98. Habermas argues that this is what distinguishes the new social movements from the New Left with its false revolutionary ideals.

99. Habermas, unlike Dworkin, argues that this was true of the German antimissile protests of the late 1980s, which he interprets as a series of symbolic collective actions aimed at convincing public opinion and influencing the legislative majority and not as an elitist power play.

100. In other words, if the principle of majority rule is to be viable with regard to the normative component of legislation, where the mere counting of preferences is inadequate and it is not a question of individual rights, it must be brought back to a set of moral principles that underlie democratic theory. We addressed this under the heading of democratic legitimacy in chapter 8.

101. Like the idea of moral rights, the principle of democratic legitimacy operates as a set of counterfactual norms that the state can partly but never completely institutionalize. The state monopolizes the legitimate use of violence, but it cannot monopolize politics without becoming antidemocratic, without violating the idea of popular sovereignty and the democratic legitimacy linked to it.

Index